CLASSICAL MUSIC RECORDINGS

CLASSICAL MUSIC RECORDINGS

FOR HOME AND LIBRARY

Richard Sweeney Halsey

American Library Association
Chicago 1976

016.789912
H19c

BN

Library of Congress Cataloging in Publication Data
Halsey, Richard S   1929–
   Classical music recordings for home and library.
   Includes index.
   1. Phonorecord collecting. 2. Phonorecord librar-
ies. 3. Music-Discography. I. Title.
ML111.5.H34   016.7899'12   75–40205
ISBN 0-8389-0188-3

Printed in the United States of America

To C. Vincent Bleecker

Contents

Preface

Standards for school and public library programs have been completely revised in recent years because of extensive changes in contemporary education
and society. Many cultural and social events and expressions have now been
best preserved in other than the traditional printed formats. Acknowledgment
of this fact has led to the publication of guidelines calling for large quantities
of motion picture films, slides, art reproductions, sound recordings, and other
nonprint resources to be integrated into collections.

Although qualitative controls and an effective network of reviews and selection tools treat the printed word, the other media lack guides of comparable
reliability and currency. Dissatisfaction with this neglect prompted preparation
of this guide for organizations and individuals concerned with collecting and
organizing, playing and caring for sound recordings.

Its chief purpose is to ease the way for those who want to build, enlarge, or
upgrade their collections. The second chapter provides a comprehensive title
listing of classical musical works identified in terms of popularity, aesthetic
worth, and listening level. Recorded performances are cited for all compositions which have had interpretations represented in recent issues of the
Schwann-I and *Schwann-II Records and Tapes* guides.

A second reason for preparing this book is that most recordings far surpass
in artistry and fidelity to the composer's intentions most concert hall interpretations. Rare is the superlative moment when composer, performer, and
listener attain an absolute union of insight because restricted rehearsal time,
normal acoustics, normal artistic temperament and fallibility, and normal
audience disengagement conspire against its consummation. In contrast, because
time, tape editing, money, and musicians are committed to rise to the challenge, the recorded performance is often better. Although nostalgic humanists
may deplore the calculated intervention of the recording studio, the public and
the art of music benefit. This guide has been prepared to promote the widest
possible distribution of that benefit to listeners of all ages. As Charles Edward
Ives observed, a composer must deal with real and imperfect musical instruments and voices, and, at the least, a successful sound recording reduces compromise with the muse before the music goes forth to the listener. That one
ineluctable barrier, the instrument itself, is quite enough as Ives' protestation
reveals:

> My God! What has sound got to do with music! The waiter
> brings the only fresh egg he has, but the man at breakfast sends

it back because it doesn't fit his eggcup. Why can't music go out in the same way it comes in to a man, without having to crawl over a fence of sounds, thoraxes, catguts, wire, wood, and brass? Consecutive fifths are as harmless as blue laws compared with the relentless tyranny of the "media." The instrument!—there is the perennial difficulty—there is music's limitation.[1]

Subjective judgments have been assiduously avoided in the assignment of ratings to compositions in chapter 2. Value assessments were derived from a comprehensive statistical analysis of the production and market status of 42,943 different recorded versions of musical works issued on long-playing records during the years 1961–69[2] and updated by thorough monitoring of subsequent musical and recording activity between 1970 and the present.

All highly recommended issues, those keyed with double asterisks in the chapter 2 lists, have been favorably reviewed in at least 80 percent of the critical literature examined by the author. Only reviewers who had attained a reputation for sustained probity and dependability of musical judgment were counted in this opinion survey.

Although this guide will usually be employed as a selection and collection development aid, other uses are foreseen. It could serve as a title reservoir for program planners in schools, public libraries, radio stations, or listening clubs. The accessibility ratings could serve as directional markers for buyers hesitant to explore strange listening channels in the fields of chamber music, lieder, or other genres. For example, composers Schoenberg, Carter, and Ives whose prime works have dense textures, abstruse rhythms, or brash harmonies may be tolerated and later make a connection if the listener will savor the relatively accessible works first and progress in a logical sequence towards the more unyielding and enigmatic musical statements.

Alternatively, haphazard exposure to helpings of unfamiliar contemporary music can actually depreciate its value. The result may resemble the discomfiture suffered by persons who indiscriminately overindulge in exotic food or love-making. Discredit may be cast both upon lovers and the objects of their affection.

This book contains information of interest to home and library audiences. The reader will note that chapters 1, 2, 3, and 6 comprise the core of advice on collection development, reviews, equipment and listening environments which should have value for both institutional and private consumers. Chapters 4 and 5 will be of especial interest to those who organize and administer collections for others.

Many individuals and organizations assisted in the compilation of supportive data for this guide. Robert Conrad, program manager of radio station WCLV, Cleveland, Ohio, provided access to catalogs of WCLV's record holdings;

---

1. Charles Ives, *Essays before a Sonata and Other Writings* (New York: W. W. Norton & Co., 1961), p.84.
2. Richard S. Halsey, "A Bibliometric Analysis of the Serious Music Literature on Long Playing Records" (Ph.D. diss., Case Western Reserve University, 1972). In this study, the techniques and perspectives of information science and the aesthetics of music were joined in an investigation of the relationship between musical worth, market viability, and production frequency.

Larry Lake, program manager of the Canadian Broadcasting Corporation, Toronto, Ontario, granted permission to examine the files of CBC's central sound recordings library. Jack Saul, president of the Sir Thomas Beecham Society, loaned out-of-print catalogs; and Helene Stern, music librarian at Case Western Reserve University, Cleveland, located bibliographic and human resources needed to document and verify statistical and textual information.

Editors of the following journals responded to requests for information about their publications: *American Record Guide, American Recorder, American String Teacher, Audio, Booklist, Children's Record Critique, Choral Journal, Clavier, English Dance and Song, Fono Forum, Gramophone, Harpsichord, Hi-Fi News and Record Review, High Fidelity* and *Musical America, Hillandale News, Jazz Hot, Jazz Journal, Monthly Letter, Music in Education, Musica e Dischi, Opera Canada, Record Retailer, Record World, Rolling Stone, Sing Out!, Sound and Picture Tape Recording Magazine, Stereo Review, Storyville,* and *Views and Reviews Magazine.*

The Trade Service Publications, Incorporated, supplied courtesy subscriptions to *Phonolog Reporter* and *List-O-Tapes* services, and Ivan March donated copies of the Long-Playing Record Library publication, *The Stereo Record Guide.*

To Denise Dunn and Gwenyth Zilm, former graduate students at the Faculty of Library Science, University of Toronto, and Philip Casey, graduate student at the School of Library and Information Science, State University of New York at Albany, who confirmed timings, proofread, and offered valuable suggestions and criticism, I am grateful.

Contributions of the above and unnamed others permitted this work to reach completion.

Rachel, Gabriela, Pat, and Willy merit especial appreciation for their patience during a season of unflown kites, untrained grapes, and unflung bones.

Music, Education, and Recordings

In this chapter a synopsis of the history of Western music, an analysis of the role of appreciation in the schools, and description of different ways in which the challenge of selection may be met are offered to form a backdrop for what follows in the remainder of this guide.

Western Music

The past three hundred years has seen fundamental changes in the content and purpose of European and American music. Audience, composer, performer relationships, and attitudes have been drastically altered since an earlier time when compositions could be immediately recognized as being either in a folk or serious idiom. Until the nineteenth century, *all* written scores had been "classical." "Popular" music came in when a leisurely Victorian era permitted the bourgeoisie to indulge in artistic pastimes. For the first time, the fashionable and playful could compete with solid, fortifying church music.

Today, as the advent of recorded sound nears its centenary, the acquisition of audio recordings and high-fidelity equipment has billowed into a conspicuous consumption phenomenon on a par with the big car and swimming pool affluence test rituals of a previous decade. The two billion dollar market of recording consumers divides into strata. A vast majority of purchased discs and tapes are within the jazz, rock, folk, popular, country and western categories with less than 10 percent of total sales falling within the classical field. The genuine music lover who also buys discriminately in the upper-quality ranges represented in this book is almost as rare as the barking bird. Much more common are the various subspecies, such as the fancier of operatic and vocal rarities. A third large but unstable group straddles the serious and popular genres. This fad-conscious constituency is governed in its buying habits almost entirely by the endorsements of friends and leaders in its peer group. Young adults and members of the counterculture tend to adopt this pattern. Yet another segment of buyers gravitates to great music selections promoted on television or radio. These are the masterpieces which should be owned by all who aspire to life styles with a modicum of refinement. The Mozart *Requiem* and Brahms' set

of four symphonies, the *Rasumovsky* Quartets and *Firebird, La Mer*, and the *Brandenburgs* would be placed on any such list. Record clubs often advertise these keys to the kingdom of civilized taste.

Other strictly nonmusical factors which influence buyers are performer name, dazzling sonics, and commercial propaganda. Purchasers of "anything by Ozawa," quadraphonic versions of the *1812* Overture with added cannons, brass bands, choirs and cathedral bells, and the "Greatest Hits of ———" are exhibiting this form of behavior. There is little doubt that those who take a liking to classical music first heard on sound tracks of motion picture films are advanced beyond this automatic reflex reaction. Even if the original scores have been inflated by arrangers and united with irrelevant imagery, the customers are exercising critical muscle. A milestone on the road to appreciation has been reached. In our time this road is unsafe because culture, consumerism, and technology vie with one another for a claim upon our being. This welter of production and audience values did not exist before this century.

In Mozart's time, a music appreciator was either a member of the church congregation or the court. Composers and performers were shadowy figures, not artists but artisans. With Beethoven came the sudden awareness of the composer's personality. Beethoven cracked the classical glaze and brought in the hot wind of human affairs. It was not very long before grief, exaltation, unrequited love, domestic bliss, personal philosophies, and patriotic fervor were aired in public.

Ironically, as composers gained psychological freedom their audiences lost their physical freedom. During the earliest periods of its development, *all* music had been communal, contemporary, religious, or personally expressive. The dance had been predominant in initial Western civilizations in Asia, Africa, and ancient Greece. Attendance at the symphony or chamber concert as we practice it is a horribly confining and unnatural experience, a denial by the dead hand of formality of the expressive use of our bodies. The idea of people paying for the privilege of sitting solemnly in tiers like banks of artificial flowers at a funeral to listen to music out of the past would have bemused a William Byrd or Palestrina. They would have expected us to produce our own music and use it to celebrate our homage to God.

During the nineteenth century, as the concert audiences became larger, more heterogeneous and less discriminating, they paid for and demanded a show for their money. Two-thousand voice choirs, virtuosi who played their instruments in inverted positions, live ammunition and bells for the *1812* Overture, and multimedia spectaculars became popular. In 1911, Alexander Scriabin's *A Poem of Fire* included a color keyboard to project changing hues to go with the shifting musical moods. Two years later, Arnold Schoenberg, in his frenetic monodrama *Die Glückliche Hand*, scored a coordinated orchestral and color crescendo. As the orchestral sound broadened and intensified, a red-brown-green-purple sequence of projected lights provided synchronized heightening of the emotional crises in the music. After Schoenberg came the other innovators with silent music, modified and electronic instruments, toy machine guns and radios, nude cellists in cellophane wrappers, and ever more radical experimentation with players, audiences, and instruments. To escort and ornament these works, the composers have donated written and verbal tattoos of playful and pompous polemics.

2

Four kinds of composers are writing music today. There are the isolated academic theoreticians whose scores impress those familiar with esoteric techniques but whose music means little to those not in the inner circle. At the other extreme, there are the slick writers who confirm a barrenness of imagination and disdainful view of their audience by offering up facile and empty technical displays with carefully plotted emotional prescriptions. Much Soviet music is like this. And there are the snake-oil salesmen who lure us with "innovative" collateral and slight of hand to compensate for a lack of technical facility and creativity. Finally, if one listens intently, one may hear a genuine spokesman of the art.

Critics and our own good sense are the best guides through this musical rogues' gallery. There is no *sure* passage and the first meeting with any new piece, be it significant or not, is generally uncomfortable. We are like spies dropped onto alien land where the speech is strange. We must work quickly to decipher the language as we wish neither to remain ignorant nor to waste time decoding banalities or nonsense before being whisked away. If frustration forces premature indifference, a message of vital importance may be missed because what appears to be empty or arbitrary cacophony might with patient exploration have disclosed an original or valuable communication.

Music which immediately reveals its charms, like a woman of easy virtue, usually lacks character. Charles Ives, the "George Washington of American music," correctly observed that "when a new or unfamiliar work is accepted as beautiful on its first hearing, its fundamental quality is one that tends to put the mind to sleep. A narcotic is not always unnecessary, but it is seldom a basis of progress—that is, wholesome evolution in any creative experience." Modern music no doubt has its many faceless opportunists who dole out the vulgar, meaningless, and narcotic. The listener's task is to bypass the sludge and tap the veins of superior musical imagination and uncompromised personal conviction. Speculation and mistakes are unavoidable in this drilling operation.

New works are necessary because the familiar and accustomed faces of even the masterpieces become exhausted clichés within the channels of remembrance and survive only because surrounding flood waters temporarily enshroud them and our responses are allowed to rest. Paradoxically we are later enabled to redeem and appreciate more deeply the very substance that had supposedly been swept away by the tide of change. This central artery, bequeathed by over two thousand years of skilled and inspired craftsmen may be senescent or it may be metamorphosing into a reconstituted essence. One hopes that the frantic chase after newly minted, "green" forms, modes, and materials for saltatory evolution has not precluded the gradual accumulation of changes capable of generating normal, organic growth by the main body.

During a brief three-year interval, 1937–39, the world witnessed premieres of Shostakovich's Fifth Symphony (1937); Kodály's *Peacock Variations* (1939); Stravinsky's *Jeu de Cartes* (1937); Walton's Violin Concerto (1939); Hindemith's *Nobilissima Visione* (1937); Bartók's Music for Strings, Percussion, and Celesta (1937), Sonata for Two Pianos and Percussion (1938), Violin Concerto (1939), and String Quartet no. 6 (1939); Vaughan Williams' *Riders to the Sea* (1937); Webern's Cantata, op. 29 (1939); Prokofiev's *Alexander Nevsky* (1939); Roy Harris' Third Symphony (1938); Charles Ives' *Concord*

Sonata (first performance in 1939); Copland's *Billy the Kid* (1938); Douglas Moore's *Devil and Daniel Webster* (1938); Piston's *Incredible Flutist* (1938); Marc Blitzstein's *The Cradle Will Rock* (1937); and Samuel Barber's Essay for Orchestra no. 1 and Adagio for Strings (both 1938).

From the 1940s until very recently, we have seen the continuing popularity of Stravinsky and firm establishment of Britten's skein of competently crafted compositions across all genres. But it is difficult to discern within the past quarter of a century any concentrations of works comparable to the 1937–39 and earlier twentieth century auroral displays. At this point in time, the many acclaimed masterpieces born during the past thirty years appear to have lacked the staying power possessed by their predecessors in the progression.

Our appreciative sensitivity may not be up to our intellectual pretensions or the music may be below both. Most likely the failure is in the social milieu. There has been no call for human justice and compassion to inspire artistic celebration within these years. Acceptance of indifference and inaction, despoilation of man and environment, may have encouraged creators' retreat from connectivity. History has demonstrated that whenever men have joined together in common causes resonated by universal aspirations (for example, countering the effects and assisting casualties of poverty, corrupt government, or natural disaster), artists and musicians *have* joined the crusades and spoken eloquently.

It is unfortunate that the new serious music is little played and dependent not upon the public's good will or enjoyment but upon sponsorship by the academy. The captive audience of our age has become an elitist caste which thrives upon separatism and isolation. The outer world of musicmaking remains untouched and is antagonistic to the avant-garde enclave. The symphony orchestras and other performing groups, the pianists, and touring and recording artists have detached themselves from the current composers who have in turn ceased to write for the usual concert media. A modus vivendi must be fashioned or musical organizations may become museums for reconstituting the past with sound recordings providing the only outlet for young writers.

Channels to the Love of Music

Music as a Form of Communication

Classical music in the Western tradition embodies three components: (1) structure, (2) tonal language, and (3) psychological value. The first measure of worth, structure, resides in the score. One may ask whether the notation is lodged in a tonal or atonal system with a musical dialectic, grammar, and syntax. Can one discern an organic unity of tempi; a cadential and rhythmic order? Is there conformity to compositional logic? Without a coherent system of harmonic, contrapuntal, and rhythmic elements; without an organized body composed of mutually connected parts, there can be no lasting value. However, structure in itself is no guarantee of musical power. For example, Mussorgsky is an exception to this rule, *Boris Godounov*, *Nursery*, and *Songs and Dances of Death* drawing most of their strength from the other two sectors.

A second value determinant is tonal language. If a work has a simple, transparent, universally understood vocabulary, its innovative importance will be very small but its musical significance or impact may be major. Stamitz, Telemann, and most of the music piped into offices and supermarkets is at the primary language level. The Rolling Stones, Ravel's *Boléro*, and Carl Orff's *Carmina Burana* are sure audience pleasers because their simple and comfortable idioms do not impede their considerable psychological wallop.

Whenever a piece resists our comprehension, there may be one of three causes for the communication block. The composer may have renovated a universally comprehended form. Mozart and Beethoven did this to the symphonic structure, their personal views being imprinted in careful evolutionary adjustments. The screen or comprehension shield erected by the extension and enrichment of existing vocabularies and grammars may be so transparent as to be barely perceptible while the psychological intensity of the music increases dramatically. With the late Beethoven and Elliott Carter quartets the screen is an opaque barrier for those unaccustomed to the composers' usage of the language. The audience must ingest a portion of this separator each time it rehears these "difficult" works. As the barrier is absorbed, the listener's interior vision is deepened. A third kind of language fence is interposed by the composer who is ahead of his time. In the sixteenth century, Gesualdo's futurism was premature and confused his audience. Therefore his advanced harmonic progressions, dissonances, tone colors, and chromaticism were shunted aside and not readmitted into service until Liszt and Wagner appropriated them for their escape from the framework of the symphonic form created by Joseph Haydn.

Music may also sound meaningless because it is meaningless. A composer's playfulness, indifference, dependence upon esoteric devices to camouflage incompetence, or psychological ailments may be responsible. In all of these instances, our repeated hearings will reduce unfamiliarity but cannot recompense us with added insight. We recognize the piece on the street but cannot summon up fondness for it. It may be that the composer is an avowed iconoclast like John Cage who seeks to shock, punish, or ridicule his listeners and their settled expectations. Cage has criticized Edgard Varèse, himself regarded as an important innovator, for being reluctant to treat sound as an abstracted, isolated phenomenon and for taking his audience seriously.

Beyond the domains of structure and tonal language, there lies the third and most vital zone of musical meaning; the psychic dimension. A piece with an adequate structure, transparent texture, attractive vocabulary, and pleasurable message will be certain of instantaneous success if it is given a dedicated reading. Whether the work endures in the repertory will depend upon the meanings behind its pleasant mask. The emotional efferent of sound flows directly into our conscious mind with no intervening particulate analysis. Message conduits to the human brain carry over one hundred times as much psychic voltage per second as they do cognitive bits of musical data (harmonic changes, shifts in instrumentation, dynamic variations, etc.) because only these latter structural identities must be sorted prior to registration at the brain's central desk. Therefore, the psychic dimension must become part of the performer or diminution and mutilation of a work's spirit will result.

Paradoxically, susceptibility to interpretive mangling decreases as a com-

poser's distinction of personality increases. Beethoven, Stravinsky, and Bach are less likely to be ruined by misinterpretation than lesser men because their technical control, clarity of language, and the bigness of their personalities cannot be disguised or bedimmed by the most inspired incompetence. At the other extreme, popular music and jazz are almost wholly dependent upon the performer for their success or failure. Their structure and vocabulary are far less crucial than the personality of the interpreter. The score is just a base camp for an improvizational journey. The language of jazz may be couched in an obscure tonal or atonal, or even aleatoric syntax but its basic code of communication remains more open and connotative than denotative or it fails. "Great" jazz recordings endure because of the personal insight creative performing artists breathe into often mediocre or maudlin notes and words. Serious music does not in similar fashion profit from personalization because the composer is the leading partner in the composer-performer team; the performer is only an executant and *re*-creative artist.

Although the running times of recorded Beethoven symphonies and piano sonatas vary in excess of 50 percent above and below a modal norm, and phrasing, dynamic, and internal tempo deviations increase this distance from the composer's conception, the term *faithful rendition* may be empirically demonstrated. As Ludwig Wittgenstein observed in his *Tractatus Logico-Philosophicus*, musical idea, score, interpretation of the musical idea, recording, and sound waves are derivations or projections of the singular personal energy of the creator. His manner of speaking or psychic radiation profile is as distinctive as a finger or voice print. In Beethoven's case, this ideational impulse is so pungent that artistic miscalculation becomes immediately apparent. An accustomed listener unerringly identifies which three among thirty Fifth Symphony recordings ring true and the great interpreters, notably Toscanini, sustain preternaturally uniform tempi throughout their concert careers with running times varying less than 1 percent across a span of hundreds of performances. Manfred Clynes' hypothesis that proximity to the inner pulse of an original work can be measured may be confirmed in future experiments. According to Clynes, all of a composer's works exhibit in performance a consistent pulse pattern measurable by a computer of average transients (CAT), a sophisticated device analogous to the EKG. He found that the pulse pattern exhibited by a pianist performing early, middle, or late Beethoven remains identical.

> According to Clynes, the consistency of the inner pulse form for a particular composer is not simply the result of tradition or style. "Mozart and Haydn have very different pulse forms," says Clynes. "So have Debussy and Ravel." Clynes himself has difficulty explaining the phenomenon. He speculates that each composer has somehow translated a characteristic brain program into an arrangement of sounds and silences for which the standard musical notation is only a rough approximation. Through some manner not yet understood the sensitive performer grasps this implicit brain program and is able to re-create it so that the sensitive listener says, "Yes, that is Mozart."[1]

1. Gerald Jonas, "Manfred Clynes and the Science of Sentics," *Saturday Review* 55:51 (May 13, 1973).

If indeed the Clynes argument could be substantiated, the tired dispute between those who uphold a performer's right to tailor scores to suit the times and his own feelings, and those who believe in definitive renditions might be resolved in favor of the "purists." In this author's opinion, the three components of music's value are an organically unified taxonomy. Structure, tonal language, and psychological wealth represent a rising succession of value and without power in the uppermost sector a piece cannot achieve greatness. Arnold Schoenberg, Paul Hindemith, Béla Bartók, and Wolfgang Amadeus Mozart each reveal a differing contour of strengths and weaknesses to illustrate this definition.

Schoenberg's post World War I atonal compositions move rapidly and provide so few clues for the listener that their irreproachable structural integrity remains undisclosed to persons unfamiliar with serial language or the scores. Only those who can trace the threads of sound as they turn tail, invert themselves, change speed, and rub against each other, can appreciate his music. These works resemble architecture and sculpture; they must be *seen* to be structurally comprehended. In Schoenberg's second sector, the listener is frustrated by arbitrary and unnatural language. However, because of his mordant personality, the insistent dissonance and frantic linear motion establish a mood of hysterical urgency. I have never found Schoenberg's music aseptic or neutral. Unlike the contrived works of his disciples and some of the later total serialists, his music invariably contains a few ounces of overpowering egoistic essence. One can hear Schoenberg the sorcerer wresting control of the magical broom from the apprentice for a few sweeps of his own.

Hindemith's music provides an instructive counterexample. His work abides by orderly and genial conventions of the past, logically extended into the twentieth century, but his convictions and spirit are not attuned to our times. The structure is compatible with the demands of the human ear and chordal tensions and resolutions are plotted out to satisfy listeners' auditory and dramatic expectations. Though his compositional logic and tonal vocabulary yield their secrets to the attentive, Hindemith has not maintained his position as a favored modernist. As Howard Hanson is a teetotaler's Sibelius, so Hindemith lacks the personal heat, tensile strength, and charm of Johannes Brahms, a composer who had a similar high regard for the craft of composition. It is regrettable that the muted lyricism, simplicity, economy of means, and wholesomeness of Hindemith's later works, especially the requiem *When Lilacs Last in the Dooryard Bloom'd*, has been unappreciated in the years after his death. Perhaps this has happened to his better works because so much of his remaining output of strictly systematized compositions is dryly impersonal and denies us the insight and warmth we seek.

In Bartók and Mozart, the three values we have been discussing approach perfect apportionment and calibration. Mozart's voice and style were fully formed during his childhood and, within a serene classical mold, his music gathered strength. It was not necessary to develop novel structures and harmonies to personify his thought. Bartók, in contrast, began his career in a milieu which venerated Lisztian fireworks and grandiloquence. In the sequence of Bartók's works there is a gradual disentanglement from cheap rhetoric and clichés, the lush and loose-jointed early pieces bearing little likeness to those of his maturity. Bartók's analyses of Hungarian, Serbo-Croatian, and Romanian

folk music, painstakingly transcribed from recordings made during his visits to peasant villages, were infused into the mellow, highly refined writing of the last decade of his life. Rhythmic vigor, terseness and humor; the modal freedom of the folk song were alchemized into a creative outpouring which culminated in the final three string quartets, Music for Strings, Percussion, and Celesta, Concerto no. 3 for Piano, Sonata for Two Pianos and Percussion, and popular Concerto for Orchestra. Unlike Schoenberg, Bartók did not feel that it was necessary to frame legislation to cradle and control the flow of his ideas. Technique and style were freed to evolve in a sustained ascending arc, each work attaining a higher degree of artistic excellence than its predecessor.

In Mozart, we confront a miracle of human accomplishment. Structure, musical grammar, existential intimations are unified from the onset and his sounds are those of a celestial lute.

> Whenever Mozart is serious—and music is to him the only serious affair in life—he speaks no dialect, only the purest language in the world. It is no Esperanto, no international speech-currency. It is Mozartian language—the clearest, brightest, most transparent speech in the music of the second half of the eighteenth century, distilled from a myriad of sounds, conceived by the finest ear and the most critical taste that is recorded in the entire history of music. It is, to use a favorite expression of Goethe's from the realm of alchemy, "cohobated" music.[2]

In summary, as one listens to recordings of music by these four composers or any others, a fair criticism and response should take into account the above delineated factors. It is suggested here that great works, because of their integrity and elegance of fabrication will intrigue the intellect no matter how often they are heard. These works are also based upon the Pythagorean or some other tonal system which provides a functional musical dialect. And above all, the personal belief of the composer must be revealed and this revelation should add to our sense of the universe. Any patient listener can tell the difference between a composer who has something deep-reaching to share and a composer whose statements are juiced with nice sentiments but thin and not fully alive. All music has two psychological layers—a pretty, superficially attractive epidermis and beyond this, an inner skin. The masterpiece has recesses which carry unfathomable meanings. One never wholly penetrates nor comprehends and it continues to mean different things to different people. Great music inspires hidden being and points, across and beyond local conventions of individuals and groups towards an attainable possibility. Such music can be a lodestar of human ethical conduct.

Music Education, U.S.A.

Without an apostolate of lobbyists who know and respect the intrinsic validity and powers of the beauteous, good music would lose its tenure in our

---

2. Alfred Einstein, *Greatness in Music* (New York: Oxford Univ. Pr., 1941), p. 28.

society. Music appreciation is an American invention, an attempt to compensate for cultural lag. The moderately well-off, European man-in-the-street can immediately recognize important composers of his country if he hears them on the radio, television, or in live performance; an American with equivalent education and means cannot claim this ability. Elliott Carter, Charles Ives, and George Crumb may be prominent but they are not household names at any level of our society. We remain hostile or deaf to good music because it has been apologetically and obliquely dealt with by our public schools. Current musicals and sentimental favorites monopolize the secondary school calendar of events while serious music remains in penumbra. In the elementary school only about 100 minutes a day are committed to academic instruction. Language development, mathematics, science, and art consume all save a few seconds of this time. Unless a district is adequately staffed with music specialists and its library media centers stocked with sound recordings, the incidence of contact with good music must be negligible.

American civilization is engaged to the practical and immediate; our affiliation with the aesthetic has been intermittent and diffused. The Puritans and Horace Mann added music to the school program primarily because of its salutary value. In the mid-nineteenth century singing was prescribed as preventive medicine because it stimulated the circulation and purified the blood, aided digestion and combatted tuberculosis by increasing resistance to infection. A second dividend was promised by the transfer theorists who predicted that music's harmonic relations and progressions, its mathematical elements would somehow enhance the child's sense of structure and order. Mastery of arithmetic, algebra, and geometry would be a less arduous experience. Overriding these arguments was the expectation that music would act as a moral leaven. Here was an inexpensive counter to youth's bad manners and incontinence. Classroom discipline and esprit de corps would benefit by the singing of simple folk songs and patriotic music, and the cost to the public would be negligible because neither instruments nor skilled performers would be needed.

To this day progressive educators have continued to stress the socialization function of music to the extreme that *any* musical doing has been deemed superior to inaction. Here we have an aberrant oversimplification because John Dewey had never accepted, as have so many of his disciples, indiscriminate doing as being any more than the yeast to start artistic accomplishment. Children do not intuit a priori that which is best for them aesthetically any better than they select nutritious food if left on their own. As they have no homing instinct to direct them to that which is worth hearing, adults must assist and monitor each child's experimentation. Teacher and parent must by their own celebration of the connections between life and art serve as magnetic conductors. Only then is it possible for them to help the child progress beyond trivial poking, blowing, and strumming and towards an enlargement of his sensibility and humanity.

Another disservice to music has accrued from educators' ambitious attempt to interrelate disciplines. In the humanities this may create more problems than it solves when applied to evolution of the arts. Raphael and Mozart, Michelangelo and Beethoven, though three centuries distant from each other, are comparable in scale and style. Bach's baroque masterpieces were performed in Balthazar Neumann's effusively rococo church; Michelangelo was a con-

temporary of Lassus, Victoria, and Palestrina but his technique and breadth of expression are more closely approximated in Beethoven. Music has generally lagged two centuries behind the plastic and graphic arts and it takes a teacher of uncommon ability to illumine the crosshatching of political movements, scientific invention, and events in the humanities. And a teacher's ability to verbalize about Beethoven and Napoleon or Michelangelo and Pope Julius may be irrelevant because awareness of an artist's place in history does not advance appreciation of the content and expressive power of the sound or sight of his creations. Rarely do descriptive data and blueprints, pedigrees, and secondhand evidence move people to accept or reject houses, dogs, or friends. So it is with music. Personal hearing is the convincing proof.

Worst of the offenses perpetrated by the old-time music education was its disproportionate emphasis upon children's technical prowess. The enticement of public relations puffs led music supervisors to plan their programs around razzle dazzle display pieces requiring the least possible rehearsal time. Precision and dexterity were falsely equated with musical accomplishment so that much of this activity became spiritless drill. Youngsters became so engrossed with coordination and control that they began to perform like prisoners eating by the numbers (four steps from plate to mouth, four steps from mouth to plate . . .) in a fine restaurant. The mechanical action had become more important than the meal. Children are ripe for such exploitation because the gap between their ability to perform and ability to experience widens as they move through adolescence, motor skills moving far in advance of musicality. As soon as exterior motivation is removed these youngsters drop out without being touched by new musical insights.

Infatuation with competitive cultural events has lessened but not vanished because the American school still emulates industry. Europe has modeled its schools after the garden or farm, environments which foster organic growth; America has copied the factory operation. Efficiency, accountability, cost effectiveness, criterion-based performance; the terminology of business management has been affectionately embraced by boards of education and teacher-training institutions.

In summary, music education has been hampered by three energizers of our society: scientism, materialism, and activism. The disdain of ontology and axiology, the excessive concern with prospects and challenges, and the absence of cultural ambience in our history have made it difficult for good music to find a place in the daily lives of our children. That this is about to change is obvious because the energizers must soon be modified or replaced. Benjamin Franklin's classic suggestion that schools concentrate upon science, history, and physical education and build the traits of ingenuity, humor, and industry has become glaringly deficient in the twentieth century. Enlightened self-interest has been magnified into corporate greed and the attitudes and platitudes of colonial America won't work anymore because the characteristics of agrarian society have been literally turned upside down. Underpopulation, manpower deficiencies, a scale which allowed any poor but honest person to attain political leadership, unlimited opportunity—these descriptions and a simplistic "world beater" philosophy of education have become dangerously anachronistic. The harbingers of change are on the horizon because the financing of music education has proportionately increased as private and government sup-

port for the arts has expanded during the recent recession. This has occurred despite a deceleration of total educational expenditures. A new era of intrinsic education which will place creativity, art, the dance, and music within or close to its curricular core may be near at hand.

Pathways to Appreciation

Music will make a permanent imprint upon a child's consciousness only if most of the following conditions are met: (1) The quality of the music should be good; (2) the performance should achieve the technical and inspirational standard established for the adult audience; (3) the program should be appropriate for young listeners; (4) the environment should be congenial; (5) friends and adults should approve and reinforce the listening habit; and (6) easily available and inexpensive contact with fine music should become an ordinary element in the child's daily life. These conditions all affect the germination probability. Table 1 illustrates three hypothetical "seeding" operations in which a ten-year-old is introduced to music. The exposures are to (1) a live performance during school hours, (2) a disc jockey promotion on the radio during his free time, and (3) a movie in which music is used in conjunction with animation. Adequacy of the music and conditions for its acceptance are quantified on a 5-point scale for each situation. A "5" signifies the ideal; a "1" the lowest rating. For illustrative purposes, a total of 18 points has been set as the minimum required for the music to "stay" with the child.

Table 1. Conditional Factors and Music Appreciation

Musical title	Brahms Symphony no. 4, Scherzo	Popular hit	Tchaikovsky, "Nutcracker Suite"
Listening location	Concert hall	Home or street	Movie theater
Listening source	Live performance	Radio	Soundtrack

Conditional Factor	Factor Weights		
Quality of music	4	1	3
Performance quality	3	3	4
Program accessibility	4	5	5
Environment congeniality	1	3	4
Reinforcement probability	1	5	3
Ease of availability	2	5	3
Total Factor Weights	15	22	22

NOTE: Factor weights indicate following conditions: 1 = very poor, 2 = inferior, 3 = adequate, 4 = good, 5 = excellent

11

In the first example, the child is taken to the concert hall as part of the school's cultural uplift program. After the visitors have settled down, a master of ceremonies begins an informal dialogue. Functions of the concert master, conductor, and families of instruments, basic musical forms, and biographical sketches are gone over with the audience. Then a series of short selections and excerpts are presented by the orchestra, usually with the lights left on. Finally the flock files out. The program is well selected and the performance is adequate though lacking the customary bloom and bite one associates with the orchestra's playing. A second-string conductor who underestimates the critical capacity of the children may be responsible for the perfunctory interpretations. The elimination of the concert ritual trivializes the event so that bus trip, hall, and the master of ceremonies' forced jollity become the high points in memory.

The fifth condition, reinforcement, will probably be absent in the child's post-concert environment because the likelihood that parents, teachers, and friends will contribute additional exposure to Brahms is remote. The outlook for on-demand availability of good music is similarly dim. If the child's family doesn't already have discriminating taste, the commercial media and a musically barren home environment will soon dry out his desire to hear more good music. Commercial and educational television provide debased and feeble fare. Although some television graphics have become tasteful and imaginative, music has remained a shabby Cinderella being called upon merely to establish moods and neglected as an independent art. Parents have removed themselves from their children's cultural life and the schools, commercial media, and friends in the same age group (the most influential force) have by default assumed the responsibility for taste cultivation. In Japan, a father or mother often learns to play an instrument with a child. In the United States, the Suzuki method's failure to attract a larger following than it has can be ascribed to parental reluctance to participate in the learning process. Sissifying connotations and fear of appearing clumsy have inhibited many. Jack Benny's self-deprecatory scraping has been a mirror of national opinion on the subject of serious music-making and those in high places in our government have seldom been cultural leaders. Thomas Jefferson was the last public official to play an instrument tolerably well and the presidential taste has never risen above fondness for the sentimental or stirring, for example, *Home on the Range* and Sousa marches, the *Missouri Waltz*, *Oh Promise Me*, and *The Rosary*, *Victory at Sea*, and the *Warsaw* Concerto.

Returning to Table 1, a total of 15 points is the estimate of the "taking" potential of the Brahms Symphony no. 4 Scherzo heard in the concert hall. As this is below the 18-point arbitrary minimum requirement, the Brahms has failed the test.

The next example illustrates the common experience of children and adolescents in our culture. Popular music is recorded, ruthlessly promoted, and highlighted on the radio. The music may be execrable but direct exploitation of trite sentiments and insistent repetition insure its success. The performance is up to the requirements of the audience and music, and the environment rates a "3" in spite of the inferior sonics of transistor radios because the listener is not restricted by the behavioral code of the concert hall. Friend and adult approval is a near certainty and follow-up reinforcement is inescapable

because of the cashbox mentality and promotional efficiency of the commercial music business. Blessed with these advantages, such music stakes its claim to a front row seat in the child's mind.

The third situation succeeds for different reasons. Here the child peripherally encounters the music while sitting through the Disney-Stokowski *Fantasia* with its pastorale symphony prettified by bowdlerized nymphs and satyrs cavorting in a pastel Arcadia. Sometimes, given this confectionary coating, even the Beethoven sticks, while Mussorgsky's *Night on Bald Mountain*, Tchaikovsky's *Sugar Plum Fairy*, and Dukas' *Sorcerer's Apprentice* almost always persist in the memory. The Saturday afternoon occasion is comfortable; popcorn, squirming, and chatter are tolerated. *Fantasia* is wholesome entertainment and has brought these favorites of the concert hall to a much wider audience than could have otherwise been possible. It reappears periodically and continues to attract new "camp" followers a quarter of a century after its premiere.

Teachers and parents may improve children's aesthetic chances by concentrating upon the first four of the above illustrated conditions, those within their sphere of influence. Alteration of the remaining two is a desirable, long-range hope. School and home should encourage independence and individuality in taste formation and assist the child's progress up the ladder of musical skills and understandings. The gifted child does not concern us here; we are describing the youngster with usual rather than exceptional genetic and environmental advantages. From early childhood up to age seven or eight, rhythmic movement and manipulation of a wide variety of percussion, woodwind and other instruments, simple singing and mimicry are the vehicles of activity. The aim, during this formative stage, is to direct energy so that it becomes consciously musical. Otherwise, it will remain a predominantly kinetic rather than aesthetic form of motion. By the time a child is eight, he should have acquired basic listening skills. He should be able to identify the difference between chordal and scalar patterns; he should be able to hear doubled and halved tempi in relation to a basic rhythmic pulse, discern the difference between a faulty and musically satisfying accompaniment, and recognize fundamental forms such as the simple song and minuet. Common orchestral instruments and the ranges of the human voice should be identifiable by name. If a child has these skills, the elementary level titles with access ratings of "1" and "2" in chapter 2 will be comprehensible and enjoyable because of their straightforward and attractive melodic, rhythmic, harmonic, orchestral, and stylistic features.

At the secondary level, music should receive as much academic attention as prose, poetry, and the visual arts. If Shakespeare, Goethe, Melville, Robert Penn Warren, Steinbeck, Berryman, and Proust are required reading, Mozart, Beethoven, Ives, Carter and Copland, Crumb, and Debussy should be required listening. They are not, and the sciences, social studies, and literature are stressed much more than music. This difference in emphasis should narrow as the curriculum designers reshape schools' programs to fit contemporary societal needs. Though proficiency in music does not by some miraculous osmosis confer upon the learner a better command of mathematics, the two disciplines have a kinship. Both have symbolic notations and the physical phenomena of periodicity, frequency, harmonic motion are implicitly respected

in any musical score. The compositions of Mozart and Stravinsky are in their seeming simplicity and inspired logic like elegant mathematical proofs. As it is with mathematical statements, so it is with music; compositions with abstruse textures will not yield their secrets to quick inspection. Stravinsky's Symphony of Psalms, Mussorgsky's *Boris Godounov*, Beethoven's String Quartet no. 14 in c sharp, op. 131, and Palestrina's *Missa Papae Marcellus* are masterpieces which require an intense concentration. Orff's *Carmina Burana*, Leoncavallo's *Pagliacci*, Grieg's *Peer Gynt* Suite, and most of Telemann's works though much more elementary and approachable, lack the ontological weight of the first group of titles. Introduction to the more inaccessible works should take place only after the teenager has begun to comprehend and enjoy the more easily assimilated works, those assigned a "1" or "2" access rating in chapter 2. During this stage it is difficult for adults with firmly rooted tastes to act in a manner that is unpatronizing, that mutes the sharpness of their own convictions without compromising their honesty, and that keeps the lines of communication between the generations open. The best they can do is offer clues, suggestions, and a personal example so that the adolescent may be environmentally stimulated to make his way out of the stultifying mire of most popular culture as he merges into adulthood. The aim is to advance freedom of aesthetic choice, to allow an authentic taste, truly of his own making, to take its form and enrich his living.

As there is an enormous repertory of sound recordings of good music congenial to any normal child or teenager, its absence from the home, schools, or library is inexcusable. To keep out meaningful music is to add to the shrinkage of human worth already accomplished by mechanization, noise, and defilement of the natural environment. Taste has an outer boundary which changes with age like a naturally supple elastic; it may be stretched to enclose more if treated with a gentle, firm, and competent hand. Young people are slow to accept delayed gratification by the less than obvious. And great music never grants immediate satisfaction. One cannot appreciate the development of sections of a Beethoven symphony until a proprietary curiosity is awakened, a tie is formed with the fortunes of themes as they define themselves, develop, mix with other themes, and travel towards their destiny.

One involves oneself with the musical event or misses the composer's message. The Bach Mass in b is deeply religious, the adagio of Beethoven's Ninth Symphony and last movement of Bartók's Sixth String Quartet are mystical revelations, Charles Ives' Fourth Symphony is quintessentially American, and Sibelius' symphonies are steeped in the Finnish landscape. It is within a composer's power to communicate meaning and being that elude normal descriptive language because music is not the literal transcription of thought. Music differs from all the other arts in that it does not copy observed phenomena. The listener who rejects Stravinsky, Beethoven, or Mozart is rejecting a man rather than misreading a musical language. With justification, Sir Thomas Beecham has claimed that the man who has never heard Mozart deserves pity but the man who knows Mozart and dislikes him deserves our contempt. It is foolish to expect that Beethoven's affirmation of human dignity and freedom will ever be heard by those for whom such issues are irrelevant or trivial. Conversely, Beethoven's transmission of what is essentially the spirit of the Kantian categorical imperative can reach many who have not fathomed the

14

nettlesome prose of Kant's philosophical treatises. Interpreted in this way music can be identified as an indirect, auxiliary form of education.

The appreciation of music develops a courageous attitude because it is the sharing of a composer's bravery in forsaking the safety of stale formulas and the commonplace. The listener learns how to accept the uneasiness that can come from making up his own mind and develops the self-confidence to renounce the apish phoniness of popular, commercial music. Exposure to the best of human creations is not the imposition of a strait jacket; it is an invitation. Although this may not mean the exclusion of rock and popular music, it does mean that the Mount Everests of the musical art must be brought to young listeners in the school and home so that they do not remain isolated in self-satisfied ignorance. As explorers, they may observe the lesser landmarks, move into exotic regions, develop a reliable and enriching personal taste only after having been introduced to the complete map of music. To distort this global geography by offering children junior versions of classical music or to ignore its existence is to derogate adult responsibility and block the free flow of cultural information. Though the bromide that one must "start where the children are" is sensible (what else can one do?), too many of us also *stop* at this same point because of insecurity, prejudice, or want of knowledge. After a connection with simple but beautiful music is established, the movement towards more challenging music, particularly the masterpieces, should proceed. A knowledge of great music, an awareness of the conditions necessary for its appreciation, a consistent plan for guiding and encouraging learners—these are required of anyone who would lead a child to the love of music.

Sound Recordings

Value and Use

In the history of human communications technology, the invention of the sound recording was comparable to that of the printing press. It permitted man to preserve sonic events and legendary performances within a physical form just as the printing press had five centuries earlier allowed him to transform handwritten and oral tradition into typeset. The owner of a recording has at his disposal a slice of significant time which he may consult almost as conveniently as an edition of a printed work. For today's composers of revolutionary and bewildering scores which require unusual skills or large numbers of performers for their execution, the recording has become an insurance policy, a secondary defense against oblivion. Much of the contemporary music literature had not been heard by the general public before 1950, the time of the 33–⅓ r.p.m. long-playing record's initial penetration into the market. Before World War II, one very rarely ran into recordings of new music so that producing composers had a small, select audience. One spent the time and money to attend the annual meetings of the International Society for Contemporary Music, lived in New York City, Los Angeles, Paris, or one of the other few large metropolitan areas where such music was premiered, or

missed out. Even the professional musicians, with the exception of those associated with innovative performing organizations or conservatories, had no contact with ongoing trends in twentieth century composition.

To its credit, the sound recording industry has multiplied at least one-hundred fold the young composer's opportunity to reach new listeners. Like the internal combustion engine, telephone, and book, the recording lost its innocence as soon as it became a marketplace commodity. Recorded music has become either a nuisance, necessity, or nicety for most of us. Greed and creativity, technology, and human need have contended with each other here as they have in the automotive and garment industries. Some companies conscientiously cater to general or special tastes while others create with clever advertising artificial needs. New machines, speeds, and novel formats may constitute genuine technological breakthroughs or they may be strategems to stimulate more sales. However, aside from these suspicions about industrial ethics, there still remain shortcomings of the medium which require attention.

Canned music's predictability, the lack of audience-performer interaction, and the depreciation of live musicianship are the three most commonly cited negative aspects. The recorded performance *is* unchanging and the pleasures of discovery dim after the first hearings. Repeated exposure to interpretation of any exciting work will lessen its detonative charge. The romantic composer wrote scores which combine dramatic and musical impact. Beethoven owes his immense popularity to his ability to rivet any new listener's attention to a series of musical events which are simultaneously unexpected and inevitable. The shifts in the relative security of our anticipations are as important as the logic of the underlying harmony and counterpoint. This persuasive power disappears as we repeatedly encounter the same piece unless its notes convey a universality of meaning or formal logic which commands our spirit even after we know the plot by heart. Lacking a firm structural foundation, most romantic orchestral pieces pall after only a few hearings. Recordings compound this depreciation of interest because they limit one to the accents and nuances of a single performance to which the listener may become fanatically loyal to the extreme of rejecting all other versions. Mozart's music along with that of Vivaldi, Bach, and Haydn remains relatively impervious to this kind of response because self-expression is restrained by stringent rules of craftsmanship. These composers were celebrants and sounding boards of God's world. In a reverse frame of reference, Beethoven, Mahler, Wagner, and Schoenberg saw themselves as creators for whom craftsmanship was subordinate to self-expression. For this reason the latter are seldom selected for background music. The baroque, classical, and impressionist composers are more suitable for conditioning the tedium and pain of household chores, driving, and the dentist's drill because their works are discreet and don't have the "heart on the sleeve" heroics of Tchaikovsky, Mahler, or Berlioz who leap upon the listener like affectionate collies. The earlier writers wear well if listened to attentively or if only sensed as audio wallpaper.

Although repeatability is an asset for classical and baroque music, it has become a necessity for most modern music. Economy of means, understatement, avoidance of redundancy characterize the new works and the composers express themselves in cryptic languages which may be puzzling to unfamiliar listeners. During live performance the score flashes by like a fast freight train

and even though conductors and performers may repeat particularly perplexing pieces, this courtesy is no more helpful than an instant replay (without the assistance of the sports commentator) of a complicated football pattern for the person who knows neither players, positions, nor the rules of the game. Multiple hearings of new music are often necessary before one may fairly assess its form, style, and inner essence, and sound recordings grant us as many reruns as we need at very low cost.

Sound recordings also greatly enlarge the musical power of the classroom teacher. Fumbling or strained misrepresentations of good music or, worse yet, the playing of prosaic pieces written for the unaccomplished teacher-pianist cannot compete with fine recorded renditions of Ravel, Bartók, Chopin, Grieg, and Kabalevsky. With historically important figures be they political or artistic, vocal inflections add immeasurably to our insight. Musician, poet, and statesman are revealed in the round only after one has sensed their individual sound. The dynamism and hypnotic force of a Toscanini, Landowska, and Casals; Sandburg, Dylan Thomas, and Martin Luther King; Hitler, Roosevelt, or Churchill cannot be believed until one has witnessed with one's ears their persuasion. The sound recording extends this recapture privilege on an egalitarian basis. The high price of admission to the concert hall, exclusion by cliques, geographical isolation from live performances, sickness, inclement weather, and unavailable babysitters no longer cut off access to the very best listening. The predictability and constancy of the sound recording is a virtue when viewed in this light.

A second complaint about the recording is its mechanical and unresponsive nature. As the performing arts depend upon a dialogue between entertainers and entertained, this is a threatening objection. Fortunately it is not entirely valid because of the special conditions which attach to the production of an audio-recording. The performer's self-evaluation prior to the release of the tape, the response of those present during the recording sessions, and the reviewers insure that no artist can become insulated from his audience for very long and survive. Even though the immediacy and ambience associated with the live performance are lost, an enormous outer audience is gained by the recording artist. If he takes this route he saves himself countless harassments. He does not have to contend with booking agencies, program managers and PR-minded impresarios, union restrictions, out-of-tune pianos, musical politics, poor acoustics, foul weather, or transportation breakdowns. Glenn Gould, a pianist who has put on record conspicuously fine Bach and Schoenberg performances, has forsaken the concert circuit to concentrate upon refinement and extension of his recorded repertory. So much satisfaction has come from his being able to perfect earlier interpretations and record neglected and new music; so much frustration had formerly stemmed from forced repetition of live audience favorites that the common platitude that mass reproduction deteriorates culture has been virtually stood on its head by Mr. Gould.

A related advantage should appeal to parents with active small children. Sound recordings are less physically restricting than books, television, or the concert hall because free movement is limited only by the range of the tape or record player's sound. Coordination with plays, physical exercise, and dancing; language self-instruction, familiarization of amateurs with professional performance models are among the many contexts of use. The exceptional,

convalescent, and retarded child can also benefit from hearing fine music. Clearly the values of machine-made sound depend upon our ingenuity and taste and any arbitrariness is of our own making.

This brings us to the third objection leveled against canned music, that it will discourage and ultimately displace human performance. There are those who predict that the conservatories will close, and chamber, opera, and symphonic groups will disappear by century's end with mechanical simulations replacing flesh and blood musicians. This is possible but very unlikely. Elitist groups will continue to seek ways in which to discriminate between those worthy of "club" membership and those "beyond the pale." Both sham and genuine connoisseurs in this upper stratum of society will retain one of their long-established public rites, going to concerts. Apart from this and common to all social classes, there is the human desire to gather together. Just as video tape cassettes viewed in the home cannot replace the crowd warmth or salubrious change of pace of the visit to the downtown movie theater, so recordings cannot completely satisfy the tastes of the dedicated music lover.

As we move further into a style of life which grants increased leisure and shortened work weeks, much of our effort to accumulate goods and services will be redirected towards a mastery of contemplative and creative skills. If a minimum income is legislated, lethargy and boredom, drug addiction and destructive behavior will surely rise to intolerable levels unless the population can develop more skills of artistic production and aesthetic appreciation. If educational leaders anticipate this change in the requirements of mature adulthood, serious musicians and other creative artists could once more find themselves in a healthy profession connected to the well-being of the general public.

Whether or not so-called high culture ever succeeds in overthrowing the dictatorship of popular culture, the artists will never be satisfied with merely meeting the inspirational and technical standards set by others. Pinnacles of pianistic and vocal achievement continually rise as do the Olympic records. Paderewski, Caruso, and Gieseking, though legends in their own times, have been bettered by Glenn Gould, Luciano Pavarotti, and Arturo Michelangeli, who, in turn, will be followed by others in the evolutionary cycle. It is evident that the sound recording, like the book, is only a product of human invention and that men, not their products, are the stimulators or inhibitors of artistic progress. To infer that the recording deters the development of musicianship makes as much sense as blaming droughts upon weather instruments because the rain will fall in its own time and the weatherman can do no more than attend and record the fact.

The recording is a marvelous mechanical handmaiden, a receptable and preserver of the ceremonials of human spirit and will. However, the very abundance of good music on tape and discs may have helped to diminish its appeal to the buyer. We know that earthquakes and epicurian feasts, memorable music and love-making have an effect upon those on the scene which weakens with expansion of temporal and sensual distance. Television, because it transmits images inexpensively and to a global audience, diminishes the significance of violence, space walks, and artistic expression. By imposing a singular perspective and commentary, it purblinds the individual's inner vision. Regardless of how one feels about the relative arbitrariness or dictatorial nature of media, it cannot be denied that the wide availability of performances

by Gieseking, Toscanini, and other great artists on cheap reissues has tended to deflate their marketplace value.

James Goodfriend, the discriminating and outspoken critic of *Stereo Review*, has suggested that classical music discs and tapes be issued in limited editions and the masters *destroyed!* Reduced availability would lift "landmark" recordings into the same category of object as limited editions of engravings and literary works. Therefore, a Picasso lithograph and a great recording of the past would be equally rare and cherished collectors' items. Museums of sound could be erected and the faithful invited to listen to legendary performers for a reasonable fee. The cost of the limited editions could be high enough to produce comfortable royalties for performer, producer, and composer. Classical music broadcasting would be prohibited and pirating vigorously prosecuted. Hopefully the attraction of pride of ownership of "original editions" would be stronger than the temptation to produce illegal makeshift tapes.

Although the Goodfriend proposal was considered quixotic and subversive by many of his readers, his suggestion makes sense if the appreciation of good music is indeed attainable by only a minute proportion of the population. As human potential is conditioned by environment and heredity, the proportion of the society that can enjoy good music may increase or decrease as we modify the quality and extent of growing children's musical surroundings. Proponents of extrinsic motivation and the status quo should like the Goodfriend proposal; those who believe that a higher order of environment can lift the level of mankind and that communication between man and the world is a dynamic and mutually lifting-lowering phenomenon will find this idea as repellent as Goodfriend did.

Selection

Most adults who listen with regularity to serious music have developed a selective taste. Typically they prefer music written between 1700 and 1900 and concentrate upon no more than two or three genres, for example, orchestral tone poems, concerti, and symphonies; chamber music; and art songs. Musically omniverous tastes are exhibited by teenagers but after this time of life, most of us tend to become less open in our aesthetic attitudes. We lose the elasticity and patience to come to terms with new music and we miss significant areas of earlier composers' contributions because of our exclusive attention to only a few musical forms. Schubert and Haydn, Beethoven and Britten, Stravinsky and Mozart have expressed themselves in vocal, instrumental, orchestral chamber pieces which as a totality provide the only fair hearing of each man's genius. It is a salutary experience to sharpen our awareness by noting composers' ways of handling the textures, tone colors, palette options afforded by different combinations of voices and instruments.

A successful collection needs sufficient forms, styles, and periods to supply it with body. Like a balanced ale, a collection should additionally have purity and flavor. "Purity" denotes in this context the exclusion of poor arrangements and distortions of Beethoven, Schubert, Mozart, Tchaikovsky, and other great composers especially produced at discount prices for the children's market. Though children respond according to their position on a maturity gradient, folk music preceding instrumental music, program music coming be-

fore abstract music, the obviously rhythmic pieces preceding the primarily melodic and more formal works, shorter preceding longer, there is no justification for not buying the very best interpretations of music within a child's reach. If symphonies cannot be absorbed by small children, it is still possible to play whole movements, for example, the Scherzo from Beethoven's Ninth Symphony and march movement from Tchaikovsky's *Pathétique*. Retardation of a child's development is accomplished by exposure to the coy and syrupy biographies in sound that have inundated public and school library collections. Once these inferior products find their foothold, buyers' and listeners' incentive to learn to like what they don't know is lost.

It is the selector's responsibility to seek out superior recordings and bring to an end the monopoly of shabbiness in most library sound recordings collections. In the pioneer days of the long-playing record industry, 1949–53, collectors had been able to rely upon the Columbia, RCA, Angel, and Deutsche Grammophon Gesellschaft classical divisions to provide an excellent miscellany of interpretations across all genres. Later, as the recording industry expanded into a massive business empire, the amenities of the small-scale enterprise were sacrificed. Inviting listening booths and knowledgeable sales personnel vanished. Supermarkets and department stores, discount houses and self-service outlets which now account for most sales do not have to personally assist customers to make a profit. At the same time the character of the record industry's production has radically changed. The large companies, those with which the buyer is most familiar, have redirected their energies to satisfying and cultivating the whims of the undiscriminating mass market, while the smaller companies have dedicated themselves to serving a select, loyal audience of connoisseurs with firmly settled tastes. Accordingly, the recording reviews and guides have assumed a more influential role.

In desperation some public schools have rotated the responsibility for selection among various staff members other than the librarian. In most of these cases, the balance, quality, and growth of the collections suffer. Electronic music, acid rock, ethnic music, Broadway hits, spoken word have their innings in successive years and continuity of development is difficult to maintain. In district-wide operations, disparities between building holdings are exacerbated and the librarians may end up acting as caretakers of dead appendage, cemetery collections as a consequence of the futile attempt to keep up with fluctuating mass market enthusiasms. The content may become indistinguishable from what is available outside the school, thereby adding nothing significant to the student experience and reinforcing a situation which educators should strive to change. Worse yet, such vacillation invites censorship. If a library caves in to popularity polls and preferences of outsiders, this pliability and willingness to heed demands for any *in*clusion implies an even-handed willingness to *ex*clude anything not wanted by unreasonable parents, board members, or other self-appointed arbiters within or outside the library.

There is a method of selection which has the advantage of countering this brand of pressure and accusations of idiosyncratic bias. Standard lists and critical consensus can be used to justify each selection decision and an elaborate weighting priority scheme devised so that the choosing process becomes almost wholly automatic. Selection of books has been negotiated in this way for many years by thousands of libraries. However, a similar approach for

sound recordings fails because standard selection tools are incomplete and out-of-date in their handling of this medium. One of the most respected lists contains no recordings of Schubert, Haydn, Debussy, Mendelssohn, Bartók, Beethoven, or Stravinsky—composers who wrote music eminently suitable for a child's or adolescent's listening. Composers Griffes, Harris, and Copland are the only "contemporary" Americans and the majority of other entries have been superseded by artistically and technically superior versions. No denigration of such basic lists is intended because their benefit to the book selector may be substantial. However, the compilers usually possess only slight knowledge of the qualities of sound recordings and therefore choose only the safe and established titles to meet the minima for nonprint materials set forth in current library program standards. Exclusive dependence upon such tools would deny a collection freshness and flavor, the third of the trinity of essential qualities to be encouraged. The especial evaluation requirements and gyrations of the field force the selector of sound recordings to depend upon reviews, advice from experts, and authoritative discographies as preferred sources of assistance.

In conclusion, the selector should strive to intensify the ambience of culture and make less tenuous the listener's growing affiliation with the beautiful and intrinsically valuable. The selector should interpret local requirements armed with recognition of individual differences among listeners, the world of sound recordings, listening equipment and environments, repertories of various genres, and fine interpretations needed to strengthen supposition of an axiological universe.

The Collection 2

The title and label lists in this chapter are limited to classical composition. Popular, folk, rock, country and western, and the other informal idioms differ from serious music in content and durability. Because monetary reward more than inspiration, and transient social mores rather than enduring cultural values are associated with popular music's production and enjoyment, particular titles' relevance and importance for an audience are momentary. In contrast, a recording in the classical field may remain highly desirable for more than twenty years, and the work itself may stay in the standard concert repertory for generations.

The guide numbers associated with works in this book provide a unique identification code for each classical composition for which one or more recordings have been cited. Whenever newly composed or neglected works are recorded in acceptable versions, they will be assigned guide numbers to be intercalated in future editions of this guide. Deceased composers with significant quantities of unrecorded music and particularly prolific or promising living composers have been allotted sufficient "open" space to accommodate integration of additional works without sacrificing either the alphabetization of titles or the numerical sequence of guide numbers in the Composer-Title List (pp. 45–150). Titles will retain the same guide numbers from edition to edition.

Listening Programs

A sound recordings session in the home or library is like an automobile trip or walk through the zoo. There are no best itineraries. A car trip may concentrate upon historical landmarks, foliage and natural scenery, exploration of back roads; a zoo excursion may focus upon a few species or a cross section of the complete animal kingdom. Whether one begins with birds, seals, or reptiles is not important. What is important is that the expenditure of energy and time remains within the boundaries of the spectator's capacity. Zoo visitations, car trips, and concerts can go on so long that heavy-lidded drowsiness or squirmy irritability may transform the enjoyable into the unendurable. There is a simple way to estimate maximal dosages of music. Multiply the audience's

age by five and the resulting figure will be close to the upper margin of tolerance. Using this rule of thumb, a six-year-old cannot take more than about 30 minutes and a twelve-year-old can absorb only about an hour. Intermissions are essential for adult and child alike. Concerts of chamber, keyboard, choral, vocal, and orchestral music usually last between 75 and 105 minutes, exclusive of intermissions. With the exception of operas, musicals, and the expansive orchestral and chamber tapestries of the romantics, the 2-hour figure is rarely surpassed. Works which exceed an hour's length are usually coupled with fillers or presented as single attractions; for example, Beethoven's Ninth Symphony (1 hour, 6 minutes) is often partnered with his Eighth Symphony (26 minutes) while Berlioz' *Damnation of Faust* (2 hours) and Mahler's Eighth Symphony (1 hour, 19 minutes), because of their even greater running times and draining emotionality, monopolize an entire program.

The conventional orchestral program is made up of three to five works, balanced in weight, flavor, and texture. A brilliant curtain raiser (appetizer) is succeeded by an established masterpiece (entrée), usually a symphony. After this, a challenging piece is brought in (exotic side dish or adventuresome salad) and the concert concludes with an amiable, affirmative statement (dessert). Appetizer and/or side dish may be omitted from the meal if entrée and dessert have enough substance and flavor to stand alone. Ten sample programs are illustrated below. Guide numbers, timings, age minima, aesthetic significance, and accessibility ratings are identified for these titles. (See pp. 42–44 for an explanation of ratings.)

GUIDE NO.	COMPOSER	TITLE	AGE MIN	AES SIG	AC-CESS
386,750	Boyce	Symphony no. 8 in d (11 min.)	S	3	2
536,774	Mozart	Concerto no. 24 in c, K. 491 for Piano and Orchestra (28 min.)	S	1	2
974,250	Carter	Concerto for Orchestra (24 min.)	A	1	5
617,750	Debussy	*Ibéria* (no. 2 from *Images* pour Orchestre) (20 min.)	S	2	2
749,750	Rossini	*Thieving Magpie* Overture (9 min.)	E	4	2
424,250	Haydn	Symphony no. 101 in D (28 min.)	E	2	1
711,000	Milhaud	*Le Boeuf sur le toit* (15 min.)	S	3	2
586,000	Bartók	Concerto for Orchestra (37 min.)	S	2	1
620,250	Debussy	*Prélude à l'après-midi d'un faune* (9 min.)	E	2	1
574,750	Walton	Concerto for Viola and Orchestra (25 min.)	A	3	3
633,000	Fauré	*Pelléas et Mélisande*, op. 80 (18 min.)	S	2	2
630,000	Elgar	*Enigma* Variations, op. 36 (30 min.)	S	2	1
758,250	Schubert	Overture in C—in the Italian style (7 min.)	S	3	1
498,500	Bartók	Concerto no. 3 for Piano (25 min.)	A	1	2
275,750	Berg	*Lyric Suite* for String Quartet (27 min.)	A	2	4
736,750	Ravel	*Daphnis et Chloé*: Suite no. 2 (16 min.)	S	2	1

GUIDE NO.	COMPOSER	TITLE	AGE MIN	AES SIG	AC-CESS
760,500	Schumann	*Manfred* Overture, op. 115 (12 min.)	S	4	2
429,250	Ives	Symphony no. 2 (1897–1902) (41 min.)	S	2	2
378,000	Beethoven	Symphony no. 5 in c, op. 67 (32 min.)	E	1	1
661,000	Handel	*Water Music*: Suite no. 1 (29 min.)	E	2	1
501,750	Berg	Concerto for Violin and Orchestra (24 min.)	A	2	4
737,250	Ravel	*Ma Mère l'Oye* (ballet) (28 min.)	E	2	2
450,000	Mozart	Symphony no. 35 in D, K. 385 (*Haffner*) (18 min.)	S	2	2
551,750	Schoenberg	Concerto for Piano and Orchestra, op. 42 (20 min.)	A	3	4
465,000	Schumann	Symphony no. 1 in B flat, op. 38 (*Spring*) (31 min.)	S	3	1
378,750	Beethoven	Symphony no. 8 in F, op. 93 (26 min.)	S	2	2
379,250	Beethoven	Symphony no. 9 in d, op. 125 (1 hour, 6 min.)	S	1	4
392,000	Bruckner	Symphony no. 9 in d (59 min.)	A	3	2
76,250	Purcell	*Come Ye Sons of Art* (26 min.)	S	3	2
54,500	Haydn	*Creation* (oratorio) (1 hour, 47 min.)	S	1	3

The preceding programs, though well balanced, fail to capitalize upon a bonus which the sound recording medium confers upon its user, the ability to mix performance genres. While this is sometimes attempted in the concert hall, it very rarely succeeds because acoustics, hall size, and crowd psychology conspire against the successive presentation of chamber, keyboard, orchestral, and solo works from the same stage to the same audience. Sound recordings surmount this problem because superior high-fidelity equipment can reproduce with equal ease the intimacy of the clavichord or grandiosity of *Götter-dämmerung*. There are multitudinous ways in which recorded music can be arranged to illustrate relationships between compositions. Several of these options are suggested below.

First, there are composers with the capacity to handle a wide gamut of forms, instrumentation, and feeling. A whole program of their works will hold one's attention. For purposes of demonstrating this point, I have placed composers in one-, two-, and three-night categories. The three-night composers include Bach, Bartók, Beethoven, Brahms, Haydn, Schubert, and Stravinsky. Debussy, Handel, Hindemith, Ives, Prokofiev, Ravel, and Shostakovich fall into the two-night class, and Berg, Britten, Chopin, Copland, Elgar, Fauré, Franck, Gershwin, Grieg, Mendelssohn, Mussorgsky, Poulenc, Schumann, Schoenberg, Sibelius, Richard Strauss, and Vaughan Williams have enough variety for an evening's entertainment. Programs for ten of these multigenre composers are offered as illustrations:

1. Igor Stravinsky (three-night composer)

GUIDE NO.	TITLE	AGE MIN	AES SIG	AC-CESS
787,200	Suite no. 2 for Small Orchestra (6 min.)	S	4	3
782,200	*Apollo* (*Apollon Musagète*) (ballet) (22 min.)	A	3	3
87,500	*Symphony of Psalms* (1930) (22 min.)	A	1	3
785,400	*Petrouchka* (complete ballet) (34 min.)	S	2	2
876,600	Four Russian Songs for Flute, Harp, Guitar, and Soprano (5 min.)	E	3	3
876,700	*In Memoriam Dylan Thomas* for Tenor, 4 Trombones, and String Quartet (7 min.)	A	3	4
87,750	*Threni* (*Lamentations of Jeremiah*) (1957–58) (30 min.)	A	2	5
557,750	Concerto in D for Violin and Orchestra (21 min.)	A	2	3
475,000	Symphony in Three Movements (21 min.)	S	2	2
955,250	*Renard* (16 min.)	E	4	2
361,500	Octet for Wind Instruments (15 min.)	S	2	2
785,200	*Orpheus* (ballet) (31 min.)	A	2	3
784,000	*Firebird*: Suite (22 min.)	E	3	1

2. Ludwig van Beethoven (three-night composer)

GUIDE NO.	TITLE	AGE MIN	AES SIG	AC-CESS
590,500	*Coriolanus* Overture, op. 62 (8 min.)	S	2	2
121,750	Sonata no. 14 in c sharp, op. 27, no. 2 (*Moonlight*) (15 min.)	S	2	1
266,750	Quartet no. 14 in c sharp, op. 131 (38 min.)	A	1	4
378,500	Symphony no. 7 in A, op. 92 (37 min.)	S	2	2
591,000	*Fidelio* Overture, op. 72c (7 min.)	S	2	1
263,250	Octet in E Flat for Winds, op. 103 (22 min.)	S	2	1
125,250	Sonata no. 28 in A, op. 101 (20 min.)	A	2	3
377,500	Symphony no. 3 in E Flat, op. 55 (*Eroica*) (50 min.)	S	1	3
591,503	*Leonore 3*, op. 72b: Overture (13 min.)	S	1	1
271,250	Sonata no. 9 in A, op. 47 (*Kreutzer* for Violin and Piano) (31 min.)	A	2	1
815,600	*An die ferne Geliebte*, op. 98 (14 min.)	A	3	3
378,000	Symphony no. 5 in c, op. 67 (32 min.)	E	1	1

3. Claude Debussy (three-night composer)

GUIDE NO.	TITLE	AGE MIN	AES SIG	AC-CESS
620,250	*Prélude à l'après-midi d'un faune* (9 min.)	E	2	1
292,000	*Syrinx,* for Flute Unaccompanied (2 min.)	S	3	2
291,000	Quartet in g, op. 10 (24 min.)	S	2	2

GUIDE NO.	TITLE	AGE MIN	AES SIG	AC-CESS
512,000	*Première Rapsodie* for Clarinet (8 min.)	S	3	2
291,250	Sonata no. 1 in d for Cello and Piano (12 min.)	A	2	2
617,750	*Ibéria* (no. 2 from *Images* pour Orchestre) (20 min.)	S	2	2
619,250	*Nuages and Fêtes* (from *Nocturnes*) (15 min.)	S	2	1
163,500	*Fille aux cheveux de lin* (3 min.)	E	2	1
163,750	*Cathédrale engloutie* (7 min.)	E	2	1
164,000	*Danse de Puck* (3 min.)	E	2	2
164,750	*Puerta del Vino* (3 min.)	E	2	2
165,250	*Feux d'artifice* (4 min.)	S	2	3
827,500	*Trois ballades de François Villon* (10 min.)	A	2	4
291,250	Sonata no. 1 in d for Cello and Piano (12 min.)	A	2	2
619,000	*La Mer* (24 min.)	E	1	2
161,750	*L'Isle joyeuse* (6 min.)	S	1	2
291,750	Sonata no. 3 in g for Violin and Piano (1916–17) (12 min.)	A	2	3
826,750	*Chansons de Bilitis* (3) Song cycle (10 min.)	A	3	2
162,500	Preludes for Piano, Book 1 (1910) (vary) (approximately 37 min.)	S	2	2
511,500	*Danse sacrée et danse profane* for Harp and Orchestra (10 min.)	A	2	2
512,250	*Rapsodie* for Saxophone and Orchestra (10 min.)	S	4	2

4. Paul Hindemith (two-night composer)

GUIDE NO.	TITLE	AGE MIN	AES SIG	AC-CESS
311,250	Theme and 4 variations, *Four Temperaments* for Piano and String Orchestra (27 min.)	A	3	3
182,750	Sonata no. 3 for Piano (18 min.)	A	3	3
57,250	*When Lilacs Last in the Dooryard Bloom'd*, an American Requiem (Walt Whitman) for Solo Voices, Chorus, and Orchestra (1 hour)	A	2	3
426,000	*Mathis der Maler* (symphony) (27 min.)	A	1	2
668,000	Concert Music for Strings and Brass, op. 50 (16 min.)	A	2	2
834,900	*Marienleben*, op. 27 (14 min.)	A	3	4
525,500	Concerto for Violin and Orchestra (31 min.)	A	3	3
312,750	Sonata for Harp (9 min.)	A	3	2
669,000	Symphonic Metamorphosis of Themes by Weber (19 min.)	A	3	2

5. Charles Ives (two-night composer)

GUIDE NO.	TITLE	AGE MIN	AES SIG	AC-CESS
678,000	*Browning* Overture (20 min.)	A	4	3
183,250	Sonata no. 2 for Piano (*Concord, Mass., 1840–1860*) (1909–15)	A	2	5

GUIDE NO.	TITLE	AGE MIN	AES SIG	AC-CESS
429,250	Symphony no. 2 (1897–1902) (41 min.)	S	2	2

GUIDE NO.	TITLE	AGE MIN	AES SIG	AC-CESS
680,250	*Unanswered Question* (6 min.)	A	2	2
678,500	*Circus Band March* (4 min.)	E	4	2
59,500	*Harvest Home* Chorales (3) (1898–1912) (8 min.)	S	2	2
835,300	*Ann Street* (1 min.)	A	3	3
836,000	*A Farewell to Land* (1 min.)	A	3	3
836,200	*General William Booth Enters Heaven* (6 min.)	S	2	1
315,500	Quartet no. 2 (26 min.)	A	3	5
183,750	Variations on *America* for Organ (1891) (7 min.)	E	4	2
429,750	Symphony no. 4 (1910–16) (31 min.)	S	2	3

6. Benjamin Britten (one-night composer)

GUIDE NO.	TITLE	AGE MIN	AES SIG	AC-CESS
607,800	Young Person's Guide to the Orchestra, op. 34 (19 min.)	E	3	1
284,500	Nocturnal for Guitar, op. 70 (18 min.)	S	3	2
284,750	Sonata in C for Cello and Piano, op. 65 (19 min.)	A	3	3
824,500	Serenade for Tenor, Horn, Strings, op. 31 (24 min.)	A	2	3
606,000	*Peter Grimes*: 4 Sea Interludes and Passacaglia (17 min.)	S	2	2

7. Aaron Copland (one-night composer)

GUIDE NO.	TITLE	AGE MIN	AES SIG	AC-CESS
615,500	*El Salón México* (11 min.)	E	2	1
613,250	*Lincoln Portrait* (15 min.)	E	3	1
825,800	*Twelve Poems of Emily Dickinson* (27 min.)	A	3	3
153,000	Piano Variations (1930) (12 min.)	S	3	3
611,750	*Appalachian Spring* (ballet suite) (25 min.)	E	2	1

8. Edward Elgar (one-night composer)

GUIDE NO.	TITLE	AGE MIN	AES SIG	AC-CESS
629,750	*Cockaigne* Overture, op. 40 (1901) (15 min.)	S	3	1
630,500	Introduction and Allegro for Strings, op. 47 (14 min.)	S	3	2
514,500	Concerto for Cello, op. 85 (30 min.)	S	2	2
630,751	*Pomp and Circumstance* March, op. 39, no. 1 (7 min.)	E	3	1
630,000	*Enigma* Variations, op. 36 (30 min.)	S	2	1

9. Arnold Schoenberg (one-night composer)

GUIDE NO.	TITLE	AGE MIN	AES SIG	AC-CESS
757,500	*Verklärte Nacht*, op. 4 (30 min.)	S	3	1
224,500	Suite for Piano, op. 25 (13 min.)	A	3	3
851,900	*Pierrot Lunaire*, op. 21 (34 min.)	A	2	4
757,250	Variations for Orchestra, op. 31 (21 min.)	A	4	4
551,750	Concerto for Piano and Orchestra, op. 42 (20 min.)	A	3	4

10. Jean Sibelius (one-night composer)

GUIDE NO.	TITLE	AGE MIN	AES SIG	AC-CESS
762,250	*Finlandia*, op. 26 (8 min.)	E	3	1
765,000	*Valse triste* (from *Kuolema*, op. 44) (5 min.)	S	3	1
870,000	*Autumn Evening* (5 min.)	A	3	3
870,100	*Black Roses* (2 min.)	S	3	2
870,200	*The Diamond on the March Snow* (2 min.)	S	3	2
870,300	*The Maiden Returned from Her Tryst* (3 min.)	S	3	1
472,000	Symphony no. 4 in a, op. 63 (35 min.)	A	2	3
554,750	Concerto in d for Violin, op. 47 (30 min.)	S	3	2

In the preceding programs, the most daring and significant (indicated by "1" or "2" ratings in the Aes Sig column) compositions are generally in the penultimate position and followed by brilliant, more accessible works to bring each listening session to a rousing close. Note that the age minimum and access numbers reflect this sequence, the works with E (elementary) or S (secondary), and lower access numbers being concentrated at beginnings and ends.

Another shared feature which can generate a good program is musical style; classicist, neoromanticist, expressionist, rococo, and so on. As an example, impressionism can bring under its umbrella chronologically separated but stylistically kindred Couperin and Debussy, Delius and Bax, Griffes and Loeffler, and other masters of gossamer texture and coloristic suggestion. The following program illustrates this:

GUIDE NO.	COMPOSER	TITLE	AGE MIN	AES SIG	AC-CESS
155,000	Couperin, François	*Le Rossignol en amour* (2 min.)	S	3	2
155,100	———	*Le Carillon de Cythère* (3 min.)	S	3	2
154,300	———	*Les Barricades Mystérieuses* (2 min.)	S	3	1
622,500	Delius, Frederick	*On Hearing the First Cuckoo in Spring* (6 min.)	E	3	1
655,500	Griffes, Charles Tomlinson	"White Peacock" (from *Roman Sketches*) (5 min.)	E	3	1
224,750	Schoenberg, Arnold	3 Pieces for Piano, op. 11 (15 min.)	A	3	4

GUIDE NO.	COMPOSER	TITLE	AGE MIN	AES SIG	AC-CESS
990,400	Messiaen, Olivier	*L'Ascension* (4 meditations) (26 min.)	S	3	3
849,850	Ravel, Maurice	*Shéhérazade* (16 min.)	S	3	2
741,250	Respighi, Ottorino	*Pines of Rome* (15 min.)	E	2	1

The above composers offer a sequence of decreasing abstraction and increasing literal-mindedness leading from natural history (Couperin) to personal introspection (Schoenberg) and religious ecstasy (Messiaen), from human love (Ravel) to the martial splendor of the Roman legions (Respighi). Examples of impressionism are innumerable because of composers' persistent desire to evoke subjective feelings about real and imagined worlds. Stravinsky's *Firebird*, Holst's *Perfect Fool* and the ubiquitous *Till Eulenspiegel*, the forest warbling and night sounds in the middle movements of Bartók's second and third piano concerti and his Music for Strings, Percussion, and Celesta, Webern's subtly shaded pointillism capture emotional immediacy in sound.

Electronic, aleatoric, and total serial compositions (see category 11, New and Experimental Music, page 146) may be beaded to form sonic ringlets to intrigue and tease the ear. Electronic composers who have more than a charivari of buzzes, burps, beeps, screams, and jet engines with which to serenade listeners include the deceased Edgard Varèse, Otto Luening, and Vladimir Ussachevsky (patriarchs of the electronic movement), Pierre Henry, Iannis Xenakis, Luciano Berio, Charles Wuorinén, Milton Babbitt, Henk Badings, Donald Erb, Mauricio Kagel, György Ligeti, Bruno Maderna, Karlheinz Stockhausen, Henri Pousseur, Morton Feldman, Melvin Powell, and Morton Subotnick. John Cage's and Harry Partch's experiments and effects call for mixes of invented, modified, and crossbred instruments.

A third option for the program planner is exploration of national styles, for example, those of Czechoslovakia, Poland, Hungary, Russia, and Spain. Contemporary American music may be examined in considerable depth because its representation on sound recordings has been generously supported by federal and private grants and recording company chieftains whose concern for the survival of young writers has not been entirely stifled by the profit motive. Seven labels which deserve commendation for championing unknowns are Columbia, Composers Recordings, Inc., Desto, Mainstream, Nonesuch, Turnabout, and Vox.

Forty American composers are represented below. The first group of twenty is easier to assimilate, more eclectic and melodious than the more radical writers in the second list.

Twenty Conservative American Composers

COMPOSER	REPRESENTATIVE WORK	GUIDE NO.
Antes, John (1740–1811)	Trios (3) for 2 Violins and Cello, op. 3	247,500
Barber, Samuel (1910–)	*Adagio for Strings* (from Quartet, op. 11) (1936)	584,500
Bernstein, Leonard (1918–)	*Chichester Psalms*, for Chorus and Orchestra (1965)	29,500

COMPOSER	REPRESENTATIVE WORK	GUIDE NO.
Billings, William (1746–1800)	Hymns and Anthems	30,000
Blitzstein, Marc (1905–1964)	*Regina*	908,250
Chanler, Theodore (1902–1961)	*Epitaphs* (1937; 1940)	825,400
Copland, Aaron (1900–)	*Billy the Kid* (ballet suite) (1938)	612,000
Dello Joio, Norman (1913–)	*Meditations on Ecclesiastes* (1956)	624,000
Gershwin, George (1898–1937)	*Rhapsody in Blue* (1924)	517,250
Gottschalk, Louis Moreau (1829–1869)	*Gran Tarantella* for Piano and Orchestra	518,750
Gould, Morton (1913–)	*Spirituals for Orchestra* (1941)	648,500
Griffes, Charles Tomlinson (1884–1920)	*Poem* for Flute and Orchestra	519,500
Grofé, Ferde (1892–1972)	*Grand Canyon Suite* (1931)	656,000
Harris, Roy (1898–)	Symphony no. 3 (1938)	404,250
Harrison, Lou (1917–)	*Four Strict Songs* for 8 Baritones and Orchestra (1956)	54,000
Hovhaness, Alan (1911–)	*Mysterious Mountain*, op. 132	673,500
MacDowell, Edward (1861–1908)	Concerto no. 2 in d for Piano, op. 23 (1890)	530,752
Piston, Walter (1894–)	*Incredible Flutist* (ballet suite) (1938)	729,000
Rorem, Ned (1923–)	*Some Trees: Songs*	850,700
Schuman, William (1910–)	*Credendum* (1955)	759,250

Twenty Avant-Garde American Composers

COMPOSER	REPRESENTATIVE WORK	GUIDE NO.
Babbitt, Milton (1916–)	Composition for Synthesizer (1964)	965,600
Brant, Henry (1913–)	*Fourth Millennium* (*Millennium IV*)	969,500
Brown, Earle (1926–)	Quartet (1965)	970,750
Cage, John (1912–)	*Fontana Mix-Feed*	972,250
Carter, Elliott (1908–)	Quartet no. 2	285,750
————	Quartet no. 3	286,000
Crumb, George (1929–)	*Ancient Voices of Children*	976,250
Davidovsky, Mario (1934–)	Synchronisms no. 6; Electronic Study no. 3 (1965); Synchronisms no. 5	977,500
Druckman, Jacob (1928–)	String Quartet no. 2 (1966)	981,000
Feldman, Morton (1926–)	*King of Denmark*	982,000
Foss, Lukas (1922–)	*Time Cycle*	983,500
Partch, Harry (1901–)	*Delusion of the Fury*	992,200

COMPOSER	REPRESENTATIVE WORK	GUIDE NO.
Powell, Melvin (1923–)	*Events, M*	993,400
Reich, Steve (1936–)	*Come Out*	993,700
Riegger, Wallingford (1885–1961)	Symphony no. 4 (1957)	458,500
Ruggles, Carl (1876–1971)	*Sun-Treader* (1932)	753,000
Sessions, Roger (1896–)	Concerto for Violin (1935)	553,500
Subotnick, Morton (1933–)	*Silver Apples of the Moon* for Electronic Music Synthesizer	996,400
Wolff, Christian (1934–)	*For 1, 2, or 3 People* (1964)	998,100
Wolpe, Stefan (1902–1972)	String Quartet (1968–69)	998,250
Wuorinén, Charles (1938–)	*Time's Encomium* for Electronic-Music Synthesizer	998,400

A fourth means of selecting titles is particularly well suited for children's record concerts. Portraits in sound of storybook characters, animals, places, and nature can be pulled together. The following small sample of such works includes the favorites along with exotic and lesser-known possibilities.

Story Book Characters

COMPOSER		GUIDE NO.
Bizet, Georges	*Jeux d'Enfants*, op. 22	600,000
Debussy, Claude	*Boîte à Joujoux* (children's ballet) (1913)	617,000
———	*Children's Corner* Suite (1906–8)	158,250
Dukas, Paul	*Sorcerer's Apprentice* (1897)	625,250
Humperdinck, Engelbert	*Hansel and Gretel*	924,750
Liadov, Anatol	*Baba Yaga*, op. 56 (1904)	691,000
Mussorgsky, Modest	*Night on Bald Mountain*	725,500
———	*Pictures at an Exhibition*	725,750
Poulenc, Francis	*Babar, Story of the Elephant* (1940)	730,000
Prokofiev, Serge	*Cinderella*, op. 87	730,750
———	*Peter and the Wolf*, op. 67 (1936)	732,000
Ravel, Maurice	*L'Enfant et les sortilèges*	944,750
———	*Ma Mère l'Oye* (ballet) (1915)	737,250
Respighi, Ottorino	*Boutique Fantasque* (ballet, after Rossini) (1919)	740,500
Saint-Saëns, Camille	*Carnival of the Animals*	753,250
Strauss, Richard	*Till Eulenspiegel*, op. 28 (1895)	781,000
Stravinsky, Igor	*Petrouchka*: Suite	785,600
———	*Renard* (1922)	955,250
Tchaikovsky, Peter Ilyitch	*Nutcracker Suite*, op. 71A	792,000

Birds

COMPOSER		GUIDE NO.
Daquin, Louis-Claude	*Coucou* (piece for harpsichord)	157,000
Gibbons, Orlando	*Silver Swan*	47,750

31

COMPOSER		GUIDE NO.
Jannequin, Clement	*Le Chant des Oiseaux*	4,800
Kodály, Zoltan	Variations on a Hungarian Folksong (*Peacock* Variations)	687,000
Messiaen, Olivier	*Oiseaux Exotiques* (1955–56); *Réveil des Oiseaux* (1953); *Catalogue d'Oiseaux* no. 9, *La Buscarle* (1956–58)	991,100
Mussorgsky, Modest	*Ballet of the Unhatched Chicks* (from *Pictures at an Exhibition*)	725,750
Respighi, Ottorino	*Pines of the Janiculum* (from *Pines of Rome*)	741,250
———	*Gli Uccelli* (*The Birds*) (1927)	742,000
Saint-Saëns, Camille	*The Aviary* (from *Carnival of the Animals*)	753,250
Schuller, Gunther	*The Twittering Machine* (from *Seven Studies on Themes of Paul Klee*) (1959)	994,600
Stravinsky, Igor	*Renard* (opening song of the cock) (1922)	955,250
Vivaldi, Antonio	*The Seasons*, op. 8 (*Spring*)	572,001
Wagner, Richard	*Siegfried: Forest Murmers*	806,250

Places

COMPOSER	THE AMERICAN SCENE	GUIDE NO.
Barber, Samuel	*Knoxville: Summer of 1915* (1948)	814,750
Copland, Aaron	*Appalachian Spring*: Suite	611,750
———	*Our Town* (suite) (1940)	613,750
———	*Quiet City* for Trumpet, English Horn, Orchestra (1940)	614,250
———	*Tender Land* (orchestral suite) (1954)	616,000
Foster, Stephen	*Jeannie with the Light Brown Hair*	833,300
———	*Swanee River*	833,900
Grofé, Ferde	*Grand Canyon Suite* (1931)	656,000
Ives, Charles	*Central Park in the Dark* (1898–1907)	678,250
———	Sonata no. 2 (*Concord, Mass., 1840–1860*) (1909–15)	183,250
———	*Three Places in New England* (1903–14)	680,000
Schuman, William	*New England Triptych*, 3 Pieces for Orchestra (1956)	759,750
Thomson, Virgil	*Louisiana Story*: Suite (1948)	796,250
———	*Plow That Broke the Plains* (1939)	796,300
———	*The River*: Suite (1942)	796,350

COMPOSER	OTHER PLACES	GUIDE NO.
Albeniz, Isaac	*Iberia* (suite, orchestration by Arbós)	578,000
Balakirev, Mily	*Islamey* (*Oriental Fantasy*)	112,000
Borodin, Alexander	*In the Steppes of Central Asia*	603,000
Canteloube, Joseph	*Songs of the Auvergne*	825,200
Chabrier, Emmanuel	*España*	609,000
Chávez, Carlos	*Sinfonia India*	393,000
Coates, Eric	*London Suite* (1933)	611,250
Debussy, Claude	*Pagodes* and *Soirées dans Granada* (from *Estampes* for Piano) (1903)	159,500
———	*Jardin sous la pluie* (from *Estampes* for Piano) (1903)	159,750
———	*Ibéria* (no. 2 from *Images* pour Orchestre)	617,750
Elgar, Edward	*Cockaigne* Overture, op. 40 (1901)	629,750
Falla, Manuel de	*Nights in the Gardens of Spain* (1909–15)	515,000
Gershwin, George	*American in Paris* (1928)	640,000
Gottschalk, Louis Moreau	*Nuit des Tropiques* (symphony poem)	647,000
Holst, Gustav	*Planets*, op. 32 (1914–16)	670,500
Ibert, Jacques	*Escales* (*Ports of Call*) (1922)	675,500
Ippolitov-Ivanov, Mikhail	*Caucasian Sketches*, op. 10 (1894)	676,000
Milhaud, Darius	*Suite Française* (1944)	712,000
Mussorgsky, Modest	*Great Gates of Kiev* (from *Pictures at an Exhibition*)	725,750
Ravel, Maurice	*Chansons Madécasses* (1925–26)	849,250
Sibelius, Jean	*Finlandia*, op. 26 (1899)	762,250
Smetana, Bedřich	*Moldau* (*Vltava*)	766,500
Vaughan Williams, Ralph	Symphony no. 2 (*London*) (1914, rev. 1920)	480,250
———	Symphony no. 7 (*Antarctica*) (1951–52)	481,500

Water

COMPOSER		GUIDE NO.
Britten, Benjamin	*Peter Grimes*: 4 Sea Interludes and Passacaglia	606,000
Debussy, Claude	*Images* pour Piano, Book I	160,750
———	*Reflets dans l'eau*	161,000
———	*La Mer* (1903–5)	619,000
Elgar, Edward	*Sea Pictures*	831,300
Handel, George Frideric	*Water Music*: Suite	661,000
Hovhaness, Alan	*And God Created Great Whales*	673,000
Liadov, Anatol	*Enchanted Lake*	691,500
Ravel, Maurice	*Jeux d'Eau* (1901)	215,225

COMPOSER		GUIDE NO.
Rimsky-Korsakov, Nikolai	*Scheherazade*, op. 35	746,250
Sibelius, Jean	*Oceanides*, op. 73 (1914)	736,000
Smetana, Bedřich	*Moldau* (*Vltava*)	766,500

A fifth common ground upon which to build a program is humor. The selections in the next group are unified by this thread and range from the fanciful and subtle (Ravel) to pratfall rudeness (Ibert and Schickele).

Humor

COMPOSER		GUIDE NO.
Ibert, Jacques	*Divertissement* (1930)	675,000

Broad-stroked assassinations of the Strauss waltz, Offenbach can-can, and Mendelssohn *Wedding* March with a wild, rushing Mack Sennett chase conclusion.

Ives, Charles — Symphony no. 2 (1897–1902) — 429,250
Columbia the Gem of the Ocean, Bringing in the Sheaves, and other traditional American themes are unceremoniously slammed together in a helter-skelter run to the cacophonous, nose-thumbing, final chord.

——— Variations on *America* for Organ (1891) — 183,750
Ives scandalized the proper folks in church and got the choir boys giggling with this bit of silliness.

Milhaud, Darius — *Le Boeuf sur le toit* (1919) — 711,000
Ingenious and amiable buffoonery.

Mozart, Wolfgang Amadeus *Magic Flute*, K. 620 — 934,500
Cosmic yet childlike, the sublime and ridiculous coexist in this music of amazing grace and refinement.

Piston, Walter — *Incredible Flutist* (ballet suite) (1938) — 729,000
Nicolas Slonimsky has referred to this as "a ballet to a story about a versatile flutist in the circus band who can charm not only snakes but also snake charmers with boisterous music in all moods, from mock-romantic to vulgarly Lisztian, and all idioms, from simple diatonic to twelve-tone themes, luxuriously orchestrated and further enhanced by shouting."

Ravel, Maurice — *L'Enfant et les Sortilèges* (1920–25) — 944,750
A Ravel-Colette collaboration. Mistreated toys and wounded trees, love-sick cats and babbling mathematicians, fox-trotting crockery and a naughty boy are personified in pellucid and fragrant music. The jazz, like that in the Walton below, now seems very quaint.

Saint-Saëns, Camille — *Carnival of the Animals* — 753,250
The elephants, pianists, and wild asses are funniest. Clever writing that wears better without a narrator.

COMPOSER		GUIDE NO.
Schickele, Peter	*P. D. Q. Bach* and *Stoned Guest*	755,825
	Wurst of P. D. Q. Bach	755,925

Schickele's inspired musicological lunacy is halfway between Ibert and the immortal Spike Jones.

Strauss, Richard	*Till Eulenspiegel*, op. 28 (1895)	781,000

A swarm of orchestral colors is in this skillful sketch of Till's careening, capricious misadventures.

Walton, William	*Façade* (1922)	808,200

1920s popular dance tunes and recitation of Dame Edith Sitwell's elegantly absurd poems combine to make a perennial pleaser.

Add as a postscript the patter songs and good-natured skullduggery of the Gilbert and Sullivan operettas, guide numbers 917,250–919,000.

Drama attains an added qualitative dimension through the mediation of the composer's art. Shakespeare and Goethe have been favored by the strongest musical elaboration. *Romeo and Juliet*, *Hamlet*, and *Faust*, plays which vividly project our preoccupations with love and lust, the familial and the eternal, have been set to music in a variety of forms: opera, oratorio, cantata, incidental and ballet scores, symphonic poems, and so on. The Orpheus and Don Juan legends, along with Maurice Maeterlinck's static, veiled vision of love and death, Pelléas et Mélisande, have also inspired music writers.

For readers who desire to explore and compare musical settings, a list of titles represented in this guide follows:

COMPOSER	ROMEO AND JULIET SETTINGS	GUIDE NO.
Berlioz, Hector	*Roméo et Juliette*, op. 17 (choral symphony)	28,750
Gounod, Charles	*Roméo et Juliette* (opera) (1867)	920,750
Prokofiev, Serge	*Romeo and Juliet* (ballet)	732,250
Tchaikovsky, Peter Ilyitch	*Romeo and Juliet* (overture-fantasy) (1870)	793,000

COMPOSER	HAMLET SETTINGS	GUIDE NO.
Liszt, Franz	*Hamlet* (Symphonic Poem no. 10)	692,250
Shostakovich, Dmitri	*Hamlet*: Incidental Music, op. 32 (1932)	762,000
Tchaikovsky, Peter Ilyitch	*Hamlet* (Fantasy Overture, op. 67a)	791,000
Walton, William	*Hamlet* (film music)	808,350

COMPOSER	FAUST SETTINGS	GUIDE NO.
Berlioz, Hector	*La Damnation de Faust*, op. 24 (cantata)	28,000
Boito, Arrigo	*Mefistofele* (opera)	908,500
Gounod, Charles	*Faust* (opera) (1859)	920,500

COMPOSER	FAUST SETTINGS	GUIDE NO.
Liszt, Franz	*Faust* Symphony (choral and symphonic work)	62,000
Mahler, Gustav	Symphony no. 8 in E flat (*Symphony of a Thousand*) (includes setting of final scene of Goethe's *Faust*, part 2) (1907)	436,250
Wagner, Richard	*Eine Faust Ouverture* (1840)	803,000

COMPOSER	ORPHEUS SETTINGS	GUIDE NO.
Gluck, Christoph Willibald	*Orfeo ed Euridice* (opera)	920,250
Liszt, Franz	*Orpheus* (Symphonic Poem no. 4)	694,500
Monteverdi, Claudio	*L'Orfeo* (opera)	930,750
Offenbach, Jacques	*Orpheus in Hades* (opera)	936,250
Schuman, William	*A Song of Orpheus* (fantasy) for Cello and Orchestra (1961)	552,250
Stravinsky, Igor	*Orpheus* (ballet) (1948)	785,200

COMPOSER	DON JUAN SETTINGS	GUIDE NO.
Dargomizhsky, Alexander	*The Stone Guest* (opera)	913,250
Gluck, Christoph Willibald	*Don Juan* (ballet)	646,000
Mozart, Wolfgang Amadeus	*Don Giovanni* (opera)	933,250
Strauss, Richard	*Don Juan*, op. 20 (tone poem) (1888)	779,500

COMPOSER	PELLÉAS ET MÉLISANDE SETTINGS	GUIDE NO.
Debussy, Claude	*Pelléas et Mélisande* (opera) (1892–1902)	913,500
Fauré, Gabriel	*Pelléas et Mélisande*, op. 80 (incidental music) (1898)	633,000
Schoenberg, Arnold	*Pelleas und Melisande*, op. 5 (incidental music) (1902)	756,500
Sibelius, Jean	*Pelléas et Mélisande*, op. 46 (incidental music) (1905)	763,250

The majesty and nobility of Greek tragedy have kindled countless composers' imaginations. The eight works which follow are moderately significant and listenable, and may be purchased in first-rate recorded versions.

COMPOSER	GREEK TRAGEDY	GUIDE NO.
Barber, Samuel	*Medea's Meditation and Dance of Vengeance*, op. 23A (from ballet)	585,250
Cherubini, Luigi	*Medea* (opera rescued from oblivion by Maria Callas' supremely vital performance) (1797)	912,000
Milhaud, Darius	*Choëphores* (incidental music) (1915–16)	65,500

COMPOSER	GREEK TRAGEDY	GUIDE NO.
Orff, Carl	*Antigonae* (opera) (1949)	937,250
————	*Oedipus der Tyrann* (opera) (1959)	938,000
Satie, Erik	*Socrate* (opera) (1919)	851,500
Strauss, Richard	*Elektra*, op. 58 (opera) (1906–8)	953,250
Stravinsky, Igor	*Oedipus Rex* (opera-oratorio) (1927)	954,500

Another intriguing exercise is the comparison of arrangements and original untouched compositions. Notable and popular transformations of modest scores into more sartorially elegant orchestral works are cited below.

ORIGINAL MUSIC	ARRANGER OR BORROWER	NEW TITLE	GUIDE NO.
American hymns and folk music	Charles Ives	Violin sonatas, symphonies, and songs include borrowings from his American heritage. See particularly the works associated with cited guide nos.	183,000– 183,750 315,000– 316,750 429,000– 431,000 678,000– 680,750 835,300– 836,400
Anon: *Dies Irae* (medieval mass)	Hector Berlioz	*Symphonie Fantastique*	381,250
————: *Dies Irae* (medieval mass)	Franz Liszt	*Todtentanz* for Piano and Orchestra	530,250
————: *Dies Irae* (medieval mass)	Modest Mussorgsky	*Trepak* (from *Songs and Dances of Death*)	846,500
————: *Dies Irae* (medieval mass)	Sergei Rachmaninoff	*Isle of the Dead*	734,000
————: *Dies Irae*	Camille Saint-Saëns	*Danse Macabre*	753,500
————: *Dies Irae*	Peter Ilyitch Tchaikovsky	Suite no. 3 for Orchestra	793,700
Auvergne folk songs	Joseph Canteloube	*Songs of the Auvergne*	825,200
J. S. Bach: Cantata no. 60 (*Es ist genug*)	Alban Berg	Concerto for Violin and Orchestra, Finale	501,750
————: *Jesu, Joy of Man's Desiring* (from Cantata no. 147)	Leopold Stokowski	Same as original	23,347
————: *Sheep May Safely Graze* (from Cantata no. 208)	Leopold Stokowski	Same as original	583,750
————: Toccata and Fugue in d for Organ, S. 565	Leopold Stokowski	Same as original	584,250
————: *Brandenburg* Concerto no. 3	Walter Carlos (Moog Synthesizer)	Same as original	583,253
————: Various works	William Walton	*Wise Virgins* (ballet suite)	808,800

ORIGINAL MUSIC	ARRANGER OR BORROWER	NEW TITLE	GUIDE NO.
Mahler: *Das Lied von der Erde*	George Crumb	*Ancient Voices of Children*	976,250
Mussorgsky: *Pictures at an Exhibition*	Maurice Ravel	Same as original	725,750
Pergolesi: Various works	Igor Stravinsky	*Pulcinella*	785,800; 786,000
Rossini: Various works	Ottorino Respighi	*Boutique Fantasque*	740,500
———: Overture to *William Tell*	Dmitri Shostako-vich	Symphony no. 15 in A, op. 141 (1971)	471,000
D. Scarlatti: Various works	Vincenzo Tomma-sini	*Good-humored Ladies*	797,000
Tallis: Theme from English Hymnal	Ralph Vaughan Williams	Fantasia on a Theme by Tallis	800,200
Wagner: *Der Ring des Nibelungen*	Dmitri Shostako-vich	Symphony no. 15 in A, op. 141 (1971)	471,000

An eighth approach which most fully exploits the medium is to select works rarely heard in live performance because of their extreme difficulty, uncommon instrumentation, or lack of general appeal. A sampling of these neglected but superior pieces follows:

COMPOSER	TITLE	GUIDE NO.
Bartók, Béla	Quartet no. 6 (1939)	261,500
———	Sonata for 2 Pianos and Percussion (1937)	261,750
Beethoven, Ludwig van	*Fidelio,* op. 72	905,500
———	Octet in E Flat for Winds, op. 103	263,250
———	Sextet in E Flat for Winds, op. 71	268,750
———	Quartet no. 16 in F, op. 135	267,250
Berg, Alban	*Wozzeck* (1914–21)	907,000
Brahms, Johannes	*Alto Rhapsody,* op. 53	31,000
Britten, Benjamin	*War Requiem,* op. 66 (1962)	36,000
———	*Serenade* for Tenor, Horn, Strings, op. 31 (1943)	824,500
Byrd, William	Mass in 3 parts; Mass in 4 parts; Mass in 5 parts	1,100; 1,200; 1,300
Dallapiccola, Luigi	*Canti di Prigionia*	976,750
Debussy, Claude	*Pelléas et Mélisande* (1892–1902)	913,500
———	Sonata no. 2 for Flute, Viola and Harp (1916)	291,500
Dvořák, Antonin	Serenade in E for Strings, op. 22	628,000
Falla, Manuel de	Concerto in D for Harpsichord, Flute, Oboe, Clarinet, Violin, and Cello	296,000
Gesualdo, Don Carlo	Italian Madrigals	45,250
Handel, George Frideric	*Acis and Galatea*	48,500
———	*Alexander's Feast*	48,750
———	*Ode for St. Cecilia's Day*	52,000
Hindemith, Paul	Requiem *For Those We Love* (1946)	57,250

COMPOSER	TITLE	GUIDE NO.
Honegger, Arthur	Symphony *Di tre re*	428,750
Ives, Charles	Sonata no. 2 (*Concord, Mass., 1840–1860*) (1909–15)	183,250
———	Songs	835,300–836,400
———	Symphony no. 4 (1910–16)	429,750
Machaut, Guillaume de	Ballades, Rondeaux, Virelais . . .	6,000
Mendelssohn, Felix	Octet in E Flat for Strings, op. 20	325,000
Monteverdi, Claudio	*L'Orfeo*	930,750
Purcell, Henry	*Come Ye Sons of Art*	76,250
Ravel, Maurice	*Chansons madécasses* (1925–26)	849,250
———	*Introduction and Allegro* for Harp, Flute, Clarinet, and String Quartet (1905–6)	348,000
Schoenberg, Arnold	*Five Pieces for Orchestra,* op. 16 (1909, rev. 1949)	756,250
———	*Gurre-Lieder* (1901–13)	80,000
———	*Pierrot Lunaire,* op. 21 (1912)	851,900
Schubert, Franz	Quintet in C, op. 163, D. 956	354,250
Stravinsky, Igor	Mass (1948)	86,750
———	Octet for Wind Instruments (1923)	361,500
———	*Oedipus Rex* (1927)	954,500
———	*Rake's Progress* (1951)	955,000
———	*Renard* (1922)	955,250
———	*Song of the Nightingale* (opera)	955,500
———	*Symphonies of Wind Instruments*	787,400
———	*Symphony of Psalms*	87,500
Tallis, Thomas	*Lamentations of Jeremiah*	16,500
Taverner, John	Mass (*The Western Wynde*)	16,900
Varèse, Edgard	*Ionisation*	799,600
Villa-Lobos, Heitor	*Bachianas Brasileiras* no. s 1–8	802,000; 877,600

New works by Elliott Carter, George Crumb, Lou Harrison, Hans Werner Henze, Leon Kirchner, Olivier Messiaen, Krzysztof Penderecki, Roger Sessions, and Sir Michael Tippett may also be placed within this category.

Composer-Title List

The 4,101 musical works listed in this chapter were selected from two sources: (1) 4,626 compositions represented on 42,943 recordings issued in the United States during the years 1961 through 1969[1] and (2) newly composed or formerly neglected works recorded between 1970 and 1975.

1. Richard S. Halsey, *"A Bibliometric Analysis of the Serious Music Literature on Long Playing Records"* (Ph.D. diss., Case Western Reserve University, 1972).

Within the first grouping, approximately two thousand trivial or transient works were eliminated. Most of these discards remained on the market for less than three years and none were well received by critics of either the live or recorded premieres. The winnowing process was not as severe as might be implied from a face value interpretation of the above 42,943 to 4,101 ratio because of excessive duplications. During a nine-year span, the Chopin Minute Waltz was recorded 44 times, Handel's *Messiah* 32 times, Berlioz' *Symphonie Fantastique* 26 times, *Un Furtiva Lagrima* from *L'Elisir d'Amore* 21 times, and Bartók's Concerto for Orchestra 13 times. In direct contrast, 95 important works are included in the composer-title listing despite the scant attention granted them by the recording industry during the past fourteen years. These neglected but notable works include Lassus' *Penitential Psalms*, Handel's *Semele*, Roger Sessions' Mass, Hindemith's Theme and 4 Variations, *Four Temperaments* for Piano and String Orchestra, Villa-Lobos' *Chôros* no. 4 for 3 Horns and Trombones, Mussorgsky's *Nursery* (song cycle), Dallapiccola's *Il prigionere*, Marc Blitzstein's *Regina*, and Honegger's Fifth Symphony. It is hoped that corrective action will be taken by the recording manufacturers so that superior versions of these works may again become available to the general listening public.

The composer-title section is divided into eleven categories which demarcate major genres within serious music. Category 1, "Early Music," includes works written by composers born before 1550 A.D. Victoria, Palestrina, and Lassus; Byrd, Tallis, and Taverner; Binchois and Dufay, Milan and Morales, Jannequin, Sermisy, LeJeune, Costeley, and Isaac fall within this grouping. Although many of the English madrigalists (e.g., Dowland, Gibbons, and Morley) are closely related to the previous figures, they are placed in some other category because of their post-1550 A.D. birthdates. The 1550 line separates transitional composers Hassler, Schütz, Sweelinck, Monteverdi, Frescobaldi, Giovanni Gabrieli, and Peri who straddle the renaissance and baroque periods, from the vast majority of pre-1500 writers whose styles are wholly ensconced in the earlier era.

The second category, "Choral Music," includes music performed by a chorus or choral ensemble with more than one singer assigned each vocal part. Monophonic and polyphonic compositions with and without instrumental accompaniments are included. Music in which no individual vocal line is soloistically prominent has been placed in this category along with borderline cases where insufficient evidence concerning the recorded performances could be located. Madrigals written by composers born after 1550 A.D. are also represented in this section.

Category 3, "Keyboard Instruments," is limited to works played by one or more keyboard instruments without accompaniment. Accordingly, Bartók's Sonata for Two Pianos and Percussion belongs in category 4, "Chamber Music," while Debussy's *En blanc et noir* for two pianos is placed in category 3.

"Chamber Music," category 4, includes works for no more than fourteen instruments which do not belong in categories 1 or 3.

Categories 5, 6, and 7 take in all orchestral music. Category 5, "Symphonies," contains works which have both a symphonic form and orchestral scoring. The Stravinsky *Symphony of Psalms*, a primarily choral work, is

placed in category 2 while Beethoven's Ninth Symphony and Mahler's Second Symphony belong in 5 even though sections of the latter two works are chorally enriched. The sinfonias of pre-Haydn composers appear in category 7 or 9 depending upon their instrumentation. The earliest qualifying work for inclusion in 5 is Sammartini's Symphony in G, JC50.

Category 6 includes pieces for one to five solo instruments (other than keyboard) and orchestra.

"Other Orchestral Works," category 7, encompasses tone poems, suites, program music, concerti for orchestra, orchestrally scored oddities that cannot properly be classed elsewhere.

Category 8, "Songs and Other Works Scored for Single Voice and Accompaniment," is self-explained. Art songs and lieder, madrigals not found in category 1, and arrangements in which a solo vocal line is presumed to be prominent appear here.

"Popular Arias," category 9, does not include aesthetic significance ratings because no aria can be validly appraised when divorced from the context of the opera from which it has been excerpted. This sectional listing is useful for directing those who don't know much about opera. Arias are generally somewhat longer than songs and may in the interest of dramatic effect or vocal fit sacrifice literal interpretation of the text. Most of the arias in the section exhibit features which please the operagoer—these being their deliberate difficulty, wide dynamic and vocal range, and projection of passionate feelings. Verdi, Mozart, Puccini excelled in the genre; Donizetti, Bellini, and Handel were close competitors. Wagner and Verdi discarded this expressive device as they neared the zenith of their careers, Verdi's *Falstaff* and *Otello*, and Wagner's *Tristan und Isolde* substituting the less artificial leitmotiv to evoke recurrent ideas, passions, characters, situations in a more realistic and subtle way. Though arias are not intellectually demanding, they may act as musical aperitifs preparing the unaccustomed palate for abstract symphonic, chamber, and keyboard music. Generally acclaimed recordings of artists' aria recitals are cited in the addendum to category 9.

In the tenth category, "Opera," the criteria for inclusion are consistent with the policy adopted by Schwann. Therefore *Porgy and Bess*, the *Three Penny Opera, Renard*, and Ezra Pound's *Le Testament* are placed here for the convenience of the record hunter even though their qualifications as operas may be open to question.

The final category, "New and Experimental Music," is limited to composers born after 1920 whose association with avant-garde movements has been unambiguous. Electronic and radically offbeat compositions are included. Access and aesthetic significance ratings are omitted because their assignment would call upon precognitive powers which this author cannot claim. Therefore, only titles, manufacturers' numbers, and timings are provided for these composers' pieces.

Composer and performer names are as they appear in Schwann. Early music writers' birth and death years were verified in *Baker's Biographical Dictionary of Musicians* and *Die Musik in Geschichte und Gegenwart*. The *ASCAP (American Society of Composers, Authors, and Publishers) Biographical Dictionary of Composers, Authors, and Publishers*, Broadcast Music, Inc. (BMI) publications, the American Music Center, Inc., and data sent to the

author by recording companies were consulted for confirmation of contemporary composers' vital statistics. Keys of work titles such as "c# minor" and "b♭ major" appear as "c sharp" and "E flat" respectively. The capital letters indicate major and small letters represent the minor keys; accidentals are written out. This procedure is identical to that used by Schwann and Harrison catalogs consulted by most record purchasers.

The timings which appear in parentheses immediately following most titles are modal or representative. Whenever no consistent figure could be confirmed, an average value has been substituted. These figures have been taken from the files of the Canadian Broadcasting Company in Toronto, Radio Station WCLV in Cleveland, and the British Broadcasting Company catalogs and supplemented by personal audition. T. C. York's *How Long Do They Play?* (London: Oxford Univ. Pr., 1929) and the ASCAP, BMI, and Edwin Fleischer Private Collection of Orchestral Music catalogs were useful supplementary sources.

Several caveats should condition the reader's interpretation of these timings. First, contemporary performances have a quickened tempo so that the running times quoted in the Fleischer and other earlier catalogs are generally longer than those cited in this guide. Second, observance or omission of da capos can have a drastic effect. Finally, electronic and aleatoric compositions in category 11 are exempt from this variability. Electronic music is programmed directly onto tape and divergence from the composer's intention cannot occur; aleatoric music must remain unpredictable or lose its special trademark.

This said, it is evident that the real and perceived passage of time has perplexed the philosophers and scientists from Saint Augustine until the present. A metaphor may clarify its several meanings for music listeners. Imagine a man, stopwatch in hand, standing on a railroad station platform observing trains which pass by on an oval track. He measures instantaneous velocities at various points on the track and totals up the time it takes each train to circle the platform. If the trains are Beethoven's Fifth "specials," he will discover that most experienced conductors take about 32 minutes to transport their passengers the full distance and it is this time that is given for selections in this guide.

A second "time" is experienced by the passenger who is "transported." This subjective "time" differs according to the traveler's familiarity with the Fifth and with other rolling stock built by Beethoven. As the passenger takes his trip, he reacts to the landscape and interior furnishing. As the soundscape passes he senses as in a mirror the anticipated and remembered images. The more removed the experience from his "mental mirror" expectation the greater will be his aesthetic satisfaction and the narrower the seeming girth of experienced time. The passenger may become so accustomed to train and soundscape that the trip becomes a bromide. Only an inspired conductor and the passage of real time can redeem his attention by contradicting his remembrance.

The third "time" is molded by the conductor and suspensions, ritardandos, dynamic inflections, and internal elasticity are its substance. The second and third "times" are psychoplasmic; the first "time" is external and objectively measurable. All are experienced by any completely involved listener.

A minimum age level is suggested for each title in the list; adult (A),

secondary (S), or elementary (E). The (E) and (S) ratings were arrived at by combining personal choices, recommendations of music educators, and preferences expressed by children's and young adult audiences. Abstract or deep works lacking surface appeal have been coded for adults (A).

Aesthetic significance ratings are based upon statistical findings which correlate with expert musical opinion. It was confirmed by the author that titles with moderately high duplication and low deletion rates in manufacturers' catalogs include most of the works labeled as masterpieces by music critics. There is a direct correlation between musical quality and title longevity on the long-playing record market. Recorded works divide into two categories and the recording industry maintains an ecological balance. It performs a dual role, acting both as a cultural preservation/dissemination agency for a loyal, small band of educated listeners and as caterer to a much larger general public with a less stable but seemingly insatiable appetite for favorites and fads of the concert hall. In Beethoven's case the dichotomy is clear. There is one set of works comprising the reliable attractions (*Moonlight, Appassionata, Pathétique, Kreutzer* sonatas; Fifth Symphony, *Emperor* Concerto, and so on) and a second set which has as front runners the final five quartets, late piano sonatas, *Missa Solemnis, Eroica* Symphony, and *Fidelio.* This same pattern has been confirmed in the recorded works of Béla Bartók, Claude Debussy, and Arnold Schoenberg. It is a systemic, generally pervasive condition. This evidence in combination with the testimony of critics, biographers, and historians of music stands behind the aesthetic significance ratings.

The aesthetic significance scale reflects the following appraisals:

1 = A masterpiece.
2 = Very well-crafted music of lesser magnitude.
3 = Solidly or cleverly designed but deficient in proportions, integrity of expression, internal consistency, clarity, or depth of meaning.
4 = Weaker than 3; nondescript.
5 = Flawed or insubstantial. Of sufficient interest to be considered only by those who wish to build a comprehensive collection.

The access scale ratings are also predicated upon statistical evidence. A very few recorded compositions which are audience favorites compete with a vast numerical majority in accordance with a log-log or hyperbolic distribution, title replication frequencies plotting as a straight line on log rank–log percentage. A production homostasis is achieved because the pressure to record well-known staples of the repertory is balanced by a discriminating audience's demand for a very large number of obscure but respected or innovative compositions. Those pieces which are recorded most frequently have been assigned the lowest or easiest access rating of 1. Approximately 21 percent of the total of the titles falls within this rating group. The author's calculations of performance frequencies correlate very closely with those identified in other sources. These include Emil E. E. Folgmann, "An Experimental Study of Composer-Preferences of Four Outstanding Symphony Orchestras," *Journal of Experimental Psychology* 16: 709–24 (1933); Kate Hevner Mueller, *Twenty-Seven Major American Symphony Orchestras: A History and Analysis of Their Repertoires (Seasons 1842–43 through 1969–70),* Indiana University

Studies (Bloomington: Indiana University Pr., 1973); Abraham Moles, *Information Theory and Esthetic Perception* (Urbana: University of Illinois Pr., 1966); W. Schwann Inc.'s series of catalogs and annual summaries of recording production activity; the Record Industry Association of America, Inc.'s statistical monographs; *Billboard* magazine; and listener preference surveys conducted by radio station WCLV in Cleveland, Ohio.

The access scale indicates the following degrees of listenability:

1 = Work commands attention; an immediate connection is made.
2 = May require a second or third hearing but the message is in an easily comprehended musical language.
3 = More subtle and/or less directly appealing than 2.
4 = Dull or unfathomable. If it is incomprehensible, the communication barrier may yield after repeated hearings. Concentration and patience may be required.
5 = Austere, esoteric, or too arbitrary for most listeners. Familiarity with the score may be prerequisite to proper appreciation *or* work may be musically empty.

Recommended recordings are provided for most of the titles in the composer-title list. A double asterisk indicates that a recording is definitive or contains a landmark interpretation; a single asterisk indicates that it is one among several acceptable though unremarkable versions. Lack of an asterisk means that the recording may have technical or interpretive shortcomings but is the only one that could be purchased through normal trade channels at the time this book went to press.

All recommendations have been painstakingly screened. Behind each stands the collective endorsement of critics noted for their authority and musicality. Journals most often referred to for this purpose were *Gramophone, High Fidelity, Hi-Fi News and Record Review, Monthly Letter,* the *New Records,* and *Stereo Review.* Especially handy cumulative sources were the EMG Hand-Made Gramophones Ltd., *Art of Record Buying* (1974 and 1975 editions); Consumers Union Reviews, *Classical Recordings* (Mount Vernon, N.Y.: Consumers Union, 1972); Bernard H. Haggin, *New Listener's Companion and Record Guide,* 3d ed. (New York: Horizon Pr., 1974); and Edward Greenfield et al., *Stereo Record Guide,* 9 vols. (London: Long Playing Record Library Ltd., 1960–74).

Composer-Title List

1. Early Music

GUIDE NO.	COMPOSER AND TITLE	AGE MIN	AES SIG	AC-CESS
	ADAM DE LA HALLE (c.1237–1287)			
100	*Le jeu de Robin et Marion* (7 min.) **(Tel. 6.41219)	S	3	2
	ARCADELT, JACOB (c.1514–c.1568)			
200	*Missa Noe, Noe*; Secular Music (Lyr. 7199)	S	3	4
	ATTAIGNANT, PIERRE (15??–1552)			
300	Dances (vary) *(RCA VICS–1362); *(Turn. 34137)	E	4	2
	BINCHOIS, GILLES (c.1400–1460)			
400	Secular Chansons and Instrumental Pieces (about 3 min. ea.) **(None. H–71010); **(None. H–71058)	S	4	2
	BYRD, WILLIAM (1543–1623)			
500	*Ave verum corpus* (5 min.) *(Argo 5226)	A	1	4
600	*Cantiones Sacrae* in 5 and 6 Voices (complete) (*3–Oiseau S–311/3)	A	2	3
700	Fantasies for Strings (vary) (Tel. 6.41201)	A	3	4
800	Keyboard Musick (varies) *(Col. MS–7326)	A	2	4
900	Madrigals (vary) (Lyr. 7156)	S	2	3
1000	*Magnificat* (10 min.) *(Argo 5226)	A	1	4
1100	Mass in 3 parts (20 min.) **(Argo 5362)	A	1	4
1200	Mass in 4 parts (26 min.) **(Argo 5362)	A	1	3
1300	Mass in 5 parts (18 min.) *(Argo 5226)	A	1	4
1400	*Nunc Dimittis* *(Argo 5226)	A	2	4
	CABEZON, ANTONIO DE (c.1510–1566)			
1500	*Obras de musica para tecla, arpa y vihuela* (vary) *(None. H–71098); *(Turn. 34097)	S	3	2
	COSTELEY, GUILLAUME (c.1531–1606)			
1700	Chansons (vary) (*Mignonne, allon voir si la rose* and *Allon, gay Bergères*) **(Bach SRV–298 SD)	S	3	2
	DES PREZ, JOSQUIN (c.1440–1521)			
1800	*Adieu, mes amours, Allégez-moy,* and *Vive le Roi*	S	3	3
	(2–3 min. ea.) **(None. H–71012)			
1900	*La Déploration de Johan Okeghem* (5 min.) *(Argo ZRG–681)	A	2	4
2000	Instrumental Pieces (vary) *(Argo ZRG–681)	S	2	3
2100	*Missa Ave Maris Stella* (20 min.) *(None. H–71216)	A	1	4
2200	*Missa Hercules dux Ferrariae* (Mus. –Lib. 7075)	A	2	4
2300	*Missa L'Homme armé* *(Van. HM–3 SD)	A	2	4
2400	*Missa Pange Lingua* (32 min.) *(Turn. 34431)	A	1	4
2500	Motets (vary) **(DG ARC–2533110); *(None. H–71216)	A	1	4
2600	*Parfons regretz* (3 min.) **(Bach SRV 298 SD)	S	2	3
2700	Secular Works (vary) **(None. H–71261)	A	3	3
	DUFAY, GUILLAUME (c.1400–1474)			
2800	Hymns, Choruses and Songs, Sacred and Secular *(Tel. 6.41058)	A	2	4
2900	*Missa (L'Homme armé)* (28 min.) (Lyr. 7150)	A	1	4
3000	*Missa (Se la face ay pale)* (Van. HM–2 SD)	A	1	4
3100	Motets (vary) (Lyr. 7190)	A	2	4
3200	Sacred Songs (vary) (*Lamentatio sanctae matris Ecclesiae constantinopolitanae* and *Vergine bella*) **(None. H–71058)	A	2	4
3300	Secular Songs (vary) (*Adieu, m'amour, adieu ma joie* and *Pour l'amour de ma doulce amye*) **(None. H–71120)	S	2	3
3400	Secular Songs (vary) (*Donnés l'assault à la forteresse* and *Les doleurs dont me sens*) **(None. H–71010)	S	2	3
	DUNSTABLE, JOHN (c.1385–1453)			
3500	Latin Church Music (varies) *(Argo ZRG–681)	A	2	4
3600	*O rosa bella* *(Argo ZRG–681)	S	2	3
	GABRIELI, ANDREA (c.1520–1586)			
3700	Ricercare and Sacred Works (24 min.) **(Ang. S–36443)	A	1	4
	GREGORIAN CHANT (4th–6th century A.D.)			
3800	Lent and Easter Music (varies) **(Turn. 34070)	S	1	2

GUIDE NO.	COMPOSER AND TITLE	AGE MIN	AES SIG	AC-CESS
3900	Midnight Mass for Christmastide (47 min.) **(DG ARC–198153)	S	1	2
4000	Music of the Mass (varies) **(Oiseau 60040); **(Tel. 6.41213)	S	1	2
	ISAAC, HEINRICH (c.1450–1517)			
4100	*Innsbruck, ich muss dich lassen* (4 min.) *(2–Tel. 26.35052)	S	2	3
4200	*Missa carminum* (24 min.) (None. H–71084)	A	2	4
4300	*Missa super o praeclara;* Motets and Chansons **(Tel. 6.41247)	A	2	4
4400	Music for the Court of Lorenzo the Magnificent; *A la bataglia* (4 min.) **(MCA 2508); *(MCA 2513)	A	2	3
	JANNEQUIN, CLEMENT (c.1475–c.1560)			
4500	*Au joly boys* (2 min.) **(Bach SRV 298 SD)	S	3	2
4600	*Le bataille de Marignan* or *La Guerre* (6 min.) **(Bach SRV 298 SD)	S	3	2
4700	*Le Chant de l'Alouette* (3 min.) **(Bach SRV 298 SD)	S	4	2
4800	*Le Chant des oiseaux* (6 min.) **(Bach SRV 298 SD)	S	2	2
4900	*Ce Moys de May* (1 min.) **(Bach SRV 298 SD)	E	3	2
	LANDINI, FRANCESCO (c. 1335–1397)			
5000	Madrigals, Cacce, Ballate, etc. (vary) **(Argo ZRG 642)	A	5	3
	LASSUS, ORLANDUS (1532–1594)			
5100	Chansons (*Mon coeur se recommende à vous* (2 min.) and *La nuit froide et sombre*) (3 min.) **(Bach SRV 298 SD)	S	2	3
5200	Madrigals (vary) . *(MCA 2513)	S	2	3
5300	Mass (*Ecce nunc benedicite Dominum*) (20 min.) (None. H–71053)	A	2	4
5500	Motets (vary) (None. H–71084)	A	2	4
5700	*Prophetiae Sibyllarum* (28 min.) (None. H–71053)	A	3	4
	LE JEUNE, CLAUDE (c.1530–1600)			
5800	Chansons (vary) (None. H–71001)	A	4	3
	LEONIN (12th century)			
5900	*Notre Dame Organa* (varies) *(2–Tel. 26.35010)	A	1	3
	MACHAUT, GUILLAUME DE (c.1300–1377)			
6000	Ballades, Rondeaux, Virelais (vary) *(Oiseau S–310)	S	2	2
6100	*Comment qu'a moy* (2 min.) **(Bach SRV 298 SD)	S	2	2
6200	*De petit po* (3 min.) *(MCA 2516)	S	2	2
6500	*Se je souspir parfondement* (3 min.) *(MCA 2516)	S	2	2
6600	*S'il estoit nulz* (3 min.) (EA S–83)	S	2	3
6800	*Très douce dame* (2 min.) *(Oiseau S–310)	S	2	2
6900	Mass (*Notre-Dame*) (38 min.) **(Tel. 6.41125); *(Oiseau S–310)	A	2	4
	MILAN, LUIS (c.1500–after 1561)			
7100	6 Pavanas *(DG 139365)	A	3	3
	MORALES, CRISTOBAL DE (c.1500–1553)			
7200	*Ave Maria* **(None. H–71016)	A	2	4
7300	*Lamentabatur Jacob* **(None. H–71016)	A	2	4
7400	*Magnificat septimi toni* **(None. H–71016)	A	2	4
7500	*Missa Quaeramus cum pastoribus* **(BASF 20343)	A	2	4
7600	*Missus est Gabriel angelus* (7 min.) **(None. H–71016); *(Dover 97271E) -mono	A	2	4
7700	*Motet Exaltata est Sancta Dei Genitrix* **(BASF 20343)	A	2	4
7800	*O magnum mysterium* (None. H–71026)	A	2	4
	OBRECHT, JACOB (c.1450–1505)			
7900	*Missa Fortuna desperata* **(MCA 2508)	A	3	5
8000	*Missa Sub tuum praesidium* (21 min.) (DG ARC–198406); (Van. HM–2 SD)	A	3	5
	OCKEGHEM, JOHANNES (c.1425–1495)			
8100	*Alma redemptoris Mater* (Lyr. 7213)	A	3	4
8200	*Ave Maria* (Lyr. 7213)	A	3	4
8300	*Ma bouche rit* (Lyr. 7213)	A	3	3
8400	*Ma maitresse* (Lyr. 7213)	A	3	3
8500	*Missa Caput* (Lyr. 7213)	A	3	4
8700	*Missa Ecce ancilla* **(BASF–21512)	A	3	4
8800	*Missa Mi-mi* (DG ARC–198406)	A	3	4
8900	*Motet Intemerata Dei Mater* **(BASF–21512)	A	3	4
9000	*Petite camusette* (Lyr. 7213)	A	3	3
9100	*Salve Regina* (Lyr. 7213)	A	3	4
	PALESTRINA, GIOVANNI (1525–1594) Madrigals			
9200	*Ahi che quest'occhi miei* (Count. 5602)	A	3	3

GUIDE NO.	COMPOSER AND TITLE	AGE MIN	AES SIG	AC-CESS
9300	Da cosi dotta man (Count. 5602)	A	3	3
9400	Il dolce sonno (Count. 5602)	A	3	3
9500	Il tempo vola (Count. 5602)	A	3	3
9600	Io son ferito (Count. 5602)	A	3	3
9700	Se fra quest'erb'e fiore (Count. 5602)	A	3	3
9800	Vestiva i colli (Count. 5602)	A	3	3
	Masses			
9900	Aeterna Christi munera (Argo 5186)	A	2	4
10,000	Ascendo ad patrem (24 min.) (Odys. 32160122)	A	1	4
10,100	Assumpta est Maria **(Argo ZRG–690)	A	1	4
10,200	De beata virgine (Turn. 34309)	A	1	4
10,300	Ecce ego Joannes (Oiseau S–269)	A	1	4
10,400	In festis apostolorum (26 min.) (Odys. 32160122)	A	1	4
10,500	Missa brevis (25 min.) **(Argo ZRG–690); **(Sera. S–60187)	A	1	3
10,600	Papae Marcelli (29 min.) **(Sera. S–60187); (Ang. S–36022)	A	1	3
10,700	Sine nomine (21 min.) (Oiseau S–269)	A	1	3
10,800	Veni sponsa Christe *(Argo ZRG–578)	A	1	3
	Motets			
10,900	Adjuro vos filiae *(Van. HM–9 SD)	A	1	4
11,000	Ave maris stella (Count. 5602)	A	1	4
11,100	Ave Regina (Oiseau S–283)	A	1	4
11,200	Cantantibus organis (5 min.) (Odys. 32160122)	A	1	4
11,300	Conditur alme siderum *(Argo ZRG–578)	A	1	4
11,400	Descendi in hortum meam *(Van. HM–9 SD)	A	1	4
11,500	Dilectus meus descendit *(Van. HM–9 SD)	A	1	4
11,600	Dilectus meus mihi *(Van. HM–9 SD)	A	1	4
11,700	Duo ubera tua *(Van. HM–9 SD)	A	1	4
11,800	Ecce tu pulcher es *(Van. HM–9 SD)	A	1	4
11,900	Exaltabo te (Count. 5602)	A	1	4
12,000	Exultate Deo *(Argo ZRG–578); (Count. 5602)	A	1	3
12,100	Fasciculus myrrae *(Van. HM–9 SD)	A	1	4
12,200	Hodie beata virgo *(Argo 5398)	A	1	4
12,300	Introduxit me rex *(Van. HM–9 SD)	A	1	4
12,400	Jesu Rex admirabilis *(Argo ZRG–578)	A	1	4

GUIDE NO.	COMPOSER AND TITLE	AGE MIN	AES SIG	AC-CESS
12,500	Lauda Sion salvatorum (Turn. 34309)	A	1	4
12,600	Litaniae de beata vergine Maria (15 min.) *(Argo 5398)	A	1	4
12,700	Magnificat I toni *(Argo 5398); (Oiseau S–283)	A	1	3
12,800	Magnificat IV toni *(Argo ZRG–578); (Count. 5602)	A	1	4
13,000	Martibus suis dixerunt (Count. 5602)	A	1	4
13,100	Nigra sum *(Van. HM–9 SD)	A	1	4
13,200	O magnum mysterium (Turn. 34309)	A	1	4
13,300	Osculetur me *(Van. HM–9 SD)	A	1	4
13,400	Quam pulchri sunt *(Van. HM–9 SD)	A	1	4
13,500	Salvete flores martyrum (Count. 5602)	A	1	4
13,600	Senex puerum portabat *(Argo 5398)	A	1	4
13,700	Sicut cervus (5 min.) (Count. 5602)	A	1	4
13,800	Sicut lilium *(Van. HM–9 SD)	A	1	4
13,900	Si ignoras te *(Van. HM–9 SD)	A	1	4
14,000	Stabat Mater (10 min.) *(Argo 5398)	A	1	3
14,100	Surgam et circuibo civitatem *(Van. HM–9 SD)	A	1	4
14,200	Surge, amica mea (2 min.) *(Van. HM–9 SD); (Odys. 32160122)	A	1	3
14,300	Surge illuminare (Count. 5602); (Oiseau S–283)	A	1	3
14,400	Tota pulchra es *(Van. HM–9 SD)	A	1	4
14,500	Tua Jesu dilectio *(Argo ZRG–578)	A	1	4
14,600	Tu es Petrus (6 min.) (Turn. 34309)	A	1	4
14,700	Vineam meam *(Van. HM–9 SD)	A	1	4
14,800	Veni sancte spiritus (Oiseau S–283)	A	1	4
14,900	Veni sponsa Christi *(Argo ZRG–578); *(Van. HM–9 SD); (Count. 5602)	A	1	3
15,000	Vox dilecti mei *(Van. HM–9 SD)	A	1	4
15,100	Vulnerasti cor meum *(Van. HM–9 SD)	A	1	4
	Ricercari			
15,200	Ricercar del IV tono (Count. 5602)	A	1	4
15,300	Ricercar del VI tono (Count. 5602)	A	1	4
15,400	Ricercar del VIII tono (Count. 5602)	A	1	4
	PEROTIN (c.1155–c.1200)			
15,500	Sederunt Principes (Van. HM–1 SD)	A	1	3
15,600	Viderunt Omnes (Van. HM–1 SD)	A	1	3

GUIDE NO.	COMPOSER AND TITLE	AGE MIN	AES SIG	AC-CESS
15,700	PLAY OF DANIEL (12th century miracle play with music) (40 min.) **(MCA 2504)	S	2	2
15,800	PLAY OF HEROD (medieval music drama) (1 hr., 30 min.) *(2–MCA 2–10008)	S	3	2
	RHAW, GEORG (1488–1548)			
15,900	*Ach Elslein, liebes Elselein* *(DG ARC–2533066)	A	3	3
16,000	*Entlaubet ist der Walde* *(DG ARC–2533066)	A	3	3
16,100	*Mir ist ein feins brauns Maidelein* *(DG ARC–2533066)	A	3	3
16,200	SUMER IS ICUMEN IN, LHUDE SING CUCCU (written by anonymous composer, 1240–1310 A.D.) *(Argo ZRG–5443)	E	3	2
	SUSATO, TIELMAN (?–c.1561)			
16,300	*The Danserye* (vary) **(Ang. S–36851)	E	3	2
	TALLIS, THOMAS (c.1505–1585)			
16,400	*Cantiones sacrae* (vary) (Tel. 6.41201)	A	2	4
16,500	*Lamentations of Jeremiah* (13 min.) **(Argo 5479)	A	1	4
16,600	Mass for 4 Voices (*Missa sine titulo ad quator voces inaequales*) (18 min.) (MCA 2505)	A	2	4
16,700	*Spem in alium* (40 part motet) **(Argo 5436)	A	2	5
	TAVERNER, JOHN (c.1495–1545)			
16,800	*Kyrie Le roy* (4 min.) **(Argo 5316)	A	2	4
16,900	Mass (*The Western Wynde*) (45 min.) **(Argo 5316)	A	1	4
	VICTORIA, TOMAS LUIS DE (1548–1611) Motets and Hymns			
17,000	*Anima mea* (Oiseau S–283)	A	2	4
17,100	*Ascendens Christus in altem* *(Argo ZRG–570)	A	2	4
17,200	*Ave Maria* (3 min.) *(Argo ZRG–570); (Oiseau S–283)	A	2	3
17,300	*Estote fortes in bello* **(Argo ZRG–620)	A	2	4
17,400	*Gaudent in coelis* *(Argo ZRG–570)	A	2	4
17,500	*Hic vir despiciens mundum* **(Argo ZRG–620)	A	2	4
17,600	*Iste sanctus pro lege Dei* **(Argo ZRG–620)	A	2	4
17,700	*Jesu dulcis memoria* (2 min.) (Oiseau S–283)	S	2	3
17,800	*Lauda Sion Salvatorum* (Oiseau S–283)	A	2	4

GUIDE NO.	COMPOSER AND TITLE	AGE MIN	AES SIG	AC-CESS
17,900	*Litaniae de beata Virgine* **(Argo ZRG–620)	A	2	4
18,000	Magnificat I toni (11 min.) **(Argo ZRG–620); (Oiseau S–283)	A	2	4
18,100	*O magnum mysterium* (4 min.) *(Argo ZRG–570); *(Oiseau S–270)	A	2	4
18,200	*O quam gloriosum* (4 min.) **(Argo ZRG–620); *(Oiseau S–270)	A	2	4
18,300	*Veni sponsa Christi* **(Argo ZRG–620)	A	2	4
	Masses			
18,400	*O magnum mysterium* *(Oiseau S–270)	A	2	4
18,500	*O quam gloriosum* **(Argo ZRG–620); *(Oiseau S–270)	A	2	4
18,600	Requiem Mass for the Empress Maria *(Argo ZRG–570)	A	1	5
	WERT, GIACHES DE (JAKOB VAN WERT) (1535–1596)			
18,800	Madrigals; Canzonets; Motets; etc. (vary) *(Van. VCS–10083)	A	3	4
	WILLAERT, ADRIAN (c.1490–1562)			
18,900	Music of Willaert (varies) *(CSP C32160202)	A	3	4

Anthologies of Early Music

GUIDE NO.	TITLE OF ALBUM	AGE MIN	AES SIG	AC-CESS
19,000	*Ars Antiqua: Organum, Motets, Conductus, and Other Early Polyphony* **(2–Tel. 26.35010)	S	2	3
19,200	*Carmina Burana: The Original 20 Songs from the Illuminated Manuscript, 1300 A.D.* **(Tel. 6.41184)	A	3	3
19,300	*Carmina Burana, Volume II: 13 Songs after the Benediktbeurn Manuscript, c.1300 A.D.* **(Tel. 6.41234)	A	3	3
19,500	*Ceremonial Music of the Renaissance: Ciconia, Geragut, Dufay, Encina, Isaac, Mouton, anon.* **(Tel. 6.41087)	S	3	3
19,700	*Chansons des Troubadours: Songs and Instrumental Music of the 13th Century* **(Tel. 6.41126)	S	3	2
19,900	*Dance Music of the Renaissance: Gulielmus, Torre, Attaignant, Milan, Mudarra, Susato, et. al.* **(DG ARC–2533150)	E	4	2
20,100	*Medieval and Renaissance Music for the Irish and Medieval Harps, Viele, Recorders, and Tambourin* **(Turn. 34019)	S	4	3

GUIDE NO.	TITLE OF ALBUM	AGE MIN	AES SIG	AC-CESS
20,300	*Missa Tournai and Motets, c.1320 A.D.* **(Tel. 6.41230)	A	2	4
20,500	*Music from the Time of Christopher Columbus* **(Phi. 839714)	S	3	2
20,700	*Music of Shakespeare's Time: Vocal and Instrumental Works of Elizabethan England* **(2–None. HB–73010)	S	2	3
20,900	*Music of the Crusades: Songs of Love and War* **(Argo ZRG–673)	S	4	2

GUIDE NO.	TITLE OF ALBUM	AGE MIN	AES SIG	AC-CESS
21,100	*Music of the Early Renaissance: John Dunstable and His Contemporaries* **(Turn. 34058)	A	3	4
21,300	*Music of the Spanish Renaissance* *(Turn. 34264)	A	3	4
21,700	*Secular Vocal Music of the Renaissance from Spain, Italy, and France* **(Dover 5262)	S	3	3
21,900	*Songs of the Spanish Renaissance* **(Ang. S–35888)	S	2	2

2. Choral Music

GUIDE NO.	COMPOSER AND TITLE	AGE MIN	AES SIG	AC-CESS
	ANERIO, GIOVANNI FRANCESCO (c.1567–1630)			
22,000	*Missa pro defunctis* **(Oiseau 60042)	A	3	3
	BACH, JOHANN SEBASTIAN (1685–1750)			
23,004	Cantata no. 4 (*Christ lag in Todesbanden*) (20 min.) **(DG ARC–198465)	S	1	3
23,008	Cantata no. 8 (*Liebster Gott, wann werd' ich sterben*) (21 min.) (2–Tel. 26.35028)	A	2	3
23,010	Cantata no. 10 (*Meine Seele 'erhebt den Herrn*) (22 min.) *(2–Tel. 26.35029)	A	2	3
23,018	Cantata no. 18 (*Gleich wie der Regen*) (14 min.) *(DG ARC–198441)	A	1	2
23,021	Cantata no. 21 (*Ich hatte viel Bekümmernis*) (44 min.) **(DG ARC–2533049)	A	1	2
23,026	Cantata no. 26 (*Ach wie flüchtig, ach wie nichtig*) (15 min.) **(DG ARC–198402)	A	1	3
23,050	Cantata no. 50 (*Nun ist das Heil und die Kraft*) (5 min.) *(Van. HM–22 SD)	S	4	1
23,051	Cantata no. 51 (*Jauchzet Gott in allen Landen*) (19 min.) *(DG ARC–198027)	S	2	2
23,056	Cantata no. 56 (*Ich will den Kreuzstab gerne tragen*) (21 min.) *(DG ARC–198477)	A	2	2
23,057	Cantata no. 57 (*Selig ist der Mann*) (26 min.) **(None. H–71029)	S	2	3
23,060	Cantata no. 60 (*O Ewigkeit du Donnerwort*) (18 min.) **(DG ARC–198331)	S	2	2

GUIDE NO.	COMPOSER AND TITLE	AGE MIN	AES SIG	AC-CESS
23,065	Cantata no. 65 (*Sie werden aus Saba alle kommen*) (17 min.) (Van. SRV–226 SD)	S	2	2
23,067	Cantata no. 67 (*Halt im Gedächtnis Jesum Christ*) (16 min.) *(Lon. OS 26098)	A	1	3
23,078	Cantata no. 78 (*Jesu der du meine Seele*) (25 min.) *(Ang. S–36354)	S	2	2
23,080	Cantata no. 80 (*Ein feste Burg ist unser Gott*) (29 min.) *(DG ARC–198407)	S	2	2
23,082	Cantata no. 82 (*Ich habe genug*) (24 min.) *(DG ARC–198477)	S	2	2
23,106	Cantata no. 106 (*Gottes Zeit ist die allerbeste Zeit*) (20 min.) **(DG ARC–198402); *(Tel. 6.41060)	S	2	2
23,206	Sinfonia (6 min.) **(DG ARC–198402); *(Tel. 6.41060)	S	1	1
23,240	Cantata no. 140 (*Wachet auf!*) (29 min.) **(None. H–71029); *(DG ARC–198407)	S	1	2
23,247	Cantata no. 147 (*Herz und Mund und Tat und Leben*) (33 min.) **(Ang. S–36804); **(DG ARC–198331)	S	2	2
23,347	*Jesu Joy of Man's Desiring* (4 min.) **(Ang. S–36804); **(DG ARC–198331)	E	2	1
23,359	Cantata no. 159 (*Sehet, wir geh'n hinauf*) (17 min.) *(Oiseau S–295)	S	2	1
23,370	Cantata no. 170 (*Vergnügte Ruh', beliebte Seelenlust*) (24 min.) *(Oiseau S–295)	A	2	3

GUIDE NO.	COMPOSER AND TITLE	AGE MIN	AES SIG	AC-CESS
23,372	Cantata no. 172 (*Erschallet, ihr Lieder*) (24 min.) (None. H–71256)	S	2	2
23,382	Cantata no. 182 (*Himmelskönig, sei willkommen*) (30 min.) *(Tel. 6.41060)	A	2	2
23,398	Cantata no. 198 (*Lass Fürstin, lass noch einen Strahl*) (38 min.) *(Tel. 6.41215)	A	2	3
23,402	Cantata no. 202 (*Weichet nur, betrübe Schatten*) (*Wedding* Cantata) (22 min.) *(DG ARC–198027); *(Turn. 34042)	S	3	2
23,406	Cantata no. 206 (*Schleicht, spielende Wellen*) (44 min.) *(Tel. 6.41047)	A	2	2
23,408	Cantata no. 208 (*Was mir behagt, ist nur die muntre Jagd*) (35 min.) *(Tel. 6.41050); (Sera. S–60121)	A	3	3
23,409	Cantata no. 209 (*Non sa che sia dolore*) (23 min.) *(Tel. 6.41067)	A	3	2
23,411	Cantata no. 211 (*Coffee* Cantata) (28 min.) *(Tel. 6.41079)	A	3	2
23,412	Cantata no. 212 (*Mer hahn en neue Oberkeet*) (*Peasant* Cantata) (30 min.) *(Tel. 6.41079)	A	3	2
23,750	*Christmas* Oratorio, S. 248 (2 hr., 43 min.) **(3–Tel. 36.35022)	A	2	2
24,000	*Easter* Oratorio, S. 249 (47 min.) **(Lon. OS 26100)	A	2	2
24,250	*Magnificat* in D, S. 243 (29 min.) *(Ang. S–36615)	S	2	2
24,500	*Mass* in b, S. 232 (2 hr.) **(3–DG ARC–2710001)	A	1	3
24,750	*Motets* (6), S. 225–30 (1 hr., 16 min.) *(2–RCA VICS–6037)	A	3	2
25,000	*Motet* no. 3 (*Jesu, meine Freude*, S. 227) (24 min.) *(Argo–5234)	A	2	2
25,250	*St. John Passion*, S. 245 (1 hr., 56 min.) **(3–Tel. 36.35018)	A	2	3
25,500	*St. Matthew Passion*, S. 244 (3 hr., 13 min.) **(4–Lon. OSA 1431)	A	1	2
	BARTÓK, BÉLA (1881–1945)			
26,000	*Cantata Profana* (*Enchanted Deer*) (1930) (17 min.) (Bartok 312)-*mono*	A	2	4
	BEETHOVEN, LUDWIG VAN (1770–1827)			
26,500	*Christus am Oelberg*, op. 85 (oratorio) (56 min.) (West. WGS–8206)	A	4	4
26,750	*Fantasia* in c for Piano, Chorus, and Orchestra, op. 80 (19 min.) *(Col. MS–6616)	A	4	4
27,000	*Mass* in C, op. 86 (45 min.) *(Ang. S–36775)	A	3	4
27,250	*Meeresstille und glückliche Fahrt*, op. 112 (Col. M–30085)	A	4	3
27,500	*Missa Solemnis* in D, op. 123 (1 hr., 20 min.) **(2–Ang. S–3679)	A	1	3
	BERLIOZ, HECTOR (1803–1869)			
28,000	*La damnation de Faust*, op. 24 (2 hr.) **(3–Phi. 6703042)	A	2	3
28,250	*L'Enfance du Christ*, op. 25 (1 hr., 33 min.) *(2–Oiseau 60032/3)	S	3	2
28,500	*Requiem*, op. 5 (*Grande Messe des Mort*) (1 hr., 26 min.) **(2–DG 2707032)	A	3	3
28,750	*Roméo et Juliette*, op. 17 (1 hr., 35 min.) **(2–Phi. 839716/7)	A	3	2
29,000	*Te Deum*, op. 22 (49 min.) (Phi. 839790)	A	2	3
	BERNSTEIN, LEONARD (1918–)			
29,500	*Chichester Psalms* for Chorus and Orchestra (1965) (18 min.) **(Col. MS–6792)	S	3	2
	BILLINGS, WILLIAM (1746–1800)			
30,000	*Chester* (2 min.) **(Col. MS–7277)	S	4	2
30,250	*David's Lamentation* (2 min.) **(Col. MS–7277)	S	4	2
30,500	*Hymns and Anthems* (vary) **(Col. MS–7277)	S	4	2
30,750	*When Jesus Wept* (2 min.) **(Col. MS–7277)	S	4	2
	BRAHMS, JOHANNES (1833–1897)			
31,000	*Alto Rhapsody*, op. 53 (13 min.) **(Rich. R 23183)-*mono*	A	3	2
31,250	*German Requiem*, op. 45 (1 hr., 8 min.) **(2–Ang. S–3624)	A	2	3
31,500	*Liebeslieder* Waltzes, op. 52 (24 min.) *(RCA LSC–2864)	S	4	1
31,750	*Liebeslieder* Waltzes, op. 65 (20 min.) *(RCA LSC–2864)	S	4	1
32,000	*Schicksalslied*, op. 54 (15 min.) *(Lon. OS 26106)	A	3	2
32,250	*Zigeunerlieder*, op. 103 (12 min.) *(None. H–71228)	A	4	1
	BRITTEN, BENJAMIN (1913–)			
33,000	*Cantata Academica*, op. 62 (20 min.) **(Oiseau 60037)	A	3	3
33,500	*Cantata Misericordium*, op. 69 (1963) (20 min.) **(Lon. OS 25937)	A	3	3

GUIDE NO. COMPOSER AND TITLE	AGE MIN	AES SIG	AC-CESS
34,000 *Ceremony of Carols*, op. 28 (1942) (21 min.) *(Argo 5440); *(Sera. S–60217)	A	3	3
34,500 *Missa brevis* in D, op. 63 *(Argo 5440); *(Sera. S–60217)	A	4	3
35,000 *Rejoice in the Lamb*, op. 30 (1943) (18 min.) *(Argo 5440)	A	3	3
35,500 *Spring* Symphony (1949) (44 min.) **(Lon. OS 25242)	S	3	2
36,000 *War Requiem*, op. 66 (1962) (1 hr., 22 min.) **(2–Lon. OSA 1255)	A	2	2
BRUCKNER, ANTON (1824–1896)			
37,000 Mass no. 3 in f (*Great*) (1 hr., 30 min.) *(DG 138829)	A	3	4
37,250 Motets (*Afferentur; Os justi; Inveni David; Pange lingua; Ecce sacerdos*) (7 min.) **(Argo ZRG–760)	A	3	3
37,500 Motet (*Ave Maria*) (4 min.) (Argo ZRG–523)	A	3	2
38,000 *Te Deum* (22 min.) **(2–Phi. 802759/60)	A	2	4
BUXTEHUDE, DIETRICH (c.1637–1707)			
38,500 *Magnificat* (10 min.) (Turn. 34173)	A	3	4
CARISSIMI, GIACOMO (1605–1674)			
39,000 *Jephte* **(Turn. 34089)	A	4	3
COPLAND, AARON (1900–)			
40,000 *In the Beginning* (1947) (16 min.) *(Ev. 3129)	S	4	2
DEBUSSY, CLAUDE (1862–1918)			
41,250 *Trois Chansons de Charles d'Orléans* (1908) (6 min.) *(Argo ZRG–523)	A	4	3
DELIUS, FREDERICK (1862–1934)			
41,500 *Requiem* **(Sera. S–60147)	A	3	3
41,750 *Sea Drift* (30 min.) **(Ang. S–37011)	A	3	3
42,000 *A Village Romeo and Juliet* (1907) **(2–Ang. S–3784X)	A	4	3
DEMANTIUS, CHRISTOPH (1567–1643)			
42,250 *Prophecy of the Suffering and Death of Jesus Christ* (12 min.) *(Turn. 34175)	A	4	4
DVOŘÁK, ANTONIN (1841–1904)			
42,500 Requiem, op. 89 (1 hr., 34 min.) **(2–Lon. OSA 1281)	A	3	4

GUIDE NO. COMPOSER AND TITLE	AGE MIN	AES SIG	AC-CESS
42,750 *Stabat Mater*, op. 58 (1 hr., 28 min.) *(2–DG 2707014)	A	4	4
ELGAR, EDWARD (1857–1934)			
43,000 *Dream of Gerontius* (1900) (1 hr., 41 min.) **(2–Ang. S–3660)	A	3	3
FAURÉ, GABRIEL (1845–1924)			
43,250 Requiem, op. 48 (1887) (38 min.) **(Ang. S–35974)	S	2	1
FOSS, LUKAS (1922–)			
43,500 *Parable of Death* (cantata) (31 min.) **(CSP AML–4859)-*mono*	A	3	3
GABRIELI, GIOVANNI (1551–1612)			
44,000 *Hodie Christus natus est* (4 min.) *(Col. MS–7071)	A	2	4
44,500 *In ecclesiis benedicite Domino* (7 min.) *(Col. MS–7071)	A	2	4
45,000 *Timor et tremor* (6 min.) *(Ang. S–36443)	A	2	4
GESUALDO, DON CARLO (c.1560–1613)			
45,250 Italian Madrigals (vary) **(Phi. 839789)	A	2	4
45,500 *Ahi, gia mi discoloro* (3 min.) **(Phi. 839789)	A	2	3
45,750 *Dolcissima mia vita* (4 min.) **(Phi. 839789)	A	2	4
46,000 *Ecco moriro . . .* (2 min.) **(Phi. 839789)	A	2	3
46,250 *Invan dunque, a crudele* (3 min.) **(Phi. 839789)	A	2	4
46,500 *Io tacero, ma nel silentio mio* (3 min.) **(Phi. 839789)	A	2	3
46,750 *Itene o miei sospiri* (3 min.) *(None. H–71277)	A	2	4
47,000 Motet (*O vos omnes*) (3 min.) *(None. H–71277); *(Tel. 6.41266)	A	2	4
GOUNOD, CHARLES (1818–1893)			
48,000 *Messe Solennelle* (St. Cecilia) (47 min.) **(Ang. S–36214)	S	5	2
48,250 Soldiers' Chorus from *Faust* (4 min.) *(Ang. S–35827)	S	4	2
HANDEL, GEORGE FRIDERIC (1685–1759)			
48,500 *Acis and Galatea* (1 hr., 26 min.) **(2–Oiseau 60011/2)	S	3	2
48,750 *Alexander's Feast* (1 hr., 39 min.) (2–Van. SRV–282/3 SD)	S	2	2

51

GUIDE NO.	COMPOSER AND TITLE	AGE MIN	AES SIG	AC-CESS
49,000	*L'Allegro ed il Penseroso* (1 hr., 38 min.) (2–Oiseau 60025/6)	A	2	3
49,250	Anthems (4) for the Coronation of George II (vary) **(Argo 5369)	A	3	3
49,500	*The King Shall Rejoice* (12 min.) **(Argo 5369)	A	3	2
49,750	*Let Thy Hand Be Strengthened* (9 min.) **(Argo 5369)	A	4	3
50,000	*Zadok the Priest* (6 min.) **(Argo 5369)	A	3	2
50,125	Chandos Anthem 1 (*O Be Joyful in the Lord*) *(Van. SRV–229 SD)	A	3	3
50,250	Chandos Anthem 2 (*In the Lord Put I My Trust*) (26 min.) *(Van. SRV–228 SD)	A	3	3
50,500	Chandos Anthem 3 (*Have Mercy upon Me*) (26 min.) *(Van. SRV–228 SD)	A	3	3
50,625	Chandos Anthem 5 (*I Will Magnify Thee*) *(Van. SRV–229 SD)	A	3	3
50,750	Chandos Anthem 6 (*As Pants the Hart*) (23 min.) *(Argo ZRG–541); *(Van. SRV–227 SD)	A	2	3
51,000	*Dettingen Te Deum* (42 min.) (None. H–71003)	A	3	3
51,250	*Dixit Dominus* (38 min.) *(Ang. S–36331)	A	3	3
51,500	*Israel in Egypt* (oratorio) (1 hr., 27 min.) **(2–DG ARC–2708020)	A	4	4
51,750	*Messiah* (oratorio) (2 hr., 26 min.) **(3–Phi. SC71AX300)	S	3	1
52,000	*Ode for St. Cecilia's Day* (1 hr.) *(Argo S–563)	S	2	2
52,750	*Saul* (2 hrs.) *(3–Van. HM–24/5/6 SD)	A	3	3
53,000	*Semele* (2 hr., 38 min.) *(3–Oiseau S–111E)-*mono*	A	4	3
53,250	*Solomon* (1 hr., 40 min.) **(2–Sera. S–6039)	A	5	3

HANSON, HOWARD (1896–)

53,750	*Lament for Beowulf* (1925) (20 min.) (Mer. 75007)	S	5	3

HARRISON, LOU (1917–)

54,000	*4 Strict Songs for 8 Baritones and Orchestra* (1956) (16 min.) *(Lou. 58–2)-*mono*	A	3	3

HAYDN, (FRANZ) JOSEPH (1732–1809)

54,500	*Creation* (oratorio) (1 hr., 47 min.) **(2–DG 2707044)	S	1	2
55,000	Mass no. 5 in B flat (*Little Organ*) (20 min.) *(Turn. 34132)	A	3	3
55,250	Mass no. 7 (*Missa in tempore belli*) (*Paukenmesse*)	A	2	3

GUIDE NO.	COMPOSER AND TITLE	AGE MIN	AES SIG	AC-CESS
	(40 min.) **(Argo ZRG–634)			
55,500	Mass no. 8 in B flat (*Heiligmesse*) (38 min.) *(Argo ZRG–542)	A	3	3
55,750	Mass no. 9 in d (*Missa Solemnis*) (*Nelson Mass*) (39 min.) *(Argo 5325)	A	2	3
56,000	Mass no. 10 in B flat (*Theresien-Messe*) (44 min.) **(Argo 5500)	A	3	3
56,250	Mass no. 11 in B flat (*Creation*) (50 min.) *(Argo ZRG–598)	A	3	3
56,500	Mass no. 12 in B flat (*Harmoniemesse*) (46 min.) **(Argo Z–515)	S	2	2
56,750	*Seasons* (oratorio) (2 hr., 20 min.) **(3–None. HC–73009)– (in German); **(3–Phi. 839719/21)–(in English)	S	1	2

HINDEMITH, PAUL (1895–1963)

57,250	*Requiem* (*For Those We Love*) (1949) (1 hr.) **(CSP AMS–6573)	A	2	3

HOLST, GUSTAV (1874–1934)

57,750	*Choral Hymns* from the *Rig-Veda*, op. 26 (1910) (10 min.) **(Argo ZNF–6)	A	4	3
58,250	Medieval Lyrics; Part Songs, op. 44 **(Argo 5495)	A	3	3

HONEGGER, ARTHUR (1892–1955)

58,500	*Christmas Cantata* (25 min.) *(Lon. OS 25320)	A	3	3
59,000	*Roi David* (1921) (1 hr., 15 min.) *(2–Van. VSD 2117/8)	S	4	3

IVES, CHARLES (1874–1954)

59,500	*Harvest Home Chorales* (3) (1898–1912) (8 min.) *(Col. MS–6921)	S	2	2
59,750	*Psalms 24, 67, 90, 100, 150* (10 min.) *(Col. MS–6921)	S	3	2

JANÁČEK, LEOŠ (1854–1928)

60,500	*Slavonic Mass* (*M'ša Glagolskaja*) (1927) (41 min.) *(DG 138954)	A	3	3

KODÁLY, ZOLTÁN (1882–1967)

61,000	Hungarian Folksongs (20) (arranged by Bartók and Kodály) (19 min.) *(Ang. S–36334)	S	3	1
61,250	*Missa brevis* (1945) (35 min.) *(Lyr. 7144)	S	4	3
61,500	*Psalmus Hungaricus*, op. 13 (1923) (23 min.) **(Lon. OS 26186)	S	4	1

GUIDE NO.	COMPOSER AND TITLE	AGE MIN	AES SIG	ACCESS
	LISZT, FRANZ (1811–1886)			
62,000	*Faust* Symphony (1 hr., 7 min.) *(2–Sera. S–6017)	S	4	1
62,250	*Missa choralis* in a (32 min.) **(Argo ZRG–760)	S	4	2
	MAHLER, GUSTAV (1860–1911)			
63,000	*Das klagende Lied* (complete original version with *Wald-märchen* movement) (1 hr., 15 min.) **(2–Col. M2–30061)	A	3	2
	MARENZIO, LUCA (1553–1599)			
63,500	Madrigal (*Ahi, dispietate morte*) (3 min.) *(Ev. 3179E)-mono	A	3	3
64,000	Madrigal (*Scendo dal paradiso*) (8 min.) *(Ev. 3179E)-mono	A	2	3
	MENDELSSOHN, FELIX (1809–1847)			
65,250	*Elijah*, op. 70 (oratorio) (2 hr., 18 min.) *(3–Ang. S–3738)	A	4	2
	MILHAUD, DARIUS (1892–1974)			
65,500	*Choëphores* (1915–16) (34 min.) **(CSP AMS–6396)	S	3	2
	MONTEVERDI, CLAUDIO (1567–1643)			
66,000	*Il ballo delle ingrate* (42 min.) **(Phi. 6500457)	A	2	3
66,500	*Lagrime d'Amante* (from Madrigals, Book VI) (23 min.) *(Van. SRV–297 SD)	A	2	2
67,000	*Lamento d'Arianna* (16 min.) *(Van. SRV–297 SD)	A	2	2
67,500	*Lamento della ninfa* (4 min.) **(Argo ZRG–668)	A	1	2
68,000	Madrigals (vary) **(Argo ZRG–668); **(5–Phi. 6799006)	A	3	3
68,500	*Madrigali guerrieri et amorosi* (50 min.) **(5–Phi. 6799006)	A	3	3
69,000	*Magnificat a 6 voci* (from *Vespro*, 1610) (19 min.) *(Oiseau S–263)	A	2	4
69,500	Mass in 4 Parts (1640) **(Argo 5494)	A	2	4
70,000	Mass in 4 Parts (1651) **(Argo 5494)	A	2	4
70,500	*Laudate pueri* (7 min.) **(Argo 5494)	A	2	4
71,000	*Ut queant laxis* (3 min.) **(Argo 5494)	A	2	4
71,500	*Vespro della Beata Vergine* (1 hr., 50 min.) *(2–Tel. 26.35045)	A	2	4
	MOZART, WOLFGANG AMADEUS (1756–1791)			
72,000	*Ave, verum corpus*, K. 618 (3 min.) **(Phi. 6500271)	A	2	2
72,250	Mass in C, K. 317 (*Coronation*) (26 min.) **(None. H–71041)	A	3	3
72,500	Mass in c, K. 427 (*The Great*) (57 min.) *(DG 138124)	A	2	3
72,750	*Missa brevis* in C, K. 259 (16 min.) *(Turn. 34132)	A	2	3
73,000	Requiem, K. 626 (56 min.) **(Phi. 802862)	A	1	3
73,250	*Vesperae Solennes de Confessore* in C, K. 339 (27 min.) **(Phi. 6500271); *(None. H–71041)	A	3	2
	ORFF, CARL (1895–)			
73,500	*Carmina Burana* (scenic cantata) (1935–36) (1 hr.) **(Ang. S–36333)	S	4	1
73,750	*Catulli Carmina* (scenic cantata) (1943) (37 min.) *(DG 2530074)	S	4	2
	PARKER, HORATIO (1863–1919)			
74,000	*Hora Novissima*, op. 30 (1893) (1 hr., 2 min.) (2–Desto S–6413/4E)-mono	A	5	2
	PERGOLESI, GIOVANNI BATTISTA (1710–1736)			
74,250	*Stabat Mater* (41 min.) **(DG ARC–2533114); *(Lon. OS 25921)	A	3	2
	PILKINGTON, FRANCIS (c.1562–?)			
74,500	*Rest Sweet Nymphs* (4 min.) *(None. H–71097)	S	3	2
	POULENC, FRANCIS (1899–1963)			
74,750	*Gloria in G* (1961) (24 min.) *(Ang. S–35953)	A	4	2
75,000	*Mass in G* (1937) (17 min.) *(Sera. S–60085)	A	3	2
75,250	*Motets (4) pour un temps de pénitence* (1939) (14 min.) *(Ang. S–36121)	A	2	3
75,500	*Stabat Mater* (1951) (31 min.) *(Ang. S–36121)	A	2	2
	PROKOFIEV, SERGE (1891–1953)			
75,750	*Alexander Nevsky*, op. 78 (1939) (40 min.) **(Mel./Ang. S–40010)	S	2	2
	PURCELL, HENRY (c.1659–1695)			
76,000	Anthems (vary) **(Argo 5444)	S	3	2
76,250	*Come Ye Sons of Art* (26 min.) **(Oiseau S–102E)-mono	S	3	2
76,500	*Jubilate* in D (8 min.) *(Argo ZRG–724)	S	3	2
76,750	Music for the Funeral of Queen Mary (1695) (12 min.) *(Argo ZRG–724)	S	3	2

GUIDE NO.	COMPOSER AND TITLE	AGE MIN	AES SIG	AC- CESS
77,000	*Ode for St. Cecilia's Day* (55 min.) **(DG ARC–2533042)	S	2	2
77,250	*Te Deum* (14 min.) *(Argo ZRG–724)	A	3	2
	RACHMANINOFF, SERGEI (1873–1943)			
77,500	*The Bells*, op. 35 (1913) (35 min.) *(Mel./Ang. S–40114)	A	4	2
	ROSSINI, GIOACCHINO (1792–1868)			
77,750	*Stabat Mater* (54 min.) **(Lon. OS 26250)	S	3	2
	SCHEIDT, SAMUEL (1587–1654)			
78,000	*Psalm 103* **(Argo ZRG–576)	A	3	3
	SCHEIN, JOHANN HERMANN (1586–1630)			
78,200	*Freue dich* **(Argo ZRG–576)	A	3	3
78,400	*Ich beschwöre* **(Argo ZRG–576)	A	3	3
78,600	*Zion spricht* **(Argo ZRG–576)	A	3	3
	SCHMITT, FLORENT (1870–1958)			
79,000	*Psalm XLVII*, op. 38 *(Ang. S–36953)	A	3	2
	SCHOENBERG, ARNOLD (1874–1951)			
79,500	*De Profundis*, for Chorus a cappella, op. 50b (1951) (5 min.) *(2–Col. M2S–780)	A	4	4
79,750	*Friede auf Erden*, op. 13 (1907) (9 min.) *(Argo ZRG–523)	A	5	2
80,000	*Gurre-Lieder* (1901–13) (2 hr., 10 min.) **(2–DG 2726046)	A	5	3
80,250	*Song of the Wood Dove* (13 min.) **(2–DG 2726046)	A	4	2
80,500	*6 Pieces for Men's Chorus*, op. 35 (1930) (15 min.) **(Ang. S–36480); *(2–Col. M2S–780)	A	4	5
80,750	*Survivor from Warsaw*, op. 46 (1947) *(2–Col. M2S–679)	A	3	4
	SCHUBERT, FRANZ (1797–1828)			
81,002	*Mass no. 2 in G*, D. 167 (25 min.) (MCA 2529)	S	4	2
81,006	*Mass no. 6 in E flat*, D. 950 (51 min.) (Lyr. 776)	S	2	2
	SCHÜTZ, HEINRICH (1585–1672)			
82,250	*Cantiones sacrae 1625* (complete) **(3–Tel. 36.35009)	A	3	4
82,500	*Christmas Oratorio* (30 min.) **(Turn. 34088)	A	3	3
82,750	*Deutsches Magnificat* (1671) **(Argo ZRG–666)	A	3	3
83,000	*Easter Oratorio* (48 min.) **(Turn. 34231); *(Argo ZRG–639)	A	3	3
83,250	*Kleine geistliche Konzerte a 1–5* (4 hrs.) *(2–None. HB–73012); *(4–None. HD–73024)	A	3	3
83,500	*Magnificat* (14 min.) *(Turn. 34099)	A	2	2
83,750	*Motets* (vary) *(None. H–71062)	A	3	3
84,000	*Psalms of David*, op. 2 (1619) (vary) **(Argo ZRG–666)	A	3	3
84,125	*Psalm 24* **(Argo ZRG–576)	A	3	3
84,250	*St. Luke Passion* (36 min.) *(Tel. 6.41193)	A	2	4
84,500	*St. Matthew Passion* (54 min.) **(Argo ZRG–689)	A	2	4
84,750	*Seven Words from the Cross* (21 min.) *(Tel. 6.41193)	A	2	4
85,000	*Symphoniae Sacrae; Small Sacred Concerti* (vary) *(None. H–71160); *(None. H–71196)	A	3	3
	SHOSTAKOVICH, DMITRI (1906–1975)			
85,500	*Song of the Forests*, op. 81 (oratorio) **(Mel./Ang. S–40214)	S	5	3
	STAINER, JOHN (1840–1901)			
85,750	*Crucifixion* (53 min.) **(Argo ZRG–5320)	A	5	3
	STRAVINSKY, IGOR (1882–1971)			
86,000	*Cantata* (1952) (26 min.) *(Col. MS–6992); *(Oiseau S–265)	A	2	4
86,250	*Canticum Sacrum* **(CSP CMS–6022)	A	2	4
86,750	*Mass* (1948) *(Col. MS–6992); *(Oiseau S–265)	A	2	4
87,000	*Les Noces* (1917–23) (24 min.) *(Lon. CS 6219)	S	2	3
87,250	*A Sermon, a Narrative, and a Prayer* (1961) *(Col. MS–7054)	A	4	4
87,500	*Symphony of Psalms* (1930) (22 min.) **(Lon. CS 6219); *(Col. MS–6548)	A	1	3
	TELEMANN, GEORG PHILIPP (1681–1767)			
88,000	*Canary Cantata* (17 min.) (Sera. S–60121)	S	4	3
88,250	*Cantata* (*Machet die Tore weit*) (17 min.) (None. H–71182)	S	4	3
88,500	*Der Tag des Gerichts* (oratorio) **(2–Tel. 26.35044)	A	5	3
	TIPPETT, MICHAEL (1905–)			
89,000	*Child of our Time* (oratorio) (1944) **(2–Argo ZDA–19/20)	A	3	3

GUIDE NO.	COMPOSER AND TITLE	AGE MIN	AES SIG	AC- CESS
89,250	*The Weeping Babe* for Chorus and Soprano Solo (11 min.) **(Argo ZRG–535)	A	2	3
	VAUGHAN WILLIAMS, RALPH (1872–1958)			
89,500	*Benedicite* (1929) **(Ang. S–36751)	S	4	2
89,625	*Dona nobis pacem* (1936) *(Ang. S–36972)	S	4	2
89,750	*Flos Campi,* Suite for Viola, Orchestra, and Chorus (1925) (15 min.) **(Ang. S–36699)	S	4	2
90,000	*Magnificat* (1932) (18 min.) **(Ang. S–36819)	S	4	2
90,250	*Mass in g* (1923) (30 min.) **(Ang. S–36590)	S	2	2
90,500	*Sancta Civitas* (oratorio) (22 min.) **(Ang. S–36751)	S	4	2
90,750	*Serenade to Music* (1937–38) **(Ang. S–36902)	S	3	2
	VERDI, GIUSEPPE (1813–1901)			
91,000	*Choruses* (vary) (Lon. OS 25893)	S	3	2
91,500	*Pezzi sacri* (4) (1898) (41 min.) **(Ang. S–36125)	A	2	3
91,750	*Requiem Mass,* in memory of Manzoni (1874)	A	1	2

GUIDE NO.	COMPOSER AND TITLE	AGE MIN	AES SIG	AC- CESS
	(1 hr., 20 min.) **(2–RCA LM–6018)-*mono*; *(2–Ang. S–3649); *(2–DG 2707065)			
	VIVALDI, ANTONIO (1678–1741)			
92,750	*Gloria in D* (31 min.) **(Argo Z–505); **(Turn. 34029)	S	2	2
	WALTON, WILLIAM (1902–)			
93,250	*Belshazzar's Feast* (1931) (36 min.) **(Ang. S–35681); *(Ang. S–36861)	S	3	1
	WEBERN, ANTON (1883–1945)			
93,500	*Das Augenlicht,* op. 26 (1935) (cantata for chorus and orchestra) (6 min.) (4–CSP CK4L–232)-*mono*	A	2	5
93,750	*Cantata,* op. 29 (1940) (8 min.) **(Lon. CS 6612)	A	2	5
94,250	*Entflieht auf leichten Kähnen,* op. 2 (1908) (MGM S–4722)	S	4	4
	WEELKES, THOMAS (c.1575–1623)			
94,500	*Church Music* (varies) **(Argo 5237)	A	2	3

3. Keyboard Instruments

GUIDE NO.	COMPOSER AND TITLE	AGE MIN	AES SIG	AC- CESS
	ALBÉNIZ, ISAAC (1860–1909)			
94,750	*Cantos de España,* op. 232 (23 min.) **(2–Lon. CSA 2235)	S	4	4
95,000	*Cordoba* only (4 min.) **(2–Lon. CSA 2235)	S	4	4
95,250	*Seguidillas* only (4 min.) **(2–Lon. CSA 2235)	S	4	3
95,500	*Under Palm Tree* only (5 min.) **(2–Lon. CSA 2235)	S	4	4
96,000	*Iberia* (complete) **(2–Lon. CSA 2235)	S	3	3
96,250	Book I, *Evocación* (7 min.) **(2–Lon. CSA 2235)	S	3	3
96,500	Book I, *El puerto* (4 min.) **(2–Lon. CSA 2235)	S	3	3
96,750	Book I, *Fête-Dieu à Séville* (7 min.) **(2–Lon. CSA 2235)	S	3	3
97,000	Book II, *Almeria* (9 min.) **(2–Lon. CSA 2235)	S	3	3
97,250	Book II, *Triana* (5 min.) **(2–Lon. CSA 2235)	S	3	2
97,500	Book III, *El Albaicin* (7 min.) **(2–Lon. CSA 2235)	S	3	3
97,750	Book IV, *Málaga, Jérez, and Eritaña* (22 min.) **(2–Lon. CSA 2235)	S	3	3

GUIDE NO.	COMPOSER AND TITLE	AGE MIN	AES SIG	AC- CESS
	D'ANGLEBERT, JEAN-HENRI (c.1628–1691)			
98,500	*Tombeau de M. de Chambonnières* (4 min.) (RCA VICS–1370)	A	4	3
	BACH, CARL PHILLIP EMANUEL (1714–1788)			
98,750	*Sonata in g* for Organ (15 min.) *(Tel. 6.41085)	A	4	3
99,000	Variations for Harpsichord (*Les Folies d'Espagne* W. 118) (9 min.) *(Argo ZRG–577)	A	4	3
	BACH, JOHANN CHRISTOPH (1642–1703)			
99,250	Chorale Prelude (*Warum betrubst du dich*) (2 min.) **(Tel. 6.41113)	A	4	4
	BACH, JOHANN MICHAEL (1754–?)			
99,500	Chorale Prelude (*Wenn wir in höchsten Noten*) (2 min.) **(Tel. 6.41113)	A	4	4
	BACH, JOHANN SEBASTIAN (1685–1750)			
100,000	*Art of the Fugue,* S. 1080	A	2	5

GUIDE NO.	COMPOSER AND TITLE	AGE ADMIN	AES SIG	ACCESS
	(1 hr., 3 min.)			
	**(2–Ang. S–3766);			
	*(3–Odys. 32360020)			
100,250	Canonic Variations for	A	4	5
	Organ, S. 769 (12 min.)			
	*(2–Tel. 26.35077)			
100,500	Capriccio for Harpsichord,	S	3	3
	S. 992 (12 min.)			
	*(Tel. 6.41065)			
	*(Tel. 6.41130)			
100,767	Chorale Partita, S. 767 for	A	3	4
	Organ (14 min.)			
	*(DG 139387)			
101,000	Chorale Preludes (*Orgel-*	A	3	3
	büchlein, S. 599–644) 1–5			
	min. ea.)			
	*(2–DG ARC–2708023);			
	(4–None. HD–73015)			
101,599	Chorale Prelude, S. 599	A	3	3
	for Organ (*Nun komm*			
	der Heiden Heiland)			
	(1 min.)			
	*(2–DG ARC–2708023);			
	(4–None. HD–73015)			
101,604	Chorale Prelude, S. 604	A	3	3
	for Organ (*Gelobet seist*			
	du, Jesu Christ) (2 min.)			
	*(2–DG ARC–2708023);			
	(4–None. HD–73015)			
101,607	Chorale Prelude, S. 607	A	3	3
	for Organ (*Vom Himmel*			
	kam der Engel Schar)			
	(1 min.)			
	*(2–DG ARC–2708023);			
	(4–None. HD–73015)			
101,608	Chorale Prelude, S. 608	A	3	2
	for Organ (*In dulci*			
	jubilo) (2 min.)			
	*(2–DG ARC–2708023);			
	(4–None. HD–73015)			
101,610	Chorale Prelude, S. 610	A	3	3
	for Organ (*Jesu, meine*			
	Freude) (3 min.)			
	*(2–DG ARC–2708023);			
	(4–None. HD–73015)			
101,615	Chorale Prelude, S. 615	A	3	3
	for Organ (*In dir ist*			
	Freude) (3 min.)			
	*(2–DG ARC–2708023);			
	(4–None. HD–73015)			
101,622	Chorale Prelude, S. 622	A	2	2
	for Organ (*O Mensch,*			
	bewein' dein' Sünde			
	gross) (6 min.)			
	*(2–DG ARC–2708023);			
	(4–None. HD–73015)			
102,640	Chorale Preludes: *Schübler*	A	2	2
	Chorales, S. 645–50			
	(2–4 min. ea.)			
	*(Argo 5419);			
	*(3–Vox SVBX–5445)			
102,645	Chorale Prelude, S. 645	A	2	1
	(*Wachet auf, ruft uns*			
	die Stimme) (4 min.)			
	**(DG 139321);			
	*(3–Vox SVBX–5445)			
102,646	Chorale Prelude, S. 646	A	3	2
	(*Wo soll ich fliehen hin*)			
	(2 min.)			
	*(Argo 5419);			
	*(3–Vox SVBX–5445)			
102,647	Chorale Prelude, S. 647	A	3	2
	(*Wer nur den lieben*			

GUIDE NO.	COMPOSER AND TITLE	AGE ADMIN	AES SIG	ACCESS
	Gott lässt walten)			
	(3 min.)			
	*(Argo 5419);			
	*(3–Vox SVBX–5445)			
102,648	Chorale Prelude, S. 648	A	3	2
	(*Meine Seele erhebet*			
	den Herren) (3 min.)			
	*(Argo 5419);			
	*(3–Vox SVBX–5445)			
102,649	Chorale Prelude, S. 649	A	3	1
	(*Ach bleib' bei uns, Herr*			
	Jesu Christ) (3 min.)			
	**(Tel. 6.41061);			
	*(Argo 5419);			
	*(3–Vox SVBX–5445)			
102,650	Chorale Prelude, S. 650	A	3	3
	(*Kommst du nun, Jesu,*			
	vom Himmel herunter)			
	(4 min.)			
	**(DG 139321);			
	*(3–Vox SVBX–5445)			
103,650	Chorale Settings for Organ,	A	2	3
	S. 651–68 (3–9 min. ea.)			
	*(2–DG ARC–2708023);			
	(4–None. HD–73015)			
103,651	S. 651 (*Komm, heiliger*	A	2	2
	Geist-Fantasia) (6 min.)			
	*(2–DG ARC–2708023);			
	(4–None. HD–73015)			
103,652	S. 652 (*Komm, heiliger*	A	2	3
	Geist) (9 min.)			
	*(2–DG ARC–2708023);			
	(4–None. HD–73015)			
103,653	S. 653 (*An Wasserflüssen*	A	2	2
	Babylon) (5 min.)			
	*(2–DG ARC–2708023);			
	(4–None. HD–73015)			
103,654	S. 654 (*Schmücke dich,*	A	3	2
	o liebe Seele) (9 min.)			
	*(2–DG ARC–2708023);			
	(4–None. HD–73015)			
103,656	S. 656 (*O Lamm Gottes*	A	3	2
	unschuldig) (8 min.)			
	*(2–DG ARC–2708023);			
	(4–None. HD–73015)			
103,658	S. 658 (*Von Gott will ich*	A	3	2
	nicht lassen) (5 min.)			
	*(2–DG ARC–2708023);			
	(4–None. HD–73015)			
103,659	S. 659 (*Nun komm der*	A	2	2
	Heiden Heiland)			
	(5 min.)			
	*(2–DG ARC–2708023);			
	(4–None. HD–73015)			
103,668	S. 668 (*Von deinen*	A	2	2
	Thron) (4 min.)			
	*(2–DG ARC–2708023);			
	(4–None. HD–73015)			
104,660	German Organ Mass (part	A	2	2
	3 of *Clavierübung*),			
	S. 669–89 (1–7 min. ea.)			
	*(3–Vox SVBX–5445)			
104,669	S. 669 Kyrie (*Gott Vater*	A	3	3
	in Ewigkeit) (3 min.)			
	*(3–Vox SVBX–5445)			
104,670	S. 670 (*Christe, alle Welt*	A	3	3
	trost) (4 min.)			
	*(3–Vox SVBX–5445)			
104,671	S. 671 Kyrie (*Gott heiliger*	A	3	3
	Geist) (5 min.)			
	*(3–Vox SVBX–5445)			
104,675	S. 675 (*Allein Gott in der*	A	3	3
	Hoh' sei Ehr) (3 min.)			
	*(3–Vox SVBX–5445)			

GUIDE NO.	COMPOSER AND TITLE	AGE	AES MIN	AC- CESS
104,677	S. 677 (*Allein Gott in der Hoh' sei Ehr*) (1 min.)	A	3	3
	*(3–Vox SVBX–5445)			
104,678	S. 678 (*Dies sind die heil'gen zehn Gebot'*) (5 min.)	A	3	3
	*(3–Vox SVBX–5445)			
104,680	S. 680 (*Wir glauben all' an einem Gott*) (4 min.)	A	3	2
	*(3–Vox SVBX–5445)			
104,682	S. 682 (*Vater unser im Himmelreich*) (7 min.)	A	3	3
	*(3–Vox SVBX–5445)			
104,683	S. 683 (*Vater unser im Himmelreich*) (1 min.)	A	3	3
	*(3–Vox SVBX–5445)			
104,684	S. 684 (*Christ, unser Herr, zum Jordan kam*) (4 min.)	A	3	3
	*(3–Vox SVBX–5445)			
104,685	S. 685 (*Christ, unser Herr, zum Jordan kam*)(1 min.)	A	3	3
	*(3–Vox SVBX–5445)			
104,687	S. 687 (*Aus tiefer Not schrei' ich zu dir*) (5 min.)	A	3	3
	*(3–Vox SVBX–5445)			
104,689	S. 689 (*Jesu Christus, unser Heiland*) (4 min.)	A	3	3
	*(3–Vox SVBX–5445)			
	Other Chorale Prelude			
104,712	S. 712 (*In dich hab' ich gehoffet, Herr*) (3 min.)	A	3	3
	**(Tel. 6.41061)			
104,903	Chromatic Fantasy and Fugue in d, Harpsichord S. 903 (12 min.)	S	2	2
	*(Tel. 6.41130); (3–Vox SVBX–5438)			
105,800	English Suites (6) for Harpsichord, S. 806–11 (12 min.)	A	2	3
	(3–Vox SVBX–5438)			
105,806	English Suite no. 1 for Harpsichord, S. 806 (21 min.)	A	3	3
	(3–Vox SVBX–5438)			
105,807	English Suite no. 2 for Harpsichord, S. 807 (21 min.)	A	3	3
	(3–Vox SVBX–5438)			
105,808	English Suite no. 3 for Harpsichord, S. 808 (18 min.)	A	3	3
	(3–Vox SVBX–5438)			
105,809	English Suite no. 4 for Harpsichord, S. 809 (19 min.)	A	3	3
	(3–Vox SVBX–5438)			
105,810	English Suite no. 5 for Harpsichord, S. 810 (19 min.)	A	3	3
	(3–Vox SVBX–5438)			
105,811	English Suite no. 6 for Harpsichord, S. 811 (23 min.)	A	3	3
	(3–Vox SVBX–5438)			
105,904	Fantasia and Fugue in a for Harpsichord, S. 904 (8 min.)	A	3	3
	*(Tel. 6.41130)			
106,250	Fantasia and Fugue in c for Harpsichord, S. 562 (5 min.)	A	2	3
	(DG 2530035)			
106,537	Fantasia and Fugue in c for Organ, S. 537 (10 min.)	A	2	3
	**(DG ARC–198305)			
106,750	Fantasia and Fugue in g for Organ, S. 542 (13 min.)	A	1	1
	**(Sera. S–60196); *(3–Vox SVBX–5445) *(DG 2530035)			
107,572	Fantasia in G for Organ, S. 572 (9 min.)	A	3	3
	**(2–Tel. 26.35082)			
107,812	French Suite no. 1 in d for Harpsichord, S. 812 (13 min.)	A	3	3
	*(Oiseau 60039)			
107,813	French Suite no. 2 in c for Harpsichord, S. 813 (14 min.)	A	3	3
	*(Oiseau 60039)			
107,814	French Suite no. 3 in b for Harpsichord, S. 814 (14 min.)	A	3	3
	*(Oiseau 60039)			
107,815	French Suite no. 4 in E flat for Harpsichord, S. 815 (13 min.)	A	3	3
	*(Oiseau 60039)			
107,816	French Suite no. 5 in G for Harpsichord, S. 816 (17 min.)	A	2	2
	*(Oiseau 60039)			
107,817	French Suite no. 6 in E for Harpsichord, S. 817 (15 min.)	A	3	3
	*(Oiseau 60039)			
107,988	Goldberg Variations for Harpsichord, S. 988 (1 hr., 6 min.)	A	1	4
	**(Col. MS–7096E)-*mono*; **(3–Odys. 32360020); *(2–Ang. S–3796); *(DG 139455)			
108,000	Inventions, 2 and 3 part, S. 772–801 (51 min.)	A	2	3
	**(None. H–71144)			
108,250	Italian Concerto in F for Harpsichord, S. 971 (13 min.)	A	2	2
	**(DG ARC–198032); (3–Vox SVBX–5438)			
108,500	Partita in b, S. 831 (28 min.)	A	2	3
	**(DG ARC–198032)			
108,825	Partita no. 1 in B flat, S. 825 (14 min.)	S	2	2
	*(2–Col. M2S–693)			
108,826	Partita no. 2 in c, S. 826 (18 min.)	A	3	3
	*(2–Col. M2S–693)			
108,827	Partita no. 3 in a, S. 827 (13 min.)	A	3	3
	*(2–Col. M2S–693)			
108,828	Partita no. 4 in D, S. 828 (24 min.)	S	1	2
	*(2–Col. M2S–693)			
108,829	Partita no. 5 in G, S. 829 (13 min.)	A	3	3
	*(2–Col. M2S–693)			
108,830	Partita no. 6 in e, S. 830 (24 min.)	A	2	3
	*(2–Col. M2S–693)			
109,000	Passacaglia and Fugue in c for Organ, S. 582 (14 min.)	A	2	2
	**(DG ARC–198305);			

GUIDE NO.	COMPOSER AND TITLE	AGE AES ADMIN SIG	AC-CESS
	**(Phi. 6500214); **(Sera. S–60196)		
109,250	Pastorale in F for Organ, S. 590 (11 min.) **(2–Tel. 26.35082)	A 3	3
109,532	Prelude and Fugue for Organ, S. 532 (11 min.) **(Phi. 6500214)	A 2	3
109,534	Prelude and Fugue for Organ, S. 534 *(3–Vox SVBX–5445)	A 3	3
109,536	Prelude and Fugue for Organ, S. 536 *(3–Vox SVBX–5445)	A 3	3
109,543	Prelude and Fugue for Organ, S. 543 **(DG 139321); **(Phi. 6500214)	A 2	1
109,544	Prelude and Fugue for Organ, S. 544 **(DG 139321)	A 2	2
109,552	Prelude and Fugue for Organ, S. 552 (16 min.) *(3–Vox SVBX–5445)	A 2	2
109,554	Prelude and Fugue (little) for Organ, S. 554 (4 min.) **(Tel. 6.41061)	A 3	2
110,000	Toccata, Adagio and Fugue in C for Organ, S. 564 (16 min.) **(DG ARC–198304)	A 2	2
110,250	Toccata and Fugue in d for Organ, S. 538 (13 min.) **(DG ARC–198304)	A 2	3
110,500	Toccata and Fugue in d for Organ, S. 565 (9 min.) **(DG ARC–198304); **(Phi. 6500214); **(Sera. S–60196)	E 2	2
110,750	Toccata and Fugue in F for Organ, S. 540 (14 min.) **(DG 139325); **(DG ARC–198304)	A 2	2
110,911	Toccata in c, S. 911 (14 min.) *(Ang. S–36055)	A 3	3
110,912	Toccata in D, S. 912 (11 min.) *(Ang. S–36055)	A 3	3
110,915	Toccata in g, S. 915 (8 min.) *(DG 2530035)	A 3	3
111,525	Trio Sonata no. 1 for Organ, S. 525 (12 min.) **(2–Tel. 26.35076); *(2–Phi. 6700059)	A 2	3
111,526	Trio Sonata no. 2 for Organ, S. 526 (13 min.) **(2–Tel. 26.35076); *(2–Phi. 6700059)	A 2	3
111,527	Trio Sonata no. 3 for Organ, S. 527 (14 min.) **(2–Tel. 26.35076); *(2–Phi. 6700059)	A 2	3
111,528	Trio Sonata no. 4 for Organ, S. 528 (10 min.) **(2–Tel. 26.35076); *(2–Phi. 6700059)	A 2	3
111,529	Trio Sonata no. 5 for Organ, S. 529 (14 min.) **(2–Tel. 26.35076); *(2–Phi. 6700059)	A 2	3
111,530	Trio Sonata no. 6 for Organ, S. 530 (14 min.) **(2–Tel. 26.35076); *(2–Phi. 6700059)	A 2	3

GUIDE NO.	COMPOSER AND TITLE	AGE AES ADMIN SIG	AC-CESS
	Well-Tempered Clavichord, Book I		
111,846	Prelude and Fugue no. 1, S. 846 (5 min.) **(2–DG 2707015); *(Col. MS–6408); *(3–Col. D3S–733)	A 2	2
111,847	Prelude and Fugue no. 2, S. 847 (3 min.) **(2–DG 2707015); *(Col. MS–6408); *(3–Col. D3S–733)	A 2	2
111,848	Prelude and Fugue no. 3, S. 848 (4 min.) **(2–DG 2707015); *(Col. MS–6408); *(3–Col. D3S–733)	A 2	2
111,849	Prelude and Fugue no. 4, S. 849 (8 min.) **(2–DG 2707015); *(Col. MS–6408); *(3–Col. D3S–733)	A 2	3
111,850	Prelude and Fugue no. 5, S. 850 (3 min.) **(2–DG 2707015); *(Col. MS–6408); *(3–Col. D3S–733)	A 2	2
111,851	Prelude and Fugue no. 6, S. 851 (4 min.) **(2–DG 2707015); *(Col. MS–6408); *(3–Col. D3S–733)	A 2	2
111,852	Prelude and Fugue no. 7, S. 852 (6 min.) **(2–DG 2707015); *(Col. MS–6408); *(3–Col. D3S–733)	A 2	4
111,853	Prelude and Fugue no. 8, S. 853 (10 min.) **(2–DG 2707015); *(Col. MS–6408); *(3–Col. D3S–733)	A 2	2
111,854	Prelude and Fugue no. 9, S. 854 (3 min.) **(2–DG 2707015); *(Col. MS–6538); *(3–Col. D3S–733)	A 2	2
111,855	Prelude and Fugue no. 10, S. 855 (3 min.) **(2–DG 2707015); *(Col. MS–6538); *(3–Col. D3S–733)	A 2	2
111,856	Prelude and Fugue no. 11, S. 856 (2 min.) **(2–DG 2707015); *(Col. MS–6538); *(3–Col. D3S–733)	A 2	2
111,857	Prelude and Fugue no. 12, S. 857 (7 min.) **(2–DG 2707015); *(Col. MS–6538); *(3–Col. D3S–733)	A 2	4
111,858	Prelude and Fugue no. 13, S. 858 (4 min.) **(2–DG 2707015); *(Col. MS–6538); *(3–Col. D3S–733)	A 2	3
111,859	Prelude and Fugue no. 14, S. 859 (5 min.) **(2–DG 2707015); *(Col. MS–6538); *(3–Col. D3S–733)	A 2	4
111,860	Prelude and Fugue no. 15, S. 860 (4 min.) **(2–DG 2707015);	A 2	3

GUIDE NO.	COMPOSER AND TITLE	AGE MIN	AES SIG	ACCESS
	*(Col. MS–6538);			
	*(3–Col. D3S–733)			
111,861	Prelude and Fugue no. 16,	A	2	3
	S. 861 (5 min.)			
	**(2–DG 2707015);			
	*(Col. MS–6538);			
	*(3–Col. D3S–733)			
111,862	Prelude and Fugue no. 17,	A	2	2
	S. 862 (4 min.)			
	**(2–DG 2707015);			
	*(Col. MS–6776);			
	*(3–Col. D3S–733)			
111,863	Prelude and Fugue no. 18,	A	2	3
	S. 863 (5 min.)			
	**(2–DG 2707015);			
	*(Col. MS–6776);			
	*(3–Col. D3S–733)			
111,864	Prelude and Fugue no. 19,	A	2	3
	S. 864 (4 min.)			
	**(2–DG 2707015);			
	*(Col. MS–6776);			
	*(3–Col. D3S–733)			
111,865	Prelude and Fugue no. 20,	A	2	2
	S. 865 (6 min.)			
	**(2–DG 2707015);			
	*(Col. MS–6776);			
	*(3–Col. D3S–733)			
111,866	Prelude and Fugue no. 21,	A	2	2
	S. 866 (3 min.)			
	**(2–DG 2707015);			
	*(Col. MS–6776);			
	*(3–Col. D3S–733)			
111,867	Prelude and Fugue no. 22,	A	2	2
	S. 867 (7 min.)			
	**(2–DG 2707015);			
	*(Col. MS–6776);			
	*(3–Col. D3S–733)			
111,868	Prelude and Fugue no. 23,	A	2	3
	S. 868 (4 min.)			
	**(2–DG 2707015);			
	*(Col. MS–6776);			
	*(3–Col. D3S–733)			
111,869	Prelude and Fugue no. 24,	A	2	3
	S. 869 (10 min.)			
	**(2–DG 2707015);			
	*(Col. MS–6776);			
	*(3–Col. D3S–733)			
	Well-Tempered Clavichord, Book II			
111,870	Prelude and Fugue no. 1,	A	2	2
	S. 870 (5 min.)			
	**(3–DG 2709019);			
	*(Col. MS–7099);			
	*(Col. D3M–31525)			
111,871	Prelude and Fugue no. 2,	A	2	3
	S. 871 (4 min.)			
	**(3–DG 2709019);			
	*(Col. MS–7099);			
	*(Col. D3M–31525)			
111,872	Prelude and Fugue no. 3,	A	2	3
	S. 872 (5 min.)			
	**(3–DG 2709019);			
	*(Col. MS–7099);			
	*(Col. D3M–31525)			
111,873	Prelude and Fugue no. 4,	A	2	3
	S. 873 (7 min.)			
	**(3–DG 2709019);			
	*(Col. MS–7099);			
	*(Col. D3M–31525)			
111,874	Prelude and Fugue no. 5,	A	2	2
	S. 874 (7 min.)			
	**(3–DG 2709019);			
	*(Col. MS–7099);			
	*(Col. D3M–31525)			
111,875	Prelude and Fugue no. 6,	A	2	2
	S. 875 (4 min.)			
	**(3–DG 2709019);			
	*(Col. MS–7099);			
	*(Col. D3M–31525)			
111,876	Prelude and Fugue no. 7,	A	2	2
	S. 876 (6 min.)			
	**(3–DG 2709019);			
	*(Col. MS–7099);			
	*(Col. D3M–31525)			
111,877	Prelude and Fugue no. 8,	A	2	3
	S. 877 (8 min.)			
	**(3–DG 2709019);			
	*(Col. MS–7099);			
	*(Col. D3M–31525)			
111,878	Prelude and Fugue no. 9,	A	2	3
	S. 878 (8 min.)			
	**(3–DG 2709019);			
	*(Col. MS–7409);			
	*(Col. D3M–31525)			
111,879	Prelude and Fugue no. 10,	A	2	3
	S. 879 (7 min.)			
	**(3–DG 2709019);			
	*(Col. MS–7409);			
	*(Col. D3M–31525)			
111,880	Prelude and Fugue no. 11,	A	2	2
	S. 880 (5 min.)			
	**(3–DG 2709019);			
	*(Col. MS–7409);			
	*(Col. D3M–31525)			
111,881	Prelude and Fugue no. 12,	A	2	1
	S. 881 (9 min.)			
	**(3–DG 2709019);			
	*(Col. MS–7409);			
	*(Col. D3M–31525)			
111,882	Prelude and Fugue no. 13,	A	2	4
	S. 882 (7 min.)			
	**(3–DG 2709019);			
	*(Col. MS–7409);			
	*(Col. D3M–31525)			
111,883	Prelude and Fugue no. 14,	A	2	4
	S. 883 (8 min.)			
	**(3–DG 2709019);			
	*(Col. MS–7409);			
	*(Col. D3M–31525)			
111,884	Prelude and Fugue no. 15,	A	2	2
	S. 884 (4 min.)			
	**(3–DG 2709019);			
	*(Col. MS–7409);			
	*(Col. D3M–31525)			
111,885	Prelude and Fugue no. 16,	A	2	3
	S. 885 (7 min.)			
	**(3–DG 2709019);			
	*(Col. MS–7409);			
	*(Col. D3M–31525)			
111,886	Prelude and Fugue no. 17,	A	2	3
	S. 886 (7 min.)			
	**(3–DG 2709019);			
	*(Col. M–30537);			
	*(Col. D3M–31525)			
111,887	Prelude and Fugue no. 18,	A	2	3
	S. 887 (7 min.)			
	**(3–DG 2709019);			
	*(Col. M–30537);			
	*(Col. D3M–31525)			
111,888	Prelude and Fugue no. 19,	A	2	3
	S. 888 (4 min.)			
	**(3–DG 2709019);			
	*(Col. M–30537);			
	*(Col. D3M–31525)			
111,889	Prelude and Fugue no. 20,	A	2	2
	S. 889 (4 min.)			
	**(3–DG 2709019);			
	*(Col. M–30537);			
	*(Col. D3M–31525)			

GUIDE NO.	COMPOSER AND TITLE	AGE	AES MIN SIG	AC-CESS
111,890	Prelude and Fugue no. 21, S. 890 (5 min.)	A	2	3
	**(3–DG 2709019); *(Col. M–30537); *(Col. D3M–31525)			
111,891	Prelude and Fugue no. 22, S. 891 (9 min.)	A	2	3
	**(3–DG 2709019); *(Col. M–30537); *(Col. D3M–31525)			
111,892	Prelude and Fugue no. 23, S. 892 (6 min.)	A	2	3
	**(3–DG 2709019); *(Col. M–30537); *(Col. D3M–31525)			
111,893	Prelude and Fugue no. 24, S. 893 (4 min.)	A	2	3
	**(3–DG 2709019); *(Col. M–30537); *(Col. D3M–31525)			
	BALAKIREV, MILY (1837–1910)			
112,000	*Islamey* (*Oriental Fantasy*) (8 min.)	A	4	3
	*(Lon. STS–15086)			
	BARBER, SAMUEL (1910–)			
112,500	Sonata for Piano, op. 26 (18 min.)	A	4	3
	*(RCA LSC–3229)			
	BARTÓK, BÉLA (1881–1945)			
113,000	*Allegro barbaro* for Piano (2 min.)	E	4	2
	**(Turn. 34167)			
113,250	15 Hungarian Peasant Songs (13 min.)	E	4	2
	**(3–Vox SVBX–5426)			
113,500	*For Children* (set of pieces) (1 hr., 3 min.)	E	4	2
	**(3–Vox SVBX–5426)			
113,750	*Improvisations* (8), op. 20 (12 min.)	E	4	3
	*(3–Vox SVBX–5427)			
113,800	*Mikrokosmos* (153 progressive piano pieces) in 6 Volumes (2 hrs., 28 min.)	S	3	2
	*(3–Vox SVBX–5425)			
113,801	Volume I (pieces 1–36) (21 min.)	E	3	2
	*(3–Vox SVBX–5425)			
113,802	Volume II (pieces 37–66) (21 min.)	E	3	2
	*(3–Vox SVBX–5425)			
113,803	Volume III (pieces 67–96) (26 min.)	E	3	2
	*(3–Vox SVBX–5425)			
113,804	Volume IV (pieces 97–121) (28 min.)	E	3	2
	*(3–Vox SVBX–5425)			
114,097	no. 97 (*Notturno*) (2 min.)	E	2	1
	*(3–Vox SVBX–5425)			
114,100	no. 100 (*In the Style of a Folk Song*) (1 min.)	E	2	1
	*(3–Vox SVBX–5425)			
114,102	no. 102 (*Harmonics*) (1 min.)	S	2	2
	*(3–Vox SVBX–5425)			
114,109	no. 109 (*From the Island of Bali*) (2 min.)	S	2	2
	*(3–Vox SVBX–5425)			
114,113	no. 113 (*Bulgarian Rhythm*) (1 min.)	E	2	1
	*(3–Vox SVBX–5425)			
114,120	Volume V (pieces 122–39) (20 min.)	S	3	2
	*(3–Vox SVBX–5425)			
114,226	no. 126 (*Change of Time*) (1 min.)	S	3	2
	*(3–Vox SVBX–5425)			
114,227	no. 127 (*New Hungarian Folk Song*) (1 min.)	S	3	2
	*(3–Vox SVBX–5425)			
114,229	no. 129 (*Alternating Thirds*) (1 min.)	E	3	2
	*(3–Vox SVBX–5425)			
114,231	no. 131 (*Fourths*) (1 min.)	E	3	2
	*(3–Vox SVBX–5425)			
114,232	no. 132 (*Major Seconds Broken and Together*) (2 min.)	S	3	3
	*(3–Vox SVBX–5425)			
114,235	no. 135 (*Perpetuum Mobile*) (1 min.)	E	3	2
	*(3–Vox SVBX–5425)			
114,239	no. 139 (*Merry Andrew*) (1 min.)	E	3	2
	*(3–Vox SVBX–5425)			
114,250	Volume VI (pieces 140–53) (25 min.)	S	3	2
	*(Phi. 6500013); *(3–Vox SVBX–5425)			
114,342	no. 142 (*From the Diary of a Fly*) (2 min.)	E	3	2
	*(Phi. 6500013); *(3–Vox SVBX–5425)			
114,344	no. 144 (*Minor Seconds, Major Sevenths*) (3 min.)	S	3	2
	*(Phi. 6500013); *(3–Vox SVBX–5425)			
114,346	no. 146 (*Ostinato*) (2 min.)	S	3	2
	*(Phi. 6500013); *(3–Vox SVBX–5425)			
114,350	nos. 148–53 (Six Dances in Bulgarian Rhythm) (9 min.)	S	3	2
	*(Phi. 6500013); *(3–Vox SVBX–5425)			
114,500	*Out of Doors* (15 min.)	A	3	4
	**(3–Vox SVBX–5426); *(Phi. 6500013); *(Turn. 34167)			
114,750	Sonata for Piano (13 min.)	A	2	3
	**(3–Vox SVBX–5426)			
115,000	Suite for Piano, op. 14 (9 min.)	A	3	3
	*(3–Vox SVBX–5427)			
115,250	Suite for 2 Pianos, op. 4b (30 min.)	A	4	2
	(Conn. S–2033)			
115,500	Three Etudes, op. 18 (8 min.)	A	4	3
	*(3–Vox SVBX–5427)			
	BEETHOVEN, LUDWIG VAN (1770–1827)			
116,000	*Andante favori* in F, K. 57 (8 min.)	S	3	3
	**(DG 138934)			

GUIDE NO.	COMPOSER AND TITLE	AGE MIN	AES SIG	AC-CESS
116,250	Bagatelles, op. 33 (20 min.) *(Turn. 34077)	A	3	2
116,500	Bagatelles, op. 119 (15 min.) **(Col. MS–6838); *(Turn. 34077)	A	3	3
116,750	Bagatelles, op. 126 (18 min.) **(DG 138934); *(Turn. 34077)	A	1	2
117,000	Fantasia in g for Piano, op. 77 (10 min.) *(Turn. 34402); (Col. M–32294)	A	3	2
117,250	*Für Elise* (3 min.) **(DG 138934)	E	3	1
117,500	Minuet in G (3 min.) *(Col. MS–7326)	E	3	1
117,750	Rondo a capriccio in G, op. 129 (*Rage over a Lost Penny*) (6 min.) **(DG 138934)	S	3	1
118,000	Rondo in C, op. 51, no. 1 (6 min.) **(DG 138934)	S	4	2
118,250	Rondo in G, op. 51, no. 2 (6 min.) **(DG 138934)	S	4	2
118,500	Sonata no. 1 in f for Piano, op. 2, no. 1 (18 min.) *(DG 138935); *(Van. VCS 10084)	S	3	3
118,750	Sonata no. 2 for Piano, op. 2, no. 2 in A (24 min.) *(Van. VCS 10084)	S	3	3
119,000	Sonata no. 3 in C, op. 2, no. 3 for Piano (25 min.) **(RCA LSC–2812)	S	3	3
119,250	Sonata no. 4 in E flat, op. 7 for Piano (28 min.) **(13–Phi. 6747035); *(Van. VCS–10085)	S	3	3
119,500	Sonata no. 5 in c, op. 10, no. 1 (18 min.) **(13–Sera. 6063/6)-*mono*; *(Phi. 6500179); *(Van. VCS–10085)	S	3	2
119,750	Sonata no. 6 in F, op. 10, no. 2 (12 min.) **(Phi. 839749)	S	3	2
120,000	Sonata no. 7 in D, op. 10, no. 3 (25 min.) **(Phi. 6500417); **(13–Phi. 6747035)	S	3	2
120,250	Sonata no. 8 in c, op. 13 (*Pathétique*) (19 min.) **(Col. M–31811); **(Phi. 6599308); **(RCA LSC–2654); *(DG 138941); *(DG 139300); *(Phi. 6500315); (Col. MS–6945)	S	2	1
120,500	Sonata no. 9 in E, op. 14, no. 1 (14 min.) **(13–Phi. 6747035); **(12–RCA VICS–9000); *(Col. MS–6945)	S	3	3
120,750	Sonata no. 10 in G, op. 14, no. 2 (17 min.) **(DG 138938); (Col. MS–6945)	A	3	3
121,000	Sonata no. 11 in B flat, op. 22 (26 min.) (Col. M–32294)	A	3	3
121,250	Sonata no. 12 in A flat, op. 26 (*Funeral March*) (20 min.) **(13–Phi. 6747035); **(13–Sera. 6063/6)-*mono*; *(DG 138935)	S	3	2
121,500	Sonata no. 13 in E flat, op. 27, no. 1 (15 min.) **(13–Sera. 6063/6)-*mono*; *(Van. VCS–10055)	A	3	3
121,750	Sonata no. 14 in c sharp, op. 27, no. 2 (*Moonlight*) (15 min.) **(13–Sera. 6063/6)-*mono*; *(Phi. 6500417); *(Phi. 6599308); (Col. M–31811); (DG 138941); (DG 139300); (RCA LSC–2654)	S	2	1
122,000	Sonata no. 15 in D, op. 28 (*Pastoral*) (22 min.) **(13–Sera. 6063/6)-*mono*; *(DG 138941)	A	3	3
122,250	Sonata no. 16 in G, op. 31, no. 1 (23 min.) (Col. M–32349)	S	3	3
122,500	Sonata no. 17 in d, op. 31, no. 2 (*Tempest*) (24 min.) **(13–Sera. 6063/6)-*mono*; *(Ang. S–35679); *(DG 138942); (Col. M–32349)	S	3	2
122,750	Sonata no. 18 in E flat, op. 31, no. 3 (23 min.) (Col. M–32349)	S	3	2
123,000	Sonata no. 19 in g, op. 49, no. 1 (8 min.) **(13–Sera. 6063/6)-*mono*; *(DG 138935)	S	3	2
123,250	Sonata no. 20 in G, op. 49, no. 2 (7 min.) **(13–Sera. 6063/6)-*mono*; *(DG 138935)	S	3	2
123,500	Sonata no. 21 in C, op. 53 (*Waldstein*) (24 min.) **(13–Sera. 6063/6)-*mono*; *(12–RCA VICS–9000)	S	2	1
124,000	Sonata no. 23 in f, op. 57 (*Appassionata*) (24 min.) **(DG 139300); *(Col. M–31811); (RCA LSC–2812); (Phi. 6599308)	S	3	1
124,250	Sonata no. 24 in F sharp, op. 78 (9 min.) **(DG 138941); **(13–Phi. 6747035); **(13–Sera. 6063/6)-*mono*; (Van. VSC–10055); (Col. M–32294)	S	3	2
124,500	Sonata no. 25 in G, op. 79 (9 min.) **(13–Sera. 6063/6)-*mono*; *(Phi. 6500417)	S	3	2
124,750	Sonata no. 26 in E flat, op. 91A (*Les Adieux*) (16 min.) **(DG 139300); **(13–Sera. 6063/6)-*mono*; (RCA LSC–2654)	S	2	2
125,000	Sonata no. 27 in e, op. 90 (13 min.) **(Sera. S–60016); **(13–Sera. 6063/6)-*mono*; *(13–Phi. 6747035)	S	2	2

GUIDE NO.	COMPOSER AND TITLE	AGE ADMIN	AES SIG	AC-CESS
125,250	Sonata no. 28 in A, op. 101 (21 min.) *(DG 138942); *(13–Phi. 6747035); *(12–RCA VICS–9000)	A	2	3
125,500	Sonata no. 29 in B flat, op. 106 (*Hammerklavier*) (45 min.) *(DG 138944)	A	2	4
125,750	Sonata no. 30 in E, op. 109 (22 min.) **(13–Sera. 6063/6)-*mono*; **(Van. VSD 71172); (DG 138944)	A	2	3
126,000	Sonata no. 31 in A flat, op. 110 (20 min.) **(13–Sera. 6063/6)-*mono*; *(13–Phi. 6747035); *(Van. VCS–10055)	A	1	3
126,250	Sonata no. 32 in c, op. 111 (27 min.) **(13–Sera. 6063/6)-*mono*; *(Van. VSD 71172)	A	1	4
126,500	Variations and Fugue in E flat, op. 35 (*Eroica*) (24 min.) **(Phi. 839743); **(3–Sera. 6067)-*mono*	A	3	3
126,750	Variations in c (32 var.), G. 191 (11 min.) **(Phi. 839743)	A	2	3
127,000	Variations in F on an Original Theme, op. 34 (14 min.) **(Phi. 839743); **(3–Sera. 6067)-*mono*	A	4	3
127,250	Variations on a Theme by Diabelli, op. 120 (47 min.) **(CSP AML–5246)-*mono*; **(3–Sera. 6067)-*mono*	A	1	4

BRAHMS, JOHANNES (1833–1897)

GUIDE NO.	COMPOSER AND TITLE	AGE ADMIN	AES SIG	AC-CESS
127,501	Ballade, op. 10, no. 1 in d (4 min.) *(Lon. CS 6444)	A	4	3
127,502	Ballade, op. 10, no. 2 in D (6 min.) *(Lon. CS 6444)	A	5	3
127,503	Ballade, op. 10, no. 3 in b (4 min.) *(Lon. CS 6444)	A	4	3
127,504	Ballade, op. 10, no. 4 in B (7 min.) *(Lon. CS 6444)	A	4	3
127,750	Chorale-Preludes, op. 122 *(Turn. 34422)	A	3	2
128,250	Hungarian Dances nos. 1–10 (25 min.) **(Lon. CS 6473)	S	3	2
128,500	8 Intermezzi and Capriccios, op. 76 (27 min.) **(2–Lon. CS 6396, 6404)	A	3	3
128,750	op. 116, nos. 1–6 (21 min.) **(2–Lon. CS 6396, 6404)	A	2	3
129,000	op. 117, nos. 1–3 (16 min.) **(Lon. CS 6716); **(2–Lon. CS 6396, 6404)	A	2	3
129,100	op. 118, nos. 1–6 (25 min.) **(2–Lon. CS 6396, 6404)	A	2	2
129,200	op. 119, nos. 1–4 (16 min.) **(2–Lon. CS 6396, 6404)	A	2	3
129,501	Rhapsody, op. 79, no. 1 in b (8 min.)	A	2	3

GUIDE NO.	COMPOSER AND TITLE	AGE ADMIN	AES SIG	AC-CESS
	**(Lon. CS 6716); *(Lon. CS 6444)			
129,502	Rhapsody, op. 79, no. 2 in g (6 min.) *(Lon. CS 6444)	A	2	3
129,750	Sonata in f for 2 Pianos, op. 34A (37 min.) **(Lon. CS 6533)	A	4	3
129,800	Sonata no. 1 in C, op. 1 (26 min.) **(Lon. CS 6410)	A	5	4
129,850	Sonata no. 2 in f sharp, op. 2 (25 min.) **(Lon. CS 6410)	A	5	4
129,900	Sonata no. 3 in f, op. 5 (39 min.) **(Lon. CS 6482)	A	5	4
129,935	Variations on a Theme by Paganini, op. 35 (23 min.) *(Lon. STS–15150)	A	4	3
129,950	Waltzes, op. 39 (13 min.) *(Lon. CS 6444)	A	3	2

BULL, JOHN (c.1562–1628)

GUIDE NO.	COMPOSER AND TITLE	AGE ADMIN	AES SIG	AC-CESS
130,000	Keyboard Music I (varies) **(Oiseau S–255)	A	3	3

BUSONI, FERRUCCIO (1866–1924)

GUIDE NO.	COMPOSER AND TITLE	AGE ADMIN	AES SIG	AC-CESS
130,500	*Elegies* (6) (23 min.) *(Argo ZRG–741)	A	4	4

BUXTEHUDE, DIETRICH (c.1637–1707)

GUIDE NO.	COMPOSER AND TITLE	AGE ADMIN	AES SIG	AC-CESS
131,000	Chorale Preludes (vary) (None. H–71188)	A	3	3
131,250	Fugue in C for Organ (3 min.) (None. H–71188)	A	3	3
131,500	Organ Music (varies) (9–Vox SVBX–527/9)	A	2	3
131,750	Partita on the chorale, 'Auf meinen lieben Gott' (5 min.) (Tel. 6.41057)	A	2	3
132,000	Passacaglia in d (6 min.) (None. H–71188)	A	2	3
132,250	Prelude, Fugue, and Chaconne in C (5 min.) (Col. MS–6944)	A	2	3
132,500	Toccatas (vary) (9–Vox SVBX–527/9)	A	3	3

CHABRIER, EMMANUEL (1841–1894)

GUIDE NO.	COMPOSER AND TITLE	AGE ADMIN	AES SIG	AC-CESS
132,750	*Bourrée fantasque* (5 min.) *(3–Vox SVBX–5400)	S	4	1
133,000	*Dix Piéces pittoresques* (1880) (39 min.) *(3–Vox SVBX–5400)	S	3	2
133,250	*Trois Valses romantiques* for 2 pianos (13 min.) (Turn. 34241)	A	3	2

CHOPIN, FRÉDÉRIC (1810–1849)

GUIDE NO.	COMPOSER AND TITLE	AGE ADMIN	AES SIG	AC-CESS
133,500	Andante Spianato and Grande Polonaise, op. 22 (14 min.) **(2–RCA LSC–7037)	S	4	3
133,750	Ballade no. 1 in g, op. 23 (9 min.)	S	2	2

GUIDE NO.	COMPOSER AND TITLE	AGE MIN	AES SIG	AC-CESS
	**(Lon. CS 6422);			
	**(RCA LSC–2370);			
	*(Turn. 34271)			
133,800	Ballade no. 2 in F, op. 38 (7 min.)	S	3	3
	**(Lon. CS 6422);			
	**(RCA LSC–2370);			
	*(Turn. 34271)			
133,850	Ballade no. 3 in A flat, op. 47 (7 min.)	S	3	2
	**(Lon. CS 6422);			
	**(RCA LSC–2370);			
	*(Turn. 34271)			
133,900	Ballade no. 4 in f, op. 52 (11 min.)	S	1	2
	**(Lon. CS 6422);			
	**(RCA LSC–2370);			
	*(Turn. 34271)			
134,000	Barcarolle in f sharp, op. 60 (9 min.)	S	3	2
	**(Lon. CS 6562);			
	**(Phi. 6500393);			
	**(RCA LSC–2889)			
134,250	Berceuse in D flat, op. 57 (1843) (5 min.)	E	3	1
	**(RCA LSC–2889)			
134,500	Études, op. 10 (30 min.)	S	3	2
	*(DG 136454);			
	*(DG 2530291);			
	*(Sera. S–60081)			
134,750	op. 10, no. 3 in E (4 min.)	S	3	1
	*(DG 136454);			
	*(DG 2530291);			
	*(Sera. S–60081)			
134,800	op. 10, no. 4 in c sharp (2 min.)	S	3	2
	*(DG 136454);			
	*(DG 2530291);			
	*(Sera. S–60081)			
134,850	op. 10, no. 5 in G flat (2 min.)	S	3	1
	*(DG 136454);			
	*(DG 2530291);			
	*(Sera. S–60081)			
134,900	op. 10, no. 12 in c (*Revolutionary Etude*) (3 min.)	E	3	1
	*(DG 136454);			
	*(DG 2530291);			
	*(Sera. S–60081)			
135,000	Études, op. 25 (31 min.)	S	3	2
	*(DG 136454);			
	*(DG 2530291);			
	*(Sera. S–60081)			
135,050	op. 25, no. 1 in A flat (*Aeolian Harp*) (2 min.)	S	3	1
	*(DG 136454);			
	*(DG 2530291);			
	*(Sera. S–60081)			
135,100	op. 25, no. 7 in c sharp (5 min.)	S	2	2
	*(DG 136454);			
	*(DG 2530291);			
	*(Sera. S–60081)			
135,150	op. 25, no. 9 in G flat (*Butterfly Etude*) (1 min.)	S	3	1
	*(DG 136454);			
	*(DG 2530291);			
	*(Sera. S–60081)			
135,200	op. 25, no. 11 in a (*Winter Winds*) (4 min.)	S	3	2
	*(DG 136454);			
	*(DG 2530291);			
	*(Sera. S–60081)			
135,250	op. 25, no. 12 in c (3 min.)	S	3	2
	*DG 136454);			
	*(DG 2530291);			
	*(Sera. S–60081)			
135,500	Fantaisie Impromptu no. 4 in c sharp, op. 66 (5 min.)	S	3	1
	**(2–RCA LSC–7037)			
135,750	Fantaisie in f, op. 49 (12 min.)	S	2	2
	**(RCA LSC–2889);			
	*(Turn. 34271)			
135,800	Impromptu no. 2 in F sharp, op. 36 (6 min.)	S	3	2
	**2–RCA LSC–7037)			
136,000	Mazurkas (51) (vary)	S	3	2
	**(3–RCA LSC–6177)			
136,350	op. 6, no. 3 (2 min.)	S	3	2
	**(3–RCA LSC–6177)			
136,500	op. 6, no. 4 (1 min.)	A	3	2
	**(3–RCA LSC–6177)			
136,750	op. 7, no. 1 (2 min.)	S	3	2
	**(3–RCA LSC–6177)			
137,000	op. 7, no. 2 (3 min.)	S	3	2
	**(3–RCA LSC–6177)			
137,250	op. 7, no. 3 (3 min.)	S	3	2
	**(3–RCA LSC–6177)			
137,500	op. 17, no. 2 (2 min.)	S	3	2
	**(3–RCA LSC–6177)			
137,750	op. 17, no. 4 (4 min.)	S	3	1
	**(3–RCA LSC–6177)			
138,000	op. 24, no. 1 (3 min.)	S	3	2
	**(3–RCA LSC–6177)			
138,250	op. 24, no. 2 (2 min.)	S	3	2
	**(3–RCA LSC–6177)			
138,500	op. 24, no. 4 (5 min.)	S	3	1
	**(3–RCA LSC–6177)			
138,750	op. 30, no. 2 (1 min.)	S	3	2
	**(3–RCA LSC–6177)			
139,000	op. 30, no. 4 (4 min.)	S	3	1
	**(3–RCA LSC–6177)			
139,250	op. 41, no. 2 (2 min.)	S	3	2
	**(3–RCA LSC–6177)			
139,500	op. 50, no. 3 (5 min.)	S	3	1
	**(3–RCA LSC–6177)			
139,750	op. 59, no. 1 (4 min.)	S	3	2
	**(3–RCA LSC–6177)			
140,000	op. 63, no. 3 (2 min.)	S	3	2
	**(3–RCA LSC–6177)			
140,250	op. 67, no. 4 (3 min.)	S	3	2
	**(3–RCA LSC–6177)			
140,500	op. 68, no. 2 (3 min.)	T	3	1
	**(3–RCA LSC–6177)			
140,750	op. 68, no. 4 (3 min.)	S	3	2
	**(3–RCA LSC–6177)			
141,000	Nocturnes (19) (vary)	S	3	2
	*(2–RCA LSC–7050)			
141,250	op. 9, no. 2 (4 min.)	S	3	1
	*(2–RCA LSC–7050)			
141,500	op. 9, no. 3 (6 min.)	S	3	1
	*(2–RCA LSC–7050)			
141,750	op. 15, no. 1 (4 min.)	S	3	2
	*(2–RCA LSC–7050)			
142,000	op. 15, no. 2 (4 min.)	S	3	1
	*(2–RCA LSC–7050)			
142,250	op. 27, no. 1 (5 min.)	A	2	2
	*(2–RCA LSC–7050)			
142,500	op. 27, no. 2 (5 min.)	S	2	1
	*(2–RCA LSC–7050)			
142,750	op. 37, no. 1 (6 min.)	S	3	2
	*(2–RCA LSC–7050)			

GUIDE NO.	COMPOSER AND TITLE	AGE	AES SIG	AC-CESS
143,000	op. 37, no. 2 (5 min.) *(2–RCA LSC–7050)	S	3	1
143,250	op. 48, no. 1 (6 min.) *(2–RCA LSC–7050)	S	3	1
143,500	op. 55, no. 1 (5 min.) *(2–RCA LSC–7050)	S	3	1
143,750	op. 55, no. 2 (5 min.) *(2–RCA LSC–7050)	S	3	2
144,000	op. 62, no. 1 (6 min.) **(Phi. 6500393); *(2–RCA LSC–7050)	S	3	1
144,250	op. 62, no. 2 (5 min.) **(Phi. 6500393); *(2–RCA LSC–7050)	S	3	2
144,500	op. 72, no. 1 (4 min.) *(2–RCA LSC–7050)	S	3	2
144,750	Nouvelles études (3) (6 min.) **(RCA LSC–2889); *(Lon. CS 6422)	A	3	3
145,000	Polonaise Fantaisie, op. 61 (12 min.) **(2–Ang. S–3794); **(Phi. 6500393); **(2–RCA LSC–7037)	A	1	3
145,250	Polonaise in A, op. 40, no. 1 (*Military*) (5 min.) **(2–Ang. S–3794); **(2–RCA LSC–7037)	S	3	1
145,500	Polonaise in A flat, op. 53 (*Heroic*) (7 min.) **(2–Ang. S–3794); **(2–RCA LSC–7037)	E	3	1
145,750	Polonaise in c, op. 40, no. 2 (6 min.) **(2–Ang. S–3794); **(2–RCA LSC–7037)	A	3	2
146,000	Polonaise in c sharp, op. 26, no. 1 (8 min.) **(2–Ang. S–3794); **(2–RCA LSC–7037)	A	3	2
146,250	Polonaise in e flat, op. 26, no. 2 (7 min.) **(2–Ang. S–3794); **(2–RCA LSC–7037)	A	3	2
146,500	Polonaise in f sharp, op. 44 (11 min.) **(2–Ang. S–3794); **(2–RCA LSC–7037)	A	2	2
146,750	Preludes (24), op. 28 (36 min.) *(RCA LM–1163)-*mono* *(Vox 510940E)	S	3	2
147,001	no. 1 in C (1 min.) *(RCA LM–1163)-*mono* *(Vox 510940E)	S	3	2
147,002	no. 2 in a (2 min.) *(RCA LM–1163)-*mono* *(Vox 510940E)	A	3	3
147,003	no. 3 in G (1 min.) *(RCA LM–1163)-*mono* *(Vox 510940E)	S	3	2
147,004	no. 4 in e (2 min.) *(RCA LM–1163)-*mono* *(Vox 510940E)	S	2	2
147,005	no. 5 in D (1 min.) *(RCA LM–1163)-*mono* *(Vox 510940E)	S	3	2
147,006	no. 6 in b (2 min.) *(RCA LM–1163)-*mono* *(Vox 510940E)	S	3	1
147,007	no. 7 in A (1 min.) *(RCA LM–1163)-*mono* *(Vox 510940E)	S	3	1
147,008	no. 8 in f sharp (2 min.) *(RCA LM–1163)-*mono* *(Vox 510940E)	S	2	3
147,009	no. 9 in E (2 min.) *(RCA LM–1163)-*mono* *(Vox 510940E)	S	3	2
147,010	no. 10 in c sharp (1 min.) *(RCA LM–1163)-*mono* *(Vox 510940E)	A	4	3
147,011	no. 11 in B (1 min.) *(RCA LM–1163)-*mono* *(Vox 510940E)	S	4	2
147,012	no. 12 in g sharp (1 min.) *(RCA LM–1163)-*mono* *(Vox 510940E)	S	3	2
147,013	no. 13 in F sharp (3 min.) *(RCA LM–1163)-*mono* *(Vox 510940E)	S	2	3
147,014	no. 14 in e flat (½ min.) *(RCA LM–1163)-*mono* *(Vox 510940E)	S	3	2
147,015	no. 15 in D flat (*Raindrop*) (5 min.) *(RCA LM–1163)-*mono* *(Vox 510940E)	S	2	1
147,016	no. 16 in b flat (1 min.) *(RCA LM–1163)-*mono* *(Vox 510940E)	S	2	2
147,017	no. 17 in A flat (4 min.) *(RCA LM–1163)-*mono* *(Vox 510940E)	S	3	2
147,018	no. 18 in f (1 min.) *(RCA LM–1163)-*mono* *(Vox 510940E)	S	3	2
147,019	no. 19 in E flat (1 min.) *(RCA LM–1163)-*mono* *(Vox 510940E)	S	2	2
147,020	no. 20 in c (2 min.) *(RCA LM–1163)-*mono* *(Vox 510940E)	S	3	1
147,021	no. 21 in B flat (2 min.) *(RCA LM–1163)-*mono* *(Vox 510940E)	S	2	3
147,022	no. 22 in g (1 min.) *(RCA LM–1163)-*mono* *(Vox 510940E)	S	3	2
147,023	no. 23 in F (1 min.) *(RCA LM–1163)-*mono* *(Vox 510940E)	A	2	3
147,024	no. 24 in d (2 min.) *(RCA LM–1163)-*mono* *(Vox 510940E)	A	1	2
147,250	Prelude in c sharp, op. 45 (4 min.) **(Lon. CS 6562)	A	3	4
147,500	Rondo in C, op. 73 for 2 Pianos (9 min.) *(Sera. S–60109)	A	4	3
147,751	Scherzo no. 1, op. 20 (9 min.) **(Lon. CS 6562); **(RCA LSC–2368)	S	3	2
147,752	Scherzo no. 2, op. 31 (10 min.) **(Lon. CS 6562); **(RCA LSC–2368)	S	3	2
147,753	Scherzo no. 3, op. 39 (7 min.) **(Lon. CS 6562); **(RCA LSC–2368)	S	3	1
147,754	Scherzo no. 4, op. 54 (11 min.) **(Lon. CS 6562); **(RCA LSC–2368)	S	3	2

GUIDE NO.	COMPOSER AND TITLE	AGE MIN	AES SIG	AC-CESS
148,000	Sonata no. 2 in b flat for Piano, op. 35 (22 min.) ** (RCA LSC–3194); * (Lon. STS–15050) * (Vox 510940E)	S	2	1
148,250	Sonata no. 3 in b for Piano, op. 58 (25 min.) ** (RCA LSC–3194); * (Lon. STS–15050) Waltzes (14) ** (Odys. 32160058)-*mono*	S	3	2
148,501	op. 18, no. 1 in E flat (5 min.) ** (Odys. 32160058)-*mono*; * (RCA LSC–2726)	E	3	1
148,502	op. 34, no. 1 in A flat (5 min.) ** (Odys. 32160058)-*mono*; * (RCA LSC–2726)	E	3	1
148,503	op. 34, no. 2 in a (5 min.) ** (Odys. 32160058)-*mono*; * (RCA LSC–2726)	S	3	2
148,504	op. 34, no. 3 in F (2 min.) ** (Odys. 32160058)-*mono*; * (RCA LSC–2726)	S	3	2
148,505	op. 42, no. 5 in A flat (4 min.) ** (Odys. 32160058)-*mono*; * (RCA LSC–2726)	S	3	1
148,506	op. 64, no. 1 in D flat (*Minute Waltz*) (2 min.) ** (Odys. 32160058)-*mono*; * (RCA LSC–2726)	E	3	1
148,507	op. 64, no. 2 in c sharp (3 min.) ** (Odys. 32160058)-*mono*; * (RCA LSC–2726)	E	3	1
148,508	op. 64, no. 3 in A flat (3 min.) ** (Odys. 32160058)-*mono*; * (RCA LSC–2726)	S	3	2
148,509	op. 69, no. 1 in A flat (4 min.) ** (Odys. 32160058)-*mono*; * (RCA LSC–2726)	S	3	2
148,510	op. 69, no. 2 in b (4 min.) ** (Odys. 32160058)-*mono*; * (RCA LSC–2726)	S	3	2
148,511	op. 70, no. 1 in G flat (2 min.) ** (Odys. 32160058)-*mono*; * (RCA LSC–2726)	S	3	2
148,512	op. 70, no. 2 in f (3 min.) ** (Odys. 32160058)-*mono*; * (RCA LSC–2726)	S	3	2
148,513	op. 70, no. 3 in D flat (3 min.) ** (Odys. 32160058)-*mono*; * (RCA LSC–2726)	S	3	2
148,514	Waltz no. 14 in e (no opus no.) (3 min.) ** (Odys. 32160058)-*mono*; * (RCA LSC–2726)	S	3	2
148,750	Waltz no. 15 in E (posth. op.) (2 min.) (Sera. S–60093)	S	3	2
	CIMAROSA, DOMENICO (1749–1801)			
149,000	2 Sonatas for Harpsichord (vary) * (None. H–71117)	S	4	3

GUIDE NO.	COMPOSER AND TITLE	AGE MIN	AES SIG	AC-CESS
	CLEMENTI, MUZIO (1752–1832)			
149,250	Sonata, op. 7, no. 3 in g * (2–Oiseau S–306/7)	S	4	2
149,500	Sonata, op. 24, no. 2 in B flat * (2–Oiseau S–306/7)	S	4	2
149,750	Sonata, op. 25, no. 4 in A * (2–Oiseau S–306/7)	S	4	2
150,000	Sonata, op. 25, no. 5 in f sharp * (2–Oiseau S–306/7)	S	4	2
150,250	Sonata, op. 33, no. 1 in A * (2–Oiseau S–306/7)	S	4	2
150,500	Sonata, op. 33, no. 3 in C * (2–Oiseau S–306/7)	S	4	2
150,750	Sonata, op. 40, no. 2 in b * (2–Oiseau S–306/7)	S	4	2
151,000	Sonata, op. 50, no. 3 in g (*Didone Abbandonata*) (23 min.) * (2–Oiseau S–306/7)	S	3	2
	COPLAND, AARON (1900–)			
152,000	*The Cat and the Mouse* (4 min.) (Orion. 7280)	S	4	3
152,250	*Danzón Cubano* (1942) (6 min.) (RCA VICS–1419)	A	3	2
152,500	Passacaglia for Piano (1922) (6 min.) (Lyr. 7104)	A	4	3
152,750	Piano Fantasy (1957) (31 min.) * (Odys. 32160040)	A	2	4
153,000	Piano Variations (1930) (11 min.) (Lyr. 7104)	A	3	4
153,250	Sonata for Piano (1941) (22 min.) (Lyr. 7104)	A	3	3
	COUPERIN, FRANÇOIS (1668–1733) Pieces de clavecin			
154,100	Ordre no. 1 (27 min.) (3–Vox SVBX–5448)	S	3	2
154,200	Ordre no. 2 (31 min.) (3–Vox SVBX–5448)	S	3	2
154,300	Ordre no. 6 (no. 5 *Les Barricades mystérieuses*) (2 min.) (None. H–71037); (3–Vox SVBX–5448)	S	3	1
154,400	Ordre no. 6 (no. 8 *Le Moucheron*) (2 min.) (3–Vox SVBX–5448)	S	3	2
154,500	Ordre no. 8 (26 min.) * (Argo ZRG–632); (3–Vox SVBX–5448)	S	3	3
154,600	Ordre no. 8 (no. 8 Passacaille) (7 min.) * (Argo ZRG–632); (3–Vox SVBX–5448)	S	1	2
154,700	Ordre no. 11 (no. 5 *Les Fastes de la grande et ancienne Ménestrandise* [pts. i–v]) (10 min.) (None. H–71037)	S	3	2
154,800	Ordre no. 13 (no. 4 *Les Folies françoises, ou Les Dominos*) (7 min.) (None. H–71037)	S	2	3

GUIDE NO.	COMPOSER AND TITLE	AGE	AES MIN SIG	AC- CESS
154,900	Ordre no. 14 (14 min.) *(Argo ZRG–632)	S	3	2
155,000	Ordre no. 14 (no. 1 *Le Rossignol-en-amour*) (3 min.) *(Argo ZRG–632); (None. H–71037)	S	3	2
155,100	Ordre no. 14 (no. 6 *Le Carillon de Cythère*) (3 min.) *(Argo ZRG–632); (None. H–71037)	S	3	2
155,200	Ordre no. 18 (no. 6 *Le Tic-toc-choc, ou Les Maillotins*) (2 min.) (None. H–71037)	S	3	1
155,300	Ordre no. 19 (no. 1 *Les Calotins et les calotines, ou La Pièce à tretous*) (3 min.) (None. H–71037)	S	3	2
155,400	Ordre no. 21 (12 min.) *(Argo ZRG–632); *(3–None. HC–73014)	S	3	2
155,500	Ordre no. 26 (no. 1 *La Convalescente*) (4 min.) (None. H–71265)	S	2	2
155,600	Ordre no. 26 (no. 4 *L'Épineuse*) (4 min.) (None. H–71265)	S	3	2
155,700	Ordre no. 26 (no. 5 *La Pantomine*) (2 min.) (None. H–71265)	S	3	2
155,800	Pieces d'orgue consistantes en deux Messes (43–55 min.) **(Turn. 34074)	A	3	3
	COUPERIN, LOUIS (c. 1626–1661)			
156,000	*Tombeau de M. de Chambonnières* (5 min.) (RCA VICS–1370)	A	2	3
	DAQUIN, LOUIS (1694–1772)			
157,000	*Le Coucou* (2 min.) *(Col. MS–7326)	E	4	1
	DEBUSSY, CLAUDE (1862–1918)			
158,000	*Arabesques* (2) (1888) (7 min.) **(DG 139458); (3–Vox SVBX–5433)	E	4	1
158,250	*Children's Corner* Suite (1906–8) (15 min.) **(Ang. 35067)-*mono*; **(DG 2530196); **(3–Odys. 32360021)-*mono*; (3–Vox SVBX–5433)	E	2	2
158,750	*Claire de Lune* (from *Suite bergamasque*) (5 min.) **(Ang. 35067)-*mono*; **(3–Odys. 32360021)-*mono*; **(DG 139458)	E	2	1
159,000	*En blanc et noir*, for 2 pianos (1915) (15 min.) *(Turn. 34234)	A	2	3
159,250	*Epigraphes antiques* (6) (1918) (14 min.) *(Turn. 34235)	A	3	3
159,500	*Estampes*, for Piano (1903) (13 min.) *(Ang. 35065)-*mono*;	A	2	3

GUIDE NO.	COMPOSER AND TITLE	AGE	AES MIN SIG	AC- CESS
	*(Ang. S–36874); (3–Vox SVBX–5433)			
159,750	*Jardin sous la pluie* (3 min.) *(Ang. 35065)-*mono*; *(Ang. S–36874); (3–Vox SVBX–5433)	A	2	2
160,000	Études for Piano (1915) (3–Vox SVBX–5433)	A	3	4
160,250	Book 1 (21 min.) (3–Vox SVBX–5433)	A	3	4
160,500	Book 2 (23 min.) (3–Vox SVBX–5433)	A	3	4
160,750	*Images* pour Piano, Book 1 (1905) (15 min.) **(DG 2530196); *(Ang. 35065)-*mono*; *(Ang. S–36874); (3–Vox SVBX–5433)	A	2	3
161,000	*Reflets dans l'eau* (5 min.) **(DG 2530196); *(Ang. 35065)-*mono*; *(Ang. S–36874); (3–Vox SVBX–5433)	A	1	2
161,250	*Images* pour piano, Book 2 (1907) (12 min.) **(DG 2530196); *(Ang. 35065)-*mono*; *(Ang. S–36874); (3–Vox SVBX–5433)	A	2	3
161,500	*Poissons d'or* (4 min.) **(DG 2530196); *(Ang. 35065)-*mono*; *(Ang. S–36874); (3–Vox SVBX–5433)	A	2	2
161,750	*L'Isle joyeuse* (6 min.) **(DG 139458); (3–Vox SVBX–5433)	S	1	2
162,000	*La plus que lente* (4 min.) **(DG 139458); (3–Vox SVBX–5433)	A	3	2
162,250	*Pour le piano* (suite) (1896–1901) **(DG 139458); *(Ang. S–36874); *(Ang. 35065)-*mono*; (3–Vox SVBX–5433)	S	3	3
162,500	Preludes for Piano, Book 1 (1910) (vary) **(2–Ang. 35066)-*mono*; **(3–Odys. 32360021)-*mono*; (3–Vox SVBX–5433)	S	2	2
162,750	*Cathédrale engloutie* (7 min.) **(Ang. 35066)-*mono*; **(3–Odys. 32360021)-*mono*; (3–Vox SVBX–5433)	E	1	1
163,000	*La danse de Puck* (3 min.) **(Ang. 35066)-*mono*; **(3–Odys. 32360021)-*mono*; (3–Vox SVBX–5433)	E	2	2
163,250	*Danseuses de Delphes* (3 min.) **(2–Ang. 35066)-*mono*; **(3–Odys. 32360021)-*mono*; (3–Vox SVBX–5433)	S	2	3
163,500	*Des pas sur la neige* (4 min.) **(Ang. 35066)-*mono*; **(3–Odys. 32360021)-	S	2	2

GUIDE NO.	COMPOSER AND TITLE	AGE MIN	AES SIG	AC- CESS
	mono; (3–Vox SVBX–5433)			
163,750	*La Fille aux cheveux de lin* (2 min.) **(Ang. 35066)-*mono*; **(3–Odys. 32360021)- *mono*; (3–Vox SVBX–5433)	E	2	1
164,000	*Voiles* (3 min.) **(2–Ang. 35066)-*mono*; **(3–Odys. 32360021)- *mono*; (3–Vox SVBX–5433)	E	2	3
164,250	Preludes for Piano, Book 2 (1910–13) (vary) **(Ang. 35249)-*mono*; **(3–Odys. 32360021)- *mono*; (3–Vox SVBX–5433)	A	3	3
164,500	*Feuilles mortes* (3 min.) **(Ang. 35249)-*mono*; **(3–Odys. 32360021)- *mono*; (3–Vox SVBX–5433)	A	2	3
164,750	*Feux d'artifice* (4 min.) **(Ang. 35249)-*mono*; **(3–Odys. 32360021)- *mono*; (3–Vox SVBX–5433)	S	2	2
165,000	*Ondine* (3 min.) **(Ang. 35249)-*mono*; **(3–Odys. 32360021)- *mono*; (3–Vox SVBX–5433)	S	2	3
165,250	*Puerta del vino* (3 min.) **(Ang. 35249)-*mono*; **(3–Odys. 32360021)- *mono*; (3–Vox SVBX–5433)	S	2	3
165,500	*Rêverie* (4 min.) (3–Vox SVBX–5433)	E	4	1
165,750	*Suite bergamasque* for piano (1890–1905) (16 min.) **(Ang. 35067)-*mono*; **(DG 139458); **(3–Odys. 32360021)- *mono*; (3–Vox SVBX–5433)	S	3	1
	DELLO JOIO, NORMAN (1913–)			
166,000	Sonata no. 3 for Piano (1947) (13 min.) **(Con.–Disc 217)	S	4	3
	FAURÉ, GABRIEL (1845–1924)			
167,000	*Barcarolle* no. 10 in a, op. 104 (6–Vox SVBX–5423/4 [2 vols.])	A	3	3
167,250	*Nocturne* no. 10 in e, op. 99 (4 min.) (6–Vox SVBX–5423/4)	A	3	3
167,500	*Nocturne* no. 13 in b, op. 119 (6–Vox SVBX–5423/4)	A	2	3
	FIELD, JOHN (1782–1837) Nocturnes (vary)			
168,002	no. 2 in c *(None. H–71195)	A	4	2
168,003	no. 3 in A flat *(None. H–71195)	A	4	2
168,004	no. 4 in A *(None. H–71195)	A	4	2

GUIDE NO.	COMPOSER AND TITLE	AGE MIN	AES SIG	AC- CESS
168,005	no. 5 in B flat *(None. H–71195)	A	4	2
168,006	no. 6 in F *(None. H–71195)	A	4	2
168,009	no. 9 in E flat *(None. H–71195)	A	4	2
168,010	no. 10 in e *(None. H–71195)	A	4	2
168,012	no. 12 in G *(None. H–71195)	A	4	2
168,013	no. 13 in d *(None. H–71195)	A	4	2
168,015	no. 15 in C *(None. H–71195)	A	4	2
168,017	no. 17 in E *(None. H–71195)	A	4	2
168,018	no. 18 in E *(None. H–71195)	A	4	2
	FRANCK, CÉSAR (1822–1890) Chorales (3) for Organ			
169,001	no. 1 in e (15 min.) *(Mer. 75006)	A	4	3
169,002	no. 2 in b (14 min.) **(Argo 5339); *(Mer. 75006)	A	4	2
169,003	no. 3 in a (13 min.) *(Mer. 75006)	A	4	3
169,250	Grande pièce symphonique, op. 17 (25 min.) *(Lon. STS–15104)	A	5	4
169,500	*Pastorale* (8 min.) *(Lon. STS–15105)	A	4	3
169,750	*Pièce heroïque* (8 min.) **(Argo 5339); *(Lon. STS–15103); *(Mer. 75006)	A	5	3
170,000	*Prélude, Choral, et Fugue* for Piano (19 min.) (Sera. S–60103)	A	3	2
	FRESCOBALDI, GIROLAMO (1583–1643)			
171,000	Keyboard Music (varies) **(Tel. 6.41076)	A	2	3
	FROBERGER, JOHANN JAKOB (1616–1667)			
172,000	*Suites de Claveçin* (vary) **(Oiseau 60038); **(Tel. 6.41128)	A	3	3
172,250	Suite no. 26 (6 min.) **(Odys. Y–30289)	A	3	3
	GERSHWIN, GEORGE (1898–1937)			
173,000	*Preludes* (3) for Piano (1926) (6 min.) **(Col. MS–7518)	E	4	1
	GIBBONS, ORLANDO (1583–1625)			
174,000	*The Lord of Salisbury his Pavin* (3 min.) *(Turn. 34017)	A	2	3
	GINASTERA, ALBERTO (1916–)			
175,000	Sonata for Piano (1952) (15 min.) *(Gene. 1008)	A	3	3
	GOTTSCHALK, LOUIS MOREAU (1829–1869)			
176,000	Piano Music *(2–Van. VSD–723/4)	S	5	3

67

GUIDE NO. COMPOSER AND TITLE	AGE MIN	AES SIG	AC- CESS	GUIDE NO. COMPOSER AND TITLE	AGE MIN	AES SIG	AC- CESS
GRANADOS, ENRIQUE (1867–1916)				181,521 Sonata no. 21 in C (14 min.) (3–Vox SVBX–574)	S	4	2
177,000 *Goyescas* (49 min.) (Sera. S–60178)	S	4	2	181,522 Sonata no. 22 in E (10 min.) *(3–Oiseau S–273/5);	S	3	2
177,250 Piano Music *(Arc. Piano X–909)	S	4	2	(3–Vox SVBX–574) 181,523 Sonata no. 23 in F (10 min.)	S	3	1
177,500 *Spanish Dances*, op. 37 (25 min.) *(Arc. Piano X–909)	S	4	2	*(3–Oiseau S–273/5) 181,527 Sonata no. 27 in G (10 min.) (3–Vox SVBX–576)	E	3	1
177,750 no. 5 in e (4 min.) *(Arc. Piano X–909)	S	4	1	181,528 Sonata no. 28 in E flat (12 min.) *(3–Oiseau S–273/5)	S	2	2
GRIEG, EDVARD (1843–1907)				181,530 Sonata no. 30 in A (10 min.) *(3–Oiseau S–273/5)	A	2	2
178,000 Lyric Pieces (10 sets, op. 12, 38, 43, 47, 54, 57, 62, 65, 68, 71) (vary) (3–Vox SVBX–5457); (3–Vox SVBX–5458)	S	4	1	181,531 Sonata no. 31 in E (9 min.) *(3–Oiseau 273/5) 181,534 Sonata no. 34 in e (10 min.) (3–Vox SVBX–575)	A A	2 2	2 2
178,250 *Butterfly*, op. 43, no. 1 (2 min.) (3–Vox SVBX–5457)	E	4	1	181,535 Sonata no. 35 in C (12 min.) (3–Vox SVBX–575) 181,536 Sonata no. 36 in c sharp	E A	3 2	1 2
178,500 *March of the Dwarfs*, op. 54, no. 3 (3 min.) (3–Vox SVBX–5457)	E	4	1	(12 min.) (3–Vox SVBX–575) 181,537 Sonata no. 37 in D (11 min.) (3–Vox SVBX–575)	E	3	2
178,750 *Notturno*, op. 54, no. 4 (3 min.) (3–Vox SVBX–5457)	E	4	1	181,538 Sonata no. 38 in E flat (12 min.) *(3–Oiseau S–273/5); (3–Vox SVBX–575)	A	4	2
179,000 *To the Spring*, op. 43, no. 6 (3 min.) (3–Vox SVBX–5457)	E	4	1	181,540 Sonata no. 40 in G (8 min.) *(3–Oiseau S–273/5); (3–Vox SVBX–574)	S	3	2
179,250 *Wedding Day at Tröldhaugen*, op. 65, no. 6 (3 min.) (3–Vox SVBX–5458)	E	4	1	181,544 Sonata no. 44 in g (15 min.) (3–Vox SVBX–575) 181,545 Sonata no. 45 in E flat (3–Vox SVBX–575)	A S	2 2	3 2
179,500 Norwegian Peasant Dances (*Slätter*), op. 72 (1902) (vary) (3–Vox SVBX–5457)	S	4	1	181,546 Sonata no. 46 in A flat (15 min.) *(3–Oiseau S–273/5); (3–Vox SVBX–575)	A	1	2
HANDEL, GEORGE FRIDERIC (1685–1759)				181,548 Sonata no. 48 in C (10 min.) *(Lon. STS–15041); *(3–Oiseau S–273/5); (3–Vox SVBX–574)	S	3	2
180,000 Suites for Harpsichord nos. 1–4 *(Oiseau S–152E)-*mono*	A	4	3	181,549 Sonata no. 49 in E flat (23 min.) (3–Vox SVBX–576)	S	2	3
180,250 Suite II (9 min.) *(Oiseau S–152E)-*mono*	S	3	3	181,550 Sonata no. 50 in C (14 min.) (3–Vox SVBX–576)	A	1	2
180,500 Suite V, Set 1 (*Harmonious Blacksmith*) (5 min.) *(Col. MS–7326)	S	3	3	181,551 Sonata no. 51 in D (3–Vox SVBX–574) 181,552 Sonata no. 52 in E flat	A A	2 1	3 3
180,750 Suite VIII (12 min.) (Tel. 6.41045)	A	3	3	(18 min.) *(Lon. STS–15041); (3–Vox SVBX–575)			
HAYDN, (FRANZ) JOSEPH (1732–1809)							
181,000 *Andante and Variations* in f (10 min.) *(Lon. STS–15041); *(RCA LSC–2635)	S	1	1	HINDEMITH, PAUL (1895–1963) 182,250 Sonata no. 1 for Piano (23 min.) *(Col. M–32350)	A	3	4
181,250 *Fantasia* in C (5 min.) (Lon. STS–15041)	A	2	2	182,500 Sonata no. 2 for Piano (11 min.) *(Col. M–32350)	A	3	2
181,502 Sonata no. 2 in B flat *(3–Vox SVBX–573)	S	3	2	182,750 Sonata no. 3 for Piano (18 min.) *(Col. M–32350)	A	3	3
181,506 Sonata no. 6 in G (12 min.) *(3–Oiseau S–273/5); *(3–Vox SVBX–573)	S	2	2				
181,508 Sonata no. 8 in G (12 min.) *(3–Vox SVBX–573)	E	3	1	IVES, CHARLES (1874–1954)			
181,512 Sonata no. 12 in A (7 min.) *(3–Vox SVBX–573)	E	3	1	183,000 Sonata no. 1 for Piano (1909) (22 min.) **(Odys. 32160059)-*mono*	A	3	3
181,513 Sonata no. 13 in E **(Odys. Y–30289); *(3–Vox SVBX–573)	E	3	1	183,250 Sonata no. 2 for Piano (1909–15) (*Concord, Mass., 1840–1860*)	A	2	5
181,514 Sonata no. 14 in D (11 min.) *(3–Vox SVBX–573)	E	3	1				
181,520 Sonata no. 20 in c (14 min.) *(3–Oiseau S–273/5); (3–Vox SVBX–575)	A	2	3				

GUIDE NO.	COMPOSER AND TITLE	AGE MIN	AES SIG	AC-CESS
	(37–47 min.)			
	**(Col. MS–7192)			
183,500	*Three-page Sonata* for Piano (1905) (6 min.)	A	3	4
	*(Cam. 1804)			
183,750	Variations on *America*, for Organ (1891) (7 min.)	E	4	2
	**(Col. MS–6161)			
	LISZT, FRANZ (1811–1886)			
185,000	*Années de pèlerinage: 1st Year* (*Switzerland**) (44 min.)	A	4	2
	(Dover–7257)			
185,250	*Années de pèlerinage: 2nd Year* (*Italy**) (50 min.)	A	4	2
	*(Phi. 6500420)			
185,500	*Années de pèlerinage: 3d Year* (52 min.)	S	3	2
	(3–Vox SVBX–5454)			
185,750	*Années de pèlerinage: Years 1 and 2* (excerpts)	A	4	2
	**(Turn. 34385E)-*mono*			
	(3–Vox SVBX–5448)			
186,000	*Ballade* no. 2 in b for Piano (7 min.)	S	5	2
	**(Phi. 802906)			
186,250	Fantasia and Fugue on *Ad nos* for Organ (12 min.)	A	3	3
	**(Argo Z–503); **(Phi. 6500215); **(Phi. 6500376)			
186,500	*Funérailles* (10 min.)	A	2	3
	*(Turn. 34414E)-*mono*			
186,507	*Harmonies poétiques et religieuses*	A	3	3
	*(Turn. 34414E)-*mono* (includes only nos. 1, 3, 4, 7, 10)			
186,750	*Hungarian Rhapsodies* (19) for Piano	S	4	1
	**(3–DG 2709044)			
187,000	*Hungarian Rhapsody* no. 2 (10 min.)	E	4	1
	**(3–DG 2709044); **(RCA LM–2584)-*mono*			
187,250	*Liebestraum* no. 3 (4 min.)	S	4	1
	**(Lon. CS 6693)			
187,500	*Mephisto-Waltz* (Version no. 1 for Piano Solo)	S	3	2
	**(Ang. S–36820); **(Lon. CS 6719); **(Sera. S–60170)			
187,600	*Mephisto-Waltz* (Version no. 3 for Piano Solo)	S	3	2
	*(Sera. S–60170)			
187,750	Opera Transcriptions (Verdi)	A	5	2
	**(Phi. 6500368)			
188,000	*Prelude and Fugue on B-A-C-H* for Organ (12 min.)	A	5	2
	**(Argo Z–503); **(Phi. 6500376)			
188,250	*Réminiscences de Don Juan* (after Mozart) (17 min.)	S	4	1
	**(Sera. S–60088)			
188,500	Sonata in b for Piano (29 min.)	S	3	1
	**(Lon. CS 6371); **(Lon. CS 6693); **(Phi. 6500043)			
188,750	*Transcendental Etudes* (6) after Paganini for Piano	S	3	1
	**(Ang. S–36820)			
189,000	Etude No. 3 (*Campanella*) (5 min.)	S	4	1
	**(Ang. S–36820)			
189,250	*Transcendental Etudes* (12) for Piano (1 hr.)	S	3	1
	**(Lon. CS 6719)			
	LUTOSLAWSKI, WITOLD (1913–)			
190,000	Variations on a Theme of Paganini (1941) (5 min.)	A	3	4
	**(Lon. CS 6434)			
	MENDELSSOHN, FELIX (1809–1847)			
192,000	Fantasy in f sharp (*Sonate éccossaise*) op. 28 (15 min.)	A	4	2
	*(RCA LSC–3239)			
192,250	*Rondo capriccioso* in E, op. 14 (7 min.)	S	4	2
	(Mon. MCS 2128)			
192,500	Sonata no. 1 for Organ, op. 65 (10 min.)	S	4	2
	(CSP AMS–6087)			
192,750	*Songs without Words* (8 books, op. 19b, 30, 38, 53, 62, 67, 85, 102) (vary)	S	3	1
	**(Ang. 35428)-*mono*			
193,000	*Variations sérieuses*, op. 54 (12 min.)	S	3	2
	**(RCA LSC–3239)			
	MILHAUD, DARIUS (1892–1974)			
194,000	*Scaramouche* Suite, op. 165b (1937) (9 min.)	E	4	1
	**(Lon. CS 6434)			
	MOZART, WOLFGANG AMADEUS (1756–1791)			
195,250	Adagio in b, K. 540 (6 min.)	A	2	3
	**(4–Sera. 6047)-*mono*			
195,500	Andante in F, K. 616 (6 min.)	S	2	2
	*(DG 138949)			
195,750	Fantasia in c, K. 396 (9 min.)	A	4	2
	*(Van. VCS–10043)			
196,000	Fantasia in c, K. 475 (12 min.)	A	1	2
	*(Turn. 34178); (Vox SVBX–5429)			
196,250	Fantasia in d, K. 397 (6 min.)	S	3	1
	*(DG 2530061)			
196,500	Fantasia in f for Organ, K. 608 (12 min.)	A	1	2
	**(Oiseau S–335); *(Turn. 34087)			
196,750	Rondo in a for Piano, K. 511 (10 min.)	A	2	3
	**(Lon. CS 6659); *(DG 139318); *(Van. VCS–10043)			
196,850	Sonata in D for 2 Pianos, K. 448 (19 min.)	A	3	2
	**(Turn. 34064); *(Lon. CS 6411)			
196,950	Sonata in F, K. 533 (14 min.)	S	2	2
	(Vox SVBX–5429)			
197,000	Sonata no. 1 in C, K. 279 (12 min.)	S	3	2
	(Vox SVBX–5428)			
197,250	Sonata no. 2 in F, K. 280 (11 min.)	E	3	1
	(Vox SVBX–5428)			

GUIDE NO. COMPOSER AND TITLE	AGE MIN	AES SIG	AC-CESS
197,500 Sonata no. 3 in B flat, K. 281 (13 min.) *(DG 2530061); (Vox SVBX–5428)	S	3	2
197,750 Sonata no. 4 in E flat, K. 282 (11 min.) (Vox SVBX–5428)	S	2	1
198,000 Sonata no. 5 in G, K. 283 (12 min.) (Vox SVBX–5428)	S	2	1
198,500 Sonata no. 7 in C, K. 309 (16 min.) (Vox SVBX–5428)	S	3	2
198,750 Sonata no. 8 in a, K. 310 (17 min.) **(Lon. CS 6659); *(DG 2530061); *(Van. VCS–10043); (Vox SVBX–5428)	S	2	2
199,000 Sonata no. 9 in D, K. 311 (15 min.) (Vox SVBX–5428)	S	3	2
199,250 Sonata no. 10 in C, K. 330 (17 min.) *(DG 139318); (Vox SVBX–5428)	S	2	2
199,500 Sonata no. 11 in A, K. 331 (18 min.) *(DG 139318); (Vox SVBX–5429)	E	2	1
199,750 Sonata no. 12 in F, K. 332 (14 min.) *(DG 138949); (Vox SVBX–5429)	S	2	2
200,000 Sonata no. 13 in B flat, K. 333 (17 min.) *(DG 138949); (Vox SVBX–5429)	S	2	2
200,250 Sonata no. 14 in e, K. 457 (18 min.) *(Turn. 34178); (Vox SVBX–5429)	A	1	2
200,500 Sonata no. 15 in C, K. 545 (10 min.) *(Mace S–9060); (Vox SVBX–5429)	E	2	1
200,750 Sonata no. 16 in B flat, K. 570 (17 min.) (Conn. S–2002); (Vox SVBX–5429)	A	3	2
201,000 Sonata no. 17 in D, K. 576 (14 min.) **(Lon. CS 6659); (Vox SVBX–5429)	S	2	2
201,750 Variations on a Minuet by Duport, K. 573 (8 min.) *(Van. VCS–10043)	S	2	2
202,000 Variations (12) on *Ah, vous dirai-je, Maman*, K. 265 (8 min.) **(Odys. Y–30289); *(DG 138949)	S	3	1
202,250 Variations on *Unser dummer Poebel meint*, K. 455 (14 min.) (Vox SVBX–5407)	S	2	2
MUSSORGSKY, MODEST (1839–1881)			
203,000 *Pictures at an Exhibition* (piano version) (32 min.) **(Odys. Y–32223)-*mono*; **(RCA LM–2357)-*mono*	E	2	2

GUIDE NO. COMPOSER AND TITLE	AGE MIN	AES SIG	AC-CESS
PACHELBEL, JOHANN (1653–1706)			
205,000 Organ Music (varies) **(Tel. 6.41090); *(Tel. 6.41084)	A	4	4
POULENC, FRANCIS (1899–1963)			
206,000 Sonata for Piano, 4 Hands (1916) (6 min.) **(Lon. CS 6434)	S	4	2
PROKOFIEV, SERGE (1891–1953)			
207,000 *Sarcasms*, op. 17 (11 min.) *(3–Vox SVBX–5408)	S	3	3
207,250 Sonata no. 2 in d, op. 14 (1912) (18 min.) *(3–Vox SVBX–5408)	S	4	3
207,500 Sonata no. 3 in a, op. 28 (1917) (7 min.) *(3–Vox SVBX–5408)	S	4	3
207,750 Sonata no. 4 in c, op. 29 (15 min.) *(3–Vox SVBX–5408)	S	3	3
208,000 Sonata no. 6 in A, op. 82 (1940) (27 min.) *(RCA LSC–3229)	A	3	3
208,250 Sonata no. 7 in B flat, op. 83 (1942) (17 min.) **(DG 2530225); **(Lon. CS 6573); **(2–RCA LM–6014)-*mono*	S	2	2
208,500 Sonata no. 8 in B flat, op. 84 (1944) (29 min.) *(Lon. CS 6573)	A	3	3
208,750 *Suggestion Diabolique*, op. 4 (3 min.) *(3–Vox SVBX–5408)	S	4	2
209,000 Toccata, op. 11 (4 min.) *(3–Vox SVBX–5408)	S	3	1
209,250 *Visions fugitives* (20) op. 22 (1915–17) (16 min.) *(3–Vox SVBX–5408)	S	3	3
PURCELL, HENRY (c.1659–1695)			
210,000 Suites for Harpsichord (vary) *(Oiseau 149E)-*mono*	S	3	3
RACHMANINOFF, SERGEI (1873–1943)			
211,000 Prelude in B flat, op. 23, no. 2 (4 min.) **(DG 138076); *(Mel./Ang. S–40235)	S	3	2
211,250 Prelude in b flat, op. 32, no. 2 (3 min.) **(DG 138076); *(Mel./Ang. S–40235)	S	4	2
211,500 Prelude in C, op. 32, no. 1 (3 min.) **(DG 138076); *(Mel./Ang. S–40235)	S	3	2
211,750 Prelude in c, op. 23, no. 7 (3 min.) **(DG 138076); *(Mel./Ang. S–40235)	S	3	2
212,000 Prelude in c sharp, op. 3, no. 2 (4 min.) **(RCA LM–2587)-*mono*	S	3	1
212,250 Prelude in D, op. 23, no. 4 (4 min.) **(DG 138076); *(Mel./Ang. S–40235)	S	3	2

GUIDE NO.	COMPOSER AND TITLE	AGE	AES MIN SIG	AC-CESS
212,500	Prelude in f sharp, op. 23, no. 1 (4 min.) *(Mel./Ang. S–40235)	S	3	2
213,000	Prelude in g, op. 23, no. 5 (4 min.) **(DG 138076); *(Mel./Ang. S–40235)	S	´3	1
213,500	Prelude in g sharp, op. 32, no. 12 (3 min.) *(Mel./Ang. S–40235)	S	3	1
213,750	Suite 2 for 2 pianos, op. 17 (25 min.) **(Lon. CS 6434)	S	4	2
	RAMEAU, JEAN PHILIPPE (1683–1764)			
214,000	*Pièces de clavecin* (vary) (None. H–71278)	S	4	2
214,250	Suite in e for Harpsichord (20 min.) (None. H–71278)	S	4	2
214,750	*Tambourin* (2 min.) (None. H–71278)	E	4	1
	RAVEL, MAURICE (1875–1937)			
215,000	*Gaspard de la nuit* (1908) (22 min.) **(Lon. CS 6472); **(3–Odys. 32360003)-*mono*; *(Turn. 34397)	A	2	3
215,225	*Jeux d'eau* (1901) (5 min.) *(3–Odys. 32360003)-*mono*	S	2	2
215,500	*Ma Mère l'Oye* (4-hand piano suite) (14 min.) *(3–Odys. 32360003)-*mono*	E	3	1
215,750	*Miroirs* (1905) (27 min.) *(3–Odys. 32360003)-*mono*	A	4	2
216,000	*Pavane pour une infante défunte* (1899) (6 min.) *(3–Odys. 32360003)-*mono*	S	3	1
216,250	*Sonatine* for Piano (1903–5) (11 min.) *(3–Odys. 32360003)-*mono*	S	2	2
216,500	*Le Tombeau de Couperin* (1914–17) (24 min.) *(3–Odys. 32360003)-*mono*	A	3	3
216,750	*Valses nobles et sentimentales* (1911) (14 min.) *(3–Odys. 32360003)-*mono*; *(Turn. 34397)	S	3	3
	REUBKE, JULIUS (1834–1858)			
217,000	Sonata on 94th Psalm for Organ (23 min.) **(Oiseau S–335)	A	5	3
	ROUSSEL, ALBERT (1869–1937)			
217,500	Sonatine for Piano, op. 16 (11 min.) (Oiseau 60052)	A	4	3
	SATIE, ERIK (1866–1925)			
218,000	*Avant-dernières pensées* (3 min.) **(Ang. S–36482)	S	4	2
218,250	*Automatic Descriptions* (5 min.) **(Ang. S–36459)	S	4	2
218,500	*Chapters Turned Every Which Way* (5 min.) **(Ang. S–36459)	S	4	2
218,750	*Dessicated Embryoe* (5 min.) **(Ang. S–36485)	S	4	2

GUIDE NO.	COMPOSER AND TITLE	AGE	AES MIN SIG	AC-CESS
219,000	*Dream of Pantagreul's Childhood* (2 min.) **(Ang. S–36485)	S	4	2
219,250	*Eccentric Beauty* (6 min.) **(Ang. S–36459)	S	4	2
219,500	*Flabby Preludes* (3 min.) **(Ang. S–36459)	S	4	2
219,750	*In Riding Habit* (7 min.) **(Ang. S–36459)	S	4	2
220,000	*Old Sequins and Old Cuirasses* (4 min.) **(Ang. S–36459)	S	4	2
220,250	*Passacaglia* (3 min.) **(Ang. S–36485)	S	4	2
220,500	*Puppets Are Dancing* (1 min.) **(Ang. S–36485)	S	4	2
220,750	*Sports and Entertainments* (13 min.) **(Ang. S–36459)	S	3	2
221,000	*3 Distinguished Waltzes of the Disabused Affected Man* (2 min.) **(Ang. S–36482)	S	4	2
221,250	*Unpleasant Glimpses* (4 min.) **(Ang. S–36459)	S	4	2
221,500	*Veritable Flabby Preludes* (3 min.) **(Ang. S–36459)	S	4	2
221,750	*Gnossiennes* (6) (18 min.) **(Ang. S–36714)	S	4	2
222,000	Sonatine bureaucratique (4 min.) **(Ang. S–36811)	S	4	2
222,250	*Trois Gymnopédies* (3 min. ea.) **(Ang. S–36482)	E	3	1
222,500	*Trois morceaux en forme de poire* (1903) (14 min.) **(Ang. S–36482)	S	4	2
	SCARLATTI, DOMENICO (1685–1757)			
223,010	Sonata in A, L. 238 (2 min.) **(2–Odys. 32260007)-*mono*	S	2	3
223,020	Sonata in A, L. 391 (3 min.) **(Col. MS–6658)	S	3	3
223,030	Sonata in A, L. 428 (2 min.) **(2–Odys. 32260007)-*mono*	E	3	1
223,040	Sonata in a, L. 241 (4 min.) **(Col. MS–6658); **(2–Odys. 32260007)-*mono*	S	3	2
223,050	Sonata in a, L. 378 (3 min.) **(2–Odys. 32260007)-*mono*	S	3	2
223,060	Sonata in a, L. 429 (2 min.) **(2–Odys. 32260007)-*mono*	S	3	1
223,070	Sonata in B flat, L. 497 (3 min.) **(2–Odys. 32260012E)-*mono*	S	2	2
223,080	Sonata in C, L. 255 (3 min.) **(None. H–71094)	S	3	2
223,090	Sonata in C, L. 457 (4 min.) **(2–Odys. 32260007)-*mono*	S	2	2
223,100	Sonata in c, L. 10 (3 min.) **(2–Odys. 32260007)-*mono*	S	3	2
223,110	Sonata in D, L. 107 (2 min.) **(2–Odys. 32260007)-*mono*	S	3	2
223,120	Sonata in D, L. 146 (3 min.) **(Col. MS–6658)	S	3	2
223,130	Sonata in D, L. 164 (5 min.) **(2–Odys. 32260012E)-*mono*	E	3	1
223,140	Sonata in D, L. 206 (5 min.) **(2–Odys. 32260012E)-*mono*	S	2	3

GUIDE NO.	COMPOSER AND TITLE	AGE	AES MIN SIG	AC-CESS
223,150	Sonata in D, L. 415 (3 min.)	E	2	1
	**(2–Odys. 32260007)-*mono*			
223,160	Sonata in D, L. 424 (3 min.)	S	3	2
	**(Col. MS–6658)			
223,170	Sonata in D, L. 465 (2 min.)	S	2	1
	**(Col. MS–6658);			
	**(2–Odys. 32260007)-*mono*			
223,180	Sonata in d, L. 215 (2 min.)	E	3	2
	**(2–Odys. 32260007)-*mono*			
223,190	Sonata in d, L. 266 (3 min.)	S	3	3
	**(None. H–71094)			
223,200	Sonata in E, L. 21 (4 min.)	S	3	2
	**(Col. MS–6658);			
	**(None. H–71094)			
223,210	Sonata in E, L. 23 (4 min.)	S	2	2
	**(DG ARC–2533072)			
223,220	Sonata in E, L. 323 (4 min.)	S	2	3
	**(2–Odys. 32260007)-*mono*			
223,230	Sonata in E, L. 373 (2 min.)	S	3	2
	**(2–Odys. 32260007)-*mono*			
223,240	Sonata in E flat, L. 203 (3 min.)	S	3	3
	**(Col. MS–6658)			
223,250	Sonata in e, L. 22 (3 min.)	S	3	2
	**(Col. MS–6658)			
223,260	Sonata in F, L. 188 (3 min.)	S	3	3
	**(Col. MS–6658);			
	**(DG ARC–2533072)			
223,270	Sonata in f, L. 118 (3 min.)	S	3	2
	**(Col. MS–6658)			
223,280	Sonata in f, L. 187 (3 min.)	S	3	3
	**(Col. MS–6658)			
223,290	Sonata in f, L. 281 (3 min.)	S	2	1
	**(2–Odys. 32260007)-*mono*			
223,300	Sonata in f, L. 475 (3 min.)	S	3	2
	**(2–Odys. 32260012E)-*mono*			
223,310	Sonata in G, L. 204 (3 min.)	E	3	1
	**(2–Odys. 32260007)-*mono*			
223,320	Sonata in G, L. 209 (4 min.)	S	3	3
	**(DG ARC–2533072)			
223,330	Sonata in G, L. 304 (4 min.)	S	2	2
	**(2–Odys. 32260012E)-*mono*			
223,340	Sonata in G, L. 349 (3 min.)	S	3	2
	**(Col. MS–6658);			
	**(None. H–71094)			
223,500	Sonatas (L. 18, L. 21, L. 22, L. 64, L. 88, L. 187, L. 203, L. 241, L. 349, L. 391, L. 424, L. 465) (vary)	S	2	2
	**(Col. MS–6658)			
223,501	Sonatas (L. 12, L. 23, L. 31, L. 35, L. 108, L. 126, L. 127, L. 165, L. 188, L. 209, L. 225, L. 283, L. 443, L. 456, L. 459, Suppl. L. 16, Suppl. L. 45)	S	3	3
	**(DG ARC–2533072)			
223,502	Sonatas (L. 10, L. 25, L. 27, L. 38, L. 103, L. 107, L. 124, L. 204, L. 215, L. 238, L. 241, L. 267, L. 273, L. 281, L. 282, L. 323, L. 373, L. 378, L. 379, L. 397, L. 407, L. 415, L. 416, L. 428, L. 429, L. 432, L. 452, L. 457, L. 461, L. 465)	S	3	3
	**(2–Odys. 32260012E)-*mono*			
223,503	Sonatas (L. 2, L. 3, L. 8, L. 12, L. 14, L. 24, L. 65, L. 82, L. 116, L. 119, L. 128, L. 164, L. 172, L. 206, L. 252, L. 266,	S	3	3

GUIDE NO.	COMPOSER AND TITLE	AGE	AES MIN SIG	AC-CESS
	L. 275, L. 286, L. 287, L. 304, L. 321, L. 324, L. 359, L. 427, L. 454, L. 466, L. 470, L. 475, L. 497, L. 500)			
	**(2–Odys. 32260012E)-*mono*			

SCHOENBERG, ARNOLD (1874–1951)

GUIDE NO.	COMPOSER AND TITLE	AGE	AES MIN SIG	AC-CESS
224,000	*Five Piano Pieces*, op. 23 (10 min.)	A	2	4
	*(Col. MS–7098);			
	*(Turn. 34378)			
224,250	*Six Little Pieces for Piano* (1911), op. 19 (5 min.)	A	3	3
	*(Col. MS–7098);			
	*(Turn. 34378)			
224,500	*Suite* for Piano, op. 25 (13 min.)	A	3	4
	*(Col. MS–7098);			
	*(Turn. 34378)			
224,750	*Three Pieces for Piano*, op. 11 (15 min.)	A	3	3
	*(Col. MS–7098);			
	*(Turn. 34378)			
225,000	*Variations on a Recitative* for Organ, op. 40 (1943) (2–Col. M2S–767)	A	5	4

SCHUBERT, FRANZ (1797–1828)

GUIDE NO.	COMPOSER AND TITLE	AGE	AES MIN SIG	AC-CESS
226,000	*Fantasia in f*, op. 103, D. 940 (18 min.)	A	2	2
	*(Phi. 802817)			
226,250	*German Dances*, op. 33 (11 min.)	E	4	1
	*(Turn. 34006)			
226,500	*Impromptus*, op. 90, nos. 1–4 (24 min.)	E	3	2
	**(DG 139149);			
	**(Turn. 34481);			
	*(Phi. 6500415)			
226,501	op. 90, no. 1 (9 min.)	S	3	2
	**(DG 139149);			
	**(Turn. 34481);			
	*(Phi. 6500415)			
226,502	op. 90, no. 2 (5 min.)	S	3	2
	**(DG 139149);			
	**(Sera. 60115)-*mono*;			
	**(Turn. 34481);			
	*(Phi. 6500415)			
226,503	op. 90, no. 3 (6 min.)	E	3	1
	**(DG 139149);			
	**(Lon. CS 6416);			
	**(Turn. 34481);			
	*(Phi. 6500415)			
226,504	op. 90, no. 4 (7 min.)	E	3	1
	**(DG 139149);			
	**(Lon. CS 6416);			
	**(Sera. 60115)-*mono*;			
	**(Turn. 34481);			
	*(Phi. 6500415)			
226,700	*Impromptus*, op. 142, nos. 1–4 (27 min.)	S	3	2
	**(DG 139149);			
	**(Turn. 34481)			
226,701	op. 142, no. 1 (10 min.)	S	3	2
	**(DG 139149);			
	**(Turn. 34481)			
226,702	op. 142, no. 2 (5 min.)	S	3	2
	**(DG 139149);			
	**(Turn. 34481)			
226,703	op. 142, no. 3 (9 min.)	E	3	1
	**(DG 139149);			
	**(Turn. 34481)			

GUIDE NO.	COMPOSER AND TITLE	AGE MIN	AES SIG	AC-CESS
226,704	op. 142, no. 4 (7 min.) **(DG 139149); **(Turn. 34481)	E	3	1
227,000	Moments musicaux, op. 94, D. 780 (24 min.) **(DG 139372); **(Phi. 6500418); **(Turn. 34475)	S	3	2
227,250	Sonata in A for Piano, op. 120, D. 664 (18 min.) **(Lon. CS 6500); *(Ang. S–36150)	S	3	3
227,500	Sonata in A for Piano (posth. op.) D. 959 (36 min.) *(Col. MS–6849)	A	2	3
228,000	Sonata in a for Piano, op. 143, D. 784 (18 min.) **(Lon. CS 6500); **(Phi. 6500418)	A	2	4
228,250	Sonata in B flat for Piano (posth. op.) D. 960 (32 min.) **(Phi. 6500285)	A	1	3
228,750	Sonata in c for Piano (posth. op.) D. 958 (29 min.) *(Phi. 6500415)	A	2	4
229,000	Sonata in D for Piano, op. 53, D. 850 (31 min.) **(Lon. CS 6416)	A	3	2
229,250	Sonata in E flat for Piano, op. 122, D. 568 (26 min.) (RCA LSC–2955)	A	3	2
229,750	Waltzes (vary) *(Turn. 34006)	E	4	1
230,000	Wanderer Fantasie for Piano, op. 15, D. 760 (22 min.) **(DG 139372); **(Phi. 6500285); *(Ang. S–36150)	S	3	2

SCHUMANN, ROBERT
(1810–1856)

GUIDE NO.	COMPOSER AND TITLE	AGE MIN	AES SIG	AC-CESS
230,250	Album für die Jugend, op. 68, no. 8 (Wilder Reiter) *(3–Vox SVBX–5468)	E	4	1
230,500	Album für die Jugend, op. 68, no. 10 (Fröhlicher Landmann) *(3–Vox SVBX–5468)	E	4	1
231,000	Andante and Variations in B flat, op. 46 *(Lon. CS 6411)	A	5	2
231,250	Arabeske for Piano, op. 18 (6 min.) **(Phi. 839709); *(3–Vox SVBX–5468)	S	4	2
232,000	Carnaval, op. 9 (25 min.) **(Phi. 802746); **(RCA LSC–2669); *(DG 2530185); *(Turn. 34164E)-mono; *(3–Vox SVBX–5468)	E	2	2
232,250	Davidsbundlertänze, op. 6 (27 min.) **(Phi. 6500178)	S	3	2
232,500	Fantasia in C, op. 17 (30 min.) **(Lon. CS 6471); **(Phi. 802746); *(Ang. S–35679); *(DG 2530185); *(Gene. 1030)	S	3	2

GUIDE NO.	COMPOSER AND TITLE	AGE MIN	AES SIG	AC-CESS
232,750	Fantasiestücke, op. 12 (27 min.) **(Phi. 6500423); *(RCA LSC–2669)	E	3	1
233,000	op. 12, no. 2 (Auf- schwung) (4 min.) **(Phi. 6500423); *(RCA LSC–2669)	E	3	1
233,250	op. 12, no. 3 (Warum?) (3 min.) **(Phi. 6500423); *(RCA LSC–2669)	E	3	1
233,500	op. 12, no. 4 (Grillen) (3 min.) **(Phi. 6500423)	E	3	1
233,750	Faschingsschwank aus Wien, op. 26 (19 min.) **(Phi. 839709); *(Ang. S–36104); (3–Vox SVBX–5468)	S	4	2
234,000	Kinderscenen, op. 15 (18 min.) *(Turn. 34164E)-mono	E	3	2
234,250	op. 15, no. 1 (Von fremden Ländern und Menschen) (3 min.) *(Turn. 34164E)-mono	E	3	2
234,500	op. 15, no. 7 (Traümerei) (3 min.) *(Turn. 34164E)-mono	E	2	1
234,750	op. 15, no. 8 (Am Camin) (3 min.) *(Turn. 34164E)-mono	E	3	1
235,000	op. 15, no. 9 (Ritter vom Steckenpferd) (2 min.) *(Turn. 34164E)-mono	E	4	1
235,750	Kreisleriana, op. 16 (30 min.) **(Col. MS–7264); **(Lon. CS 6749); **(DG 2530317); **(Phi 6500394)	S	3	2
236,000	Novelettes, op. 21 (50 min.) **(Phi. 6500396)	S	4	2
236,250	Papillons, op. 2 (12 min.) *(Ang. S–36104); *(Turn. 34164E)-mono	E	4	1
236,500	Sonata no. 1 in f sharp for Piano, op. 11 (28 min.) **(Phi. 802793)	A	5	3
236,750	Sonata no. 3 in g for Piano, op. 22 (27 min.) **(Phi. 6500394); *(Ang. S–36104)	A	4	3
237,000	Symphonic Etudes, op. 13 (31 min.) **(DG 2530317); **(Lon. CS 6471); *(Phi. 6500130); (3–Vox SVBX–5468)	A	4	2
237,250	Toccata, op. 7 (6 min.) **(Col. MS–6411); (3–Vox SVBX–5468)	S	4	2
237,500	Waldszenen, op. 82 (20 min.) **(Phi. 6500423); (RCA LSC–2955)	S	4	2
237,750	op. 82, no. 7 (Vogel als Prophet) (3 min.) **(Phi. 6500423); (RCA LSC–2955)	E	3	1

SCRIABIN, ALEXANDER
(1872–1915)

GUIDE NO.	COMPOSER AND TITLE	AGE MIN	AES SIG	AC-CESS
238,000	Preludes (24), op. 11 (30 min.) (Desto 7145)	S	4	2

GUIDE NO. COMPOSER AND TITLE	AGE MIN	AES SIG	AC-CESS
238,250 Sonata no. 3 in f sharp, op. 23 (19 min.) *(RCA LM–2005)-*mono*	A	3	1
SEIXAS, (JOSE ANTONIO) CARLOS DE (1704–1742)			
239,750 Sonatas, Fugues, and Dances for the Harpsichord (vary) (Can. 31020)	A	4	2
SOLER, PADRE ANTONIO (1729–1783)			
240,000 Concerti for 2 (solo) Keyboard Instruments (organ or harpsichord) (vary) *(Turn. 34136)	S	4	2
240,250 no. 1 in g (5 min.) *(Turn. 34136)	S	4	2
240,500 no. 2 in a (11 min.) *(Turn. 34136)	S	4	2
240,750 no. 3 in G (11 min.) *(Turn. 34136)	S	4	2
241,000 no. 4 in F (5 min.) *(Turn. 34136)	S	4	2
241,250 no. 5 in A (8 min.) *(Turn. 34136)	S	4	2
241,500 no. 6 in D (9 min.) *(Turn. 34136)	S	4	2
241,750 Sonatas for Harpsichord (vary) (Turn. 34366)	S	4	2
STRAVINSKY, IGOR (1882–1971)			
242,000 Concerto for 2 Solo Pianos (1935) (21 min.) **(DG 2530225); *(CSP AMS–6333)	A	4	3

GUIDE NO. COMPOSER AND TITLE	AGE MIN	AES SIG	AC-CESS
242,250 *5 Pièces faciles* (6 min.) *(CSP AMS–6333)	E	3	1
242,500 *Ragtime for Piano* (5 min.) *(None. H–71212)	E	4	2
242,750 Serenade in A for Piano (1925) (13 min.) *(None. H–71212)	A	3	4
243,000 Sonata for Piano (1924) (11 min.) *(None. H–71212)	A	3	3
243,250 Sonata for 2 Pianos (11 min.) *(CSP AMS–6333)	A	4	2
243,500 *3 Pièces faciles* (4 min.) *(CSP AMS–6333)	E	3	1
SWEELINCK, JAN PIETERSZOON (1562–1621)			
243,750 Organ Music (varies) (Cam. 3508)	A	3	3
TCHAIKOVSKY, PETER ILYITCH (1840–1893)			
244,500 Piano Music (varies) (3–Vox SVBX–5455); (3–Vox SVBX–5459)	S	5	1
WEBERN, ANTON (1883–1937)			
245,250 Variations for Piano Solo, op. 27 (1926) (6 min.) (Dover 7285)	A	2	5
WIDOR, CHARLES MARIE (1844–1937)			
245,750 Symphony no. 5 in f for Organ, op. 42, no. 1, Toccata only (5 min.) *(None. H–71210)	S	4	1

4. Chamber Music

GUIDE NO. COMPOSER AND TITLE	AGE MIN	AES SIG	AC-CESS
ALBÉNIZ, ISAAC (1860–1909)			
Suite española			
246,000 *Granada* (4 min.) **(DG 2530230)	S	3	1
246,250 *Sevillanas* (4 min.) **(Ang. S–36020)	S	3	1
246,500 *Asturias* (*Leyenda*) (6 min.) **(DG 2530159)	S	3	1
246,750 *Torre bermeja* **(DG 2530159)	S	3	1
247,000 Tango in D, op. 165, no. 2 (3 min.) **(Col. M–30057)	S	3	1
ALBINONI, TOMASO (1671–1750)			
247,250 Sonata in a for Flute and Harpsichord, op. 6, no. 6 (8 min.) *(Orion 7149)	S	4	2
ANTES, JOHN (1740–1811)			
247,500 Trio no. 1 for 2 Violins and Cello, op. 3 (13 min.) *(Odys. 32160340)	A	3	3
ARENSKY, ANTON (1861–1906)			
247,750 Trio in d for Violin, Cello, Piano, op. 32 (28 min.) *(Can. 31029)	A	4	3

GUIDE NO. COMPOSER AND TITLE	AGE MIN	AES SIG	AC-CESS
BACH, CARL PHILIPP EMANUEL (1714–1788)			
248,000 6 Sonatas for Flute and Harpsichord (40 min.) **(None. H–71034)	S	3	2
248,250 Sonata in a for Flute Unaccompanied (11 min.) *(Tel. 6.41011)	A	4	3
248,500 Sonata in G for Harp, W. 139 (13 min.) (None. H–71098)	S	4	2
BACH, JOHANN CHRISTIAN (1735–1782)			
248,750 Quintet for Flute, Oboe, Violin, Viola and Cello no. 6 in D (12 min.) **(Tel. 6.41062)	A	4	3
BACH, JOHANN SEBASTIAN (1685–1750)			
250,000 Sonata in a for Unaccompanied Flute, S. 1013 (11 min.) *(2–Odys. Y2–31925)	A	4	4
250,250 Sonata no. 1 in b for Flute, Harpsichord, S. 1030 (19 min.) **(Ang. S–36337); *(2–Odys. Y2–31925)	A	3	3
250,500 Sonata no. 2 in E flat for Flute, Harpsichord, S. 1031 (11 min.)	A	2	3

GUIDE NO.	COMPOSER AND TITLE	AGE	AES ADMIN SIG	AC- CESS
	**(Ang. S–36350);			
	*(2–Odys. Y2–31925)			
250,750	Sonata no. 3 in A for Flute, Harpsichord, S. 1032 (12 min.)	A	3	3
	**(Ang. S–36337);			
	*(2–Odys. Y2–31925);			
	*(Tel. 6.41011)			
251,000	Sonata no. 4 in C for Flute, Harpsichord, S. 1033 (9 min.)	A	2	3
	**(Ang. S–36350);			
	*(2–Odys. Y2–31925)			
251,250	Sonata no. 5 in e for Flute, Harpsichord, S. 1034 (14 min.)	A	3	3
	**(Ang. S–36337);			
	*(2–Odys. Y2–31925)			
251,500	Sonata no. 6 in E for Flute, Harpsichord, S. 1035 (12 min.)	A	4	3
	**(Ang. S–36350);			
	*(2–Odys. Y2–31925)			
251,750	Sonata no. 7 in g for Flute, Harpsichord, S. 1020 (11 min.)	A	3	3
	**(Ang. S–36350);			
	*(2–Odys. Y2–31925)			
252,000	Sonata no. 1 for Viola da Gamba and Harpsichord, S. 1027 in G (14 min.)	A	3	3
	*(DG ARC–2533055);			
	*(Tel. 6.41242)			
252,250	Sonata no. 2 for Viola da Gamba and Harpsichord, S. 1028 in D (15 min.)	A	3	3
	*(DG ARC–2533055);			
	*(Tel. 6.41242)			
252,500	Sonata no. 3 for Viola da Gamba and Harpsichord, S. 1029 in g (15 min.)	A	3	3
	*(DG ARC–2533055);			
	*(Tel. 6.41242)			
252,750	Sonata no. 1 in g for Violin Unaccompanied S. 1001 (17 min.)	A	1	4
	**(3–Bach BG 627/9)-*mono*;			
	**(3–DG 2709028);			
	**(Phi. 835198);			
	**(3–Phi. 835198/200)			
253,000	Partita no. 1 in b for Violin Unaccompanied S. 1002 (21 min.)	A	1	4
	**(3–Bach BG 627/9)-*mono*;			
	(3–DG 2709028);			
	**(Phi. 835198);			
	**(3–Phi. 835198/200)			
253,250	Sonata no. 2 in a for Violin Unaccompanied S. 1003 (21 min.)	A	1	4
	**(3–Bach BG 627/9)-*mono*;			
	**(3–DG 2709028);			
	**(Phi. 835199);			
	**(3–Phi. 835198/200)			
253,500	Partita no. 2 in d for Violin Unaccompanied S. 1004 (26 min.)	A	1	4
	**(3–Bach BG 627/9)-*mono*;			
	**(3–DG 2709028);			
	**(Phi. 835199);			
	**(3–Phi. 835198/200)			
253,750	Sonata no. 3 in C for Violin Unaccompanied S. 1005 (22 min.)	A	1	4
	**(3–Bach BG 627/9)-*mono*;			

GUIDE NO.	COMPOSER AND TITLE	AGE	AES ADMIN SIG	AC- CESS
	**(3–DG 2709028);			
	**(Phi. 835200);			
	**(3–Phi. 835198/200)			
254,000	Partita no. 3 in E for Violin Unaccompanied A. 1006 (16 min.)	A	1	4
	**(3–Bach BG 627/9)-*mono*;			
	**(3–DG 2709028);			
	**(Phi. 835200);			
	**(3–Phi. 835198/200)			
254,250	Sonata for Violin and Harpsichord in b, S. 1014, no. 1 (14 min.)	A	2	3
	**(2–Ang. S–3629)			
254,500	Sonata for Violin and Harpsichord in A, S. 1015, no. 2 (14 min.)	A	2	3
	**(2–Ang. S–3629)			
254,750	Sonata for Violin and Harpsichord in E, S. 1016, no. 3 (18 min.)	A	2	3
	**(2–Ang. S–3629)			
255,000	Sonata for Violin and Harpsichord in c, S. 1017, no. 4 (15 min.)	A	2	3
	**(2–Ang. S–3629)			
255,225	Sonata for Violin and Harpsichord in f, S. 1018, no. 5 (14 min.)	A	2	3
	**(2–Ang. S–3629)			
255,500	Sonata no. 6 for Violin and Harpsichord in G, S. 1019 (16 min.)	A	2	3
	**(2–Ang. S–3629)			
255,750	Suite no. 1 for Cello Unaccompanied, S. 1007 (17 min.)	A	1	3
	**(2–Ang. 3786)-*mono*;			
	*(DG ARC–198186)			
256,000	Suite no. 2 for Cello Unaccompanied, S. 1008 (19 min.)	A	1	3
	**(2–Ang. 3786)-*mono*;			
	*(DG ARC–198186)			
256,250	Suite no. 3 for Cello Unaccompanied, S. 1009 (17 min.)	A	1	3
	**(2–Ang. 3786)-*mono*;			
	*(DG ARC–198187)			
256,500	Suite no. 4 for Cello Unaccompanied, S. 1010 (20 min.)	A	1	3
	**(2–Ang. 3786)-*mono*;			
	*(DG ARC–198187)			
256,750	Suite no. 5 for Cello Unaccompanied, S. 1011 (22 min.)	A	1	3
	**(2–Ang. 3786)-*mono*;			
	*(DG ARC–198188)			
257,000	Suite no. 6 for Cello Unaccompanied, S. 1012 (26 min.)	A	1	3
	**(2–Ang. 3786)-*mono*;			
	*(DG ARC–198188)			
257,250	Suite for Lute in C, S. 997	S	2	2
	**(DG 2530462);			
	**(RCA LSC–2896)			
257,500	Suite for Lute in e, S. 996 (17 min.)	S	2	2
	**(DG 2530462);			
	**(RCA LSC–2896)			
258,000	Trio Sonata no. 2 in C, S. 1037 (13 min.)	A	2	3
	*(Oiseau S–319)			

GUIDE NO.	COMPOSER AND TITLE	AGE MIN	AES SIG	AC-CESS
258,250	Trio Sonata no. 3 in G, S. 1038 (9 min.) *(Oiseau S–171)	A	2	2
258,500	Trio Sonata no. 4 in G, S. 1039 (13 min.) *(Tel. 6.41242)	A	2	3
	BARBER, SAMUEL (1910–)			
259,000	*Summer Music* for Wood-wind Quintet, op. 31 (12 min.) *(CSP AMS–6114)	A	3	3
	BARTÓK, BÉLA (1881–1945)			
260,000	*Contrasts* for Clarinet, Violin, Piano (17 min.) **(Odys. 32160220E)-*mono*	A	2	4
260,250	Quartet no. 1 in a, op. 7 (30 min.) **(3–Col. D3S–717)	A	4	3
260,500	Quartet no. 2 in a, op. 17 (28 min.) **(3–Col. D3S–717)	A	4	3
260,750	Quartet no. 3 in C sharp (1927) (15 min.) **(3–Col. D3S–717)	A	4	4
261,000	Quartet no. 4 in C (1928) (22 min.) **(3–Col. D3S–717)	A	2	4
261,250	Quartet no. 5 in B flat (1934) (30 min.) **(3–Col. D3S–717)	A	2	4
261,500	Quartet no. 6 in D (1939) (28 min.) **(3–Col. D3S–717)	A	1	3
261,750	Sonata for 2 Pianos and Percussion (25 min.) **(Lon. CS 6583)	A	2	4
262,000	Sonata for Solo Violin (1944) (25 min.) *(Lon. STS–15153)	A	3	4
262,250	Sonata no. 1 for Violin and Piano (32 min.) *(Col. M–30944)	A	3	4
262,500	Sonata no. 2 for Violin and Piano (20 min.) **(2–Van. SRV–304/5SD)-*mono*; *(Col. M–30944)	A	2	4
	BEETHOVEN, LUDWIG VAN (1770–1827)			
263,000	Grosse Fuge in B flat, op. 133 for Quartet (15 min.) **(Phi. 839795); *(Van. VCS–10097)	A	3	4
263,500	Quartet no. 1 in F, op. 18, no. 1 (27 min.) *(Phi. 6500181); *(3–Sera. S–6005)	A	3	2
263,750	Quartet no. 2 in G, op. 18, no. 2 (22 min.) *(3–Sera. S–6005)	A	3	3
264,000	Quartet no. 3 in D, op. 18, no. 3 (21 min.) *(Phi. 6500181); *(3–Sera. S–6005)	A	3	3
264,250	Quartet no. 4 in c, op. 18, no. 4 (22 min.) *(Dover 7280); *(3–Sera. S–6005)	A	4	3
264,500	Quartet no. 5 in A, op. 18, no. 5 (25 min.) *(3–Sera. S–6005)	A	4	3
264,750	Quartet no. 6 in B flat,	A	4	3
	op. 18, no. 6 (25 min.) *(3–Sera. S–6005)			
265,000	Quartet no. 7 in F, op. 59, no. 1 (*Rasumovsky*) (38 min.) *(3–Sera. S–6006)	A	2	3
265,250	Quartet no. 8 in e, op. 59, no. 2 (*Rasumovsky*) (35 min.) *(3–Sera. S–6006)	A	2	3
265,500	Quartet no. 9 in C, op. 59, no. 3 (*Rasumovsky*) (28 min.) *(3–Sera. S–6006)	A	2	2
265,750	Quartet no. 10 in E flat, op. 74 (*Harp*) (30 min.) **(Phi. 6500180); *(3–Sera. S–6006)	A	2	3
266,000	Quartet no. 11 in f, op. 95 (21 min.) **(Phi. 6500180); *(3–Sera. S–6006); *(Dover 7280)	A	2	2
266,250	Quartet no. 12 in E flat, op. 127 (36 min.) *(5–Col. M5S–677); *(Phi. 839745)	A	1	3
266,500	Quartet no. 13 in B flat, op. 130 (36 min.) **(Van. VCS–10096); *(5–Col. M5S–677); *(Phi. 839795)	A	1	4
266,750	Quartet no. 14 in c sharp minor, op. 131 (38 min.) **(Van. VCS–10062); *(Phi. 802915)	A	1	4
267,000	Quartet no. 15 in a, op. 132 (44 min.) **(Van. VCS–10005); *(Phi. 802806)	A	1	4
267,250	Quartet no. 16 in F, op. 135 (25 min.) *(Van. VCS–10097)	A	1	3
267,500	Quintet in C, op. 29 (30 min.) *(Col. MS–6952)	E	4	2
267,750	Quintet in E flat for Piano and Winds, op. 16 (25 min.) **(Lon. CS 6494)	S	4	3
268,250	Septet in E flat for Strings and Winds, op. 20 (42 min.) **(Oiseau 60015)	S	3	2
268,500	Serenade in D for Flute, Violin, Viola, op. 25 (22 min.) **(Phi. 6500167)	S	3	2
269,000	Sonata for Horn and Piano, op. 17 (15 min.) *(Sera. 60040)-*mono*	A	4	4
269,250	Sonata no. 1 in D, op. 12, no. 1 for Violin and Piano (19 min.) **(Van. 300E)-*mono*; **(4–Van. SRV–300/1/2/3)-*mono*; *(4–Phi. 835245/8)	A	3	2
269,500	Sonata no. 2 in A, op. 12, no. 2 for Violin and Piano (17 min.) **(Van. 300E)-*mono*; **(4–Van. SRV–300/1/2/3)-*mono*; *(4–Phi. 835245/8)	A	3	3

GUIDE NO.	COMPOSER AND TITLE	AGE MIN	AES SIG	AC-CESS
269,750	Sonata no. 3 in E flat, op. 12, no. 3 for Violin and Piano (20 min.) **(Van. 300E)-*mono*; **(4–Van. SRV–300/ 1/2/3)-*mono*; *(4–Phi. 835245/8)	A	3	3
270,000	Sonata no. 4 in a, op. 23 for Violin and Piano (20 min.) **(Van. 301E)-*mono*; **(4–Van. SRV–300/ 1/2/3)-*mono*; *(4–Phi. 835245/8)	A	4	3
270,250	Sonata no. 5 in F, op. 24 (*Spring*) for Violin and Piano (23 min.) **(Van. 302E)-*mono*; **(4–Van. SRV–300/ 1/2/3)-*mono*; *(4–Phi. 835245/8); *(RCA LSC–2377)	A	3	1
270,500	Sonata no. 6 in A, op. 30, no. 1 for Violin and Piano (24 min.) **(Van. 301E)-*mono*; **(4–Van. SRV–300/ 1/2/3)-*mono*; *(4–Phi. 835245/8)	A	3	3
270,750	Sonata no. 7 in c, op. 30, no. 2 for Violin and Piano (25 min.) **(Van. 303E)-*mono*; **(4–Van. SRV–300/ 1/2/3)-*mono*; *(4–Phi. 835245/8)	A	3	2
271,000	Sonata no. 8 in G, op. 30, no. 3 for Violin and Piano (18 min.) **(Van. 301E)-*mono*; **(4–Van. SRV–300/ 1/2/3)-*mono*; *(4–Phi. 835245/8); *(RCA LSC–2620)	A	3	2
271,250	Sonata no. 9 in A, op. 47 (*Kreutzer*) for Violin and Piano (31 min.) **(2–Van. SRV–304/5SD)-*mono*; **(4–Van. SRV–300/ 1/2/3)-*mono*; *(4–Phi. 835245/8); *(RCA LSC–2377)	A	2	1
271,500	Sonata no. 10 in G, op. 96 for Violin and Piano (27 min.) **(Van. 303E)-*mono*; **(4–Van. SRV–300/ 1/2/3)-*mono*; *(4–Phi. 835245/8)	A	2	3
272,000	Sonata no. 1 in F, op. 5, no. 1 for Violoncello and Piano (21 min.) **(3–Odys. 32360016E)-*mono*; **(2–Sera. 6075)-*mono*; *(2–Phi. 835182/3)	A	4	3
272,250	Sonata no. 2 in g, op. 5, no. 2 for Violoncello and Piano (21 min.) **(3–Odys. 32360016E)-*mono*; **(2–Sera. 6075)-*mono*; *(2–Phi. 835182/3)	A	3	3
272,500	Sonata no. 3 in A, op. 69 for Violoncello and Piano (26 min.) **(5–Col. M5–30069)-*mono*; **(3–Odys. 32360016E)-*mono*; **(2–Sera. 6075)-*mono*; *(Ang. S–36384); *(2–Phi. 835182/3)	A	2	2
272,750	Sonata no. 4 in C, op. 102, no. 1 for Violoncello and Piano (15 min.) **(3–Odys. 32360016E)-*mono*; **(2–Sera. 6075)-*mono*; *(2–Phi. 835182/3)	A	3	3
273,000	Sonata no. 5 in D, op. 102, no. 2 for Violoncello and Piano (20 min.) **(3–Odys. 32360016E)-*mono*; **(2–Sera. 6075)-*mono*; *(2–Phi. 835182/3); *(Ang. S–36384)	A	2	3
273,250	Trio in B flat, op. 11 (22 min.) *(5–Col. M5–30065)	S	3	3
273,500	Trio in D, op. 70, no. 1 (25 min.) *(5–Col. M5–30065); *(DG 2530207)	A	3	3
273,750	Trio in E flat, op. 70, no. 2 (31 min.) *(5–Col. M5–30065); *(DG 2530207)	A	3	4
274,000	Trio in G, op. 121A (*Kakadu*) (18 min.) *(5–Col. M5–30065)	S	3	2
274,250	Trio no. 1 in E flat, op. 1, no. 1 (29 min.) *(5–Col. M5–30065)	A	3	3
274,500	Trio no. 2 in G, op. 1, no. 2 (31 min.) *(5–Col. M5–30065)	A	4	3
274,750	Trio no. 3 in C, op. 1, no. 3 (30 min.) **(Turn. 34490); *(Col. MS–7083); *(5–Col. M5–30065)	A	3	2
275,000	Trio no. 6 in B flat, op. 97 (*Archduke*) (41 min.) *(Col. MS–6819); *(5–Col. M5–30065); *(DG 2530147)	A	2	2
275,250	Variations in E flat, op. 44 (14 min.) *(5–Col. M5–30065)	A	3	2
	BERG, ALBAN (1885–1935)			
275,750	*Lyric Suite* for String Quartet (27 min.) **(DG 2530283); **(5–DG 2720029)	A	2	4
276,000	Quartet, op. 3 (22 min.) **(DG 2530283); **(5–DG 2720029); *(CSP CML–4737)-*mono*	A	4	3
	BLOCH, ERNEST (1880–1959)			
276,250	*Baal Shem* for Violin and Piano (14 min.) **(CSP AMS–6717)	A	4	3
276,500	Quintet for Piano and Strings (32 min.) *(Con.–Disc.–252)	S	2	2

GUIDE NO.	COMPOSER AND TITLE	AGE MIN	AES SIG	AC- CESS
	BOCCHERINI, LUIGI (1743–1805)			
276,750	Quintet in D for Guitar and Strings, op. 50, no. 4 (18 min.)	S	4	1
	**(DG 2530069)			
277,000	Quintet in e for Guitar and Strings, op. 50, no. 3 (21 min.)	S	4	1
	**(RCA LSC–3027)			
277,500	Quintet in E for Strings, op. 13, no. 5 (23 min.)	E	3	1
	*(Van. HM–43 SD)			
	BORODIN, ALEXANDER (1833–1887)			
277,750	Quartet no. 2 in D (27 min.)	S	3	2
	**(Lon. STS–15046); *(Phi. 802814)			
	BRAHMS, JOHANNES (1833–1897)			
278,000	Quartet no. 1 in c, op. 51, no. 1 (30 min.)	A	2	4
	**(2–Col. M2S–734); **(3–Phi. 6703029)			
278,250	Quartet no. 2 in a, op. 51, no. 2 (31 min.)	A	3	4
	**(2–Col. M2S–734); **(3–Phi. 6703029)			
278,500	Quartet no. 3 in B flat, op. 67 (32 min.)	A	2	3
	**(2–Col. M2S–734); **(3–Phi. 6703029)			
278,750	Quartet no. 1 in g, op. 25 for Piano and Strings (40 min.)	A	4	4
	(DG 2530133)			
279,000	Quartet no. 2 in A, op. 26 for Piano and Strings (47 min.)	A	3	4
	**(2–Odys. 32260019)-*mono*			
279,250	Quartet no. 3 in c, op. 60 for Piano and Strings (33 min.)	A	3	4
	**(Oiseau S–320)			
279,500	Quintet in b for Clarinet and Strings, op. 115 (36 min.)	A	1	3
	*(Ang. S–36280)			
279,750	Quintet in f for Piano and Strings, op. 34 (39 min.)	A	4	3
	*(Col. MS–6631)			
280,000	Quintet no. 1 in F, op. 88 (27 min.)	A	4	4
	*(DG 139430)			
280,250	Quintet no. 2 in G, op. 111 (27 min.)	A	4	4
	*(DG 139430)			
280,500	Sextet in B flat for Strings, op. 18 (35 min.)	A	3	3
	*(DG 139371)			
280,750	Sextet in G, op. 36 (38 min.)	A	4	4
	*(RCA LSC–2739)			
281,000	Sonata in e for Cello and Piano, op. 38	A	5	3
	**(Turn. 34461E)-*mono*			
281,250	Sonata in F for Cello and Piano, op. 99 (26 min.)	A	3	3
	**(5–Col. M5–30069)-*mono*; **(Lon. CS 6814); **(Turn. 34461E)-*mono*			
281,500	Sonata no. 1 for Clarinet (or Viola) and Piano,	A	3	2

GUIDE NO.	COMPOSER AND TITLE	AGE MIN	AES SIG	AC- CESS
	op. 120 in f (21 min.) (Sera. 60011)-*mono*			
281,750	Sonata no. 2 for Clarinet (or Viola) and Piano, op. 120 in E flat (20 min.)	A	3	2
	(Sera. 60011)-*mono*			
282,000	Sonata no. 1 for Violin and Piano, op. 78 in G (27 min.)	A	3	3
	**(Lon. CS 6549); *(RCA LSC–2620)			
282,250	Sonata no. 2 for Violin and Piano, op. 100 in A (19 min.)	A	2	3
	**(Lon. CS 6549); *(RCA LSC–2619)			
282,500	Sonata no. 3 for Violin and Piano, op. 108 in d (21 min.)	A	2	2
	**(Lon. CS 6549); **(Mel./Ang. S–40121); *(RCA LSC–2619)			
282,750	Trio in a for Clarinet, Cello, Piano, op. 114 (24 min.)	A	2	3
	*(DG 139398)			
283,000	Trio in B for Violin, Cello, Piano, op. 8 (37 min.)	A	4	3
	**(Lon. CS 6611)			
283,250	Trio in E flat for Horn, Violin, Piano, op. 40 (29 min.)	A	2	2
	**(Lon. CS 6628); *(DG 139398)			
283,500	Trio no. 2 in C for Violin, Cello, Piano, op. 87 (29 min.)	A	2	3
	**(Lon. CS 6814)			
283,750	Trio no. 3 in c for Violin, Cello, Piano, op. 101 (21 min.)	A	3	3
	**(Lon. CS 6611)			
	BRITTEN, BENJAMIN (1913–)			
284,000	Fantasy for Oboe and Strings, op. 2 (13 min.)	A	4	3
	(Van. VCS–10064)			
284,250	*Gloriana*: Courtly Dances (10 min.)	S	3	2
	*(RCA LSC–2730)			
284,500	*Nocturnal* for Guitar, op. 70 (18 min.)	S	3	2
	*(RCA LSC–2964)			
284,750	Sonata in C for Cello and Piano, op. 65 (19 min.)	A	3	3
	**(Lon. CS 6237)			
	CARTER, ELLIOTT (1908–)			
285,250	Eight Etudes and a Fantasy (21 min.)	A	4	5
	*(Can. 31016)			
285,500	Quartet no. 1 (37 min.)	A	3	5
	**(None. H–71249)			
285,750	Quartet no. 2 (20 min.)	A	2	5
	**(None. H–71249); *(Col. M–32738)			
286,000	Quartet no. 3	A	2	5
	*(Col. M–32738)			
286,250	Sonata for Cello	A	3	5
	(None. H–71234)			
286,500	Sonata for Flute, Oboe, Cello and Harpsichord (16 min. ch.)	A	3	5
	(None. H–71234)			

GUIDE NO.	COMPOSER AND TITLE	AGE ADMIN	AES SIG	ACCESS
286,750	Woodwind Quintet (8 min. ch.) *(Can. 31016)	A	3	5
	CHÁVEZ, CARLOS (1899–)			
287,000	Toccata for Percussion (12 min.) (CSP AMS–6447)	E	3	2
	CHOPIN, FRÉDÉRIC (1810–1849)			
287,250	*Introduction and Polonaise* for Piano and Cello, op. 3 (9 min.) (Mon. MC(S)–2119)-*mono*	A	4	2
287,500	Sonata in g for Cello and Piano, op. 65 (23 min.) **(Ang. S–36937)	A	5	3
	COPLAND, AARON (1900–)			
287,750	Quartet for Piano and Strings (21 min.) **(Col. M–30376)	A	4	4
288,000	Sonata for Violin and Piano (19 min.) *(Col. M–32737)	A	3	3
288,250	*Vitebsk*, Study on a Jewish Theme (12 min.) **(Col. M–30376)	A	3	2
	CORELLI, ARCANGELO (1653–1713)			
288,500	Sonata in A for Violin and Continuo, op. 5, no. 9 (9 min.) *(DG ARC–2533132)	A	4	3
288,750	Sonata in B flat for Violin and Continuo, op. 5, no. 2 (10 min.) *(DG ARC–2533132)	A	4	3
	COUPERIN, FRANÇOIS (1668–1733)			
289,000	*Concerts royaux*, no. 2 in D (10 min.) *(Van. VCS–10029)	A	3	3
289,250	*Concerts royaux*, no. 4 in e (16 min.) *(3–None. HC–73014)	A	4	3
289,500	*Les Nations*: 1 in e (*La Françoise*) (19 min.) **(2–Tel. 26.48009); *(2–Oiseau S–137/8)	A	3	2
289,750	*Les Nations*: 2 in c (*L'Espagnole*) (28 min.) **(2–Tel. 26.48009); *(2–Oiseau S–137/8)	A	3	2
290,000	*Les Nations*: 3 in d (*L'Impériale*) (28 min.) **(2–Tel. 26.48009); *(2–Oiseau S–137/8)	A	3	2
290,250	*Les Nations*: 4 in g (*La Piémontaise*) (24 min.) **(2–Tel. 26.48009); *(2–Oiseau S–137/8)	A	3	2
	DANZI, FRANZ (1763–1826)			
290,500	Quintet for Woodwind, op. 56, no. 1 (13 min.) *(None. H–71108)	A	4	3
290,750	Quintet for Woodwind, op. 56, no. 2 (14 min.) *(Con.–Disc 205); *(None. H–71108)	A	4	3
	DEBUSSY, CLAUDE (1862–1918)			
291,000	Quartet in g, op. 10 (1893) (24 min.) **(None. H–71007); *(Phi. 835361)	S	2	2
291,250	Sonata no. 1 in d for Cello and Piano (1915) (12 min.) **(Lon. CS 6237); *(DG 2530049)	A	2	2
291,500	Sonata no. 2 for Flute, Viola, and Harp (1916) (17 min.) **(Oiseau 60048); *(DG 2530049)	A	3	3
291,750	Sonata no. 3 in g for Violin and Piano (1916–17) (12 min.) **(2–Van. SRV–304/5SD)-*mono*; *(DG 2530049)	A	2	3
292,000	*Syrinx*, for Flute Unaccompanied (1912) (2 min.) *(DG 2530049)	S	3	2
	DIAMOND, DAVID (1915–)			
292,250	String Quartet no. 9 (1968) **(CRI S–294)	A	4	3
	DOWLAND, JOHN (1562–1626)			
292,500	Dances for Lute **(RCA LSC–2987)	S	3	2
	DVOŘÁK, ANTONIN (1841–1904)			
293,500	Quartet no. 2 in d, op. 34 (29 min.) (3–Vox SVBX–549)	A	3	3
293,750	Quartet no. 3 in E flat, op. 51 (31 min.) (3–Vox SVBX–549)	A	4	4
294,000	Quartet no. 6 in F, op. 96 (*American*) (24 min.) *(Phi. 802814)	A	2	3
294,250	Quartet no. 7 in A flat, op. 105 (RCA LSC–2887)	A	3	3
294,375	Quartet no. 13 in G, op. 106 (36 min.) **(DG 2530480)	A	2	3
294,500	Quintet in A, op. 81 (Piano) (36 min.) **(Lon. CS6357); **(2–Odys. 32260019)-*mono*	A	3	3
294,750	Quintet in G, op. 77 (orig. op. 18) (34 min.) (DG 2530214)	A	4	4
295,000	Quintet no. 3 in E flat, op. 97 (strings) (31 min.) *(Col. MS–6952); **(Lon. STS–15242)	A	3	2
295,250	Trio in e, op. 90 (*Dumky*) (32 min.) **(Phi. 802918)	A	2	2
	ELGAR, EDWARD (1857–1934)			
295,500	Quartet in c, op. 83 (23 min.) (None. H–71140)	A	4	4
	ENESCO, GEORGES (1881–1955)			
295,750	Sonata no. 3 in a for Violin and Piano, op. 25 (24 min.) *(Ang. S–36418)	A	3	3

GUIDE NO.	COMPOSER AND TITLE	AGE ADMIN	AES SIG	AC- CESS
	FALLA, MANUEL DE (1876–1946)			
296,000	Concerto in D for Harpsichord, Flute, Oboe, Clarinet, Violin and Cello (15 min.) (Phi. 6505001)	A	3	4
	FAURÉ, GABRIEL (1845–1924)			
296,250	Berceuse for Violin and Piano, op. 16 (3 min.) (Mon. MC(S)–2017)	S	4	3
296,500	*Impromptu*, op. 86 for Harp (8 min.) **(Oiseau S–308)	S	4	3
296,750	Quartet (piano) in c, op. 15 (30 min.) **(Oiseau S–289); (3–Vox SVBX–5100)	A	3	3
296,850	Quartet in e, op. 121 (24 min.) (3–Vox SVBX–5100)	A	2	4
297,000	Sonata no. 1 in A for Violin, op. 13 (23 min.) (RCA LM–2074)-*mono*	A	3	2
297,250	Sonata no. 2 in e for Violin, op. 108 (24 min.) (Ev. 3140E)-*mono*	A	2	1
297,500	Trio (piano), op. 120 (22 min.) **(Oiseau S–289); (3–Vox SVBX–5100)	A	2	1
	FRANÇAIX, JEAN (1912–)			
297,875	Divertissement for Oboe, Clarinet and Bassoon (1947) **(Ang. S–36586); **(CSP AMS–6213)	A	3	3
298,000	Quintet for Woodwinds (20 min.) *(Turn. 34507); (Orion 73123)	A	4	4
	FRANCK, CÉSAR (1822–1890)			
299,000	Quintet in f for Piano and Strings (39 min.) *(RCA LSC–2739)	A	3	2
299,500	Sonata in A for Violin and Piano (27 min.) **(Lon. CS 6628); **(Mel./Ang. S–40121); *(Ang. S–36937)	S	3	1
	HANDEL, GEORGE FRIDERIC (1685–1759)			
300,000	Sonata 2 in G for Flute and Continuo, op. 1 (8 min.) **(Tel. 6.41044); *(2–Odys. Y2–32370)	S	4	3
300,250	Sonata 4 in a for Flute and Continuo, op. 1 (9 min.) **(Tel. 6.41044); *(2–Odys. Y2–32370)	S	4	3
300,500	Sonata 5 in G for Flute and Continuo, op. 1 (9 min.) *(2–Odys. Y2–32370)	S	4	3
300,750	Sonata 7 in C for Flute and Continuo, op. 1 (11 min.) **(Tel. 6.41044); *(2–Odys. Y2–32370)	S	4	3
301,000	Sonata 9 in b for Flute and Continuo, op. 1 (7 min.) *(2–Odys. Y2–32370)	S	4	3

GUIDE NO.	COMPOSER AND TITLE	AGE ADMIN	AES SIG	AC- CESS
301,250	Sonata 11 in F for Flute and Continuo, op. 1 (6 min.) **(Tel. 6.41044); *(2–Odys. Y2–32370)	S	4	3
301,500	Sonata 15 for Violin and Continuo, op. 1 (9 min.) *(None. H–71238)	S	4	3
	HARRIS, ROY (1898–)			
301,750	Quintet for Piano and Strings (1936) **(Contem. 8012)	S	3	2
	HAYDN (FRANZ) JOSEPH (1732–1809)			
302,000	Divertimento 45 in D for Baryton, Viola, and Cello (12 min.) *(None. H–71049)	A	4	3
302,250	Quartet, op. 1, no. 3 (13 min.) *(Lon. STS–15168)	S	3	3
302,500	Quartet, op. 2, no. 2 (20 min.) **(Haydn HS–7–9078)	S	3	3
302,750	Quartet, op. 2, no. 4 (19 min.) **(Haydn HS–7–9079)	A	3	3
303,000	Quartet, op. 3, no. 5 (15 min.) *(Lon. CS 6385)	S	2	3
303,250	Serenade only (4 min.) *(Lon. CS 6385)	E	2	1
303,500	Quartet, op. 20, no. 4 (24 min.) **(Haydn HS–7–9087)	S	2	3
303,750	Quartet, op. 20, no. 5 (21 min.) **(Haydn HS–7–9088)	A	2	2
304,000	Quartet, op. 20, no. 6 (22 min.) **(Haydn HS–7–9088)	A	3	2
304,250	Quartet, op. 33, no. 2 (18 min.) *(Lon. CS 6385)	A	2	2
304,500	Quartet, op. 33, no. 3 (17 min.) **(Haydn HS–7–9015)	A	2	2
304,750	Quartet, op. 33, no. 5 (17 min.) (3–Vox SVBX–556)	A	2	3
305,000	Quartet, op. 50, no. 4 (18 min.) **(Haydn HS–7–9090)	A	2	4
305,250	Quartet, op. 54, no. 1 (19 min.) *(DG 2530302)	A	2	3
305,500	Quartet, op. 54, no. 2 (20 min.) *(DG 2530302)	A	2	3
305,750	Quartet, op. 54, no. 3 (20 min.) (3–Vox SVBX–559)	A	3	3
306,000	Quartet, op. 55, no. 1 (16 min.) (3–Vox SVBX–559)	A	3	3
306,250	Quartet, op. 55, no. 2 (20 min.) (3–Vox SVBX–559)	A	3	3
306,500	Quartet, op. 55, no. 3 (18 min.) (3–Vox SVBX–559)	A	3	3
306,750	Quartet, op. 64, no. 4 (17 min.) (3–Vox SVBX–597)	S	2	1

GUIDE NO.	COMPOSER AND TITLE	AGE MIN	AES SIG	AC-CESS
307,000	Quartet, op. 64, no. 5 (*The Lark*) (18 min.) (3–Vox SVBX–597)	S	2	2
307,250	Quartet, op. 74, no. 1 (20 min.) (Van. HM–42 SD)	A	2	1
307,500	Quartet, op. 74, no. 2 (22 min.) (Van. HM–42 SD)	A	2	2
307,750	Quartet, op. 74, no. 3 (20 min.) (Van. HM–42 SD)	A	2	1
308,000	Quartet, op. 76, no. 1 (21 min.) (CSP AML–4922)-*mono*	A	2	2
308,250	Quartet, op. 76, no. 2 (19 min.) **(Haydn HS–7–9015); *(Lon. CS 6385); (CSP AML–4922)-*mono*	A	2	2
308,500	Quartet, op. 76, no. 3 (23 min.) (DG 138886); (CSP AML–4923)-*mono*	S	3	1
308,750	Quartet, op. 76, no. 4 (21 min.) (CSP AML–4923)-*mono*	A	2	2
309,000	Quartet, op. 76, no. 5 (20 min.) (CSP AML–4924)-*mono*	A	1	2
309,250	Quartet, op. 76, no. 6 (20 min.) (CSP AML–4924)-*mono*	A	2	2
309,500	Quartet, op. 77, no. 1 (19 min.) *(DG 138980); *(Haydn HS–7–9095)	A	2	2
309,750	Quartet, op. 77, no. 2 (20 min.) *(Haydn HS–7–9095)	A	1	2
310,000	Quartet, op. 103 (*Unfinished*) (11 min.) (3–Vox SVBX–595)	A	4	3
310,250	Trios (piano) (31) (9–16 min.) **(Phi. 6500400, 6500401, 6500023, 6500522, 6500521)	A	2	3

HINDEMITH, PAUL
(1895–1963)

311,500	*Kammermusik no. 2*, op. 36, no. 1 (20 min.) (Lou. S–684)	A	4	4
311,750	*Kammermusik no. 3*, op. 36, no. 2 (18 min.) (3–Tel. 36.35008)	A	3	2
312,000	*Kammermusik no. 4*, op. 36, no. 3 (20 min.) *(Mel./Ang. S–40068)	A	3	3
312,250	*Kleine Kammermusik*, op. 24, no. 2 (12 min.) *(Con.–Disc 205)	S	3	2
312,500	Sonata for Flute and Piano (13 min.) (Lyr. 7185)	A	3	3
312,750	Sonata for Harp (9 min.) **(Oiseau S–308)	A	3	2

HUMMEL, JOHANN NEPOMUK (1778–1837)

313,000	Septet in d, op. 74 (32 min.) **(Oiseau S–290)	A	4	3

IBERT, JACQUES
(1890–1962)

314,500	*Trois pièces brèves* (7 min.) *(Turn. 34507)	S	3	2

IVES, CHARLES
(1874–1954)

315,000	Largo for Violin, Clarinet, and Piano (1902) (6 min.) (Col. M–30230)	A	4	4
315,250	Quartet no. 1 (22 min.) **(Col. MS–7027); *(Turn. 34157)	A	4	4
315,500	Quartet no. 2 (26 min.) **(Col. MS–7027); *(Turn. 34157)	A	3	5
315,750	Sonata no. 1 for Violin and Piano (21 min.) (2–None. HB–73025)	A	4	4
316,000	Sonata no. 2 for Violin and Piano (14 min.) (2–None. HB–73025)	A	3	4
316,250	Sonata no. 3 for Violin and Piano (26 min.) (2–None. HB–73025)	A	4	5
316,500	Sonata no. 4 for Violin and Piano (10 min.) (2–None. HB–73025)	S	5	2
316,750	Trio for Violin, Cello, and Piano (28 min.) (Col. M–30230)			

JANÁČEK, LEOS
(1854–1928)

317,000	Sextet for Wind Instruments (*Youth*) (18 min.) (Desto 6428)	A	3	2

KIRCHNER, LEON
(1919–   )

318,000	Quartet no. 3 for Strings and Electronic Tape (16 min.) **(3–Vox SVBX–5306)	A	3	4

KODÁLY, ZOLTÁN
(1882–1967)

319,000	Sonata for Cello and Piano, op. 4 (18 min.) **(3–Per. 1093)-*mono*	A	4	3
319,250	Sonata for Cello Unaccompanied, op. 8 (26 min.) **(3–Per. 1093)-*mono*	S	2	2

LAWES, WILLIAM
(1602–1645)

322,000	*Great Consort* Consort Studies and Sonatas **(Argo ZRG–555)	A	4	3

LECLAIR, JEAN MARIE
(1697–1764)

323,000	Sonata for Violin and Piano, op. 9, no. 3 (11 min.) *(RCA VICS–1058)	S	4	2

LOCATELLI, PIETRO
(1695–1764)

324,000	Sonata for Violin, op. 6, no. 7 *(RCA VICS–1058)	S	4	2

MENDELSSOHN, FELIX
(1809–1847)

325,000	Octet in E flat for Strings, op. 20 (31 min.) *(Col. MS–6848)	S	2	1
325,500	Quartet no. 2, op. 13 (28 min.) *(RCA LSC–2948)	S	4	2

GUIDE NO.	COMPOSER AND TITLE	AGE MIN	AES SIG	AC-CESS
326,000	Sonata no. 2 for Cello and Piano, op. 58 (26 min.) *(3–Vox SVBX–582)	S	4	3
326,250	Trio No. 1 in d (piano), op. 49 (27 min.) *(Col. MS–7083); *(3–Vox SVBX–582)	S	3	2
326,500	Trio no. 2 in c (piano), op. 66 (28 min.) *(3–Vox SVBX–582)	S	3	3
	MILHAUD, DARIUS (1892–1974)			
327,000	*Cheminée du Roi René*, op. 205 (13 min.) (CSP AMS–6213); (Ev. 3092)	S	3	2
	MOZART, WOLFGANG AMADEUS (1756–1791)			
327,500	Divertimento in E flat for String Trio, K. 563 (40 min.) **(Phi. 802803)	A	1	4
328,000	Divertimento no. 8 in F, K. 213 (9 min.) **(Phi. 6500002)	E	4	2
328,250	Divertimento no. 14 in B flat, K. 270 (11 min.) *(Phi. 6500004)	S	4	3
328,500	Divertimento no. 15 in B flat, K. 287 for Strings and 2 Horns (39 min.) *(DG 139004)	S	3	3
329,000	Duo no. 1 for Violin and Viola, K. 423 (15 min.) **(Lon. CS 6377); *(Phi. 839747)	A	2	4
329,250	Duo no. 2 for Violin and Viola, K. 424 (19 min.) *(Phi. 839747)	A	2	4
329,500	Quartet for Flute and Strings, K. 285 in D (14 min.) **(Phi. 6500034); *(DG 138997)	E	3	3
329,750	Quartet for Flute and Strings, K. 298 in A (11 min.) **(Phi. 6500034); *(DG 138997)	E	4	3
330,000	Quartet in F for Oboe and Strings, K. 370 (14 min.) *(DG 138996); *(Turn. 34035); *(Van. HM–40 SD)	S	2	1
330,250	Quartet (piano) in E flat, K. 493 (26 min.) *(Col. MS–6683); *(Oiseau S–285); *(Van. SRV–284 SD)	A	2	2
330,500	Quartet (piano) in g, K. 478 (25 min.) *(Col. MS–6683); *(Oiseau S–285); *(Van. SRV–284 SD)	A	1	2
330,750	Quartet no. 14 in G, K. 387 (28 min.) **(3–Odys. Y3–31242)-*mono*	S	2	2
331,000	Quartet no. 15 in d, K. 421 (26 min.) **(3–Odys. Y3–31242)-*mono*	A	1	3
331,250	Quartet no. 16 in E flat, K. 428 (24 min.) **(3–Odys. Y3–31242)-*mono*	A	2	3
331,500	Quartet no. 17 in B flat, K. 458 (*Hunting*) (25 min.) **(3–Odys. Y3–31242)-*mono*; *(DG 138886)	S	3	2
331,750	Quartet no. 18 in A, K. 464 (31 min.) **(3–Odys. Y3–31242)-*mono*	A	2	3
332,000	Quartet no. 19 in C, K. 465 (*Dissonant*) (28 min.) **(3–Odys. Y3–31242)-*mono*	A	2	3
332,250	Quartet no. 20 in D, K. 499 (24 min.) **(Lon. STS–15116); **(Phi. 6500241)	A	2	3
332,500	Quartet no. 21 in D, K. 575 (23 min.) **(Phi. 6500241)	A	2	3
332,750	Quartet no. 22 in B flat, K. 589 (23 min.) **(Lon. STS–15116); **(Phi. 6500225)	A	3	3
333,000	Quartet no. 23 in F, K. 590 (24 min.) **(Phi. 6500225)	A	3	3
333,250	Quintet in C, K. 515 (31 min.) *(5–Tel. 56.35017); *(Van. HM–29 SD)	S	1	3
333,500	Quintet in D, K. 593 (26 min.) *(5–Tel. 56.35017); *(Van. SRV–194 SD)	A	1	3
333,750	Quintet in E flat, K. 614 (25 min.) *(5–Tel. 56.35017); *(Van. SRV–194 SD)	A	3	3
334,000	Quintet in g, K. 516 (32 min.) *(5–Tel. 56.35017); *(Van. HM–29 SD)	A	1	3
334,250	Quintet in A for Clarinet and Strings, K. 581 (30 min.) **(Ang. S–36241); *(DG 138996); *(Phi. 6500073); *(5–Tel. 56.35017)	A	1	1
334,500	Quintet in E flat for Horn and Strings, K. 407 (16 min.) *(5–Tel. 56.35017); *(Turn. 34035)	A	4	3
334,750	Quintet in E flat for Piano and Winds, K. 452 (23 min.) **(Lon. CS 6494)	A	3	2
335,000	Serenade no. 10 in B flat for 13 Wind Instruments, K. 361 (42 min.) **(Ang. S–36247); *(DG 2530136); *(Phi. 839734)	S	2	2
335,250	Serenade no. 11 in E flat, K. 375 for Winds (24 min.) *(BASF 29312); *(Phi. 802907)	A	2	3
335,500	Serenade no. 12 in c, K. 388 for Winds *(BASF 29312); *(Phi. 802907)	A	2	3
335,750	Sonata for Violin and Piano, K. 296 in C (16 min.) **(Col. MS–7064); *(3–Van. SRV–262/3/4 SD)	A	4	3

GUIDE NO.	COMPOSER AND TITLE	AGE	AES MIN SIG	AC-CESS
336,000	Sonata for Violin and Piano, K. 304 in e (12 min.) **(Col. MS–7064); **(3–Van. SRV–262/3/4 SD)	S	2	2
336,250	Sonata for Violin and Piano, K. 376 in F (17 min.) **(Col. MS–7064); *(3–Van. SRV–265/6/7 SD)	S	3	1
336,500	Sonata for Violin and Piano, K. 377 in F (19 min.) *(3–Van. SRV–262/3/4 SD)	S	2	1
336,750	Sonata for Violin and Piano, K. 378 in B flat (18 min.) *(3–Van. SRV–265/6/7 SD)	A	3	3
337,000	Sonata for Violin and Piano, K. 379 in G (16 min.) *(3–Van. SRV–265/6/7 SD)	A	3	3
337,250	Sonata for Violin and Piano, K. 454 in B flat (22 min.) *(Phi. 6500055); *(3–Van. SRV–265/6/7 SD)	A	1	1
337,500	Sonata for Violin and Piano, K. 481 in E flat (23 min.) *(Phi. 6500055); *(3–Van. SRV–265/6/7 SD)	A	2	3
337,750	Sonata for Violin and Piano, K. 526 in A (21 min.) *(3–Van. SRV–265/6/7 SD)	A	2	3
338,000	Trio in E flat for Clarinet, Viola, Piano, K. 498 (20 min.) **(Ang. S–36241); *(Phi. 6500073); *(Van. HM–40 SD)	A	2	3
338,250	Trio (piano) no. 1, K. 254 in B flat (16 min.) (3–Vox SVBX–568)	A	3	3
338,500	Trio (piano) no. 3, K. 496 in G (26 min.) (3–Vox SVBX–568)	A	2	3
338,750	Trio (piano) no. 4, K. 502 in B flat (24 min.) (3–Vox SVBX–568)	A	3	3
339,000	Trio (piano) no. 5, K. 542 in E (19 min.) (3–Vox SVBX–568)	A	3	3
339,250	Trio (piano) no. 6, K. 548 in C (16 min.) (3–Vox SVBX–568)	A	3	3
339,500	Trio (piano) no. 7, K. 564 in G (17 min.) (3–Vox SVBX–568)	A	3	3

NIELSEN, CARL (1865–1931)

| 340,000 | Quintet, op. 43 for Winds (24 min.) *(CSP AMS–6114) | A | 4 | 3 |

PAGANINI, NICCOLO (1782–1840)

| 341,000 | Caprices (24), op. 1 for Solo Violin **(Lon. CS 6163) | A | 4 | 3 |

POULENC, FRANCIS (1899–1963)

342,000	Sextuor for Piano and Woodwind Quintet (18 min.) **(CSP AMS–6213); *(Turn. 34507)	A	3	2
342,125	Sonata for Clarinet and Bassoon (1922) **(Ang. S–36586)	A	3	2
342,250	Sonata for Flute and Piano (12 min.) *(Tel. 6.41011)	S	2	1
342,500	Sonata for Oboe and Piano (13 min.) *(None. H–71033)	A	3	2
342,750	Trio for Oboe, Bassoon, and Piano (13 min.) **(Ang. S–36586)	A	3	2

PROKOVIEV, SERGE (1891–1953)

343,000	Quartet, op. 92 (21 min.) **(Phi. 6500103)	A	2	3
343,250	Quintet for Winds and Strings, op. 39 (19 min.) **(Oiseau S–267)	A	3	2
343,500	Sonata for Cello and Piano, op. 119 (24 min.) **(Argo ZRG–727)	A	3	4
343,750	Sonata no. 1 for Violin, op. 80 (28 min.) *(RCA LSC–3118)	A	3	4
344,000	Sonata no. 2 for Violin, op. 94-bis (23 min.) *(RCA LSC–3118)	A	3	2

RACHMANINOFF, SERGEI (1873–1943)

| 345,000 | Sonata in g for Cello and Piano, op. 19 (35 min.) (2–GC 40899) | A | 4 | 3 |

RAMEAU, JEAN PHILIPPE (1683–1764)

346,000	*Pièce de claveçin en concert* no. 1 (8 min.) **(None. H–71063)	A	3	2
346,250	*Pièce de claveçin en concert* no. 2 (13 min.) **(None. H–71063)	A	3	2
346,500	*Pièce de claveçin en concert* no. 3 (10 min.) **(None. H–71063)	A	3	2
346,750	*Pièce de claveçin en concert* no. 4 (7 min.) **(None. H–71063)	A	3	2
347,000	*Pièce de claveçin en concert* no. 5 (8 min.) **(None. H–71063)	A	3	2

RAVEL, MAURICE (1875–1937)

348,000	*Introduction and Allegro* for Harp, Flute, Clarinet, and String Quartet (10 min.) **(Ang. S–36586); **(Sera. S–60142); *(DG 139304); *(Oiseau 60048)	S	1	1
348,250	*Pièce en forme de Habañera* for Violin and Piano (3 min.) (Mon. MC(S)–2017)	S	3	2
348,500	Quartet in F (28 min.) **(None. H–71007); **(Phi. 835361)	S	2	2
348,750	Trio in a (piano) (28 min.) *(RCA LM–1119)-*mono*	A	1	2

SCHOENBERG, ARNOLD (1874–1951)

| 350,000 | *Phantasy* for Violin and Piano, op. 47 (10 min.) (2–Col. M2S–767) | A | 4 | 5 |
| 350,250 | Quartet no. 1 in d, op. 7 (42 min.) **(DG 2530329); **(5–DG 2720029) | A | 4 | 4 |

GUIDE NO.	COMPOSER AND TITLE	AGE MIN	AES SIG	AC-CESS
350,500	Quartet no. 2 in f sharp, op. 10 (29 min.) **(5–DG 2720029); *(CSP AML–4736)-*mono*; *(Turn. 34032)	A	4	4
350,750	Quartet no. 3, op. 30 (30 min.) **(CSP AML–4736)-*mono*; **(5–DG 2720029)	A	3	5
351,000	Quartet no. 4, op. 37 (32 min.) **(5–DG 2720029); *(CSP AML–4737)-*mono*	A	2	5
351,250	Quintet for Flute, Oboe, Clarinet, Horn, and Bassoon, op. 26 (37 min.) (2–Col. M2S–762); (GC/NEC102)	A	4	5

SCHUBERT, FRANZ
(1797–1828)

GUIDE NO.	COMPOSER AND TITLE	AGE MIN	AES SIG	AC-CESS
352,000	*Nocturne* in E flat, op. 148, D. 897 (9 min.) *(BASF 20314)	A	4	2
352,250	Octet in F for Strings and Winds, op. 166, D. 803 (56 min.) **(Lon. CS 6051); *(Ang. S–36529); *(DG 139102)	A	2	3
352,500	Phantasie in C for Violin and Piano, op. 159, D. 934 (23 min.) *(3–Vox SVBX–569)	A	2	2
352,750	Quartet no. 9 in g, D. 173 (21 min.) (DG 139194)	A	3	3
353,000	Quartet no. 12 in c (*Quartettsatz*) D. 703 (10 min.) **(Lon. CS 6357); *(DG 139103); *(RCA LSC–3285)	A	2	3
353,250	Quartet no. 13 in a, op. 29, D. 804 (34 min.) *(RCA LSC–3285); (DG 139194)	A	1	3
353,500	Quartet no. 14 in d, "Death and the Maiden," D. 810 (37 min.) *(RCA ARL 1–0483)	S	2	2
353,750	Quartet no. 15 in G, op. 161, D. 887 (37 min.) *(DG 139103)	A	2	3
354,000	Quintet in A (piano), op. 114 (*Trout*) D. 667 (36 min.) **(Lon. CS 6090); **(Van. VSD 71145); (BASF 20314)	S	2	2
354,250	Quintet in C, op. 163, D. 956 (46 min.) **(Col. MS–6536); **(5–Col. MS–30069)-*mono*	A	1	3
354,500	*Rondo brillant* in b for Violin and Piano, op. 70 (16 min.) *(Van. VSD 71146); (3–Vox SVBX–569)	A	4	3
354,750	Sonata for Arpeggione and Piano, D. 821 (20 min.) **(Lon. CS 6649); (3–Vox SVBX–569)	A	4	3
355,000	Sonata in A for Violin and Piano, op. 162 D. 574	S	3	2

GUIDE NO.	COMPOSER AND TITLE	AGE MIN	AES SIG	AC-CESS
	(20 min.) *(Van. VSD 71146); (3–Vox SVBX–569)			
355,250	Trio no. 1 in B flat (piano), op. 99, D. 898 (32 min.) *(Col. MS–6716)	A	1	1
355,500	Trio no. 2 in E flat (piano), op. 100, D. 929 (43 min.) *(Col. MS–7419)	A	2	1

SCHUMANN, ROBERT
(1810–1856)

GUIDE NO.	COMPOSER AND TITLE	AGE MIN	AES SIG	AC-CESS
356,000	Adagio and Allegro for Horn, op. 70 (10 min.) *(Sera. 60040)-*mono*	A	4	3
356,250	*Fantasiestücke* for Cello and Piano, op. 73 (11 min.) (Crys. S–134)	A	4	3
356,500	Quartet, op. 41, no. 1 in a (26 min.) **(3–Phi. 6703029)	A	4	3
356,750	Quartet, op. 41, no. 2 in F (22 min.) **(3–Phi. 6703029)	A	5	3
357,000	Quartet, op. 41, no. 3 in A (31 min.) **(3–Phi. 6703029)	A	4	3
357,250	Quartet in E flat for Piano and Strings, op. 47 (28 min.) **(Oiseau S–320)	S	4	2
357,500	Quintet in E flat for Piano and Strings, op. 44 (30 min.) **(2–Odys. 32260019)-*mono*; *(2–Col. M2S–734)	S	2	2
357,750	Romance for Oboe, op. 94, no. 2 in A (4 min.) (Lyr. 7193)	A	4	3
358,000	*Stücke* (5) *im Volkston* for Cello, op. 102 (18 min.) **(Lon. CS 6237)	A	3	2

SESSIONS, ROGER
(1896–   )

GUIDE NO.	COMPOSER AND TITLE	AGE MIN	AES SIG	AC-CESS
358,250	Sonata for Violin Solo (26 min.) (Orion 73110)	A	3	5

SHOSTAKOVICH, DMITRI
(1906–1975)

GUIDE NO.	COMPOSER AND TITLE	AGE MIN	AES SIG	AC-CESS
358,500	Quartet no. 4 in D, op. 83 (25 min.) **(6–Sera. S–6034/5)	A	2	3
358,750	Quartet no. 8 in c, op. 110 (20 min.) **(Lon. STS–15046); **(6–Sera. S–6034/5)	A	3	2
359,000	Quartet no. 10, op. 118 (23 min.) **(6–Sera. S–6034/5)	A	2	2
359,250	Quintet for Piano and Strings, op. 57 (32 min.) **(Mel./Ang. S–40085); (Oiseau S–267)	S	2	2
359,500	Sonata for Cello and Piano, op. 40 (26 min.) **(Mon. MCS 2021)-*mono*	A	4	3
359,750	Trio no. 2 in e (piano), op. 67 (26 min.) *(Mel./Ang. S–40091)	A	4	3

SIBELIUS, JEAN
(1865–1957)

GUIDE NO.	COMPOSER AND TITLE	AGE MIN	AES SIG	AC-CESS
360,000	Quartet in d, op. 56	A	5	3

GUIDE NO.	COMPOSER AND TITLE	AGE	AES SIG	AC- MIN CESS
	(*Voces intimae*) (28 min.)			
	*(None. H–71140)			
	SMETANA, BEDŘICH			
	(1824–1884)			
360,250	Quartet no. 1 in e (*From My Life*) (27 min.) (RCA LSC–2887)	S	2	1
	SOR, FERNANDO (1778–1839)			
360,500	Variations on a Theme of Mozart, op. 9 for Guitar (7 min.) **(Col. MS–7195); **(DG 139366)	S	4	1
	SPOHR, LUDWIG (1784–1859)			
360,750	Nonet in F, op. 31 (29 min.) (Lon. STS–15074)	S	3	1
	STRAVINSKY, IGOR (1882–1971)			
361,000	*Duo concertant* for Violin and Piano (15 min.) *(Sera. 60183)-*mono*	A	3	4
361,250	*Histoire du soldat*: Suite (25 min.) **(Col. MS–6272); **(Col. MS–7093)	S	2	2
361,500	Octet for Wind Instruments (15 min.) **(Col. MS–30579); **(Col. MS–6272)	S	2	2
361,750	Septet for Piano and Strings and Wind Instruments (11 min.) **(Col. MS–7054)	A	4	5
362,000	3 Pieces for String Quartet (7 min.) **(Mel./Ang. S–40085)	A	5	4
	TARTINI, GIUSEPPE (1692–1770)			
362,250	Sonata in g for Violin (*Devil's Trill*) (15 min.) **(DG ARC 2533086); **(RCA VICS–1037)	A	4	2
362,500	Sonata no. 10 (*Didone Abbandonata*) for Violin with Cello and Cembalo, op. 1 (12 min.) *(2–Tel. 26.48002)	A	5	3
	TCHAIKOVSKY, PETER ILYITCH (1840–1893)			
362,750	Quartet no. 1, op. 11 (25 min.) *(Mel./Ang. S–40222)	S	4	2
363,000	Andante Cantabile only (6 min.) *(Mel./Ang. S–40222)	S	2	1
363,250	*Souvenir de Florence*, op. 70 (31 min.) *(Mel./Ang. S–40036)	A	5	2
363,500	Trio (piano) in a, op. 50 (42 min.) **(Phi. 6500132)	A	4	2
	TELEMANN, GEORG PHILIPP (1681–1767)			
363,750	Quartet no. 4 in b for Flute, Violin, Violoncello, and Continuo (9 min.) **(Tel. 6.41183)	A	3	2
364,000	Sonata in d for Flute, Oboe, and Continuo (8 min.) *(None. H–71061)	A	3	2
364,250	Trio in C, for Flute, Recorder, and Cembalo (13 min.) *(Orion 7149)	A	3	2
364,500	Trio in E flat for 2 Violins, Cello, and Continuo (13 min.) *(None. H–71004)	A	3	2
364,750	Trio Sonata in E flat for Oboe, Harpsichord, and Continuo (9 min.) **(DG ARC–198198); *(None. H–71061)	A	3	2
365,000	Trio Sonata in e for Flute, Oboe, and Continuo (9 min.) *(None. H–71061)	A	3	2
	TURINA, JOAQUÍN (1882–1949)			
365,250	*Fandanguillo*, op. 36, for Guitar (5 min.) **(Col. MS–6608)	S	4	1
365,500	*Hommage à Tarrega* (5 min.) **(Col. MS–6608)	S	4	1
365,750	*Sevillana-Fantasia*, op. 29 for Guitar (6 min.) **(MCA 2532)	S	4	1
	VARÈSE, EDGARD (1883–1965)			
366,000	*Density 21.5* (4 min.) *(Col. MS–6146)	A	3	3
366,250	*Octandre* (7 min.) *(Col. MS–6146)	S	3	4
	VILLA-LOBOS, HEITOR (1887–1959)			
366,500	*Bachianas Brasileiras* no. 6, Flute and Bassoon (10 min.) *(Ang. 35547)-*mono*	A	3	3
366,750	*Chôros* no. 1 for Guitar (4 min.) **(2–RCA VICS–7057)	S	3	2
367,000	*Estudio* no. 1 in e (2 min.) **(DG 2530140)	S	3	1
367,250	*Estudio* no. 11 in e (4 min.) **(DG 2530140)	S	3	1
367,500	*Prelude* no. 1 in e (4 min.) **(DG 2530140)	S	3	1
367,750	*Prelude* no. 2 in E for Guitar (3 min.) **(DG 2530140)	S	3	1
368,000	*Prelude* no. 3 in a (5 min.) **(DG 2530140)	S	3	1
368,250	*Prelude* no. 4 in e (3 min.) **(DG 2530140)	S	3	1
368,500	*Prelude* no. 5 in D (4 min.) **(DG 2530140)	S	3	1
368,750	*Quintette en forme de Chôros* (11 min.) (Orion 73123)	A	3	3
	VITALI, TOMMASO ANTONIO (c.1665–??)			
369,000	*Ciaccona* for Violin (10 min.) **(DG ARC–2533086)	A	3	3
	VIVALDI, ANTONIO (1678–1741)			
369,250	*Pastor fido*, op. 13, no. 1 in c (9 min.) **(DG ARC–2533117)	A	4	3
369,500	*Pastor fido*, op. 13, no. 2 in C (6 min.) **(DG ARC–2533117)	A	4	3

GUIDE NO. COMPOSER AND TITLE	AGE MIN	AES SIG	AC-CESS
369,750 *Pastor fido*, op. 13, no. 3 in G (10 min.) **(DG ARC–2533117)	A	4	3
370,000 *Pastor fido*, op. 13, no. 4 in a (10 min.) **(DG ARC–2533117)	A	4	3
370,250 *Pastor fido*, op. 13, no. 5 in C (12 min.) **(DG ARC–2533117)	A	4	3
370,500 *Pastor fido*, op. 13, no. 6 in g (7 min.) **(DG ARC–2533117)	A	4	3
370,750 Sonata no. 1 in e for Cello and Harpsichord, op. 14 (9 min.) (Tel. 6.41108)	A	3	2
WEBER, CARL MARIA VON (1786–1828)			
371,250 Quintet (clarinet) in B flat, op. 34 (25 min.) *(Turn. 34151)	A	3	2

GUIDE NO. COMPOSER AND TITLE	AGE MIN	AES SIG	AC-CESS
WEBERN, ANTON (1883–1945)			
371,500 Concerto for 9 Instruments, op. 24 (8 min.) (Ev. 3232)	A	4	5
371,750 Five Movements for String Quartet (11 min.) **(DG 2530284); **(5–DG 2720029); **(Phi. 6500105); *(CSP AML–4737)-*mono*	A	2	5
372,250 Quartet, op. 28 (8 min.) **(DG 2530284); **(5–DG 2720029); **(Phi. 6500105)	A	3	5
WIENIAWSKI, HENRYK (1835–1880)			
372,500 *Scherzo-Tarantelle*, op. 16 (4 min.) *(Lon. STS–15049)	A	4	3

5. Symphonies

GUIDE NO. COMPOSER AND TITLE	AGE MIN	AES SIG	AC-CESS
ANTHEIL, GEORGE (1900–1959)			
372,750 Symphony no. 4 (1942) (27 min.) (Ev. 3013)	S	4	2
BACH, CARL PHILLIPP EMANUEL (1714–1788)			
373,000 Symphony in B, no. 2, W. 182 (12 min.) **(Phi. 839741)	E	4	2
373,250 Symphony in b, no. 5, W. 182 (15DA) (13 min.) **(Phi. 839741)	E	4	2
√ 373,500 Symphony in C, no. 3, W. 182 (12DA) (11 min.) **(Phi. 839741)	E	4	2
373,750 Symphony in E flat, W. 183 (10 min.) *(Argo ZRG–577); *(Tel. S–9440)	E	4	2
374,250 Symphony in e, W. 177 **(Phi. 839741)	E	4	2
BACH, JOHANN CHRISTIAN (1735–1782)			
√ 375,000 Symphony in g, op. 6, no. 6 (20DA) (12 min.) **(BASF 20309)	S	4	2
BALAKIREV, MILY (1837–1910)			
√ 375,500 Symphony no. 1 in C (42 min.) **(Sera. S–60062)	S	4	2
BARBER, SAMUEL (1910–)			
√ 375,750 *Symphony no. 1 in One Movement*, op. 9 (19 min.) *(Mer. 75012)	S	4	2
BAZELON, IRWIN (1922–)			
376,000 Short Symphony (*Testament to a Big City*) (16 min.) (Lou. S–664)	S	5	2

GUIDE NO. COMPOSER AND TITLE	AGE MIN	AES SIG	AC-CESS
BEESON, JACK (1921–)			
√376,250 Symphony no. 1 in A (1959) (19 min.) (CRI S–196)	A	4	3
376,500 Symphony no. 5 (1967) (28 min.) (CRI S–287)	S	4	2
BEETHOVEN, LUDWIG VAN (1770–1827)			
√377,000 Symphony no. 1 in C, op. 21 (25 min.) **(RCA VICS–1654E)-*mono*; **(8–RCA VIC 8000)-*mono*; **(3–Sera. 6015)-*mono*; *(Phi. 6500087); *(DG 138801)	E	3	2
√377,250 Symphony no. 2 in D, op. 36 (32 min.) **(Ang. S–35509); **(RCA VICS–1654E)-*mono*; *(DG 138801)	S	2	2
√377,500 Symphony no. 3 in E flat, op. 55 (*Eroica*) (50 min.) **(Ang. S–35853); **(RCA VICS–1655E)-*mono*; *(Ang. S–36461)	S	1	3
√377,750 Symphony no. 4 in B flat, op. 60 (33 min.) **(Ang. S–36461); **(7–Odys. Y7–30051); **(Phi. 6500089); **(3–Sera. 6015)-*mono*; *(DG 138803); *(Lon. CS 6512); (Ang. S–35661)	S	2	2
√378,000 Symphony no. 5 in c, op. 67 (32 min.) **(2–Col. MG–30371); **(RCA VICS–1648E)-*mono*; *(Phi. 802769)	E	1	1

GUIDE NO.	COMPOSER AND TITLE	AGE MIN	AES SIG	AC- CESS
378,250	Symphony no. 6 in F, op. 68 (*Pastoral*) (41 min.) **(Ang. S–35711); **(DG 2530142); **(7–Odys. Y7–30051); **(RCA VICS–1654E)-*mono*; **(3–Sera. 6015)-*mono*; **(7–Sera. S–6071)	E	2	2
378,500	Symphony no. 7 in A, op. 92 (37 min.) **(RCA VIC–1502)-*mono*; **(Sera. S–60038); *(Lon. CS 6777)	S	2	2
378,750	Symphony no. 8 in F, op. 93 (26 min.) **(DG 139015); *(Phi. 6500087)	S	2	2
379,250	Symphony no. 9 in d, op. 125 (1 hr., 6 min.) **(Lon. OSA 1159); **(Odys. 32160322E)-*mono*; **(7–Odys. Y7–30051); **(RCA VIC–1607)-*mono*; *(2–Lon. CSP–8)	S	1	4

BERLIOZ, HECTOR
(1803–1869)

381,250	*Symphonie Fantastique*, op. 14 (52 min.) **(Phi. 835188/200)	S	2	2
381,750	*Symphonie funèbre et triomphale*, op. 15 (35 min.) **(Phi. 802913)	S	4	3

BERNSTEIN, LEONARD
(1918–)

382,000	*Jeremiah* Symphony (26 min.) **(Col. MS–6303)	S	5	2
382,250	Symphony no. 2 (*Age of Anxiety*) (30 min.) **(Col. MS–6885)	S	4	2
382,500	Symphony no. 3 (*Kaddish*) (1963) (Col. KS–6605)	S	5	2

BERWALD, FRANZ
(1796–1868)

382,750	Symphony no. 1 in g (*Sérieuse*) (30 min.) *(None. H–71087)	A	3	3
383,250	Symphony no. 3 in C (*Singulière*) (1845) (25 min.) *(None. H–71087)	A	2	3

BIZET, GEORGES
(1838–1875)

384,000	Symphony no. 1 in C (28 min.) **(Sera. S–60192); *(Argo ZRG–719); *(Lon. CS 6208); *(None. H–71183)	E	3	1

BOCCHERINI, LUIGI
(1743–1805)

384,250	Six Symphonies, op. 35 (about 20 min. ea.) *(3–Tel. 36.35021)	S	4	2

BORODIN, ALEXANDER
(1833–1887)

384,500	Symphony no. 2 in b (27 min.) *(Lon. STS–15149); (Mel./Ang. S–40056)	S	4	2

GUIDE NO.	COMPOSER AND TITLE	AGE MIN	AES SIG	AC- CESS
384,750	Symphony no. 3 in a (17 min.) *(Lon. STS–15149)	S	5	3

BOYCE, WILLIAM
(1710–1779)

385,000	Symphony no. 1 in B flat (6 min.) **(Van. HM–23 SD); *(Ang. S–36951)	S	3	2
385,250	Symphony no. 2 in A (5 min.) **(Van. HM–23 SD); *(Ang. S–36951)	S	3	2
385,500	Symphony no. 3 in C (5 min.) **(Van. HM–23 SD); *(Ang. S–36951)	S	3	2
385,750	Symphony no. 4 in F (6 min.) **(Van. HM–23 SD); *(Ang. S–36951)	S	3	2
386,000	Symphony no. 5 in D (8 min.) **(Van. HM–23 SD); *(Ang. S–36951)	S	3	2
386,250	Symphony no. 6 in F (6 min.) **(Van. HM–23 SD); *(Ang. S–36951)	S	3	2
386,500	Symphony no. 7 in B flat (7 min.) **(Van. HM–23 SD); *(Ang. S–36951)	S	3	2
386,750	Symphony no. 8 in d (11 min.) **(Van. HM–23 SD); *(Ang. S–36951)	S	3	2

BRAHMS, JOHANNES
(1833–1897)

387,000	Symphony no. 1 in c, op. 68 (43 min.) **(Ang. S–35481); **(Odys. Y–30311); **(Phi. 6500519)	A	1	3
387,500	Symphony no. 2 in D, op. 73 (41 min.) **(Odys. Y–31924); **(4–RCA VIC–6400)-*mono*; *(DG 138925); *(Ang. S–35532)	S	2	2
388,000	Symphony no. 3 in F, op. 90 (35 min.) **(Ang. S–35545); **(Odys. Y–32225); *(Col. MS–6685)	S	2	2
388,500	Symphony no. 4 in e, op. 98 (39 min.) **(Phi. 6500389); *(Ang. S–35546)	A	1	3
388,750	3d movement only *(Odys. Y–32373)	E	1	1

BRANT, HENRY
(1913–)

389,000	Symphony no. 1 (1931) (25 min.) (Desto 6416E)-*mono*	A	3	4

BRITTEN, BENJAMIN
(1913–)

389,250	*Simple Symphony* for Strings, op. 4 (1934) (17 min.) **(Lon. CS 6618)	S	3	2

GUIDE NO.	COMPOSER AND TITLE	AGE MIN	AES SIG	AC-CESS
389,500	1st movement only (4 min.) **(Lon. CS 6618)	E	3	2
	BRUCKNER, ANTON (1824–1896)			
389,750	Symphony no. 0 in d (44 min.) *(Phi. 802724)	A	4	4
390,000	Symphony no. 1 in c (Linz version) (46 min.) **(Phi. 6500439); *(DG 139131)	A	4	3
390,250	Symphony no. 2 in c (59 min.) **(Phi. 802912)	A	5	3
390,500	Symphony no. 3 in d (55 min.) **(Col. MS–6897); **(Lon. CS 6717)	A	4	3
390,750	Symphony no. 4 in E flat (*Romantic*) (1 hr., 14 min.) **(Ang. S–36245); **(Odys. Y–32981); **(Phi. 835385)	A	3	2
391,000	Symphony no. 5 in B flat (1 hr., 12 min.) **(2–Phi. 6700055); *(2–Ang. S–3709)	A	4	4
391,250	Symphony no. 6 in A (54 min.) **(Ang. S–36271)	A	5	3
391,500	Symphony no. 7 in E (1 hr., 1 min.) *(2–Phi. 802759/60)	A	4	3
391,750	Symphony no. 8 in c (1 hr., 19 min.) **(2–Phi. 6700020)	A	4	4
392,000	Symphony no. 9 in d (59 min.) *(Phi. 835381)	A	3	2
	CANNABICH, CHRISTIAN (1731–1798)			
392,250	Symphony no. 5 in B flat (18 min.) (Mace S–9069)	A	5	3
	CHAUSSON, ERNEST (1855–1899)			
392,750	Symphony in B flat, op. 20 (35 min.) (Mer. 75029)	A	3	1
	CHÁVEZ, CARLOS (1899–)			
393,000	*Sinfonia India* (12 min.) *(Col. MS–6514); (Ev. 3029)	S	3	2
393,250	Symphony no. 4 (*Romantica*) (21 min.) (Ev. 3029)	A	4	3
	CHERUBINI, LUIGI (1760–1842)			
393,500	Symphony in D (28 min.) **(Phi. 6500154)	S	4	2
	CLEMENTI, MUZIO (1752–1832)			
393,750	Symphony in D (19 min.) *(Mace S–9051)	S	3	2
	COPLAND, AARON (1900–)			
394,000	*Dance Symphony* (1922–25) (18 min.) **(Col. MS–7223)	S	4	2
394,250	*Short Symphony* (1934) (15 min.) **(Col. MS–7223)	S	4	2
394,500	Symphony no. 1 for Organ and Orchestra (1925) (25 min.) *(Col. MS–7058)	S	3	2
394,750	Symphony no. 3 (1946) (41 min.) *(Ev. 3018)	S	3	2
	COWELL, HENRY (1897–1965)			
395,000	Symphony no. 5 (1949) (24 min.) (Desto S–6406E)-*mono*	S	3	3
395,250	Symphony no. 15 (*Thesis*) (21 min.) (Lou. 622)-*mono*	S	4	3
	DVOŘÁK, ANTONIN (1841–1904)			
396,000	Symphony no. 1 in c (*Bells of Zlonice*) op. 3 (51 min.) **(Lon. CS 6523)	A	4	2
396,250	Symphony no. 2 in B flat, op. 4 (54 min.) **(Lon. CS 6524)	A	4	2
396,500	Symphony no. 3 in E flat, op. 10 (36 min.) **(Lon. CS 6525)	A	5	2
396,750	Symphony no. 4 in d, op. 13 (40 min.) **(Lon. CS 6526)	A	4	2
397,000	Symphony no. 5 in F, op. 76 (old no. 3) (37 min.) **(Lon. CS 6511)	A	3	2
397,250	Symphony no. 6 in D, op. 60 (old no. 1) (43 min.) **(Lon. CS 6495)	A	5	2
397,500	Symphony no. 7 in d, op. 70 (old no. 2) (37 min.) *(Lon. STS–15157)	A	3	2
398,000	Symphony no. 8 in G, op. 88 (old no. 4) (35 min.) **(DG 139181); **(Lon. CS 6358); **(Turn. 34525E)-*mono*	S	2	2
398,250	Symphony no. 9 in e, op. 95 (*New World*) (old no. 5) (43 min.) **(Lon. CS 6527); **(RCA VICS–1249E)-*mono*; *(Ang. S–35615); *(2–Col. MG–30371); *(Odys. Y–30045)	S	2	1
	EFFINGER, CECIL (1914–)			
398,750	*Little Symphony* (1945) (11 min.) (CSP AMS–6597)	A	4	2
	ELGAR, EDWARD (1857–1934)			
399,000	Symphony no. 1 in A flat, op. 55 (1908) (55 min.) **(Sera. S–60068)	S	3	2
399,250	Symphony no. 2 in E flat, op. 63 (1911) (52 min.) **(Col. M–31997); **(2–Sera. S–6033)	S	4	3
	FINE, IRVING (1914–1962)			
400,000	Symphony (1962) (23 min.) *(Desto 7167)	A	3	4

GUIDE NO.	COMPOSER AND TITLE	AGE MIN	AES SIG	AC-CESS
	FINNEY, ROSS LEE (1906–)			
400,250	Symphony no. 1 (*Communiqué*) (1943) (20 min.) (Lou. 652)-*mono*	A	3	4
400,500	Symphony no. 2 (20 min.) (Lou. 625)-*mono*	A	4	5
400,750	Symphony no. 3 (1964) (19 min.) (Lou. S–672)	A	4	5
	FRANCK, CESAR (1822–1890)			
401,000	Symphony in d (39 min.) **(RCA LSC–2514); **(Sera. S–60012); *(Ang. S–36729); *(Lon. CS 6222)	S	2	1
	FRICKER, PETER RACINE (1920–)			
401,250	Symphony no. 1, op. 9 (1948–49) (34 min.) (Lou. S–675)	A	3	4
	GADE, NIELS (1817–1890)			
401,500	Symphony no. 1 in c, op. 5 (36 min.) (Turn. 34052E)	A	5	3
	GERHARD, ROBERTO (1896–1970)			
402,000	Symphony no. 4 (1967) (35 min.) **(Argo ZRG–701)	A	3	4
	GLIÈRE, REINHOLD (1875–1956)			
402,500	Symphony no. 3, op. 42 (*Ilya Murometz*) (1909–11) (47 min.) (RCA LSC–3246)	S	3	2
	GOLDMARK, KARL (1830–1915)			
402,750	Symphony, op. 26 (*Rustic Wedding*) (42 min.) **(Col. MS–7261)	S	3	2
	GOULD, MORTON (1913–)			
403,000	Symphony no. 4 for Band (*West Point*) (1952) (20 min.) (Mark 21360)	S	5	1
	GUTCHE, GENE (1907–)			
403,250	Symphony no. 5 (1962) (20 min.) (CRI S–189)	A	4	4
	HANSON, HOWARD (1896–)			
403,500	Symphony no. 2, op. 30 (*Romantic*) (1930) (24 min.) *(Mer. 75007)	S	4	1
404,000	Symphony no. 6 (1968) (25 min.) (Turn. 34534)	A	5	2
	HARRIS, ROY (1898–)			
404,250	Symphony no. 3 (1938) (16 min.) *(Col. MS–6303); (Desto 6404E)-*mono*	S	2	2
404,500	Symphony no. 5 (1943) (23 min.) (Lou. S–655)	A	5	1
	HARRISON, LOU (1917–)			
404,750	Symphony on G (1954–66) (39 min.) (CRI S–236)	A	3	3
	HAYDN, (FRANZ) JOSEPH (1732–1809)			
405,750	Symphony no. 1 in D (13 min.) **(6–Lon. STS–15310/15); (Mace. S–9098)	S	4	2
406,000	Symphony no. 2 in C (9 min.) **(6–Lon. STS–15310/15)	S	4	2
406,250	Symphony no. 3 in G (17 min.) **(6–Lon. STS–15310/15); **(None. H–71096)	S	4	2
406,500	Symphony no. 5 in A (15 min.) **(6–Lon. STS–15310/15)	S	4	2
406,750	Symphony no. 6 in D (*Le Matin*) (19 min.) **(6–Lon. STS–15310/15); **(None. H–71015)	S	3	2
407,000	Symphony no. 7 in C (*Le Midi*) (23 min.) **(6–Lon. STS–15310/15); **(None. H–71015)	E	3	2
407,250	Symphony no. 8 in G (*Le Soir*) (21 min.) **(6–Lon. STS–15310/15); **(None. H–71015)	A	4	2
407,500	Symphony no. 9 in C (13 min.) **(6–Lon. STS–15310/15)	A	4	2
407,750	Symphony no. 10 in D (16 min.) **(6–Lon. STS–15310/15)	A	4	2
408,000	Symphony no. 11 in E flat (17 min.) **(6–Lon. STS–15310/15)	A	4	2
408,250	Symphony no. 12 in E (14 min.) **(6–Lon. STS–15310/15); **(None. 71083)	S	4	2
408,500	Symphony no. 13 in D (17 min.) **(6–Lon. STS–15310/15); **(None. H–71121)	S	3	2
408,750	Symphony no. 14 in A (13 min.) **(6–Lon. STS–15310/15)	E	3	1
409,000	Symphony no. 15 in D (18 min.) **(6–Lon. STS–15310/15)	S	4	2
409,250	Symphony no. 16 in B flat (12 min.) **(6–Lon. STS–15310/15)	S	4	2
409,500	Symphony no. 17 in F (13 min.) **(6–Lon. STS–15310/15)	S	4	2
409,750	Symphony no. 18 in G (15 min.) **(6–Lon. STS–15310/15)	E	4	3
410,000	Symphony no. 19 in D (19 min.) **(6–Lon. STS–15310/15); **(None. H–71031)	S	4	2
410,250	Symphony no. 20 in C (17 min.) **(6–Lon. STS–15257/62)	A	4	2
410,500	Symphony no. 21 in A (15 min.)	S	4	2

GUIDE NO.	COMPOSER AND TITLE	AGE MIN	AES SIG	AC-CESS
	**(6–Lon. STS–15257/62); *(None. H–71101)			
410,750	Symphony no. 22 in E flat (*Der Philosoph*) (18 min.)	A	3	2
	**(6–Lon. STS–15257/62); *(Phi. 839796); (Van. VSD 71126)			
411,000	Symphony no. 26 in d (*Lamentatione*) (15 min.)	A	3	3
	**(6–Lon. STS–15257/62); **(None. H–71083); (Van. VSD 71126)			
411,250	Symphony no. 28 in A (16 min.)	S	4	2
	**(6–Lon. STS–15257/62)			
411,500	Symphony no. 29 in E	S	4	2
	**(6–Lon. STS–15257/62); **(None. H–71121)			
411,750	Symphony no. 31 in D (*Hornsignal*) (24 min.)	S	3	2
	**(6–Lon. STS–15257/62); **(None. H–71031)			
412,000	Symphony no. 34 in d (16 min.)	A	4	2
	**(6–Lon. STS–15257/62); **(None. H–71106)			
412,250	Symphony no. 35 in B flat	A	4	2
	**(6–Lon. STS–15257/62); *(None. H–71131)			
412,500	Symphony no. 36 in E flat (21 min.)	S	4	2
	**(6–Lon. STS–15249/54)			
412,750	Symphony no. 39 in g (16 min.)	A	3	3
	**(6–Lon. STS–15249/54); **(None. H–71096); **(Phi. 839796)			
413,000	Symphony no. 43 in E flat (22 min.)	S	4	2
	**(6–Lon. STS–15249/54); *(None. H–71131)			
413,250	Symphony no. 44 in e (*Trauer*) (22 min.)	A	3	2
	**(6–Lon. STS–15249/54); (None. H–71032)			
413,500	Symphony no. 45 in f sharp (*Farewell*) (27 min.)	E	3	2
	**(6–Lon. STS–15249/54); **(None. H–71031)			
413,750	Symphony no. 46 in B (17 min.)	S	4	2
	**(6–Lon. STS–15249/54); **(Oiseau S–135)			
414,000	Symphony no. 47 in G (18 min.)	S	4	2
	**(6–Lon. STS–15249/54); *(Phi. 839796)			
414,250	Symphony no. 48 in C (*Maria Theresa*) (22 min.)	S	4	2
	**(6–Lon. STS–15249/54); **(Phi. 6500194); *(None. H–71101)			
414,500	Symphony no. 49 in f (*La Passione*) (22 min.)	A	3	2
	**(4–Lon. STS–15127/30); (None. H–71032)			
414,750	Symphony no. 52 in c (22 min.)	A	4	2
	**(4–Lon. STS–15127/30); **(Oiseau S–135); **(Phi. 6500114); **(Van. HM–27 SD)			
415,000	Symphony no. 54 in G	S	4	2
	(27 min.) **(4–Lon. STS–15127/30); **(None. H–71106)			
415,250	Symphony no. 55 in E flat (*Schoolmaster*) (22 min.)	S	4	2
	**(4–Lon. STS–15127/30)			
415,500	Symphony no. 56 in C (27 min.)	S	4	2
	**(4–Lon. STS–15127/30)			
415,750	Symphony no. 57 in D (23 min.)	S	3	2
	**(4–Lon. STS–15131/4)			
416,000	Symphony no. 59 in A (*Fire*) (21 min.)	A	3	2
	**(4–Lon. STS–15131/4); *(Van. VSD 71161)			
416,250	Symphony no. 60 in C (*Il Distraito*) (25 min.)	S	4	2
	**(4–Lon. STS–15131/4); **(Van. HM–27 SD)			
416,500	Symphony no. 61 in D (23 min.)	S	3	2
	**(4–Lon. STS–15131/4); *(None. H–71168)			
416,750	Symphony no. 63 in C (*La Roxolane*) (20 min.)	A	4	2
	**(4–Lon. STS–15131/4)			
417,000	Symphony no. 64 in A (21 min.)	S	4	2
	**(4–Lon. STS–15131/4); **(None. H–71121)			
417,250	Symphony no. 67 in F (23 min.)	S	4	2
	**(4–Lon. STS–15135/8)			
417,500	Symphony no. 70 in D (17 min.)	A	4	3
	**(4–Lon. STS–15135/8); **(Phi. 6500194); *(Van. VSD 71161)			
417,750	Symphony no. 72 in D (20 min.)	E	4	2
	**(4–Lon. STS–15135/8)			
418,000	Symphony no. 73 in D (21 min.)	S	3	3
	**(4–Lon. STS–15182/5); **(None. H–71096)			
418,250	Symphony no. 75 in D (21 min.)	S	4	2
	**(4–Lon. STS–15182/5); **(None. H–71106)			
418,500	Symphony no. 77 in B flat (18 min.)	S	4	2
	**(4–Lon. STS–15182/5); *(None. H–71168)			
418,750	Symphony no. 78 in c (19 min.)	S	4	2
	**(4–Lon. STS–15182/5)			
419,000	Symphony no. 80 in d (21 min.)	S	4	2
	**(4–Lon. STS–15182/5); *(None. H–71131)			
419,250	Symphony no. 81 in G (26 min.)	A	3	2
	**(4–Lon. STS–15182/5)			
419,500	Symphony no. 82 in C (*L'Ours*) (24 min.)	S	4	2
	**(6–Lon. STS–15229/34); *(3–Col. D3S–769); (None. H–71101)			
419,750	Symphony no. 83 in g (*La Poule*) (21 min.)	S	3	2
	**(6–Lon. STS–15229/34); **(None. H–71083); *(3–Col. D3S–769)			

90

GUIDE NO.	COMPOSER AND TITLE	AGE MIN	AES SIG	AC-CESS
420,000	Symphony no. 84 in E flat (25 min.) **(6–Lon. STS–15229/34); *(3–Col. D3S–769)	S	3	1
420,250	Symphony no. 85 in B flat (*La Reine*) (22 min.) **(6–Lon. STS–15229/34); *(3–Col. D3S–769)	S	3	2
420,500	Symphony no. 86 in D (28 min.) **(6–Lon. STS–15229/34); *(3–Col. D3S–769)	S	3	1
420,750	Symphony no. 87 in A (25 min.) **(6–Lon. STS–15229/34); *(3–Col. D3S–769)	S	3	2
421,000	Symphony no. 88 in G (21 min.) **(6–Lon. STS–15229/34); *(Ang. S–36346)	S	3	1
421,250	Symphony no. 89 in F (22 min.) **(6–Lon. STS–15229/34)	S	4	2
421,500	Symphony no. 90 in C (25 min.) **(6–Lon. STS–15229/34); *(DG 2530398)	S	3	2
421,750	Symphony no. 91 in E flat (25 min.) **(6–Lon. STS–15229/34)	S	3	2
422,000	Symphony no. 92 in G (*Oxford*) (26 min.) **(6–Lon. STS–15229/34)	S	2	2
422,250	Symphony no. 93 in D (23 min.) **(CSP AML–4374)	S	3	2
422,500	Symphony no. 94 in G (*Surprise*) (24 min.) **(CSP AML–4453)-*mono*; **(Lon. STS–15085); **(Lon. STS–15178)	E	2	1
422,750	Symphony no. 95 in c (20 min.) *(Col. M–30366); *(DG 2530420)	S	3	2
423,000	Symphony no. 96 in D (*Miracle*) (23 min.) *(Col. M–30366); *(DG 2530420)	E	3	2
423,250	Symphony no. 97 in C (26 min.) *(Col. M–30646); *(DG 2530420)	S	3	2
423,500	Symphony no. 98 in B flat (26 min.) *(Ang. S–35872); *(Col. M–30646)	S	2	1
423,750	Symphony no. 99 in E flat (24 min.) **(Lon. STS–15085); *(Van. SRV–211 SD)	S	2	2
424,000	Symphony no. 100 in G (*Military*) (23 min.) *(Van. SRV–187 SD)	S	3	2
424,250	Symphony no. 101 in D (*Clock*) (28 min.) **(Lon. STS–15178); *(Ang. S–35872); *(Van. SRV–187 SD)	E	2	1
424,500	Symphony no. 102 in B flat (25 min.) *(Van. SRV–211 SD)	S	1	1
424,750	Symphony no. 103 in E flat (*Drum Roll*) (29 min.)	A	2	1
	**(CSP AML–4453)-*mono*; *(Van. SRV–166 SD)			
425,000	Symphony no. 104 in D (*London*) (27 min.) *(Ang. S–36346); *(Van. SRV–166 SD)	S	2	1
425,100	Toy Symphony (Movements 3, 4, 7 of L. Mozart's *Cassatio*) **(Ang. S–35638); (Turn. 34134)	E	3	1
	HINDEMITH, PAUL (1895–1963)			
426,000	*Mathis der Maler* (symphony) (1934) (27 min.) **(DG 2530246); **(Lon. CS 6665); *(Ang. S–35949)	A	1	2
426,250	*Symphonia Serena* (1947) (33 min.) *(Ang. S–35491)	A	4	3
426,500	Symphony in B flat for Band (1951) (17 min.) *(Sera. S–60005)	A	3	3
426,750	Symphony in E flat (1941) (32 min.) *(Col. MS–7426)	A	4	3
	HOLZBAUER, IGNAZ (1711–1783)			
427,000	Symphony, op. 4/3 (16 min.) (Mace S–9069)	A	3	3
	HONEGGER, ARTHUR (1892–1955)			
428,000	Symphony no. 2 for String Orchestra (1942) (24 min.) *(DG 2530068)	A	3	2
428,250	Symphony no. 3 (*Liturgique*) (1946) (29 min.) **(Lon. OS 25320); *(DG 2530068)	A	3	3
428,500	Symphony no. 4 (*Deliciae Basiliensis*) (1947) (25 min.) **(Lon. OS 25320)	A	4	3
428,750	Symphony no. 5 (*Di tre re*) (1951) (21 min.)	A	2	2
	IVES, CHARLES (1874–1954)			
429,000	Symphony (*Holidays*) (42 min.) *(Col. MS–7147)	S	3	3
429,250	I. *Washington's Birthday* (11 min.) *(Col. MS–7147)	S	3	3
429,500	II. *Decoration Day* (9 min.) **(Col. MS–6843); *(Col. MS–7147)	S	3	3
429,750	III. *Fourth of July* (6 min.) **(Col. MS–6889); *(Col. MS–7147)	S	3	3
430,000	IV. *Thanksgiving Day* (15 min.) *(Col. MS–7147)	S	3	4
430,250	Symphony no. 1 in d (1896–98) (36 min.) *(RCA LSC–2893); (3–Van. VCS–10032/3/4)	A	4	3
430,500	Symphony no. 2 (1897–1902) (41 min.)	S	2	2

91

GUIDE NO. COMPOSER AND TITLE	AGE	AES SIG	AC-MIN CESS
**(Col. MS–6889);			
(3–Van. VCS–10032/3/4)			
430,750 Symphony no. 3 (1901–4)	S	3	3
(24 min.)			
**(Col. MS–6843);			
(3–Van. VCS–10032/3/4)			
431,000 Symphony no. 4 (1910–16)	S	2	3
(31 min.)			
**(Col. MS–6775);			
(3–Van. VCS–10032/3/4)			
JOSTEN, WERNER			
(1885–1963)			
431,250 Symphony in F (1936)	A	5	3
(16 min.)			
(CRI S–225)			
KABALEVSKY, DMITRI			
(1904–)			
431,500 Symphony no. 4 (40 min.)	S	5	2
*(Mon. MC 2007)-*mono*			
KALINNIKOV, VASSILI			
SERGEIEVITCH (1866–1901)			
431,750 Symphony no. 1 in g	A	4	3
(37 min.)			
*(Mel./Ang. S–40173)			
432,000 Symphony no. 2 in A	A	3	3
(45 min.)			
**(Mel./Ang. S–40132)			
KHACHATURIAN, ARAM			
(1903–)			
432,500 Symphony no. 3 (1947)	A	5	3
(23 min.)			
*(RCA LSC–3067)			
KHRENNIKOV, TIKHON			
(1913–)			
432,750 Symphony no. 1 in B flat	A	4	3
minor, op. 4 (22 min.)			
(Mon. MC(S)2077)-*mono*			
KUPFERMAN, MEYER			
(1926–)			
433,000 *Chamber Symphony* (1950)	A	4	5
(20 min.)			
(Ser. 12017)			
433,250 *Lyric Symphony* (1956)	A	4	5
(23 min.)			
(Ser. 12000)			
LALO, ÉDOUARD			
(1823–1892)			
433,750 Symphony in g (27 min.)	S	4	3
**(Sera. S–60192)			
LUKE, RAY (1928–)			
434,000 Symphony no. 2 (16 min.)	A	4	4
(Lou. S–634)			
MAGNARD, ALBÉRIC			
(1865–1914)			
434,250 Symphony no. 3 (1902)	S	4	3
(38 min.)			
*(Lon. CS 6615)			
MAHLER, GUSTAV			
(1860–1911)			
434,500 Symphony no. 1 in D (1888)	S	2	2
(52 min.)			
**(Lon. CS 6401);			
**(None. H–71240);			
**(Odys. Y–30047);			
*(Phi. 6500342)			
434,750 Symphony no. 2 in c (*Resur-*	S	3	3
rection) (1894) (1 hr.,			
24 min.)			
**(2–Ang. S–3634);			
**(2–Col. M2–32681);			
**(2–Odys. Y2–30848)			
435,000 Symphony no. 3 in d	A	4	3
(1895) (1 hr., 38 min.)			
**(2–Phi. 802711/2);			
*(2–Col. M2S–675);			
*(2–None. HB–73023)			
435,250 Symphony no. 4 in G	S	2	2
(1900) (55 min.)			
**(Col. MS–6833);			
*(Ang. S–35829);			
*(Sera. S–60105)			
435,500 Symphony no. 5 in c sharp	A	3	3
(1902) (1 hr., 8 min.)			
**(2–Odys. 32260016E)-			
mono;			
*(2–Ang. S–3760);			
*(2–Col. M2S–698)			
435,750 Symphony no. 6 in a (1904)	A	4	3
(1 hr., 17 min.)			
*(3–Col. M3S–776)			
436,000 Symphony no. 7 in e (1905)	A	4	3
(1 hr., 21 min.)			
**(2–Phi. 6700036);			
**(2–Van. VSD–71141/2)			
436,250 Symphony no. 8 in E flat	A	4	3
(*Symphony of a Thousand*)			
(1907) (1 hr., 19 min.)			
**(2–Lon. OSA 1295)			
436,500 Symphony no. 9 in D	A	3	2
(1909) (1 hr., 20 min.)			
**(2–Ang. S–3708);			
**(2–Odys. Y2–30308);			
*(3–Col. M3S–776);			
*(2–Phi. 6700021)			
436,750 Symphony no. 10 (Adagio	A	3	3
only) (1910) (26 min.)			
*(2–Col. M2S–735)			
MARTINŮ, BOHUSLAV			
(1890–1959)			
437,500 Symphony no. 5 (1948)	A	4	3
(27 min.)			
(Lou. 663)-*mono*			
MENDELSSOHN, FELIX			
(1809–1847)			
438,000 Symphony no. 1 in c, op. 11	A	4	3
(29 min.)			
**(2–Phi. 802856/7)			
438,250 Symphony no. 2 in B flat,	A	4	4
op. 52 (*Lobgesang*) with			
voices (1 hr., 5 min.)			
**(2–Phi. 802856/7)			
438,500 Symphony no. 3 in a, op. 56	S	3	2
(*Scotch*) (38 min.)			
**(Lon. STS–15091);			
*(DG 2530126);			
*(Phi. 802858)			
438,750 Symphony no. 4 in A,	S	2	1
op. 90 (*Italian*) (27 min.)			
*(Ang. S–35629);			
*(Phi. 802718);			
(Lon. CS 6436)			
439,000 4th movement (*Taran-*	E	2	1
tella) (6 min.)			
**(DG 138684);			
*(Ang. S–35629);			
*(Phi. 802718)			
439,250 Symphony no. 5 in d, op. 107	S	4	2
(*Reformation*) (27 min.)			
*(Phi. 802718)			
(Lon. CS 6436)			
439,500 Symphony no. 9 for String	S	4	3
Orchestra (26 min.)			
*(Argo 5467)			

GUIDE NO.	COMPOSER AND TITLE	AGE MIN	AES SIG	AC-CESS
439,750	Symphony no. 10 for String Orchestra in b (9 min.) *(Argo 5467)	S	4	3
440,000	Symphony no. 12 in g for String Orchestra (19 min.) *(Argo 5467)	S	4	3
	MENNIN, PETER (1923–)			
440,250	Symphony no. 3 (1946) (20 min.) *(CRI S–278E)-*mono*	A	4	3
440,500	Symphony no. 5 (1951) (22 min.) (Mer. 75020)	A	4	4
440,750	Symphony no. 6 (1953) (22 min.) (Lou. 545–3)-*mono*	A	4	4
	MOZART, WOLFGANG AMADEUS (1756–1791)			
441,000	Symphony in F, K. 75 (15 min.) *(8–Phi. 6747099)	E	4	2
441,250	Symphony in F, K. 76 (15 min.) *(8–Phi. 6747099)	E	4	2
441,500	Symphony no. 4 in D, K. 19 (10 min.) *(Phi. 6500532); *(8–Phi. 6747099)	E	4	2
441,750	Symphony no. 5 in B flat, K. 22 (7 min.) *(8–Phi. 6747099)	E	4	2
442,000	Symphony no. 6 in F, K. 43 (14 min.) *(8–Phi. 6747099)	E	4	2
442,250	Symphony no. 7 in D, K. 45 (12 min.) *(8–Phi. 6747099)	E	4	2
443,000	Symphony no. 8 in D, K. 48 (13 min.) *(8–Phi. 6747099)	E	4	2
443,250	Symphony no. 9 in C, K. 73 (12 min.) *(8–Phi. 6747099)	E	4	2
443,500	Symphony no. 10 in G, K. 74 (9 min.) *(Phi. 6500532); *(8–Phi. 6747099)	E	4	2
444,250	Symphony no. 11 in D, K. 84 (11 min.) *(8–Phi. 6747099)	E	4	2
444,500	Symphony no. 12 in G, K. 110 (16 min.) *(8–Phi. 6747099)	E	4	2
444,750	Symphony no. 13 in F, K. 112 (13 min.) **(Argo ZRG–594); *(8–Phi. 6747099)	E	4	2
445,000	Symphony no. 14 in A, K. 114 (17 min.) **(Argo ZRG–594); *(8–Phi. 6747099); (Mace S–9031)	S	4	2
445,250	Symphony no. 15 in G, K. 124 (12 min.) **(Argo ZRG–594); *(8–Phi. 6747099)	E	4	2
445,500	Symphony no. 16 in C, K. 128 (11 min.) **(Argo ZRG–594); *(8–Phi. 6747099)	E	4	2
445,750	Symphony no. 18 in F, K. 130 (18 min.) *(8–Phi. 6747099)	S	4	2
446,000	Symphony no. 19 in E flat, K. 132 (20 min.) *(8–Phi. 6747099)	S	4	2
446,250	Symphony no. 20 in D, K. 133 (18 min.) *(8–Phi. 6747099)	S	3	2
446,500	Symphony no. 21 in A, K. 134 (20 min.) *(DG 139405)	S	4	2
446,750	Symphony no. 22 in C, K. 162 (9 min.) *(DG 139405)	E	4	2
447,000	Symphony no. 23 in D, K. 181 (10 min.) **(Argo ZRG–653); *(DG 139405)	S	3	2
447,250	Symphony no. 24 in B flat, K. 182 (10 min.) **(Argo ZRG–653); *(DG 139405)	E	4	2
447,500	Symphony no. 25 in g, K. 183 (19 min.) **(Argo ZRG–706); *(7–DG 2721007); *(DG 2530120)	A	2	2
447,750	Symphony no. 26 in E flat, K. 184 (9 min.) **(Argo ZRG–653); **(DG 139159); **(DG 2530120); *(7–DG 2721007)	S	3	3
448,000	Symphony no. 27 in G, K. 199 (15 min.) **(Argo ZRG–706); **(DG 2530120); *(7–DG 2721007)	S	4	3
448,250	Symphony no. 28 in C, K. 200 (21 min.) **(Oiseau S–266); *(Col. MS–6858); *(7–DG 2721007)	S	2	2
448,500	Symphony no. 29 in A, K. 201 (23 min.) **(Argo ZRG–706); *(Ang. S–36329); *(7–DG 2721007)	S	2	2
448,750	Symphony no. 30 in D, K. 202 (18 min.) *(7–DG 2721007)	S	3	2
449,000	Symphony no. 31 in D, K. 297 (*Paris*) (18 min.) **(Ang. S–36216); **(DG 139159); *(7–DG 2721007)	S	2	3
449,250	Symphony no. 32 in G, K. 318 (9 min.) *(Ang. S–36216); *(7–DG 2721007); *(Lon. STS–15087)	S	3	2
449,500	Symphony no. 33 in B flat, K. 319 (23 min.) *(Ang. S–36329); *(Col. MS–6858); *(7–DG 2721007)	S	3	1
449,750	Symphony no. 34 in C, K. 338 (21 min.) **(Ang. S–36216); **(DG 139159); **(Phi. 802769); *(7–DG 2721007)	S	3	2
450,000	Symphony no. 35 in D, K. 385 (*Haffner*) (18 min.) **(Col. MS–6255); **(3–Col. D3S–691);	S	2	2

GUIDE NO. COMPOSER AND TITLE	AGE MIN	AES SIG	AC-CESS
*(Ang. S–36512);			
*(7–DG 2721007)			
√450,250 Symphony no. 36 in C,	S	2	2
K. 425 (*Linz*) (27 min.)			
**(Col. MS–6493);			
**(3–Col. D3S–691);			
*(DG 139160);			
*(7–DG 2721007)			
√450,500 Symphony no. 38 in D,	S	1	1
K. 504 (*Prague*) (25 min.)			
**(Ang. S–36129);			
**(Col. MS–6494);			
**(3–Col. D3S–691);			
**(Oiseau S–266);			
*(Ang. S–36512);			
*(7–DG 2721007);			
*(Lon. STS–15087)			
450,750 Symphony no. 39 in E flat,	E	1	1
K. 543 (25 min.)			
**(Ang. S–36129);			
**(Col. MS–6493);			
**(3–Col. D3S–691);			
*(DG 139160);			
*(7–DG 2721007)			
√451,000 Symphony no. 40 in g,	E	1	2
K. 550 (26 min.)			
**(Ang. S–36183);			
**(Col. MS–6494);			
**(3–Col. D3S–691);			
**(DG 138815);			
*(7–DG 2721007)			
√451,500 Symphony no. 41 in C,	E	1	2
K. 551 (*Jupiter*) (28 min.)			
**(Ang. S–36183);			
**(Col. MS–6255);			
**(3–Col. D3S–691);			
*(DG 138815);			
*(7–DG 2721007)			
NEUBAUR, FRANZ			
CHRISTOPH (1760–1795)			
452,000 Symphony, op. 11 (*Bataille*	A	4	3
de Martinestie) (25 min.)			
(None. H–71146)			
NIELSEN, CARL			
(1865–1931)			
√452,500 Symphony no. 2 (*Four*	A	4	3
Temperaments) (32 min.)			
*(Turn. 34049)			
√452,750 Symphony no. 3, op. 27 ·	A	4	3
(*Sinfonia Expansiva*)			
(36 min.)			
(Col. MS–6769)			
√453,000 Symphony no. 4, op. 29	A	3	3
(*Inextinguishable*)			
(37 min.)			
*(Col. M–30293);			
(RCA LSC–2958)			
√453,250 Symphony no. 5, op. 50	A	3	2
(32 min.)			
**(None. H–71236)			
√453,500 Symphony no. 6 (*Sinfonia*	A	3	3
Semplice) (33 min.)			
(Turn. 34182)			
PINKHAM, DANIEL			
(1923–)			
454,250 Symphony no. 2 (15 min.)	A	4	3
(Lou. 652)-*mono*			
PISTON, WALTER			
(1894–)			
√454,500 Symphony no. 2 (26 min.)	A	4	3
*(DG 2530103)			
√454,875 Symphony no. 4 (23 min.)	S	2	2
(CSP AML–4992)-*mono*			
455,000 Symphony no. 5 (21 min.)	A	4	3
(Lou. S–653)			
PORTER, QUINCY			
(1897–1966)			
455,250 Symphony no. 2 (22 min.)	A	4	3
(Lou. 642)-*mono*			
PROKOFIEV, SERGE			
(1891–1953)			
√455,500 Symphony in D, op. 25	E	2	1
(*Classical*) (14 min.)			
*(Argo ZRG–719);			
*(Lon. CS 6679);			
(Sera. S–60172)			
455,750 Symphony no. 2, op. 40	A	5	2
(32 min.)			
*(Ev. 3214)			
√456,000 Symphony no. 3, op. 44	A	3	2
(34 min.)			
*(Lon. CS 6679)			
√456,250 Symphony no. 5, op. 100	S	2	2
(41 min.)			
**(Lon. CS 6406);			
*(DG 139040)			
√456,500 Symphony no. 6, in e flat,	A	3	3
op. 111 (39 min.)			
*(Mel./Ang. S–40046)			
√456,750 Symphony no. 7, op. 131	A	3	3
(32 min.)			
*(Ev. 3214)			
RACHMANINOFF, SERGEI			
(1873–1943)			
√457,000 Symphony no. 1 in d, op. 13	S	4	2
(44 min.)			
*(Col. MS–6986);			
*(Lon. CS 6803)			
√457,250 Symphony no. 2 in e, op. 27	S	3	1
(48 min.)			
**(Ang. S–36954)			
RAWSTHORNE, ALAN			
(1905–)			
457,750 Symphony no. 3 (32 min.)	A	4	3
**(Argo ZRG–553)			
RICHTER, FRANZ			
XAVIER (1709–1789)			
458,250 Symphony in G (12 min.)	A	5	3
(Mace S–9069)			
RIEGGER, WALLINGFORD			
(1885–1961)			
458,500 Symphony no. 4 (29 min.)	A	3	4
(Lou. S–646)-*mono*			
RIMSKY–KORSAKOV,			
NIKOLAI (1844–1908)			
√458,750 Symphony no. 1 in e, op. 1	S	5	2
(28 min.)			
(Mel./Ang. S–40094)			
459,000 Symphony no. 2, op. 9 (*Antar*	S	3	1
[symphonic suite])			
(30 min.)			
*(Mel./Ang. S–40230)			
ROCHBERG, GEORGE			
(1918–)			
459,250 Symphony no. 1 (27 min.)	A	4	3
(Lou. S–634)			
459,500 Symphony no. 2 (30 min.)	A	4	3
(CSP AMS–6379)			
ROREM, NED (1923–)			
459,750 Symphony no. 3 (23 min.)	S	5	3
*(Turn. 34447)			

GUIDE NO. COMPOSER AND TITLE	AGE MIN	AES SIG	AC- CESS
ROUSSEL, ALBERT (1869–1937)			
460,000 Symphony no. 3 in g, op. 42 (24 min.) (Lon. STS–15025)	A	3	3
460,250 Symphony no. 4 in A, op. 53 (23 min.) (Lon. STS–15025)	A	3	2
SAINT-SAËNS, CAMILLE (1835–1921)			
460,500 Symphony no. 3 in c, op. 78 (*Organ*) (34 min.) **(Lon. STS–15154); *(RCA LSC–2341)	S	4	1
SAMMARTINI, GIOVANNI BATTISTA (1701–1775)			
460,750 Symphony in G, JC50 (9 min.) (Dover 5247)-*mono*	S	4	2
SANDERS, ROBERT L. (1906–)			
461,000 *Little Symphony* no. 1 in C (15 min.) (Lou. 635)-*mono*	S	4	3
SCHOENBERG, ARNOLD (1874–1951)			
461,250 Chamber Symphony in E flat, op. 9 (20 min.) **(Lon. CS 6612)	A	4	3
461,500 Chamber Symphony no. 2, op. 38 (19 min.) (Ang. S–36480)	A	4	5
SCHUBERT, FRANZ (1797–1828)			
461,750 Symphony no. 1 in D, D. 82 (28 min.) **(Lon. CS 6772)	E	3	2
462,000 Symphony no. 2 in B flat, D. 125 (28 min.) **(Lon. CS 6772); (Ang. S–36453)	E	3	2
462,250 Symphony no. 3 in D, D. 200 (24 min.) (Turn. 34361)	E	4	2
462,500 Symphony no. 4 in c (*Tragic*), D. 417 (27 min.) (Turn. 34361)	S	3	2
462,750 Symphony no. 5 in B flat, D. 485 (27 min.) **(Col. MS–6218); **(DG 139162)	S	2	1
463,000 Symphony no. 6 in C (*Little*), D. 589 (29 min.) *(Ang. S–36453)	E	4	1
463,250 Symphony no. 8 in b (*Unfinished*), D. 759 (23 min.) **(Col. MS–6218); **(DG 139162); (Ang. S–36609)	E	1	1
463,500 Symphony no. 9 in C (*The Great*), D. 944 (50 min.) *(Lon. STS–15140); *(Sera. S–60194)	S	1	1
SCHUMAN, WILLIAM (1910–)			
463,750 Symphony no. 3 (31 min.) *(Col. MS–7442)	A	3	2
464,000 Symphony no. 5 (*Symphony for Strings*) (1943) (17 min.) *(Col. MS–7442)	A	3	2
464,250 Symphony no. 6 (24 min.) (CSP AML–4992)-*mono*	A	3	3
464,500 Symphony no. 7 (26 min.) *(Turn. 34447)	A	3	3
464,750 Symphony no. 9 (23 min.) (RCA LSC–3212)	A	3	3
SCHUMANN, ROBERT (1810–1856)			
465,000 Symphony no. 1 in B flat, op. 39 (*Spring*) (31 min.) **(3–Odys. Y3–30844); *(Lon. STS–15019); (Ang. S–36353); (Lon. CS 6696)	S	3	1
465,250 Symphony no. 2 in C, op. 61 (31 min.) **(3–Odys. Y3–30844)	S	3	2
465,500 Symphony no. 3 in E flat, op. 97 (*Rhenish*) (33 min.) **(3–Odys. Y3–30844)	S	4	2
465,750 Symphony no. 4 in d, op. 120 (27 min.) **(3–Odys. Y3–30844); *(Ang. S–35629)	S	3	1
SCRIABIN, ALEXANDER (1872–1915)			
466,000 Symphony no. 1 in E, op.·26 (49 min.) *(Mel./Ang. S–40113)	A	5	2
466,250 Symphony no. 2, op. 29 (49 min.) *(Mel./Ang. S–40118)	S	5	2
466,500 Symphony no. 4, op. 54 (*Poème d'Extase*) (20 min.) **(Lon. CS 6552); *(DG 2530137); *(Mel./Ang. S–40019); (Ev. 3032)	S	4	1
466,750 Symphony no. 5, op. 60 (*Prometheus*) (20 min.) **(Lon. CS 6732)	S	4	2
SESSIONS, ROGER (1896–)			
467,000 Symphony no. 2 (26 min.) *(CRI S–278E)-*mono*	A	4	4
467,250 Symphony no. 8 *(Argo ZRG–702)	A	3	3
SHOSTAKOVICH, DMITRI (1906–1975)			
467,500 Symphony no. 1 in F, op. 10 (30 min.) **(Col. MS–6124); *(Lon. STS–15180)	S	3	1
468,250 Symphony no. 4, op. 43 (1 hr., 1 min.) *(Col. MS–6459)	S	4	2
468,500 Symphony no. 5, op. 47 (46 min.) **(Mel./Ang. S–40163); **(RCA LSC–2866)	S	1	1
468,750 Symphony no. 6, op. 54 (27 min.) *(Ev. 3007)	A	3	3
469,000 Symphony no. 7, op. 60 (1 hr., 15 min.) (2–Mel./Ang. S–4107)	A	4	3
469,250 Symphony no. 8 in c, op. 65 (55 min.) (Ev. 3250)	A	4	3

GUIDE NO. COMPOSER AND TITLE	AGE AES AC- MIN SIG CESS
✓469,500 Symphony no. 9, op. 70 (25 min.) *(Mel./Ang. S–40000)	A 3 3
✓469,750 Symphony no. 10 in e, op. 93 (50 min.) *(Mel./Ang. S–40025)	A 2 3
✓470,000 Symphony no. 11 (1 hr., 1 min.) *(Mel./Ang. S–40244)	A 5 3
470,250 Symphony no. 12 (*Lenin*) (37 min.) *(Phi. 6580012)	A 5 3
✓470,500 Symphony no. 13, op. 113 (55 min.) *(RCA LSC–3162)	S 4 3
✓470,750 Symphony no. 14, op. 135 (49 min.) **(Mel./Ang. S–40147)	S 3 3
471,000 Symphony no. 15 in A, op. 141 (1971) (Mel./Ang. S–40213)	A 4 3
SIBELIUS, JEAN (1865–1957)	
✓471,250 Symphony no. 1 in e, op. 39 (36 min.) **(Lon. CS 6375)	S 3 1
✓471,500 Symphony no. 2 in D, op. 43 (44 min.) **(Lon. CS 6408); **(RCA VIC–1510)-*mono*; *(Phi. 835306)	S 3 1
✓471,750 Symphony no. 3 in C, op. 52 (27 min.) *(Lon. CS 6591)	A 4 3
✓472,000 Symphony no. 4 in a, op. 63 (35 min.) **(Lon. CS 6592)	A 2 3
✓472,250 Symphony no. 5 in E flat, op. 82 (33 min.) *(Col. MS–6749); (Lon. CS 6488)	S 2 1
✓472,500 Symphony no. 6 in d, op. 104 (26 min.) *(Lon. CS 6591)	A 5 3
✓472,750 Symphony no. 7 in C, op. 105 (23 min.) *(Lon. CS 6488); (Ang. S–35458)	A 3 2
SIEGMEISTER, ELIE (1909–)	
✓473,000 Symphony no. 3 (19 min.) (CRI S–185)	A 4 3
STAMITZ, JOH. WENZEL ANTON (1717–1757)	
473,250 Symphony in A (*Spring*) (18 min.) (None. H–71076)	A 4 3
STRAUSS, RICHARD (1864–1949)	
✓473,750 *Eine Alpensinfonie*, op. 64 (50 min.) **(RCA LSC–2923)	A 5 3
✓474,000 *Symphonia domestica*, op. 53 (44 min.) **(RCA VICS–1104)	A 4 2
STRAVINSKY, IGOR (1882–1971)	
✓474,500 Symphony in C (27 min.) *(Col. MS–6548)	S 3 3

GUIDE NO. COMPOSER AND TITLE	AGE AES AC- MIN SIG CESS
474,750 Symphony in E flat, op. 1 (40 min.) **(Col. MS–6989)	S 4 3
✓475,000 Symphony in Three Movements (21 min.) **(Col. MS–6331)	S 2 2
TCHAIKOVSKY, PETER ILYITCH (1840–1893)	
✓475,500 Symphony no. 1 in g, op. 13 (*Winter Dreams*) (42 min.) *(Lon. CS 6426)	S 4 2
✓475,750 Symphony no. 2 in c, op. 17 (*Little Russian*) (33 min.) *(Lon. CS 6427)	S 3 2
✓476,000 Symphony no. 3 in D, op. 29 (*Polish*) (40 min.) *(Lon. CS 6428)	S 4 2
✓476,250 Symphony no. 4 in f, op. 36 (42 min.) **(Lon. CS 6429)	S 2 1
✓476,500 Symphony no. 5 in e, op. 64 (45 min.) *(Lon. CS 6409)	S 2 1
✓476,750 Symphony no. 6 in b, op. 74 (*Pathétique*) (45 min.) **(Sera. 60231)-*mono*; *(DG 138921); *(Phi. 6500081); *(Sera. S–60031)	S 2 1
✓477,000 Symphony no. 7 in E flat (reconstructed S. Bagatyryev) (39 min.) (Col. MS–6349)	S 5 2
THOMPSON, RANDALL (1899–)	
✓477,250 Symphony no. 2 (27 min.) (Desto S–6406E)-*mono*	A 4 2
VAUGHAN WILLIAMS, RALPH (1872–1958)	
✓480,000 Symphony no. 1 (*Sea*) (1 hr., 5 min.) *(2–Ang. S–3739); **(RCA LSC–3170)	S 3 1
✓480,250 Symphony no. 2 (*London*) (45 min.) **(Ang. S–36838)	S 3 1
✓480,500 Symphony no. 3 (*Pastoral*) (35 min.) **(Ang. S–36532)	S 4 1
✓480,750 Symphony no. 4 in f (34 min.) *(Ang. S–36557)	A 2 2
✓481,000 Symphony no. 5 in D (37 min.) **(Ang. S–35952); *(Ang. S–36698)	S 3 1
✓481,250 Symphony no. 6 in e (35 min.) *(RCA LSC–3114)	A 2 2
481,500 Symphony no. 7 (*Antarctica*) (44 min.) *(Ang. S–36763)	S 4 1
✓481,750 Symphony no. 8 in d (28 min.) *(Ang. S–36625); *(RCA LSC–3114)	A 4 2
✓482,000 Symphony no. 9 in e (38 min.) *(Ang. S–36742)	A 4 2

GUIDE NO.	COMPOSER AND TITLE	AGE MIN	AES SIG	AC- CESS
	WAGENAAR, BERNARD (1894–)			
482,250	Symphony no. 4 (29 min.) (Desto 6415E)-*mono*	A	4	3
	WALTON, WILLIAM (1902–)			
482,750	Symphony no. 2 (27 min.) *(Ang. S–37001)	A	4	3
	WARD, ROBERT (1917–)			
483,000	Symphony no. 1 (14 min.) (Desto 6405E)-*mono*	A	5	3
483,250	Symphony no. 2 (21 min.) (CRI 127)-*mono*	A	4	3
483,500	Symphony no. 3 (23 min.) (CRI 206)-*mono*	A	4	3

GUIDE NO.	COMPOSER AND TITLE	AGE MIN	AES SIG	AC- CESS
	WEBER, CARL MARIA VON (1786–1826)			
483,750	Symphony no. 1 in C (24 min.) **(Phi. 6500154)	A	4	3
	WEBERN, ANTON (1883–1945)			
484,000	Symphony, op. 21 (9 min.) (in complete works) (4–CSP CK4L–232)-*mono*	S	3	5
	WEILL, KURT (1900–1950)			
485,000	Symphony no. 1 (*Berliner*) (25 min.) **(Argo ZRG–755)	A	4	3
485,250	Symphony no. 2 (25 min.) **(Argo ZRG–755)	A	4	3

---

6. Concerti and Other Works for Solo Instruments and Orchestra

GUIDE NO.	COMPOSER AND TITLE	AGE MIN	AES SIG	AC- CESS
	ADDINSELL, RICHARD (1904–)			
491,500	*Warsaw Concerto* (8 min.) (Ang. S–36062)	E	4	1
	ALBINONI, TOMASO (1671–1750)			
491,750	Adagio for Strings and Organ (attrib) (7 min.) *(Turn. 34135)	S	3	2
492,000	Concerto for Oboe and Orchestra, op. 7/6 in D (8 min.) *(Van. HM–40 SD); *(Van. VSD 2036)	S	3	2
492,252	Concerto for Oboe and Orchestra, op. 9/2 in d (14DA) (12 min.) *(RCA VICS–1691)	S	3	2
492,270	Concerto for Oboe and Orchestra, op. 9/11 (12 min.)	S	3	3
492,500	Concerto for Trumpet and Strings in C (9 min.) *(Argo ZRG–585); (Turn. 34057)	S	3	2
	ARENSKY, ANTON (1861–1906)			
492,750	Concerto for Piano, op. 2 (27 min.) (Can. 31029)	A	5	3
	BACH, CARL PHILIPP EMANUEL (1714–1788)			
493,000	Concerto for Flute and Strings in d, W. 22 (25 min.) **(Lon. CS 6739); (DG ARC–198435)	S	4	3
493,750	Concerto in d for Harpsichord, W. 23 (18DA) (26 min.) *(RCA VICS–1463)	S	5	3
494,000	Concerto in E flat for Oboe, W. 165 *(RCA VICS–1463)	S	4	3

GUIDE NO.	COMPOSER AND TITLE	AGE MIN	AES SIG	AC- CESS
	BACH, JOHANN CHRISTIAN (1735–1782)			
494,500	Sinfonia Concertante for Flute, Oboe, Violin, Cello, and Orchestra in C (21 min.) *(None. H–71165)	S	4	3
	BACH, JOHANN SEBASTIAN (1685–1750)			
494,750	Concerto in a for Flute, Violin, Harpsichord, and Strings, S. 1044 (22 min.) *(Oiseau S–171)	S	3	2
495,000	Concerto no. 1 in d for Harpsichord, S. 1052 (24 min.) *(Ang. S–37010); *(DG ARC–198013); (Lon. CS 6440)	S	2	1
495,002	Concerto no. 2 in E for Harpsichord, S. 1053 (21 min.) *(Ang. S–37010); *(DG ARC–198013)	S	2	2
495,004	Concerto no. 3 in D for Harpsichord, S. 1054 (18 min.) *(Ang. S–36790)	S	3	2
495,006	Concerto no. 4 in A for Harpsichord, S. 1055 (14 min.) *(Ang. S–36790); *(Oiseau S–171)	S	2	1
495,008	Concerto no. 5 in f for Harpsichord, S. 1056 (10 min.) (Ang. S–36762)	S	2	1
495,010	Concerto no. 6 in F for Harpsichord, S. 1057 (17 min.) *(Ang. S–36790)	S	3	1
495,012	Concerto no. 7 in g for Harpsichord, S. 1058 (14 min.) *(Ang. S–36762)	S	3	1

GUIDE NO.	COMPOSER AND TITLE	AGE MIN	AES SIG	AC-CESS
495,014	Concerto no. 8 in d for Harpsichord, S. 1059 (11 min.) (Tel. 6.41190)	S	3	2
495,250	Concerto no. 1 in c for 2 Harpsichords, S. 1060 (14 min.) *(Ang. S–36762); *(Bach 70659); *(DG ARC–198321)	S	3	2
495,252	Concerto no. 2 in C for 2 Harpsichords, S. 1061 (19 min.) *(Ang. S–36762)	S	3	2
495,254	Concerto no. 3 in c for 2 Harpsichords, S. 1062 (14 min.) (None. H–71019)	S	3	3
495,500	Concerto no. 1 in d for 3 Harpsichords, S. 1063 (16 min.) (None. H–71019); (Tel. 6.41190)	S	3	1
495,502	Concerto no. 2 in C for 3 Harpsichords, S. 1064 (18 min.) (None. H–71019); (Tel. 6.41190)	S	3	2
495,750	Concerto in a for 4 Harpsichords, S. 1065 (11 min.) (None. H–71019)	S	3	1
496,000	Concerto no. 1 in a for Violin, S. 1041 (15 min.) *(Tel. 6.41227)	S	1	2
496,002	Concerto no. 2 in E for Violin, S. 1042 (18 min.) *(Tel. 6.41227)	S	1	2
496,250	Concerto in d for 2 Violins, S. 1043 (16 min.) *(Tel. 6.41227) (DG 138714)	S	1	2
496,500	Concerto in D for 3 Violins (arr. of S. 1064) (20 min.) (None. H–71057)	S	3	1
496,750	Concerto in c for Violin and Oboe, S. 1060 (14 min.) *(Ang. S–36103); *(DG ARC–198321)	S	3	2
	BARBER, SAMUEL (1910–)			
497,500	Concerto for Piano and Orchestra, op. 38 (26 min.) **(Col. MS–6638)	A	4	3
498,000	Concerto for Violin and Orchestra, op. 14 (25 min.) *(Col. MS–6713)	A	3	3
	BARTÓK, BÉLA (1881–1945)			
498,496	Concerto no. 1 for Piano (24 min.) *(Turn. 34065); (Col. MS–6405)	A	3	4
498,498	Concerto no. 2 for Piano (28 min.) **(DG 138111)	S	2	3
498,500	Concerto no. 3 for Piano (25 min.) **(DG 138111); *(Lon. CS 6487)	A	1	2
498,750	Concerto for Viola and Orchestra (22 min.) *(Ang. S–36438)	A	4	3

GUIDE NO.	COMPOSER AND TITLE	AGE MIN	AES SIG	AC-CESS
499,000	Concerto for Violin and Orchestra (1938) (37 min.) *(Ang. S–36360); *(Phi. 6500021)	A	2	2
499,250	Concerto no. 1 for Violin and Orchestra (posth. op.) (22 min.) *(Ang. S–36438)	A	5	1
499,500	Rhapsody for Piano and Orchestra, op. 1 (23 min.) *(Turn. 34130)	S	5	1
499,700	Rhapsody for Violin and Orchestra, no. 1 (10 min.) *(Ang. S–36360); *(Col. MS–6373)	S	5	1
499,701	Rhapsody for Violin and Orchestra no. 2 (11 min.) **(2–Van. SRV 304/5SD)-*mono*; *(Col. MS–6373)	S	5	1
	BEETHOVEN, LUDWIG VAN (1770–1827)			
499,994	Concerto no. 1 in C for Piano and Orchestra, op. 15 (37 min.) **(4–Col. M4X–30052); *(DG 138774); *(4–Lon. CSA 2404); *(Phi. 839749); *(Phi. 6500179); (Col. MS–6838)	S	2	2
499,996	Concerto no. 2 in B flat for Piano and Orchestra, op. 19 (28 min.) **(3–Sera. 6043)-*mono*; *(4–Col. M4X–30052); *(DG 138775); *(4–Lon. CSA 2404)	S	3	3
499,998	Concerto no. 3 in c for Piano and Orchestra, op. 37 (35 min.) *(4–Lon. CSA 2404); (4–Col. M4X–30052); (Phi. 6500315)	S	2	3
500,000	Concerto no. 4 in G for Piano and Orchestra, op. 58 (32 min.) **(4–Col. M4X–30052); *(DG 138775); *(4–Lon. CSA 2404)	S	1	3
500,002	Concerto no. 5 in E flat, op. 73 (38 min.) *(4–Col. M4X–30052); *(DG 138777); *(4–Lon. CSA 2404)	S	2	1
500,250	Concerto in D for Violin, op. 61 (45 min.) **(6–Col. M6X–31513); **(Odys. Y–30042)	A	1	3
500,500	Concerto in C for Violin, Cello, and Piano, op. 56 (34 min.) *(Ang. S–36727)	S	3	2
500,750	Romance no. 1 for Violin and Orchestra, op. 40 (7 min.) *(Lon. CS 6656); *(Sera. 60135)-*mono*; (DG 138714); (Phi. 6580047)	S	4	2
501,000	Romance no. 2 for Violin and Orchestra, op. 50 (9 min.)	S	4	2

GUIDE NO. COMPOSER AND TITLE	AGE MIN	AES SIG	AC-CESS
*(Lon. CS 6656); (DG 138714); (Phi. 6580047)			
BELLINI, VINCENZO (1801–1835)			
501,250 Concerto in E flat for Oboe and Orchestra, (9 min.) *(DG 139152); *(Oiseau S–277)	S	4	2
BENDA, FRANZ (1709–1786)			
501,500 Concerto in e for Flute and Orchestra (20 min.) *(Orion 7264)-*mono*	S	4	2
BERG, ALBAN (1885–1935)			
501,750 Concerto for Violin and Orchestra (24 min.) *(Col. MS–6373)	A	2	4
BERLIOZ, HECTOR (1803–1869)			
502,000 *Harold in Italy*, for Viola and Orchestra, op. 16 (44 min.) **(CSP CML–4542)-*mono*	A	3	3
BLOCH, ERNEST (1880–1959)			
502,500 Concerto for Violin and Orchestra (37 min.) **(Ang. S–36192)	A	4	2
502,750 *Schelomo* (Rhapsody for Cello and Orchestra) (21 min.) **(Lon. CS 6661)	A	3	1
503,000 *Voice in the Wilderness*, with Cello Obbligato (27 min.) **(Lon. CS 6661)	A	4	1
BOCCHERINI, LUIGI (1743–1805)			
503,250 Concerto in B flat for Cello and Orchestra (22 min.) **(Phi. 18110CAA)-cassette; *(None. H–71071); (Ang. S–36439); (Mace. S–9077)	S	3	1
503,500 Concerto in D for Cello and Orchestra, op. 34 (17 min.) *(Tel. 6.41197)	A	5	3
BOIELDIEU, FRANÇOIS (1775–1834)			
504,000 Concerto in C for Harp (21 min.) **(DG 138118)	S	3	2
BOISMORTIER, JOSEPH BODIN DE (1691–1755)			
504,250 Concerto in D for Bassoon, op. 26 (8 min.) (None. H–71080)	S	4	2
BRAHMS, JOHANNES (1883–1897)			
504,500 Concerto no. 1 in d for Piano, op. 15 (47 min.) **(Lon. CS 6329); *(Col. MS–7143)	S	2	1
504,501 Concerto no. 2 in B flat for Piano, op. 83 (47 min.) **(Col. MS–6967)	S	1	1

GUIDE NO. COMPOSER AND TITLE	AGE MIN	AES SIG	AC-CESS
504,750 Concerto in D for Violin, op. 77 (40 min.) **(Ang. S–35836); *(Ang. S–36033); *(Phi. 6500299)	S	2	2
505,000 Concerto in a for Violin and Cello, op. 102 (34 min.) **(Col. MS–6158); *(Ang. S–36032)	A	3	3
BRITTEN, BENJAMIN (1913–)			
505,500 Symphony for Cello and Orchestra, op. 68 (34 min.) **(Lon. CS 6419)	A	2	4
BRUCH, MAX (1838–1920)			
506,000 Concerto no. 1 in g for Violin, op. 26 (24 min.) *(Ang. S–35730); *(Ang. S–36920); *(RCA LSC–4011); (Col. MS–7003)	S	3	1
506,250 *Kol Nidrei* for Cello and Orchestra, op. 47 (10 min.) (Mer. 75045)	S	4	1
506,500 *Scottish Fantasy* for Violin and Orchestra, op. 46 (25 min.) **(Lon. CS 6337); (RCA LSC–2603)	S	4	2
CARULLI, FERDINANDO (1770–1841)			
506,750 Concerto in A for Guitar and Orchestra (9 min.) **(DG 139417)	S	4	2
CASTELNUOVO-TEDESCO, MARIO (1895–1968)			
507,000 Concerto in D for Guitar, op. 99 (19 min.) **(Col. MS–6834)	E	4	1
CHAUSSON, ERNEST (1855–1899)			
507,250 *Poème* for Violin and Orchestra, op. 25 (16 min.) **(Phi. 802708)	S	4	1
CHOPIN, FRÉDÉRIC (1810–1849)			
507,500 Concerto no. 1 in e for Piano, op. 11 (39 min.) **(Sera. 60007)-*mono*; **(Sera. S–60066); *(RCA LSC–2575); (RCA VICS–1030)	S	3	1
507,502 Concerto no. 2 in f for Piano, op. 21 (31 min.) *(DG 136452); *(Lon. CS 6440); *(Phi. 6500309); (Sera. S–60109)	S	3	1
507,750 Grand Fantasy on Polish Airs, op. 13 (14 min.) *(Phi. 6500422)	S	5	2
508,000 *Krakowiak*, Rondo, op. 14, for Piano and Orchestra (14 min.) *(Phi. 6500309)	S	5	2
CIMAROSA, DOMENICO (1749–1801)			
508,250 Concerto for 2 Flutes in G **(Lon. CS 6739); *(Turn. 34307)	S	3	2

GUIDE NO. COMPOSER AND TITLE	AGE MIN	AES SIG	AC- CESS
508,500 Concerto for Oboe and Strings (11 min.) *(DG 139152); *(RCA VICS–1691); (Van. VSD 2036)	E	3	2
CLARKE, JEREMIAH (c.1673–1707)			
508,750 Trumpet Voluntary (*Prince of Denmark's March*) (3 min.) **(Van. HM–31SD)	E	3	1
COPLAND, AARON (1900–)			
509,000 Concerto for Clarinet and Orchestra (17 min.) **(Col. MS6497)	S	4	3
509,500 Concerto for Piano and Orchestra (16 min.) **(Col. MS–6698); (Van. VSD 2094)	S	4	2
510,000 *Quiet City* for Trumpet, English Horn, Orchestra (9 min.) **(Col. MS–7375)	S	3	2
CORRETTE, MICHEL (1709–1795)			
510,250 Concerto in e for Flute, op. 4, no. 6 (8 min.) *(Turn. 34010)	E	3	1
510,500 Concerto in G for Flute, op. 3, no. 6 (9 min.) *(Turn. 34307); (None. H–71080)	E	3	1
511,000 Concerto in d for Flute, Harpsichord, and Strings, op. 26, no. 6 (9 min.) *(Turn. 34010); *(Turn. 34135)	E	4	2
DEBUSSY, CLAUDE (1862–1918)			
511,500 *Danse sacrée et danse profane*, for Harp and Orchestra (10 min.) **(Sera. S–60142); *(DG 139304)	A	2	2
511,750 Fantasie for Piano and Orchestra (24 min.) **(Lon. CS 6657); (Can. 31069)	A	5	2
512,000 Première rapsodie for Clarinet (8 min.) *(Lon. CS 6437); (Can. 31069); (Col. MS–6659); (Van. VSD 71167)	S	3	2
512,250 Rapsodie for Saxophone and Orchestra (10 min.) (Can. 31069); (Col. MS–6659)	S	4	2
DELLO JOIO, NORMAN (1913–)			
512,500 Fantasy and Variations for Piano and Orchestra (21 min.) (RCA LSC–2667)	A	4	3
D'INDY, VINCENT (1851–1931)			
512,600 *Symphony on a French Mountain Air*, op. 25 (25 min.) *(Odys. Y–31274)	S	4	1

GUIDE NO. COMPOSER AND TITLE	AGE MIN	AES SIG	AC- CESS
DITTERSDORF, KARL DITTERS VON (1739–1799)			
512,700 Concerto in A for Harp and Orchestra (19 min.) *(Turn. 34005); (DG 139112)	S	4	1
512,800 Concerto in E for Double-Bass (16 min.) *(Turn. 34005)	A	5	3
512,900 Sinfonia Concertante for Double-Bass and Viola (16 min.) *(Turn. 34005)	S	5	2
DOHNANYI, ERNST VON (1877–1960)			
513,000 Variations on a Nursery Song, op. 25 (23 min.) **(Lon. CS 6153)	S	3	1
DONIZETTI, GAETANO (1797–1848)			
513,100 Concertino in G for English Horn and Orchestra (12 min.) *(DG 139152)			
DVOŘÁK, ANTONIN (1841–1904)			
513,250 Concerto in b for Cello, op. 104 (39 min.) **(DG 138755); *(Ang. S–35417); *(Col. MS–6714); *(Phi. 802892); (Mer. 75045)	S	2	1
513,500 Concerto in g for Piano, op. 33 (36 min.) **(West. WGS–8165)	A	5	3
513,750 Concerto in a for Violin, op. 53 (32 min.) *(Ang. S–36011); (Col. MS–6876)	S	4	2
514,000 Romance for Violin and Orchestra, op. 11 (13 min.) (Col. MS–6876)	S	5	3
EICHNER, ERNST (1740–1777)			
514,250 Concerto no. 1 for Harp (14 min.) (DG 139112)	S	4	3
ELGAR, EDWARD (1857–1934)			
514,500 Concerto for Cello, op. 85 (30 min.) **(Ang. S–36338)	S	2	2
514,750 Concerto for Violin, op. 61 (48 min.) *(Ang. S–36330)	S	3	2
FALLA, MANUEL DE (1876–1946)			
515,000 *Nights in the Gardens of Spain* (23 min.) **(Lon. CS 6046)	S	3	1
FASCH, JOHANN FRIEDRICH (1688–1758)			
515,250 Concerto in D for Trumpet, 2 Oboes, and Strings (7 min.) *(Argo ZRG–585); *(None. H–71148)	S	4	1

GUIDE NO.	COMPOSER AND TITLE	AGE	AES MIN	AC-CESS SIG
	FAURÉ, GABRIEL (1845–1924)			
515,500	*Ballade* for Piano and Orchestra, op. 19 (13 min.) *(Col. MS–6377)	S	3	2
515,750	*Elégie* for Cello and Orchestra, op. 24 (7 min.) (Ang. S–35417)	S	4	2
	FRANCK, CÉSAR (1822–1890)			
516,500	Symphonic Variations for Piano and Orchestra (14 min.) *(Lon. CS 6157); *(Odys. Y–31274); (Lon. CS 6818)	S	3	1
	GERSHWIN, GEORGE (1898–1937)			
516,750	Concerto in F for Piano (32 min.) *(Ang. S–36810)	E	3	1
517,000	*I Got Rhythm* Variations for Piano and Orchestra (8 min.) *(Ang. S–36070)	E	4	1
517,250	*Rhapsody in Blue* (16 min.) **(Col. MS–6091); *(Ang. S–36810); (Lon. CS 6633)	E	3	1
	GINASTERA, ALBERTO (1916–)			
517,750	Concerto for Piano and Orchestra (27 min.) (RCA LSC–3029)	A	4	3
	GIULIANI, MAURO (1781–1828)			
518,000	Concerto in A for Guitar and Strings, op. 30 (24 min.) **(DG 139417); **(RCA LSC–2487)	S	4	2
	GLAZOUNOV, ALEXANDER (1865–1936)			
518,200	Concerto in a for Violin, op. 82 (19 min.) *(RCA LSC–4011); *(Ang. S–36011)	A	4	2
518,250	Concerto no. 1 in f for Piano, op. 92 (28 min.) (Mon. MC–2131)-*mono*	A	5	2
	GOTTSCHALK, LOUIS MOREAU (1829–1869)			
518,750	Gran Tarantella for Piano and Orchestra (7 min.) *(Turn. 34449); (Van. SRV–275SD)	S	5	2
	GRIEG, EDVARD (1843–1907)			
519,250	Concerto in a for Piano, op. 16 (29 min.) **(Odys. 32160141)-*mono*; *(Lon. CS 6157); (Sera. S–60032)	E	3	1
	GRIFFES, CHARLES TOMLINSON (1884–1920)			
519,500	Poem for Flute and Orchestra (9 min.) *(Mer. 75020)	E	3	2
	HANDEL, GEORGE FRIDERIC (1685–1759)			
520,225	Concerto in B flat for Harp and Orchestra, op. 4, no. 6 (14 min.) **(Oiseau 60013); *(DG 139304)	S	3	1
520,256	Concerto in F for Harp and Orchestra, op. 4, no. 5 (9 min.) **(Oiseau 60013)	S	4	2
520,500	Concerto for Oboe in B flat, no. 1 (8 min.) *(Ang. S–36103); *(Argo. 5442); (Van. HM–40SD)	S	3	3
520,502	Concerto for Oboe in B flat, no. 2 (9 min.) *(Ang. S–36103); *(Argo. 5442); (Van. HM–40SD)	S	3	3
520,504	Concerto in g for Oboe, no. 3 (9 min.) *(Ang. S–36103); *(Argo. 5442); (Van. VSD–2036)	S	3	3
520,700	Concerto for Organ and Strings in F (*Cuckoo and the Nightingale*) (15 min.) **(2–BASF–29050); (Col. MS–6439)	S	3	1
520,750	Concerto for Organ and Strings, op. 4, no. 1 in g (11 min.) **(2–BASF–29050)	S	3	1
520,754	Concerto for Organ and Strings, op. 4, no. 4 in F (15 min.) **(2–BASF–29050)	S	3	1
520,755	Concerto for Organ and Strings, op. 4, no. 5 in F (9 min.) **(2–BASF–29050); (Col. MS–6439)	S	3	2
520,756	Concerto for Organ and Strings, op. 4, no. 6 in B flat (10 min.) **(2–BASF–29050)	S	3	2
521,000	Concerto for Organ and Strings, op. 7, no. 1 in B flat (17 min.) **(2–BASF–29050)	S	3	2
521,002	Concerto for Organ and Strings, op. 7, no. 2 in A (13 min.) **(2–BASF–29050)	S	3	2
521,003	Concerto for Organ and Strings, op. 7, no. 3 in G flat (13 min.) **(2–BASF–29050)	S	3	3
521,004	Concerto for Organ and Strings, op. 7, no. 4 in d (16 min.) **(2–BASF–29050)	S	3	3
521,005	Concerto for Organ and Strings, op. 7, no. 5 in g (13 min.) **(2–BASF–29050)	S	3	3
521,006	Concerto for Organ and Strings, op. 7, no. 6 in B flat (9 min.) **(2–BASF–29050)	S	3	3
521,014	Concerto for Organ and Strings no. 14 in A	S	3	3

GUIDE NO.	COMPOSER AND TITLE	AGE	AES MIN SIG	AC-CESS
	(17 min.)			
	**(2–BASF–29050);			
	(Turn. 34135)			
521,015	Concerto for Organ and Strings no. 15 in d, (11 min.)	S	3	3
	**(2–BASF–29050)			
521,016	Concerto for Organ and Strings no. 16 in F, (17 min.)	S	3	2
	(Col. MS–6439)			
	HAYDN, JOSEPH (1732–1809)			
521,500	Concerto in C for Cello (26 min.)	S	3	2
	**(Lon. CS 6419);			
	**(Phi. 18110CAA);			
	*(Ang. S–36439);			
	*(DG 139358)			
521,750	Concerto in D for Cello, op. 101 (27 min.)	S	2	1
	**(None. H–71071);			
	*(DG 139358)			
522,250	Concerto for Harpsichord in D, op. 21 (21 min.)	S	3	2
	*(Sera. S–60132)			
522,500	Concerto in F for Harpsichord (13 min.)	S	4	3
	*(Sera. S–60132)			
522,750	Concerto in G for Harpsichord (20 min.)	S	4	3
	*(Sera. S–60132)			
523,000	Concerto no. 1 in D for Horn (16 min.)	S	3	2
	**(Argo. 5498);			
	*(RCA VICS–1324)			
523,002	Concerto no. 2 in D for Horn (16 min.)	S	3	2
	**(Argo 5498)			
523,250	Concerto no. 1 in C for 2 Liras (14 min.)	S	4	3
	**(Turn. 34055)			
523,253	Concerto no. 3 in G for 2 Liras (15 min.)	S	4	3
	**(Turn. 34055)			
523,255	Concerto no. 5 in F for 2 Liras (13 min.)	S	4	3
	**(Turn. 34055)			
523,500	Concerto in C for Oboe and Orchestra (attrib.) (24 min.)	S	3	3
	*(Van. VSD–2036)			
523,750	Concerto no. 1 in C for Organ (20 min.)	S	4	2
	*(Argo ZRG–631);			
	*(2–Phi. 6700052);			
	(None. H–71024)			
523,752	Concerto no. 2 in C for Organ (13 min.)	S	4	3
	*(2–Phi. 6700052)			
523,753	Concerto no. 3 in C for Organ (13 min.)	S	4	3
	*(2–Phi. 6700052)			
524,000	Concerto in E flat for Trumpet and Orchestra (15 min.)	E	2	1
	**(DG ARC–198415)			
524,250	Concerto no. 1 in C for Violin (19 min.)	S	4	2
	*(Ang. S–36190)			
524,253	Concerto no. 3 in A for Violin (26 min.)	S	4	2
	*(Tel. 6.41241)			

GUIDE NO.	COMPOSER AND TITLE	AGE	AES MIN SIG	AC-CESS
	HAYDN, MICHAEL (1737–1806)			
524,500	Concerto in D for Trumpet (10 min.)	S	3	2
	**(DG ARC–198415)			
	HENSELT, ADOLPH VON (1814–1889)			
524,750	Concerto in f for Piano and Orchestra, op. 16 (28 min.)	S	5	2
	(Col. MS–7252)			
	HERTEL, JOHANN WILHELM (1727–1789)			
525,000	Concerto in D for Trumpet, 2 Oboes, 2 Bassoons, and Strings (14 min.)	S	4	2
	*(Argo ZRG–585)			
	HINDEMITH, PAUL (1895–1963)			
525,250	Concerto for Horn and Orchestra (15 min.)	A	5	3
	*(Ang. S–35491)			
525,500	Concerto for Violin and Orchestra (31 min.)	A	3	3
	**(Lon. CS 6337);			
	*(Col. MS–6713)			
525,750	*Schwanendreher* (viola concerto) (26 min.)	A	2	3
	*(Odys. 32160368)			
526,000	*Trauermusik* for Viola and Strings (7 min.)	S	4	2
	*(Ang. S–36484)			
	HOFFMANN, JOHANN (flourished end of 18th century)			
526,200	Concerto in D for Mandolin and Orchestra (19 min.)	A	5	3
	*(Turn. 34003)			
	HUMMEL, JOHANN NEPOMUK (1778–1837)			
526,400	Concerto in F for Bassoon and Orchestra (26 min.)	S	5	3
	(Turn. 34348)			
526,600	Concerto in E flat for Trumpet and Orchestra (17 min.)	S	4	1
	*(Lon. CS 6603);			
	*(Tel. 6.41241)			
	JANÁČEK, LEOŠ (1854–1928)			
527,250	Concertino for Piano and Chamber Orchestra (17 min.)	A	3	3
	*(Turn. 34130)			
	KABALEVSKY, DMITRI (1904–)			
527,500	Concerto no. 3 for Piano and Orchestra (17 min.)	S	5	2
	*(Mon. MC(S)–2061)-*mono*			
	KHACHATURIAN, ARAM (1903–)			
527,750	Concerto for Piano and Orchestra (37 min.)	S	4	1
	*(Lon. CS 6818)			
528,000	Concerto for Violin and Orchestra (36 min.)	S	5	1
	*(RCA VICS–1153)			

GUIDE NO.	COMPOSER AND TITLE	AGE MIN	AES SIG	AC-CESS
	KROMMER, FRANZ (1759–1851)			
528,250	Concerto in E flat for Clarinet and Orchestra, op. 36 (21 min.) (Van. VSD–71167)	A	5	3
	LALO, ÉDOUARD (1823–1892)			
528,750	*Symphonie espagnole* for Violin and Orchestra, op. 21 (33 min.) (Col. MS–7003)	S	4	2
	LAMONTAINE, JOHN (1920–)			
529,000	Concerto for Piano and Orchestra, op. 9 (26 min.) (CRI S–189)	A	4	3
	LECLAIR, JEAN MARIE (1697–1764)			
529,250	Concerto in C for Oboe and Orchestra, op. 7, no. 3 (14 min.) **(Phi. 6500413)	A	4	3
	LEO, LEONARDO (1694–1744)			
529,500	Concerto in A for Cello (5 min.) *(Turn. 34236)	A	4	3
	LISZT, FRANZ (1811–1886)			
529,750	Concerto no. 1 in E flat for Piano and Orchestra (18 min.) **(Phi. 835474)	S	3	1
529,752	Concerto no. 2 in A for Piano and Orchestra (20 min.) **(Phi. 835474)	S	3	1
530,000	Hungarian Fantasia for Piano and Orchestra (16 min.) *(Phi. 6500095); (DG 138692)	S	4	1
530,250	*Totentanz* for Piano and Orchestra (15 min.) *(Phi. 6500095); (Col. MS–7252)	S	4	1
	LITOLFF, HENRY (1818–1891)			
530,500	*Concerto Symphonique* no. 4 in d, op. 102: Scherzo (7 min.) **(Lon. CS 6157)	S	3	1
	MACDOWELL, EDWARD (1861–1908)			
530,750	Concerto no. 1 in a for Piano (25 min.) (West. WGS–8156)	S	4	1
530,752	Concerto no. 2 in d for Piano, op. 23 (27 min.) (West. WGS–8156)	S	3	1
	MANFREDINI, FRANCESCO (c.1680–1748)			
531,250	Concerto in D for 2 Trumpets (9 min.) *(Turn. 34057)	S	4	2
	MARCELLO, ALESSANDRO (c.1684–c.1750)			
531,500	Concerto for Oboe and Strings in c (arranged by Benelli) (11 min.) **(Phi. 6500413); *(RCA VICS–1691)	S	3	1
	MENDELSSOHN, FELIX (1809–1847)			
532,250	*Capriccio brillant* for Piano and Orchestra, op. 22 (10 min.) *(RCA VICS–1030)	S	4	2
532,500	Concerto no. 1 in g for Piano, op. 25 (20 min.) *(Col. MS–6128); *(Kla. 531)	S	4	3
532,502	Concerto no. 2 in d for Piano, op. 40 (25 min.) *(Col. MS–6128); *(Kla. 531)	S	5	3
532,750	Concerto in a for Piano and String Orchestra in a (posth. op.) (33 min.) *(Argo ZRG–605); (Turn. 34170)	S	5	3
533,000	Concerto in A flat for 2 Pianos and Orchestra (31 min.) (None. H–71099)	S	5	2
533,250	Concerto in E for 2 Pianos and Orchestra (29 min.) *(Argo ZRG–605)	S	5	2
533,500	Concerto in e for Violin, op. 64 (27 min.) *(Ang. S–35730); *(Ang. S–36850); *(Phi. 6500465)	E	2	1
533,750	Concerto in d for Violin, Piano, and Orchestra (38 min.) *(Ang. S–36850); *(Phi. 6500465)	S	5	3
534,000	*Rondo brillant* for Piano and Orchestra, op. 29 (11 min.) *(Kla. 531); (Turn. 34170)	S	5	2
534,250	*Serenade and Allegro giojoso* for Piano and Orchestra, op. 43 (13 min.) (Turn. 34170)	S	5	2
	MENOTTI, GIAN CARLO (1911–)			
534,500	Concerto in F for Piano (33 min.) (Van. VSD–2094)	A	5	3
	MOZART, LEOPOLD (1719–1787)			
534,750	Concerto in D for Trumpet (13 min.) *(Lon. CS 6603)	A	3	1
	MOZART, WOLFGANG AMADEUS (1756–1791)			
535,000	Andante in C for Flute and Orchestra, K. 315 (6 min.) *(None. H–71126); *(Phi. 6500378)	S	4	3
535,250	Concerto in B flat for Bassoon, K. 191 (18 min.) *(DG 2530411); *(Phi. 6500378)	S	4	2
535,500	Concerto in A for Clarinet, K. 622 **(Lon. CS 6178); *(DG 2530411); *(Lon. STS–15071); *(Phi. 6500378)	S	1	2
535,750	Concerto no. 1 in G for Flute, K. 313 (26 min.)	S	4	2

GUIDE NO.	COMPOSER AND TITLE	AGE MIN	AES SIG	ACCESS
	*(None. H–71126); *(Phi. 6500379)			
535,752	Concerto no. 2 in D for Flute, K. 314 (also scored for oboe) (19 min.) *(Phi. 6500174)-oboe version; *(Phi. 6500379)-oboe version; *(Van. HM–40SD)	S	3	2
536,000	Concerto in C for Flute and Harp, K. 299 (29 min.) **(DG 138853); **(Turn. 34087); *(Lon. STS–15071)	S	3	2
536,250	Concerto no. 1 for Horn, K. 412 (9 min.) **(Ang. 35092); *(Ang. S–35689); *(Lon. CS 6178); *(Lon. CS 6403)	S	4	3
536,252	Concerto no. 2 for Horn, K. 417 (14 min.) **(Ang. 35902); *(Ang. S–35689); *(Lon. CS 6403)	S	3	2
536,253	Concerto no. 3 for Horn, K. 447 (15 min.) **(Ang. 35092); *(Ang. S–35689); *(Lon. CS 6178); *(Lon. CS 6403)	S	2	2
536,254	Concerto no. 4 for Horn, K. 495 in E flat (17 min.) **(Ang. 35092); *(Ang. S–35689); *(Lon. CS 6403)	S	3	2
536,500	Concerto-Rondo for Piano, K. 386 (8 min.) **(Lon. CS 6501)	S	4	2
536,756	Concerto no. 7 in B flat, K. 238 for Piano and Orchestra (21 min.) **(Lon. CS 6579); *(DG 138824)	S	4	2
536,758	Concerto no. 8 in C, K. 246 for Piano and Orchestra (22 min.) **(Lon. CS 6501); *(BASF 29311)	S	4	2
536,759	Concerto no. 9 in E flat, K. 271 for Piano and Orchestra (32 min.) **(Lon. CS 6501)	S	3	1
536,761	Concerto no. 11 in F, K. 413 for Piano and Orchestra (24 min.) *(Turn. 34027); (Col. M–31728)	S	4	2
536,762	Concerto no. 12 in A, K. 414 for Piano and Orchestra (24 min.) (Col. M–31728)	S	3	2
536,763	Concerto no. 13 in C, K. 415 for Piano and Orchestra (26 min.) (CSP P11816)	S	3	2
536,764	Concerto no. 14 in E flat, K. 449 for Piano and Orchestra (21 min.) *(Col. MS–6844); (CSP P11817); (Turn. 34095)	A	4	3
536,765	Concerto no. 15 in B flat, K. 450 for Piano and Orchestra (26 min.) *(Turn. 34027)	S	2	2
536,766	Concerto no. 16 in D, K. 451 for Piano and Orchestra (22 min.) (DG 138870)	S	3	2
536,767	Concerto no. 17 in G, K. 453 for Piano and Orchestra (30 min.) *(Col. MS–6844); *(Turn. 34080); (CSP P11817)	S	2	1
536,768	Concerto no. 18 in B flat, K. 456 for Piano and Orchestra (31 min.) (CSP P11817); (Turn. 34503)	S	3	2
536,769	Concerto no. 19 in F, K. 459 for Piano and Orchestra (28 min.) *(Turn. 34080)	S	3	2
536,770	Concerto no. 20 in d, K. 466 for Piano and Orchestra (30 min.) **(RCA LSC–2635); *(RCA ARL1–0610); *(Turn. 34095); *(Lon. CS 6579)	S	1	3
536,771	Concerto no. 21 in C, K. 467 for Piano and Orchestra (28 min.) **(Ang. 35931)-*mono*; *(Phi. 6500431); *(RCA ARL1–0610); *(RCA LSC–2634)	S	1	2
536,772	Concerto no. 22 in E flat, K. 482 for Piano and Orchestra (34 min.) *(DG 138824); (Turn. 34233)	S	2	2
536,773	Concerto no. 23 in A, K. 488 for Piano and Orchestra (26 min.) *(RCA LSC–2634); (DG 138870)	S	1	1
536,774	Concerto no. 24 in c, K. 491 for Piano and Orchestra (28 min.) *(Turn. 34178)	S	1	2
536,775	Concerto no. 25 in C, K. 503 for Piano and Orchestra (32 min.) *(Phi. 6500431); *(Turn. 34129); (Ang. S–36536)	S	1	3
536,776	Concerto no. 26 in D, K. 537 (*Coronation*) for Piano and Orchestra (29 min.) *(BASF 29311)	S	3	1
536,777	Concerto no. 27 in B flat, K. 595 for Piano and Orchestra (31 min.) *(Turn. 34129)	S	2	1
537,000	Concerto no. 10 in E flat for 2 Pianos, K. 365 (25 min.) **(Turn. 34064)	S	2	2
537,250	Concerto in F for 3 Pianos, K. 242 (24 min.) *(None. H–71028)	S	4	3
537,500	Concerto for Violin no. 1 in B flat, K. 207 (19 min.)	A	4	3

GUIDE NO. COMPOSER AND TITLE	AGE MIN	AES SIG	AC-CESS
**(Phi. 835136);			
*(Ang. S–36231)			
537,502 Concerto for Violin no. 2 in D, K. 211	A	4	3
**(Phi. 835256);			
*(Ang. S–36231)			
537,503 Concerto for Violin no. 3 in G, K. 216 (25 min.)	A	3	3
**(Phi. 835112);			
*(Ang. S–35745);			
*(Col. MS–6063)			
537,504 Concerto for Violin no. 4 in D, K. 218 (22 min.)	A	3	3
**(Phi. 835112);			
*(Ang. S–36152);			
*(Col. MS–6063);			
*(RCA LSC–3265)			
537,505 Concerto for Violin no. 5 in A, K. 219 (29 min.)	A	2	2
**(RCA LSC–3265);			
*(Ang. S–35745);			
*(Phi. 835112);			
*(Phi. 6500537)			
537,506 Concerto for Violin no. 6 in E flat, K. 268 (26 min.)	A	5	3
*(Ang. S–36240)			
537,507 Concerto for Violin no. 7 in D, K. 271A (28 min.)	S	4	2
*(Ang. S–36152)			
537,750 *Concertone* for 2 Violins, Oboe, and Cello, K. 190 (29 min.)	A	4	2
*(Ang. S–36240);			
*(Col. MS–6848)			
537,875 Rondo in D for Piano and Orchestra, K. 382 (10 min.)	S	4	2
(Turn. 34233)			
538,000 *Sinfonia Concertante* in D flat for Oboe, Clarinet, Bassoon, Horn, and Strings, K. Anh. 9 (297b) (33 min.)	A	3	2
**(DG 139156)			
538,250 *Sinfonia Concertante* in D flat for Violin and Viola, K. 364 (31 min.)	A	1	2
**(Lon. CS 6377);			
(Phi. 835256);			
(Ang. S–36190);			
*(DG 139156)			
538,500 Sonata for Organ and Orchestra in E flat, K. 67 (3 min.)	S	4	3
*(2–Phi. 6700061)			
538,510 Sonata for Organ and Orchestra, K. 68 (3 min.)	S	4	3
*(2–Phi. 6700061)			
538,520 Sonata for Organ and Strings, K. 69 (3 min.)	S	4	3
*(2–Phi. 6700061)			
538,530 Sonata for Organ and Strings, K. 144 (3 min.)	S	4	3
*(2–Phi. 6700061);			
(Turn. 34135)			
538,540 Sonata for Organ and Strings, K. 224e (5 min.)	S	4	3
*(2–Phi. 6700061)			
538,550 Sonata for Organ and Strings, K. 244 (4 min.)	S	4	3
*(Phi. 6700061)			
538,560 Sonata for Organ and Strings, K. 245 (4 min.)	S	4	3
*(2–Phi. 6700061)			
538,570 Sonata for Organ and Strings, K. 274 (4 min.)	S	4	3
*(2–Phi. 6700061)			
538,580 Sonata for Organ and Strings, K. 278 (4 min.)	S	4	3
*(2–Phi. 6700061)			
538,590 Sonata for Organ and Strings, K. 328 (5 min.)	S	4	3
*(2–Phi. 6700061)			
538,600 Sonata for Organ and Strings, K. 329 (4 min.)	S	4	3
*(2–Phi. 6700061)			
538,610 Sonata for Organ and Strings, K. 336 (5 min.)	S	4	3
*(2–Phi. 6700061)			
NAUDOT, JEAN JACQUES (?–1762)			
539,500 Concerto in G for Recorder, Strings, op. 17, no. 5 (11 min.)	S	4	2
**(Tel. 6.41095)			
NIELSEN, CARL (1865–1931)			
539,750 Concerto for Clarinet, op. 57 (23 min.)	A	3	2
*(Col. MS–7028)			
540,000 Concerto for Flute (18 min.)	S	3	2
*(Col. MS–7028)			
PAGANINI, NICCOLO (1782–1840)			
540,750 Concerto no. 1 in D for Violin, op. 6 (29 min.)	S	4	1
**(DG 139424);			
*(Ang. S–36836)			
540,752 Concerto no. 2 in b for Violin, op. 7 (27 min.)	S	4	1
**(DG 139424)			
541,000 *Moto perpetuo* for Violin and Orchestra, op. 11 (4 min.)	S	4	2
(Sera. S–60199)			
PERGOLESI, GIOVANNI BATTISTA (1710–1736)			
541,250 Concerto in D for Flute and Strings (attrib.) (11 min.)	S	3	2
**(Lon. CS 6395)			
541,500 Concerto in G for Flute and Strings (attrib.) (13 min.)	S	3	1
**(Lon. CS 6395)			
541,750 Sinfonia in F for Cello and Continuo (attrib.)	S	4	2
(None. H–71119)			
PERSICHETTI, VINCENT (1915–)			
542,000 *Sinfonia: Janiculum* (Symphony No. 9)	S	4	3
(RCA LSC–3212)			
POULENC, FRANCIS (1899–1963)			
542,250 *Aubade*, for Piano and 18 Instruments (21 min.)	A	3	2
*(Ang. S–36426);			
*(None. H–71033)			
542,500 *Concert champêtre* for Harpsichord and Orchestra (27 min.)	A	3	2
**(Ang. S–35993)			

GUIDE NO.	COMPOSER AND TITLE	AGE MIN	AES SIG	AC-CESS
542,750	Concerto in g for Organ, Strings, and Timpani (23 min.) **(Ang. S–35953)	S	3	1
543,000	Concerto for 2 Pianos and Orchestra (19 min.) **(Ang. S–35993)	A	3	1
	PROKOFIEV, SERGE (1891–1953)			
544,000	Concerto no. 1 in D flat for Piano, op. 10 (14 min.) **(Col. MS–6925); (Mon. S–2131E)-*mono*	A	4	3
544,002	Concerto no. 2 in g for Piano, op. 16 (30 min.) (RCA VICS–1071)	A	4	3
544,003	Concerto no. 3 in C for Piano (28 min.) **(DG 139349); *(Col. MS–6925); *(Lon. CS 6633); (Mer. 75019); (Mon. MC(S)–2061)-*mono*	S	2	1
544,004	Concerto no. 4 for left hand, op. 53 (23 min.) *(Col. MS–6405)	A	4	2
544,250	Concerto no. 1 in D for Violin, op. 19 (21 min.) **(Col. MS–6635); *(Mel./Ang. S–40068)	S	2	2
544,252	Concerto no. 2 in g for Violin, op. 63 (26 min.) **(Col. MS–6635); **(RCA LSC–4010)	S	2	1
544,500	Sinfonia Concertante for Cello, op. 125 (38 min.) *(Sera. S–60171)	A	4	2
	PURCELL, HENRY (c.1659–1695)			
544,750	Sonata in D for Trumpet and Strings (7 min.) **(Van. HM–31SD)	S	3	1
	QUANTZ, JOHANN JOACHIM (1697–1773)			
545,250	Concerto no. 17 in D for Flute (17 min.) *(Oiseau S–279)	S	4	2
	RACHMANINOFF, SERGEI (1873–1943)			
545,500	Concerto no. 1 in f sharp for Piano, op. 1 (25 min.) **(3–RCA LM–6123)-*mono*; *(Mer. 75019); (RCA VICS–1101)	S	3	1
545,502	Concerto no. 2 in c for Piano, op. 18 (33 min.) **(3–RCA LM–6123)-*mono*; *(Lon. CS 6390)	S	2	1
545,503	Concerto no. 3 in d for Piano, op. 30 (43 min.) **(RCA LSC–2355); **(3–RCA LM–6123)-*mono*	S	3	1
545,504	Concerto no. 4 in g for Piano, op. 40 (26 min.) **(3–RCA LM–6123)-*mono*; *(Ang. S–35567)	S	4	2
545,750	*Rhapsody on a Theme* of Paganini, op. 43 (22 min.) **(3–RCA LM–6123)-*mono*; *(Lon. CS 6153)	S	3	1
	RAVEL, MAURICE (1875–1937)			
546,000	Concerto in D for the Left Hand (18 min.) *(Lon. CS 6633)	S	4	2
546,250	Concerto in G for Piano and Orchestra (21 min.) **(Ang. S–35567); **(DG 139349); *(Col. MS–6043); *(Lon. CS 6487); (RCA VICS–1071)	S	2	1
546,500	*Tzigane* for Violin and Orchestra (10 min.) **(Phi. 802708)	S	3	1
	REINECKE, CARL (1824–1910)			
546,750	Concerto in e for Harp, op. 182 (22 min.) **(DG 138853)	S	4	2
	RIEGGER, WALLINGFORD (1885–1961)			
547,000	*Variations* for Piano and Orchestra (16 min.) (Lou. 545–3)-*mono*	A	4	4
	RODRIGO, JOAQUIN (1902–)			
548,000	Concert-Serenade for Harp and Orchestra (23 min.) **(DG 138118)	S	4	1
548,250	*Concierto de Aranjuez* for Guitar and Orchestra (21 min.) **(Col. MS–6834); **(Lon. STS–15199); *(RCA LSC–2730)	S	4	1
548,500	*Fantasia para un gentil-hombre* for Guitar (22 min.) **(Lon. STS–15199); *(Col. MS–7063)	S	3	1
	RUBINSTEIN, ANTON (1829–1894)			
549,000	Concerto no. 4 in d for Piano and Orchestra, op. 70 (33 min.) (Can. 31023)	A	5	2
	SAINT-SAËNS, CAMILLE (1835–1921)			
549,250	Concerto no. 1 in a for Cello and Orchestra, op. 33 (19 min.) *(Ang. S–36642)	S	3	1
549,252	Concerto no. 2 in g for Piano and Orchestra, op. 22 (23 min.) **(3–Sera. S–6081)	S	3	1
549,254	Concerto no. 4 in c for Piano and Orchestra, op. 44 (25 min.) **(3–Sera. S–6081); *(Col. MS–6377); *(Phi. 6500095)	S	4	1
549,500	Concerto no. 3 in b for Violin and Orchestra, op. 61 (27 min.) (Lon. STS–15142)	S	4	2
549,750	*Havanaise* for Violin and Orchestra (10 min.) **(Lon. CS 6165); *(RCA VICS–1153)	S	4	1

GUIDE NO. COMPOSER AND TITLE	AGE MIN	AES SIG	AC-CESS
550,000 *Introduction and Rondo Capriccioso*, op. 28 (9 min.) **(Lon. CS 6165)	S	3	1
SALIERI, ANTONIO (1750–1825)			
550,250 Concerto in C for Flute, Oboe, and Orchestra (20 min.) *(DG 139152); *(Turn. 34307)	S	4	2
SAMMARTINI, GIUSEPPE (c.1693–c.1770)			
550,500 Concerto in F for Recorder and String Orchestra (14 min.) **(Tel. 6.41095)	A	4	2
SARASATE, PABLO DE (1844–1908)			
550,750 *Carmen Fantasy*, op. 25 for Violin and Orchestra (11 min.) **(Lon. CS 6165); *(Ang. S–36836)	S	5	1
551,000 *Zigeunerweisen*, op. 20, no. 1 for Violin and Orchestra (8 min.) **(Lon. CS 6165)	S	4	1
SCARLATTI, ALESSANDRO (1660–1725)			
551,502 Concerto grosso no. 2 (9 min.) (DG ARC–198442)	S	4	2
551,503 Concerto grosso no. 3 (8 min.) (DG ARC–198442)	S	4	2
551,504 Concerto grosso no. 4 (8 min.) (DG ARC–198442)	S	4	2
551,505 Concerto no. 3 in F (8 min.) *(None. H–71052)	S	4	2
SCHOENBERG, ARNOLD (1874–1951)			
551,750 Concerto for Piano and Orchestra, op. 42 (20 min.) *(DG 2530257)	A	3	4
552,000 Concerto for Violin and Orchestra, op. 36 (29 min.) *(DG 2530257)	A	3	5
SCHUMAN, WILLIAM (1910–)			
552,250 *A Song of Orpheus* (Fantasy) for Cello and Orchestra (21 min.) *(Col. MS–6638)	S	3	2
SCHUMANN, ROBERT (1810–1856)			
552,500 Concerto in a for Cello and Orchestra, op. 129 (25 min.) (Ang. S–36642)	S	3	2
552,750 Concerto in a for Piano and Orchestra, op. 84 (30 min.) **(Lon. STS–15176E)-*mono*; *(Odys. 32160141)-*mono*	S	2	2
553,000 Introduction and Allegro in G (*Konzertstück*), op. 92 (16 min.) *(None. H–71044)	S	4	3
553,250 *Konzertstück* in F for 4 Horns and Orchestra,	S	5	3

GUIDE NO. COMPOSER AND TITLE	AGE MIN	AES SIG	AC-CESS
op. 86 (19 min.) *(None. H–71044)			
SESSIONS, ROGER (1910–)			
553,500 Concerto for Violin (29 min.) *(CRI S–220)	A	3	5
SHOSTAKOVICH, DMITRI (1906–1975)			
554,000 Concerto in E flat for Cello, op. 107 (27 min.) **(Col. MS–6124)	A	3	3
554,250 Concerto no. 1 for Piano, Trumpet, and Orchestra, op. 35 (22 min.) **(Sera. 60161)-*mono*; *(Argo ZRG–674)	S	3	1
554,252 Concerto no. 2 for Piano and Orchestra, op. 102 (19 min.) *(Col. MS–6043); *(Sera. 60161)-*mono*	S	4	2
554,500 Concerto no. 1 in a for Violin and Orchestra, op. 99 (38 min.) *(Ang. S–36964)	A	2	3
554,502 Concerto no. 2 in c sharp for Violin, op. 129 (30 min.) *(Mel./Ang. S–40064)	A	2	3
SIBELIUS, JEAN (1865–1957)			
554,750 Concerto in d for Violin, op. 47 (30 min.) **(RCA LSC–4010); *(Lon. CS 6710); (Lon. STS–15054)	S	3	1
SPOHR, LUDWIG (1784–1859)			
555,000 Concerto no. 3 for Violin, *Gesangscene* (17 min.) *(RCA LM–2860)-*mono*	A	4	2
STAMITZ, KARL (1745–1801)			
555,250 Concerto no. 3 in B flat for Clarinet and Orchestra (16 min.) (None. H–71148)	A	4	2
555,500 Concerto no. 1 in D for Viola and Orchestra (22 min.) *(Turn. 34221)	A	4	3
STÖLZEL, GOTTFRIED HEINRICH (1690–1749)			
555,750 Concerto in D for 6 Trumpets, 4 Kettledrums, 2 Harpsichords, and Double String Orchestra (11 min.) (Turn. 34090)	S	4	2
STRAUSS, RICHARD (1864–1949)			
556,000 *Burleske* in d for Piano and Orchestra (21 min.) *(RCA VICS–1101)	S	4	3
556,250 Concerto no. 1 in E flat for Horn, op. 11 (16 min.) **(Lon. CS 6519)	A	3	2
556,500 Concerto for Oboe and Orchestra (23 min.) *(Phi. 6500174)	A	3	1

GUIDE NO. COMPOSER AND TITLE	AGE MIN	AES SIG	AC-CESS
556,750 *Don Quixote*, op. 35 (41 min.)	S	3	2
**(RCA VICS–1561); *(DG 139009); *(Odys. Y–32224)			
557,000 *Festival Prelude* for Organ and Orchestra, op. 61 (13 min.)	S	5	2
*(DG 138866)			
STRAVINSKY, IGOR (1882–1971)			
557,250 *Capriccio* for Piano and Orchestra (17 min.)	A	4	3
*(Argo ZRG–674); (Turn. 34130)			
557,500 Concerto for Piano and Wind Orchestra (20 min.)	A	3	3
*(Turn. 34065)			
557,750 Concerto in D for Violin and Orchestra (21 min.)	A	2	3
*(Col. MS–6331)			
558,000 *Movements for Piano and Orchestra* (9 min.)	A	3	5
*(Col. MS–6272)			
TARTINI, GIUSEPPE (1692–1770)			
558,500 Concerto in A for Cello and Strings (15 min.)	S	4	2
*(Turn. 34236)			
559,000 Concerto in d for Violin (15 min.)	S	3	2
(Col. MS–6953)			
TCHAIKOVSKY, PETER ILYITCH (1840–1893)			
559,250 Concerto no. 1 in b flat for Piano and Orchestra, op. 23 (33 min.)	E	2	1
**(RCA LM–2319)-*mono*; *(RCA VICS–1039); *(RCA LSC–2252); (Sera. 56–6020)			
559,252 Concerto no. 2 in G for Piano and Orchestra, op. 44 (43 min.)	S	2	3
(Col. MS–6755)			
559,253 Concerto no. 3 in E flat for Piano and Orchestra, op. 75	S	5	3
(Col. MS–6755)			
559,500 Concerto in D for Violin and Orchestra, op. 35 (33 min.)	S	2	1
*(DG 139028)			
559,750 *Sérénade mélancolique* for Violin, op. 26 (8 min.)	S	5	2
*(Lon. STS–15054); (Phi. 6580047)			
560,000 *Variations on a Rococo Theme* for Cello, op. 33 (18 min.)	A	3	1
(Col. MS–6714)			
TELEMANN, GEORG PHILIPP (1681–1767)			
560,500 Concerto in D for Horn and Orchestra (7 min.)	S	4	3
*(None. H–71148)			
561,500 Concerto in F for 2 Horns, 2 Violins, and Continuo (17 min.)	S	4	3
*(None. H–71066)			
562,500 Concerto in A for Oboe d'Amore and Strings	S	4	3

GUIDE NO. COMPOSER AND TITLE	AGE MIN	AES SIG	AC-CESS
(14 min.) *(None. H–71066)			
563,500 Concerto in C for Recorder and Strings (16 min.)	S	4	3
**(Tel. 6.41095)			
564,000 Concerto in e for Recorder, Flute, and Strings (14 min.)	S	4	3
*(Tel. 6.41039)			
564,500 Concerto in D for Trumpet and Strings (8 min.)	S	3	1
*(None. H–71066)			
565,000 Concerto in D for Trumpet, 2 Oboes, and Continuo (15 min.)	S	3	2
*(None. H–71132); *(Argo ZRG–585)			
565,500 Concerto in D for 3 Trumpets, 2 Oboes, and Orchestra (11 min.)	S	3	1
*(None. H–71132)			
566,000 Concerto in G for Viola (15 min.)	S	4	2
*(Oiseau S–276); *(Turn. 34288)			
566,500 Concerto in G for 2 Solo Violas, and Strings (13 min.)	S	4	2
*(Turn. 34288)			
567,000 Concerto in a for Violin (11 min.)	S	4	2
*(None. H–71052)			
568,000 Concerto in F for 3 Violins and Orchestra (17 min.)	S	4	2
*(Turn. 34288)			
569,500 Suite in a for Flute and Strings (26 min.)	S	2	1
*(Tel. 6.41039); *(Tel. 6.41225); (Orion 7264)-*mono*			
VAUGHAN WILLIAMS, RALPH (1872–1958)			
570,000 Concerto for Piano (also arranged for 2 pianos) (24 min.)	S	4	2
*(Ang. S–36625)			
570,250 *The Lark Ascending* (romance for violin and orchestra) (15 min.)	S	4	3
**(Ang. S–36902); *(Argo ZRG–696)			
VIEUXTEMPS, HENRI (1820–1881)			
570,500 Concerto no. 4 for Violin, op. 31 (25 min.)	A	5	1
**(Phi. 802708)			
570,505 Concerto no. 5 in a for Violin, op. 37 (19 min.)	A	4	1
*(RCA LSC–2603)			
VIOTTI, GIOVANNI BATTISTA (1755–1824)			
570,750 Concerto no. 22 in a for Violin (26 min.)	S	5	2
*(Turn. 34229)			
VIVALDI, ANTONIO (1678–1741) (*L'Estro Armonico*)			
571,005 no. 5 in A for 2 Violins, P. 212 (3–Van. HM 37/8/9SD)	S	3	2

GUIDE NO.	COMPOSER AND TITLE	AGE MIN	AES SIG	AC-CESS
571,008	no. 8 in a for 2 Violins, P. 2 (12 min.) *(DG 138714); (Col. M–32230); (3–Van. HM–37/8/9SD)	S	2	2
571,010	no. 10 in b for 4 Violins and Cello, P. 148 (10 min.) *(Ang. S–36103); *(Oiseau S–276); (Col. M–32230); (3–Van. HM–37/8/9SD)	S	2	2
571,011	no. 11 in d for 2 Violins and Cello, P. 250 (11 min.) *(None. H–71052); (Col. M–32230); (3–Van. HM–37/8/9SD) Concerti from op. 4 (*La stravaganza*)—all for solo violin	S	2	2
571,501	no. 1 in B flat, P. 327 (9 min.) (3–Vox SVBX–531E)-*mono*	S	3	3
571,502	no. 2 in e, P. 98 (11 min.) (3–Vox SVBX–531E)-*mono*	S	3	3
571,503	no. 3 in G, P. 99 (9 min.) (3–Vox SVBX–531E)-*mono*	S	3	3
571,504	no. 4 in a, P. 3 (9 min.) (3–Vox SVBX–531E)-*mono*	S	3	3
571,505	no. 5 in A, P. 213 (10 min.) (3–Vox SVBX–531E)-*mono*	S	3	3
571,506	no. 6 in g, P. 328 (10 min.) (3–Vox SVBX–531E)-*mono*	S	3	2
571,507	no. 7 in C, P. 4 (9 min.) (3–Vox SVBX–531E)-*mono*	S	3	2
571,508	no. 8 in d, P. 253 (7 min.) (3–Vox SVBX–531E)-*mono*	S	3	3
571,509	no. 9 in F, P. 251 (8 min.) (3–Vox SVBX–531E)-*mono*	S	3	3
571,510	no. 10 in c, P. 413 (9 min.) (3–Vox SVBX–531E)-*mono*	S	3	3
571,511	no. 11 in D, P. 149 (7 min.) (3–Vox SVBX–531E)-*mono*	S	3	3
571,512	no. 12 in G, P. 100 (11 min.) (3–Vox SVBX–531E)-*mono* Concerti from op. 8 (*Trial of Harmony and Invention*)	S	3	3
572,000	(no. 1–4 [*The 4 Seasons*]) (43 min.) **(Phi. 6500017); *(Ang. S–35877)	E	2	1
572,001	no. 1 in E (*La primavera*), P. 241 (11 min.) **(Phi. 6500017); *(Ang. S–35877)	E	2	1
572,002	no. 2 in g (*Estate*), P. 336 (11 min.) **(Phi. 6500017); *(Ang. S–35877)	E	2	1
572,003	no. 3 in F (*Autonno*), P. 257 (12 min.) **(Phi. 6500017); *(Ang. S–35877)	E	2	1
572,004	no. 4 in f (*L'inverno*), P. 442 (9 min.) **(Phi. 6500017); *(Ang. S–35877)	E	2	1
572,005	op. 8, no. 5 in E flat (*La tempesta di mare*), P. 415 (Col. M–32693)	S	2	2
572,012	op. 8, no. 12 in C (also for oboe), P. 8 (Col. M–32840) Concerti from op. 9 (*La Cetra*)	S	2	2
572,504	no. 4 in E, P. 242 (12 min.) (Van. SRV–159SD)	S	3	2
572,508	no. 8 in d, P. 260 (10 min.) (Van. SRV–159SD)	S	3	2
572,509	no. 9 in B flat, P. 341 (10 min.) (Van. SRV–159SD)	S	3	2
572,512	no. 12 in G, P. 154 (14 min.) (Van. SRV–159SD) Concerti for Flute and Orchestra, op. 10	S	2	2
573,001	no. 1 in F (*La tempesta di mare*), P. 261 (8 min.) *(3–Col. D3S–770); *(DG ARC–2533044); *(None. H–71042)	S	4	3
573,002	no. 2 in g (*La notte*), P. 342 (10 min.) *(3–Col. D3S–770); *(None. H–71042)	S	3	2
573,003	no. 3 in D (*Il gardellino*), P. 155 (10 min.) *(3–Col. D3S–770); *(None. H–71042)	S	2	2
573,004	no. 4 in G, P. 104 (8 min.) *(3–Col. D3S–770); *(None. H–71042)	S	4	3
573,005	no. 5 in F, P. 262 (9 min.) *(3–Col. D3S–770); *(None. H–71042); (Tel. 6.41217)	S	3	3
573,006	no. 6 in G, P. 105 (9 min.) *(3–Col. D3S–770); *(None. H–71042)	S	3	2
573,500	Concerto in C for Violin, 2 String Choirs, 2 Harpsichords in C (*Per la S.S. Assunzione di Maria Vergine*), P. 14 *(Van. HM–16SD)	S	2	2
574,043	P. 43. Concerto in C for Oboe (12 min.) (Odys. 32160214)	S	4	2
574,070	P. 70. Concerto in a for Bassoon (10 min.) (Turn. 34025)	S	3	2
574,074	P. 74. Concerto in C for 2 Oboes and 2 Clarinets (12 min.) *(DG ARC–2533044); (Odys. 32160012)	S	3	2
574,075	P. 75. Concerto in C for 2 Trumpets (7 min.) *(Argo. ZRG–644); *(Turn. 34057); *(Van. HM–31SD)	S	3	1
574,077	P. 77. Concerto in a for Recorder (8 min.) **(Tel. 6.41239) (None. H–71148)	S	3	2
574,078	P. 78. Concerto in C for Flute (11 min.) *(3–Col. D3S–770); *(Turn. 34009)	S	3	2

GUIDE NO. COMPOSER AND TITLE	AGE	AES MIN	AC- SIG CESS
574,079 P. 79. Concerto in C for Piccolo (10 min.) *(3–Col. D3S–770); *(DG ARC–198318)	S	3	1
574,083 P. 83. Concerto in a for Piccolo (11 min.) *(Turn. 34009); (Odys. 32160012)	S	3	1
574,133 P. 133. Concerto for 2 Mandolins in G (12 min.) *(Van. HM–16SD)	S	3	1
574,134 P. 134. Concerto in C for Mandolin (8 min.) **(DG 139417)	S	3	1
574,137 P. 137. Concerto in e for Bassoon (11 min.) *(None. H–71104)	S	4	1
574,209 P. 209. Concerto in D for Lute (10 min.) **(DG 139417); *(RCA LSC–2730)	S	3	1
574,222 P. 222. Concerto in D for 2 Violins (16 min.) *(DG ARC–198318)	S	3	2
574,266 P. 266. Concerto in d for Viola d'amore and lute (12 min.) *(DG ARC–198318); *(None. H–71104); *(Turn. 34009)	S	2	1
574,278 P. 278. Concerto in F for 3 Violins (11 min.) (Col. M–32032)	S	3	2
574,288 P. 288. Concerto in d for Viola d'amore (10 min.) *(Turn. 34009)	S	3	2
574,320 P. 320. Concerto in F for 2 Horns (10 min.) *(DG ARC–2533044); (None. H–71091)	S	3	1
574,321 P. 321. Concerto in F for 2 Horns (8 min.) *(DG ARC–2533044); *(None. H–71091); *(Tel. 6.41217)	S	3	1
574,342 P. 342. Concerto in g for Flute and Bassoon (8 min.) *(Van. HM–16SD); (Odys. 32160012)	S	3	2

GUIDE NO. COMPOSER AND TITLE	AGE	AES MIN	AC- SIG CESS
574,434 P. 434. Concerto in c for Cello (11 min.) *(DG ARC–198318); *(Oiseau S–277)	S	3	2
574,440 P. 440. Concerto in c for Recorder (8 min.) **(Tel. 6.41095); *(3–Col. D3S–770)	S	3	2
WALTON, WILLIAM (1902–)			
574,750 Concerto for Viola and Orchestra (25 min.) **(Ang. S–36719); (Odys. 32160368)	A	3	2
575,000 Concerto for Violin and Orchestra (29 min.) **(Ang. S–36719)	A	2	3
WEBER, CARL MARIA VON (1786–1826)			
575,250 Concertino for Clarinet and Orchestra, op. 26 (9 min.) *(Ang. S–36589); *(Turn. 34151); (Van. VSD–71167)	S	3	2
575,500 Concerto in F for Bassoon and Orchestra, op. 75 (18 min.) *(Lon. CS 6603)	S	5	3
575,750 Concerto no. 1 in f for Clarinet, op. 73 (21 min.) *(Ang. S–36589); *(Turn. 34151)	S	3	1
575,752 Concerto no. 2 in E flat for Clarinet, op. 74 (22 min.) *(Oiseau 60035)	S	4	2
576,000 *Konzertstück* in f for Piano and Orchestra, op. 79 (16 min.) **(Sera. S–60020)	S	3	1
WIENIAWSKI, HENRYK (1835–1880)			
576,252 Concerto no. 2 in d for Violin and Orchestra, op. 22 (24 min.) *(Ang. S–36903)	A	5	1
576,500 *Légende* for Violin and Orchestra, op. 17 (8 min.) (Phi. 6580047)	A	5	2

7. Other Orchestral Works

GUIDE NO. COMPOSER AND TITLE	AGE	AES MIN	AC- SIG CESS
ADAM, ADOLPHE- CHARLES (1803–1856)			
577,000 *Diable à quatre* (ballet) (57 min.) **(Lon. CS 6454)	A	5	2
577,250 *Giselle* (complete ballet) (1 hr., 18 min.) **(2–Lon. CSA 2226)	A	4	2
577,300 *Giselle*: Suite (48 min.) *(Lon. STS–15010)	A	4	2
577,500 *If I Were King*: Overture (8 min.) (Lon. STS–15021)	S	4	2

GUIDE NO. COMPOSER AND TITLE	AGE	AES MIN	AC- SIG CESS
ALBÉNIZ, ISAAC (1860–1909)			
578,000 *Iberia* (suite) (orchestration by Arbós) (31 min.) (None. H–71189)	E	3	2
578,500 *Suite española* (47 min.) *(Lon. CS 6581)	E	3	1
ALBINONI, TOMASO (1671–1750)			
579,000 *Concerti à cinque*, op. 5, no. 5 (8 min.) *(Oiseau S–264)	S	4	3

GUIDE NO. COMPOSER AND TITLE	AGE MIN	AES SIG	AC-CESS
ALFVÉN, HUGO (1872–1960)			
579,500 *Midsommarvaka* (Swedish Rhapsody no. 1) (9 min.) (Col. MS–6196)	S	5	1
AMIROV, FIKRET (1922–)			
579,750 *Azerbaijan Mugam* (13 min.) (Ev. 3032)	A	4	2
ANTHEIL, GEORGE (1900–1959)			
580,000 *Ballet mécanique* (1924) (18 min.) (CSP AML–4956)-*mono*	S	4	2
ARENSKY, ANTON (1861–1906)			
580,500 *Variations* on a Theme by Tchaikovsky, op. 35a (15 min.) *(Ang. S –36269)	S	4	2
AUBER, DANIEL-FRANÇOIS (1782–1871)			
581,000 *Domino Noir* Overture (7 min.) (Lon. STS–15021)	S	5	1
BACH, JOHANN CHRISTIAN (1735–1782)			
581,500 Sinfonia in D no. 3 for Double Orchestra (14 min.) **(None. H–71165)	S	4	2
582,000 Sinfonia in E flat, op. 9, no. 2 (14 min.) (Lon. CS 6621)	S	4	2
582,500 Sinfonia in E flat for Double Orchestra, op. 18, no. 1 (14 min.) *(Oiseau S–317)	S	4	2
582,750 Sinfonietta in C (10 min.) (Mace S–9098)	S	5	2
BACH, JOHANN SEBASTIAN (1685–1750)			
583,000 *Art of the Fugue,* S. 1080 (1 hr. 28 min.) **(2–Lon. CSA 2215)	A	1	4
583,251 Brandenburg Concerto no. 1 in F, S. 1046 (21 min.) *(2–Ang. S–3787); *(2–RCA VICS–6023)	A	1	3
583,252 Brandenburg Concerto no. 2 in F, S. 1047 (12 min.) *(2–Ang. S–3787); *(2–RCA VICS–6023)	S	1	2
583,253 Brandenburg Concerto no. 3 in G, S. 1048 (12 min.) *(2–Ang. S–3787); *(2–RCA VICS–6023)	S	2	3
583,254 Brandenburg Concerto no. 4 in G, S. 1049 (17 min.) *(2–Ang. S–3787); *(2–RCA VICS–6023)	S	2	3
583,255 Brandenburg Concerto no. 5 in D, S. 1050 (23 min.) *(2–Ang. S–3787); *(2–RCA VICS–6023)	S	2	2
583,256 Brandenburg Concerto no. 6 in B flat, S. 1051 (18 min.) *(2–Ang. S–3787); *(2–RCA VICS–6023)	A	3	3
583,500 *Musical Offering,* S. 1079 (46 min.) **(DG ARC–198320); **(Lon. STS–15063)	A	2	1

GUIDE NO. COMPOSER AND TITLE	AGE MIN	AES SIG	AC-CESS
584,001 Suite no. 1 in C, S. 1066 for Orchestra (21 min.) *(2–Sera. S–6085); *(2–Tel. 26.35046)	S	2	2
584,002 Suite no. 2 in b for Flute and Strings, S. 1067 (22 min.) *(2–Sera. S–6085); *(2–Tel. 26.35046)	S	2	1
584,003 Suite no. 3 in D, S. 1068 (21 min.) *(2–Sera. S–6085); *(2–Tel. 26.35046)	S	2	2
584,013 *Air on the G String* (6 min.) *(2–Sera. S–6085); *(2–Tel. 26.35046)	E	2	1
584,014 Suite no. 4 in D, S.1069 (21 min.) *(2–Sera. S–6085); *(2–Tel. 26.35046)	S	2	1
584,250 *Toccata and Fugue in d,* S. 565 (orchestra version) (13 min.) (Col. MS–6180)	E	2	1
BARBER, SAMUEL (1910–)			
584,500 *Adagio for Strings* (from Quartet, op. 11) (8 min.) *(Mer. 75012); *(Odys. Y–33230)	S	2	1
585,000 *Medea,* op. 23 (ballet suite) (1946) (25 min.) *(Mer. 75012)	S	3	2
585,250 *Medea's Meditation and Dance of Vengeance,* op. 23a (13 min.) *(Odys. Y–33230)	S	3	1
585,500 *Overture to the School of Scandal,* op. 5 (8 min.) *(Mer. 75012); *(Odys. Y–33230)	S	4	2
BARTÓK, BÉLA (1881–1945)			
586,000 Concerto for Orchestra (1943) (37 min.) **(Lon. CS 6784); **(RCA VICS–1110); *(Ang. S–37059)	S	2	1
586,250 *Dance Suite* (1923) (17 min.) **(Lon. CS 6784); **(Lon. CS 6407)	E	4	1
586,500 *Deux Images* for Orchestra, op. 10 (1910) (17 min.) *(Bartok 307)-*mono*	S	5	1
586,750 *Divertimento* for String Orchestra (1939) (25 min.) (Argo ZRG–657)	S	3	2
587,000 Hungarian Sketches (11 min.) *(RCA VICS–1620)	S	5	1
587,250 *The Miraculous Mandarin* (ballet) (18 min.) **(Lon. CS 6783); *(Mer. 75030); (Turn. 34086)	S	3	3
587,500 *Music for Strings, Percussion and Celesta* (1935) (30 min.) **(Lon. 6783); *(Ang. S–35949); *(DG 2530065); *(RCA VICS–1620); (Argo ZRG–657)	A	1	4

GUIDE NO.	COMPOSER AND TITLE	AGE MIN	AES SIG	AC-CESS
587,750	Roumanian Folk Dances (1915) (6 min.) *(Lon. CS 6407)	E	4	1
588,250	*Two Portraits for Orchestra*, op. 4 (14 min.) *(Lon. CS 6407)	S	4	1
588,500	*Wooden Prince*, op. 13 (41 min.) (Turn. 34086)	A	4	2
	BATH, HUBERT (1883–1945)			
588,750	*Cornish Rhapsody* (6 min.) (RCA LSC–2380)	S	5	1
	BAX, ARNOLD (1883–1953)			
589,500	*Tintagel* (15 min.) **(Ang. S–36415)	S	3	2
	BEETHOVEN, LUDWIG VAN (1770–1827)			
590,000	*Consecration of the House* Overture, op. 124 (11 min.) **(Ang. S–35661); *(Lon. CS 6512)	S	2	3
590,250	*Contra Dances* (12), G. 141 **(Lon. CS 6656)	E	4	1
590,500	*Coriolanus* Overture, op. 62 (8 min.) *(Col. MS–6966); (DG 139015)	S	2	2
590,750	*Egmont* Overture, op. 84 (9 min.) *(Col. MS–6966)	S	2	2
591,000	*Fidelio*, op. 72c: Overture, (7 min.) **(Ang. S–35711); *(DG 139015)	S	4	2
591,200	*Grosse Fuge* in B flat, op. 133 (orchestra arrangement) (16 min.) (DG 2530066)	A	3	4
591,250	*King Stephen*, op. 117: Overture (8 min.) *(Col. MS–6966)	S	4	2
591,501	*Leonore 1* in C, op. 138 (Overture) (8 min.) **(Phi. 6500089)	S	3	2
591,502	*Leonore 2* in C, op. 72a (Overture) (14 min.) *(Col. MS–6966)	S	2	2
591,503	*Leonore 3*, op. 72b (Overture) (14 min.) **(Phi. 6500089); *(DG 139015)	S	1	1
591,750	*Prometheus* (ballet music), op. 43 (52 min.) *(CSP AM–30082)	A	3	2
592,000	*Prometheus* (Overture) (5 min.) *(Ang. S–35658)	S	2	2
592,250	*Ruins of Athens*: Incidental Music, op. 113 (33 min.) **(Ang. S–35509)	A	5	3
592,500	*Turkish March* (2 min.) **(Ang. S–35509)	E	3	1
592,750	*Wellington's Victory*, op. 91 (15 min.) *(West. WGS–8192)	S	5	2
	BERG, ALBAN (1885–1935)			
593,000	*Chamber Concerto* for Piano, Violin, and 13 Wind Instruments (32 min.) (Col. MS–7179)	A	3	4

GUIDE NO.	COMPOSER AND TITLE	AGE MIN	AES SIG	AC-CESS
593,250	*Lulu* Suite (34 min.) **(DG 2530146)	A	4	4
593,750	Three Pieces for Orchestra, op. 6 (20 min.) **(DG 2530146); (Col. MS–7179)	A	3	4
	BERLIOZ, HECTOR (1803–1869)			
594,000	*Corsaire* (Overture) (8 min.) (Phi. 835367)	E	3	1
594,750	*Dance of the Sylphs* from *Damnation of Faust* (3 min.) *(Odys. Y–31017)	E	3	1
595,000	*Les Francs-Juges* (Overture) (13 min.) **(Phi. 835367)	S	4	2
595,250	*King Lear* (Overture) (15 min.) **(Phi. 835367)	S	3	2
595,300	*Rackoczy* March from *Damnation of Faust* (14 min.) *(Odys. Y–31017)	E	3	1
595,500	*Roman Carnival* (Overture) (9 min.) **(Phi. 835367); **(RCA VIC–1244)-*mono*	E	3	1
595,750	*Waverley* (Overture) (10 min.) **(Phi. 835367)	S	4	2
	BERNSTEIN, LEONARD (1918–)			
597,000	*Candide* (Overture) (4 min.) *(Col. MS–6677); (Turn. 34459)	E	3	1
597,500	*Facsimile* (18 min.) *(Col. MS–6792)	A	4	1
598,000	*Fancy Free* (1944) (24 min.) *(Col. MS–6677)	S	4	1
598,500	*Serenade for Violin, Strings, Harp, and Percussion* (31 min.) *(Col. MS–7058)	A	4	2
	BIZET, GEORGES (1838–1875)			
599,000	*L'Arlésienne*: Suite 1 (18 min.) *(Col. MS–6877); *(Lon. STS–15052); *(Lon. SPC 21023)	E	2	1
599,250	*L'Arlésienne*: Suite 2 (18 min.) *(Lon. STS–15052); *(Lon. SPC 21023)	E	2	1
599,500	*Carmen* Suite (24 min.) *(Lon. STS–15052); *(Lon. SPC 21023)	E	3	1
599,750	*Carmen* Suite no. 1 (9 min.) *(Col. M–31800)	E	3	1
600,000	*Jeux d'Enfants*, op. 22 (11 min.) **(Lon. STS–15093); **(Lon. CS 6208); *(None. H–71183)	E	2	1
600,250	*Jolie fille de Perth*: Suite (12 min.) **(Lon. CS 6208)	S	3	1
600,500	Overture: *Patrie*, op. 19 (12 min.) *(None. H–71183)	S	5	2

BLISS, ARTHUR
(1891–1975)

01,000	Things to Come: Suite (15 min.) *(Lon. STS–15112)	S	4	1
01,250	Welcome to the Queen (7 min.) *(Lon. STS–15112)	E	4	1

BLOCH, ERNEST
(1880–1959)

01,500	Concerto grosso no. 1 for Strings and Piano Obbligato (24 min.) *(Mer. 75017)	S	2	2
01,750	Trois Poèmes Juifs (23 min.) (Desto 6409E)-mono	S	4	2

BOCCHERINI, LUIGI
(1743–1803)

02,000	Serenade in D (13 min.) *(Mace S–9051)	S	3	2

BORODIN, ALEXANDER
(1833–1887)

03,000	In the Steppes of Central Asia (8 min.) *(Mel./Ang. S–40056)	E	3	1
03,250	Nocturne for String Orchestra (from Quartet no. 2) (9 min.) (Col. MS–6575)	S	3	1
03,500	Overture: Prince Igor (11 min.) **(Lon. CS 6785); *(Lon. STS–15149); (Mer. 75016)	E	3	1
03,750	Prince Igor: Polovtsian Dances (13 min.) **(Lon. CS 6785); *(Lon. SPC 21003); (Mer. 75016)	E	3	1

BRAHMS, JOHANNES
(1833–1897)

04,000	Academic Festival Overture, op. 80 (10 min.) **(Odys. Y–32225); *(Ang. S–35545)	E	3	1
04,251	Hungarian Dance no. 1 (3 min.) *(Lon. STS–15009); *(Mer. 75024)	E	3	1
04,252	Hungarian Dance no. 2 (3 min.) *(Mer. 75024)	E	3	2
04,253	Hungarian Dance no. 3 (2 min.) *(Mer. 75024)	E	3	2
04,254	Hungarian Dance no. 4 (4 min.) *(Mer. 75024)	E	3	2
04,255	Hungarian Dance no. 5 (3 min.) *(Lon. STS–15009); *(Mer. 75024)	E	3	1
04,256	Hungarian Dance no. 6 (3 min.) *(Lon. STS–15009); *(Mer. 75024)	E	3	1
04,257	Hungarian Dance no. 7 (2 min.) *(Lon. STS–15009); *(Mer. 75024)	E	3	2
04,260	Hungarian Dance no. 10 (2 min.)	E	3	2

	*(Lon. STS–15009); *(Mer. 75024)			
604,261	Hungarian Dance no. 11 (4 min.) *(Mer. 75024)	E	3	2
604,267	Hungarian Dance no. 17 (4 min.) *(Mer. 75024)	E	3	1
604,268	Hungarian Dance no. 18 (4 min.) *(Mer. 75024)	E	3	2
604,269	Hungarian Dance no. 19 (2 min.) *(Lon. STS–15009); *(Mer. 75024)	E	3	2
604,270	Hungarian Dance no. 20 (3 min.) *(Mer. 75024)	E	3	2
604,271	Hungarian Dance no. 21 (2 min.) *(Lon. STS–15009); *(Mer. 75024)	E	3	1
604,501	Serenade no. 1 in D, op. 11 (47 min.) *(Lon. CS 6567)	S	4	2
604,502	Serenade no. 2 in A, op. 16 (32 min.) **(Lon. CS 6594)	S	3	2
604,750	Tragic Overture, op. 81 (13 min.) **(Ang. S–35532); **(Col. MS–6158); **(3–Sera. 6015)-mono; *(Odys. Y–31924)	S	2	1
605,000	Variations and Fugue on a Theme by Handel, op. 24 (25 min.) (Col. MS–7298)	A	4	2
605,250	Variations on a Theme by Haydn, op. 56a (17 min.) **(Col. MS–30069)-mono; *(Col. MS–6685); (Col. MS–7298)	S	2	1

BRITTEN, BENJAMIN
(1913–   )

606,000	Peter Grimes: 4 Sea Interludes and Passacaglia (17 min.) *(Lon. CS 6179)	S	2	2
606,900	Sinfonia da Requiem, op. 20 (19 min.) **(Lon. OS 25937); (Odys. Y–31016)	A	4	3
607,500	Variations on a Theme by Frank Bridge (27 min.) **(Lon. CS 6671)	A	3	2
607,800	Young Person's Guide to the Orchestra, op. 34 (19 min.) **(Lon. CS 6671)	E	3	1

CARPENTER, JOHN ALDEN
(1876–1951)

608,000	Skyscrapers (ballet) (1926) (15 min.) (Desto 6407E)	S	4	2

CHABRIER, EMMANUEL
(1841–1894)

608,500	Bourrée fantasque (6 min.) (Sera. S–60108)	E	4	1
608,750	Danse Slave (5 min.) *(Lon. CS 6438)	E	5	1

GUIDE NO.	COMPOSER AND TITLE	AGE MIN	AES SIG	AC-CESS
609,000	*España* (6 min.) *(Lon. CS 6006); *(Lon. CS 6438); *(Sera. S–60177); (Sera. S–60108)	E	4	1
609,250	*Fête Polonaise* (8 min.) *(Lon. CS 6438); (Sera. S–60108)	E	4	1
609,500	*Gwendoline* Overture (9 min.) (Sera. S–60108)	S	4	1
609,750	*Marche Joyeuse* (4 min.) *(Lon. CS 6438); (Sera. S–60108)	E	4	1
610,000	*Suite Pastorale* (19 min.) *(Lon. CS 6438)	S	4	1

CHADWICK, GEORGE WHITEFIELD (1854–1931)

610,250	*Tam O'Shanter:* Symphonic Ballad (20 min.) (Desto 6421E)-*mono*	S	5	2

CHÁVEZ, CARLOS (1899–   )

610,500	*Toccata* for Percussion (12 min.) (CSP AMS–6447)	S	4	2

CHOPIN, FRÉDÉRIC (1810–1849)

610,750	*Les Sylphides* (29 min.) *(DG 136257)	S	3	1

COATES, ERIC (1886–1957)

611,250	*London* Suite (14 min.) (RCA LSC–2719)	S	4	1

COPLAND, AARON (1900–   )

611,750	*Appalachian Spring:* Suite (25 min.) **(Col. M–30649); *(Col. MS–6355); *(RCA LSC–2401); (Ev. 3002)	E	2	1
612,000	*Billy the Kid* (ballet suite) (20 min.) **(Col. MS–6175)	E	2	1
612,250	*Connotations* for Orchestra (19 min.) **(Col. MS–7431)	A	4	4
612,500	*Danzón Cubano* (7 min.) *(Col. MS–6514)	E	2	1
612,750	*Fanfare for the Common Man* (3 min.) **(Col. M–30649); *(Col. MS–6684)	E	4	1
613,250	*Lincoln Portrait* (15 min.) **(Col. MS–6684); *(Col. M–30649)	E	3	1
613,500	*Music for the Theater* (22 min.) **(Col. MS–6698)	S	2	1
613,750	*Our Town* (suite) (11 min.) **(Col. MS–7375)	S	4	1
614,000	*Outdoor* Overture (10 min.) **(Col. MS–7375); (Pol. 245006)	S	4	1
614,250	*Quiet City* (10 min.) **(Col. MS–7375); (Turn. 34398)	S	4	1
614,500	*Red Pony* Suite (24 min.) *(Odys. Y–31016)	E	4	1
614,750	*Rodeo* (19 min.) **(Col. MS–6175)	E	3	1

GUIDE NO.	COMPOSER AND TITLE	AGE MIN	AES SIG	AC-CES
615,000	*Hoedown* only (3 min.) **(Col. MS–6175)	E	3	1
615,250	*Night Waltz* only (4 min.) **(Col. MS–6175)	E	3	2
615,500	*El Salón México* (11 min.) *(Col. MS–6355)	E	2	1
615,750	*Statements* for Orchestra (18 min.) *(Col. M–30374)	A	4	2
616,000	*Tender Land* (orchestral suite) (1954) (18 min.) *(RCA LSC–2401)	S	5	2

CORELLI, ARCANGELO (1653–1713)

616,251	Concerto grosso, op. 6, no. 1 (14 min.) **(3-Argo ZRG–773/5); *(Oiseau S–277)	S	3	3
616,252	Concerto grosso, op. 6, no. 2 (11 min.) **(3-Argo ZRG–773/5); *(Ang. S–36130)	S	3	2
616,253	Concerto grosso, op. 6, no. 3 (11 min.) **(3-Argo ZRG–773/5)	S	3	3
616,254	Concerto grosso, op. 6, no. 4 (10 min.) **(3-Argo ZRG–773/5)	S	3	2
616,255	Concerto grosso, op. 6, no. 5 (11 min.) **(3-Argo ZRG–773/5)	S	3	3
616,256	Concerto grosso, op. 6, no. 6 (13 min.) **(3-Argo ZRG–773/5); *(Ang. S–36130)	S	3	3
616,257	Concerto grosso, op. 6, no. 7 (10 min.) **(3-Argo ZRG–773/5); *(Ang. S–36130)	S	3	1
616,258	Concerto grosso, op. 6, no. 8 (*Christmas*) (16 min.) **(3-Argo ZRG–773/5); *(Ang. S–36130); (DG 2530070)	S	3	1
616,259	Concerto grosso, op. 6, no. 9 (10 min.) **(3-Argo ZRG–773/5)	S	3	3
616,260	Concerto grosso, op. 6, no. 10 (13 min.) **(3-Argo ZRG–773/5)	S	3	3
616,261	Concerto grosso, op. 6, no. 11 (11 min.) **(3-Argo ZRG–773/5)	S	3	3
616,262	Concerto grosso, op. 6, no. 12 (12 min.) **(3-Argo ZRG–773/5); *(3–DG ARC–2710011)	S	3	3

COUPERIN, FRANÇOIS (1668–1733)

616,500	*Apothéose de Lully* (24 min.) **(Oiseau S–300); *(DG ARC–2533067)	S	3	3
616,750	*Le Parnasse* (*Apothéose de Corelli*) (15 min.) *(DG ARC–2533067)	S	3	3

DEBUSSY, CLAUDE (1862–1918)

617,000	*Boîte à joujoux* (children's ballet) (29 min.) *(Lon. STS–15042)	A	3	3

GUIDE NO.	COMPOSER AND TITLE	AGE MIN	AES SIG	AC- CESS
17,250	Clair de lune (orchestra arrangement) (4 min.) (Col. MS–6575)	E	3	1
17,500	Danse (1890) (orchestration by Ravel) (Tarantelle styrienne) (5 min.) *(Lon. STS–15022)	S	4	2
17,750	Ibéria (no. 2 from Images pour orchestre) (20 min.) **(RCA VIC–1246)-mono; (None. H–71189); (RCA VICS–1025)	S	2	2
18,000	Images pour orchestre (3) (complete) (37 min.) **(Lon. CS 6225)	S	2	3
18,250	Gigues (8 min.) **(Lon. CS 6225)	S	3	3
18,500	Rondes de Printemps (8 min.) **(Lon. CS 6225)	S	3	3
18,750	Jeux-Poeme dansé (17 min.) *(Lon. STS–15022)	A	4	3
19,000	La Mer (24 min.) **(RCA VIC 1246)-mono; *(Ang. S–35977); *(DG 138923); *(Odys. Y–31928); (Lon. CS 6437)	E	1	2
19,250	Nocturnes (Nuages, Fêtes, Sirènes) (24 min.) *(Ang. S–35977); *(Sera. S–60104)	S	2	1
19,500	Nuages only (9 min.) *(Ang. S–35977); *(Sera. S–60104)	S	2	1
19,750	Fêtes only (6 min.) *(Ang. S–35977); *(Sera. S–60104)	S	2	1
20,000	Sirènes only (10 min.) *(Ang. S–35977); *(Sera. S–60104)	S	2	1
20,250	Prélude à l'après-midi d'un faune (9 min.) *(DG 138923); *(RCA VICS–1323); *(Sera. S–60177)	E	2	1
20,500	Printemps (15 min.) *(Lon. STS–15042)	A	5	3
	DELIBES, LÉO (1836–1891)			
21,000	Coppélia (complete ballet) (1 hr., 28 min.) *(2–Lon. CSA 2229)	E	4	1
21,100	Coppélia: Suite (23 min.) *(DG 136257); *(Ev. 3116)	E	4	1
21,250	Sylvia: Procession of Bacchus (7 min.) *(Ev. 3116)	E	4	1
21,500	Sylvia: Suite (17–22 min.) *(Ev. 3116)	E	4	1
	DELIUS, FREDERICK (1862–1934)			
21,750	Brigg Fair (18 min.) **(Sera. S–60185)	A	4	3
22,000	In a Summer Garden (15 min.) **(Ang. S–36588)	A	4	3
22,250	Irmelin Prelude (6 min.) **(Sera. S–60000); *(Ang. S–36415)	A	4	2
22,500	On Hearing the First Cuckoo in Spring (7 min.) **(Sera. S–60185); *(Ang. S–36588)	S	3	2

GUIDE NO.	COMPOSER AND TITLE	AGE MIN	AES SIG	AC- CESS
622,750	Over the Hills and Far Away (14 min.) **(Sera. S–60212)	A	4	2
623,000	Paris (24 min.) *(Ang. S–36870)	A	5	3
623,250	Song of Summer (11 min.) **(Ang. S–36415)	A	5	3
623,500	Summer Night on the River (7 min.) **(Sera. S–60185); *(Ang. S–36588)	A	4	3
623,750	Walk to the Paradise Garden (10 min.) **(Ang. S–36415)	S	3	2
	DELLO JOIO, NORMAN (1913–)			
624,000	Meditations on Ecclesiastes (26 min.) (CRI 110)-mono	S	3	3
624,250	Serenade (18 min.) (2–Desto 6413/4E)-mono	S	4	3
	DIAMOND, DAVID (1915–)			
624,500	Romeo and Juliet (1947) (18 min.) (CRI 216)	S	4	3
	DUKAS, PAUL (1865–1935)			
625,000	La Péri (17 min.) *(Lon. STS–15022)	E	4	2
625,250	Sorcerer's Apprentice (11 min.) **(RCA VIC–1267)-mono; *(Lon. CS 6367); *(Lon. STS–15005); *(Sera. S–60177); (Col. MS–6943)	E	3	1
	DUTILLEUX, HENRI (1916–)			
625,500	Loup (ballet) (1953) (20 min.) *(Ang. S–35932)	A	4	3
	DVOŘÁK, ANTONIN (1841–1904)			
626,000	Amid Nature, op. 91 (overture) (14 min.) **(Lon. CS 6526)	S	3	2
626,250	Carnival Overture, op. 92 (9 min.) **(Lon. CS 6495); **(RCA VICS–1424)	S	3	1
626,500	Golden Spinning Wheel, op. 109 (symphonic poem) (21 min.) **(Lon. CS 6721)	S	3	2
626,750	Husitska (dramatic overture) op. 67 (14 min.) **(Lon. CS 6525); **(Lon. CS 6746)	S	5	1
626,800	My Home, op. 62 (overture) (9 min.) **(Lon. CS 6511)	S	4	2
627,000	Noonday Witch, op. 108 (14 min.) **(Lon. CS 6746)	S	4	1
627,250	Othello: Overture, op. 93 (16 min.) **(Lon. CS 6527)	A	3	2
627,750	Scherzo Capriccioso, op. 66 (12 min.) **(Lon. CS 6358); *(Sera. S–60098)	A	3	2

GUIDE NO.	COMPOSER AND TITLE	AGE MIN	AES SIG	ACCESS
628,000	Serenade in E for Strings, op. 22 (27 min.) *(Lon. STS–15037)	S	2	1
628,250	Serenade in d, op. 44 (25 min.) **(Lon. CS 6594)	S	3	2
628,500	*Slavonic Dances,* op. 46, (complete) nos. 1–8 (38 min.) *(Col. MS–7208)	E	3	2
628,501	*Slavonic Dance,* op. 46, no. 1 (4 min.) *(Lon. STS–15009)	E	3	1
628,503	*Slavonic Dance,* op. 46, no. 3 (5 min.) *(Lon. STS–15009)	E	3	1
628,508	*Slavonic Dance,* op. 46, no. 8 (4 min.) *(Lon. STS–15009)	E	3	1
628,750	*Slavonic Dances,* op. 72 (complete) 9–16 (36 min.) *(Col. MS–7208)	E	4	2
628,751	*Slavonic Dance,* op. 72, no. 1 (4 min.) *(Col. MS–7208); *(Lon. STS–15009)	E	4	1
628,752	*Slavonic Dance,* op. 72, no. 2 (6 min.) *(Col. MS–7208); *(Lon. STS–15009)	E	4	1
628,757	*Slavonic Dance,* op. 72, no. 7 (3 min.) *(Col. MS–7208)	E	4	1
629,000	*Symphonic Variations,* op. 78 (23 min.) **(Lon. CS 6721)	A	3	2
	ELGAR, EDWARD (1857–1934)			
629,750	*Cockaigne* Overture, op. 40 (1901) (15 min.) *(Ang. S–36120)	S	3	1
630,000	*Enigma Variations,* op. 36 (30 min.) *(Ang. S–36120); *(Ang. S–36799)	S	2	1
630,250	*Falstaff* (symphonic study), op. 68 (35 min.) **(2–Sera. S–6033)	A	2	3
630,500	*Introduction and Allegro* for Strings, op. 47 (14 min.) **(Ang. S–36101); *(Lon. CS 6618)	S	3	2
630,751	*Pomp and Circumstance* March, op. 39, no. 1 (7 min.) *(Ang. S–36403); *(Lon. STS–15112)	E	3	1
630,752	*Pomp and Circumstance* March, op. 39, no. 2 (5 min.) *(Ang. S–36403); *(Lon. STS–15112)	E	4	2
630,753	*Pomp and Circumstance* March, op. 39, no. 3 (6 min.) *(Ang. S–36403); *(Lon. STS–15112)	E	4	2
630,754	*Pomp and Circumstance* March, op. 39, no. 4 (6 min.) *(Ang. S–36403); *(Lon. STS–15112)	E	3	1
630,755	*Pomp and Circumstance* March, op. 39, no. 5	E	3	2
	*(Ang. S–36403); *(Lon. STS–15112)			
631,000	Serenade in e for Strings, op. 20 (13 min.) **(Ang. S–36101)	S	4	2
	ENESCO, GEORGES (1881–1955)			
631,251	*Roumanian Rhapsody* no. 1, op. 11 (11 min.) *(Mer. 75018); (Van. SRV–160SD)	E	4	1
631,252	*Roumanian Rhapsody* no. 2, op. 11 (11 min.) *(Mer. 75018); (Van. SRV–160SD)	E	5	2
	FALLA, MANUEL DE (1876–1946)			
631,500	*Ritual Fire Dance* from *El Amor Brujo* (4 min.) *(Ang. S–36385)	E	3	1
631,750	*Three Cornered Hat* (complete ballet) (38 min.) *(Ang. S–36235); (Lon. CS 6224)	E	3	2
632,000	*Vida breve:* Dance no. 1 (3 min.) *(Lon. CS 6224)	E	3	1
632,250	*Vida breve:* Interlude and Dance, no. 1 (8 min.) *(Lon. CS 6224)	E	3	2
	FAURÉ, GABRIEL (1845–1924)			
632,500	*Dolly,* op. 56 (orchestral version) (18 min.) **(Sera. S–60084)	E	4	2
632,750	*Pavane,* op. 50 (7 min.) **(Sera. S–60134)	E	3	2
633,000	*Pelléas et Mélisande,* op. 80 (18 min.) *(Odys. Y–31017)	S	2	2
	FRANCK, CÉSAR (1822–1890)			
633,500	*Chasseur maudit* (symphonic poem) (14 min.) *(Lon. CS 6222)	S	4	2
	GABRIELI, GIOVANNI (1551–1612)			
636,250	*Canzona primi toni a 8* (4 min.) *(Argo ZRG–644)	S	3	3
637,250	*Canzona noni toni* (3 min.) *(Oiseau S–276)	S	3	3
637,600	*Sonata pian' e forte* (5 min.) (None. H–71118)	S	3	2
	GEMINIANI, FRANCESCO (1687–1762)			
638,000	Concerto grosso, op. 2, no. 3 (6 min.) (None. H–71052)	A	4	1
638,250	Concerto grosso, op. 3, no. 2 (9 min.) (Mace. S–9077)	A	4	1
638,253	Concerto grosso, op. 3, no. 3 (10 min.) *(Oiseau S–277)	A	4	1
	GERHARD, ROBERTO (1896–1970)			
639,000	Concerto for Orchestra (22 min.) *(Argo ZRG–553)	A	4	3

GUIDE NO.	COMPOSER AND TITLE	AGE MIN	AES SIG	AC-CESS
	GERMAN, EDWARD (1862–1936)			
639,500	Three dances from *Henry VIII* (8 min.) (RCA LM–1803)-*mono*	E	4	1
	GERSHWIN, GEORGE (1898–1937)			
640,000	*American in Paris* (18 min.) *(Col. MS–6091); *(Ang. S–36810)	E	4	1
640,250	*Cuban Overture* (11 min.) *(Ang. S–36070)	E	5	2
640,500	*Porgy and Bess* (symphonic picture) (25 min.) *(Ang. S–36070); (RCA LSC–3130)	E	3	1
	GINASTERA, ALBERTO (1916–)			
641,000	*Estancia* (ballet suite) (12 min.) (Ev. 3013)	S	4	3
641,500	*Variaciones Concertantes* (1953) (12 min.) (RCA LSC–3029)	S	3	3
	GLAZOUNOV, ALEXANDER (1865–1936)			
642,000	*Seasons*, op. 67 (36 min.) *(Lon. CS 6509)	E	3	2
642,500	*Autumn* (9 min.) (Lon. CS 6509)	E	3	1
	GLIÈRE, REINHOLD (1875–1956)			
643,000	*Red Poppy*, op. 70 (ballet suite) (18–28 min.) (Mel./Ang. S–40089); (Turn. 34218)	S	5	2
643,500	*Russian Sailors' Dance* (5 min.) (Mel./Ang. S–40089); (Turn. 34218)	E	4	1
	GLINKA, MIKHAIL (1804–1857)			
644,000	*Jota Aragonesa* (9 min.) *(Mel./Ang. S–40081); (Col. M–30390)	S	5	1
644,250	*Kamarinskaya* (7 min.) *(Mel./Ang. S–40081)	S	4	1
644,500	*Russlan and Ludmila*: Overture (5 min.) **(Lon. CS 6785)	E	3	1
645,000	*Valse-Fantaisie* (9 min.) *(Mel./Ang. S–40081)	S	5	2
	GLUCK, CHRISTOPH WILLIBALD (1714–1787)			
646,000	*Don Juan* (ballet) (27 min.) **(Lon. STS–15169)	S	4	2
646,500	*Iphigénie en Aulide*: Overture (11 min.) (Ang. S–36175)	S	3	2 .
	GOTTSCHALK, LOUIS MOREAU (1829–1869)			
647,000	*Nuit des Tropiques* (symphonic poem) (6 min.) (Van. SRV–275 SD)	S	5	3
	GOULD, MORTON (1913–)			
648,000	*American Salute* (5 min.) (Turn. 34459)	E	4	1
648,250	*Latin American Symphonette* (21 min.) (Van. SRV–275SD)	E	4	2
648,500	*Spirituals* for Orchestra (19 min.) (Ev. 3002)	E	4	1
	GOUNOD, CHARLES (1818–1893)			
649,000	*Faust* (ballet music) (17 min.) *(DG 2530199); *(Lon. CS 6780)	E	4	1
	GRÉTRY, ANDRÉ (1741–1813)			
651,000	*Céphale et Procris* (15 min.) *(Oiseau S–297)	E	4	2
651,500	*L'Épreuve villageoise* (ballet music) (10 min.) *(Oiseau S–297)	E	4	2
	GRIEG, EDVARD (1843–1907)			
652,000	*Holberg* Suite, op. 40 (18 min.) *(Van. VCS–10067); (Lon. STS–15044)	S	3	1
652,250	*Homage* March (9 min.) *(DG 2530243)	E	4	1
652,750	*Jorsalfar* Suite (14 min.) *(DG 2530243)	S	4	2
653,000	*Last Spring* (arr.) (6 min.) *(Van. VCS–10067)	E	4	1
653,250	*Lyric Suite*, op. 54 (15 min.) (Sera. S–60032)	E	4	1
653,500	*Notturno* (4 min.) (Sera. S–60032)	E	4	1
653,750	*Norwegian Dance* no. 2, op. 35 (3 min.) *(Ang. S–36803); (Sera. S–60032)	E	4	1
654,000	*Peer Gynt* Suite no. 1, op. 46 (14 min.) *(Ang. S–36803); *(Col. MS–6877); *(Col. M–31800); *(DG 2530243) (Col. MS–6196)	E	3	1
654,250	*Peer Gynt* Suite no. 2, op. 55 (16 min.) *(Ang. S–36803); *(Col. M–31800); *(DG 2530243)	E	3	1
654,500	*Symphonic Dances*, op. 64 (27 min.) (Vox 510330)	E	4	2
654,750	*Two Elegiac Melodies*, op. 34 (9 min.) *(Van. VCS–10067)-no. 1 only; (Vox 510330)	E	4	1
	GROFÉ, FERDE (1892–1972)			
656,000	*Grand Canyon Suite* (32 min.) (Col. M–31824)	E	4	1
	GUARNIERI, CAMARGO (1907–)			
657,000	*Dansa Brasileira* (2 min.) *(Col. MS–6514)	E	3	1

117

GUIDE NO.	COMPOSER AND TITLE	AGE MIN	AES SIG	AC- CESS
	HANDEL, GEORGE FRIDERIC (1685–1759)			
659,000	Ballet Music: *Alcina, Ariodante, Il Pastor Fido* **(Argo ZRG–686)	S	2	2
659,200	*Berenice* (overture) (8 min.) *(Argo 5442); *(Lon. CS 6586)	A	4	2
659,250	Concerti grossi (6), op. 3 (vary) **(DG ARC–2533116)	S	3	2
659,751	Concerto grosso, op. 6, no. 1 (13 min.) *(DG ARC–2533088); *(3–Lon. CSA 2309); *(Oiseau S–264); *(3–Phi. SC71AX302)	S	2	1
659,752	Concerto grosso, op. 6, no. 2 (13 min.) *(DG ARC–2533088); *(3–Lon. CSA 2309); *(3–Phi. SC71AX302)	S	2	2
659,753	Concerto grosso, op. 6, no. 3 (13 min.) *(DG ARC–2533141); *(3–Lon. CSA 2309); *(3–Phi. SC71AX302)	S	2	2
659,754	Concerto grosso, op. 6. no. 4 (13 min.) *(DG ARC–2533141); *(3–Lon. CSA 2309); *(Oiseau S–276); *(3–Phi. SC71AX302)	S	2	1
659,755	Concerto grosso, op. 6, no. 5 (16 min.) *(DG ARC–2533142); *(3–Lon. CSA 2309); *(3–Phi. SC71AX302)	S	3	2
659,756	Concerto grosso, op. 6, no. 6 (17 min.) *(DG ARC–2533159); *(3–Lon. CSA 2309); *(3–Phi. SC71AX302)	S	2	1
659,757	Concerto grosso, op. 6, no. 7 (15 min.) *(DG ARC–2533159); *(3–Lon. CSA 2309); *(3–Phi. SC71AX302)	S	2	2
659,758	Concerto grosso, op. 6, no. 8 (15 min.) *(DG ARC–2533142); *(3–Lon. CSA 2309); *(3–Phi. SC71AX302)	S	2	2
659,759	Concerto grosso, op. 6, no. 9 (15 min.) *(DG ARC–2533142); *(3–Lon. CSA 2309); *(3–Phi. SC71AX302)	S	2	2
659,760	Concerto grosso, op. 6, no. 10 (16 min.) *(DG ARC–2533088); *(3–Lon. CSA 2309); *(3–Phi. SC71AX302)	S	2	2
659,761	Concerto grosso, op. 6, no. 11 (18 min.) *(DG ARC–2533141); *(3–Lon. CSA 2309); *(3–Phi. SC71AX302)	S	2	2
659,762	Concerto grosso, op. 6, no. 12 (14 min.) *(DG ARC–2533088); *(3–Lon. CSA 2309); *(3–Phi. SC71AX302)	S	2	1
659,800	Concerto in C (*Alexanderfest*) (13 min.) **(Oiseau 60013); *(DG ARC–2533159)	S	3	2
660,000	*Faithful Shepherd* Suite (arranged by Beecham) (25 min.) **(CSP AML–4374)-*mono*	E	2	1
660,500	*Royal Fireworks* Music (14–24 min.) **(Lon. CS 6236); *(Argo ZRG–697); *(BASF 2020350); *(DG ARC–2533151)	E	2	2
660,750	Sinfonia: *Jephtha* (3 min.) *(Lon. CS 6586)	E	2	1
661,000	*Water Music* (complete) (49 min.) *(Ang. S–36173); *(Argo ZRG–697); *(BASF 20341)	S	2	1
662,000	*Water Music*: Suite (29 min.) **(Lon. CS 6236)	E	2	1
	HARRISON, LOU (1917–)			
663,000	Suite for Symphonic Strings (32 min.) (Lou. 621)-*mono*	A	4	3
	HAYDN, (FRANZ) JOSEPH (1732–1809)			
664,500	Overture no. 14 in B flat (*Armida*) (5 min.) *(None. H–71032)	A	4	1
664,750	Overture no. 16 in B flat (*Orlando Paladino*) (3 min.) *(Van. VSD 71126)	A	4	2
665,000	Sinfonia Concertante in B flat, op. 84 (22 min.) *(DG 2530398); *(6–Lon. STS–15229/34); *(None. H–71024)	S	3	2
	HÉROLD, LOUIS JOSEPH F. (1791–1833)			
667,000	Overture to *Zampa* (8 min.) (Col. M–31815); (Lon. STS–15021)	E	5	1
	HINDEMITH, PAUL (1895–1963)			
668,000	*Concert Music* for Strings and Brass, op. 50 (16 min.) **(DG 2530246); *(Sera. S–60005)	A	2	2
668,500	Five Pieces for String Orchestra, op. 44, no. 4 (13 min.) *(Argo ZRG–763)	A	3	3
669,000	*Symphonic Metamorphoses of Themes by Weber* (19 min.) **(Col. MS–7166); *(Col. MS–7426)	A	3	2
669,500	March only (4 min.) **(Col. MS–7166); *(Col. MS–7426)	E	3	1
	HOLST, GUSTAV (1874–1934)			
670,500	*The Planets*, op. 32 (49 min.) **(Ang. S–36420); *(Ang. S–36991); *(Lon. CS 6244)	E	3	2

GUIDE NO.	COMPOSER AND TITLE	AGE MIN	AES SIG	AC- CESS
570,750	Mercury only (5 min.) **(Ang. S–36420); *(Ang. S–36991); *(Lon. CS 6244)	E	2	1
571,000	St. Paul's Suite for Strings (13 min.) *(Ang. S–36883)	S	4	2
571,250	Suite no. 1 for Band (9 min.) (Cornell U. 5)	S	4	2
	HONEGGER, ARTHUR (1892–1955)			
572,000	Pacific 231 (6 min.) *(Lon. CS 6367); (Col. MS–6659); (Van. SRV–274 SD)	E	3	2
572,250	Pastorale d'été (8 min.) (Col. MS–6659)	S	3	2
572,500	Rugby (7 min.) (Col. MS–6659)	S	4	3
	HOVHANESS, ALAN (1911–)			
573,000	And God Created Great Whales (12 min.) *(Col. M–30390)	E	4	1
573,250	Fra Angelico (15 min.) (Orion 7268)	S	4	2
573,500	Mysterious Mountain, op. 132 (19 min.) *(RCA LSC–2251)	S	4	2
	HUMPERDINCK, ENGEL-BERT (1854–1921)			
574,000	Dream Pantomime from Hansel and Gretel (9 min.) (Ang. S–36175)	E	3	2
574,250	Hansel and Gretel (over-ture) (8 min.) (Ang. S–36175)	E	3	2
574,500	Hansel and Gretel (prayer) (3 min.) (Ang. S–36175)	E	3	1
	IBERT, JACQUES (1890–1962)			
575,000	Divertissement (15 min.) **(Lon. STS–15093)	E	2	1
575,500	Escales (Ports of Call) (15 min.) *(RCA VICS–1323)	E	3	2
	IPPOLITOV-IVANOV, MIKHAIL (1859–1935)			
576,000	Caucasian Sketches, op. 10 (22 min.) (Mel./Ang. S–40119); (Turn. 34218)	E	4	2
576,250	In the Village only (5 min.) (Mel./Ang. S–40119); (Turn. 34218)	E	4	1
576,500	Procession of the Sardar only (4 min.) (Mel./Ang. S–40119); (Turn. 34218)	E	3	1
	IRELAND, JOHN (1879–1962)			
577,000	London Overture (12 min.) **(Ang. S–36415)	S	3	1
	IVES, CHARLES (1874–1954)			
578,000	Browning Overture (20 min.)	A	4	3

GUIDE NO.	COMPOSER AND TITLE	AGE MIN	AES SIG	AC- CESS
	*(Col. MS–7015); (Van. VCS–10013)			
678,250	Central Park in the Dark (17 min.) **(Col. MS–6843)	A	4	3
678,500	Circus Band March (4 min.) (Van. VCS–10013)	E	4	2
678,750	Decoration Day from Holidays (9 min.) **(Col. MS–6843); (Lou. 621)-mono	A	3	2
679,000	Fourth of July from Holidays (6 min.) **(Col. MS–6889)	A	4	3
679,250	From the Steeples and the Mountains (4 min.) *(Col. MS–7318); (Turn. 34398)	A	4	3
679,500	Halloween (2 min.) (Cam. 1804); (3–Van. VCS–10032/3/4)	S	4	2
679,750	Over the Pavements (5 min.) *(Col. MS–7318) (Cam. 1804)	A	4	3
680,000	Three Places in New England (17 min.) **(DG 2530048); (Col. MS–7015); (Col. MS–6684)	A	3	3
680,250	Unanswered Question (6 min.) **(Col. MS–6843); *(RCA LSC–2893); (Van. VCS–10013)	A	2	2
680,500	Variations on America (William Schuman orches-tration) (8 min.) *(RCA LSC–2893)	E	3	1
680,750	Washington's Birthday from Holidays (12 min.) *(Col. MS–7015)	A	3	3
	JANÁČEK, LEOŠ (1854–1928)			
681,250	Sinfonietta (22 min.) **(Col. MS–7166); *(Ang. S–36045); *(DG 2530075)			
681,500	Taras Bulba (22 min.) *(DG 2530075)	S	3	3
	KABALEVSKY, DMITRI (1904–)			
683,000	Colas Breugnon Overture, op. 24 (5 min.) *(RCA VICS–1068)	S	4	1
683,250	Comedians, op. 26 (17 min.) (RCA LSC–2398)	E	4	1
683,500	Galop only (2 min.) (RCA LSC–2398)	E	4	1
	KHACHATURIAN, ARAM (1903–)			
684,000	Gayne Ballet Suite (21–29 min.) **(Lon. CS 6322)	E	5	1
684,250	Dance of the Rose Maidens only (2 min.) **(Lon. CS 6322)	E	4	1
684,500	Lullaby only (5 min.) **(Lon. CS 6322)	E	4	1
684,750	Sabre Dance only (2 min.) **(Lon. CS 6322)	E	4	1
685,000	Masquerade Suite (15 min.) (RCA LSC–2398)	E	4	1

GUIDE NO.	COMPOSER AND TITLE	AGE MIN	AES SIG	AC-CESS
685,250	*Galop* (3 min.) (RCA LSC–2398)	E	4	1
	KODÁLY, ZOLTÁN (1882–1967)			
686,000	*Concerto for Orchestra* (21 min.) (Col. MS–7034)	S	3	2
686,250	*Galanta Dances* (16 min.) **(Lon. CS 6417); (Col. MS–7034)	S	3	1
686,500	*Háry János:* Suite (23 min.) **(Lon. CS 6417); *(Col. MS–7408)	E	2	1
686,750	*Marosszék Dances* (13 min.) (Col. MS–7034)	S	3	2
687,000	*Peacock Variations* (25 min.) **(Lon. OS 26186)	A	3	2
	LALANDE, MICHEL-RICHARD DE (1657–1726)			
688,000	*Symphonies pour les soupers du roi,* no. 1 (10 min.) (None. H–71009)	A	4	2
	LIADOV, ANATOL (1855–1914)			
691,000	*Baba Yaga,* op. 56 (3 min.) *(Lon. STS–15066); *(Mel./Ang. S–40159)	E	4	2
691,250	*Eight Russian Folksongs,* op. 58 (14 min.) *(Lon. STS–15066); *(Mel./Ang. S–40159)	E	4	2
691,500	*The Enchanted Lake* (7 min.) *(Mel./Ang. S–40159)	S	3	1
691,750	*Kikimora,* op. 63 (8 min.) *(Lon. STS–15066); *(Mel./Ang. S–40159)	S	4	2
	LISZT, FRANZ (1811–1886)			
692,000	*Hamlet,* Symphonic Poem no. 10 **(Phi. 6500046)	S	4	2
692,250	*Battle of the Huns,* Symphonic Poem no. 11 (14 min.) *(Phi. 6500189)	S	5	2
692,500	*Hungaria,* Symphonic Poem no. 9 (22 min.) **(Phi. 6500046)	S	5	3
692,750	*Hungrian Rhapsody* no. 1 in f (11 min.) (Col. M–30645)	S	3	1
693,000	*Hungarian Rhapsody* no. 2 (10 min.) *(Mer. 75018)	S	3	1
693,125	*Hungarian Rhapsody* no. 3 (6 min.) *(Mer. 75018)	S	4	1
693,250	*Hungarian Rhapsody* no. 4 (12 min.) *(DG 138692); (Col. M–30645)	S	4	1
693,500	*Hungarian Rhapsody* no. 5 (12 min.) *(DG 138692); *(Van. SRV–160)	S	4	1
693,750	*Hungarian Rhapsody* no. 6 (12 min.) *(Van. SRV–160)	S	4	1
694,000	*Mazeppa,* Symphonic Poem no. 6 (16 min.) **(Lon. CS 6738);	S	4	2
	**(Phi. 6500046); *(DG 138692)			
694,250	*Mephisto-Waltz* (11 min.) *(RCA VICS–1025)	S	4	2
694,500	*Orpheus,* Symphonic Poem no. 4 (11 min.) **(Lon. CS 6738); *(Phi. 839788)	S	4	2
694,750	*Les Préludes,* Symphonic Poem no. 3 (16 min.) *(Lon. CS 6529); (Phi. 839788)	S	4	1
695,000	*Tasso-Lament and Triumph,* Symphonic Poem no. 2 (20 min.) *(Phi. 839788)	S	5	2
	LOCATELLI, PIETRO (1695–1764)			
696,000	*Concerto grosso,* op. 1, no. 8 (*Christmas*) (19 min.) (DG 2530070)	A	3	1
696,500	*Introduzione teatrale* no. 5 in D, op. 4 no. 5 (7 min.) *(Phi. 802901)	E	3	1
	LOEFFLER, CHARLES MARTIN (1861–1935)			
697,000	*Pagan Poem* (24 min.) (Sera. S–60080)	S	4	2
	LULLY, JEAN BAPTISTE (1632–1687)			
698,250	*Marches and Fanfares* (about 2 min. each) (None. H–71009)	S	4	2
	LUTOSLAWSKI, WITOLD (1913–)			
699,000	*Concerto for Orchestra* (29 min.) *(Ang. S–36045)	S	3	2
	MACDOWELL, EDWARD (1861–1908)			
700,000	*Suite* no. 2, op. 48 (*Indian* Suite) (33 min.) *(Mer. 75026)	S	3	1
	MASCAGNI, PIETRO (1863–1945)			
704,000	*Intermezzo* from *Cavalleria Rusticana* (3 min.) *(Lon. STS–15043)	S	3	1
	MASSENET, JULES (1842–1912)			
705,000	*Le Cid* (ballet suite) (9 min.) **(Lon. STS–15051)	S	5	1
	MENDELSSOHN, FELIX (1809–1847)			
707,000	*Calm Sea and Prosperous Voyage* Overture, op. 27 (12 min.) *(Lon. STS–15076)	A	4	3
707,250	*Fair Melusina* Overture, op. 32 (11 min.) *(Lon. CS 6436); (None. H–71099)	A	4	3
707,500	*Fingal's Cave* (*Hebrides*) Overture, op. 26 (10 min.) **(Lon. STS–15091); **(RCA VICS–1424); *(DG 2530126); *(Lon. CS 6436)	A	3	1
707,750	*Midsummer Night's Dream:* Incidental Music op. 21	E	3	2

GUIDE NO.	COMPOSER AND TITLE	AGE MIN	AES SIG	AC-CESS
	and 61 (22–48 min.)			
	*(Col. MS–7002)-op. 61 only;			
	*(DG 138959)			
708,250	*Wedding March* (5 min.)	E	2	1
	*(Col. MS–7002);			
	*(DG 138959)			
708,500	*Ruy Blas* Overture (8 min.)	S	4	1
	**(Phi. 802858);			
	*(Lon. CS 6436)			
	MEYERBEER, GIACOMO (1791–1864)			
710,500	*Les Patineurs* (ballet arranged by Lambert) (13 min.)	E	3	1
	**(Lon. STS–15051)			
	MILHAUD, DARIUS (1892–1974)			
711,000	*Le Boeuf sur le toit* (15 min.)	S	3	2
	(None. H–71122)			
711,250	Concerto for Percussion and Small Orchestra (7 min.)	A	4	2
	(Can. 31013)			
711,500	*Création du monde* (16 min.)	S	3	2
	*(Ang. S–35932);			
	*(None. H–71281);			
	(None. H–71122)			
711,750	*L'Homme et son désir*, op. 48 (Ballet) (17 min.)	A	4	2
	*(Can. 31008);			
	(Van. SRV–274)			
712,000	*Suite française* (17 min.)	S	3	2
	(Coro. S–1502)			
	MOORE, DOUGLAS (1893–1969)			
713,000	*In Memoriam* (10 min.)	A	3	3
	(CRI 127)-*mono*			
	MOURET, JEAN JOSEPH (1682–1738)			
714,000	Suite de simphonïes (1) (8 min.)	A	5	3
	(None. H–71009)			
	MOZART, LEOPOLD (1719–1787)			
715,000	*Musical Sleigh Ride* (24 min.)	E	3	1
	*(Turn. 34134)			
	MOZART, WOLFGANG AMADEUS (1756–1791)			
716,000	*Abduction from the Seraglio* (*Die Entführung aus dem Serail*) Overture (6 min.)	S	3	2
	*(Sera. S–60037);			
	(Ang. S–36289)			
716,250	Adagio and Fugue in c, K. 546 (8 min.)	A	3	3
	*(Ang. S–36289);			
	*(Phi. 6500537);			
	*(5–Tel. 56.35017);			
	(DG 253006)			
716,500	Cassation 1 in G, K. 63 (22 min.)	A	4	3
	(Turn. 34373)			
716,750	Cassation 2 in B flat, K. 99 (28 min.)	A	5	3
	(Turn. 34373)			
717,000	*Cosi Fan Tutte* Overture (5 min.)	S	2	2
	*(Odys. Y–30048);			
	*(Sera. S–60037);			
	(Ang. S–36289)			

GUIDE NO.	COMPOSER AND TITLE	AGE MIN	AES SIG	AC-CESS
717,250	Divertimento no. 1 in E flat, K. 113 (12 min.)	S	3	3
	**(Lon. STS–15170)			
	Divertimenti for String Orchestra			
717,500	Divertimento no. 1 in D, K. 136 (13 min.)	S	2	2
	**(Argo ZRG–554);			
	**(Lon. STS–15170);			
	*(Phi. 6500536)			
717,750	Divertimento no. 2 in B flat, K. 137 (11 min.)	S	3	2
	**(Argo ZRG–554);			
	*(Phi. 6500536)			
718,000	Divertimento no. 3 in F, K. 138 (10 min.)	S	3	2
	**(Argo ZRG–554);			
	*(Phi. 6500536)			
718,250	Divertimento no. 10 in F, K. 247 (30 min.)	S	2	2
	*(Phi. 6500538)			
718,500	Divertimento no. 11 in D, K. 251 (24 min.)	S	2	2
	*(Lon. STS–15035);			
	*(Phi. 6500538)			
718,750	Divertimento no. 17 in D, K. 334 for Horns and Strings (44 min.)	S	2	2
	**(Van. VCS–10066);			
	*(Argo ZRG–705)			
719,000	Minuet in D for Strings only	E	2	2
	**(Sera. S–60057);			
	**(Van. VCS–10066);			
	*(Argo ZRG–705)			
719,250	*Don Giovanni* Overture (6 min.)	S	1	2
	*(Ang. S–36289);			
	*(Sera. S–60037)			
719,500	German Dances (6), K. 509 (11 min.)	E	3	2
	(Mace. S–9070)			
720,250	German Dances (3), K. 605 (7 min.)	E	3	2
	**(Sera. S–60057)			
720,500	*Impressario Overture* (4 min.)	S	3	2
	*(Odys. Y–30048);			
	*(Sera. S–60037)			
720,750	*Magic Flute* Overture (7 min.)	E	3	1
	**(3–Sera. 6015)-*mono*;			
	*(Ang. S–36289);			
	*(Odys. Y–30048);			
	*(Sera. S–60037)			
721,500	March in D, K. 408/1 (2 min.)	E	4	2
	*(None. H–71194)			
721,750	March in D, K. 408/2 (4 min.)	E	4	2
	*(None. H–71194)			
722,000	*Marriage of Figaro* Overture (4 min.)	E	2	1
	*(Col. MS–6858);			
	*(Odys. Y–30048);			
	*(Sera. S–60037);			
	*(Ang. S–36289)			
722,250	*Musical Joke*, K. 522 (18 min.)	S	4	2
	*(Turn. 34134)			
722,500	*Masonic Funeral Music*, K. 477 (6 min.)	A	3	3
	*(Ang. S–36289);			
	*(Odys. Y–30048)			

GUIDE NO.	COMPOSER AND TITLE	AGE MIN	AES SIG	AC- CESS
722,750	*Les Petits Riens* (ballet music), K. Anh. 10, K. 299b (20 min.) (Lon. STS–15044)	E	3	2
723,000	Serenade no. 4 in D, K. 203 (34 min.) *(Lon. STS–15077); *(None. H–71194)	A	3	2
723,250	Serenade no. 6 in D, K. 239 (*Serenata Notturna*) (13 min.) **(Sera. S–60057); *(Argo ZRG–554); *(Phi. 6500536)	E	3	2
723,500	Serenade no. 7 in D, K. 250 (*Haffner*) (52 min.) *(BASF 29310)	A	3	2
723,750	Serenade no. 9 in D, K. 320 (*Posthorn*) (39 min.) *(Col. MS–7273)	A	3	3
724,000	Serenade no. 12 in c, K. 388 (24 min.) (Ang. S–36536)	A	3	3
724,250	Serenade no. 13 in G, K. 525 (*Eine kleine Nachtmusik*) (17 min.) **(Phi. 6500537); **(Sera. S–60057); *(DG 139004); *(Odys. Y–30048); *(5–Tel. 56.35017); (Col. MS–7273); (Lon. STS–15141)	S	2	1
724,500	*Romanze* only **(Sera. S–60057)	E	2	1
	MUSSORGSKY, MODEST (1839–1881)			
725,250	*Khovantchina*: Prelude to Act I (5 min.) **(Lon. CS 6785)	S	3	2
725,500	*Night on Bald Mountain* (11 min.) **(Lon. CS 6785); **(RCA VICS–1068); *(DG 138033); (Col. MS–6943)	E	3	1
725,750	*Pictures at an Exhibition* (31 min.) **(DG 139010); **(RCA VIC–1273)-*mono*; *(Odys. Y–32223)	E	2	1
	NICOLAI, OTTO (1810–1849)			
726,000	*Merry Wives of Windsor* Overture (9 min.) *(Lon. CS 6605); (Col. MS–7085); (Lon. STS–15021)	S	4	1
	NIELSEN, CARL (1865–1931)			
727,000	*Saga-Dream*, op. 39 (9 min.) **(None. H–71236)	A	4	3
	OFFENBACH, JACQUES (1819–1880)			
727,200	*Barcarolle* from *Tales of Hoffmann* (4 min.) (RCA VICS–1466)	E	3	1
727,250	*La Belle Hélène* Overture (8 min.) (Kla. 517)	S	4	2
727,500	*Gaîté Parisienne* (arranged by Rosenthal) (38 min.)	S	4	1

GUIDE NO.	COMPOSER AND TITLE	AGE MIN	AES SIG	AC- CESS
	*(DG 2530199); *(Lon. CS 6780)			
727,750	*Grand Duchess of Gérolstein* Overture (Kla. 517)	S	5	3
728,000	*Orpheus in Hades* Overture (10 min.) (Col. MS–7085); (Kla. 517)	S	4	1
	PERGOLESI, GIOVANNI BATTISTA (1710–1736)			
728,500	Concertino no. 1 in f (13 min.) *(Oiseau S–156E) *mono*	A	3	2
728,750	Concertino no. 2 in G (12 min.) *(Oiseau S–156E)-*mono*	A	3	3
	PISTON, WALTER (1894–)			
729,000	*Incredible Flutist* (ballet suite) (16 min.) *(Col. MS–6943)	S	3	2
	PONCHIELLI, AMILCARE (1834–1886)			
729,250	*Gioconda: Dance of the Hours* (10 min.) *(Lon. STS–15043); (DG 2530200); (Lon. CS 6753)	E	4	1
	POULENC, FRANCIS (1899–1963)			
729,500	*Biches* (ballet suite) (19 min.) *(Ang. S–35932)	A	4	2
729,750	*Suite française* (12 min.) *(Ang. S–36519)	E	3	2
730,000	*Story of Babar, the Elephant* (25 min.) *(Ang. S–36357)	E	4	2
	PRAETORIUS, MICHAEL (1571–1621)			
730,250	*Terpsichore* (*Dance Pieces*) (5–16 min.) *(DG ARC–198166)	A	3	2
	PROKOFIEV, SERGE (1891–1953)			
730,500	*Buffoon*, Suite no. 1, op. 21 (37 min.) *(Mel./Ang. S–40017)	S	3	2
730,750	*Cinderella*, op. 87 (various ballet excerpts) (20–50 min.) *(Lon. CS 6242); (Ev. 3016)	S	3	2
731,000	*Lieutenant Kijé* Suite, op. 60 (20 min.) **(RCA LSC–2150); *(Col. MS–7408)	E	2	1
731,250	*Love for Three Oranges*: Suite, op. 33-bis (16 min.) (Mer. 75030)	S	3	2
731,500	March and Scherzo only (2 min.) (Mer. 75030)	E	3	2
731,750	*Pas d'acier*: Suite, op. 41–b (13 min.) *(Mel./Ang. S–40017)	A	4	3
732,000	*Peter and the Wolf*, op. 67 (26 min.) **(Ang. S–35638); *(Sera. S–60172)	E	3	1

122

GUIDE NO. COMPOSER AND TITLE	AGE MIN	AES SIG	AC- CESS
732,250 *Romeo and Juliet*, op. 64 (ballet) (45 min.) *(Phi. 6500640)	S	3	1
732,500 *Romeo and Juliet* (complete ballet) **(3–Lon. CSA 2312)	S	3	1
732,750 *Scythian* Suite, op. 20 (21 min.) *(Mer. 75030)	S	4	2
PURCELL, HENRY (c.1659–1695)			
733,000 *Abdelazer*: Suite (12 min.) (Van. SRV–155)	A	3	2
733,250 *Gordian Knot Untied*: Suite no. 1 and 2 (12 min.) *(None. H–71027); (Van. SRV–155 SD)	A	3	1
733,500 *Married Beau*: Suite (11 min.) (Van. SRV–155 SD)	A	3	2
733,750 *Virtuous Wife*: Suite (9 min.) *(None. H–71027); (Van. SRV–155 SD)	A	3	1
RACHMANINOFF, SERGEI (1873–1943)			
734,000 *Isle of the Dead*, op. 29 (21 min.) *(Mel./Ang. S–40019)	S	4	2
734,250 *Symphonic Dances*, op. 45 (34 min.) *(Phi. 6500362)	S	4	2
RAMEAU, JEAN PHILIPPE (1683–1764)			
735,000 *Indes galantes* (ballet suite) (24 min.) *(Oiseau 60024)	A	3	2
735,250 *Paladins*: Suite for Horn and Strings (21 min.) *(Phi. 802901)	A	4	2
735,500 *Le Temple de la Gloire*: Suite (20 min.) *(Oiseau S–297)	A	4	2
RAVEL, MAURICE (1875–1937)			
735,750 *Alborada del gracioso* (7 min.) *(Ang. S–36111); *(Lon. STS–15092)	S	3	1
736,000 *Barque sur l'océan* (8 min.) *(Ang. S–36111)	A	4	2
736,250 *Boléro* (15 min.) *(DG 139010); *(Lon. SPC 21003); *(Lon. CS 6367); *(Sera. S–60177); *(RCA VICS–1323)	E	3	1
736,500 *Daphnis et Chloé* (complete ballet) (55 min.) **(Lon. CS 6456); **(Lon. STS–15090)	S	3	3
736,750 *Daphnis et Chloé*: Suite no. 2 (16 min.) *(DG 138923); *(Lon. STS–15092); *(Odys. Y–31928); *(RCA VIC–1273)-*mono*	S	2	1
737,250 *Ma Mère l'Oye* (ballet) (28 min.) **(Ang. S–36110)	E	2	2
737,500 *Menuet antique* (6 min.) *(Ang. S–36111)	E	4	2

GUIDE NO. COMPOSER AND TITLE	AGE MIN	AES SIG	AC- CESS
737,750 *Pavane pour une infante défunte* (6 min.) **(Ang. S–36111); **(Lon. CS 6225); *(Ang. S–36385); *(Odys. Y–31928)	E	3	1
738,000 *Rapsodie espagnole* (16 min.) *(Ang. S–36385); *(Sera. S–60104)	E	4	1
738,250 *Le Tombeau de Couperin* (17 min.) **(Ang. S–36111); **(Lon. STS–15092)	S	3	2
738,500 *La Valse* (12 min.) **(Lon. CS 6367); *(RCA VICS–1323)	S	3	2
738,750 *Valse nobles et sentimentales* (16 min.) **(Ang. S–36110); **(Lon. STS–15092); *(Odys. Y–31017)	S	2	2
RESPIGHI, OTTORINO (1879–1936)			
739,750 *Ancient Airs and Dances*, Set 1 (16 min.) (Mer. 75009)	S	4	2
740,000 *Ancient Airs and Dances*, Set 2 (19 min.) (Mer. 75009)	S	4	2
740,250 *Ancient Airs and Dances*, Set 3 (19 min.) (Mer. 75009)	S	3	2
740,500 *Boutique Fantasque* (ballet after Rossini) (40 min.) *(Lon. STS–15005); *(Van. VSD–71127)	E	3	1
740,750 *Feste Romane* (24 min.) *(Col. MS–6587)	S	3	2
741,000 *Fountains of Rome* (15 min.) **(RCA VIC–1244)-*mono*; **(RCA LSC–2436); *(Lon. SPC 21024); (Col. MS–6587)	S	2	1
741,250 *Pines of Rome* (20 min.) **(RCA VIC–1244)-*mono*; **(RCA LSC–2436); *(DG 138033); *(Lon. SPC 21024); (Col. MS–6587)	S	2	1
741,500 *Rossiniana* (22 min.) *(Van. VSD–71127)	A	4	2
742,000 *Gli uccelli* (*The Birds*) (18 min.) (Col. MS–7242)	S	3	2
742,250 Prelude only (Col. MS–7242)	E	3	1
742,500 *Vetrate di Chiesa* (25 min.) (Col. MS–7242)	A	4	3
REZNIČEK, EMIL NIKOLAUS VON (1860–1945)			
742,750 *Donna Diana*: Overture (6 min.) *(Lon. CS 6605); (Col. MS–7085); (Lon. STS–15021)	S	4	1
RIEGGER, WALLINGFORD (1885–1961)			
743,000 *Dance Rhythms*, op. 58 (6 min.) (CRI 117)-*mono*	A	3	4

GUIDE NO.	COMPOSER AND TITLE	AGE	AES MIN	AC-SIG	CESS
743,250	*Dichotomy* (1932) *(Argo. ZRG–702)	A	3		4
	RIMSKY-KORSAKOV, NIKOLAI (1844–1908)				
743,750	*Capriccio espagnol,* op. 349 (15 min.) **(Lon. CS 6006); *(DG 138033); *(Mel./Ang. S–40230)	E	3		1
744,000	*Christmas Eve:* Suite (23 min.) **(Lon. CS 6036)	S	5		2
744,250	*Coq d'or:* Suite (25 min.) (Mer. 75016)	S	4		2
744,500	*Bridal Procession* only (6 min.) (Mer. 75016)	E	4		1
744,750	*Hymn to the Sun* only (4 min.) (Mer. 75016)	E	4		1
745,250	*Flight of the Bumblebee* from *Tsar Saltan* Suite (2 min.) *(Lon. CS 6036)	E	3		1
745,500	*May Night* Overture (8 min.) *(Lon. CS 6012)	S	3		1
746,000	*Russian Easter* Overture, op. 36 (14 min.) *(Lon. CS 6012)	S	4		1
746,250	*Scheherazade,* op. 35 (45 min.) **(Ang. S–35505); *(Lon. STS–15158); *(Mel./Ang. S–40112)	E	3		1
746,500	*Song of India* from *Sadko* (4 min.) *(Lon. CS 6036)	E	4		1
746,750	*Tsar Saltan:* Suite, op. 57 (20 min.) *(Lon. CS 6012)	S	4		2
	ROSSINI, GIOACCHINO (1792–1868)				
747,250	*Barber of Seville* Overture (7 min.) **(RCA VIC–1274)-*mono;* **(RCA LSC–2318); *(Lon. CS 6204); *(Sera. S–60138); (Col. MS–7085); (2–Ev. 3186)	E	3		1
747,500	*La Cenerentola* Overture (8 min.) **(RCA LSC–2318); *(Sera. S–60058); (2–Ev. 3186)	S	4		2
747,750	*La Gazza Ladra* Overture (10 min.) **(RCA LSC–2318); **(RCA VIC–1274)-*mono;* *(Col. MS–7031); *(Lon. CS 6204); *(Sera. S–60058); (2–Ev. 3186)	E	3		1
748,000	*L'Italiana in Algeri* Overture (8 min.) *(Col. MS–7031); *(Sera. S–60138); (2–Ev. 3186)	E	3		2
748,250	*La Scala de Seta* Overture (6 min.) **(RCA LSC–2318); *(Col. MS–7031); *(Lon. CS 6204); *(Sera. S–60138); (2–Ev. 3186)	E	4		1
748,500	*Semiramide* Overture (13 min.) **(RCA VIC–1274)-*mono;* *(Lon. CS 6204); *(Sera. S–60058); (2–Ev. 3186)	E	3		2
748,750	*Siege of Corinth* Overture (10 min.) (2–Ev. 3186)	S	4		3
749,000	*Signor Bruschino* Overture (5 min.) **(RCA LSC–2318); **(RCA VIC–1274)-*mono;* *(Sera. S–60138); (2–Ev. 3186)	S	3		2
749,251	Sonata no. 1 for Strings (12 min.) **(Phi. 6500243)	S	3		2
749,252	Sonata no. 2 for Strings (13 min.) **(Phi. 6500243)	S	4		2
749,253	Sonata no. 3 for Strings (12 min.) **(Phi. 6500243)	S	4		2
749,254	Sonata no. 4 for Strings **(Phi. 6500243)	S	4		2
749,255	Sonata no. 5 for Strings (15 min.) **(Phi. 6500243)	S	4		2
749,256	Sonata no. 6 for Strings (15 min.) **(Phi. 6500243)	S	3		2
749,500	*Tancredi* Overture (6 min.) *(Sera. S–60058); (2–Ev. 3186)	S	4		2
749,750	*Thieving Magpie* Overture (9 min.) *(Sera. 60134)	S	4		2
750,000	*Torvaldo e Dorliska* Overture (8 min.) (Lon. CS 6486)	S	3		2
750,250	*Turco in Italia* Overture (9 min.) *(Col. MS–7031)	S	4		2
750,500	*William Tell* Overture (12 min.) **(RCA LSC–2318); **(RCA VIC–1274); *(Lon. CS 6204); *(Sera. S–60058); (Col. M–31815); (2–Ev. 3186)	E	2		1
	RUGGLES, CARL (1876–1971)				
752,000	*Lilacs* (8 min.) (CSP AML–4986)-*mono*	A	3		5
752,250	*Men and Mountains* (9 min.) (Turn. 34398)	A	3		5
752,500	*Organum* for Orchestra (1945–46) (8 min.) (CRI 127)-*mono*	A	3		4
752,750	*Portals* (5 min.) (CSP AML–4986)-*mono*	A	3		5
753,000	*Sun-Treader* (17 min.) **(DG 2530048)	A	3		5

GUIDE NO.	COMPOSER AND TITLE	AGE MIN	AES SIG	AC-CESS
	SAINT-SAËNS, CAMILLE (1835–1921)			
753,250	*Carnival of the Animals* (21–30 min.) **(Ang. S–36421)	E	3	1
753,500	*Danse macabre,* Op. 40 (7 min.) **(Lon. STS–15093); **(RCA VIC–1244)-*mono;* *(Ang. S–37009); *(Sera. S–60177)	E	4	1
754,000	*Le Rouet d'Omphale,* op. 31 (8 min.) **(Lon. STS–15093); *(Ang. S–37009)	E	3	1
	SATIE, ERIK (1866–1925)			
754,250	*La Belle Excentrique* (4 pieces for music-hall orchestra) *(2–Van. VCS–10037/8)	S	4	2
754,500	*En habit de cheval:* Deux chorales et deux figures (3 min.) *(2–Van. VCS–10037/8)	S	4	2
754,750	*Gymnopédie* no. 1 (orchestrated by Debussy) (3 min.) *(Col. M–30294); (Lon. SPC 21062)	E	3	1
755,000	*Gymnopédie* no. 2 (orchestrated by Jones) (4 min.) (Lon. SPC 21062)	E	4	2
755,250	*Gymnopédie* no. 3 (orchestrated by Debussy) (3 min.) *(Col. M–30294)	E	3	1
755,500	*Parade* (14 min.) *(Col. M–30294)	S	3	2
755,750	*Relâche* (22 min.) *(Col. M–30294)	S	4	2
	SCHICKELE, PETER (1935–)			
755,825	*P.D.Q. Bach* and *Stoned Guest* (Van. VSD–6536)	S	5	1
755,925	*Wurst of P.D.Q. Bach* (2–Van. VSD–719/20)	S	5	1
	SCHOENBERG, ARNOLD (1874–1951)			
756,250	*Five Pieces for Orchestra,* op. 16 (16 min.) (CSP CMS–6103)	A	3	3
756,500	*Pelléas und Mélisande,* op. 5 (42 min.) (2–Col. M2S–694)	A	4	3
756,750	*Theme and Variations,* op. 43a for Band (11 min.) (Cornell U. 1)	A	5	4
757,000	*Three Little Orchestra Pieces* (1910) (1 min.) (2–Col. M2S–694)	A	5	4
757,250	*Variations for Orchestra,* op. 31 (21 min.) **(Lon. CS 6612); (2–Col. M2S–694)	A	4	4
757,500	*Verklärte Nacht,* op. 4 (30 min.) **(Lon. CS 6552); (Ang. S–36484); (2–Col. M2S–694); (Sera. S–60080)	S	3	1

GUIDE NO.	COMPOSER AND TITLE	AGE MIN	AES SIG	AC-CESS
	SCHUBERT, FRANZ (1797–1828)			
757,750	*German Dances* (15 min.) *(Lon. STS–15035); (Mace S–9070)	E	4	2
758,000	*Marche militaire,* op. 51, no. 1, D. 733 (5 min.) (RCA ARL 1–0114)	E	3	1
758,250	Overture in C—in the Italian Style (7 min.) *(Ang. S–36609)	S	3	1
758,500	Overture in D—in the Italian Style (8 min.) *(Ang. S–36609); *(Lon. STS–15076)	S	3	1
758,750	*Rosamunde:* Incidental Music, op. 26, D. 797 (25 min.) *(Col. MS–7002)	E	3	1
	SCHUMAN, WILLIAM (1910–)			
759,000	*American Festival* Overture (9 min.) (Desto 6404E)-*mono*	A	4	3
759,250	*Credendum (Article of Faith)* (17 min.) (CRI S–308)	A	3	3
759,750	*New England Triptych,* 3 Pieces for Orchestra (15 min.) *(Mer. 75020)	S	3	2
	SCHUMANN, ROBERT (1810–1856)			
760,250	*Genoveva,* op. 81: Overture (9 min.) *(DG 138955); *(Lon. STS–15076)	A	5	3
760,500	*Manfred* Overture, op. 115 (12 min.) *(Ang. S–36353)	S	4	2
760,750	*Overture, Scherzo, and Finale,* op. 52 (15 min.) *(Lon. CS 6696)	A	5	3
	SESSIONS, ROGER (1896–)			
761,000	*Black Maskers:* Suite (22 min.) (Desto 6404E)-*mono*	A	3	3
761,125	Rhapsody for Orchestra (1970) (Argo ZRG–702)	A	3	3
	SHOSTAKOVICH, DMITRI (1906–1975)			
761,250	*Age of Gold,* op. 22 (ballet suite) (23 min.) *(Lon. STS–15180)	S	3	2
761,500	Polka and Russian Dance only (6 min.) *(Lon. STS–15180)	E	3	1
761,750	*Festive* Overture, op. 96 (6 min.) (Pol. 245006)	E	5	2
762,000	*Hamlet:* Incidental Music op. 32 (21 min.) (RCA LSC–3130)	S	5	2
	SIBELIUS, JEAN (1865–1957)			
762,250	*Finlandia,* op. 26 (8 min.) **(Sera. S–60208); *(Col. MS–6732); (Col. MS–6196)	E	3	1

125

GUIDE NO.	COMPOSER AND TITLE	AGE MIN	AES SIG	AC-CESS
762,500	*Karelia* Suite, op. 11 (15 min.) **(Lon. CS 6375); **(Sera. S–60208)	E	4	2
762,750	*Lemminkäinen's Return* (6 min.) **(Sera. S–60208)	S	3	1
763,000	*The Oceanides*, op. 73 (symphonic poem) (10 min.) *(Ang. S–35458)	A	3	3
763,250	*Pelléas et Mélisande*, op. 46 (27 min.) *(Ang. S–35458); (Mel./Ang. S–40031)	A	4	3
763,500	Waltz only, 3rd movement *(Ang. S–35458); (Mel./Ang. S–40031)	A	3	1
763,750	*Pohjola's Daughter*, op. 49 (13 min.) **(Sera. S–60208); *(Col. MS–6749)	S	3	2
764,000	*Romance* in C for String Orchestra, op. 42 (6 min.) (Mel./Ang. S–40031)	A	4	3
764,250	*En Saga*, op. 9 (19 min.) *(Col. MS–6732)	S	3	1
764,500	*Swan of Tuonela* (9 min.) *(Col. MS–6732)	S	3	1
764,750	*Tapiola*, op. 112 (18 min.) **(Sera. S–60000) *(Lon. CS 6592)	A	4	3
765,000	*Valse triste* (from *Kuolema*, op. 44) (5 min.) **(Sera. S–60208); (Col. MS–6196); (Col. MS–6732); (Mel./Ang. S–40031)	S	3	1

SKALKOTTAS, NIKOS
(1904–1949)

| 765,250 | Three Greek Dances (*Epiroticos, Peloponnisiaskos,* and *Klefticos*) (7 min.) *(Col. M–30390) | E | 5 | 1 |

SMETANA, BEDŘICH
(1824–1884)

765,500	*Bartered Bride: Dance of the Comedians* (5 min.) **(Sera. S–60098)	E	3	1
765,750	*Bartered Bride: Furiant* (2 min.) **(Sera. S–60098)	E	3	1
766,000	*Bartered Bride:* Overture (6 min.) **(RCA VICS–1424)	S	3	1
766,250	*Bartered Bride:* Polka (5 min.) **(Sera. S–60098)	E	3	1
766,500	*Moldau* (*Vltava*) (from *My Fatherland*) (12 min.) (Ang. S–35615)	E	2	1
766,750	*My Fatherland* (*Ma Vlast*) (1 hr. 16 min.) *(Lon. STS–15096/7)	A	3	2

SOWERBY, LEO
(1895–1968)

| 767,750 | *Prairie* (17 min.) (Desto 6421E)-*mono* | A | 4 | 3 |

STAMITZ, JOHANN WENZEL ANTON
(1717–1757)

| 768,000 | Trio in A, op. 1, no. 2 for Orchestra (12 min.) *(Tel. 6.41062) | A | 4 | 3 |

STRAUSS, JOHANN
(1825–1899)

768,500	*Die Fledermaus* (overture) (9 min.) **(Lon. CS 6605); *(DG 139014)	E	3	1
768,750	*Graduation Ball* (ballet suite) (arranged by Dorati) (29 min.) (Lon. STS–15070)	E	4	2
769,000	*Gypsy Baron* Overture (8 min.) *(DG 139014)	S	4	2
769,500	*Perpetual Motion* (3 min.) **(3–Lon. CSA 2307); *(DG 139014)	E	3	1

WALTZES, POLKAS,
and MARCHES

769,750	*Acceleration Waltz* (8 min.) **(Lon. CS 6731)	E	3	2
770,000	*Annen* Polka (4 min.) **(Lon. CS 6731); *(DG 139014)	E	4	2
770,250	*Artists Life* Waltz (8 min.) **(Ang. S–36826); **(3–Lon. CSA 2307)	E	3	1
770,500	*Auf der Jagd* Polka (2 min.) **(Ang. S–36887); **(3–Lon. CSA 2307); *(DG 2530027)	E	4	2
770,750	*Banditen Galopp* Polka (2 min.) **(3–Lon. CSA 2307)	E	4	2
771,000	*Blue Danube* Waltz (8 min.) **(3–Lon. CSA 2307); *(DG 139014)	E	3	1
771,250	*Champagne* Polka (3 min.) **(Lon. CS 6008); **(3–Lon. CSA 2307)	E	4	2
771,500	*Egyptian* March (4 min.) *(DG 2530027)	E	4	2
771,750	*Eljen a Magyar* Polka (3 min.) **(3–Lon. CSA 2307)	E	4	2
772,000	*Kaiser* Waltz (10 min.) *(DG 139014)	E	3	1
772,250	*Morning Papers* Waltz (8 min.) **(3–Lon. CSA 2307); *(DG 2530027)	E	4	2
772,750	*Pizzicato* Polka (3 min.) **(Lon. CS 6008); **(3–Lon. CSA 2307)	E	4	2
773,000	*Roses from the South* Waltz (9 min.) **(3–Lon. CSA 2307)	E	3	1
773,250	*Tales from Vienna Woods* (5 min.) **(3–Lon. CSA 2307); *(DG 2530027)	E	3	1
773,500	*Thunder and Lightning* Polka (3 min.) **(3–Lon. CSA 2307); *(DG 2530027)	E	3	1

GUIDE NO.	COMPOSER AND TITLE	AGE MIN	AES SIG	AC-CESS
773,750	*Tritsch Tratsch* Polka (3 min.) *(DG 139014)	E	3	1
774,000	*Vienna Blood* (5 min.) **(Lon. CS 6008); **(3–Lon. CSA 2307)	E	3	1
774,250	*Vienna Bons Bons* (3 min.) **(Lon. CS 6008); **(3–Lon. CSA 2307)	E	4	2
775,000	*Voices of Spring* (6 min.) **(3–Lon. CSA 2307)	E	3	1
775,250	*Where the Citrons Bloom* Waltz (8 min.) **(3–Lon. CSA 2307)	E	4	2
775,500	*Wine, Women, and Song* (6 min.) **(Ang. S–36887)	E	3	1

STRAUSS, JOHANN, Sr.
(1804–1849)

GUIDE NO.	COMPOSER AND TITLE	AGE MIN	AES SIG	AC-CESS
775,750	*Radetzky* March, op. 228 (3 min.) **(3–Lon. CSA 2307); *(DG 139014)	E	3	1

STRAUSS, JOSEF
(1827–1870)

GUIDE NO.	COMPOSER AND TITLE	AGE MIN	AES SIG	AC-CESS
778,000	*Feuerfest* Polka (3 min.) **(3–Lon. CSA 2307)	E	4	2
778,500	*Music of the Spheres* Waltz (6 min.) **(3–Lon. CSA 2307)	E	4	1

STRAUSS, RICHARD
(1864–1949)

GUIDE NO.	COMPOSER AND TITLE	AGE MIN	AES SIG	AC-CESS
778,750	*Also sprach Zarathustra* (29–38 min.) **(DG 2530402); **(Lon. STS–15083); **(RCA VICS–1265); *(Ang. S–35994); *(Lon. CS 6609)	S	4	3
779,000	*Bourgeois gentilhomme* Suite, op. 60 (36 min.) *(Lon. CS 6537)	A	4	4
779,250	*Death and Transfiguration,* op. 24 (24 min.) *(Ang. S–35976); *(DG 2530368); *(Odys. Y–30313)	S	3	2
779,500	*Don Juan,* op. 20 (16 min.) **(RCA VIC–1267)-*mono;* *(DG 138866); *(DG 2530349); *(Lon. CS 6209); (Odys. Y–30313)	S	2	2
779,750	*Ein Heldenleben,* op. 40 (46 min.) **(Sera. S–60041); *(Lon. CS 6608); *(Phi. 6500048)	S	3	2
780,000	*Metamorphosen* (26 min.) **(Ang. S–35976); (DG 2530066)	A	4	3
780,250	*Rosenkavalier:* Suite (23 min.) *(Lon. SPC 21037)	S	3	2
780,500	*Rosenkavalier:* Waltzes (9 min.) **(RCA VICS–1561); *(Lon. CS 6537)	S	2	1
780,750	*Salome: Dance of the Seven Veils* (9 min.) **(RCA VICS–1424); *(DG 138866); *(DG 2530349)	S	3	2

GUIDE NO.	COMPOSER AND TITLE	AGE MIN	AES SIG	AC-CESS
781,000	*Till Eulenspiegel,* op. 28 (15 min.) **(RCA VIC–1267)-*mono;* *(DG 138866); *(Odys. Y–30313); (DG 2530349)	E	2	1

STRAVINSKY, IGOR
(1882–1971)

GUIDE NO.	COMPOSER AND TITLE	AGE MIN	AES SIG	AC-CESS
782,000	*Agon* (ballet) (22 min.) (RCA LSC–2879)	A	3	4
782,200	*Apollo* (*Apollon Musagète*) (ballet) (30 min.) **(Col. MS–6646); **(3–Col. D3S–761); *(Argo ZRG–575); *(DG 2530065)	A	3	3
782,400	*Le baiser de la fée* (45 min.) **(3–Col. D3S–761); *(RCA LSC–2251)	A	4	3
782,600	*Circus* Polka (3 min.). **(Col. M–31729)	E	4	2
782,800	*Concerto in D for String Orchestra* (12 min.) **(Oiseau 60050); *(Col. M–30516)	A	3	2
783,000	*Danses concertantes* (20 min.) **(Oiseau 60050); *(Col. M–30516)	A	4	3
783,200	*Dumbarton Oaks* Concerto in E flat (14 min.) **(Oiseau 60050); **(Col. M–31729)	A	4	3
783,400	*Ebony Concerto* (13 min.) **(Col. M–30579)	A	5	3
783,600	*Études* (4) for Orchestra (9 min.) **(Col. M–31729)	A	4	3
783,800	*Firebird* (complete ballet) **(Col. MS–6328); **(3–Col. D3S–705); *(Ang. S–36910)	S	3	1
784,020	*Dance of King Katchei* (5 min.) **(Col. MS–6328); **(Col. MS–7011)	E	3	1
784,060	*Finale* (7 min.) **(Col. MS–6328); **(Col. MS–7011)	E	3	1
784,100	*Firebird:* Suite (20–30 min.) **(Col. MS–7011)	E	3	1
784,200	*Fireworks,* op. 4 (4 min.) **(Col. M–7094)	S	4	3
784,400	*Greeting Prelude* (1 min.) **(Col. M–31729)	E	4	2
784,600	*Jeu de Cartes* (23 min.) **(Col. M–31921)	A	3	3
784,800	*Monumentum pro Gesualdo* (7 min.) **(CSP CKS–6318)	A	3	4
785,000	*Norwegian Moods* (4) (9 min.) **(Col. M–30516)	S	3	1
785,200	*Orpheus* (ballet) (31 min.) **(Col. MS–6646); **(3–Col. D3S–761)	A	2	3
785,400	*Petrouchka* (complete ballet) (34 min.) **(Col. MS–6332); **(3–Col. D3S–705); **(Lon. CS 6009)	S	2	2
785,600	*Petrouchka:* Suite (17 min.) **(Col. MS–7011);	S	2	2

GUIDE NO.	COMPOSER AND TITLE	AGE	AES MIN SIG	AC-CESS
	*(Col. MS–7094)-5 dances only			
785,650	*Russian Dance* only (3 min.)	E	1	1
	**(Col. MS–7011); *(Col. MS–7094)			
785,800	*Pulcinella* (ballet after Pergolesi) (1920; rev. 1949) (39 min.)	S	3	2
	*(3–Col. D3S–761)			
786,000	*Pulcinella:* Suite (1920) (22 min.)	S	3	2
	**(Col. MS–7093); *(Argo ZRG–575); *(Lon. STS–15011)			
786,200	*Le Sacre du printemps* (34 min.)	S	1	2
	**(Col. MS–6319); **(3–Col. D3S–705); *(Col. MS–6010)			
786,400	*Scherzo à la russe* (4 min.)	S	4	2
	**(Col. MS–7094)			
786,600	*Scherzo fantastique,* op. 3 (12 min.)	S	4	3
	**(Col. MS–7094)			
786,800	*Song of the Nightingale* (22 min.)	A	3	3
	**(Lon. STS–15011); **(RCA LSC–2150)			
787,000	Suite no. 1 for Small Orchestra (6 min.)	S	4	3
	**(Col. M–31729)			
787,200	Suite no. 2 for Small Orchestra (5 min.)	S	4	3
	**(Col. M–31729)			
787,400	*Symphonies of Wind Instruments* (9 min.)	A	2	4
	*(Lon. CS 6225)			
	SUK, JOSEF (1874–1935)			
788,000	Serenade in E flat for Strings, op. 6 (25 min.)	A	3	2
	*(Lon. CS 6737)			
	SUPPÉ, FRANZ VON (1819–1895)			
788,500	*Beautiful Galatea* Overture (8 min.)	E	4	2
	**(DG 2530051); (Col. MS–7085)			
788,750	*Light Cavalry* Overture (7 min.)	E	3	1
	**(DG 2530051); (Col. MS–7085)			
789,000	*Morning, Noon, and Night in Vienna* Overture (8 min.)	E	4	1
	**(DG 2530051)			
789,250	*Pique Dame* Overture (8 min.)	E	4	2
	**(DG 2530051); (Lon. STS–15021)			
789,500	*Poet and Peasant* Overture (10 min.)	E	4	1
	**(DG 2530051); (Col. M–31815)			
	TCHAIKOVSKY, PETER ILYITCH (1840–1893)			
790,000	*Capriccio italien,* op. 45 (16 min.)	S	4	1
	*(DG 139028); *(RCA LSC–2323)			
790,500	*Eugen Onegin,* op. 24: Polonaise (5 min.) (DG 2530200)	S	4	2

GUIDE NO.	COMPOSER AND TITLE	AGE	AES MIN SIG	AC-CESS
790,750	*Francesca de Rimini,* op. 32 (23 min.)	S	3	1
	**(Ev. 3011); *(Phi. 6500643)			
791,000	*Hamlet, Fantasy* Overture, op. 67a (17 min.)	S	4	2
	**(Ev. 3011)			
791,250	*Manfred,* op. 58 (symphonic poem) (58 min.)	A	4	2
	*(Mel./Ang. S–40028)			
791,500	*Marche Slave,* op. 31 (10 min.)	E	4	1
	**(RCA VICS–1676); *(Ang. S–36890); *(Phi. 6500643)			
791,750	*Nutcracker,* op. 71 (complete ballet) (1 hr. 24 min.)	E	2	1
	**(2–Lon. CSA 2203)			
792,000	*Nutcracker* Suite, op. 71A (12 min.)	E	2	1
	**(Lon. CS 6097); *(Ang. S–35680); *(DG 139030)			
792,250	*Trepak* only (1 min.)	E	3	1
	**(Lon. CS 6097); *(Ang. S–35680); *(DG 139030)			
792,500	*Waltz of the Flowers* (6 min.)	E	3	1
	**(Lon. CS 6097); *(Ang. S–35680); *(DG 139030)			
792,750	*Overture 1812,* op. 49 (17 min.)	E	3	1
	**(RCA VICS–1025); *(Ang. S–36890); *(Phi. 6500643); *(RCA LSC–3204)			
793,000	*Romeo and Juliet* (20 min.)	S	3	1
	*(Ang. S–35680); *(Ang. S–36890); *(DG 2530137); *(Lon. CS 6209)			
793,250	*Serenade* in C for Strings, op. 48 (30 min.)	A	3	1
	**(Ang. S–36269); *(DG 139030); *(Lon. STS–15141)			
793,500	*Sleeping Beauty,* op. 6 (complete ballet) (2 hrs. 31 min.)	S	3	2
	**(3–Lon. CSA 2304)			
793,600	*Sleeping Beauty* (excerpts) (21–54 min.)	E	3	1
	*(DG 2530195); (Lon. STS–15179); *(Phi. 7505040)–cassette			
793,700	Suite no. 3, op. 55 (43 min.) (Mel./Ang. S–40175)	A	4	2
793,800	Theme and Variations only (20 min.) (Mel./Ang. S–40175)	S	3	1
794,100	*Swan Lake,* op. 20 (complete ballet) (approx. 2½ hr.)	S	3	3
	**(3–Mel./Ang. S–4106); *(2–Lon. CSA 2204)			
794,200	*Swan Lake* (excerpts) (22 min.)	E	3	1
	**(Lon. CS 6127); **(Lon. CS 6218); *(DG 2530195); *(Phi. 7505040)-cassette			
794,250	Waltz from *Eugen Onegin* (6 min.) (Col. MS–7133)	S	3	1

GUIDE NO.	COMPOSER AND TITLE	AGE MIN	AES SIG	AC-CESS
	TELEMANN, GEORG PHILIPP (1681–1767)			
794,500	*Don Quichotte* (16 min.)	A	4	2
	*(7–Ev. 3194)			
794,750	*Musique de Table* (suites)	A	3	2
	(28 min. each)			
	*(2–Tel. 26.48006);			
	*(2–Tel. 26.48007);			
	*(2–Tel. 26.48008)			
795,000	Overture in C for 3 Oboes, Strings, and Continuo (20 min.)	A	4	2
	(None. H–71132)			
795,250	Overture in D (27 min.)	A	3	2
	(None. H–71091)			
795,750	*Water Music* (Overture in C, *Hamburg's Tides*) (24 min.)	A	3	2
	**(DG ARC–198198)			
	THOMAS, AMBROISE (1811–1896)			
796,000	*Mignon* (overture) (8 min.)	S	5	1
	(Col. M–31815)			
796,050	*Raymond* (overture) (8 min.)	S	5	1
	(Col. M–31815)			
	THOMSON, VIRGIL (1896–)			
796,250	*Louisiana Story: Acadian Songs and Dances* (11 min.)	E	4	2
	(Turn. 34534)			
796,300	*Plow That Broke the Plains* (14 min.)	E	4	2
	*(Van. VSD 2095)			
796,350	*The River:* Suite (25 min.)	E	4	2
	*(Van. VSD 2095); (Desto 6405E)-*mono*			
	TIPPETT, MICHAEL (1905–)			
796,500	Concerto for Double String Orchestra (22 min.)	A	3	3
	**(Argo ZRG–680)			
796,750	*Midsummer Marriage: Ritual Dances* (23 min.)	A	2	2
	**(2–Argo ZDA–19/20)			
	TOMMASINI, VINCENZO (1878–1950)			
797,000	*Good-humored Ladies* (ballet suite, after D. Scarlatti) (19 min.)	E	3	1
	*(Col. M–31241)			
	TORELLI, GIUSEPPE (1659–1709)			
797,250	Concerto grosso no. 2 in a (10 min.)	S	4	3
	(Mace. S–9031)			
797,750	Concerto grosso no. 6 in g (9 min.)	S	4	3
	(DG 2530070)			
	TURINA, JOAQUIN (1882–1949)			
798,500	*Danzas Fantásticas*, op. 22 (16 min.)	A	5	2
	*(Ang. S–36195)			
	VARÈSE, EDGARD (1883–1965)			
799,000	*Amériques* (20 min.)	A	3	3
	(Van. SRV–274 SD)			
799,200	*Arcana* (17 min.)	A	3	4
	**(Lon. CS 6752); *(Col. MS–6362)			
799,400	*Intégrales* (12 min.)	A	3	4
	**(Lon. CS 6752)			
799,600	*Ionisation* (5 min.)	S	2	4
	**(Lon. CS 6752)			
799,800	*Offrandes* (10 min.)	A	3	4
	*(Col. MS–6362)			
	VAUGHAN WILLIAMS, RALPH (1872–1958)			
800,000	*English Folk Song* Suite (10 min.)	E	4	1
	*(Ang. S–36799); (RCA LSC–2719)			
800,100	*Fantasia on a Theme by Tallis* (16 min.)	S	2	2
	**(Ang. S–36101); *(Argo ZRG–696); (RCA LSC–2719)			
800,150	Fantasia on *Greensleeves* (5 min.)	E	3	1
	**(Ang. S–36101); **(Ang. S–36902); *(Ang. S–36799); *(Argo ZRG–696); (RCA LSC–2719)			
800,350	*Job (A Masque for Dancing)* (1930) (45 min.)	S	4	2
	*(Ang. S–36773)			
800,500	*Norfolk Rhapsody* no. 1 in e (10 min.)	A	4	2
	**(Ang. S–36557); **(Ang. S–36902)			
800,650	*Serenade to Music* (13 min.)	A	4	2
	*(Ang. S–36698)			
800,800	*Wasps:* Incidental Music (Aristophanes) (26 min.)	A	4	2
	**(2–Ang. S–3739)			
	VERDI, GIUSEPPE (1813–1901)			
801,000	*Aida:* Grand March (6 min.)	E	3	1
	(DG 2530200)			
801,100	*Aida:* Ballet Music from Act II (8 min.)	E	4	1
	(DG 2530200)			
801,200	*Forza del Destino* Overture (8 min.)	S	4	1
	*(Sera. S–60138)			
801,400	*Otello:* Ballet Music, Act III (4 min.)	S	4	1
	(DG 2530200)			
801,500	*Traviata:* Prelude to Act I (4 min.)	S	4	1
	*(Sera. S–60138)			
801,600	*Traviata:* Prelude to Act III (4 min.)	S	4	1
	*(Sera. S–60138)			
801,700	*Vespri Siciliani:* Overture (9 min.)	S	4	1
	*(Sera. S–60138)			
	VILLA-LOBOS, HEITOR (1887–1959)			
802,000	*Bachianas Brasileiras* no. 2 for Orchestra (21 min.)	S	3	2
	*(Ang. S–36979)			
802,200	*Little Train of the Caipira* only (4 min.)	E	3	1
	*(Ang. S–36979)			

129

GUIDE NO.	COMPOSER AND TITLE	AGE	AES MIN SIG	AC-CESS
802,400	*Uirapurú* (18 min.) (Ev. 3016)	S	4	2
	WAGNER, RICHARD (1813–1883)			
803,000	*Eine Faust-Overtüre* (10 min.) **(Col. MS–6884); **(RCA VIC–1247)-*mono*	S	3	1
803,250	*Der Fliegende Holländer:* Overtüre **(Col. MS–6884); **(Lon. SPC 21035); *(2–Ang. S–3610 (S–36187/8)); *(Col. MS–6149)	E	2	1
803,500	*Götterdämmerung: Funeral Music* (8 min.) *(2–Ang. S–3610 (S–36187/8))	S	2	1
803,750	*Götterdämmerung: Rhine Journey* (12 min.) **(RCA VIC–1369)-*mono*; *(Ang. S–35947)	E	2	1
804,000	*Lohengrin:* Prelude to Act I (9 min.) **(Col. MS–6884); **(Odys. Y–30667); **(RCA VIC–1247)-*mono*; *(2–Ang. S–3610 (S–36187/8)); (Lon. CS 6529)	S	2	1
804,250	*Lohengrin:* Prelude to Act III (3 min.) **(Odys. Y–30667); **(RCA VIC–1247)-*mono*; *(2–Ang. S–3610 (S–36187/8)); (Lon. CS 6529)	E	2	1
804,400	*Meistersinger: Dance of the Apprentices* (7 min.) *(2–Ang. S–3610 (S–36187/8))	E	2	1
804,500	*Meistersinger:* Prelude to Act I (10 min.) **(Lon. SPC 21035); **(RCA VIC–1247)-*mono*; *(2–Ang. S–3610 (S–36187/8)); *(Col. MS–6149); (Col. MS–7291); (Lon. CS 6529)	E	1	2
804,750	*Parsifal: Good Friday Music* (11 min.) **(Col. MS–6149)	S	2	2
805,000	*Parsifal:* Prelude (14 min.) **(Col. MS–6149); *(Ang. S–35947); (Lon. CS 6529)	S	3	2
805,500	*Das Rheingold: Entrance of the Gods in Valhalla* (6 min.) *(Ang. S–35947); *(Col. MS–7291)	S	3	2
805,750	*Rienzi:* Overture (12 min.) **(Col. MS–6884); *(2–Ang. S–3610 (S–36187/8))	S	3	1
806,000	*Siegfried: Forest Murmurs* (7 min.) *(Ang. S–35947)	S	2	2
806,250	*Siegfried Idyll* (18 min.) **(Odys. Y–30667); **(RCA VIC–1247)-*mono*; (Ang. S–36484)	S	1	2
806,500	*Tannhäuser:* Overture (14 min.) *(2–Ang. S–3610 (S–36187/8))	E	2	1
806,750	*Tannhäuser:* Overture and *Venusberg Music* (23 min.) **(Odys. Y–30667); (Lon. SPC 21037)	S	2	2
807,000	*Tristan:* Prelude and *Liebestod* (17 min.) **(Lon. SPC 21035); *(2–Ang. S–3610 (S–36187/8)); *(Col. MS–7291)	S	1	1
807,250	*Walküre: Ride of the Valkyries* (5 min.) *(Ang. S–35947); *(Col. MS–7291)	E	2	1
807,500	*Walküre: Magic Fire Music* (7 min.) *(Col. MS–7291)	S	2	2
	WALDTEUFEL, ÉMIL (1837–1915)			
807,800	*Skaters Waltz* (Col. MS–7032)	E	4	1
	WALTON, WILLIAM (1902–)			
808,200	*Façade* (18 min.) *(Ang. S–36837)	S	3	2
808,300	*Valse* only *(Ang. S–36837)	E	3	1
808,350	*Hamlet:* Film Music *(Sera. S–60205)	S	3	1
808,400	*Partita* for Orchestra (16 min.) *(Ang. S–35681)	S	4	3
808,600	*Portsmouth Point* Overture (6 min.) *(Ang. S–37001)	S	4	2
808,700	*Scapino: A Comedy Overture* (8 min.) *(Ang. S–37001)	S	3	2
808,800	*Wise Virgins* (ballet suite, arranged from Bach) (21 min.) *(Col. M–31241)	S	3	2
	WEBER, CARL MARIA VON (1786–1826)			
809,000	*Abu Hassan* Overture (3 min.) **(Lon. STS–15056)	S	4	2
809,150	*Euryanthe* Overture (9 min.) **(Lon. STS–15056); (Ang. S–36175)	S	3	2
809,300	*Der Freischütz* Overture (10 min.) **(Lon. STS–15056); (Ang. S–36175)	S	3	2
809,450	*Invitation to the Dance,* op. 65 (9 min.) **(Lon. STS–15070)	S	4	1
809,600	*Oberon* Overture (9 min.) **(Lon. STS–15056); (Ang. S–36175)	S	3	2
809,750	*Preciosa* Overture (8 min.) **(Lon. STS–15056); (Lon. STS–15076)	S	4	3
	WEBERN, ANTON (1883–1945)			
810,000	Five Movements for String Quartet, op. 5 (arranged for orchestra) (11 min.)	A	3	3

GUIDE NO.	COMPOSER AND TITLE	AGE MIN	AES SIG	AC-CESS
	*(CSP CMS–6103);			
	(4–CSP CK4L–232)-*mono*			
810,200	Five Orchestral Pieces,	A	2	4
	op. 10 (4 min.)			
	(Ang. S–36480);			
	(4–CSP CK4L–232)-*mono*;			
	(Ev. 3232)			
810,400	Passacaglia for Orchestra,	A	3	3
	op. 1 (10 min.)			
	(4–CSP CK4L–232)-*mono*			
810,600	Six Pieces for Orchestra,	A	3	3
	op. 6 (11 min.)			
	(4–CSP CK4L–232)-*mono*			
810,800	Variations for Orchestra,	A	1	5
	op. 30 (6 min.)			
	(4–CSP CK4L–232)-*mono*			

GUIDE NO.	COMPOSER AND TITLE	AGE MIN	AES SIG	AC-CESS
	WEINBERGER, JAROMIR			
	(1896–1967)			
811,000	Schwanda: Polka and Fugue	E	3	1
	(8 min.)			
	**(RCA VICS–1424);			
	*(Sera. S–60098)			
	WIRÉN, DAG (1905–)			
811,200	Serenade for Strings	A	4	2
	(14 min.)			
	*(Van. VCS–10067)			
	WOLF, HUGO (1860–1903)			
811,400	Italian Serenade (1893–94)	S	2	1
	(7 min.)			
	**(Phi. 802725);			
	*(Lon. CS 6737)			

8. Complete Songs and Other Works Scored for Single Voice and Accompaniment

GUIDE NO.	COMPOSER AND TITLE	AGE MIN	AES SIG	AC-CESS
	Anonymous			
812,200	Greensleeves (4 min.)	E	3	1
	*(RCA VICS–1266)			
	ARDITI, LUIGI			
	(1822–1903)			
812,400	Il bacio (8 min.)	A	4	2
	**(Lon. OS 25777);			
	**(2–Lon. OSA 1254)			
	ARNE, THOMAS			
	(1710–1778)			
812,500	Blow, Blow Thou Winter	S	3	3
	Wind (3 min.)			
	**(Oiseau 60036)			
812,750	Come Away Death (7 min.)	S	3	3
	**(Oiseau 60036)			
813,250	Under the Greenwood Tree	S	3	2
	(2 min.)			
	**(Oiseau 60036)			
813,500	Where the Bee Sucks	S	3	2
	(2 min.)			
	**(Ang. S–36456)			
	BACH, JOHANN			
	SEBASTIAN (1685–1750)			
813,750	Bist du bei mir (3 min.)	S	3	2
	**(Lon. OS 26067);			
	**(RCA VICS–1317)			
814,000	Willst du dein Herz mir	S	3	3
	schenken (3 min.)			
	**(RCA VICS–1317)			
	BACON, ERNST (1898–)			
814,250	It's All I Have to Bring	A	3	3
	(1 min.)			
	*(2–Desto 6411/2)			
	BARBER, SAMUEL			
	(1910–)			
814,500	Hermit Songs (18 min.)	A	4	3
	*(CSP–CML–4988)-*mono*			
814,750	Knoxville: Summer of 1915	A	3	2
	(15 min.)			
	*(RCA LSC–3062)			
815,000	Sure on this Shining Night	A	3	3
	(2 min.)			
	(Cam. 2715)			

GUIDE NO.	COMPOSER AND TITLE	AGE MIN	AES SIG	AC-CESS
	BEETHOVEN, LUDWIG			
	VAN (1770–1827)			
815,200	Adelaide (6 min.)	A	3	3
	**(DG 139125);			
	**(DG 139197)			
815,600	An die ferne Geliebte,	A	3	3
	op. 98 (14 min.)			
	**(DG 139197);			
	*(Argo ZRG–664)			
815,800	Die Ehre Gottes aus der	A	3	3
	Natur, op. 48 (3 min.)			
	*(Argo ZRG–644)			
816,000	Ich liebe dich, G. 235	S	4	3
	(2 min.)			
	**(DG 139125);			
	(2–Desto 7118/9)			
816,200	Der Kuss, op. 128 (2 min.)	S	4	3
	**(DG 139125)			
	BERG, ALBAN (1885–1935)			
816,400	Altenberg Lieder, op. 4	A	3	3
	(11 min.)			
	*(CSP CMS–6103);			
	*(DG 2530146);			
	(Col. MS–7179)			
	BERLIOZ, HECTOR			
	(1803–1869)			
816,600	Mort de Cléopâtre (21 min.)	A	4	3
	*(Ang. S–36695);			
	(CSP CMS–6438)			
816,800	Nuits d'été, op. 7 (song	S	2	3
	cycle) (31 min.)			
	**(Phi. 6500009);			
	*(Ang. S–36505);			
	*(Lon. OS 25821)			
	BISHOP, HENRY			
	(1786–1855)			
817,000	Home Sweet Home (4 min.)	E	4	1
	**(Lon. OS 25777);			
	**(2–Lon. OSA 1254)			
817,200	Lo, here the gentle lark	S	4	1
	(5 min.)			
	**(Lon. OS 25777);			
	**(2–Lon. OSA 1254)			

GUIDE NO.	COMPOSER AND TITLE	AGE MIN	AES SIG	ACCESS
	BLOCH, ERNEST (1880–1959)			
817,400	*Sacred Service, Avodath Hakodesh* (about 50 min.) (Col. MS–6221)	A	4	2
	BRAHMS, JOHANNES (1833–1897)			
818,000	*Auf dem Kirchhofe*, op. 105, no. 4 (4 min.) **(Sera. 60065)-*mono*; *(CSP AM–30405)-*mono*	A	2	2
818,250	*Botschaft*, op. 47, no. 1 (2 min.) **(Rich. R 23183)-*mono*; **(Sera. 60065)-*mono*	S	2	2
818,500	*Dein blaues Auge*, op. 59, no. 8 (2 min.) *(Lon. OS 25757)	A	3	3
818,750	*Deutsche Volkslieder* (49) (Books 1–7) **(2–Ang. S–3675)	A	3	3
819,000	*Ernste Gesänge*, op. 121 (18 min.) **(Rich. R 23183)-*mono*; **(Sera. 60065)-*mono*; *(Argo ZRG–644)	A	3	3
819,250	*Feldeinsamkeit*, op. 86, no. 2 (3 min.) **(CSP AM–30405)-*mono*	A	2	3
819,500	*Immer leiser wird mein Schlummer*, op. 105, no. 2 (4 min.) *(CSP AM–30405)-*mono*	A	2	3
819,750	*Mädchenlied*, op. 95, no. 6 *(Oiseau S–268)	S	3	2
820,250	*Die Mainacht*, op. 43, no. 2 (4 min.) *(Lon. OS 25757); *(Sera. S–60034)	S	3	1
820,750	*O liebliche Wangen*, op. 47, no. 4 (2 min.) (Orion 7040)	S	3	2
821,000	*Sapphische Ode*, op. 94, no. 4 (3 min.) **(Rich. R 23183)-*mono*; **(Sera. 60065)-*mono*; *(Argo ZRG–644); *(CSP AM–30405)-*mono*; *(Sera. S–60034); (Orion 7040)	S	3	1
821,250	*Der Schmied*, op. 19, no. 4 (1 min.) *(Oiseau S–268); *(Sera. S–60034)	S	4	1
821,500	*Songs for Alto, Viola, Piano*, op. 91 (13 min.) *(Oiseau S–268)	A	3	3
821,750	*Sonntag*, op. 47, no. 3 (1 min.) **(Sera. 60065)-*mono*; *(Lon. OS 25757)	S	3	2
822,000	*Ständchen*, op. 106, no. 1 (2 min.) **(Sera. 60065)-*mono*; *(Lon. OS 25757); *(Oiseau S–268)	S	3	2
822,500	*Vergebliches Ständchen*, op. 84, no. 4 (2 min.) *(Sera. S–60087)	S	4	2
822,750	*Wie bist du meine Königin*, op. 32, no. 9 (4 min.) *(CSP AM–30405)-*mono*	S	2	1
823,000	*Wiegenlied*, op. 49, no. 4 (2 min.)	S	3	1
	**(Ang. S–36296); *(Lon. OS 25757)			
823,250	*Wie Melodien*, op. 105, no. 1 (2 min.) **(Sera. 60065)-*mono* (Orion 7040)	A	2	2
	BRITTEN, BENJAMIN (1913–)			
823,500	*Canticles* **(Argo ZRG–5277)	A	3	3
823,501	*My Beloved Is Mine*, op. 40 (7 min.) **(Argo ZRG–5277)	A	3	3
823,502	*Abraham and Isaac*, op. 51 (16 min.) **(Argo ZRG–5277)	A	3	3
823,503	*Still Falls the Rain*, op. 55 (11 min.) **(Argo ZRG–5277)	A	3	3
824,000	*Folk Songs* (various) **(RCA LSC–2718)	S	3	3
824,250	*Les Illuminations* for Solo Voice and Orchestra, op. 18 (23 min.) **(Lon. OS 26161)	A	2	3
824,500	*Serenade* for Tenor, Horn, Strings, op. 31 (24 min.) **(Lon. OS 26161)	A	2	3
824,750	*Songs* (6) *from the Chinese*, op. 58 **(RCA LSC–2718)	S	3	2
824,751	*The Autumn Wind* (1 min.) **(RCA LSC–2718)	S	3	2
824,752	*The Big Chariot* (2 min.) **(RCA LSC–2718)	S	3	2
824,753	*Dance Song* (1 min.) **(RCA LSC–2718)	S	3	2
824,754	*Depression* (2 min.) **(RCA LSC–2718)	S	3	2
824,755	*The Herb-Boy* (1 min.) **(RCA LSC–2718)	S	3	2
824,756	*The Old Lute* (3 min.) **(RCA LSC–2718)	S	3	2
	CALDARA, ANTONIO (1670–1736)			
825,000	*Cantata: Vaticini di Pace* (Christmas) (50 min.) *(Turn. 34096)	A	4	2
	CANTELOUBE, JOSEPH (1879–1957)			
825,200	*Songs of the Auvergne* (25 min.) *(Ang. S–36897)	S	3	1
	CHANLER, THEODORE (1902–1961)			
825,400	*Epitaphs* (13 min.) *(CSP AMS–6198)	S	3	3
	COPLAND, AARON (1900–)			
825,600	*Old American Songs* (23 min.) **(Col. MS–6497)	E	3	1
825,800	*Twelve Poems of Emily Dickinson* (27 min.) *(Col. M–30375)	A	3	3
	COUPERIN, FRANÇOIS (1668–1733)			
826,000	*Leçons de Ténèbres* (Lamentations of Jeremiah) (50 min.) (RCA VICS–1431)	A	3	3

GUIDE NO.	COMPOSER AND TITLE	AGE MIN	AES SIG	AC-CESS
	COWELL, HENRY (1867–1965)			
826,250	*Toccanta* for Soprano, Flute, Cello, and Piano (11 min.) (CSP AML–4986)	A	4	4
	DEBUSSY, CLAUDE (1862–1918)			
826,750	*Chansons de Bilitis* (3) Song Cycle (10 min.) *(Lon. OS 26043); (Can. 31024); (2–Desto 7118/9)	A	3	2
826,751	*La Chevelure* (3 min.) *(Lon. OS 26043); (Can. 31024)	A	3	2
826,752	*La Flûte de Pan* (3 min.) *(Lon. OS 26043); (Can. 31024)	A	2	2
827,200	*Fêtes galantes*, Set II (8 min.) *(Tel. 6.41293)	A	4	2
827,400	*Mandoline* (1 min.) **(Ang. S–36345)	A	4	1
827,600	*Noël des enfants qui n'ont plus de maisons* (3 min.) *(Tel. 6.41293)	A	3	4
827,700	*Le Promenoir des deux amants* *(Tel. 6.41293)	A	2	3
827,701	1. *Auprès de cette grotte sombre* (3 min.) *(Tel. 6.41293)	A	2	3
827,702	2. *Crois mon conseil, chère Clymène* (2 min.) *(Tel. 6.41293)	A	2	3
827,703	3. *Je tremble en voyant ton visage* (2 min.) *(Tel. 6.41293)	A	2	3
827,800	*Trois Ballades de François Villon* (10 min.) *(Tel. 6.41293)	A	2	4
	DOWLAND, JOHN (1562–1626)			
828,000	*Away with These Self-Loving Lads* (3 min.) *(Argo 5290); *(Argo ZRG–572); (Lyr. 7153)	A	3	3
828,250	*Can She Excuse My Wrong* (3 min.) *(Argo ZRG–572); *(RCA LSC 3131)	A	3	3
828,500	*Fineknacks for Ladies* (3 min.) *(Lon. OS 25896); *(None. H–71167); (Lyr. 7153)	A	3	3
828,750	*If My Complaints* (4 min.) *(Lon. OS 25896); (Lyr. 7153)	A	3	2
829,000	*In Darkness Let Me Dwell* (5 min.) **(RCA LSC–2819)	A	2	3
829,200	*I Saw My Lady Weep* *(RCA LSC–3131)	A	2	4
829,250	*Me, Me and None But Me* (4 min.) (Lyr. 7153)	A	3	3
829,500	*Say Love If Ever Thou Didst Find* (3 min.) **(RCA LSC–2819); (Lyr. 7153)	A	3	3
829,750	*Sorrow, Stay* (3 min.) **(RCA LSC–2819); *(Argo ZRG–572); *(Lon. OS 25896)	A	2	2
830,000	*Tell Me, True Love* (3 min.) (Lyr. 7153)	A	3	3
830,250	*What If I Never Speed* (3 min.) *(Argo ZRG–572); (Lon. OS 25896); (Lyr. 7153)	A	3	3
830,500	*Wilt Thou, Unkind, Thus Leave Me* (2 min.) **(RCA LSC–2819)	A	3	3
	DVOŘÁK, ANTONIN (1841–1904)			
831,200	*Songs My Mother Taught Me*, op. 55, no. 4 (3 min.) **(Ang. S–36296); *(Ang. S–35383)	E	4	1
	ELGAR, EDWARD (1857–1934)			
831,300	*Sea Pictures* (23 min.) **(Ang. S–36796)	E	4	2
	FALLA, MANUEL DE (1876–1946)			
831,400	*El amor brujo* (25 min.) *(Lon. STS–15014)	S	3	1
831,500	*Seven Popular Spanish Songs* (13 min.) **(Ang. S–36896)	S	3	1
831,600	*Three-Cornered Hat* (ballet) (39 min.) *(Lon. CS 6224)	S	3	1
	FAURÉ, GABRIEL (1845–1924)			
832,100	*La Bonne Chanson*, op. 61 (23 min.) (Tel. 6.41298)	A	3	3
832,200	*La Chanson d'Ève*, op. 95 **(Phi. 835286)	A	3	3
832,600	*Lydia*, op. 4, no. 2 (2 min.) (Oiseau S–323)	A	3	3
832,700	*Prison*, op. 83, no. 1 (2 min.) (Oiseau S–323)	A	3	3
	FOSTER, STEPHEN (1826–1864)			
833,200	*Beautiful Dreamer* (4 min.) (None. H–71268)	E	4	1
833,300	*Jeannie with the Light Brown Hair* (3 min.) (None. H–71268)	E	4	1
833,500	*My Old Kentucky Home* (3 min.) (Col. M–32577)	E	4	1
833,800	*Old Dog Tray* (4 min.) (Col. M–32577)	E	4	1
833,900	*Swanee River* (*Old Folks at Home*) (4 min.) (Col. M–32577)	E	4	1
	GLINKA, MIKHAIL (1804–1857)			
834,100	*Doubt*, for Contralto, Harp (or piano) and Violin (5 min.) **(Odys. 32160070); (2–Desto 7118/9)	A	3	3

133

GUIDE NO.	COMPOSER AND TITLE	AGE	AES SIG	AC- MIN CESS
	GRANADOS, ENRIQUE (1867–1916)			
834,300	Colección de Tonadillas, escritas en estilo antiguo (19 min.) **(2–Ang. S–3672)	A	3	2
834,400	El Tra-la-la y el Punteado (2 min.) **(2–Ang. S–3672)	A	3	2
	GRIEG, EDVARD (1843–1907)			
834,500	Songs (variable) **(Lon. OS 25103)	S	3	2
834,600	Ich liebe dich, op. 5, no. 3 (3 min.) **(Lon. OS 25103); *(Ang. S–35383); *(Ang. S–36296)	S	3	1
	HAYDN, (FRANZ) JOSEPH (1732–1809)			
834,700	Sailor's Song (2 min.) **(RCA LSC–2718)	S	3	1
834,800	She Never Told Her Love (Shakespeare) (3 min.) **(Oiseau 60036); **(RCA LSC–2718)	S	3	1
	HOPKINSON, FRANCIS (1737–1791)			
835,000	My Days Have Been So Wondrous Free (GC 7020)-mono	A	4	2
835,100	O'er the hills and far away (GC 7020)-mono	A	4	2
	IRELAND, JOHN (1879–1962)			
835,200	Land of Lost Content (Song Cycle, 1920–21) (10 min.) **(Argo 5418)	A	4	3
	IVES, CHARLES (1874–1954)			
835,300	Ann Street (1 min.) **(None. H–71209); (Cam. 1804)	A	3	3
835,400	At the River (2 min.) **(None. H–71209); (Col. M–30229)	·A	3	2
835,500	The Cage (1 min.) **(None. H–71209); (Cam. 1804)	A	4	3
835,600	Charlie Rutlage (3 min.) **(None. H–71209); (Col. M–30229)	A	3	2
835,700	The Children's Hour (Col. M–30229)	S	3	2
835,800	A Christmas Carol (2 min.) **(None. H–71209)	E	2	1
835,850	An Election (5 min.) (Cam. 1804)	A	3	3
835,900	Evening (2 min.) **(None. H–71209)	A	2	2
836,000	A Farewell to Land (1 min.) **(None. H–71209); (Cam. 1804)	A	3	3
836,100	From The Swimmers (1 min.) *(None. H–71209)	A	2	3
836,200	General William Booth Enters Heaven (6 min.) **(None. H–71209);	S	2	1

GUIDE NO.	COMPOSER AND TITLE	AGE	AES SIG	AC- MIN CESS
	*(2–Desto 6411/2); *(Cam. 1804)			
836,400	Walt Whitman (Col. M–30229)	A	3	3
	LEONCAVALLO, RUGGIERO (1858–1919)			
836,500	Mattinata (Aubade) (2 min.) **(2–Lon. OSA 1254); *(Lon. OS 25777)	A	5	2
	LISZT, FRANZ (1811–1886)			
837,000	Oh! quand je dors (5 min.) (2–Desto 7118/9)	A	3	3
	MAHLER, GUSTAV (1860–1911)			
839,000	Kindertotenlieder (25 min.) **(DG 138879); **(2–Odys. 32260016E)- mono; *(2–Col. M2S–698)	S	3	2
839,100	Des Knaben Wunderhorn (46 min.) **(Ang. S–36547); *(Lon. OS 26195)	S	4	2
839,200	Lied von der Erde (1 hr. 3 min.) **(Rich. R–23182)-mono	A	2	2
839,300	Songs from Ruckert (5) **(2–Ang. S–3760); **(DG 138879); *(Ang. S–36796)	A	3	2
839,301	Ich atmet' einen linden Duft (3 min.) **(2–Ang. S–3760); **(Ang. S–36545); **(DG 138879); *(Ang. S–36796)	A	3	2
839,302	Liebst du um Schönheit (3 min.) **(2–Ang. S–3760); **(DG 138879); *(Ang. S–36796)	A	3	2
839,304	Ich bin der Welt abhanden gekommen (7 min.) **(2–Ang. S–3760); **(DG 138879); *(Ang. S–36796)	A	2	2
839,305	Um Mitternacht (6 min.) **(2–Ang. S–3760); **(DG 138879); *(Ang. S–36796)	A	3	2
839,400	Songs of a Wayfarer (16 min.) *(Lon. OS 26195)	A	3	2
839,500	Wo die schönen Trompeten blasen (from Des Knaben Wunderhorn) (6 min.) **(Ang. S–36547); *(Lon. OS 26195)	A	3	2
	MENDELSSOHN, FELIX (1809–1847)			
840,000	Auf Flügeln des Gesänges, op. 34, no. 2 (4 min.) **(Ang. S–36296); *(Ang. S–35383)	S	3	1
840,200	Gruss, op. 63, no. 3 (vocal duet) (2 min.) **(2–Ang. S–3697)	A	3	2

GUIDE NO.	COMPOSER AND TITLE	AGE MIN	AES SIG	AC- CESS
	MONTEVERDI, CLAUDIO (1567–1643)			
841,000	*Lagrime d'Amante al* *Sepolcro dell'Amata* (21 min.) *(Van. SRV–297 SD)	A	2	3
841,200	*Lamento d'Arianna* (15 min.) *(Van. SRV–297 SD)	S	2	3
41,400	*Lamento della ninfa* (6 min.) *(Argo ZRG–668)	S	2	2
841,600	*Maladetto sia l'aspetto* (1 min.) *(Turn. 34388)	A	3	3
841,800	*Zefiro torna* (7 min.) *(Argo ZRG–645)	A	3	3
	MORLEY, THOMAS (1557–1603)			
842,250	*I Go Before, My Darling* (canzonet for two voices) (1 min.) (Van. HM–4 SD)	S	3	2
842,500	*It Was a Lover and His Lass* (air to the lute) (3 min.) *(RCA VICS–1266); *(Tel. 6.41127); (West WGS–8216)	S	2	1
842,750	*My Bonnie Lass, She Smileth* (ballet for 5 voices) (2 min.) (West WGS–8216)	S	3	2
843,250	*Now Is the Month of* *Maying* (ballet for 5 voices) (2 min.) (Van. HM–4 SD); (West WGS–8216)	S	2	1
843,500	*O grief! Even on the Bud* (canzonet for 5 voices) (2 min.) (Van. HM–4 SD)	A	3	2
843,750	*O Mistress Mine* (air to the lute) (3 min.) *(RCA VICS–1266); *(Tel. 6.41127)	A	3	2
844,000	*Sweet Nymph, O Come to* *Thy Lover* (canzonet for 2 voices) (2 min.) *(Van. VCS–10022)	A	3	2
	MOZART, WOLFGANG **AMADEUS** (1756–1791)			
844,250	*Abendempfindung*, K. 523 (5 min.) **(Ang. 35270)-*mono*; **(DG 2530319)	A	2	2
44,500	*An Chloe*, K. 524 (3 min.) **(Ang. 35270)-*mono*	A	2	3
44,750	*Exsultate, Jubilate*, K. 165 (16 min.) **(Sera. 60013)-*mono*; *(Argo ZRG–524); *(Turn. 34029)	S	2	1
45,500	*Das Veilchen*, K. 476 **(Ang. 35270)-*mono*; **(Ang. S–36545); **(DG 2530319)	A	2	2
	MUSSORGSKY, MODEST (1839–1881)			
46,000	*Nursery* (Song Cycle) (Turn. 34331)	A	3	3

GUIDE NO.	COMPOSER AND TITLE	AGE MIN	AES SIG	AC- CESS
846,250	*Song of the Flea* (4 min.) *(Sera. 60008)-*mono*; (Argo ZRG–708)	E	3	1
846,500	*Songs and Dances of Death* (Song Cycle) (21 min.) **(Sera. 60008)-*mono*	A	2	2
	POULENC, FRANCIS (1899–1963)			
846,750	*Banalités* (9 min.) **(2–Odys. 32260009)-*mono*	A	3	3
846,751	*Chanson d'Orkenise*: no. 1 of *Banalités* (1 min.) **(2–Odys. 32260009)- *mono*; *(Lon. OS 26043)	A	3	3
846,752	*Hôtel*: no. 2 of *Banalités* (2 min.) **(2–Odys. 32260009)- *mono*; *(Lon. OS 26043)	A	3	2
846,754	*Voyage à Paris*: no. 4 of *Banalités* (1 min.) **(2–Odys. 32260009)- *mono*	A	3	2
846,850	*La Fraîcher et le Feu* (8 min.) **(Phi. 802765)	A	3	2
846,900	*(Le) Travail du Peintre* (12 min.) *(Turn. 4489)-*mono*	A	3	2
	PURCELL, HENRY (c.1659–1695)			
847,000	*I Love and I Must* (3 min.) *(Van. SRV–280SD)	A	2	2
847,250	*If Music Be the Food of* *Love* (3 min.) *(Van. SRV–280SD)	A	2	2
847,500	*Music for a While* (4 min.) *(Van. SRV–280SD)	A	2	2
	RACHMANINOFF, SERGEI (1873–1943)			
847,700	*The Harvest of Sorrow* (5 min.) (Ang. S–36917)	A	3	2
847,750	*In the Silent Night*, op. 4, no. 3 (3 min.) (Ang. S–36917)	A	2	1
848,000	*Lilacs*, op. 21, no. 5 (2 min.) (Ang. S–36917)	A	3	1
848,250	*O, Cease Thy Singing Maiden* *Fair* (5 min.) (Ang. S–36917)	A	3	1
848,750	*To the Children* (4 min.) **(Ang. S–36345); (Ang. S–36917)	A	3	2
	RAINIER, PRIAULX (1903–)			
849,000	*Cycle for Declamation* (4 min.) **(Argo 5418)	S	4	2
	RAVEL, MAURICE (1875–1937)			
849,250	*Chansons madécasses* (13 min.) **(Phi. 839733)	A	3	3
849,400	*Cinq mélodies populaires* *grecques* for soprano and orchestra (7 min.) **(Phi. 839733)	S	3	2

GUIDE NO.	COMPOSER AND TITLE	AGE MIN	AES SIG	AC- CESS
849,550	Deux mélodies hébraïques (6 min.) **(Phi. 839733)	A	3	3
849,700	Don Quichotte à Dulcinée (7 min.) **(Phi. 839733)	A	3	3
849,850	Shéhérazade (16 min.) **(Ang. S–36505); *(CSP CMS–6438); *(Lon. OS 25821)	S	3	2
	ROREM, NED (1923–)			
850,000	Alleluia (3 min.) *(2–Desto 6411/12)	S	3	3
850,100	Bedlam (4 min.) *(2–Desto 6411/12)	S	3	3
850,200	For Poulenc (3 min.) (CRI S–238)	S	3	3
850,300	Lions? (13 min.) (CRI S–238)	S	3	3
850,400	Little Elegy (2 min.) (CRI S–238)	S	3	3
850,500	Look Down, Fair Moon (1 min.) (CRI S–238)	S	3	3
850,600	Night Crow (2 min.) (CRI S–238)	S	3	3
850,700	Some Trees (10 min.) (CRI S–238)	S	3	3
850,800	The Tulip Tree (2 min.) (CRI S–238)	S	3	3
850,900	What Sparks and Wiry Cries (2 min.) (CRI S–238)	S	3	3
	ROSSINI, GIOACCHINO (1792–1868)			
851,000	Péchés de vieillesse (excerpts) (27 min.) **(None. H–71089)	A	3	2
851,250	Regata Veneziana (10 min.) *(Lon. OS 26113)	A	3	2
	SATIE, ERIK (1866–1925)			
851,500	Socrate (34 min.) (Can. 31024)	A	3	2
	SCARLATTI, ALESSANDRO (1660–1725)			
851,625	Su le Sponde del Tebro (15 min.) (Van. VCS–10028)	E	4	1
	SCHOENBERG, ARNOLD (1874–1951)			
851,750	Book of the Hanging Gardens, op. 15 (29 min.) (Col. M–31311)	A	3	3
851,800	Erwartung, op. 17 (31 min.) **(2–Col. M2S–679)	A	4	4
851,850	Ode to Napoleon, op. 41 (15 min.) (2–Col. M2S–767)	A	4	4
851,900	Pierrot Lunaire, op. 21 (34 min.) *(2–Col. M2S–679)	A	2	4
851,950	Serenade for Septet and Baritone, op. 24 (32 min.) (2–Col. M2S–762)	A	4	4
	SCHUBERT, FRANZ (1797–1828)			
852,000	Abschied (3 min.) **(Ang. S–36127); *(Sera. S–60025)	S	3	3
852,250	Allmacht (4 min.) *(Sera. S–60034)	S	3	3

GUIDE NO.	COMPOSER AND TITLE	AGE MIN	AES SIG	AC- CESS
852,500	An die Laute, op. 81, no. 2, D. 905 (2 min.) **(Ang. S–36341); **(DG 139125); *(Lon. OS 26063)	S	3	3
852,750	An die Leier, D. 737 (5 min.) (Orion 7040)	S	2	2
853,000	An die Musik (3 min.) **(Ang. S–36462); **(Rich. R–23184)-mono; *(Sera. S–60025); (Orion 7040)	S	1	1
853,500	An Sylvia, D. 891 (3 min.) *(Lon. OS 25757)	S	1	1
853,750	Atlas, D. 957/8 (2 min.) **(Ang. S–36127)	A	2	3
854,000	Auf dem Wasser zu singen, D. 774 (4 min.) **(Ang. S–36342); **(Ang. S–36462)	S	1	1
854,250	Ave Maria, D. 839 (4 min.) **(Ang. S–36462); *(2–Sera. S–6083)	E	2	2
854,500	Doppelgänger (4 min.) **(Ang. S–36127); *(CSP AM–30405)-mono	S	1	2
854,750	Du bist die Ruh, D. 776 (4 min.) **(Ang. S–36341)	S	2	2
855,000	Der Einsame, D. 800 (4 min.) **(Ang. S–36345); **(2–DG 2707031)	S	1	2
855,250	Der Erlkönig, D. 328 (4 min.) **(Ang. S–36462); **(Ang. S–36545); **(DG 2530229); *(Lon. OS 25757)	S	2	1
855,750	Fischerweise, D. 881 (3 min.) **(Ang. S–36341); *(Sera. S–60034)	S	2	2
856,000	Die Forelle, D. 550 (2 min.) **(Ang. S–36341); **(Ang. S–36462); **(Ang. S–36345); **(DG 139125)	E	1	1
856,250	Frühlingsglaube, D. 686 (3 min.) **(Ang. S–36462)	S	1	1
856,750	Ganymed, D. 544 (5 min.) **(Ang. S–36462); **(Phi. 6500515)	A	2	2
857,000	Geheimes, D. 719 (2 min.) *(Sera. S–60025)	S	2	2
857,250	Gretchen am Spinnrade, D. 118 (3 min.) **(Ang. S–36462); **(Rich. R–23184)-mono; *(2–Sera. S–6083); (RCA VICS–1405)	S	1	1
857,500	Gruppe aus dem Tartarus, D. 583 (3 min.) **(DG 2530306)	A	2	2
857,750	Heidenröslein, D. 257 (2 min.) **(Ang. S–36341); **(Ang. S–36345); **(DG 2530229)	S	1	1
858,000	Der Hirt auf dem Feisen, D. 965 (12 min.) (RCA VICS–1405)	A	2	2

GUIDE NO.	COMPOSER AND TITLE	AGE MIN	AES SIG	AC- CESS
858,250	*Im Abendroth*, D. 799 (4 min.)	S	1	2
	*(Lon. OS 25757); *(Sera. S–60025)			
858,500	*Im Frühling*, D. 882 (4 min.)	S	2	1
	*(Sera. S–60025); (RCA VICS–1405)			
858,750	*Jüngling an der Quelle*, D. 300 (2 min.)	S	1	2
	**(Ang. S–36341); **(Ang. S–36345); *(Lon. OS 26063); (RCA VICS–1405)			
859,000	*Jüngling und der Tod*, D. 545 (4 min.)	A	2	2
	**(Ang. S–36342); **(DG 2530347)			
859,250	*Lachen und Weinen*, D. 777 (2 min.)	S	1	2
	**(Ang. S–36341); **(Ang. S–36462)			
859,500	*Liebe schwarmt auf' allen Wegen*, D. 239 (1 min.)	A	3	2
	**(Ang. S–36345); (2–Sera. S–6083)			
859,750	*Liebesbotschaft* (3 min.)	S	2	2
	**(Ang. S–36127)			
860,000	*Lied eines Schiffers an die Dioskuren*, D. 360 (3 min.)	S	2	2
	**(DG 139125)			
860,250	*Lindenbaum*, D. 911 (4 min.)	S	3	2
	*(CSP AM–30405)-*mono*; *(Sera. S–60025)			
860,500	*Litanei auf das Fest Aller Seelen*, D. 343 (4 min.)	A	2	2
	**(Ang. S–36342); **(Ang. S–36462)			
860,750	*Musensohn*, D. 764 (2 min.)	S	1	1
	**(Ang. S–36462); **(DG 139125); **(Rich. R–23184)-*mono*; (RCA VICS–1405)			
861,500	*Rastlose Liebe*, D. 138 (1 min.)	S	2	2
	**(DG 2530229)			
862,000	*Die Schöne Müllerin*, D. 795 (1 hr. 2 min.)	S	1	2
	*(2–Ang. S–3628)			
862,250	*Schwanengesang*, D. 744- cycle	A	3	2
	**(Ang. S–36127)			
862,500	*Seligkeit*, D. 433 (2 min.)	S	1	1
	**(Ang. S–36341); **(Ang. S–36345); (RCA VICS–1405)			
862,750	*Ständchen* (4 min.)	S	1	1
	**(Ang. S–36341); **(Ang. S–36127); *(Sera. S–60025)			
863,000	*Tod und das Mädchen*, D. 531 (3 min.)	A	1	1
	**(Ang. S–36342); **(Ang. S–36462)			
863,250	*Die Vögel*, D. 691 (1 min.)	S	3	2
	(RCA VICS–1405)			
863,750	*Der Wanderer*, D. 493 (6 min.)	S	2	1
	**(Ang. S–36342); *(CSP AM–30405)-*mono*; *(Lon. 25757)			
864,250	*Wanderers Nachtlied*, D. 224 (2 min.)	S	2	2
	**(DG 2530229); *(Sera. S–60025)			

GUIDE NO.	COMPOSER AND TITLE	AGE MIN	AES SIG	AC- CESS
864,500	*Winterreise*, D. 911 (1 hr. 34 min.)	A	1	2
	**(2–DG 2707028)			
	SCHUMANN, ROBERT (1810–1856)			
865,000	*Alte Laute* (2 min.)	S	3	2
	*(Sera. S–60025)			
865,250	*An den Sonnenschein* (2 min.)	S	3	2
	**(DG 139326)			
865,500	*Aufträge* (4 min.)	S	2	2
	*(BASF 29369)			
865,750	*Die beiden Grenadiere* (4 min.)	S	2	1
	*(Sera. S–60025)			
866,250	*Dein Angesicht* (3 min.)	A	3	2
	**(Ang. S–36545)			
866,500	*Dichterliebe*, op. 48 (29 min.)	S	1	2
	**(DG 139109); *(DG 139125)			
866,750	*Frauenliebe und Leben*, op. 42 (22 min.)	S	2	3
	*(Oiseau S–293); *(Rich. R–23184)-*mono*			
867,000	*Die Kartenlegerin* (4 min.)	A	3	2
	**(Ang. S–36545); *(BASF 29369)			
867,250	*Lehn' deine Wang'* (1 min.)	A	3	2
	**(DG 139125); **(Lon. OS 26216)			
867,500	*Liederkreis* (Song Cycle), op. 24 (20 min.)	A	3	2
	**(DG 139109)			
867,750	*Liederkreis* (Song Cycle), op. 39 (26 min.)	A	3	2
	**(Ang. S–36266)			
868,000	*Loreley* (4 min.)	S	2	2
	*(BASF 29369)			
868,250	*Die Lotosblume ängstigt sich* (3 min.)	S	2	2
	**(Lon. OS 26216)			
868,750	*Mondnacht* (3 min.)	S	2	1
	**(Ang. S–36266); *(CSP AM–30405)-*mono*; *(Sera. S–60025)			
869,000	*Der Nussbaum* (3 min.)	S	2	1
	*(BASF 29369)			
869,500	*Widmung* (3 min.)	S	2	1
	**(Rich. R–23184)-*mono*; *(BASF 29369)			
	SCHÜRMANN, GERARD (1928–)			
869,750	*Chuench'l* (Song cycle from the Chinese) (17 min.)	A	2	3
	**(None. H–71209)			
	SIBELIUS, JEAN (1865–1957)			
870,000	*Autumn Evening* (5 min.)	A	3	3
	**(Lon. OS 25005); **(Lon. OS 26030); *(Lon. OS 25942)			
870,100	*Black Roses* (2 min.)	S	3	2
	**(Lon. OS 25005); *(Lon. OS 25942)			
870,200	*The Diamond on the March Snow* (2 min.)	S	3	2
	**(Lon. OS 25005); **(Lon. OS 26030); *(Lon. OS 25942)			
870,300	*The Maiden Returned from Her Tryst* (3 min.)	S	3	1
	**(Lon. OS 25005); **(Lon. OS 26030); *(Lon. OS 25942)			

137

GUIDE NO.	COMPOSER AND TITLE	AGE MIN	AES SIG	ACCESS
	STRAUSS, RICHARD (1864–1949)			
870,500	*Ach, Weh mir unglückhaftem Mann* (2 min.) *(Lon. OS 25783); *(Sera. S–60025)	A	3	3
870,750	*Allerseelen* (3 min.) **(Ang. S–36483); *(Lon. OS 25757); *(Sera. S–60034)	A	2	3
871,000	*Aus den Liedern der Trauer* **(Ang. S–36483)	A	4	3
871,250	*Barkarole* **(Ang. S–36483)	A	4	3
871,750	*Breit über mein Haupt* (2 min.) *(Lon. OS 25783)	A	3	2
872,000	*Cäcilie* (2 min.) *(Lon. OS 25783)	A	3	2
872,250	*Four Last Songs* (20 min.) **(Ang. S–36347); (DG 2530368)	A	2	3
872,500	*Freundliche Vision* (3 min.) **(Ang. S–36347); **(3–Sera. 6041)-*mono*	A	3	2
872,750	*Die Heiligen drei Könige* (4 min.) **(Ang. S–36347)	A	3	2
873,000	*Heimliche Aufforderung* (3 min.) *(Lon. OS 25757); *(Lon. OS 25783)	A	2	3
873,500	*Ich trage meine Minne* (3 min.) *(Sera. S–60025)	A	2	3
873,750	*Lob des Leidens* **(Ang. S–36483)	A	4	3
874,000	*Morgen* (4 min.) **(Ang. S–36643); **(3–Sera. 6041)	A	2	2
874,250	*Die Nacht* (3 min.) **(Ang. S–36483); *(Sera. S–60025)	A	2	3
874,500	*Ruhe, meine Seele* (4 min.) **(Ang. S–36643); *(Lon. OS 25783)	A	2	2
874,750	*Schlechtes Wetter* (2 min.) **(3–Sera. 6041)-*mono*	A	3	3
875,000	*Ständchen* (2 min.) **(Ang. S–36483); **(3–Sera. 6041)-*mono;* *(Lon. OS 25757); *(Lon. OS 25783)	S	2	2
875,250	*Traum durch die Dämmerung* (3 min.) *(Lon. OS 25783); *(CSP AM–30405)-*mono*	A	2	3
875,500	*Waldseligkeit* (3 min.) **(Ang. S–36347)	A	3	3
876,000	*Wiegenlied* (5 min.) **(Ang. S–36643); **(3–Sera. 6041)-*mono*	A	3	3
876,250	*Zueignung* (2 min.) **(Ang. S–36347); *(CSP AM–30405)-*mono;* *(Lon. OS 25783)	S	2	1
	STRAVINSKY, IGOR (1882–1971)			
876,500	*Berceuses du chat* (4 min.) *(Col. MS–7439)	E	3	2
876,600	Four Russian Songs (5 min.) *(Col. MS–7439)	E	3	3

GUIDE NO.	COMPOSER AND TITLE	AGE MIN	AES SIG	ACCESS
876,700	*In Memoriam Dylan Thomas* *(Col. MS–6992)	A	3	3
876,800	*Pribaoutki* (4 min.) *(Col. MS–7439)	S	3	2
	TCHAIKOVSKY, PETER ILYITCH (1840–1893)			
877,000	*Again, As Before, Alone* op. 73, no. 6 (2 min.) *(Argo ZRG–707)	A	3	2
877,100	*At the Ball,* op. 38, no. 3 (3 min.) *(Argo ZRG–707)	A	3	2
877,200	*Don Juan's Serenade,* op. 38, no. 1 (3 min.) *(Argo ZRG–707)	A	2	2
877,300	*None But the Lonely Heart* op. 6, no. 6 (4 min.) *(Argo ZRG–707); (2–Desto 7118/9)	S	2	1
	TOSTI, FRANCESCO PAOLO (1846–1916)			
877,500	*Le Serenata* (4 min.) **(Lon. OS 25777); **(2–Lon. OSA 1254)	S	4	1
	VILLA-LOBOS, HEITOR (1887–1959)			
877,600	*Bachianas* no. 5 for Soprano and 8 Celli (11 min.) *(Col. MS–6514)	S	2	2
	WAGNER, RICHARD (1813–1883)			
877,800	*Wesendonck* Songs (21 min.) **(Lon. OS 25101)	A	3	2
	WOLF, HUGO (1860–1903)			
878,250	*Verschwiegene Liebe* (3 min.) *(Lon. OS 26043)	A	2	2
878,500	*Goethe* Lieder	A	2	2
878,750	*Anakreon's Grab* (4 min.) *(Lon. OS 26043)	A	2	2
879,000	*Epiphanias* **(Sera. 60179)-*mono;* *(Oiseau S–293)	A	3	2
879,250	*Kennst du das Land?* (6 min.) *(Oiseau S–293)	A	3	2
879,500	*Italienisches Liederbuch* **(2–Ang. S–3703)	A	2	2
879,750	*Auch kleine Dinge* (2 min.) **(2–Ang. S–3703); *(Oiseau S–293)	A	1	2
880,000	*Du denkst mit einem Fädchen* (2 min.) **(2–Ang. S–3703)	A	2	3
880,250	*Ihr jungen Leute* (1 min.) **(2–Ang. S–3703)	A	3	3
880,500	*Nein, junger Herr* (1 min.) **(2–Ang. S–3703)	A	2	3
880,750	*Nun lass uns Frieden schliessen* (2 min.) **(2–Ang. S–3703)	A	3	3
881,000	*Und willst du deinen Liebsten sterben sehen* (2 min.) **(2–Ang. S–3703)	A	3	3
881,250	*Mausfallensprüchlein* (2 min.) *(Oiseau S–293)	A	2	3

GUIDE NO.	COMPOSER AND TITLE	AGE MIN	AES SIG	AC- CESS
81,500	*Mörike* Lieder (46 songs)	A	3	3
	*(3–DG 2709053)			
81,750	*Auf ein altes Bild* (3 min.)	A	3	2
	**(Rich. R–23184)-*mono*;			
	*(3–DG 2709053)			
82,000	*Auf einer Wanderung*	A	2	3
	(3 min.)			
	**(Rich. R–23184)-*mono*;			
	*(Sera. S–60034)			
82,250	*Der Gärtner* (2 min.)	A	2	2
	**(Rich. R–23184)-*mono*;			
	*(3–DG 2709053);			
	*(Lon. OS 26043)			
82,500	*Gebet* (3 min.)	A	3	2
	*(3–DG 2709053);			
	*(Phi. 6500128)			
82,750	*Gesang Weyla's* (2 min.)	A	2	3
	*(3–DG 2709053);			
	*(Sera. S–60034)			
83,000	*Heimweh* (2 min.)	A	3	3
	*(3–DG 2709053);			
	*(Lon. OS 26043);			
	*(Phi. 6500128)			
83,125	*In der Frühe* (3 min.)	A	3	2
	*(3–DG 2709053);			

GUIDE NO.	COMPOSER AND TITLE	AGE MIN	AES SIG	AC- CESS
	*(Lon. OS 26043);			
	*(Phi. 6500128)			
883,250	*Nimmersatte Liebe* (2 min.)	A	3	3
	**(Ang. S–36545);			
	*(3–DG 2709053);			
	*(Phi. 6500128)			
883,500	*Schlafendes Jesuskind*	A	3	3
	(4 min.)			
	**(Sera. 60179)-*mono*;			
	*(3–DG 2709053);			
	*(Phi. 6500128)			
883,750	*Verborgenheit* (3 min.)	A	2	3
	**(Rich. R–23184)-*mono*;			
	**(Ang. S–36545);			
	*(3–DG 2709053)			
884,000	*Das verlassene Mägdlein*	A	2	3
	**(2–Ang. S–3697);			
	*(Lon. OS 26043);			
	*(Phi. 6500128)			
	Spanisches Liederbuch			
885,250	*Herr, was trägt der Boden*	A	3	3
	hier (3 min.)			
	**(Sera. 60179)-*mono*			
886,250	*Wenn du zu den Blumen*	A	3	3
	gehst (3 min.)			
	**(Ang. S–36345)			

---

9. Popular Arias

(See Choral Music and Operas, categories 2 and 10, for recommended albums of works from which arias are excerpted.)

GUIDE NO.	COMPOSER AND TITLE	AGE MIN	AC- CESS
	BELLINI, VINCENZO		
	(1801–1835)		
887,100	*Norma: Casta diva* (9 min.)	S	1
	**(Ang. S–35666);		
	**(Lon. OS 25232);		
	**(RCA LSC–2862)		
887,150	*I Puritani: A Teo cara* (3 min.)	A	3
	*(Lon. OS 25922)		
887,200	*I Puritani: Qui la Voce* (7 min.)	A	2
	**(Lon. OS 25922)		
887,250	*I Puritani: Son vergin Vezzosa*	A	3
	(4 min.)		
	**(Lon. OS 25232)		
887,300	*La Sonnambula: Ah non credea*	A	2
	mirarte (11 min.)		
	*(Lon. OS 25887)		
887,350	*La Sonnambula: Come per me*	A	3
	sereno (5 min.)		
	**(Lon. OS 25233)		
	BIZET, GEORGES		
	(1838–1875)		
887,600	*Carmen: L'amour est un oiseau*	S	1
	(Habanera) (4 min.)		
	**(Ang. S–35818)		
	BOITO, ARRIGO		
	(1842–1918)		
887,800	*Mefistofele: L'altra notte il*	A	2
	fondo (5 min.)		
	**(Lon. OS 25729);		
	*(Lon. OS 25083)		
	CHARPENTIER, GUSTAVE		
	(1860–1956)		
888,000	*Louise: Depuis le jour* (5 min.)	A	1
	**(DG 2530073)		

GUIDE NO.	COMPOSER AND TITLE	AGE MIN	AC- CESS
	DELIBES, LÉO		
	(1836–1891)		
888,050	*Lakmé: Bell Song* (7 min.)	A	2
	**(Lon. OS 25232);		
	*(Lon. OS 26201)		
	DONIZETTI, GAETANO		
	(1797–1848)		
888,450	*Lucia di Lammermoor:* Mad	A	3
	Scene (16 min.)		
	**(Lon. OS 25702)		
888,650	*Lucrezia Borgia: Brindisi*	A	3
	(4 min.)		
	(RCA LSC–3038)		
	GIORDANO, UMBERTO		
	(1867–1948)		
888,750	*Andrea Chénier: Caro mio ben*	A	3
	(3 min.)		
	*(Lon. OS 25076)		
888,800	*Andrea Chénier: Come un bel*	A	2
	di di Maggio (3 min.)		
	**(Lon. OS 25075)		
888,850	*Andrea Chénier: La Mamma*	A	2
	morta (5 min.)		
	**(Lon. OS 25729)		
	GLUCK, CHRISTOPH WILLIBALD (1714–1787)		
889,150	*Orfeo: Che farò senza Euridice?*	A	2
	(4 min.)		
	*(Lon. OS 26214)		
	GOUNOD, CHARLES		
	(1818–1893)		
889,300	*Faust: Avant de quitter* (5 min.)	S	3
	*(Lon. OS 26139)		

GUIDE NO.	COMPOSER AND TITLE	AGE MIN	AC-CESS
889,350	Faust: Il était un roi de Thule (11 min.) **(DG 2530073)	S	3
889,400	Faust: Jewel Song (5 min.) **(DG 2530073); **(Lon. OS 25233)	S	2
889,550	Roméo et Juliette: Je veux vivre (4 min.) **(DG 2530073); (Ang. S–36731)	A	2
	HALÉVY, JACQUES-FRANÇOIS-FROMENTAL-ELIAS (1799–1862)		
889,650	La Juive: Rachel, quand du Seigneur (6 min.) (RCA ARL 1–0447)	A	2
	HANDEL, GEORGE FRIDERIC (1685–1759)		
889,800	Berenice: Si tra i ceppi (4 min.) (4 min.) **(Lon. OS 25994)	A	3
889,850	Guilio Cesare: Piangerò, la sorte mia (6 min.) *(Lon. OS 25876)	A	3
	KIENZL, WILHELM (1857–1941)		
890,300	Evangelimann: Selig sind die Verfolgung leiden (3 min.) **(RCA VICS–1235)	S	3
	LEONCAVALLO, RUGGIERO (1858–1919)		
890,350	I Pagliacci: No Pagliacco non son (3 min) *(Lon. OS 25334)	A	3
890,400	I Pagliacci: Si può? (prologue) (8 min.) **(Lon. OS 25994)	A	3
	MASCAGNI, PIETRO (1863–1945)		
890,500	Cavalleria Rusticana: Lola (3 min.) **(RCA VICS–1235); *(DG 136281)	S	3
890,550	Cavalleria Rusticana: Mamma quel vino (4 min.) **(RCA VICS–1235)	S	1
890,600	Cavalleria Rusticana: Viva il vino (Brindisi) (4 min.) **(RCA VICS–1235)	S	2
	MASSENET, JULES (1842–1912)		
890,800	Le Cid: Pleurez! pleurez, mes yeux! (6 min.) **(2–Lon. OSA 1254)	A	3
890,850	Manon: Adieu, notre petite table (4 min.) (ABC ATS–20013)	S	2
	MEYERBEER, GIACOMO (1791–1864)		
891,150	L'Africaine: O Paradiso (3 min.) **(Lon. OS 25075)	A	1
891,200	Dinorah: Ombre leggiera (6 min.) **(2–Lon. OSA 1254)	A	3
891,250	Les Huguenots: Nobles seigneurs, salut! (4 min.) **(Lon. OS 25910); (Lon. OS 26239)	A	3
891,300	Les Huguenots: O beau pays de la Touraine (7 min.) **(DG 2530073); **(Lon. OS 25232)	A	3
	MOZART, WOLFGANG AMADEUS (1756–1791)		
891,500	Abduction from the Seraglio: Martern aller Arten (8 min.) **(Lon. OS 25233)	A	3
891,550	Così fan tutte: Come scoglio (6 min.) **(Ang. S–36167); **(Lon. OS 25782)	A	3
891,600	Così fan tutte: Per pietà (8 min.) **(Lon. OS 25782)	A	1
891,650	Don Giovanni: Batti, batti, bel Masetto (4 min.) *(Lon. OS 25115)	A	2
891,950	Don Giovanni: Madamina! il catalogo e questo (5 min.) *(Lon. OS 25769); **(Lon. OS 25994)	A	2
892,100	Magic Flute: Ach, Ich fühl's (5 min.) **(Lon. OS 25045); **(Lon. OS 26257)	S	2
892,150	Magic Flute: Dies Bildnis ist bezaubernd schön (4 min.) **(RCA VICS–1235)	S	2
892,250	Magic Flute: Vogelfänger bin ich ja (3 min.) **(Lon. OS 25994)	S	1
892,300	Marriage of Figaro: Deh vieni, non tardar (5 min.) **(Lon. OS 25045)	S	1
892,400	Marriage of Figaro: Non più andrai (3 min.) *(Lon. OS 25994)	S	2
892,550	Marriage of Figaro: Voi che sapete (3 min.) **(Lon. OS 25782)	S	1
	PONCHIELLI, AMILCARE (1834–1886)		
892,600	La Gioconda: Cielo e mar! (5 min.) **(Lon. OS 26162)	S	1
	PUCCINI, GIACOMO (1858–1924)		
893,000	La Bohème: Che gelida manina (5 min.) **(RCA VICS–1235); **(Ang. 36199)	S	1
893,100	La Bohème: Donde lieta uscì (3 min.) **(Lon. OS 25729); *(Ang. 36199)	S	2
893,200	La Bohème: Mi chiamano Mimi (5 min.) **(Lon. OS 25729)	S	1
893,400	La Bohème: Quando m'en vo' soletta (Musetta's Waltz) (3 min) *(Sera. 60202)-mono	S	1
893,600	Madame Butterfly: Addio fiorito asil (2 min.) **(Ang. S–35821); **(RCA VICS–1235)	S	2
893,700	Madame Butterfly: Tu, tu piccolo iddio (2 min.) **(RCA LSC–2506)	S	3
893,800	Madame Butterfly: Un bel dì, vedremo (5 min.)	S	1

140

GUIDE NO.	COMPOSER AND TITLE	AGE MIN	ACCESS
	(Lon. OS 25729);		
	(RCA LSC–2506)		
894,000	*La fanciulla del West: Ch'ella mi creda libero* (3 min.)	A	2
	*(Lon. OS 25196)		
894,100	*Manon Lescaut: Donna non vidi mai* (2 min.)	S	1
	**(Lon. OS 25075);		
	**(RCA LM–2784)-*mono*;		
	*(Lon. OS 25713)		
894,400	*Tosca: E lucevan le stelle* (3 min.)	S	1
	**(Lon. OS 25075);		
	*(Lon. OS 25218)		
894,500	*Tosca: Recondita armonia* (3 min.)	S	1
	**(Lon. OS 25075)		
894,600	*Tosca: Vissi d'arte* (3 min.)	S	1
	**(Lon. OS 25729);		
	**(RCA LSC–2506);		
	**(Sera. 60202)-*mono*		
894,700	*Turandot: In questa reggia* (6 min.)	A	3
	**(Ang. S–36537)		
894,800	*Turandot: Nessun dorma* (3 min.)	A	1
	**(RCA VICS–1235)		
894,900	*Turandot: Non piangere, Liù* (3 min.)	A	1
	**(RCA VICS–1235)		
895,000	*Turandot: Signore, ascolta* (8 min.)	A	2
	**(Lon. OS 25729);		
	**(RCA LSC–2506)		
895,100	*Turandot: Tu che di gel sei cinta* (3 min.)	A	2
	**(Lon. OS 25729);		
	**(RCA LSC–2506)		

ROSSINI, GIOACCHINO
(1792–1868)

895,200	*Barber of Seville: La Calunnia e un venticello* (4 min.)	S	3
	*(Lon. OS 26007)		
895,700	*Semiramide: Bel raggio lusinghier* (6 min.)	S	2
	**(Lon. OS 25233);		
	*(Lon. OS 26086)		

SAINT-SAËNS, CAMILLE
(1835–1921)

895,800	*Samson et Dalila: Amour, viens aider ma faiblesse* (4 min.)	A	3
	(Ang. S–36210)		

STRAUSS, JOHANN
(1825–1899)

896,100	*Die Fledermaus: Czárdás* (4 min.)	S	1
	**(Lon. OS 25923)		

STRAUSS, RICHARD
(1864–1949)

896,200	*Salome:* Final Scene (15 min.)	A	3
	**(Lon. OS 26169);		
	**(Sera. 60202)-*mono*		

THOMAS, AMBROISE
(1811–1896)

896,350	*Hamlet:* Ophelia's Mad Scene (9 min.)	A	3
	**(Lon. OS 25232)		

VERDI, GIUSEPPE
(1813–1901)

896,500	*Aïda: Celeste Aïda* (5 min.)	S	1
	**(Lon. OS 25075);		
	**(Lon. OS 25206)		

GUIDE NO.	COMPOSER AND TITLE	AGE MIN	ACCESS
896,700	*Aïda: Oh, patria mia, mai piu ti rivedro* (6 min.)	S	2
	*(RCA LSC–2506)		
896,900	*Aïda: Ritorna vincitor!* (7 min.)	S	1
	**(Sera. 60202)-*mono*;		
	*(RCA LSC–2506)		
897,000	*Un ballo in maschera: Di' tu se fedele il flutto m'aspetta* (4 min.)	A	2
	*(Lon. OS 25714)		
897,200	*Un ballo in maschera: Ma dall' avido stelo divulsa* (8 min.)	A	3
	**(RCA LSC–3182)		
897,500	*Don Carlos: Ella giammai m'amò!* (10 min.)	A	3
	**(Lon. OS 25769);		
	*(Lon. OS 26041)		
897,900	*Ernani: Come rugiada al cespite* (7 min.)	A	3
	*(RCA LSC–3035)		
898,000	*Ernani: Come Ernani! involami* (8 min.)	A	2
	**(Lon. OS 25939)		
898,200	*La Forza del Destino: O tu che in seno agli angeli* (6 min.)	A	2
	**(Lon. OS 25075);		
	*(Lon. OS 25085)		
898,600	*Luisa Miller: Quando le sere al placido* (5 min.)	A	3
	**(Lon. OS 25075);		
	*(RCA LSC–3037)		
898,800	*Otello: Ave Maria* (4 min.)	S	1
	**(RCA LSC–3209);		
	*(Lon. OS 25701)		
898,900	*Otello: Credo in un Dio crudel* (5 min.)	S	3
	**(Lon. OS 25994)		
899,100	*Otello: Willow Song* (10 min.)	S	1
	**(Lon. OS 25233)		
899,300	*Rigoletto: Caro nome* (6 min.)	S	1
	**(Lon. OS 25232);		
	**(Lon. OS 25939)		
899,500	*Rigoletto: La donna è mobile* (2 min.)	S	1
	**(RCA VICS–1235)		
899,800	*Rigoletto: Questa o quella* (2 min.)	S	1
	**(RCA VICS–1235)		
900,000	*La Traviata: Addio, del passato* (5 min.)	S	2
	**(Lon. OS 25886);		
	**(Lon. OS 25939)		
900,100	*La Traviata: Ah! fors' e lui* (8 min.)	S	1
	**(Lon. OS 25233);		
	**(Lon. OS 25939)		
900,500	*Il Trovatore: Ah! sì ben mio coll'essere* (3 min.)	S	1
	**(Lon. OS 25075);		
	(RCA LSC–3203)		
900,600	*Il Trovatore: D'amor sull' ali rosee* (5 min.)	S	2
	*(RCA LSC–2506)		
900,900	*Il Trovatore: Tacea la notte placida* (5 min.)	S	1
	*(RCA LSC–2506)		
901,000	*I Vespri Siciliani: Mercè, dilette amiche* (3 min.)	S	2
	**(Lon. OS 25939);		
	(RCA ARL1–0566)		

141

GUIDE NO. COMPOSER AND TITLE	AGE MIN	AC-CESS		GUIDE NO. COMPOSER AND TITLE	AGE MIN	AC-CESS
WAGNER, RICHARD (1813–1883)				902,600 *Tannhäuser: Allmächt'ge Jungfrau* (Elizabeth's Prayer) (6 min.) ** (Lon. OS 26299)	S	3
902,200 *Lohengrin: Elsa's dream* (6 min.) * (Ang. S–36313)	S	2				
902,300 *Lohengrin: In ferem Land* (6 min.) ** (RCA LM–2784)-*mono*	S	2		902,900 *Tristan and Isolde: Liebestod* (7 min.) ** (Sera. 60145)-*mono*	S	1
902,400 *Die Meistersinger: Am stillen Herd* (4 min.) * (Ang. S–36922)	S	3		903,000 *Die Walküre: Du bist der Lenz* (2 min.) ** (Lon. OS 26085)	S	3

10. Operas

GUIDE NO. COMPOSER AND TITLE	AGE MIN	AES SIG	AC-CESS		GUIDE NO. COMPOSER AND TITLE	AGE MIN	AES SIG	AC-CESS
BARTÓK, BÉLA (1881–1945)					BRITTEN BENJAMIN (1913–)			
905,000 *Bluebeard's Castle,* op. 11 (54 min.) ** (Lon. OSA 1158)	A	4	3		909,000 *Albert Herring* (2 hr. 16 min.) ** (3–Lon. OSA 1378)	A	4	3
BEESON, JACK (1921–)					909,250 *Billy Budd* (2 hr. 36 min.) ** (3–Lon. OSA 1390)	A	3	3
905,250 *Hello Out There* (35 min.) (Desto 6451)	A	4	3		909,500 *Burning Fiery Furnace* (1 hr. 3 min.) ** (Lon. OSA 1163)	A	3	3
BEETHOVEN, LUDWIG VAN (1770–1827)					909,750 *Curlew River* (1 hr. 6 min.) ** (Lon. OSA 1156)	A	3	3
905,500 *Fidelio,* op. 72 (2 hr. 37 min.) ** (3–Ang. S–3625)	A	2	4		910,250 *Midsummer Night's Dream* (2 hr. 23 min.) * (3–Lon. OSA 1385)	S	2	3
BELLINI, VINCENZO (1801–1835)					910,500 *Noye's Fludde* (49 min.) ** (Argo ZNF–1)	E	3	2
905,750 *Beatrice di Tenda* (2 hr. 27 min.) * (3–Lon. OSA 1384)	A	5	3		910,750 *Peter Grimes* (2 hr. 30 min.) ** (3–Lon. OSA 1305)	S	1	3
906,000 *Norma* (2 hr. 40 min.) * (3–Ang. S–3615)	A	3	2		911,000 *Rape of Lucretia* (1 hr. 47 min.) ** (2–Lon. OSA 1288)	A	3	3
906,250 *I Puritani* (2 hr. 30 min.) * (3–Lon. OSA 1373)	A	4	3		911,250 *Turn of the Screw* (1 hr. 45 min.) ** (2–Rich. RS–62021)-*mono*	A	3	4
906,500 *La Sonnambula* (2 hr. 16 min.) * (3–Lon. OSA 1365)	A	4	3		CAVALLI, PIER FRANCISCO (1602–1676)			
BERG, ALBAN (1885–1935)					911,500 *La Calisto* * (2–Argo ZNF–11/12)	A	3	3
906,750 *Lulu* (2 hr. 5 min.) * (3–DG 2709029)	A	3	5		911,750 *L'Ormindo* (2 hr. 10 min.) * (2–Argo ZNF–8/10)	A	4	3
907,000 *Wozzeck* (1 hr. 30 min.) ** (2–DG 2707023); ** (2–Odys. Y2–33126)-*mono*	A	1	4		CHERUBINI, LUIGI (1760–1842)			
BERLIOZ, HECTOR (1803–1869)					912,000 *Medea* (2 hr. 5 min.) ** (3–Ev./Cet. S–437/3)	A	4	3
907,250 *Béatrice et Bénédict* (1 hr. 26 min.) * (2–Oiseau S–256/7)	A	3	4		DEBUSSY, CLAUDE (1862–1918)			
907,500 *Les Troyens* (3 hr. 55 min.) * (5–Phi. 6709002)	A	4	4		913,500 *Pelléas et Mélisande* (2 hr. 35 min.) * (3–Lon. OSA 1379)	A	1	3
BIZET, GEORGES (1838–1875)					DELIBES, LÉO (1836–1891)			
907,750 *Carmen* (2 hr. 30 min.) ** (3–Ang. S–3613)	S	2	1		913,750 *Lakmé* (2 hr. 10 min.) * (3–Lon. OSA 1391)	A	5	2
908,000 *Les Pêcheurs de perles* (1 hr. 43 min.) (2–Ang. S–3603)	S	4	3		DONIZETTI, GAETANO (1797–1848)			
BOITO, ARRIGO (1842–1918)					913,875 *Anna Bolena* (1830) * (4–Lon. OSA 1436)	A	4	2
908,500 *Mefistofele* (2 hr. 30 min.) * (3–Lon. OSA 1307)	A	5	3		914,250 *Don Pasquale* (2 hr.) ** (2–Lon. OSA 1260)	A	4	2
BORODIN, ALEXANDER (1833–1887)					914,500 *L'elisir d'amore* (1 hr. 57 min.) (3–Lon. OSA 13101)	A	3	2
908,750 *Prince Igor* (3 hr. 15 min.) (4–Rich. SRS–64506)	A	4	3					

GUIDE NO. COMPOSER AND TITLE	AGE MIN	AES SIG	AC- CESS
14,750 *La Favorita* (2 hr. 10 min.) (3–Rich. SRS–63510)	A	4	3
915,000 *La Fille du Régiment* (1 hr. 38 min.) (2–Lon. OSA 1273)	A	4	3
915,250 *Lucia di Lammermoor* (2 hr. 5 min.) **(3–Lon. OSA 13103)	A	4	2
915,500 *Lucrezia Borgia* (2 hr. 14 min.) (3–RCA LSC–6176)	A	5	3
FALLA, MANUEL DE (1876–1946)			
916,250 *Retablo de Maese Pedro* (27 min.) **(Lon. STS–15014)	A	3	4
916,500 *Vida breve* (1 hr. 4 min.) **(2–Ang. S–3672)	A	4	3
FLOTOW, FRIEDRICH VON (1812–1883)			
916,750 *Martha* (2 hr. 9 min.) (3–Ang. 3753)	A	4	3
GERSHWIN, GEORGE (1898–1937)			
917,000 *Porgy and Bess* (1935) (2 hr. 10 min.) (3–Odys. 32360018E)-*mono*	S	2	1
GILBERT, WILLIAM S. (1836–1911) and SULLIVAN, SIR ARTHUR (1842–1900)			
917,250 *Gondoliers* (2 hr.) **(3–Lon. OSA 1323)	S	4	2
917,500 *H.M.S. Pinafore* (1 hr. 25 min.) **(2–Lon. OSA 1209)	S	4	1
917,750 *Iolanthe* (1 hr. 58 min.) **(2–Lon. OSA 1215)	S	3	2
918,000 *Mikado* (1 hr. 30 min.) **(2–Lon. OSA 1201)	S	3	1
918,250 *Pirates of Penzance* (1 hr. 28 min.) **(2–Lon. OSA 1277)	S	3	1
918,500 *Princess Ida* (1 hr. 22 min.) **(2–Lon. OSA 1262)	S	4	2
918,750 *Ruddigore* (1 hr. 30 min.) **(2–Lon. OSA 1248)	S	4	2
919,000 *The Yeomen of the Guard* (1 hr. 33 min.) **(2–Lon. OSA 1258)	S	3	2
GIORDANO, UMBERTO (1867–1948)			
919,250 *Andrea Chénier* (1 hr. 50 min.) *(3–Lon. OSA 1303)	A	5	2
GLUCK, CHRISTOPH WILLIBALD (1714–1787)			
919,750 *Alceste* (2 hr. 51 min.) *(3–Rich. SRS–63512)	A	3	3
920,250 *Orfeo ed Euridice* (1 hr. 48 min.) *(2–Lon. OSA 1285)	A	3	1
GOUNOD, CHARLES (1818–1893)			
920,500 *Faust* (3 hr. 8 min.) *(4–Ang. S–3622)	A	4	2
920,750 *Roméo et Juliette* (2 hr. 29 min.) (3–Ang. S–3734)	A	5	2

GUIDE NO. COMPOSER AND TITLE	AGE MIN	AES SIG	AC- CESS
HANDEL, GEORGE FRIDERIC (1685–1759)			
921,000 *Alcina* (2 hr. 41 min.) **(3–Lon. OSA 1361)	A	3	3
921,250 *Julius Caesar* (3 hr. 5 min.) *(3–RCA LSC–6182)	A	3	3
921,750 *Rodelinda* (2 hr. 47 min.) *(West. WGSO–8205–3)	A	3	3
922,000 *Xerxes* (2 hr. 48 min.) *(West. WGSO–8202–3)	A	4	3
HAYDN, (FRANZ) JOSEPH (1732–1809)			
923,000 *Man in the Moon* (Lyr. 7120)	A	4	3
HOLST, GUSTAV (1874–1934)			
924,500 *Sāvitri, op. 25* (33 min.) **(Argo ZNF–6)	A	4	2
HUMPERDINCK, ENGELBERT (1854–1921)			
924,750 *Hansel and Gretel* (1 hr. 40 min.) *(2–Tel. 26.35074)	E	3	1
JANÁČEK, LEOŠ (1854–1928)			
925,500 *Jenufa* (1 hr. 57 min.) (2–Ang. S–3756)	A	2	3
KODÁLY, ZOLTÁN (1882–1967)			
926,250 *Háry János* (1 hr. 58 min.) **(2–Lon. OSA 1278)	S	3	2
KŘENEK, ERNST (1900–)			
926,500 *Jonny spielt auf* (Mace S–9094)	S	4	2
LEONCAVALLO, RUGGIERO (1858–1919)			
927,000 *Pagliacci* (1 hr. 13 min.) *(3–DG 2709020); *(2–Lon. OSA 1280)	S	4	1
MASCAGNI, PIETRO (1863–1945)			
927,250 *Cavalleria Rusticana* (1 hr. 16 min.) *(3–DG 2709020)	S	4	1
MASSENET, JULES (1842–1912)			
927,500 *Don Quichotte* (1 hr. 43 min.) (2–Ev./Cet. 440/2F)	A	5	3
927,750 *Manon* (3 hr. 5 min.) *(4–ABC ATS–20007)	A	4	2
MENOTTI, GIAN-CARLO (1911–)			
928,250 *Amahl and the Night Visitors* (45 min.) **(RCA LSC–2762)	E	3	1
928,750 *The Medium* (1 hr.) *(2–Col. OSL–154)-*mono*; (Col. MS–7387)	S	4	2
929,000 *The Telephone* *(2–Col. OSL–154)-*mono*	S	5	2
MEYERBEER, GIACOMO (1791–1864)			
929,250 *Les Huguenots* (3 hr. 39 min.) (4–Lon. OSA 1437)	A	4	3

143

GUIDE NO.	COMPOSER AND TITLE	AGE MIN	AES SIG	ACCESS
	MONTEVERDI, CLAUDIO (1567–1643)			
930,000	*Ballo delle ingrate* (41 min.) *(Phi. 6500457)	A	3	3
930,250	*Combattimento di Tancredi e Clorinda* *(Phi. 6500457)	A	2	3
930,500	*Incoronazione di Poppea* (2 hr. 22 min.) *(2–Sera. S–6073)	A	2	3
930,750	*L'Orfeo* (1 hr. 40 min.) (3–Tel. 36.35020)	A	1	3
931,000	*Il ritorno d'Ulisse in patria* (2 hr. 15 min.) **(3–Vox SVBX–5211)	A	3	3
	MOORE, DOUGLAS (1893–1969)			
931,500	*Carry Nation* (3–Desto 6463/5)	A	5	3
931,750	*The Devil and Daniel Webster* (Desto 6450)	A	4	3
	MOZART, WOLFGANG AMADEUS (1756–1791)			
932,750	*La clemenza di Tito* (2 hr.) *(3–Lon. OSA 1387)	A	4	4
933,000	*Così fan tutte*, K. 588 (3 hr. 41 min.) **(4–Ang. S–3631)	S	2	2
933,250	*Don Giovanni* **(3–Turn. 4117/9)-*mono*; *(4–Ang. S–3605)	S	1	2
933,500	*Entführung aus dem Serail* (1 hr. 54 min.) **(2–Ang. S–3555); *(3–DG 2709051)	S	3	3
933,750	*La Finta giardiniera*, K. 196 (2 hr.) **(3–Phi. 6703039)	A	4	4
934,000	*Idomeneo, Rè di Creta*, K. 366 (2 hr.) (3–Sera. S–6070)	A	2	4
934,500	*Magic Flute*, K. 620 (2 hr.) **(3–Lon. OSA 1397); **(3–Turn. 4111/3)-*mono*	E	1	1
934,750	*Marriage of Figaro*, K. 492 (2 hr.) *(4–Lon. OSA 1402)	S	1	1
935,250	*Der Schauspieldirektor*, K. 486 *(3–DG 2709051)	A	3	3
	MUSSORGSKY, MODEST (1839–1881)			
935,500	*Boris Godunov* *(4–Lon. OSA 1439)	S	1	2
	OFFENBACH, JACQUES (1819–1880)			
936,000	*La Belle Hélène* (2–Ev./Cet. S–458/2E)-*mono*	S	4	1
936,750	*Tales of Hoffmann* (2 hr. 38 min.) *(3–Ang. S–3667); *(3–Lon. OSA 13106)	S	3	1
	ORFF, CARL (1895–)			
937,750	*Der Mond* *(2–Ang. S–3567)	A	3	3
	PERGOLESI, GIOVANNI BATTISTA (1710–1736)			
938,250	*La Serva padrona* (47 min.) *(Ev. S–455/1); *(None. H–71043)	S	4	2
	PONCHIELLI, AMILCARE (1834–1886)			
938,500	*La Gioconda* (2 hr. 38 min.) **(3–Lon. OSA 1388)	A	4	2
	POULENC, FRANCIS (1899–1963)			
938,750	*Les Dialogues des Carmélites* *(3–Ang. 3585)-*mono*	A	3	4
	PROKOFIEV, SERGE (1891–1953)			
939,250	*Betrothel in a Convent* (2 hr. 30 min.) (3–Ev./Cet. 465/3)	A	4	4
939,500	*The Flaming Angel* (West. WGSO–8173–3)	A	5	3
939,750	*Love for Three Oranges*, op. 33 (1 hr. 43 min.) (2–Mel./Ang. S–4109)	A	4	3
	PUCCINI, GIACOMO (1858–1924)			
940,500	*La Bohème* (1 hr. 40 min.) **(2–Sera. 6000)-*mono*; *(2–Lon. OSA 1299)	S	3	1
940,750	*La fanciulla del West* (2 hr. 13 min.) **(3–Lon. OSA 1306)	S	4	3
941,000	*Gianni Schicchi* (51 min.) *(Ang. S–35473); *(Lon. OSA 1153)	S	3	2
941,250	*Madame Butterfly* (2 hr. 20 min.) **(3–Ang. S–3702)	S	3	1
941,500	*Manon Lescaut* (1 hr. 50 min.) (3–Lon. OSA 1317)	A	4	3
941,750	*La Rondine* (1 hr. 35 min.) (2–RCA LSC–7048)	S	4	3
942,000	*Suor Angelica* (54 min.) *(Lon. OSA 1152)	A	5	3
942,250	*Il Tabarro* (49 min.) *(Lon. OSA 1151)	A	4	3
942,500	*Tosca* (1 hr. 50 min.) **(2–Ang. 3508)-*mono*; *(2–RCA ARL2–0105)	S	3	1
942,750	*Turandot* (1 hr.) *(3–Ang. S–3671)	A	2	3
	PURCELL, HENRY (c.1659–1695)			
943,000	*Dido and Aeneas* (55 min.) **(Oiseau 60047)	A	1	2
943,250	*Fairy Queen* (2 hr. 8 min.) **(3–Oiseau S–121/3E)-*mono*; *(2–Lon. OSA 1290)	A	2	3
943,500	*Indian Queen* *(Oiseau S–294)	A	2	3
943,750	*King Arthur* (1 hr. 30 min.) *(2–Oiseau 60008/9)	A	2	3
	RAMEAU, JEAN PHILIPPE (1683–1764)			
944,000	*Castor et Pollux* *(4–Tel. 46.35048)	A	4	3
944,500	*Hippolyte et Aricie* (2 hr. 22 min.) *(3–Oiseau S–286/8)	A	4	3
	RAVEL, MAURICE (1875–1937)			
944,750	*L'Enfant et les sortilèges* (43 min.) **(Rich. SR–33086)	E	3	2

GUIDE NO. COMPOSER AND TITLE	AGE MIN	AES SIG	AC-CESS
RIMSKY-KORSAKOV, NIKOLAI (1844–1908)			
46,000 *The Tsar's Bride* *(3–Mel./Ang. S–4122)	A	4	3
ROSSINI, GIOACCHINO (1792–1868)			
46,250 *Barber of Seville* (2 hr. 40 min.) *(3–Ang. S–3638); *(3–Lon. OSA 1381)	S	2	1
46,500 *Cambiale di Matrimonio* (1 hr. 18 min.) (2–Ev. S–446/2)	A	4	3
46,750 *La Cenerentola* (2 hr. 25 min.) *(3–Lon. OSA 1376)	A	3	3
47,000 *Italiana in Algeri* (2 hr. 9 min.) *(3–Lon. OSA 1375)	A	3	3
47,250 *Semiramide* (2 hr. 46 min.) *(3–Lon. OSA 1383)	A	4	3
47,500 *William Tell* (2 hr. 45 min.) *(5–Ang. S–3793)	A	4	3
SAINT-SAËNS, CAMILLE (1835–1921)			
47,750 *Samson et Dalila* (2 hr. 2 min.) *(3–Ang. S–3639)	A	5	3
SCHOENBERG, ARNOLD (1874–1951)			
49,500 *Die glückliche Hand* (17 min.) (2–Col. M2S–679)	A	5	4
49,750 *Moses and Aaron* (1 hr. 41 min.) (2–Phi. 6700084)	A	2	5
50,000 *Von Heute auf Morgen* (51 min.) (2–Col. M2S–780)	A	5	5
SHOSTAKOVICH, DIMITRI (1906–1975)			
50,750 *Katerina Ismailova*, op. 114 (2 hr. 40 min.) (3–Coll. Guild 665/7)-*mono*	A	3	3
STRAUSS, JOHANN (1825–1899)			
51,750 *Die Fledermaus* (1 hr. 50 min.) **(2–Rich. RS–62006)-*mono*; *(2–Ang. S–3790)	S	2	1
52,000 *Gypsy Baron* (1 hr. 37 min.) (2–Ang. S–3612)	S	2	1
STRAUSS, RICHARD (1864–1949)			
52,250 *Arabella* (2 hr. 50 min.) **(3–Rich. SRS–63522)	A	4	2
52,500 *Ariadne auf Naxos*, op. 60 (2 hr.) **(3–Ang. 3532)-*mono*	A	3	2
52,750 *Capriccio* (2 hr. 20 min.) *(3–DG 2709038)	A	4	4
53,250 *Elektra*, op. 58 (1 hr. 40 min.) **(2–Lon. OSA 1269)	A	3	3
53,500 *Die Frau ohne Schatten* *(4–Rich. SRS–64503)	A	3	4
53,750 *Der Rosenkavalier* (3 hr. 15 min.) **(4–Ang. S–3563); *(4–Lon. OSA 1435)	A	2	2
954,000 *Salome* (1 hr. 40 min.) **(2–Lon. OSA 1218)	A	3	3
STRAVINSKY, IGOR (1882–1971)			
954,250 *Mavra* (28 min.) *(Lon. STS–15102)	A	3	3
954,500 *Oedipus Rex* (51 min.) *(Turn. 34179)	A	2	3
955,000 *Rake's Progress* (2 hr. 25 min.) **(3–Col. M3S–710)	A	3	4
955,250 *Renard* (16 min.) *(Lon. STS–15102)	E	4	2
TCHAIKOVSKY, PETER ILYITCH (1840–1893)			
955,750 *Eugen Onegin*, op. 24 (2 hr. 29 min.) *(3–Mel./Ang. S–4115)	A	3	3
956,250 *Pique Dame*, op. 68 (2 hr. 35 min.) (3–Rich. SRS–63516)	A	4	3
THOMAS, AMBROISE (1811–1896)			
956,750 *Mignon* (3–Rich. RS–63014)-*mono*	A	5	3
TIPPETT, MICHAEL (1905–)			
957,500 *Midsummer Marriage* (2 hr. 32 min.) **(3–Phi. 6703027)	A	3	2
VERDI, GIUSEPPE (1813–1901)			
957,750 *Aïda* (2 hr. 25 min.) *(3–Lon. OSA 1393); *(3–Lon. OSA 1313)	S	3	1
958,000 *Un Ballo in maschera* (2 hr.) *(3–Lon. OSA 1328)	A	3	2
958,250 *Don Carlos* (3 hr.) *(4–Ang. S–3774)	A	4	3
958,500 *Ernani* (2 hr. 9 min.) *(3–RCA LSC–6183)	A	4	4
958,750 *Falstaff* (2 hr.) **(3–RCA LM–6111)-*mono*; *(3–Ang. S–3552); *(3–Lon. OSA 1395)	A	2	3
959,250 *La Forza del destino* (2 hr. 54 min.) *(4–Ang. S–3765)	A	3	3
959,500 *Macbeth* (1 hr. 57 min.) *(3–Lon. OSA 1380)	A	5	4
959,750 *Nabucco* (1 hr. 59 min.) **(3–Lon. OSA 1382)	A	4	2
960,000 *Otello* (1 hr. 28 min.) **(3–RCA LM–6107)-*mono*; *(3–Ang. SX–3809); *(3–Lon. OSA 1324)	A	1	2
960,250 *Rigoletto* (1 hr. 55 min.) **(3–Lon. OSA 13105)	S	2	1
960,500 *Simon Boccanegra* (2 hr. 19 min.) *(3–Ang. 3617)-*mono*	A	3	3
960,750 *La Traviata* (2 hr. 3 min.) *(3–Lon. OSA 1366)	S	3	1
961,000 *Il Trovatore* (2 hr. 8 min.) *(3–RCA LSC–6194)	S	4	1
WAGNER, RICHARD (1813–1883)			
961,250 *Der Fliegende Holländer* (2 hr. 20 min.) *(3–DG 2709040)	A	4	3

GUIDE NO.	COMPOSER AND TITLE	AGE MIN	AES SIG	ACCESS
961,500	*Götterdämmerung* (4 hr. 27 min.)	A	2	3
	**(6–Lon. OSA 1604)			
961,750	*Lohengrin* (3 hr. 35 min.)	A	3	2
	*(5–Ang. S–3641)			
962,000	*Die Meistersinger von Nürnberg* (4 hr. 21 min.)	A	1	3
	*(5–Ang. S–3776)			
962,250	*Parsifal* (3 hr. 51 min.)	A	4	3
	**(5–Rich. 65001)-*mono*; *(5–Lon. OSA 1510)			
962,500	*Das Rheingold* (2 hr. 33 min.)	A	2	3
	**(3–Lon. OSA 1309)			
962,750	*Der Ring des Nibelungen* (Das Rheingold, Die Walküre, Siegfried, Götterdämmerung)	A	2	3
	**(19–Lon. RING S)			
963,000	*Siegfried* (4 hr.)	A	2	3
	**(5–Lon. OSA 1508)			

GUIDE NO.	COMPOSER AND TITLE	AGE MIN	AES SIG	ACCESS
963,250	*Tannhäuser* (2 hr. 49 min.)	A	4	3
	*(4–Lon. OSA 1438)			
963,500	*Tristan und Isolde*	A	2	2
	**(5–Ang. 3588)-*mono*; *(5–DG 2713001)			
963,750	*Die Walküre* (3 hr. 48 min.)	A	2	3
	**(5–Lon. OSA 1509)			
	WARD, ROBERT (1917–)			
964,000	*The Crucible*	A	4	3
	*(2–CRI S–168)			
	WEBER, CARL MARIA VON (1786–1826)			
964,250	*Der Freischütz* (2 hr. 1 min.)	A	4	4
	(2–Sera S–6010)			
	WEILL, KURT (1900–1950)			
964,500	*Three Penny Opera* (1 hr. 10 min.)	S	3	2
	**(2–Odys. Y2–32977)			

11. New and Experimental Music

(Works which have received especially favorable reviews or have insinuated themselves into the standard repertoire are marked with a dagger).

GUIDE NO.	COMPOSER AND TITLE
	AREL, BULENT (1919–)
964,750	Stereo Electronic Music no. 1 (1964) (10 min.) (Col. MS–6566)
	AVNI, TZVI (1927–)
965,250	*Vocalise* (1964) (6 min.) (Turn. 34004)
	BABBITT, MILTON (1916–)
965,500	Composition for 4 Instruments (1948) (14 min.) (CRI 138)-*mono*
965,600	Composition for Synthesizer (1964) (11 min.) (Col. MS–6566)
965,700	Ensembles for Synthesizer (10 min.) (Col. MS–7051)
965,800	Quartet no. 3 (1969–70) (Turn. 34515)
	BASSETT, LESLIE (1923–)
966,000	Music for Cello and Piano (1966) (9 min.) (CRI S–311)
966,250	Variations for Orchestra (1962–3) (25 min.) (CRI S–203)
	BERIO, LUCIANO (1925–)
966,500	†*Circles* (e.e. cummings) (18 min.) (Main. 5005)
966,750	†*Differences* (1958–60) (Main. 5004)
967,250	*Sequenza* for Solo Flute (Main. 5014)
967,750	*Sinfonia* (27 min.) (Col. MS–7268)

GUIDE NO.	COMPOSER AND TITLE
	BOULEZ, PIERRE (1925–)
968,250	†*Marteau sans maître* (1955) (31 min.) *(Col. M–32160)
968,500	†*Pli selon pli*, for voice and orchestra (1960) (60 min.) *(Col. M–30296)
968,750	†Sonatas (3) for Piano (1946, 1948, 1957) (no. 1 and 2; movements only from no. 3) *(Col. M–32161)
969,250	*Structures* for 2 Pianos (1955) (Mace. S–9043)
	BRANT, HENRY (1913–)
969,500	*Fourth Millennium* (*Millenium IV*) (None. H–71222)
	BREHM, ALVIN (1925–)
969,750	Quintet for Brass (1967) (None. H–71222)
	BRESS, HYMAN (1931–)
970,000	Fantasy (Electronic) (11 min.) (Folk 3355)-*mono*
	BROWN, EARLE (1926–)
970,250	*Available Forms* I, for 18 players (1961) (RCA VICS–1239)
970,500	*Four Systems* (for 4 Amplified Cymbals) (5 min.) (Col. MS–7139)
970,750	†*Quartet* (1965) **(3–Vox SVBX–5306)
	BUSSOTTI, SYLVANO (1931–)
971,000	*Coeur pour batteur-Positively Yes* (10 min.) (Col. MS–7139)

GUIDE NO.	COMPOSER AND TITLE

71,250 *Frammento* (*Pièces de chair II* (1958–59): *Voix de femme*) (Main. 5005)

CAGE, JOHN (1922–)
71,500 *Amores* for Prepared Piano and Percussion (1943) (Main. 5011)
71,750 *Aria* (1958) with *Fontana Mix* (1958) (12 min.) (Main. 5005)
72,000 *Cartridge Music* (1960) (5 min.) (Main. 5015)
72,250 *Fontana Mix-Feed* (Col. MS–7139)
72,500 †*Imaginary Landscape no. 1* (3–Avakian S–1)-*mono*
72,750 *Solo for Voice 2* (1966) (Odys. 32160156)
73,000 †*String Quartet in 4 Parts* (1950) **(3–Vox SVBX–5306)
73,250 *Variations II* (1961) (26 min.) (Col. MS–7051)
73,500 *Variations IV* (excerpts) (1965) (Ev. 3132)
73,750 *Variations IV, vol. 2* (35 min.) (Ev. 3230)

CAGE, JOHN AND HILLER, LEJAREN (1924–)
74,000 †*HPSCHD,* for Harpsichord and Computer-Generated Sound Tape (None. H–71224)

CARTER, ELLIOTT (1908–)
74,250 †*Concerto for Orchestra* (Col. M–30112)
74,750 †*Double Concerto for Harpsichord, Piano, and 2 Chamber Orchestras* (1961) (24 min.) (Col. MS–7191)
75,000 †*Quartet no. 2* **(Col. M–32738); **(None. H–71249)
75,250 †*Quartet no. 3* **(Col. M–32738)
75,500 *Sonata for Piano* (1946) (23 min.) (Dover 7265)
75,750 †*Variations for Orchestra* (1955) (25 min.) *(Col. MS–7191)

CASTIGLIONI, NICCOLO (1932–)
976,000 *Gymel* for Flute and Piano (Main. 5014)

CRUMB, GEORGE (1929–)
976,250 †*Ancient Voices of Children* (None. H–71255)
976,500 †*Black Angels,* for Electric String Quartet (1970) **(3–Vox SVBX–5306) †*Echoes of Time and River* (20 min.) *(Lou. S–711)

DALLAPICCOLA, LUIGI (1904–1975)
976,750 †*Canti de Prigionia* (Tel. 6.41010)

DAVIDOVSKY, MARIO (1934–)
977,250 *Electronic Study no. 1* (1964) (6 min.) (Col. MS–6566)
977,500 *Synchronisms* nos. 1–3 (15 min.) (CRI S–204)

DAVIES, PETER MAXWELL (1934–)
977,750 *Eight Songs for a Mad King* (1969) (None. H–71285)

DOCKSTADER, TOD (1932–)
978,000 *Apocalypse* (19 min.) (Owl 6)
978,250 *Drone* (13 min.) (Owl 7)
978,500 *Luna Park* (11 min.) (Owl 6)
978,750 *Quartermass* (Owl 8)
979,000 *Traveling Music* (9 min.) (Owl 6)
979,250 *2 Fragments from Apocalypse* (6 min.) (Owl 7)
979,500 *Water Music* (18 min.) (Owl 7)

DONOVAN, RICHARD (1891–1970)
979,750 *Five Elizabethan Lyrics* (1932–57) (11 min.) (CRI S–290)
980,000 *Music for Six* (1961) (15 min.) (CRI S–290)
980,250 *Passacaglia on Vermont Folk Tunes* (1949) (11 min.); *Epos* (1963) (11 min.) (CRI S–203)

DRUCKMAN, JACOB (1928–)
980,750 *Animus II* (19 min.) (CRI S–255)
981,000 *String Quartet no. 2* (1966) **(3–Vox SVBX–5306)

EL DABH, HALIM (1921–)
981,250 *Leiyla and the Poet* (1962) (Col. MS–6566)

EVANGELISTI, FRANCO (1926–)
981,500 *Proporzioni* for Solo Flute (Main. 5014)

FELDMAN, MORTON (1926–)
981,750 *Chorus and Instruments* (II) (1967); *Christian Wolff in Cambridge* (1963) (Odys. 32160156)
982,000 *King of Denmark* (6 min.) (Col. MS–7139)
982,500 *Structures* for String Quartet (1951) **(3–Vox SVBX–5306)

FINNEY, ROSS LEE (1906–)
983,000 *Sonata no. 2 for Cello* (17 min.); *Chromatic Fantasy in E* (11 min.) (CRI S–311)

FOSS, LUKAS (1922–)
983,500 †*Time Cycle* (31 min.) (CSP AMS–6280)

GABURO, KENNETH (1926–)
984,000 *Antiphonie III* (*Pearl-White Moments*) (16 min.) (None. H–71199)
984,250 *Antiphonie IV* (*Poised*) (9 min.) (None. H–71199)
984,400 *Exit Music I: The Wasting of Lucrecetzia* (4 min.) (None. H–71199)
984,600 *Exit Music II: Fat Millie's Lament* (5 min.) (None. H–71199)

GUIDE
NO.   COMPOSER AND TITLE

994,350 *F sharp* (1968)
        (Op. One S–7)
994,400 *High Ice* (Or 2) (1967)
        (Op. One S–7)
994,450 *Joyeux Noel* (1967)
        (Op. One S–7)
994,500 *Quashed Culch* (1966)
        (Op. One S–7)

        SCHULLER, GUNTHER (1925–   )
994,600 †*Seven Studies on Themes of Paul Klee*
        (1959)
        (RCA LSC–2879)

        SCHÜRMANN, GERARD (1928–   )
994,700 †*Chuench'i* (song cycle from the Chinese)
        (None. H–71209)

        STOCKHAUSEN, KARLHEINZ
        (1928–   )
995,000 *Gesang der Jünglinge* (1955/56)
        (DG 138811)
995,200 *Hymnen:* Anthems for Electronic and
        Concrete Sounds
        (2–DG 2707039)
995,300 *Klavierstück IX*
        (Phi. 6500101)
995,400 *Klavierstück XI*
        (Phi. 6500101)
995,600 *Mikrophonie* I for Tamtam, 2 Micro-
        phones, 2 Filters, and Potentiometers
        (Col. MS–7355)
995,700 *Mikrophonie* II for Choir, Hammond
        Organ, and Ring Modulators
        (Col. MS–7355)
995,800 *Momente* (1963; rev. 1965)
        (None. H–71157)
995,900 no. 9 *Zyklus* for One Percussionist
        (Col. MS–7139)
996,300 *Zyklus* (1950); *Refrain* (1959)
        (Main. 5003)

        SUBOTNICK, MORTON (1933–   )
996,400 †*Silver Apples of the Moon* for Elec-
        tronic Music Synthesizer
        (None. H–71174)
996,450 †*Touch*
        (Col. MS–7316)
996,500 †*The Wild Bull*
        (None. H–71208)

        TAKEMITSU, TORU (1930–   )
996,600 *November Steps* (1967) (20 min.)
        (2–RCA LSC–7051)
996,650 *Textures* (1964)
        (Odys. 32160152)

        TANENBAUM, ELIAS (1924–   )
996,800 Improvisations and Patterns for Brass
        Quintet and Tape
        (4–Desto 6474/7)

        TATE, PHYLLIS (1911–   )
996,900 †*Apparitions* for Tenor, Harmonica,
        String Quartet, and Piano
        *(Argo ZRG–691)

        TIPPETT, MICHAEL (1905–   )
997,000 †*The Knot Garden* (1970)
        (2–Phi. 6700063)
997,200 †Symphony no. 3
        (Phi. 6500662)

GUIDE
NO.   COMPOSER AND TITLE

        TRIMBLE, LESTER (1923–   )
997,300 "Panels 1" for chamber orchestra
        (Desto 7132)

        TRYTHALL, GILBERT (1930–   )
997,400 *Entropy* for Stereo Brass, Improvisation
        Group, and Stereo Tape, op. 15
        (1967)
        (GC S–4085)

        USSACHEVSKY, VLADIMIR
        (1911–   )
997,500 *Creation-Prologue* (1962) (8 min.)
        (Col. MS–6566)
997,550 *Of Wood and Brass* (6 min.)
        (CRI S–227)
997,600 †*Piece for Tape Recorder* (1955)
        (6 min.)
        (CRI 112)-*mono*
997,650 *Sonic Contours*
        (Desto 6466)
997,700 *Wireless Fantasy* (5 min.)
        (CRI S–227)

        VAN VACTOR, DAVID (1906–   )
997,750 *Economy Band* (1968–   )
        (GC S–4085)

        WHITTENBERG, CHARLES
        (1927–   )
997,800 Quartet in One Movement
        (14 min.)
        (CRI S–257)

        WOLFF, CHRISTIAN (1934–   )
998,100 *For 1, 2, or 3 People* (1964)
        (Odys. 32160158)
998,200 *Summer*, for String Quartet (1961)
        (3–Vox SVBX–5306)

        WOLPE, STEFAN (1902–1972)
998,250 †String Quartet (1968/69)
        (3–Vox SVBX–5306)

        WUORINÉN, CHARLES (1938–   )
998,300 String Quartet (1970–71)
        (Turn. 34515)
998,400 †*Time's Encomium*, for synthesizer
        (1968–9) (32 min.)
        (None. H–71225)

        XENAKIS, IANNIS (1922–   )
998,500 †*Achorripsis* (11 min.)
        (Main. 5008)
998,550 †*Akrata* (11 min.)
        (None. H–71201)
998,600 *Bohor I* (1962)
        (None. H–71246)
998,650 *Concret P-H II* (1958)
        (None. H–71246)
998,700 *Diamorphoses II* (1958)
        (None. H–71246)
998,750 †*Eonta* for Piano and brass (1963)
        (Van. VCS–10030)
998,800 *Herma* (1960–61)
        (Main. 5000)
998,850 †*Métastasis*, for orchestra (1955)
        (written for the Phillips Pavilion
        Brussels World's Fair)
        (Van. VCS–10030)
998,900 *Orient-Occident III* (1959–60)
        (None. H–71246)
998,950 *Pithoprakta* for String Orchestra
        (None. H–71201)

Collection Development Priorities and Category Apportionments

There are many ways in which to build a collection. Librarians and individuals alike will be guided by impulse, professional advice and experience, subjective feelings about what constitutes optimal proportions and quality for the available money, their estimates of local audience needs, and listener requests.

If listeners served by a library or members of a family have not been exposed to music appreciation courses or had opportunities to hear live or broadcast classical music, works with low access numbers (1 and 2) should be purchased before works less obvious or immediate in their impact. In such circumstances enduring favorites would receive high priority consideration. Twenty-one orchestral works from category 7, "Other Orchestral Works," which have endured as the foremost orchestral concert favorites for the greater part of this century follow below. These would be the obvious first order purchases for any starting collection.

COMPOSER	TITLE	GUIDE NO.
Tchaikovsky	*Nutcracker Suite*	791,750–792,500
———	*Swan Lake*	794,100–794,200
———	*Serenade* in C for Strings, op. 48	793,250
———	*Sleeping Beauty*, op. 68	793,500–793,600
Rossini	*William Tell* Overture	750,500
Bizet	*Carmen* Suite	599,500–599,750
Grieg	*Peer Gynt* Suites 1 and 2	654,000–654,250
Wagner	*Tristan*: Prelude and *Liebestod*	807,000
Borodin	*Prince Igor*: Polovtsian Dances	603,750
Ravel	*Boléro*	736,250
Rimsky-Korsakoff	*Scheherazade, op. 35*	746,250
Bach	Toccata and Fugue in d, S. 565	584,250
Offenbach	*Gaîté Parisienne* (arranged by Rosenthal)	727,500
Mendelssohn	*Midsummer Night's Dream* (incidental music) op. 21 and 61	707,750
Ravel	*Pavane pour une infante défunte*	737,750
Mussorgsky	*Night on Bald Mountain*	725,500
Chabrier	*España*	609,000
Debussy	*Prélude à l'après-midi d'un faune*	620,250
Mussorgsky	*Pictures at an Exhibition*	725,750
Wagner	*Tannhäuser*: Overture	806,500
Bizet	*L'Arlésienne*: Suites 1 and 2	599,000–599,250

Audiences with settled tastes will require more substantial and subtle music. Using Beethoven as an example, these patrons would expect a library to stock Sonata no. 32, op. 111, Variations on a Theme by Diabelli, op. 120, and the late quartets as well as perennial favorites such as the *Leonore* Overture 3 and Fifth Symphony.

151

If a large collection has already been established and has surpassed the 5,000 recordings mark, attention should be directed to purchase of landmark (two-asterisk) versions of works which may have been accidentally overlooked during its development.

A successful collection tends to have representation across all categories of recorded sound in direct proportion to the depth of literature existing in each genre. As is the case with book collection evaluation, there are many ways of statistically appraising the quality of holdings. Formulas, standard checklists, dating techniques, and circulation frequency counts may be used singly or in combination to ascertain a collection's effectiveness. Appraisal of a thorough-bred race horse or wine poses a similar challenge. The expert's impressionistically offhand opinion may end up being the most reliable indicator of quality. Because experts who can tell whether or not a recordings collection is robust, well rounded, or "right" for its intended audience are hard to find, approximate percentage expenditure figures are presented in table 2 to guide the reader.

Table 2. Examples of Percentage per Category Distributions

(Figures in parentheses are based upon a $2,000 annual expenditure)

	Library A	Library Pa	Library Z
1. Early Music	4 ($80)	2 ($40)	1 ($20)
2. Choral Music	8 ($160)	4 ($80)	6 ($120)
3. Keyboard Instruments	7 ($140)	4 ($80)	4 ($80)
4. Chamber Music	10 ($200)	6 ($120)	12 ($240)
5. Symphonies	8 ($160)	14 ($280)	12 ($240)
6. Concerti and Other Works for Solo Instrument(s) and Orchestra	6 ($120)	11 ($220)	9 ($180)
7. Other Orchestral Works	9 ($180)	17 ($340)	14 ($280)
8. Songs and Other Works Scored for Single Voice and Accompaniment	1 ($20)	1 ($20)	3 ($60)
9. Popular Arias	1 ($20)	2 ($40)	3 ($60)
10. Operas	8 ($160)	6 ($120)	28 ($560)
11. New and Experimental Music	5 ($100)	5 ($100)	0 ($00)
Jazz	8 ($160)	8 ($160)	3 ($60)
Musical Comedy	4 $(80)	6 ($120)	1 ($20)
Folk Music	4 ($80)	4 ($80)	1 ($20)
Spoken and Documentary	7 ($140)	5 ($100)	3 ($60)
Patrons' Requests	10 ($200)	5 ($100)	0 ($00)

aPublic Library P maintains a separate budget for childrens recordings which approximates 10 percent of the illustrated allocation (about $200 a year).

They illustrate buying programs which include the familiar and esoteric, old and new, complex and simple. If the selector is inattentive to balance he will neglect important media or styles. Meanwhile his patrons may fail to voice their disappointment and slip quietly away never to return.

In table 2, Library A and Library P have established their basic collections and the percentages of dollar expenditures are supportive of maintenance and continuing growth. Library A has 10,000 recordings; Library P, 5,000; Library Z has none. The percentages are taken from budgets of libraries where patron satisfaction and high circulation attest to success. These figures also relate to market production volumes.

Percentages shown for the three libraries indicate amounts spent on each category. The number of titles per given amount will depend upon the unit prices within the category. For example, an opera album costs many times as much as a song or piano piece so that the proportional expenditure for operas must be high to achieve an effective balance.

Adherence to allocation formulae or any other guidelines should be conditioned by local circumstances without sacrificing a collection's structural integrity. For example, inner city public libraries and junior colleges would spend more on informal listening; jazz, folk music, country and western, and other types of popular music.

Manufacturer's Catalog Number-Performer List

For each recording cited in the main Composer-Title List, this second list provides (1) surnames of the key performer(s) and (2) guide numbers for other selections included on the recording.

As a case in point, if a reader is interested in purchasing Debussy's Sonata No. 2 for Flute, Viola, and Harp, he first consults the chamber music category (4) within the main Composer-Title List. Two recordings, **Oiseau 60048 and *DG 2530049 are recommended. If he is curious about performing artists and other pieces contained on the recordings, he will find this data in the Manufacturer's Catalog Number–Performer List. Under Oiseau 60048 and DG 2530049 he may confirm that the Melos Ensemble and performers Dwyer, Thomas, Fine, and Hobson are the two sets of artists. He will discover that the Melos Ensemble also offers guide number 348,000, Ravel's *Introduction and Allegro,* while the Deutsche Grammophon disc contains Debussy's three sonatas and his *Syrinx* for solo flute. This section may serve as a convenient checklist or accessions record because manufacturer's catalog number sequences are normally used for purchase orders. The list's usefulness is heightened in situations whenever there are three or more "with" titles or whenever the Schwann catalog fails to provide contents breakdowns as in individual songs, lieder, and arias.

A dagger before the manufacturer's catalog number indicates a monaural recording.

The following rules govern the arrangement of the list:

1. Each manufacturer's catalog number includes four elements: (a) alpha characters, (b) numeric characters, (c) special characters, and (d) spaces. The last two elements include periods, hyphens, spaces, and similarly ubiquitous and variable punctuation. Scanners are unlikely to recall the exact appearance of such elements within a manufacturer's catalog number. Therefore, *only the alpha and numeric characters determine the filing order.* The various series of catalog numbers are grouped by label under each manufacturer. Therefore

> RCA LSC–3414
> RCA VICS–1691
> 2–RCA LSC–2703

file in one sequence under the heading, RCA Victor.

2. Record labels are alphabetized, letter by letter, in their abbreviated forms. Counterpoint (Count.) therefore precedes Columbia Special Products (CSP).

3. Within label groupings, individual catalog numbers are arranged according to the following rules:

a. Alpha characters are filed before numeric characters:

> DG ARC–198477   RCA VICS–1691
> DG 139430   RCA VIC–1246
> 2–DG 2707044

b. Alpha fields (groups of alpha characters) are filed character by character, starting at the left:

> Argo S–4480   RCA LM–2226
> Argo ZRG–3440   RCA LSC–3414

c. Numerical fields are filed by their whole number values. For example, in multiple recording albums where discrete numbers, separated by a slash or comma, are assigned to each disc, only the initial numbers are used:

> 2–Phi. 802856/7
> 2–Phi. 6700035

Manufacturer's Catalog Number-Performer List

ABC

LABEL	PERFORMER	GUIDE NO.
ABC ATS–20013	Sills, Gedda, Souzay	890,850
4–ABC ATS–20007	Sills	*927,750
†ADV 5	electronic instruments	991,700

Angel

LABEL	PERFORMER	GUIDE NO.			
Ang. S–35383	Schwarzkopf	*831,200;	*834,600;	*840,000	
Ang. S–35417	Starker, Susskind	*513,250;	515,750		
Ang. S–35458	Beecham	472,750;	*763,000;	*763,250;	*763,500
Ang. S–35473	De Los Angeles	*941,000			
Ang. S–35481	Klemperer	**387,000			
Ang. S–35491	Hindemith	*426,250;	*525,250		
Ang. S–35505	Beecham	**746,250			
Ang. S–35509	Beecham	**377,250;	**592,250;	**592,500	
Ang. S–35532	Klemperer	*387,500;	**604,750		
Ang. S–35545	Klemperer	**388,000;	*604,000		
Ang. S–35546	Klemperer	*388,500			
Ang. S–35567	Michelangeli, Gracis	*545,504;	**546,250		
Ang. S–35615	Karajan	*398,250;	766,500		
Ang. S–35629	Klemperer	*438,750;	*439,000;	*465,750	
Ang. S–35638	Karajan	*425,100;	**732,000		
Ang. S–35658	Klemperer	*592,000			
Ang. S–35661	Klemperer	377,750;	**590,000		
Ang. S–35666	Callas, Serafin	**887,100			
Ang. S–35679	Richter	*122,500;	*232,500		
Ang. S–35680	Markevitch	*792,000;	*792,250;	*792,500;	*793,000
Ang. S–35681	Walton	** 93,250;	*808,400		
Ang. S–35689	Civil, Klemperer	*536,250;	*536,252;	*536,253;	*536,254
Ang. S–35711	Klemperer	**378,250;	**591,000		
Ang. S–35730	Milstein, Barzin	*506,000;	*533,500		
Ang. S–35818	De Los Angeles, Beecham	**887,600			
Ang. S–35821	De Los Angeles	**893,600			
Ang. S–35827	Gedda	* 48,250			
Ang. S–35836	Oistrakh, Klemperer	**504,750			
Ang. S–35853	Klemperer	**377,500			
Ang. S–35872	Klemperer	*423,500;	*424,250		
Ang. S–35877	Ferro, Mozzato, Fasano	*572,000;	*572,001;	*572,002;	*572,003;
		*572,004			
Ang. S–35888	De Los Angeles	** 21,900			
Ang. S–35932	Prêtre	*625,500;	*711,500;	*729,500	
Ang. S–35947	Klemperer	*803,750;	*805,000;	*805,500;	*806,000;
		*807,250			
Ang. S–35949	Karajan	*426,000;	*587,500		
Ang. S–35952	Barbirolli	**481,000			
Ang. S–35953	Prêtre, Duruflé	* 74,750;	**542,750		
Ang. S–35974	Cluytens	** 43,250			
Ang. S–35976	Klemperer	*779,250;	**780,000		
Ang. S–35977	Giulini	*619,000;	*619,250;	*619,500;	*619,750;
		*620,000			
Ang. S–35993	Van de Wiele, Prêtre	**542,500;	**543,000		
Ang. S–35994	Maazel	*778,750			

155

LABEL	PERFORMER	GUIDE NO.			
Ang. S–36011	Milstein, Frühbeck de Burgos	*513,750;	*518,200		
Ang. S–36020	Parkening	**246,250			
Ang. S–36022	Wagner	10,600			
Ang. S–36032	Oistrakh, Rostropovich, Szell	*505,000			
Ang. S–36033	Oistrakh, Szell	*504,750			
Ang. S–36045	Ozawa	*681,250;	*699,000		
Ang. S–36055	Kipnis	*110,911;	*110,912		
Ang. S–36062	Pennario	491,500			
Ang. S–36070	Pennario, Newman	*517,000;	*640,250;	*640,500	
Ang. S–36101	Barbirolli	**630,500;	**631,000;	**800,100;	**800,150
Ang. S–36103	Menuhin, Goosens	*496,750; *571,010	*520,500;	*520,502;	*520,504;
Ang. S–36104	Richter	*233,750;	*236,250;	*236,750	
Ang. S–36110	Cluytens	**737,250;	**738,750		
Ang. S–36111	Cluytens	*735,750; **738,250	*736,000;	*737,500;	**737,750;
Ang. S–36120	Barbirolli	629,750;	*630,000		
Ang. S–36121	Prêtre	* 75,250;	* 75,500		
Ang. S–36125	Giulini	** 91,500			
Ang. S–36127	Fischer-Dieskau	**852,000; **862,250;	**853,750; **862,750	**854,500;	**859,750;
Ang. S–36129	Klemperer	**450,500;	**450,750		
Ang. S–36130	Virtuosi di Roma	*616,252;	*616,256;	*616,257;	*616,258
Ang. S–36150	Richter	*227,250;	*230,000		
Ang. S–36152	Menuhin	*537,504;	*537,507		
Ang. S–36173	Menuhin	*661,000			
Ang. S–36175	Klemperer	646,500; 809,150;	674,000; 809,300;	674,250; 809,600	674,500;
Ang. S–36183	Klemperer	**451,000;	**451,500		
Ang. S–36190	Menuhin, Bath Festival Orchestra	*524,250;	*538,250		
Ang. S–36192	Menuhin, Kletzki	**502,500			
Ang. S–36195	Frühbeck de Burgos	*798,500			
Ang. S–36199	Freni, Gedda, Schippers	*893,000;	*893,100		
Ang. S–36210	Vickers, Prêtre	895,800			
Ang. S–36214	Lorengar	** 48,000			
Ang. S–36216	Klemperer	**449,000;	**449,250;	**449,750	
Ang. S–36231	Menuhin	*537,500;	*537,502		
Ang. S–36235	De Los Angeles, Frühbeck de Burgos	*631,750			
Ang. S–36240	Menuhin	*537,506;	*537,750		
Ang. S–36241	DePeyer	**334,250;	**338,000		
Ang. S–36245	Klemperer	**390,750			
Ang. S–36247	Klemperer	**335,000			
Ang. S–36266	Fischer-Dieskau	**867,750;	**868,750		
Ang. S–36269	Barbirolli	*580,500;	**793,250		
Ang. S–36271	Klemperer	**391,250			
Ang. S–36280	DePeyer, Melos Ensemble	*279,500			
Ang. S–36289	Klemperer	716,000; **720,750;	*716,250; *722,000;	717,000; *722,500	*719,250;
Ang. S–36296	De Los Angeles	**823,000;	**831,200;	*834,600;	**840,000
Ang. S–36313	Grümmer	*902,200			
Ang. S–36329	Klemperer	*448,500;	*449,500		
Ang. S–36330	Menuhin, Boult	*514,750			
Ang. S–36331	Willcocks	* 51,250			
Ang. S–36333	Frühbeck de Burgos	** 73,500			
Ang. S–36334	Andor	* 61,000			
Ang. S–36337	Shaffer	**250,250;	**250,750;	**251,250	
Ang. S–36338	Du Pré, Barbirolli	**514,500			

156

LABEL	PERFORMER	GUIDE NO.			
Ang. S–36341	Fischer-Dieskau	**852,500;	**854,750;	**855,750;	**856,000;
		**857,750;	**858,750;	**859,250;	**862,500;
		**862,750			
Ang. S–36342	Fischer-Dieskau	**854,000;	**859,000;	**860,500;	**863,000;
		**863,750			
Ang. S–36345	Schwarzkopf	**827,400;	**848,750;	**855,000;	**856,000;
		**857,750;	**858,750;	**859,500;	**862,500;
		**886,250			
Ang. S–36346	Klemperer	*421,000;	*425,000		
Ang. S–36347	Schwarzkopf	**872,250;	**872,500;	**872,750;	**875,500;
		**876,250			
Ang. S–36350	Shaffer	**250,500;	**251,000;	**251,500	
Ang. S–36353	Klemperer	465,000;	*760,500		
Ang. S–36354	South German Madrigal Choir	* 23,078			
Ang. S–36357	Ustinov, Prêtre	*730,000			
Ang. S–36360	Menuhin, Dorati	*499,000;	*499,700		
Ang. S–36384	Du Pré	*272,500;	*273,000		
Ang. S–36385	Giulini	*631,500;	*737,750;	*738,000	
Ang. S–36403	Barbirolli	*630,751;	*630,752;	*630,753;	*630,754;
		*630,755			
Ang. S–36415	Barbirolli	**589,500;	*622,250;	**623,250;	**623,750;
		**677,000			
Ang. S–36418	Menuhin, Menuhin	*295,750			
Ang. S–36420	Boult	**670,500;	**670,750		
Ang. S–36421	Ciccolini	**753,250			
Ang. S–36426	Tacchino, Prêtre	*542,250			
Ang. S–36438	Menuhin, Dorati	*498,750;	*499,250		
Ang. S–36439	Du Pré, Barenboim	503,250;	*521,500		
Ang. S–36443	Stevens, Ambrosian Singers	** 3,700;	* 45,000		
Ang. S–36453	Menuhin	*462,000;	*463,000		
Ang. S–36456	Baker	**813,500			
Ang. S–36459	Ciccolini	**218,250;	**218,500;	**219,250;	**219,500;
		**219,750;	**220,000;	**220,750;	**221,250;
		**221,500			
Ang. S–36461	Barbirolli	*377,500;	**377,750		
Ang. S–36462	Ludwig	**853,000;	**854,000;	**854,250;	**855,250;
		**856,000;	**856,250;	**856,750;	**857,250;
		**859,250;	**860,500;	**860,750;	**863,000
Ang. S–36480	Prausnitz, Alldis Chorus	** 80,500;	461,500;	810,200	
Ang. S–36482	Ciccolini	**218,000;	**221,000;	**222,500	
Ang. S–36483	Fischer-Dieskau	**870,750;	**871,000;	**871,250;	**873,750;
		**874,250;	**875,000;	**876,250	
Ang. S–36484	Aronowitz, Barenboim	*526,000;	757,500;	806,250	
Ang. S–36485	Ciccolini	**218,750;	**219,000;	**220,250;	**220,500
Ang. S–36505	Barbirolli	*816,800;	**849,850		
Ang. S–36512	Barenboim	*450,000;	*450,500		
Ang. S–36519	Prêtre	*729,750			
Ang. S–36529	Melos Ensemble	*352,250			
Ang. S–36532	Boult	**480,500			
Ang. S–36536	Klemperer	536,775;	724,000		
Ang. S–36537	Nilsson, Scotto	**894,700			
Ang. S–36545	Schwarzkopf	**839,301;	**845,500;	**855,250;	**867,000;
		**883,250;	**883,750		
Ang. S–36547	Schwarzkopf	**839,100;	**839,500		
Ang. S–36557	Boult	*480,750;	**800,500		
Ang. S–36586	Melos Ensemble	**297,875;	**342,125;	**342,750;	**348,000
Ang. S–36587	DePeyer	*991,200			
Ang. S–36588	Barbirolli	**622,000;	*622,500;	*623,500	
Ang. S–36589	DePeyer, Frühbeck de Burgos	*575,250;	*575,750		
Ang. S–36590	Willcocks	** 90,250			
Ang. S–36609	Menuhin	463,250;	*758,250;	*758,500	

157

LABEL	PERFORMER	GUIDE NO.			
Ang. S–36615	Popp, Barenboim	* 24,250			
Ang. S–36625	Boult	*481,750;	*570,000		
Ang. S–36642	DuPré, Barenboim	*549,250;	552,500		
Ang. S–36643	Schwarzkopf	**874,000;	**874,500;	**876,000	
Ang. S–36695	Baker	*816,600			
Ang. S–36698	Boult	*481,000;	*800,650		
Ang. S–36699	Willcocks	** 89,750			
Ang. S–36714	Ciccolini	**221,750			
Ang. S–36719	Menuhin	**574,750;	**575,000		
Ang. S–36727	Oistrakh, Rostropovich, Richter	*500,500			
Ang. S–36729	Karajan	*401,000			
Ang. S–36731	Freni, Corelli	889,550			
Ang. S–36742	Boult	*482,000			
Ang. S–36751	Willcocks	** 89,500;	** 90,500		
Ang. S–36762	Malcolm, Menuhin	*495,004;	*495,006;	*495,010	
Ang. S–36763	Burrows, Boult	*481,500			
Ang. S–36773	Boult	*800,350			
Ang. S–36775	Ameling, Giulini	* 27,000			
Ang. S–36790	Malcolm, Menuhin	*495,004;	*495,006;	*495,010	
Ang. S–36796	Baker	**831,300;	*839,300;	*839,301;	*839,302;
		*839,304;	*839,305		
Ang. S–36799	Boult	*630,000;	*800,000;	*800,150	
Ang. S–36803	Barbirolli	*653,750;	*654,000;	*654,250	
Ang. S–36804	Willcocks	** 23,247;	** 23,347		
Ang. S–36810	Previn	*516,750;	*517,250;	*640,000	
Ang. S–36811	Ciccolini	**222,000			
Ang. S–36819	Watts	** 90,000			
Ang. S–36820	Anievas	**187,500;	**188,750;	**189,000	
Ang. S–36826	Boskovsky	**770,250			
Ang. S–36836	Perlman, Foster	*540,750;	*550,750		
Ang. S–36837	Fielding, Flanders, Marriner	*808,200;	*808,300		
Ang. S–36838	Boult	**480,250			
Ang. S–36850	Menuhin, Frühbeck de Burgos	*533,500;	*533,750		
Ang. S–36851	Munrow	** 16,300			
Ang. S–36861	Previn	* 93,250			
Ang. S–36870	Groves	*623,000			
Ang. S–36874	Beroff	*159,500;	*160,750;	*161,000;	*161,250;
		*161,500;	*162,250		
Ang. S–36883	Marriner	*671,000			
Ang. S–36887	Boskovsky	**770,500;	**775,500		
Ang. S–36890	Previn	*791,500;	*792,750;	*793,000	
Ang. S–36896	De Los Angeles	**831,500			
Ang. S–36897	De Los Angeles	*825,200			
Ang. S–36902	Boult	** 90,750;	**570,250;	**800,150;	**800,500
Ang. S–36903	Perlman, Ozawa	*576,252			
Ang. S–36910	Ozawa	*783,800			
Ang. S–36917	Gedda	847,700;	847,750;	848,000;	848,250;
		848,750			
Ang. S–36920	Menuhin, Boult	*506,000			
Ang. S–36922	Kollo, Karajan	*902,400			
Ang. S–36937	Du Pré	**287,500;	*299,500		
Ang. S–36951	Menuhin	*385,000;	*385,250;	*385,500;	*385,750;
		*386,000;	*386,250;	*386,500;	*386,750
Ang. S–36953	Martinon	* 79,000			
Ang. S–36954	Previn	**457,250			
Ang. S–36964	Oistrakh, M. Shostakovich	*554,500			
Ang. S–36972	Armstrong, Boult	* 89,625			
Ang. S–36979	Capolongo	*802,000;	*802,200		
Ang. S–36991	Previn	*670,500;	*670,750		
Ang. S–37001	Previn	*482,750;	*808,600;	*808,700	

ABEL	PERFORMER	GUIDE NO.			
Ang. S–37009	Dervaux	*753,500;	*754,000		
Ang. S–37010	Malcolm, Menuhin	*495,000;	*495,002		
Ang. S–37011	Groves	** 41,750			
Ang. S–37059	Karajan	*586,000			
Ang. 35065	Gieseking	*159,500;	*160,750;	*161,000;	*161,250;
		*161,500;	*162,250		
Ang. 35066	Gieseking	**162,500;	**162,750;	**163,000;	**163,250;
		**163,500;	**163,750;	**164,000	
Ang. 35067	Gieseking	**158,250;	**158,750;	**165,750	
Ang. 35092	Brain, Karajan	**536,250;	**536,252;	**536,253;	**536,254
Ang. 35249	Gieseking	**164,250;	**164,500;	**164,750;	**165,000;
		**165,250			
Ang. 35270	Schwarzkopf	**844,250;	**844,500;	**845,500	
Ang. 35428	Gieseking	**192,750			
Ang. 35547	Dufrène, Plessier	*366,500			
Ang. 35931	Lipatti, Karajan	**536,771			
–Ang. S–3555	Marshall, Beecham	**933,500			
'–Ang. S–3567	Christ, Hotter, Sawallisch	*937,750			
–Ang. S–3603	Gedda, Dervaux	908,000			
'–Ang. S–3610	Klemperer	*803,250;	*803,500;	*804,000;	*804,250;
(S–36187/8)		*804,400;	*804,500;	*805,750;	*806,500;
		*807,000			
'–Ang. S–3612	Terkal, Gueden, Rothenberger, Kunz	952,000			
'–Ang. S–3624	Klemperer	** 31,250			
–Ang. S–3628	Fischer-Dieskau	*862,000			
'–Ang. S–3629	Menuhin	**254,250;	**254,500;	**254,750;	**255,000;
		**255,225;	**255,500		
'–Ang. S–3634	Klemperer	**434,750			
'–Ang. S–3649	Giulini	* 91,750			
'–Ang. S–3660	Barbirolli	** 43,000			
–Ang. S–3672	De Los Angeles	**834,300;	**834,400;	**916,500	
'–Ang. S–3675	Schwarzkopf, Fischer-Dieskau	**818,750			
'–Ang. S–3679	Klemperer	** 27,500			
–Ang. S–3697	Schwarzkopf	**840,200;	**884,000		
'–Ang. S–3703	Schwarzkopf, Fischer-Dieskau	**879,500;	**879,750;	**880,000;	**880,250;
		**880,500;	**880,750;	**881,000	
'–Ang. S–3708	Klemperer	**436,500			
.–Ang. S–3709	Klemperer	*391,000			
'–Ang. S–3739	Boult	**480,000;	**800,800		
'–Ang. S–3756	Prague National Theatre	925,500			
'–Ang. S–3760	Barbirolli	*435,000;	**839,300;	**839,301;	**839,302;
		**839,304;	**839,305		
.–Ang. S–3766	Rogg	**100,000			
–Ang. S–3784x	Davies	** 42,000			
–Ang. S–3787	Menuhin	*583,251;	*583,252;	*583,253;	*583,254;
		*583,255;	*583,256		
–Ang. S–3790	Gedda, Rothenberger, Holm, Boskovsky	*951,750			
–Ang. S–3794	Ohlsson	**145,000;	**145,250;	**145,500;	**145,750;
		**146,000;	**146,250;	**146,500	
–Ang. S–3796	Kipnis	*107,988			
2–Ang. 3508	Callas, D. Stefano, Gobbi, DeSabata	**942,500			
2–Ang. 3786	Casals	**255,750;	**256,000;	**256,250;	**256,500;
		**256,750;	**257,000		
–Ang. SX–3809	Freni, Vickers	*960,000			
–Ang. S–3552	Schwarzkopf, Merriman, Gobbi, Karajan	*958,750			
–Ang. S–3613	De Los Angeles, Beecham	**907,750			
–Ang. S–3615	Callas, Serafin	*906,000			
–Ang. S–3625	Ludwig, Klemperer	**905,500			

LABEL	PERFORMER	GUIDE NO.
3–Ang. S–3638	Bruscantini, De Los Angeles, Gui	*946,250
3–Ang. S–3639	Vickers, Gorr, Blanc, Prêtre	*947,750
3–Ang. S–3667	Gedda, D'Angelo, Schwarz-kopf, Cluytens	*936,750
3–Ang. S–3671	Nilsson, Scotto, Corelli, Molinari-Pradelli	*942,750
3–Ang. S–3702	Scotto, Stasio, Bergonzi, Barbirolli	**941,250
3–Ang. S–3734	Freni, Corelli, Lombard	920,750
3–Ang. S–3738	Frühbeck de Burgos	* 65,250
†3–Ang. 3532	Schwarzkopf, Seefried, Streich, Karajan	**952,500
†3–Ang. 3585	Duval, Crespin, Dervaux	*938,750
†3–Ang. 3617	Gobbi, Christoff, De Los Angeles, Santini	*960,500
3–Ang. 3753	Rothenberger, Gedda, Prey, Heger	916,750
4–Ang. S–3563	Schwarzkopf, Edelmann, Ludwig, Karajan	**953,750
4–Ang. S–3605	Giulini	*933,250
4–Ang. S–3622	De Los Angeles, Gedda, Christoff, Cluytens	*920,500
4–Ang. S–3631	Schwarzkopf, Böhm	**933,000
4–Ang. S–3765	Arroyo, Bergonzi, Cappuccilli, Gardelli	*959,250
4–Ang. S–3774	Caballé, Domingo, Verrett, Giulini	*958,250
5–Ang. S–3641	Grümmer, Ludwig, Thomas, Kempe	*961,750
5–Ang. S–3776	Adam, Donath, Evans, Karajan	*962,000
5–Ang. S–3793	Caballé, Mesplé, Taillon, Gardelli	*947,500
†5–Ang. 3588	Flagstad, Thebom, Suthaus, Furtwängler	**963,500

Archive of Piano Music

LABEL	PERFORMER	GUIDE NO.		
Arc. Piano X–909	Granados	*177,250;	*177,500;	*177,750

Argo

LABEL	PERFORMER	GUIDE NO.			
Argo S–563	Willcocks	* 52,000			
Argo ZNF–1	Rex, Del Mar	**910,500			
Argo ZNF–6	Holst, Baker	** 57,750;	**924,500		
Argo ZRG–523	Alldis Chorus	37,500;	* 41,250;	* 79,750	
Argo ZRG–524	Marriner	*844,750			
Argo ZRG–535	Davis	** 89,250			
Argo ZRG–541	Willcocks	* 50,750			
Argo ZRG–542	Guest	* 55,500			
Argo ZRG–553	Del Mar	**457,750;	*639,000		
Argo ZRG–554	Marriner	**717,500;	**717,750;	**718,000;	*723,250
Argo ZRG–555	Elizabethan Consort	**322,000			
Argo ZRG–570	Guest	* 17,100; * 18,600	* 17,200;	* 17,400;	* 18,100
Argo ZRG–572	Burgess	*828,000;	*828,250;	*829,750;	*830,250
Argo ZRG–575	Marriner	*782,200;	*786,000		

LABEL	PERFORMER	GUIDE NO.			
Argo ZRG–576	Leppard	** 78,000; ** 78,200; ** 78,400; ** 78,600; ** 84,125			
Argo ZRG–577	Malcolm	* 99,000; *373,750			
Argo ZRG–578	Guest	* 10,800; * 11,300; * 12,000; * 12,400; * 12,800; * 14,500; * 14,900			
Argo ZRG–585	Wilbraham, Marriner	*492,500; *515,250; *525,000; *565,000			
Argo ZRG–594	Marriner	**444,750; **445,250; **445,500			
Argo ZRG–598	Guest	* 56,250			
Argo ZRG–605	Ogdon, Marriner	*532,750; *533,250			
Argo ZRG–620	Guest	** 17,300; ** 17,500; ** 17,600; ** 17,900; ** 18,000; ** 18,200; ** 18,300; ** 18,500			
Argo ZRG–631	Preston, Marriner	*523,750			
Argo ZRG–632	Malcolm	*154,500; *154,600; *154,900; *155,000; *155,100; *155,400			
Argo ZRG–634	Guest	** 55,250			
Argo ZRG–639	Norrington	* 83,000			
Argo ZRG–642	Munrow	** 5,000			
Argo ZRG–644	Jones Brass Ensemble, Shirley-Quirk	574,075; *636,250; *819,000; *821,000			
Argo ZRG–645	Gardiner	*841,800			
Argo ZRG–653	Marriner	**447,000; **447,250; **447,750			
Argo ZRG–657	Marriner	586,750; 587,500			
Argo ZRG–664	Shirley-Quirk	*815,600; *815,800			
Argo ZRG–666	Norrington	** 82,750; ** 84,000			
Argo ZRG–668	Burgess	** 67,500; ** 68,000; *841,400			
Argo ZRG–673	Munrow	** 20,900			
Argo ZRG–674	Ogdon, Wilbraham, Marriner	*554,250; *557,250			
Argo ZRG–680	Marriner	**796,500			
Argo ZRG–681	Burgess	* 1,900; * 2,000; * 3,500; * 3,600			
Argo ZRG–686	Marriner	**659,000			
Argo ZRG–689	Norrington	** 84,500			
Argo ZRG–690	Guest	** 10,100; ** 10,500			
Argo ZRG–691	Lockhart, Cardiff Festival Players	*996,900			
Argo ZRG–696	Marriner	* 570,250; *800,100; *800,150			
Argo ZRG–697	Marriner	*660,500; *661,000			
Argo ZRG–701	Davis	**402,000			
Argo ZRG–702	Prausnitz	*467,250; *743,250; 761,125; 991,675			
Argo ZRG–705	Marriner	*718,750; *719,000			
Argo ZRG–706	Marriner	**447,500; **448,000; **448,500			
Argo ZRG–707	Tear	*877,000; *877,100; *877,200; *877,300			
Argo ZRG–708	Luxon	846,250			
Argo ZRG–719	Marriner	*384,000; *455,500			
Argo ZRG–724	Guest	* 76,500; * 76,750; * 77,250			
Argo ZRG–727	Isaac, Jones	**343,500			
Argo ZRG–741	Jones	*130,500			
Argo ZRG–748	Allegri Quartet	984,875; 984,950			
Argo ZRG–755	Bertini	**485,000; **485,250			
Argo ZRG–760	Guest	** 37,250; ** 62,250			
Argo ZRG–5277	Pears	**823,500; **823,501; **823,502; **823,503			
Argo ZRG–5320	Guest	** 85,750			
Argo ZRG–5443	Burgess	* 16,200			
Argo Z–503	Preston	**186,250; **188,000			
Argo Z–505	Willcocks	** 92,750			
Argo Z–515	Guest	** 56,500			
Argo 5186	Howard	9,900			
Argo 5226	Willcocks	* 500; * 1,000; * 1,300; * 1,400			
Argo 5234	Willcocks	* 25,000			
Argo 5237	Guest	** 94,500			
Argo 5290	Golden Age Singers	*828,000			

161

LABEL	PERFORMER	GUIDE NO.			
Argo 5316	Willcocks	** 16,800;	** 16,900		
Argo 5325	Willcocks	** 55,750			
Argo 5339	Preston	**169,002;	**169,750;	**990,400	
Argo 5362	Willcocks	** 1,100;	** 1,200		
Argo 5369	Willcocks	** 49,250;	** 49,500;	** 49,750;	** 50,000
Argo 5398	Willcocks	* 12,200;	* 12,600;	* 12,700;	* 13,600;
		* 14,000			
Argo 5418	Pears	**835,200;	**849,000		
Argo 5419	Simon, Preston	*102,640;	*102,646;	*102,647;	*102,648;
		*102,649			
Argo 5436	Willcocks	** 16,700			
Argo 5440	Guest	* 34,000;	* 34,500;	* 35,000	
Argo 5442	Lord, Marriner	*520,500;	*520,502;	*520,504;	*659,200
Argo 5444	Guest	** 76,000			
Argo 5447	Preston	*991,000			
Argo 5467	Marriner	*439,500;	*439,750;	*440,000	
Argo 5479	Willcocks	** 16,500			
Argo 5494	Guest	** 69,500;	** 70,000;	** 70,500;	** 71,000
Argo 5495	Holst	** 58,250			
Argo 5498	Tuckwell, Marriner	**523,000;	**523,002		
Argo 5500	Marriner	** 56,000			
2–Argo ZDA–19/20	Pritchard	** 89,000;	**796,750		
2–Argo ZNF–8/10	Wakefield, Cuénod, Leppard	*911,750			
2–Argo ZNF–11/12	Cotrubas, Leppard	*911,500			
3–Argo ZRG–773/5	Marriner	**616,251;	**616,252;	**616,253;	**616,254;
		**616,255;	**616,256;	**616,257;	**616,258;
		**616,259;	**616,260;	**616,261;	**616,262

Avakian

LABEL	PERFORMER	GUIDE NO.
†3–Avakian S–1	Tudor, Cunningham	972,500

Bach Guild

LABEL	PERFORMER	GUIDE NO.			
Bach SRV 298 SD	Deller	** 1,700;	** 2,600;	** 4,500;	** 4,600;
		** 4,700;	** 4,800;	** 4,900;	** 5,100;
		** 6,100			
†3–Bach BG 627/9	Szigeti	**252,750;	**253,000;	**253,250;	**253,500;
		**253,750;	**254,000		

Bartok

LABEL	PERFORMER	GUIDE NO.
†Bartok 307	Serly	*586,500
†Bartok 312	Susskind	26,000

BASF

LABEL	PERFORMER	GUIDE NO.	
BASF 20309	Collegium Aureum	**375,000	
BASF 20314	Demus, Coll. Aureum	*352,000;	354,000
BASF 20341	Collegium Aureum	*661,000	
BASF 20343	Segarra	** 7,500;	** 7,700
BASF 21512	Turner	** 8,700;	** 8,900
BASF 29310	Collegium Aureum	*723,500	

LABEL	PERFORMER	GUIDE NO.			
BASF 29311	Demus, Collegium Aureum	*536,758;	*536,776		
BASF 29312	Collegium Aureum Wind Ensemble	*335,250;	*335,500		
BASF 29369	Ameling	*865,500; *869,500	*867,000;	*868,000;	*869,000;
BASF 2020350	Collegium Aureum	*660,500			
2–BASF 29050	Ewerhardt	**520,700; **520,756; **521,004; **521,015	**520,750; **521,000; **521,005;	**520,754; **521,002; **521,006;	**520,755; **521,003; **521,014;

Cambridge

LABEL	PERFORMER	GUIDE NO.			
Cam. 1804	Curry, Vosgerchian	*183,500; 835,500;	679,500; 835,850;	679,750; 836,000;	*835,300; *836,200
Cam. 2715	Moore	815,000			
Cam. 3508	Leonhardt	243,750			

Candide

LABEL	PERFORMER	GUIDE NO.			
Can. 31002	Loriod, Messiaen	*991,100			
Can. 31008	Doemer, Klein, Arend, Koster, Milhaud	*711,750			
Can. 31009	Charlent	989,000;	989,100;	989,300;	989,400
Can. 31013	Daniel, Milhaud	711,250			
Can. 31016	Dorian Quintet	*285,250;	*286,750		
Can. 31020	Sebestyén	239,750			
Can. 31023	Ponti, Maga	549,000			
Can. 31024	Escribano	826,750;	826,751;	826,752;	851,500
Can. 31029	Terebesi, Littauer	*247,750;	492,750		
Can. 31069	Londeix, Froment	511,750;	512,000;	512,250	

Columbia

LABEL	PERFORMER	GUIDE NO.			
Col. KS–6605	Tourel, Bernstein	382,500			
Col. MS–6010	Bernstein	*786,200			
Col. MS–6043	Bernstein, Columbia Orchestra	*546,250;	*554,252		
Col. MS–6063	Francescatti, Walter	*537,503;	*537,504		
Col. MS–6091	Bernstein	**517,250;	*640,000		
Col. MS–6124	Ormandy	**467,500;	**554,000		
Col. MS–6128	Serkin, Ormandy	*532,500;	*532,502		
Col. MS–6146	Craft	*366,000;	*366,250		
Col. MS–6149	Walter	*803,250;	*804,500;	**804,750;	**805,000
Col. MS–6158	Francescatti, Fournier, Walter	**505,000;	**604,750		
Col. MS–6161	Biggs	**183,750			
Col. MS–6175	Bernstein	**612,000;	**614,750;	**615,000;	**615,250
Col. MS–6180	Ormandy	584,250			
Col. MS–6196	Ormandy	579,500;	654,000;	762,250;	765,000
Col. MS–6218	Walter	**462,750;	**463,250		
Col. MS–6221	Merrill, Cahn, Bernstein	817,400			
Col. MS–6255	Walter	**450,000;	**451,500		
Col. MS–6272	Stravinsky	**361,250;	**361,500;	*558,000	

163

LABEL	PERFORMER	GUIDE NO.			
Col. MS–6303	Tourel, Bernstein	**382,000;	*404,250		
Col. MS–6319	Stravinsky	**786,200			
Col. MS–6328	Stravinsky	**783,800;	**784,020;	**784,060	
Col. MS–6331	Stravinsky, Stern	**475,000;	*557,750		
Col. MS–6332	Stravinsky	**785,400			
Col. MS–6349	Ormandy	477,000			
Col. MS–6355	Bernstein	*611,750;	*615,500		
Col. MS–6362	Craft	*799,200;	*799,800		
Col. MS–6373	Stern, Bernstein	*499,700;	*499,701;	*501,750	
Col. MS–6377	Casadesus, Bernstein	*515,500;	*549,254		
Col. MS–6405	Serkin, Ormandy	498,496;	*544,004		
Col. MS–6408	Gould	*111,846;	*111,847;	*111,848;	*111,849;
		*111,850;	*111,851;	*111,852;	*111,853
Col. MS–6411	Horowitz	**237,250			
Col. MS–6439	Biggs, Boult	520,700;	520,755;	521,016	
Col. MS–6459	Ormandy	*468,250			
Col. MS–6493	Walter	**450,250;	**450,750		
Col. MS–6494	Walter	**450,500;	**451,000		
Col. MS–6497	Goodman, Copland	**509,000;	**825,600		
Col. MS–6514	Bernstein	*393,000;	*612,500;	*657,000;	*877,600
Col. MS–6536	Budapest	**354,250			
Col. MS–6538	Gould	*111,854–*111,861			
Col. MS–6548	Stravinsky	*87,500;	*474,500		
Col. MS–6566	electronic synthesizer	964,750;	965,600;	977,250;	981,250;
		989,800;	997,500		
Col. MS–6575	Ormandy	603,250;	617,250		
Col. MS–6587	Ormandy	*740,750;	741,000;	741,250	
Col. MS–6608	Williams	**365,250;	**365,500		
Col. MS–6616	Serkin, Bernstein	* 26,750			
Col. MS–6631	Serkin	*279,750			
Col. MS–6635	Stern, Ormandy	**544,250;	**544,252		
Col. MS–6638	Szell, Browning	**497,500;	*552,250		
Col. MS–6646	Stravinsky	**782,200;	**785,200		
Col. MS–6658	Horowitz	**223,020;	**223,040;	**223,120;	**223,160;
		**223,170;	**223,200;	**223,240;	**223,250;
		**223,260;	**223,270;	**223,280;	**223,340;
		**223,500			
Col. MS–6659	Drucker, Bernstein	512,000;	512,250;	672,000;	672,250;
		672,500			
Col. MS–6677	Bernstein	*597,000;	*598,000		
Col. MS–6683	Horszowski, Budapest Quartet	*330,250;	*330,500		
Col. MS–6684	Ormandy	*612,750;	**613,250;	680,000	
Col. MS–6685	Szell	*388,000;	*605,250		
Col. MS–6698	Bernstein, Copland	**509,500;	**613,500		
Col. MS–6713	Stern, Bernstein	*498,000;	*525,500		
Col. MS–6714	Rose, Ormandy	*513,250;	560,000		
Col. MS–6716	Stern, Rose, Istomin	*355,250			
Col. MS–6732	Ormandy	*762,250;	*764,250;	*764,500;	765,000
Col. MS–6749	Bernstein	*472,250;	*763,750		
Col. MS–6755	Graffman, Ormandy	559,252;	559,253		
Col. MS–6769	Bernstein	452,750			
Col. MS–6775	Stokowski	**431,000			
Col. MS–6776	Gould	*111,862–*111,869			
Col. MS–6792	Bernstein	** 29,500;	*597,500		
Col. MS–6819	Stern, Rose, Istomin	*275,000			
Col. MS–6833	Szell	**435,250			
Col. MS–6834	Williams	**507,000;	**548,250		
Col. MS–6838	Serkin	**116,500;	499,994		
Col. MS–6843	Bernstein	**429,500;	**430,750;	**678,250;	**678,750;
		**680,250			

LABEL	PERFORMER	GUIDE NO.			
Col. MS–6844	Serkin, Schneider	*536,764;	*536,767		
Col. MS–6848	Laredo, Schneider	*325,000;	*537,750		
Col. MS–6849	Serkin	*227,500			
Col. MS–6858	Szell	*448,250;	*449,500;	*722,000	
Col. MS–6876	Stern, Ormandy	513,750;	514,000		
Col. MS–6877	Szell	*599,000;	654,000		
Col. MS–6884	Szell	**803,000;	**803,250;	**804,000;	**805,750
Col. MS–6885	Entremont, Bernstein	**382,250			
Col. MS–6889	Bernstein	**429,750;	**430,500;	**679,000	
Col. MS–6897	Szell	**390,500			
Col. MS–6921	Smith Singers	* 59,500;	* 59,750		
Col. MS–6925	Graffman, Szell	**544,000;	*544,003		
Col. MS–6943	Bernstein	625,250;	725,500;	*729,000	
Col. MS–6944	Biggs	132,250			
Col. MS–6945	Gould	120,250;	*120,500;	120,750	
Col. MS–6952	Trampler, Budapest Quartet	*267,500;	*295,000		
Col. MS–6953	Francescatti, DeStoutz	559,000			
Col. MS–6966	Szell	*590,500;	*590,750;	*591,250;	*591,502
Col. MS–6967	Serkin, Szell	**504,501			
Col. MS–6986	Ormandy	*457,000			
Col. MS–6989	Stravinsky	**474,750			
Col. MS–6992	Stravinsky	* 86,000;	* 86,750;	*876,700	
Col. MS–7002	Szell	*707,750;	*758,750		
Col. MS–7003	Stern, Ormandy	506,000;	528,750		
Col. MS–7011	Stravinsky	**784,020;	**784,060;	**784,100;	**785,600;
		**785,650			
Col. MS–7015	Stokowski	*678,000;	680,000;	*680,750	
Col. MS–7027	Juilliard Quartet	**315,250;	**315,500		
Col. MS–7028	Drucker, Bernstein	*539,750;	*540,000		
Col. MS–7031	Szell	*747,750;	*748,000;	*748,250;	*750,250
Col. MS–7032	Ormandy	807,800			
Col. MS–7034	Ormandy	686,000;	686,250;	686,750	
Col. MS–7051	electronic synthesizer	965,700;	973,250;	993,300	
Col. MS–7054	Stravinsky	* 87,250;	**361,750		
Col. MS–7058	Biggs, Bernstein	*394,500;	*598,500		
Col. MS–7063	Williams, Groves	*548,500			
Col. MS–7064	Druian, Szell	**335,750;	**336,000;	**336,250	
Col. MS–7071	Smith Singers	* 44,000;	* 44,500		
Col. MS–7083	Istomin, Stern, Rose	*274,750;	*326,250		
Col. MS–7085	Bernstein	726,000;	728,000;	742,750;	747,250;
		788,500;	788,750		
Col. MS–7093	Stravinsky	**361,250;	**786,000		
Col. MS–7094	Stravinsky	**784,200;	*785,600;	*785,650;	**786,400;
		**786,600			
†Col. MS–7096E	Gould	**107,988			
Col. MS–7098	Gould	*224,000;	*224,250;	*224,500;	*224,750
Col. MS–7099	Gould	*111,870–*111,877			
Col. MS–7133	Ormandy	794,250			
Col. MS–7139	Neuhaus	970,500;	971,000;	972,250;	982,000;
		995,900			
Col. MS–7143	Serkin, Szell	*504,500			
Col. MS–7147	Bernstein	*429,000;	*429,250;	*429,500;	*429,750;
		*430,000			
Col. MS–7166	Szell	**669,000;	**669,500;	**681,250	
Col. MS–7176	Smith	989,200			
Col. MS–7179	Boulez, Barenboim	593,000;	593,750;	816,400	
Col. MS–7191	Prausnitz	974,750;	*975,750		
Col. MS–7192	Kirkpatrick	**183,250			
Col. MS–7195	Williams	**360,500			
Col. MS–7207	Mitchell's Ensemble	992,150			

165

LABEL	PERFORMER	GUIDE NO.			
Col. MS–7208	Szell	*628,500; *628,757	*628,750;	*628,751;	*628,752;
Col. MS–7223	Copland	**394,000;	**394,250		
Col. MS–7242	Ormandy	742,000;	742,250;	742,500	
Col. MS–7252	Lewenthal, Mackerras	524,750;	530,250		
Col. MS–7261	Bernstein	**402,750			
Col. MS–7264	Horowitz	*235,750			
Col. MS–7268	Swingle Singers, Berio	967,750			
Col. MS–7273	Szell	723,750;	*724,250		
Col. MS–7277	Smith	** 30,000;	** 30,250;	** 30,500;	** 30,750
Col. MS–7291	Szell	*804,500; *807,500	*805,500;	*807,000;	*807,250;
Col. MS–7298	Ormandy	605,000;	605,250		
Col. MS–7315	Riley	993,900;	993,950		
Col. MS–7316	electronic synthesizer	996,450			
Col. MS–7318	Schuller	*679,250;	*679,750		
Col. MS–7326	Kipnis	* 800;	*117,500;	*157,000;	*180,500;
Col. MS–7355	electronic equipment	995,600;	995,700		
Col. MS–7356	Boulez	990,700;	990,800		
Col. MS–7375	Copland	**510,000;	**613,750;	**614,000;	**614,250
Col. MS–7387	Resnik, Blegen, Patrick	928,750			
Col. MS–7408	Szell	*686,500;	*731,000		
Col. MS–7409	Gould	*111,878–*111,885			
Col. MS–7419	Stern, Rose, Istomin	*355,500			
Col. MS–7426	Bernstein	*426,750;	*669,000;	*669,500	
Col. MS–7431	Bernstein	**612,250			
Col. MS–7439	Lear, Berberian, Stravinsky	*876,500;	*876,600;	*876,800	
Col. MS–7442	Bernstein	*463,750;	*464,000		
Col. MS–7518	Levant	**173,000			
Col. M–30057	Williams	**247,000			
Col. M–30085	Boulez	27,250			
Col. M–30112	Bernstein	974,250			
Col. M–30229	Lear	835,400;	835,600;	835,700;	836,400
Col. M–30230	Zukofsky	316,750;	315,000		
Col. M–30293	Bernstein	*453,000			
Col. M–30294	Entremont	*754,750;	*755,250;	*755,500;	*755,750
Col. M–30296	Boulez	*968,500			
Col. M–30366	Szell	*422,750;	*423,000		
Col. M–30374	Copland	*615,750			
Col. M–30375	Addison, Miller, Hale, Copland	*825,800			
Col. M–30376	Copland	**287,750;	**288,250		
Col. M–30390	Kostelanetz	644,000;	*673,000;	*765,250	
Col. M–30516	Stravinsky	*782,800;	*783,000;	**785,000	
Col. M–30537	Gould	*111,887–*111,893			
Col. M–30579	Goodman, Stravinsky	**361,500;	**783,400		
Col. M–30645	Bernstein	692,750;	693,250		
Col. M–30646	Szell	*423,250;	*423,500		
Col. M–30649	Copland	**611,750;	**612,750;	*613,250	
Col. M–30944	Stern, Zakin	*262,250;	*262,500		
Col. M–31241	Lane	*797,000;	*808,800		
Col. M–31311	Vanni	851,750			
Col. M–31728	Serkin, Schneider	536,761;	536,762		
Col. M–31729	Stravinsky	**782,600; **787,000;	**783,200; **787,200	**783,600;	**784,400;
Col. M–31800	Bernstein	*599,750;	*654,000;	*654,250	
Col. M–31811	Serkin	**120,250;	121,750;	*124,000	
Col. M–31815	Bernstein	667,000; 796,050	750,500;	789,500;	796,000;
Col. M–31824	Bernstein	656,000			

LABEL	PERFORMER	GUIDE NO.			
Col. M–31921	Stravinsky	**784,600			
Col. M–31997	Barenboim	**399,250			
Col. M–32160	Boulez	*968,250			
Col. M–32161	Rosen	*968,750			
Col. M–32230	Zukerman, Sillito, Garcia	571,008;	571,010;	571,011;	574,278
Col. M–32294	Serkin	117,000;	121,000;	124,250	
Col. M–32349	Gould	122,250;	122,500;	122,750	
Col. M–32350	Gould	*182,250;	*182,500;	*182,750	
Col. M–32577	Smith	833,500;	833,800;	833,900	
Col. M–32693	Zukerman, English Chamber Orchestra	572,005			
Col. M–32737	Stern, Copland	*288,000			
Col. M–32738	Juilliard Quartet	*285,750;	*286,000;	**975,000;	**975,250
Col. M–32840	Zukerman, English Chamber Orchestra	572,012			
2–Col. MG–30371	Szell and Cleveland	**378,000;	*398,250		
2–Col. M2S–675	Bernstein	*435,000			
2–Col. M2S–679	Horton, Craft, Oliver	* 80,750;	**851,800;	**851,900;	949,500
2–Col. M2S–693	Gould	*108,825-830			
2–Col. M2S–694	Craft	756,500;	757,000;	757,250;	757,500
2–Col. M2S–698	Bernstein	*435,500;	*839,000		
2–Col. M2S–734	Budapest Quartet	**278,000;	**278,250;	**278,500;	**357,500
2–Col. M2S–735	Ormandy	*436,750			
2–Col. M2S–762	Gramm, Craft	351,250;	851,950		
2–Col. M2S–767	Horton, Gould	225,000;	350,000;	851,850	
2–Col. M2S–780	Schmidt, Harper, Craft	* 79,500;	* 80,500;	950,000	
2–Col. M2–30061	Boulez	** 63,000			
2–Col. M2–30576	Mitchell	992,200			
2–Col. M2–32681	Bernstein	**434,750			
†2–Col. OSL–154	Keller, Powers, Balalian	*928,750;	*929,000		
3–Col. D3S–691	Walter	**450,000;	**450,250;	**450,500;	**450,750;
		**451,000;	**451,500		
3–Col. D3S–705	Stravinsky	**783,800;	**785,400;	**786,200	
3–Col. D3S–717	Juilliard Quartet	**260,250;	**260,500;	**260,750;	**261,000;
		**261,250;	**261,500		
3–Col. D3S–733	Gould	*111,846–*111,869			
3–Col. D3S–761	Stravinsky	**782,200;	**782,400;	**785,200;	**785,800
3–Col. D3S–769	Bernstein	*419,500;	*419,750;	*420,000;	*420,250;
		*420,500;	*420,750		
3–Col. D3S–770	Rampal, Scimone	*573,001;	*573,002;	*573,003;	*573,004;
		*573,005;	*573,006;	*574,078;	*574,079;
		*574,440			
3–Col. M3S–710	Raskin, Sarfaty, Manning, Stravinsky	**955,000			
3–Col. M3S–776	Bernstein	*435,750;	*436,500		
4–Col. M4X–30052	Fleischer, Szell	**499,994;	*499,996;	499,998;	**500,000;
		*500,002			
5–Col. M5S–677	Budapest Quartet	*266,250;	*266,500		
5–Col. M5–30065	Istomin, Stern, Rose	*273,250;	*273,500;	*273,750;	*274,000;
		*274,250;	*274,500;	*274,750;	*275,000;
		*275,250			
†5–Col. M5–30069	Stern	**272,500;	**281,250;	**354,250;	**605,250
†6–Col. M6X–31513	Szigeti	**500,250			

Collectors Guild

LABEL	PERFORMER	GUIDE NO.
†3–Coll. Guild 665/7	Provatorov	950,750

Concert-Disc

LABEL	PERFORMER	GUIDE NO.	
Con.–Disc 205	New York Woodwind Quintet	*290,750;	*312,250
Con.–Disc 217	Glazer	**166,000	
Con.–Disc 252	Glazer, Fine Arts Quartet	*276,500	

Connoisseur Society

LABEL	PERFORMER	GUIDE NO.
Conn. S–2002	Moravec	200,750
Conn. S–2033	R. and J. Contiguglia	115,250

Contemporary

LABEL	PERFORMER	GUIDE NO.
Contem. 8012	J. Harris	**301,750

Cornell University

LABEL	PERFORMER	GUIDE NO.
Cornell U. 1	Cornell Wind Ensemble	756,750
Cornell U. 5	Cornell Wind Ensemble	671,250

Coronet

LABEL	PERFORMER	GUIDE NO.
Coro. S–1502	Ohio State University Band	712,000

Counterpoint/Esoteric

LABEL	PERFORMER	GUIDE NO.			
Count. 5602	Boepple	9,200;	9,300;	9,400;	9,500;
		9,600;	9,800;	11,000;	
		11,900;	12,000;	12,800;	13,000;
		13,500;	13,700;	14,300;	14,900;
		15,200;	15,300;	15,400	

Composers Recordings, Inc.

LABEL	PERFORMER	GUIDE NO.			
CRI S–185	Siegmeister	473,000			
CRI S–189	Keyes, Harrison	403,250;	529,000		
CRI S–196	Strickland	376,250			
CRI S–203	Steinberg, Krenz	966,250;	980,250		
CRI S–204	Guigui	977,500			
CRI S–213	Partch	992,100			
CRI S–219	Van Vactor, Hessian Radio Symphony; RCA Electronic Synthesizer	989,750			
CRI S–220	Zukofsky, Schuller	*553,500			
CRI S–225	Strickland	431,250			
CRI S–227	Columbia-Princeton Electronic Music Center	989,600; 993,550;	993,400; 997,550;	993,450; 997,700	993,500;
CRI S–236	Samuel	404,750			
CRI S–238	Curtin, Wolff, Gramm	850,200; 850,600;	850,300; 850,700;	850,400; 850,800;	850,500; 850,900

LABEL	PERFORMER	GUIDE NO.		
CRI S–252	Price	993,050		
CRI S–255	De Gaetani, Fitz	980,750;	994,050	
CRI S–257	Composer Quartet	997,800		
†CRI S–278E	Mitropoulos	*440,250;	*467,000	
CRI S–287	Solomon	376,500		
CRI S–290	Addison	979,750;	980,000	
CRI S–294	Composers Quartet	**292,250		
CRI S–308	Ormandy	759,250;	988,000	
CRI S–310	Hamm, University of Illinois Contemporary Chamber Players	987,750		
CRI S–311	Jelinek, Gurt	966,000;	983,000	
†CRI 110	Antonini	624,000		
†CRI 112	Luening	989,650;	989,700;	997,600
†CRI 117	Antonini	743,000		
†CRI 127	Strickland	483,250;	713,000;	752,500
†CRI 138	Wummer, Drucker, March, McCall	965,500		
†CRI 206	Buketoff	483,500		
†CRI 216	Krenz	624,500		
2 CRI S–168	Bible, Buckley, New York City Opera Company	*964,000		

Crystal

LABEL	PERFORMER	GUIDE NO.
Crys. S–134	Reese	356,250

Columbia Special Products

LABEL	PERFORMER	GUIDE NO.			
CSP AKS–6318	Stravinsky	**784,800			
†CSP AML–4374	Beecham	**422,250;	**660,000		
†CSP AML–4453	Beecham	**422,500;	**424,750		
†CSP AML–4736	Graf, Juilliard Quartet	*350,500;	*350,750		
†CSP AML–4737	Juilliard Quartet	*351,000;	*371,750		
†CSP AML–4859	Zorina	** 43,500			
†CSP AML–4922	Budapest Quartet	308,000;	308,250		
†CSP AML–4923	Budapest Quartet	308,500;	308,750		
†CSP AML–4924	Budapest Quartet	309,000;	309,250		
†CSP AML–4956	Surinach	580,000			
†CSP AML–4986	Kirkpatrick, Prausnitz, Juilliard	752,000;	752,750;	826,250	
†CSP AML–4992	Ormandy	454,875;	464,250		
†CSP AML–5246	Serkin	**127,250			
CSP AMS–6087	Biggs	192,500			
CSP AMS–6114	Philadelphia Woodwind Quintet	*259,000;	*340,000		
CSP AMS–6198	Curtin	*825,400			
CSP AMS–6213	Philadelphia Woodwind Ensemble	**297,875;	327,000;	**342,000	
CSP AMS–6280	Bernstein, Addison, Foss	983,500			
CSP AMS–6333	Gold and Fizdale	*242,000;	*242,250;	*243,000;	*243,500
CSP AMS–6379	Torkanowsky	459,500			
CSP AMS–6396	Bernstein, Zorina	** 65,500			
CSP AMS–6447	Temianka	287,000;	610,500		
CSP AMS–6573	Hindemith	** 57,250			
CSP AMS–6597	Rozsnyai	398,750			
CSP AMS–6717	Stern	**276,250			
CSP AM–30082	Lane	*591,750			
†CSP AM–30405	Kipnis	*818,000; *822,750; *868,750;	*819,250; *854,500; *875,250;	*819,500; *860,250; *876,250	*821,000; *863,750;

LABEL	PERFORMER	GUIDE NO.			
†CSP CML–4542	Primrose, Beecham	**502,000			
†CSP CML–4988	Price	*814,500			
CSP CMS–6022	Stravinsky	** 86,250			
CSP CMS–6103	Craft	756,250;	*810,000;	*816,400	
CSP CMS–6438	Tourel, Bernstein	816,600;	*849,850		
CSP C32160202	Stevens	* 18,900			
CSP P11816	Kraus, Simon	536,763;	536,768		
CSP P11817	Kraus, Simon	536,764;	536,767		
†4–CSP CK4L–232	Craft	93,500;	484,000;	810,000;	810,200;
		810,400;	810,600;	810,800	

Desto

LABEL	PERFORMER	GUIDE NO.			
†Desto S–6406E	Dixon	395,000;	477,250		
†Desto 6404E	Hendl	404,250;	759,000;	761,000	
†Desto 6405E	Dixon	483,000;	796,350		
Desto 6407E	VonZallinger	608,000			
†Desto 6409E	Hendl	601,750			
†Desto 6415E	Haefner	482,250			
†Desto 6416E	Swarowsky	389,000			
†Desto 6421E	Schoenherr	610,250;	767,750		
Desto 6428	Rudel	317,000			
Desto 6450	Aliberti	931,750			
Desto 6451	Gabriele, Waldman	905,250			
Desto 6466	Electronic tape	997,650			
Desto 7132	Trimble, New Forum Quartet	997,300			
Desto 7145	Laredo	238,000			
Desto 7167	Fine	*400,000			
Desto 7168	Comissiona	988,500			
†2–Desto S–6413/4E	Strickland	74,000			
2–Desto 6411/2	Steber	*814,250;	*836,200;	850,000;	850,100
†2–Desto 6413/4E	Swarowsky	624,250			
2–Desto 7118/9	Tourel	816,000;	826,750;	834,100;	837,000;
		877,300			
3–Desto 6463/5	New York City Opera Company	931,500			
4–Desto 6474/7	American Brass Ensemble	996,800			

Deutsche Grammophon

LABEL	PERFORMER	GUIDE NO.			
DG ARC–198013	Kirkpatrick	*495,000;	*495,002		
DG ARC–198027	Stader	* 23,051;	* 23,402		
DG ARC–198032	Kirkpatrick	**108,250;	**108,500		
DG ARC–198153	Benedictine Abbey Monks	** 3,900			
DG ARC–198166	Terpsichore Collegium	*730,250			
DG ARC–198186	Fournier	*255,750;	*256,000		
DG ARC–198187	Fournier	*256,250;	*256,500		
DG ARC–198188	Fournier	*256,750;	*257,000		
DG ARC–198198	Wenzinger	**364,750;	**795,750		
DG ARC–198304	Walcha	**110,000;	**110,250;	**110,500;	**110,750
DG ARC–198305	Walcha	**106,537;	**109,000		
DG ARC–198318	Linde, Hofmann	*574,079;	*574,222;	*574,266;	*574,434
DG ARC–198320	Richter	**583,500			
DG ARC–198321	Richter, Bilgram, Richter	*495,250;	*496,750		

LABEL	PERFORMER	GUIDE NO.
DG ARC–198331	Töpper	** 23,060; ** 23,247; ** 23,347
DG ARC–198402	Munich Bach Orchestra	** 23,026; ** 23,106; ** 23,206
DG ARC–198406	Knothe	8,000; 8,800
DG ARC–198407	St. Thomas Church Choir	** 23,080; * 23,240
DG ARC–198415	André	**524,000; **524,500
DG ARC–198441	St. Thomas' Choir	* 23,018
DG ARC–198442	Gracis, Scarlatti Orchestra	551,502; 551,503; 551,504
DG ARC–198465	Mathis	** 23,004
DG ARC–198477	Fischer-Dieskau	* 23,056; * 23,082
DG ARC–2533042	Mackerras	** 77,000
DG ARC–2533044	Stadlmair, Munich	*573,001; *574,074; *574,320; *574,321
DG ARC–2533049	Mathis	** 23,021
DG ARC–2533055	Wenzinger	*252,000; *252,250; *252,500
DG ARC–2533066	Knothe	* 15,900; * 16,000; * 16,100
DG ARC–2533067	Schadner	*616,500; *616,750
DG ARC–2533072	Kirkpatrick	**223,210; **223,260; **223,320; **223,501
DG ARC–2533086	Melkus	**362,250; **369,000
DG ARC–2533088	Richter	*659,751; *659,752; *659,760; *659,762
DG ARC–2533110	Jürgens	** 2,500
DG ARC–2533114	Freni	** 74,250
DG ARC–2533116	Richter	**659,250
DG ARC–2533117	Linde, Ensemble	**369,250; **369,500; **369,750; **370,000; **370,250; **370,500
DG ARC–2533132	Melkus	*288,500; *288,750
DG ARC–2533141	Richter	*659,753; *659,754; *659,761
DG ARC–2533142	Richter	*659,755; *659,758; *659,759
DG ARC–2533150	Ragossnig, Ulsamer	** 19,900
DG ARC–2533151	Richter	*660,500
DG ARC–2533159	Richter	*659,756; *659,757; *659,800
DG 136257	Karajan	*610,750; *621,100
DG 136281	Cossotto, Karajan	*890,500
DG 136452	Vàsàry, Kulka	*507,502
DG 136454	Vàsàry	*134,500; *134,750; *135,000; *135,250
DG 138033	Maazel	*725,500; *741,250; *743,750
DG 138076	Richter	**211,000; **211,250; **211,500; **211,750; **212,250; **213,000
DG 138111	Fricsay, Anda	**498,498; **498,500
DG 138118	Zabaleta	**504,000; **548,000
DG 138124	Fricsay	* 72,500
DG 138692	Karajan	530,000; *693,250; *693,500; *694,000
DG 138714	D. and I. Oistrakh, Goossens	496,250; 500,750; 501,000; *571,008
DG 138755	Fournier, Szell	**513,250
DG 138774	Kempff, Leitner	*499,994
DG 138775	Kempff	*499,996; *500,000
DG 138777	Kempff, Leitner	*500,002
DG 138801	Karajan	*377,000; *377,250
DG 138803	Karajan	*377,750
DG 138811	Stockhausen Ensemble	995,000
DG 138815	Böhm	**451,000; *451,500
DG 138824	Anda	*536,756; *536,772
DG 138829	Stader	* 37,000;
DG 138853	Zoeller, Zabaleta	*536,000; **546,750
DG 138866	Meyer, Böhm	*557,000; *779,500; *780,750; *781,000
DG 138870	Anda	536,766; 536,773
DG 138879	Fischer-Dieskau	**839,000; **839,300; **839,301; **839,302; **839,304; **839,305
DG 138886	Amadeus Quartet	308,500; *331,500
DG 138921	Karajan	*476,750
DG 138923	Karajan	*619,000; *620,250; *736,750

LABEL	PERFORMER	GUIDE NO.			
DG 138925	Karajan	*387,500			
DG 138934	Kempff	**116,000; **116,750; **117,250; **117,750; **118,000; **118,250			
DG 138935	Kempff	*118,500; *121,250; *123,000; *123,250			
DG 138938	Kempff	**120,750			
DG 138941	Kempff	*120,250; 121,750; *122,000; **124,250			
DG 138942	Kempff	*122,500; *125,250			
DG 138944	Kempff	*125,500; 125,750			
DG 138949	Eschenbach	*195,500; *199,750; *200,000; *202,000			
DG 138954	Kubelik	* 60,500			
DG 138959	Kubelik	*707,750			
DG 138996	Koch	*330,000; *334,250			
DG 138997	Zöller	*329,500; *329,750			
DG 139004	Karajan	*328,500; 724,250			
DG 139009	Fournier, Karajan	*556,750			
DG 139010	Karajan	**725,750; *736,250			
DG 139014	Karajan	*768,500; *769,000; *769,500; *770,000; *771,000; *772,000; *773,750; *775,750			
DG 139015	Karajan	**378,750; 590,500; *591,000; *591,503			
DG 139028	Karajan	*559,500; *790,000			
DG 139030	Karajan	*792,000; *792,250; *792,500; *793,250			
DG 139040	Karajan	*456,250			
DG 139102	Berlin Octet	*352,250			
DG 139103	Amadeus Quartet	*353,000; *353,750			
DG 139109	Fischer-Dieskau	**866,500; **867,500			
DG 139112	Zabaleta, Kuentz	512,700; 514,250			
DG 139125	Wunderlich	**815,200; **816,000; **816,200; **852,500; **856,000; **860,000; **860,750; **866,500; **867,250			
DG 139131	Jochum	*390,000			
DG 139149	Kempff	**226,500; **226,501; **226,502; **226,503; **226,504; **226,700; **226,701; **226,702; **226,703; **226,704			
DG 139152	Holliger, Maag	*501,250; *508,500; *513,100; *550,250			
DG 139156	Böhm	**538,000; *538,250			
DG 139159	Böhm	**447,750; **449,000; **449,750			
DG 139160	Böhm	*450,250; *450,750			
DG 139162	Böhm	**462,750; **463,250			
DG 139181	Kubelik	**398,000			
DG 139194	Amadeus Quartet	352,750; 353,250			
DG 139197	Fischer-Dieskau	**815,200; **815,600			
DG 139300	Kempff	*120,250; 121,750; **124,000; **124,750			
DG 139304	Zabaleta	*348,000; *511,500; *520,225			
DG 139318	Eschenbach	*196,750; *199,250; *199,500			
DG 139321	Richter	**102,645; **102,650; **109,543; **109,544			
DG 139325	Richter	**110,750			
DG 139349	Argerich	**544,003; **546,250			
DG 139358	Fournier, Baumgartner	*521,500; *521,750			
DG 139365	Yepes	* 7,100			
DG 139366	Yepes	**360,500			
DG 139371	Amadeus Quartet	*280,500			
DG 139372	Kempff	**227,000; **230,000			
DG 139387	Richter	*100,767			
DG 139398	Leister	*282,750; *283,250			
DG 139405	Böhm	*446,500; *446,750; *447,000; *447,250			
DG 139417	Behrend	**506,750; **518,000; **574,134; **574,209			
DG 139424	Ashkenasi, Esser	**540,750; **540,752			
DG 139430	Amadeus Quartet	*280,000; *280,250			
DG 139455	Kempff	*107,988			

LABEL	PERFORMER	GUIDE NO.			
G 139458	Vàsàry	**158,000;	*158,750;	**161,750;	**162,000;
		**162,250;	**165,750		
G 2530027	Karajan	*770,500;	*771,500;	*772,250;	*773,250;
		*773,500			
G 2530035	Richter	*106,250;	*110,915		
G 2530048	Thomas	**680,000;	**753,000		
G 2530049	Dwyer, Eskin, Fine, Hobson,	*291,250;	*291,500;	*291,750;	*292,000
	Silverstein, Thomas				
G 2530051	Karajan	**788,500;	**788,750;	**789,000;	**789,250;
		**789,500			
G 2530056	Eschenbach, Henze	985,600			
G 2530061	Gilels	*196,250;	*197,500;	*198,750	
G 2530065	Karajan	*587,500;	*782,200		
G 2530066	Karajan	591,200;	716,250;	780,000	
G 2530068	Karajan	*428,000;	*428,250		
G 2530069	Yepes	**276,750			
G 2530070	Karajan	616,258;	696,000;	797,750	
G 2530073	Caballé	**888,000;	**889,350;	**889,400;	**889,550;
		**891,300			
G 2530074	Jochum	* 73,750			
G 2530075	Kubelik	*681,250;	*681,500		
G 2530103	Thomas	*454,500			
G 2530120	Böhm	*447,500;	*447,750;	*448,000	
G 2530126	Karajan	*438,500;	*707,500		
G 2530133	Gilels	278,750			
G 2530136	Böhm	*335,000			
G 2530137	Abbado	*466,500;	*793,000		
G 2530140	Yepes	**367,000;	**367,250;	**367,500;	**367,750;
		**368,000;	**368,250;	**368,500	
G 2530142	Böhm	**378,250			
G 2530146	Abbado	**593,250;	**593,750;	*816,400	
G 2530147	Szeryng, Fournier, Kempff	*275,000			
G 2530159	Yepes	**246,500;	**246,750		
G 2530185	Kempff	*232,000;	*232,500		
G 2530195	Karajan	*793,600;	*794,200		
G 2530196	Michelangeli	**158,250;	**160,750;	**161,000;	**161,250;
		**161,500			
G 2530199	Karajan	*649,000;	*727,500		
G 2530200	Karajan	729,250;	790,500;	801,000;	801,100;
		801,400			
G 2530207	Szeryng, Fournier, Kempff	*273,500;	*273,750		
G 2530214	Boston Symphony Chamber	294,750			
	Players				
G 2530225	Pollini	**208,250;	**242,000		
G 2530229	Fischer-Dieskau	**855,250;	**857,750;	**861,500;	**864,250
G 2530230	Zabaleta	**246,000			
G 2530243	Karajan	*652,250;	*652,750;	*654,000;	*654,250
G 2530246	Steinberg	**426,000;	**668,000		
G 2530257	Brendel, Kubelik	*551,750;	*552,000		
G 2530261	Henze	**987,000			
G 2530283	La Salle Quartet	**275,750;	**276,000		
G 2530284	La Salle Quartet	**371,750;	**372,250		
G 2530291	Pollini	*134,500;	*134,750;	*134,800;	*134,850;
		*134,900;	*135,000;	*135,050;	*135,100;
		*135,150;	*135,200;	*135,250	
G 2530302	Amadeus Quartet	*305,250;	*305,500		
G 2530306	Fischer-Dieskau	**857,500			
G 2530317	Kempff	**235,750;	**237,000		

LABEL	PERFORMER	GUIDE NO.			
DG 2530319	Mathis	**844,250;	**845,500		
DG 2530329	La Salle Quartet	**350,250			
DG 2530347	Fischer-Dieskau	**859,000			
DG 2530349	Karajan	*779,500;	*780,750;	*781,000	
DG 2530368	Karajan	*779,250;	872,250		
DG 2530398	Böhm	*421,500;	*665,000		
DG 2530402	Karajan	**778,750			
DG 2530411	Zeman, Böhm	*535,250;	*535,500		
DG 2530462	Yepes	**257,250;	**257,500		
DG 2530480	Prague Quartet	**294,375			
2–DG ARC–2708020	Mackerras	** 51,500			
2–DG ARC–2708023	Walcha	*101,000;	*101,599;	*101,604;	*101,60
		*101,608;	*101,610;	*101,615;	*101,62
		*103,650;	*103,651;	*103,652;	*103,65
		*103,654;	*103,656;	*103,658;	*103,65
		*103,668			
2–DG 2707014	Smetáček	* 42,750			
2–DG 2707015	Kirkpatrick	**111,846;	**111,869		
2–DG 2707023	Lear, Böhm	**907,000			
2–DG 2707028	Fischer-Dieskau	**864,500			
2–DG 2707032	Munch, Schreier	** 28,500			
2–DG 2707039	Stockhausen Ensemble	995,200			
2–DG 2707044	Karajan	** 54,500			
2–DG 2707065	Karajan	* 91,750			
2–DG 2726046	Kubelik	** 80,000;	** 80,250		
3–DG ARC–2710001	Richter	** 24,500			
3–DG 2709020	Karajan	*927,000;	*927,250		
3–DG 2709028	Szeryng	**252,750;	**253,000;	**253,250;	**253,50
		**253,750;	**254,000		
3–DG 2709029	Lear, Fischer-Dieskau, Böhm	*906,750			
3–DG 2709038	Janowitz, Fischer-Dieskau, Schreier, Böhm	*952,750			
3–DG 2709040	Stewart, Jones, Riddenbusch, Böhm	*961,250			
3–DG 2709044	Szidon	**186,750;	**187,000		
3–DG 2709051	Grist, Auger, Schreier, Böhm	*933,500;	*935,250		
3–DG 2709053	Fischer-Dieskau, Barenboim	*881,500;	*881,750;	*882,000;	*882,25
		*882,500;	*882,750;	*883,000;	*883,12
		*883,250;	*883,500;	*883,750	
5–DG 2713001	Nilsson, Ludwig, Böhm	*963,500			
5–DG 2720029	La Salle Quartet	**275,750;	**276,000;	**350,250;	**350,50
		**350,750;	**351,000;	**371,750;	**372,25
7–DG 2721007	Böhm	*447,500;	*447,750;	*448,000;	*448,25
		*448,500;	*448,750;	*449,000;	*449,25
		*449,500;	*449,750;	*450,000;	*450,25
		*450,500;	*450,750;	*451,000;	*451,50

Dover

LABEL	PERFORMER	GUIDE NO.	
†Dover 5247	Jenkins	460,750	
Dover 5262	Stevens	** 21,700	
Dover 7257	Fiorentino	185,000	
Dover 7265	Webster	975,500	
Dover 7280	Bartók Quartet	*264,250;	*266,000
Dover 7285	Webster	245,250	
†Dover 97271E	Stevens	* 7,600	

Experiences Anonymes

LABEL	PERFORMER	GUIDE NO.
EA S–83	Planchart	6,600

Everest

LABEL	PERFORMER	GUIDE NO.			
Ev. S–445/1	Fasano, Scotto, Bruscantini	*938,250			
Ev. 3002	Susskind	611,750;	648,500		
Ev. 3007	Boult	*468,750			
Ev. 3011	Stokowski	**790,750;	**791,000		
Ev. 3013	Goossens	372,750;	641,000		
Ev. 3016	Stokowski	730,750;	802,400		
Ev. 3018	Copland	*394,750			
Ev. 3029	Chávez	393,000;	393,250		
Ev. 3032	Stokowski	466,500;	579,750		
Ev. 3092	New York Woodwind Quintet	327,000			
Ev. 3116	Fistoulari	*621,100;	*621,250;	*621,500	
Ev. 3129	Smith Singers	* 40,000			
Ev. 3132	electronic instruments	973,500			
†Ev. 3140E	Ferras	297,250			
†Ev. 3179E	Saraceni	* 63,500;	* 64,000		
Ev. 3214	Rozhdestvensky	*455,750;	*456,750		
Ev. 3230	electronic instruments	973,750			
Ev. 3232	Amy, Boulez Ensemble	371,500;	810,200		
Ev. 3250	Kondrashin	469,250			
Ev. 3290	Fine Arts Quartet	987,800			
†2–Ev./Cet. S–458/2E	Leibowitz	936,000			
2–Ev./Cet. 440/2F	Kaler, Danon	927,500			
2–Ev. S–446/2	Scotto, Monti, Panerai, Fasano	946,500			
2–Ev. 3186	Previtali	747,250; 748,250; 749,500;	747,500; 748,500; 750,500	747,750; 748,750;	748,000; 749,000;
3–Ev./Cet. S–437/3	Callas	**912,000			
3–Ev./Cet. 465/3	Moscow Stanislavsky Musical Theatre	939,250			
7–Ev. 3194	Brott	*794,500			

Folkways

LABEL	PERFORMER	GUIDE NO.			
Folk. 3355	Bress	970,000;	985,100		
Folk. 33436	electronic instruments	985,000; 994,000	988,100;	988,600;	990,050;
Folk. 33439	Rowe, Bonazzi, Pearlman	988,150			

Golden Crest/N.E. Conservatory

LABEL	PERFORMER	GUIDE NO.
GC NEC 102	New England Conservatory Chamber Players	351,250

Golden Crest

LABEL	PERFORMER	GUIDE NO.		
GC S–4085	Georgia State College Brass	989,850;	997,400;	997,750
†GC 7020	Myers	835,000;	835,100	
2–GC 40899	Nelsova	345,000		

Genesis

LABEL	PERFORMER	GUIDE NO.
Gene. 1008	Ruíz	*175,000
Gene. 1030	Gimpel	*232,500

Haydn Society

LABEL	PERFORMER	GUIDE NO.	
Haydn HS–7–9015	Schneider Quartet	**304,500;	**308,250
Haydn HS–7–9078	Schneider Quartet	**302,500	
Haydn HS–7–9079	Schneider Quartet	**302,750	
Haydn HS–7–9088	Schneider Quartet	**303,750;	**304,000
Haydn HS–7–9090	Schneider Quartet	**305,000	
Haydn HS–7–9095	Schneider Quartet	*309,500;	*309,750

Klavier

LABEL	PERFORMER	GUIDE NO.		
Kla. 517	Frémaux	727,250;	727,750;	728,000
Kla. 531	Ogdon, Ceccato	*532,500;	*532,502;	*534,000

London

LABEL	PERFORMER	GUIDE NO.			
Lon. CS 6006	Argenta	*609,000;	**743,750		
Lon. CS 6008	Boskovsky	**771,250;	**772,750;	**774,000;	**774,250
Lon. CS 6009	Ansermet	**785,400			
Lon. CS 6012	Ansermet	*745,500;	*746,000;	*746,750	
Lon. CS 6036	Ansermet	**744,000;	*745,250;	*746,500	
Lon. CS 6046	Soriano, Argenta	**515,000			
Lon. CS 6051	Vienna Octet	**352,250			
Lon. CS 6090	Curzon	**354,000			
Lon. CS 6097	Ansermet	**792,000;	**792,250;	**792,500	
Lon. CS 6127	Ansermet	**794,200			
Lon. CS 6153	Katchen, Boult	**513,000;	*545,750		
Lon. CS 6157	Curzon, Boult	*516,500;	*519,250;	**530,500	
Lon. CS 6163	Ricci	**341,000			
Lon. CS 6165	Ricci	**549,750;	**550,000;	**550,750;	**551,000
Lon. CS 6178	DePeyer, Maag	**535,500;	*536,250;	*536,253	
Lon. CS 6179	Britten	*606,000			
Lon. CS 6204	Gamba	*747,250;	*747,750;	*748,250;	*748,500;
		*750,500			
Lon. CS 6208	Ansermet	*384,000;	**600,000;	**600,250	

ABEL	PERFORMER	GUIDE NO.			
on. CS 6209	Karajan	*779,500;	*793,000		
on. CS 6218	Fistoulari	**794,200			
on. CS 6219	Ansermet	* 87,000;	** 87,500		
on. CS 6222	Ansermet	*401,000;	*633,500		
on. CS 6224	Ansermet, Berganza	631,750;	*632,000;	*632,250;	*831,600
on. CS 6225	Ansermet	**618,000;	**618,250;	**618,500;	**737,750;
		*787,400			
on. CS 6236	Szell	**660,500;	**662,000		
on. CS 6237	Rostropovich	**284,750;	**291,250;	**358,000	
on. CS 6242	Ansermet	*730,750			
on. CS 6244	Karajan	*670,500;	*670,750		
on. CS 6322	Khachaturian	**684,000;	**684,250;	**684,500;	**684,750
on. CS 6329	Curzon, Szell	**504,500			
on. CS 6337	Oistrakh, Horenstein	**506,500;	**525,500		
on. CS 6357	Curzon	**294,500;	**353,000		
on. CS 6358	Kertész	**398,000;	**627,750		
on. CS 6367	Ansermet	*625,250;	*672,000;	*736,250;	**738,500
on. CS 6371	Curzon	**188,500			
on. CS 6375	Maazel	**471,250;	**762,500		
on. CS 6377	Oistrakh	**329,000;	**538,250		
on. CS 6385	Janáček Quartet	*303,000;	*303,250;	*304,250;	*308,250
on. CS 6390	Ashkenazy, Kondrashin	*545,502			
on. CS 6395	Rampal	**541,250;	**541,500		
on. CS 6401	Solti	**434,500			
on. CS 6403	Tuckwell, Maag	*536,250;	*536,252;	*536,253;	*536,254
on. CS 6406	Ansermet	**456,250			
on. CS 6407	Ansermet	*586,250;	*587,750;	*588,250	
on. CS 6408	Maazel	**471,500			
on. CS 6409	Maazel	*476,500			
on. CS 6410	Katchen	**129,800;	**129,850		
on. CS 6411	Ashkenazy, Frager	*196,850;	*231,000		
on. CS 6416	Curzon	**226,503;	**226,504;	**229,000	
on. CS 6417	Kertész	**686,250;	**686,500		
on. CS 6419	Rostropovich	**505,500;	**521,500		
on. CS 6422	Ashkenazy	**133,750;	**133,800;	**133,850;	**133,900;
		*144,750			
on. CS 6426	Maazel	*475,500			
on. CS 6427	Maazel	*475,750			
on. CS 6428	Maazel	*476,000			
on. CS 6429	Maazel	**476,250			
on. CS 6434	Eden and Tamir	**190,000;	**194,000;	**206,000;	**213,750
on. CS 6436	Ansermet	438,750;	439,250;	*707,250;	*707,500;
		*708,500			
on. CS 6437	Gugholz, Ansermet	*512,000;	619,000		
on. CS 6438	Ansermet	*608,750;	*609,000;	*609,250;	*609,750;
		*610,000			
on. CS 6440	Ashkenazy, Zinman	495,000;	*507,502		
on. CS 6444	Katchen	*127,501;	*127,502;	*127,503;	*127,504;
		*129,501;	*129,502;	*129,950	
on. CS 6454	Bonynge	**577,000			
on. CS 6456	Ansermet	**736,500			
on. CS 6471	Ashkenazy	**232,500;	**237,000		
on. CS 6472	Ashkenazy	**215,000			
on. CS 6473	Katchen, Marty	**128,250			
on. CS 6482	Katchen	**129,900			
on. CS 6486	Bonynge	750,000			
on. CS 6487	Katchen, Kertész	*498,500;	*546,250		
on. CS 6488	Maazel	472,250;	*472,750		
on. CS 6494	Ashkenazy	**267,750;	**334,750		

LABEL	PERFORMER	GUIDE NO.			
Lon. CS 6495	Kertész	**397,250;	**626,250		
Lon. CS 6500	Ashkenazy	**227,250;	**228,000		
Lon. CS 6501	Ashkenazy, Kertész	**536,500;	**536,758;	**536,759	
Lon. CS 6509	Ansermet	*642,000;	642,500		
Lon. CS 6511	Kertész	**397,000;	**626,800		
Lon. CS 6512	Schmidt-Isserstedt	*377,750;	*590,000		
Lon. CS 6519	Tuckwell, Kertész	**556,250			
Lon. CS 6523	Kertész	**396,000			
Lon. CS 6524	Kertész	**396,250			
Lon. CS 6525	Kertész	**396,500;	**626,750		
Lon. CS 6526	Kertész	**396,750;	**626,000		
Lon. CS 6527	Kertész	**398,250;	**627,250		
Lon. CS 6529	Mehta	*694,750;	804,000;	804,250;	804,50◖
		805,000			
Lon. CS 6533	Eden, Tamir	**129,750			
Lon. CS 6537	Maazel	*779,000;	*780,500		
Lon. CS 6549	Suk	**282,000;	**282,250;	**282,500	
Lon. CS 6552	Mehta	**466,500;	**757,500		
Lon. CS 6562	Ashkenazy	**134,000;	**147,250;	**147,751;	**147,75◖
		**147,753;	**147,754		
Lon. CS 6567	Kertész	*604,501			
Lon. CS 6573	Ashkenazy	**208,250;	*208,500		
Lon. CS 6579	Ashkenazy, Schmidt-Isserstedt	**536,756;	536,770		
Lon. CS 6581	Frühbeck de Burgos	**578,500			
Lon. CS 6583	Eden and Tamir	**261,750			
Lon. CS 6586	Bonynge	*659,200;	*660,750		
Lon. CS 6591	Maazel	*471,750;	*472,500		
Lon. CS 6592	Maazel	**472,000;	*764,750		
Lon. CS 6594	Kertész	**604,502;	**628,250		
Lon. CS 6603	Cuvit, Ansermet	*526,600;	*534,750;	*575,500	
Lon. CS 6605	Boskovsky	*726,000;	*742,750;	**768,500	
Lon. CS 6608	Mehta	*779,750			
Lon. CS 6609	Mehta	*778,750			
Lon. CS 6611	Suk, Starker, Katchen	**283,000;	**283,750		
Lon. CS 6612	Mehta	** 93,750;	**461,250;	**757,250	
Lon. CS 6615	Ansermet	*434,250			
Lon. CS 6618	Britten	**389,250;	**389,500;	*630,500	
Lon. CS 6621	Bonynge	582,000			
Lon. CS 6628	Tuckwell, Perlman, Ashkenazy	**283,250;	**299,500		
Lon. CS 6633	Katchen, Kertész	517,250;	*544,003;	*546,000	
Lon. CS 6649	Rostropovich, Britten	**354,750			
Lon. CS 6656	Boskovsky	*500,750;	*501,000;	**590,250	
Lon. CS 6657	Kars, Gibson	**511,750			
Lon. CS 6659	Ashkenazy	**196,750;	**198,750;	**201,000	
Lon. CS 6661	Starker, Mehta	**502,750;	**503,000		
Lon. CS 6665	Kletzki	**426,000			
Lon. CS 6671	Britten	**607,500;	**607,800		
Lon. CS 6679	Abbado	*455,500;	**456,000		
Lon. CS 6693	Rogé	**187,250;	**188,500		
Lon. CS 6696	Solti	465,000;	*760,750		
Lon. CS 6710	Kyung-Wha Chung, Previn	*554,750			
Lon. CS 6716	Lupu	**129,000;	**129,501		
Lon. CS 6717	Böhm	**390,500			
Lon. CS 6719	Ashkenazy	**187,500;	**189,250		
Lon. CS 6721	Kertész	**626,500;	**629,000		
Lon. CS 6731	Boskovsky	**769,750;	**770,000		
Lon. CS 6732	Ashkenazy, Maazel	**466,750			
Lon. CS 6737	Münchinger	*788,000;	*811,400		

ABEL	PERFORMER	GUIDE NO.			
on. CS 6738	Mehta	**694,000;	**694,500		
on. CS 6739	Nicolet, Münchinger	**493,000;	**508,250		
on. CS 6746	Kertész	**626,750;	**627,000		
on. CS 6749	De Larrocha	**235,750			
on. CS 6752	Mehta	**799,200;	**799,400;	**799,600	
on. CS 6753	Solti	729,250			
on. CS 6772	Kertész	**461,750;	**462,000		
on. CS 6777	Solti	*378,500			
on. CS 6780	Solti	*649,000;	*727,500		
on. CS 6783	Solti	**587,250;	**587,500		
on. CS 6784	Solti	**586,000;	**586,250		
on. CS 6785	Solti	**603,500;	**603,750;	**644,500;	**725,250;
		**725,500			
on. CS 6786	Maazel	*727,500			
on. CS 6803	Weller	*457,000			
on. CS 6814	Starker, Katchen, Suk	**281,250;	**283,500		
on. CS 6818	De Larrocha, Frühbeck de Burgos	516,500;	*527,750		
on. OSA 1151	Tebaldi, Danieli, Del Monaco, Gardelli	*942,250			
on. OSA 1152	Tebaldi, Simionato, Gardelli	*942,000			
on. OSA 1153	Tebaldi, Gardelli	*941,000			
on. OSA 1156	Pears, Shirley-Quirk, Britten	**909,750			
on. OSA 1158	Ludwig, Kertész	**905,000			
on. OSA 1159	Schmidt-Isserstedt	**379,250			
on. OSA 1163	Pears, Shirley-Quirk, Britten	**909,500			
on. OS 25005	Flagstad	**870,000;	**870,100;	**870,200;	**870,300
on. OS 25045	Della Casa, Gueden, Kleiber	**892,100			
on. OS 25075	Bergonzi	**888,800;	**891,150;	**894,100;	**894,400;
		**894,500;	**896,500;	**898,200;	**898,600;
		**900,500			
on. OS 25076	Tebaldi, Gavazzeni	*888,750			
on. OS 25083	Tebaldi, Serafin	*887,800			
on. OS 25085	Tebaldi, Simionato, Molinari-Pradelli	*898,200			
on. OS 25101	Flagstad	**877,800			
on. OS 25103	Flagstad	**834,600			
on. OS 25115	Siepi, Corena, Krips	*891,650			
on. OS 25196	Tebaldi, Del Monaco, Capuana	*894,000			
on. OS 25206	Tebaldi, Karajan	**896,500			
on. OS 25218	Tebaldi, Del Monaco, Molinari-Pradelli	*894,400			
on. OS 25232	Sutherland	**887,100;	**887,250;	**888,050;	**891,300;
		**896,350;	**899,300		
on. OS 25233	Sutherland	**887,200;	**887,350;	**889,400;	**891,500;
		**895,700;	**899,100;	**900,100	
on. OS 25242	Pears, Britten	** 35,500			
on. OS 25320	Ansermet	* 58,500;	**428,250;	**428,500	
on. OS 25334	Tucci, Molinari-Pradelli	*890,350			
on. OS 25701	Tebaldi, Karajan	*898,800			
on. OS 25702	Sutherland, Pritchard	**888,450			
on. OS 25713	Tebaldi, Del Monaco, Molinari-Pradelli	*894,100			
on. OS 25714	Nilsson, Bergonzi, Solti	*897,000			
on. OS 25729	Tebaldi	**887,800;	**888,850;	**893,100;	**893,200;
		**893,800;	**894,600;	**895,000;	**895,100
on. OS 25757	Prey	*818,500;	*820,250;	*821,750;	*822,000;
		*823,000;	*853,500;	*855,250;	*858,250;
		*863,750;	*870,750;	*873,000;	*875,000
on. OS 25769	Ghiaurov	*891,950;	**897,500		

LABEL	PERFORMER	GUIDE NO.
Lon. OS 25777	Sutherland	**812,400; **817,000; **817,200; *836,50 **877,500
Lon. OS 25782	Berganza	**891,550; **891,600; **892,550
Lon. OS 25783	Krause	*870,500; *871,750; *872,000; *873,00 *874,500; *875,000; *875,250; *876,25
Lon. OS 25821	Crespin,Ansermet	*816,800; *849,850
Lon. OS 25876	Sutherland, Horne	*889,850
Lon. OS 25886	Sutherland, Pritchard	**900,000
Lon. OS 25887	Sutherland, Bonynge	*887,300
Lon. OS 25893	Franci	91,000
Lon. OS 25896	Pears, Bream	*828,500; *828,750; *829,750; 830,25
Lon. OS 25910	Horne	**891,250
Lon. OS 25921	Caracciolo	* 74,250
Lon. OS 25922	Sutherland, Bonynge	*887,150
Lon. OS 25923	Gueden, Resnik, Karajan	**896,100
Lon. OS 25937	Britten	** 33,500; **606,900
Lon. OS 25939	Sutherland	**898,000; **899,300; **900,000; **900,10 **901,000
Lon. OS 25942	Nilsson	*870,000; *870,100; *870,200; *870,30
Lon. OS 25994	Evans	**889,800; **890,400; *891,950; **892,25 **898,900
Lon. OS 26007	Berganza, Ghiaurov, Varviso	*895,200
Lon. OS 26030	Krause	**870,000; **870,200; **870,300
Lon. OS 26041	Tebaldi, Bumbry, Solti	*897,500
Lon. OS 26043	Crespin	*826,750; *826,751; *826,752; *846,75 846,752; *878,250; *878,750; *882,25 *883,000; *884,000
Lon. OS 26063	Krenn	*852,500; *858,750
Lon. OS 26067	Horne	**813,750
Lon. OS 26085	Nilsson, Crespin, Solti	**903,000
Lon. OS 26086	Sutherland, Horne	*895,700
Lon. OS 26098	Ansermet	* 23,067
Lon. OS 26100	Münchinger	** 24,000
Lon. OS 26106	Abbado	* 32,000
Lon. OS 26113	Tebaldi	*851,250
Lon. OS 26139	Sutherland, Bonynge	*889,300
Lon. OS 26161	Pears, Britten	**824,250; **824,500
Lon. OS 26162	Tebaldi, Bergonzi, Gardelli	**892,600
Lon. OS 26169	Nilsson, Solti	**896,200
Lon. OS 26186	Kertész	** 61,500; **687,000
Lon. OS 26195	Minton, Solti	*839,100; *839,400; *839,500
Lon. OS 26201	Bonynge, Sutherland	*888,050
Lon. OS 26214	Horne, Solti	*889,150
Lon. OS 26216	Krenn	**866,250; **867,250; **868,250
Lon. OS 26239	Sutherland, Arroyo, Bonynge	891,250
Lon. OS 26250	Kertész	** 77,750
Lon. OS 26257	Lorengar, Solti	**892,100
Lon. OS 26299	Dernesch, Ludwig, Solti	**902,600
Lon. SPC 21003	Black	*603,750; *736,250
Lon. SPS 21023	Munch	*599,000; *599,250; *599,500
Lon. SPC 21024	Munch	*741,000; *741,250
Lon. SPC 21035	Paita	**803,250; **804,500; **807,000
Lon. SPC 21037	Leinsdorf	*780,250; 806,750
Lon. SPC 21062	Herrmann	754,750; 755,000
Lon. STS–15005	Solti	*625,250; *740,500
Lon. STS–15009	Reiner	*604,251; *604,255; *604,256; *604,25 *604,260; *604,269; *604,271; *628,50 *628,503; *628,508; *628,751; *628,75
Lon. STS–15010	Martinon	*577,300
Lon. STS–15011	Ansermet	*786,000; **786,800

LABEL	PERFORMER	GUIDE NO.			
Lon. STS–15014	Gabarain	*831,400;	**916,250		
Lon. STS–15019	Krips	*465,000			
Lon. STS–15021	Wolff	577,500;	581,000;	667,000;	726,000;
		742,750;	789,250		
Lon. STS–15022	Ansermet	*617,500;	*618,750;	*625,000	
Lon. STS–15025	Ansermet	460,000;	460,250		
Lon. STS–15035	Münchinger	*718,500;	*757,750		
Lon. STS–15037	Kubelik	*628,000			
Lon. STS–15041	Backhaus	*181,000;	181,250;	*181,548;	*181,552
Lon. STS–15042	Ansermet	*617,000;	*620,500		
Lon. STS–15043	Gamba	*704,000;	*729,250		
Lon. STS–15044	Münchinger	652,000;	722,750		
Lon. STS–15046	Borodin Quartet	**277,750;	**358,750		
Lon. STS–15049	Ricci	*372,500			
Lon. STS–15050	Kempff	*148,000;	*148,250		
Lon. STS–15051	Martinon	**705,000;	**710,500		
Lon. STS–15052	Ansermet	*599,000;	*599,250;	*599,500	
Lon. STS–15054	Ricci, Fjeldstad	554,750;	*559,750		
Lon. STS–15056	Ansermet	**809,000;	**809,150;	**809,300;	809,600;
		809,750			
Lon. STS–15063	Münchinger	**583,500			
Lon. STS–15066	Ansermet	*691,000;	*691,250;	*691,750	
Lon. STS–15070	Boskovsky	768,750;	**809,450		
Lon. STS–15071	Prinz, Münchinger	*535,500;	*536,000		
Lon. STS–15074	Vienna Octet Members	360,750			
Lon. STS–15076	Münchinger	*707,000;	*758,500;	*760,250;	*809,750
Lon. STS–15077	Boskovsky	*723,000			
Lon. STS–15083	Karajan	**778,750			
Lon. STS–15085	Krips	**422,500;	**423,750		
Lon. STS–15086	Katchen	*112,000			
Lon. STS–15087	Maag	*449,250			
Lon. STS–15090	Monteux	**736,500			
Lon. STS–15091	Maag	**438,500;	**707,500		
Lon. STS–15092	Ansermet	*735,750;	*736,750;	**738,250;	**738,750
Lon. STS–15093	Martinon	**600,000;	**675,000;	**753,500;	**754,000
Lon. STS–15096/7	Kubelik	*766,750			
Lon. STS–15102	English, Watts, Carlyle, Ansermet	*954,250;	*955,250		
Lon. STS–15103	Demessieux	*169,750			
Lon. STS–15104	Demessieux	*169,250			
Lon. STS–15105	Demessieux	*169,500			
Lon. STS–15112	Bliss	*601,000;	*601,250;	*630,751;	*630,752;
		*630,753;	*630,754;	*630,755	
Lon. STS–15116	Vienna Philharmonic Quartet	**332,250;	**332,750		
Lon. STS–15140	Krips	*463,500			
Lon. STS–15141	Solti	724,250;	*793,250		
Lon. STS–15142	Campoli, Gamba	549,500			
Lon. STS–15149	Ansermet	*384,500;	*384,750;	*603,500	
Lon. STS–15150	Katchen	**129,935			
Lon. STS–15153	Ricci	*262,000			
Lon. STS–15154	Segon, Ansermet	**460,500			
Lon. STS–15157	Monteux	*397,500			
Lon. STS–15158	Monteux	*746,250			
Lon. STS–15168	Weller	*302,250			
Lon. STS–15169	Marriner	**646,000			
Lon. STS–15170	Boskovsky	**717,250;	**717,500		
Lon. STS–15176E	Lipatti, Ansermet	**552,750			
Lon. STS–15178	Monteux	**422,500;	**424,250		
Lon. STS–15179	Monteux	793,600			

LABEL	PERFORMER	GUIDE NO.			
Lon. STS–15180	Martinon	*467,500;	*761,250;	*761,500	
Lon. STS–15199	Yepes	**548,250;	**548,500		
Lon. STS–15242	Vienna Octet	**295,000			
2–Lon. CSA 2203	Ansermet	**791,750			
2–Lon. CSA 2204	Ansermet	*794,100			
2–Lon. CSA 2215	Münchinger	**583,000			
2–Lon. CSA 2226	Bonynge	**577,250			
2–Lon. CSA 2229	Bonynge	*621,000			
2–Lon. CSA 2235	De Larrocha	** 94,750; ** 96,000; ** 97,000;	** 95,000; ** 96,250; ** 97,250;	** 95,250; ** 96,500; ** 97,500;	** 95,500 ** 96,750 ** 97,750
2–Lon. CSP–8	Solti	*379,250			
2–Lon. CS 6396, 6404	Katchen	**128,500; **129,200	**128,750;	**129,000;	**129,100
2–Lon. OSA 1201	Godfrey, D'Oyly Carte	**918,000			
2–Lon. OSA 1209	D'Oyly Carte	**917,500			
2–Lon. OSA 1215	D'Oyly Carte	**917,750			
2–Lon. OSA 1218	Nilsson, Hoffman, Stolze, Solti	**954,000			
2–Lon. OSA 1248	D'Oyly Carte	**918,750			
2–Lon. OSA 1254	Sutherland	**812,400; **877,500;	**817,000; **890,800;	**817,200; **891,200	**836,500
2–Lon. OSA 1255	Britten	** 36,000			
2–Lon. OSA 1258	O'Oyly Carte	**919,000			
2–Lon. OSA 1260	Sciutti, Oncina, Kertész	**914,250			
2–Lon. OSA 1262	D'Oyly Carte	**918,500			
2–Lon. OSA 1269	Nilsson, Resnik, Krause, Solti	**953,250			
2–Lon. OSA 1273	Sutherland, Pavarotti, Bonynge	915,000			
2–Lon. OSA 1277	D'Oyly Carte	**918,250			
2–Lon. OSA 1278	Ustinov, Kertész	**926,250			
2–Lon. OSA 1280	McCracken, Lorengar, Gardelli	927,000			
2–Lon. OSA 1281	Kertész	** 42,500			
2–Lon. OSA 1285	Lorengar, Horne, Donath, Solti	*920,250			
2–Lon. OSA 1288	Baker, Harper, Britten	**911,000			
†2–Lon. OSA 1290	Vyvyan, Pear, Britten	*943,250			
2–Lon. OSA 1295	Solti	**436,250			
2–Lon. OSA 1299	Freni, Pavarotti, Karajan	*940,500			
3–Lon. CSA 2307	Boskovsky	**769,500; **771,000; **772,750; **774,000; **775,750;	**770,250; **771,250; **773,000; **774,250; **778,000;	**770,500; **771,750; **773,250; **775,000; **778,500	**770,750 **772,250 **773,500 **775,250
3–Lon. CSA 2309	Marriner	*659,751; *659,755; *659,759;	*659,752; *659,756; *659,760;	*659,753; *659,757; *659,761;	*659,754 *659,758 *659,762
3–Lon. CSA 2312	Maazel	**732,500			
3–Lon. OSA 1303	Tebaldi, Del Monaco, Gavazzeni	*919,250			
3–Lon. OSA 1305	Watson, Britten	**910,750			
3–Lon. OSA 1306	Tebaldi, Casoni, Del Monaco, Capuana	**940,750			
3–Lon. OSA 1307	Tebaldi, Del Monaco, Siepi, Serafin	*908,500			
3–Lon. OSA 1309	Flagstad, London, Svanholm, Solti	**962,500			
3–Lon. OSA 1313	Tebaldi, Simionato, Bergonzi, Karajan	*957,750			
3–Lon. OSA 1317	Tebaldi, Del Monaco, Borriello, Molinari-Pradelli	941,500			
3–Lon. OSA 1323	D'Oyly Carte	**917,250			
3–Lon. OSA 1324	Tebaldi, Del Monaco, Karajan	*960,000			
3–Lon. OSA 1328	Nilsson, Stahlman, Simionato, Solti	*958,000			

LABEL	PERFORMER	GUIDE NO.			
3–Lon. OSA 1361	Sutherland	**921,000			
3–Lon. OSA 1365	Sutherland, Bonynge	*906,500			
3–Lon. OSA 1366	Sutherland, Bergonzi, Merrill, Pritchard	*960,750			
3–Lon. OSA 1373	Sutherland, Bonynge	*906,250			
3–Lon. OSA 1375	Berganza, Alva, Corena, Varviso	*947,000			
3–Lon. OSA 1376	Simionato, Bruscantini, de Fabritiis	*946,750			
3–Lon. OSA 1378	Pears, Fisher, Britten	**909,000			
3–Lon. OSA 1379	Spoorenberg, Ansermet	*913,500			
3–Lon. OSA 1380	Nilsson, Taddei, Prevedi, Schippers	*959,500			
3–Lon. OSA 1381	Berganza, Benelli, Ghiaurov, Varviso	*946,250			
3–Lon. OSA 1382	Suliotis, Gobbi, Cava, Gardelli	**959,750			
3–Lon. OSA 1383	Sutherland, Horne, Rouleau, Bonynge	*947,250			
3–Lon. OSA 1384	Sutherland, Pavarotti, Bonynge	*905,750			
3–Lon. OSA 1385	Deller, Pears, Britten	*910,250			
3–Lon. OSA 1387	Krenn, Berganza, Popp, Kertész	*932,750			
3–Lon. OSA 1388	Tebaldi, Bergonzi, Horne, Gardelli	**938,500			
3–Lon. OSA 1390	Pears, Shirley-Quirk, Britten	**909,250			
3–Lon. OSA 1391	Sutherland, Bonynge	*913,750			
3–Lon. OSA 1393	Price, Vickers, Gorr, Solti	*957,750			
3–Lon. OSA 1395	Evans, Ligabue, Freni, Solti	*958,750			
3–Lon. OSA 1397	Lorengar, Solti	**934,500			
3–Lon. OSA 13101	Sutherland, Pavarotti, Bonynge	914,500			
3–Lon. OSA 13103	Sutherland, Milnes, Pavarotti, Bonynge	**915,250			
3–Lon. OSA 13105	Sutherland, Milnes, Pavarotti, Bonynge	**960,250			
3–Lon. OSA 13106	Sutherland, Domingo, Bacquier, Bonynge	*936,750			
4–Lon. CSA 2404	Ashkenazy, Solti	*499,994; *500,002	*499,996;	*499,998;	*500,000;
4–Lon. OSA 1402	Della Casa, Gueden, Danco, Kleiber	*934,750			
4–Lon. OSA 1431	Münchinger	** 25,500			
4–Lon. OSA 1435	Crespin, Jungwirth, Minton, Solti	*953,750			
4–Lon. OSA 1436	Suliotis, Horne, Ghiaurov, Varviso	*913,875			
4–Lon. OSA 1437	Arroyo, Sutherland, Bonynge	929,250			
4–Lon. OSA 1438	Ghiaurov, Vishnevskaya	*963,250			
4–Lon. OSA 1439	Karajan	*935,500			
4–Lon. STS–15127/30	Dorati	**414,500; **415,500	**414,750;	**415,000;	**415,250;
4–Lon. STS–15131/4	Dorati	**415,750; **416,750; **417,000	**416,000;	**416,250;	**416,500;
4–Lon. STS–15135/8	Dorati	**417,250;	**417,500;	**417,750	
4–Lon. STS–15182/5	Dorati	**418,000; **419,000; **419,250	**418,250;	**418,500;	**418,750;
5–Lon. OSA 1508	Nilsson, Windgassen, Solti	**963,000			
5–Lon. OSA 1509	Nilsson, Crespin, King, Solti	**963,750			
5–Lon. OSA 1510	Kollo, Ludwig, Solti	*962,250			
5–Lon. OSA 1604	Nilsson, Windgassen, Solti	**961,500			
5–Lon. STS–15229/34	Dorati	**419,500; **420,500; **421,500; *665,000	**419,750; **420,750; **421,750;	**420,000; **421,000; **422,000;	**420,250; **421,250;
4–Lon. STS–15249/54	Dorati	**412,750; **413,750;	**413,000; **414,000;	**413,250; **414,250	**413,500;

LABEL	PERFORMER	GUIDE NO.
6–Lon. STS–15257/62	Dorati	**410,250; **410,500; **410,750; **411,000; **411,250; **411,500; **411,750; **412,000; **412,250
6–Lon. STS–15310/15	Dorati	**405,750; **406,000; **406,250; **406,500; **406,750; **407,000; **407,250; **407,500; **407,750; **408,000; **408,250; **408,500; **408,750; **409,000; **409,250; **409,500; **409,750; **410,000
19–Lon. Ring S	Solti	**962,750

Louisville

LABEL	PERFORMER	GUIDE NO.		
Lou. S–634	Whitney	434,000;	459,250	
Lou. S–653	Whitney	455,000		
Lou. S–655	Whitney	404,500		
Lou. S–664	Whitney	376,000		
Lou. S–672	Whitney	400,750		
Lou. S–675	Whitney	401,250		
Lou. S–684	Mester	311,500		
Lou. S–711	Mester	*976,500		
Lou. S–722	Mester	992,700		
†Lou. 58–2	Whitney	* 54,000		
†Lou. 545–3	Whitney	440,750;	547,000;	990,350
†Lou. 621	Whitney	663,000;	678,750	
†Lou. 622	Whitney	395,250		
†Lou. 625	Whitney	400,500		
†Lou. 635	Whitney	461,000		
†Lou. 642	Whitney	455,250		
†Lou. 646	Whitney	458,500		
†Lou. 652	Whitney	400,250;	454,250	
†Lou. 663	Whitney	437,500		

Lyrichord

LABEL	PERFORMER	GUIDE NO.			
Lyr. 776	Moralt	81,006			
Lyr. 7104	Aitken	152,500;	153,000;	153,250	
Lyr. 7120	Hagner, Lindner	923,000			
Lyr. 7144	Whikehart Chorus	* 61,250			
Lyr. 7150	Gilchrist	2,900			
Lyr. 7153	Saltire Singers	828,000; 829,500;	828,500; 830,000;	828,750; 830,250	829,250;
Lyr. 7156	Saltire Singers	900			
Lyr. 7185	Bryan, Keys	312,500			
Lyr. 7190	Planchart	3,100			
Lyr. 7193	Shulman	357,750			
Lyr. 7199	Planchart	200			
Lyr. 7213	Planchart	8,100; 8,500;	8,200; 9,000;	8,300; 9,100	8,400

Mace

LABEL	PERFORMER	GUIDE NO.	
Mace S–9031	Mayer, Schierning	445,000;	797,250
Mace S–9043	Alfons, Kontarsky	969,250	
Mace S–9051	Commissiona	*393,750;	*602,000

LABEL	PERFORMER	GUIDE NO.		
Mace S–9060	Gulda	*200,500		
Mace S–9069	Brott	392,250;	427,000;	458,250
Mace S–9070	Brott	719,500;	757,750	
Mace S–9077	Mainardi	503,250;	638,250	
Mace S–9094	Hallreizer	926,500		
Mace S–9098	Boettcher	405,750;	582,750	

Mainstream

LABEL	PERFORMER	GUIDE NO.			
Main. 5000	Takahashi	998,800			
Main. 5003	Tudor, Caskel	988,350;	996,300		
Main. 5004	Berio	966,750;	990,000;	991,900	
Main. 5005	Berberian, Berio	966,500;	971,250;	971,750	
Main. 5008	Travis	998,500			
Main. 5011	Manhattan Percussion Ensemble	971,500			
Main. 5014	Gazzelloni	967,250;	976,000;	981,500;	989,950;
		990,100;	990,900		
Main. 5015	Cage	972,000			

Mark

LABEL	PERFORMER	GUIDE NO.
Mark 21360	Baker	403,000

MCA

LABEL	PERFORMER	GUIDE NO.		
MCA 2504	Greenberg	** 15,700		
MCA 2505	Greenberg	16,600		
MCA 2508	Greenberg	** 4,400;	**	7,900
MCA 2513	Greenberg	* 4,400;	*	5,200
MCA 2516	New York Pro Musica	* 6,200;	*	6,500
MCA 2529	Froitzheim	81,002		
MCA 2532	Segovia	**365,750		
2–MCA 2–10008	Greenberg	* 15,800		

Melodiya/Angel

LABEL	PERFORMER	GUIDE NO.			
Mel./Ang. S–40000	Kondrashin	*469,500			
Mel./Ang. S–40010	Svetlanov	** 75,750			
Mel./Ang. S–40017	Rozhdestvensky	*730,500;	*731,750		
Mel./Ang. S–40019	Svetlanov	*466,500;	*734,000		
Mel./Ang. S–40025	Svetlanov	*469,750			
Mel./Ang. S–40028	Svetlanov	*791,250			
Mel./Ang. S–40031	Rozhdestvensky	763,250;	763,500;	764,000;	765,000
Mel./Ang. S–40036	Borodin Quartet	*363,250			
Mel./Ang. S–40046	Rozhdestvensky	*456,500			
Mel./Ang. S–40056	Svetlanov	384,500;	*603,000		
Mel./Ang. S–40064	Oistrakh, Kondrashin	*554,502			
Mel./Ang. S–40068	I. Oistrakh	*312,000;	*544,250		
Mel./Ang. S–40081	Svetlanov	*644,000;	*644,250;	*645,000	
Mel./Ang. S–40085	Edlina, Borodin Quartet	**359,250;	**362,000		
Mel./Ang. S–40089	Fayer	643,000;	643,500		

LABEL	PERFORMER	GUIDE NO.			
Mel./Ang. S–40091	Vaiman, Rostropovich, Serebryakov	*359,750			
Mel./Ang. S–40094	Khaikin	458,750			
Mel./Ang. S–40112	Svetlanov	*746,250			
Mel./Ang. S–40113	Svetlanov	*466,000			
Mel./Ang. S–40114	Kondrashin	* 77,500			
Mel./Ang. S–40118	Svetlanov	*466,250			
Mel./Ang. S–40119	Rozhdestvensky	676,000;	676,250;	676,500	
Mel./Ang. S–40121	Oistrakh	**282,500;	**299,500		
Mel./Ang. S–40132	Svetlanov	**432,000			
Mel./Ang. S–40147	Miroshnikova	**470,750			
Mel./Ang. S–40159	Svetlanov	*691,000;	*691,250;	*691,500;	*691,750
Mel./Ang. S–40163	Shostakovich	**468,500			
Mel./Ang. S–40173	Kondrashin	*431,750			
Mel./Ang. S–40175	Kondrashin	793,700;	793,800		
Mel./Ang. S–40213	Shostakovich	471,000			
Mel./Ang. S–40214	Ivanovsky	** 85,500			
Mel./Ang. S–40222	Borodin Quartet	*362,750;	*363,000		
Mel./Ang. S–40230	Ivanov	*459,000;	*743,750		
Mel./Ang. S–40235	Richter	*211,000;	*211,250;	*211,500;	*211,750;
		*212,250;	*212,500;	*213,000;	*213,500
Mel./Ang. S–40244	Kondrashin	*470,000			
2–Mel./Ang. S–4107	Svetlanov	469,000			
2–Mel./Ang. S–4109	Dalgat, Moscow Radio Orchestra	939,750			
3–Mel./Ang. S–4106	Rozhdestvensky	**794,100			
3–Mel./Ang. S–4115	Vishevskaya, Sinyavskaya, Tûgarinova, Rostropovich	*955,750			
3–Mel./Ang. S–4122	Nesterenko, Vishnevskaya, Atlantov, Mansurov	*946,000			

Mercury

LABEL	PERFORMER	GUIDE NO.			
Mer. 75006	Dupré	*169,001;	*169,002;	*169,003;	*169,750
Mer. 75007	Hanson	53,750;	*403,500		
Mer. 75009	Dorati	739,750;	740,000;	740,250	
Mer. 75012	Hanson	*375,750;	*584,500;	*585,000;	*585,500
Mer. 75016	Dorati	603,500;	603,750;	744,250;	744,500
		744,750			
Mer. 75017	Hanson	*601,500			
Mer. 75018	Dorati	*631,251;	*631,252;	*693,000;	*693,125
Mer. 75019	Janis, Kondrashin	544,003;	*545,500		
Mer. 75020	Hanson	440,500;	*519,500;	*759,750;	990,300
Mer. 75024	Dorati	*604,251;	*604,252;	*604,253;	*604,254
		*604,255;	*604,256;	*604,257;	*604,260
		*604,261;	*604,267;	*604,268;	*604,269
		*604,270;	*604,271		
Mer. 75026	Hanson	*700,000			
Mer. 75029	Paray	392,750			
Mer. 75030	Dorati	*587,250;	731,250;	731,500;	*732,750
Mer. 75045	Starker	506,250;	513,250		

MGM

LABEL	PERFORMER	GUIDE NO.
MGM S–4722	Gottwald	94,250

Monitor

LABEL	PERFORMER	GUIDE NO.		
Mon. MC(S)–2017	Nadien	296,250;	348,250	
†Mon. MCS–2021	Rostropovich, Shostakovich	**359,500		
†Mon. MC(S)–2061	Gilels, Kabalevsky	*527,500;	544,003	
†Mon. MC(S)–2077	Gauk	432,750		
†Mon. MC(S)–2119	Rostropovich	287,250		
Mon. MCS–2128	Kuerti	192,250		
†Mon. MC–2007	Kabalevsky	*431,500		
†Mon. MC–2131	Richter, Kondrashin	518,250		

Music Library

LABEL	PERFORMER	GUIDE NO.
Mus. Lib. 7075	Aird	2,200

Nonesuch

LABEL	PERFORMER	GUIDE NO.			
None. H–71001	Kreder	5,800			
None. H–71003	Telemann Society Orchestra	51,000			
None. H–71004	London Harpsichord Ensemble	*364,500			
None. H–71007	Stuyvesant Quartet	**291,000;	**348,500		
None. H–71009	Douatte	688,000;	698,250;	714,000	
None. H–71010	Société de la musique d'autrefois	** 400;	** 3,400		
None. H–71012	Roger Blanchard Ensemble, Poulteau Consort	** 1,800			
None. H–71015	Ristenpart	**406,750;	**407,000;	**407,250	
None. H–71016	Blanchard	** 7,200;	** 7,300;	** 7,400;	** 7,600
None. H–71019	Neumeyer, Berger, Ristenpart	495,254;	495,500;	495,502;	495,750
None. H–71024	Ristenpart	523,750;	*665,000		
None. H–71026	Canby	7,800			
None. H–71027	Kehr	*733,250;	*733,750		
None. H–71028	Sancan, Pommier, Silie	*537,250			
None. H–71029	Ristenpart	** 23,057;	** 23,240		
None. H–71031	Jones	**410,000;	**411,750;	**413,500	
None. H–71032	Jones	413,250;	414,500;	*664,500	
None. H–71033	Pierlot	*342,500;	*542,250		
None. H–71034	Rampal	**248,000			
None. H–71037	Van de Wiele	154,300;	154,700;	154,800;	155,000;
		155,100;	155,200;	155,300	
None. H–71041	Ristenpart	** 72,250;	* 73,250		
None. H–71042	Eustache, Douatte	*573,001;	*573,002;	*573,003;	*573,004;
		*573,005;	*573,006		
None. H–71043	Milano Teatro Nuovo, Gracis	*938,250			
None. H–71044	Boutry, Ristenpart	*553,000;	*553,250		
None. H–71049	Salzburger Trio	*302,000			
None. H–71052	London Soloists Ensemble	*551,505;	*567,000;	*571,011;	638,000
None. H–71053	Venhoda	5,300;	5,700		
None. H–71057	Hendel, Ristenpart	496,500			
None. H–71058	Roger Blanchard Ensemble, Poulteau Consort	** 400;	** 3,200		
None. H–71061	Larrieu Quartet	*364,000;	*364,750;	365,000	
None. H–71062	Träder	* 83,750			
None. H–71063	Veyron-Lacroix	**346,000;	**346,250;	**346,500;	**346,750;
		**347,000			

LABEL	PERFORMER	GUIDE NO.			
None. H–71066	Barboteu, Coursier, Auriacombe	*561,500;	*562,500;	*564,500	
None. H–71071	Navarra	*503,250;	**521,750		
None. H–71076	Stadlmair	473,250			
None. H–71080	Allard, Wahl	504,250;	510,500		
None. H–71083	Jones	**408,250;	**411,000;	**419,750	
None. H–71084	Träder, Hahn	4,200;	5,500		
None. H–71087	Schmidt-Isserstedt	*382,750;	*383,250		
None. H–71089	Devallier	**851,000			
None. H–71091	Douatte	574,320;	*574,321;	795,250	
None. H–71094	Sgrizzi	**223,080;	**223,190;	**223,200;	**223,340
None. H–71096	Jones	**406,250;	**412,750;	**418,000	
None. H–71097	Träder	* 74,500			
None. H–71098	Jamet	* 1,500;	*248,500		
None. H–71099	Billard, Azaïs	533,000;	707,250		
None. H–71101	Ristenpart	*410,500;	*414,250;	*419,500	
None. H–71104	Allard, Ristenpart	*574,137;	*574,266		
None. H–71106	Jones	**412,000;	**415,000;	**418,250	
None. H–71108	New York Woodwind Quartet	*290,500;	*290,750		
None. H–71117	Sgrizzi	*149,000			
None. H–71118	London Brass	637,600			
None. H–71119	Collegium Musicum Saarensis	541,750			
None. H–71120	Buetens Lute Ensemble	** 3,300			
None. H–71121	Jones	**408,500;	**411,500;	**417,000	
None. H–71122	Milhaud	711,000;	711,500		
None. H–71126	Marion, Ristenpart	*535,000;	*535,750		
None. H–71131	Jones	*412,250;	*413,000;	*419,000	
None. H–71132	André, Winschermann	*565,000;	*565,500;	795,000	
None. H–71140	Claremont Quartet	295,500;	*360,000		
None. H–71144	Malcolm	**108,000			
None. H–71146	Jenkins	452,000			
None. H–71148	André, Winschermann	*515,250;	555,250;	*560,500;	574,077
None. H–71157	Stockhausen	995,800			
None. H–71160	Rilling	* 85,000			
None. H–71165	Jones	*494,500;	**581,500		
None. H–71167	Leppard	*828,500			
None. H–71168	Jones	*416,500;	*418,500		
None. H–71174	electronic synthesizer	996,400			
None. H–71182	Stich-Randall	88,250			
None. H–71183	Munch	*384,000;	*600,000;	*600,500	
None. H–71188	Hansen	131,000;	131,250;	132,000	
None. H–71189	Munch	578,000;	617,750		
None. H–71194	Ristenpart	*721,500;	*721,750;	*723,000	
None. H–71195	Lee	*168,002;	*168,003;	*168,004;	*168,005;
		*168,006;	*168,009;	*168,010;	*168,012;
		*168,013;	*168,015;	*168,017;	*168,018
None. H–71196	Rilling	* 85,000			
None. H–71198	electronic synthesizer	994,100			
None. H–71199	New Music Choral Ensemble	984,000;	984,250;	984,400;	984,600
None. H–71201	Zukofsky, Foss	992,300;	992,500;	998,550;	998,950
None. H–71208	electronic synthesizer	996,500			
None. H–71209	Nixon	**835,300;	**835,400;	**835,500;	**835,600;
		**835,800;	**835,900;	**836,000;	**836,100;
		**836,200;	**869,750;	**994,700	
None. H–71210	Ellsasser	*245,750			
None. H–71212	Lee	*242,500;	*242,750;	*243,250	
None. H–71216	Hunter	* 2,100;	* 2,500		
None. H–71222	American Brass Quartet	969,500;	969,750;	993,150	
None. H–71224	Tudor	974,000;	988,200		
None. H–71225	synthesized and processed synthesized sound	998,400			

LABEL	PERFORMER	GUIDE NO.			
None. H–71228	Rilling	* 32,250			
None. H–71231	Keach, Rifkin	994,200			
None. H–71234	Krosnick	286,250;	286,500		
None. H–71236	Horenstein	**453,250;	**727,000		
None. H–71237	Turetzky, Turetzky, George	992,050			
None. H–71238	Lautenbacher	*301,500			
None. H–71240	Horenstein	**434,500			
None. H–71246	electro-acoustic musical instruments	998,600;	998,650;	998,700;	998,900
None. H–71249	Composers Quartet	**285,500;	**285,750;	**975,000	
None. H–71255	De Gaetani	976,250			
None. H–71256	Buckel	23,372			
None. H–71261	Rifkin	** 2,700			
None. H–71265	Fuller	155,500;	155,600;	155,700	
None. H–71268	De Gaetani	833,200;	833,300		
None. H–71277	Stevens	* 46,750;	* 47,000		
None. H–71278	Fuller	214,000;	214,250;	214,750	
None. H–71281	Weisberg	*711,500			
None. H–71285	Davies	977,750			
2–None. HB–73010	Leppard	** 20,700			
2–None. HB–73012	Ehmann	* 83,250			
2–None. HB–73023	Horenstein	*435,000			
2–None. HB–73025	Zukofsky	315,750;	316,000;	316,250;	316,500
3–None. HC–73009	Goehr	** 56,750			
3–None. HC–73014	Rondeau de Paris	*155,400;	*289,250		
4–None. HD–73015	Rilling	101,000; 101,608; 103,650; 103,654; 103,668	101,599; 101,610; 103,651; 103,656;	101,604; 101,615; 103,652; 103,658;	101,607; 101,622; 103,653; 103,659;
4–None. HD–73024	Ehmann, Westphalian Ensemble	* 83,250			

Odyssey

LABEL	PERFORMER	GUIDE NO.			
Odys. Y–30042	Francescatti	**500,250			
Odys. Y–30045	Walter	*398,250			
Odys. Y–30047	Walter	**434,500			
Odys. Y–30048	Walter	*717,000; *722,500;	*720,500; *724,250	*720,750;	*722,000;
Odys. Y–30289	Kipnis	**172,250;	*181,513;	**202,000	
Odys. Y–30311	Walter	**387,000			
Odys. Y–30313	Szell	*779,250;	*779,500;	*781,000	
Odys. Y–30667	Walter	**804,000;	**804,250;	**806,250;	**806,750
Odys. Y–31016	Previn	606,900;	*614,500		
Odys. Y–31017	Munch	*594,750;	*595,300;	*633,000;	*738,750
Odys. Y–31274	Casadesus, Ormandy	*512,600;	*516,500		
Odys. Y–31924	Walter	**387,500;	*604,750		
Odys. Y–31928	Szell	*619,000;	*736,750;	*737,750	
†Odys. Y–32223	Richter, Szell	**203,000;	*725,750		
Odys. Y–32224	Fournier, Szell	*556,750			
Odys. Y–32225	Walter	**388,000;	**604,000		
Odys. Y–32373	Walter	*388,750			
Odys. Y–32981	Walter	**390,750			
Odys. Y–33230	Schippers	*584,500;	*585,250;	*585,500	
Odys. 32160012	Arner, Smyles	574,074;	574,083;	574,342	
Odys. 32160040	Masselos	*152,750			
†Odys. 32160058	Lipatti	**148,501; **148,505; **148,509; *148,513;	**148,502; **148,506; **148,510; *148,514	**148,503; **148,507; **148,511;	**148,504; **148,508; **148,512;

LABEL	PERFORMER	GUIDE NO.			
†Odys. 32160059	Masselos	*183,000			
Odys. 32160070	Tourel	*834,100			
Odys. 32160122	Martin	10,000;	10,400;	11,200;	14,200
†Odys. 32160141	Lipatti	**519,250;	*552,750		
Odys. 32160152	Iwaki	996,650			
Odys. 32160156	Lucier	972,750;	981,750;	987,900;	989,500
Odys. 32160158	Tudor	988,300;	991,650;	998,100	
Odys. 32160160	electronic equipment	990,150;	992,000;	993,700	
Odys. 32160214	Krilov, Shulman, Goberman	574,043			
†Odys. 32160220E	Goodman, Szigeti, Bartók	**260,000			
†Odys. 32160322E	Walter	**379,250			
Odys. 32160340	Fine Arts Quartet	*247,500			
Odys. 32160368	Doktor, Downes	*525,750;	574,750		
2–Odys. Y2–30308	Walter	**436,500			
2–Odys. Y2–30848	Walter	**434,750			
2–Odys. Y2–31925	Rampal	*250,000;	*250,250;	*250,500;	*250,750;
		*251,000;	*251,250;	*251,500;	*251,750
2–Odys. Y2–32370	Rampal	*300,000;	*300,250;	*300,500;	*300,750;
		*301,000;	*301,250		
2–Odys. Y2–32977	Lenya, Schellow, Hesterberg, Brückner-Rüggeberg	**964,500			
2–Odys. Y2–33126	Mitropoulos, Farrell, Jagel	**907,000			
†2–Odys. 32260007	Kirkpatrick	**223,010;	**223,030;	**223,040;	**223,050;
		**223,060;	**223,090;	**223,100;	**223,110;
		**223,150;	**223,170;	**223,180;	**223,220;
		**223,230;	**223,290;	**223,310;	**223,502
†2–Odys. 32260009	Bernac	**846,750;	**846,751;	**846,752;	**846,754
†2–Odys. 322600012E	Kirkpatrick	**223,070;	**223,130;	**223,140;	**223,300;
		**223,330;	**223,503		
†2–Odys. 32260016E	Walter	**435,500;	**839,000		
†2–Odys. 32260019	Curzon	**279,000;	**294,500;	**357,500	
3–Odys. Y3–30844	Szell	**465,000;	**465,250;	**465,500;	**465,750
†3–Odys. Y3–31242	Budapest Quartet	**330,750;	**331,000;	**331,250;	**331,500;
		**331,750;	**332,000		
†3–Odys. 32360003	Casadesus	**215,000;	*215,225;	*215,500;	*215,750;
		*216,000;	*216,250;	*216,500;	*216,750
†3–Odys. 32360016E	Casals	**272,000;	**272,500;	**272,750;	**273,000
†3–Odys. 32360018E	Williams, Engel	917,000			
3–Odys. 32360020	Rosen	*100,000;	**107,988		
†3–Odys. 32360021	Gieseking	**158,250;	**158,750;	**162,500;	**162,750;
		**163,000;	**163,250;	**163,500;	**163,750;
		**164,000;	**164,250;	**164,500;	**164,750;
		**165,000;	**165,250;	**165,750	
7–Odys. Y7–30051	Walter	**377,750;	**378,250;	**379,250	

Oiseau-Lyre

LABEL	PERFORMER	GUIDE NO.		
†Oiseau S–102E	Deller	** 76,250		
Oiseau S–135	Newstone	**413,750;	**414,750	
†Oiseau S–152E	Dart	*180,000;	*180,250	
†Oiseau S–156E	Columbo	*728,500;	*728,750	
Oiseau S–171	Dart, Adney, Jones	*258,250;	*494,750;	*495,006
Oiseau S–255	Dart	**130,000		
Oiseau S–263	Malcolm	* 69,000		
Oiseau S–264	Marriner, St. Martin's	*579,000;	*659,751	
Oiseau S–265	Davis	* 86,000;	* 86,750	
Oiseau S–266	Davis	**448,250;	**450,500	
Oiseau S–267	Melos Ensemble	**343,250;	359,250	
Oiseau S–268	Watts	*819,750;	*821,250;	*821,500; *822,000

LABEL	PERFORMER	GUIDE NO.			
Oiseau S–269	McCarthy	10,300;	10,700		
Oiseau S–270	McCarthy	* 18,100;	* 18,200;	* 18,400;	* 18,500
Oiseau S–276	Marriner	*566,000;	*571,010;	*637,250;	*659,754
Oiseau S–277	Lord, Marriner	*501,250;	*574,434;	*616,251;	*638,253
Oiseau S–279	Monteux, Marriner	*545,250			
Oiseau S–283	McCarthy	11,100; 17,000; 18,000	12,700; 17,200;	14,300; 17,700;	14,800; 17,800;
Oiseau S–285	Pro Arte Piano Quartet	*330,250;	*330,500		
Oiseau S–289	Pro Arte Piano Quartet	**296,750;	**297,500		
Oiseau S–290	Melos Ensemble	**313,000			
Oiseau S–293	Watts	*866,750; *881,250	*879,000;	*879,250;	*879,750;
Oiseau S–294	Cantelo, Brown, Tear, Mackerras	*943,500			
Oiseau S–295	Marriner	* 23,359;	* 23,370		
Oiseau S–297	Leppard	*651,000;	*651,500;	*735,500	
Oiseau S–300	Leppard	**616,500			
Oiseau S–308	Ellis	**296,500;	**312,750		
Oiseau S–310	Purcell	* 6,000;	* 6,800;	* 6,900	
Oiseau S–317	Davis	*582,500			
Oiseau S–319	Goldsbrough Ensemble	*258,000			
Oiseau S–320	Pro Arte Piano Quartet	**279,250;	**357,250		
Oiseau S–323	Burrows	832,600;	832,700		
Oiseau S–335	Herrick	**196,500;	**217,000		
†Oiseau 149E	Nef	*210,000			
Oiseau 60013	Ellis, Jones	**520,225;	**520,256;	**659,800	
Oiseau 60015	Melos Ensemble	**268,250			
Oiseau 60024	Froment	*735,000			
Oiseau 60035	De Peyer, Davis	*575,752			
Oiseau 60036	Cantelo	**812,500;	**812,750;	**813,250;	**834,800
Oiseau 60037	Malcolm	** 33,000			
Oiseau 60038	Dart	**172,000			
Oiseau 60039	Dart	*107,812;	*107,817		
Oiseau 60040	McCarthy	** 4,000			
Oiseau 60042	Malcolm	** 22,000			
Oiseau 60047	Baker, Clark, Sinclair, Lewis	***943,000			
Oiseau 60048	Melos Ensemble	**291,500;	*348,000		
Oiseau 60050	Davis	**782,800;	**783,000;	**783,200	
Oiseau 60052	Petit	217,500			
2–Oiseau S–137/8	Dart	*289,500;	*289,750;	*290,000;	*290,250
2–Oiseau S–256/7	Veasey, Davis	*907,250			
2–Oiseau S–306/7	Crowson	*149,250; *150,250;	*149,500; *150,500;	*149,750; *150,750;	*150,000; *151,000
2–Oiseau 60008/9	Morison, Harper, Thomas, Lewis	*943,750			
2–Oiseau 60011/2	Boult	** 48,500			
2–Oiseau 60025/6	Pears	49,000			
2–Oiseau 60032/3	Davis	* 28,250			
†3–Oiseau S–111E	Lewis	* 53,000			
†3–Oiseau S–121/3E	Morison, Vyvyan, Pears, Lewis	***943,250			
3–Oiseau S–286/8	Tear, Hickey, Baker, Lewis	*944,500			
3–Oiseau S–273/5	Balsam	*181,506; *181,528; *181,540;	*181,520; *181,530; *181,546;	*181,522; *181,531; *181,548	*181,523; *181,538;
3–Oiseau S–311/3	Howard	* 600			

Opus One

LABEL	PERFORMER	GUIDE NO.			
Op. One S–7	Kohon Quartet	994,300; 994,500	994,350;	994,400;	994,450;

Orion

LABEL	PERFORMER	GUIDE NO.			
Orion 7040	Enns	820,750; 853,000	821,000;	823,250;	852,750;
Orion 7149	Rampal, Gilbert	*247,250;	*364,250		
†Orion 72640	Rampal, Paris Festival	*501,500;	569,500		
Orion 7268	Torkanowsky	673,250			
Orion 7280	Silverman	152,000			
Orion 73110	Gross	358,250			
Orion 73123	Woodwind Arts Quintet	298,000;	368,750		

Owl

LABEL	PERFORMER	GUIDE NO.		
Owl 6	electronic equipment	978,000;	978,500;	979,000
Owl 7	electronic equipment	978,250;	979,250;	979,500
Owl 8	electronic equipment	978,750		

Period

LABEL	PERFORMER	GUIDE NO.	
†3–Per. 1093	Starker	**319,000;	**319,250

Philips

LABEL	PERFORMER	GUIDE NO.		
Phi. 18110 CAA	Gendron, Casals	**503,250;	**521,500	
Phi. 802708	Grumiaux, Rosenthal	**507,250;	**546,500;	**570,500
Phi. 802718	Sawallisch	*438,750;	*439,000;	*439,250
Phi. 802724	Haitink	*389,750		
Phi. 802746	Arrau	**232,000;	**232,500	
Phi. 802765	Souzay	**846,850		
Phi. 802769	Szell	*378,000;	**449,750	
Phi. 802793	Arrau	**236,500		
Phi. 802803	Grumiaux Trio	**327,500		
Phi. 802806	Italiano Quartet	*267,000		
Phi. 802814	Italiano Quartet	*277,750;	*294,000	
Phi. 802817	Haebler, Hoffmann	*226,000		
Phi. 802858	Sawallisch	*438,500;	**708,500	
Phi. 802862	Davis	** 73,000		
Phi. 802892	Gendron, Haitink	*513,250		
Phi. 802901	Leppard	*696,500;	*735,250	
Phi. 802906	Arrau	**186,000		
Phi. 802907	De Waart	*335,250;	*335,500	
Phi. 802912	Haitink	**390,250		
Phi. 802913	Davis	**381,750		
Phi. 802915	Italiano Quartet	*266,750		
Phi. 802918	Beaux Arts Trio	**295,250		
Phi. 835112	Grumiaux, Davis	**537,503;	**537,504;	*537,505
Phi. 835136	Grumiaux, Davis	**537,500		
Phi. 835188	Davis	**381,250		
Phi. 835198	Grumiaux	**252,750;	**253,000	
Phi. 835199	Grumiaux	**253,250;	**253,500	
Phi. 835200	Grumiaux	**253,750;	**254,000	
Phi. 835256	Grumiaux, Davis	**537,502;	538,250	
Phi. 835286	Souzay	**832,200		
Phi. 835306	Szell	*471,500		
Phi. 835361	Italiano Quartet	*291,000;	**348,500	

LABEL	PERFORMER	GUIDE NO.
Phi. 835367	Davis	594,000; **595,000; **595,250; **595,500; **595,750
Phi. 835381	Haitink	*392,000
Phi. 835385	Haitink	**390,750
Phi. 835474	Richter, Kondrashin	**529,750; **529,752
Phi. 839709	Arrau	**231,250; *233,750
Phi. 839714	Beckett	** 20,500
Phi. 839733	Souzay	**849,250; **849,400; **849,550; **849,700
Phi. 839734	De Waart	*335,000
Phi. 839741	Leppard	**373,000; **373,250; **373,500; **374,250
Phi. 839743	Arrau	**126,500; **126,750; **127,000
Phi. 839745	Italiano Quartet	*266,250
Phi. 839747	Grumiaux, Pelliccia	*329,000; *329,250
Phi. 839749	Arrau	**119,750; 499,994
Phi. 839788	Haitink	*694,500; 694,750; *695,000
Phi. 839789	Voorberg	** 45,250; ** 45,500; ** 45,750; ** 46,000; ** 46,250; ** 46,500
Phi. 839790	Davis	29,000
Phi. 839795	Italiano Quartet	**263,000; *266,500
Phi. 839796	Leppard	*410,750; *412,750; *414,000
Phi. 900027	Souzay	**831,000; **831,020; **831,030; **831,040; **831,050; **031,060; **831,070; **831,080; **831,090; **831,100; **831,110; **831,120
Phi. 6500002	De Waart	**328,000
Phi. 6500004	De Waart	**328,250
Phi. 6500009	Armstrong, Veasey, Davis	**816,800
Phi. 6500013	Bishop	*114,250; *114,342; *114,344; **114,346; *114,350; *114,500
Phi. 6500017	Michelucci	**572,000; **572,001; **572,002; **572,003; **572,004
Phi. 6500021	Szeryng, Haitink	*499,000
Phi. 6500023	Beaux Arts Trio	**310,250
Phi. 6500034	Bennett	**329,500; **329,750
Phi. 6500043	Arrau	**188,500
Phi. 6500046	Haitink	**692,000; **692,500; **694,000
Phi. 6500048	Haitink	*779,750
Phi. 6500055	Szeryng, Haebler	*337,250; *337,500
Phi. 6500073	Brymer	*334,250; *338,000
Phi. 6500081	Haitink	*476,750
Phi. 6500087	Jochum	*377,000; *378,750
Phi. 6500089	Jochum	**377,750; **591,501; **591,503
Phi. 6500095	Campanella, Ceccato	*530,000; *530,250; *549,254
Phi. 6500101	Bucquet	995,300; 995,400
Phi. 6500103	Novak Quartet	**343,000
Phi. 6500105	Italiano Quartet	**371,750; **372,250
Phi. 6500114	Marriner	**414,750
Phi. 6500128	Ameling	*882,500; *883,000; *883,125; *883,250; *883,500; *884,000
Phi. 6500130	Arrau	**237,000
Phi. 6500132	Beaux Arts Trio	**363,500
Phi. 6500154	Boettcher	**393,500; **483,750
Phi. 6500167	Larrieu	**268,500
Phi. 6500174	Holliger, De Waart	*535,752; *556,500
Phi. 6500178	Arrau	**232,250
Phi. 6500179	Bishop	*119,500; *499,994
Phi. 6500180	Italiano Quartet	**265,750; **266,000
Phi. 6500181	Italiano Quartet	*263,500; *264,000
Phi. 6500189	Haitink	*692,250
Phi. 6500194	Leppard	**414,250; **417,500
Phi. 6500214	Chorzempa	**109,000; **109,532; **109,543; **110,500

LABEL	PERFORMER	GUIDE NO.
Phi. 6500215	Chorzempa	**186,250
Phi. 6500225	Italiano Quartet	**332,750; **333,000
Phi. 6500241	Italiano Quartet	**332,250; **332,500
Phi. 6500243	Musici	**749,251; **749,252; **749,253; **749,254; **749,255; **749,256
Phi. 6500271	Davis	** 72,000; ** 73,250
Phi. 6500285	Brendel	**228,250; **230,000
Phi. 6500299	Grumiaux, Davis	*504,750
Phi. 6500309	Arrau, Inbal	*507,502; *508,000
Phi. 6500315	Bishop	*120,250; 499,998
Phi. 6500342	Haitink	*434,500
Phi. 6500362	De Waart	*734,250
Phi. 6500368	Arrau	**187,750
Phi. 6500376	Chorzempa	**186,250; **188,000
Phi. 6500378	Monteux, Marriner	*535,000; *535,250; *535,500
Phi. 6500379	Monteux, Marriner	*535,750; *535,752
Phi. 6500389	Haitink	**388,500
Phi. 6500393	Bishop	**134,000; **144,000; **144,250; **145,000
Phi. 6500394	Arrau	**235,750; **236,750
Phi. 6500396	Arrau	**236,000
Phi. 6500400	Beaux Arts Trio	**310,250
Phi. 6500401	Beaux Arts Trio	**310,250
Phi. 6500413	Holliger	**529,250; **531,500
Phi. 6500415	Brendel	*226,500; *226,501; *226,502; *226,503; *226,504; *228,750
Phi. 6500417	Brendel	**120,000; *121,750; *124,500
Phi. 6500418	Brendel	**227,000; **228,000
Phi. 6500420	Brendel	*185,250
Phi. 6500422	Arrau, Inbal	*507,750
Phi. 6500423	Arrau	**232,750; **233,000; **233,250; **233,500; **237,500; **237,750
Phi. 6500431	Bishop, Davis	*536,771; *536,775
Phi. 6500439	Haitink	**390,000
Phi. 6500457	Leppard	** 66,000; *930,000; *930,250
Phi. 6500465	Grumiaux, Krenz	*533,500; *533,750
Phi. 6500515	Ameling	*856,750
Phi. 6500519	Haitink	**387,000
Phi. 6500521	Beaux Arts Trio	**310,250
Phi. 6500522	Beaux Arts Trio	**310,250
Phi. 6500532	Marriner	*441,500; *443,500
Phi. 6500536	Musici	*717,500; *717,750; *718,000; *723,250
Phi. 6500537	Musici	*537,505; *716,250; **724,250
Phi. 6500538	Musici	*718,250; *718,500
Phi. 6500640	De Waart	*732,250
Phi. 6500643	Haitink	*790,750; *791,500; *792,750
Phi. 6500662	Davis	997,200
Phi. 6505001	Mackerras, Puyana	296,000
Phi. 6580012	Durjan	*470,250
Phi. 6580047	Grumiaux, De Waart	500,750; 501,000; 559,750; 576,500
Phi. 6599308	Arrau	**120,250; *121,750; 124,000
Phi. 7505040 cassette	Fistoulari	793,600; *794,200
2–Phi. 802711/2	Haitink	**435,000
2–Phi. 802759/60	Ameling, Haitink	** 38,000; *391,500
2–Phi. 802771/2	Woytowicz	992,900
2–Phi. 802856/7	Sawallisch	**438,000; **438,250
2–Phi. 835182/3	Rostropovich	*272,000; *272,500; *272,750; *273,000
2–Phi. 839716/7	Davis	** 28,750
2–Phi. 6700020	Haitink	**391,750

LABEL	PERFORMER	GUIDE NO.			
2–Phi. 6700021	Haitink	*436,500			
2–Phi. 6700036	Haitink	**436,000			
2–Phi. 6700052	Chorzempa, Winschermann	*523,750;	*523,752;	*523,753	
2–Phi. 6700055	Haitink	**391,000			
2–Phi. 6700059	Chorzempa	*111,525;	*111,526;	*111,527;	*111,528;
		*111,529;	*111,530		
2–Phi. 6700061	Chorzempa, Winschermann	*538,500;	*538,510;	*538,520;	*538,530;
		*538,540;	*538,550;	*538,560;	*538,570;
		*538,580;	*538,590;	*538,600;	*538,610
2–Phi. 6700063	Gomez, Tear, Davis	997,000			
2–Phi. 6700084	Reich, Devos, Gielen	949,750			
3–Phi. SC71AX300	Davis	** 51,750			
3–Phi. SC71AX302	Leppard	*659,751;	*659,752;	*659,753;	*659,754;
		*659,755;	*659,756;	*659,757;	*659,758;
		*659,759;	*659,760;	*659,761;	*659,762
3–Phi. 835198/200	Grumiaux	**252,750;	**253,000;	**253,250;	**253,500;
		**253,750;	**254,000		
3–Phi. 839719/21	Davis	** 56,750			
3–Phi. 6703027	Remedios, Carlyle, Herincx, Davis	**957,500			
3–Phi. 6703029	Italiano Quartet	**278,000;	**278,250;	**278,500;	**356,500;
		**356,750;	**357,000		
3–Phi. 6703039	Unger, Donath, Hollweg, Schmidt-Isserstedt	**933,750			
3–Phi. 6703042	Veasêy, Davis	** 28,000			
4–Phi. 835245/8	Oistrakh	*269,250;	*269,500;	*269,750;	*270,000;
		*270,250;	*270,500;	*270,750;	*271,000:
		*271,250;	*271,500		
5–Phi. 6709002	Lindholm, Davis	*907,500			
5–Phi. 6799006	Leppard	** 68,000;	** 68,500		
8–Phi. 6747099	Marriner	*441,000;	*441,250;	*441,500;	*441,750;
		*442,000;	*442,250;	*443,000;	*443,250;
		*443,500;	*444,250;	*444,500;	*444,750;
		*445,000;	*445,250;	*445,500;	*445,750;
		*446,000;	*446,250		
13–Phi. 6747035	Arrau	**119,250;	**120,000;	**120,500;	**121,250:
		**124,250;	*125,000;	*125,250;	*126,000

Polydor

LABEL	PERFORMER	GUIDE NO.	
Pol. 245006	Fiedler	614,000;	761,750

RCA Victor

LABEL	PERFORMER	GUIDE NO.			
RCA ARL 1–0114	Ormandy	758,000			
RCA ARL 1–0447	Arroyo, Moffo	889,650			
RCA ARL 1–0483	Cleveland Quartet	*353,500			
RCA ARL 1–0566	Arroyo, Domingo, Levine	901,000			
RCA ARL 1–0610	Anda, Vienna	*536,770;	*536,771		
†RCA LM–1119	Rubinstein, Heifetz, Piatigorsky	*348,750			
†RCA LM–1163	Rubinstein	*146,750;	*147,001;	*147,002;	*147,003;
		*147,004;	*147,005;	*147,006;	*147,007;
		*147,008;	*147,009;	*147,010;	*147,011;
		*147,012;	*147,013;	*147,014;	*147,015;
		*147,016;	*147,017;	*147,018;	*147,019;
		*147,020;	*147,021;	*147,022;	*147,023;
		*147,024			
†RCA LM–2005	Horowitz	*238,250			
†RCA LM–2074	Heifetz	297,000			
†RCA LM–2319	Horowitz, Toscanini	**559,250			
†RCA LM–2357	Horowitz	**203,000			

LABEL	PERFORMER	GUIDE NO.			
†RCA LM–2584	Horowitz	**187,000			
†RCA LM–2587	Rachmaninoff	**212,000			
†RCA LM–2784	Bjoerling	**894,100;	**902,300		
†RCA LM–2860	Heifetz, Solomon	*555,000			
RCA LSC–2150	Reiner	**731,000;	**786,800		
RCA LSC–2251	Reiner	*673,500;	*782,400		
RCA LSC–2252	Cliburn, Kondrashin	*559,250			
RCA LSC–2318	Reiner	**747,250;	**747,500;	**747,750;	**748,250;
		**749,000;	**750,500		
RCA LSC–2341	Zamkochian, Munch	*460,500			
RCA LSC–2355	Cliburn, Kondrashin	**545,503			
RCA LSC–2368	Rubinstein	**147,751;	**147,752;	**147,753;	**147,754
RCA LSC–2370	Rubinstein	**133,750;	**133,800;	**133,850;	**133,900
RCA LSC–2377	Szeryng	*270,250;	*271,250		
RCA LSC–2380	Boston Pops	588,750			
RCA LSC–2398	Kondrashin	683,250;	683,500;	685,000;	685,250
RCA LSC–2401	Copland	*611,750;	*616,000		
RCA LSC–2436	Reiner	**741,000;	**741,250		
RCA LSC–2487	Bream	**518,000			
RCA LSC–2506	Price	**893,700;	**893,800;	**894,600;	**895,000;
		**895,100;	*896,700;	*896,900;	*900,600;
		*900,900			
RCA LSC–2514	Monteux	**401,000			
RCA LSC–2575	Rubinstein, Skrowaczewski	*507,500			
RCA LSC–2603	Heifetz, Sargent	506,500;	*570,505		
RCA LSC–2619	Szeryng	*282,250;	*282,500		
RCA LSC–2620	Szeryng	*271,000;	*282,000		
RCA LSC–2634	Rubinstein, Wallenstein	*536,771;	*536,773		
RCA LSC–2635	Rubinstein	*181,000;	**536,770		
RCA LSC–2654	Rubinstein	**120,250;	121,750;	124,750	
RCA LSC–2669	Rubinstein	**232,000;	*232,750;	*233,000;	*233,250
RCA LSC–2718	Pears	**824,000;	**824,750;	**824,751;	**824,752;
		**824,753;	**824,754;	**824,755;	**824,756;
		**834,700;	**834,800		
RCA LSC–2719	Gould	611,250;	800,000;	800,100;	800,150
RCA LSC–2726	Rubinstein	*148,501;	*148,502;	*148,503;	*148,504;
		*148,505;	*148,506;	*148,507;	*148,508;
		*148,509;	*148,510;	*148,511;	*148,512;
		*148,513;	*148,514		
RCA LSC–2730	Bream	*284,250;	*548,250;	*574,209	
RCA LSC–2739	Heifetz	*280,750;	*299,000		
RCA LSC–2762	Yaghjian, King, Patrick	**928,250			
RCA LSC–2812	Rubinstein	**119,000;	124,000		
RCA LSC–2819	Pears, Bream	**829,000;	**829,500;	**829,750;	**830,500
RCA LSC–2862	Caballé	**887,100			
RCA LSC–2864	Endich	* 31,500;	* 31,750		
RCA LSC–2866	Previn	**468,500			
RCA LSC–2887	Guarneri Quartet	294,250;	360,250		
RCA LSC–2889	Rubinstein	**134,000;	**134,250;	**135,750;	**144,750
RCA LSC–2893	Gould	*430,250;	*680,250;	*680,500	
RCA LSC–2896	Bream	**257,250;	**257,500		
RCA LSC–2923	Kempe	**473,750			
RCA LSC–2948	Guarneri Quartet	*325,500			
RCA LSC–2955	Serkin	229,250;	237,500;	237,750	
RCA LSC–2964	Bream	*284,500			
RCA LSC–2987	Bream	**292,500			
RCA LSC–3027	Bream	**277,000			
RCA LSC–3029	Martins	517,750;	641,500		
RCA LSC–3035	Price, Bergonzi, Schippers	*897,900			

LABEL	PERFORMER	GUIDE NO.			
RCA LSC–3037	Moffo, Bergonzi, Cleva	*898,600			
RCA LSC–3062	Price	*814,750			
RCA LSC–3067	Stokowski	*432,500			
RCA LSC–3114	Previn	*481,250;	*481,750		
RCA LSC–3118	Perlman	*343,750;	*344,000		
RCA LSC–3130	Fiedler	640,500;	762,000		
RCA LSC–3131	Pears	*828,250;	*829,200		
RCA LSC–3162	Krause, Ormandy	*470,500			
RCA LSC–3170	Previn	**480,000			
RCA LSC–3182	Domingo, Milnes	**897,200			
RCA LSC–3194	Rubinstein	**148,000;	**148,250		
RCA LSC–3203	Price, Domingo, Mehta	900,500			
RCA LSC–3204	Ormandy	*792,750			
RCA LSC–3212	Ormandy	464,750;	542,000		
RCA LSC–3229	Cliburn	*112,500;	*208,000		
RCA LSC–3239	DeLarrocha, Kalichstein	*192,000;	**193,000		
RCA LSC–3246	Ormandy	402,500			
RCA LSC–3265	Heifetz	*537,504;	**537,505		
RCA LSC–3285	Guarneri Quartet	*353,000;	*353,250		
RCA LSC–4010	Heifetz, Munch	**544,252;	**554,750		
RCA LSC–4011	Heifetz, Hendl	*506,000;	*518,200		
RCA VICS–1025	Reiner	617,750;	*694,250;	**792,750	
RCA VICS–1030	Graffman, Munch	507,500;	*532,250		
RCA VICS–1039	Gilels, Reiner	*559,250			
RCA VICS–1058	Oistrakh	*323,000;	*324,000		
RCA VICS–1068	Reiner	683,250;	**725,500		
RCA VICS–1071	Henriot-Schweitzer, Munch	544,002;	546,250		
RCA VICS–1101	Janis, Reiner	545,500;	*556,000		
RCA VICS–1104	Reiner	**474,000			
RCA VICS–1110	Reiner	**586,000			
RCA VICS–1153	Kogan, Monteux	*528,000;	*549,750		
RCA VICS–1235	Wunderlich	**890,300; **890,500; **890,550; **890,600; **892,150; **893,000; **893,600; **894,800; **894,900; **899,500; **899,800			
RCA VICS–1239	Maderna	970,250;	993,000;	993,200	
†RCA VICS–1249E	Toscanini	**398,250			
RCA VICS–1265	Reiner	**778,750			
RCA VICS–1266	Deller	*812,200;	*842,500;	*843,750	
RCA VICS–1317	Ameling	**813,750;	**814,000		
RCA VICS–1323	Munch	*620,250;	*675,500;	*736,250;	*738,500
RCA VICS–1362	Gerwig	* 300			
RCA VICS–1370	Leonhardt	98,500;	156,000		
RCA VICS–1405	Ameling	857,250; 858,000; 858,500; 858,750; 860,750; 862,500; 863,250			
RCA VICS–1419	Vronsky, Babin	152,250			
RCA VICS–1424	Reiner	**626,250; **707,500; **766,000; **780,750; **811,000			
RCA VICS–1431	Deller, Chapuis	826,000			
RCA VICS–1463	Leonhardt, Collegium Aureum	*493,750;	*494,000		
RCA VICS–1466	Fiedler	727,200			
RCA VICS–1561	Janigro, Reiner	**556,750;	**780,500		
RCA VICS–1620	Reiner	*587,000;	*587,500		
†RCA VICS–1648E	Toscanini	**378,000			
†RCA VICS–1654E	Toscanini	**377,000;	**377,250;	**378,250	
†RCA VICS–1655E	Toscanini	**377,500			
RCA VICS–1676	Reiner	**791,500			
RCA VICS–1691	Pierlot, Scimone	*492,252;	*508,500;	*531,500	
†RCA VIC–1244	Toscanini	**595,500;	**741,000;	**741,250;	**753,500
†RCA VIC–1246	Toscanini	**617,750;	**619,000		

LABEL	PERFORMER	GUIDE NO.			
†RCA VIC–1247	Toscanini	**803,000;	**804,000;	**804,250;	**804,500
		**806,250			
†RCA VIC–1267	Toscanini	**625,250;	**779,500;	**781,000	
†RCA VIC–1273	Toscanini	**725,750;	*736,750		
†RCA VIC–1274	Toscanini	**747,250;	**747,750;	**748,500;	**749,000
		**750,500			
†RCA VIC–1369	Toscanini	**803,750			
†RCA VIC–1502	Toscanini	**378,500			
†RCA VIC–1510	Koussevitsky	*471,500			
†RCA VIC–1607	Toscanini	**379,250			
2–RCA ARL2–0105	Price, Domingo, Milnes	*942,500			
†2–RCA LM–6014	Horowitz	**208,250			
†2–RCA LM–6018	Toscanini	** 91,750			
2–RCA LSC–7037	Rubinstein	**133,500;	**135,500;	**135,800;	**145,000
		**145,250;	**145,500;	**145,750;	**146,000
		**146,250;	**146,500		
2–RCA LSC–7048	Moffo, Sciutti, Barioni, Molinari-Pradelli	941,750			
2–RCA LSC–7050	Rubinstein	*141,000;	*141,250;	*141,500;	*141,750
		*142,000;	*142,250;	*142,500;	*142,750
		*143,000;	*143,250;	*143,500;	*143,750
		*144,000;	*144,250;	*144,500	
2–RCA LSC–7051	Ozawa	991,300;	996,600		
2–RCA VICS–6023	Collegium Aureum	*583,251;	*583,252;	*583,253;	*583,254
		*583,255;	*583,256		
2–RCA VICS–6037	Kahlhöfer	* 24,750			
†3–RCA LM–6107	Nelli, Toscanini	**960,000			
†3–RCA LM–6111	Valdengo, Toscanini	**958,750			
†3–RCA LM–6123	Rachmaninoff, Ormandy, Stokowski	**545,500;	**545,502;	**545,503;	**545,504
		**545,750			
3–RCA LSC–6176	Caballé, Verrett, Kraus, Perlea	915,500			
3–RCA LSC–6177	Rubinstein	**136,000;	**136,350;	**136,500;	**136,750
		**137,000;	**137,250;	**137,500;	**137,750
		**138,000;	**138,250;	**138,500;	**138,750
		**139,000;	**139,250;	**139,500;	**139,750
		**140,000;	**140,250;	**140,500;	**140,750
3–RCA LSC–6182	Sills, Wolf	*921,250			
3–RCA LSC–6183	Price, Bergonzi, Sereni, Schippers	**958,500			
3–RCA LSC–6194	Price, Cossotto, Domingo, Mehta	**961,000			
†8–RCA VIC–8000	Toscanini	**377,000			
12–RCA VICS–9000	Frank	**120,500;	*123,500;	*125,250	

Richmond

LABEL	PERFORMER	GUIDE NO.			
†Rich. R–23182	Ferrier, Walter	**839,200			
†Rich. R–23183	Ferrier, Krauss	** 31,000;	**818,250;	**819,000;	**821,000
†Rich. R–23184	Ferrier	**853,000;	**857,250;	**860,750;	**866,750;
		**869,500;	**881,750;	**882,000;	**882,250;
		**883,750			
Rich. SR–33086	Danco, Cuénod, Ansermet	**944,750			
†2–Rich. RS–62006	Gueden, Lipp, Patzak, Krauss	**951,750			
†2–Rich. RS–62021	Vyvyan, Pears, Britten	**911,250			
†3–Rich. RS–63014	Micheau, DeLuca, Sebastian	956,750			
3–Rich. SRS–63510	Simionato, Bastianini, Erede	914,750			
3–Rich. SRS–63512	Flagstad, Lowe, Jones	**919,750			
3–Rich. SRS–63516	Heybalova, Bugarinovich, Marinkovich, Baranovich	956,750			
3–Rich. SRS–63522	Della Casa, Gueden, London, Solti	952,250			
4–Rich. SRS–64503	Rysanek, Höngen, Goltz, Böhm	*953,500			

LABEL	PERFORMER	GUIDE NO.			
4–Rich. SRS–64506	Popovich, Danon	908,750			
5–Rich. RS–65001	Mödl, London, Windgassen, Knappertsbusch	**962,250			

Serenus

LABEL	PERFORMER	GUIDE NO.
Ser. 12000	Watanabe	433,250
Ser. 12017	Farberman	433,000

Seraphim

LABEL	PERFORMER	GUIDE NO.			
Sera. S–60000	Beecham	**622,250;	**764,750		
Sera. S–60005	Hindemith	*426,500;	*668,000		
Sera. S–60012	Beecham	**401,000			
Sera. S–60016	Solomon	**125,000			
Sera. S–60020	Arrau, Galliera	559,250;	**576,000		
Sera. S–60025	Hotter	*852,000;	*853,000;	*857,000;	*858,250;
		*858,500;	*860,250;	*862,750;	*864,250;
		*865,000;	*865,750;	*868,750;	*870,500;
		*873,500;	*874,250		
Sera. S–60031	Giulini	*476,750			
Sera. S–60032	Weldon	519,250;	653,250;	653,500;	653,750
Sera. S–60034	Ludwig	*820,250;	*821,000;	*821,250;	*852,250;
		*855,750;	*870,750;	*882,000;	*882,750
Sera. S–60037	Davis	*716,000;	*717,000;	*719,250;	*720,500;
		*720,750;	*722,000		
Sera. S–60038	Cantelli	**378,500			
Sera. S–60041	Beecham	**779,750			
Sera. S–60057	Davis	**719,000;	**720,250;	**723,250;	**724,250;
		**724,500			
Sera. S–60058	Giulini	*747,500;	*747,750;	*748,500;	*749,500;
		*750,500			
Sera. S–60062	Beecham	**375,500			
Sera. S–60066	Pollini, Kletzki	**507,500			
Sera. S–60068	Barbirolli	**399,000			
Sera. S–60080	Stokowski	697,000;	757,500		
Sera. S–60081	Anievas	*134,500;	*134,750;	*134,800;	*134,850;
		*134,900;	*135,000;	*135,050;	*135,100;
		*135,150;	*135,200;	*135,250	
Sera. S–60084	Beecham	**632,500			
Sera. S–60085	Iseler	* 75,000			
Sera. S–60087	Ludwig	*822,500			
Sera. S–60088	Ogden	**188,250			
Sera. S–60093	Orozco	148,750			
Sera. S–60098	Kempe	*627,750;	**765,500;	**765,750;	**766,250;
		*811,000			
Sera. S–60103	Malcuzynski	170,000			
Sera. S–60104	Stokowski	*619,250;	*619,500;	*619,750;	*620,000;
		*738,000			
Sera. S–60105	Kletzki	*435,250			
Sera. S–60108	Dervaux	608,500;	609,000;	609,250;	609,500;
		609,750			
Sera. S–60109	François	*147,500;	507,502		
Sera. S–60121	Fischer-Dieskau	23,408;	88,000		
Sera. S–60132	Veyron-LaCroix	*522,250;	*522,500;	*522,750	
Sera. S–60134	Beecham	**632,750			
Sera. S–60138	Giulini	*747,250;	*748,000;	748,250;	749,000;
		*801,200;	*801,500;	*801,600;	*801,700

199

LABEL	PERFORMER	GUIDE NO.			
Sera. S–60142	Grandjany	**348,000;	**511,500		
Sera. S–60147	Davies	** 41,500			
Sera. S–60170	Ogdon	**187,500;	**187,600		
Sera. S–60171	Rostropovich, Sargent	*544,500			
Sera. S–60172	Flanders, Kurtz	455,500;	*732,000		
Sera. S–60177	Dervaux	*609,000;	*620,250;	*625,250;	*736,250
		*753,500			
Sera. S–60178	Ciccolini	177,000			
Sera. S–60185	Beecham	**621,750;	**622,500;	**623,500	
Sera. S–60187	Willcocks	** 10,500;	** 10,600		
Sera. S–60192	Beecham	**384,000;	**433,750		
Sera. S–60194	Barbirolli	*463,500			
Sera. S–60196	Germani	**106,750;	**109,000;	**110,500	
Sera. S–60199	Rabin	541,000			
Sera. S–60205	Walton	*808,350			
Sera. S–60208	Barbirolli	**762,250;	**762,500;	**762,750;	**763,750
		**765,000			
Sera. S–60212	Beecham	**622,750			
Sera. S–60217	Willcocks	* 34,000;	* 34,500		
†Sera. 60007	Lipatti	**507,500			
†Sera. 60008	Christoff	*846,250;	*846,500		
†Sera. 60011	Primrose	281,500;	281,750		
†Sera. 60013	Schwarzkopf	**844,750			
†Sera. 60040	Brain	*269,000;	*356,000		
†Sera. 60065	Hotter	**818,000;	**818,250;	**819,000;	**821,000
		**821,750;	**822,000;	**823,250	
†Sera. 60115	Schnabel	**226,502;	**226,504		
Sera. 60134	Beecham	*749,750			
†Sera. 60135	Menuhin, Furtwängler	*500,750			
†Sera. 60145	Flagstad, Thebom, Fischer-Dieskau	**902,900			
†Sera. 60161	Shostakovich, Vaillant, Cluytens	**554,250;	*554,252		
†Sera. 60179	Schwarzkopf	**879,000;	**883,500;	**885,250	
†Sera. 60183	Dushkin, Stravinsky	*361,000			
†Sera. 60202	Welitsch	*893,400;	**894,600;	**896,200;	**896,900
2–Sera. S–6010	Grümmer, Otto, Schock, Keilberth	964,250			
2–Sera. S–6017	Beecham	* 62,000			
2–Sera. S–6033	Barbirolli	**399,250;	**630,250		
2–Sera. S–6039	Beecham	** 53,250			
2–Sera. S–6073	Laszlo, Lewis, Dominguez, Pritchard	*930,500			
2–Sera. S–6083	Baker	*854,250;	*857,250;	*859,500	
2–Sera. S–6085	Menuhin	*584,001;	*584,002;	*584,003;	*584,013
		*584,014			
†2–Sera. 6000	De Los Angeles, Bjoerling, Beecham	**940,500			
†2–Sera. 6075	Fournier	**272,000;	**272,250;	**272,500;	**272,750
		**273,000			
3–Sera. S–6005	Hungarian Quartet	*263,500;	*263,750;	*264,000;	*264,250
		*264,500;	*264,750		
3–Sera. S–6006	Hungarian Quartet	*265,000;	*265,250;	*265,500;	*265,750
		*266,000			
3–Sera. S–6070	Jurinac, Simoneau, Pritchard	934,000			
3–Sera. S–6081	Ciccolini, Baudo	**549,252;	**549,254		
†3–Sera. 6015	Toscanini	**377,000;	**377,750;	**378,250;	**604,750
		**720,750			
†3–Sera. 6041	Schuman	**872,500;	**874,000;	**874,750;	**875,000
		**876,000			
†3–Sera. 6043	Schnabel, Dobrowen	**499,996			
†3–Sera. 6067	Schnabel	**126,500;	**127,000;	**127,250	

LABEL	PERFORMER	GUIDE NO.			
†4–Sera. 6047	Gieseking	**195,250			
6–Sera. S–6034/5	Borodin Quartet	**358,500;	**358,750;	**359,000	
7–Sera. S–6071	Cluytens	**378,250			
†13–Sera. 6063/6	Schnabel	**119,500;	**121,250;	**121,500;	**121,750;
		**122,000;	**122,500;	**123,000;	**123,250;
		**123,500;	**124,250;	**124,500;	**124,750;
		**125,000;	**125,750;	**126,000;	**126,250

Telefunken

LABEL	PERFORMER	GUIDE NO.			
Tel. 6.41010	Jürgens	976,750			
Tel. 6.41011	Nicolet	*248,250;	*250,750;	*342,250;	*990,900
Tel. 6.41039	Brüggen, Vester, Rieu	*564,000;	*569,500		
Tel. 6.41044	Brüggen	**300,000;	**300,250;	**300,750;	**301,250
Tel. 6.41045	Leonhardt	180,750			
Tel. 6.41047	Rieu	* 23,406			
Tel. 6.41050	Rieu	* 23,408			
Tel. 6.41057	Kee	**131,750			
Tel. 6.41058	Munich Capella Antiqua	* 2,800			
Tel. 6.41060	Jürgens	* 23,106;	* 23,206;	* 23,382	
Tel. 6.41061	Klerk	**102,649;	**104,712;	**109,554	
Tel. 6.41062	Vienna Concentus Musicus	**248,750;	*768,000		
Tel. 6.41065	Leonhardt	*100,500			
Tel. 6.41067	Giebel	* 23,409			
Tel. 6.41076	Leonhardt	**171,000			
Tel. 6.41079	Harnoncourt	* 23,411;	* 23,412		
Tel. 6.41084	Tachezi	*205,000			
Tel. 6.41085	Leonhardt	* 98,750			
Tel. 6.41087	Ruhland	** 19,500			
Tel. 6.41090	Hildenbrand	**205,000			
Tel. 6.41095	Harnoncourt	**539,500;	**550,500;	**563,500;	**574,440
Tel. 6.41108	Bylsma, Woodrow, Leonhardt Consort	370,750;	495,014;	495,500;	495,502
Tel. 6.41113	Krumbach	** 99,250;	** 99,500		
Tel. 6.41125	Ruhland	** 6,900			
Tel. 6.41126	Binkley	** 19,700			
Tel. 6.41127	Rogers, Dombois, Harnoncourt	*842,500;	*843,750		
Tel. 6.41128	Leonhardt	**172,000			
Tel. 6.41130	Leonhardt	*100,500;	*104,903;	*105,904	
Tel. 6.41183	Amsterdam Quadro	**363,750			
Tel. 6.41184	Binkley	** 19,200			
Tel. 6.41190	Leonhardt	495,014;	495,500;	495,502	
Tel. 6.41193	Jürgens, Leonhardt Consort	* 84,250;	* 84,750		
Tel. 6.41197	Bylsma, Schroeder	*503,500			
Tel. 6.41201	Leonhardt Consort	700;	16,400		
Tel. 6.41213	Munich Capella Antiqua	** 4,000			
Tel. 6.41215	Jürgens	* 23,398			
Tel. 6.41217	Baumann, Van Wouldenberg	573,005;	*574,321		
Tel. 6.41219	Early Music Studio	** 100			
Tel. 6.41225	Brüggen, Harnoncourt	*569,500			
Tel. 6.41227	Harnoncourt	*496,000;	*496,002;	*496,250	
Tel. 6.41230	Ruhland	** 20,300			
Tel. 6.41234	Early Music Quartet	** 19,300			
Tel. 6.41239	Brüggen	**574,077			
Tel. 6.41241	Groot, Schröder	*524,253;	*526,600		
Tel. 6.41242	Harnoncourt	*252,000;	*252,250;	*252,500;	*258,500
Tel. 6.41247	Ruhland	** 4,300			
Tel. 6.41266	Venhoda	* 47,000			

LABEL	PERFORMER	GUIDE NO.			
Tel. 6.41293	Kruysen	*827,200;	*827,600;	*827,700;	*827,701;
		*827,702;	*827,703;	*827,800	
Tel. 6.41298	Kruysen	832,100			
2–Tel. 26.35010	Ruhland	* 5,900;	** 19,000		
2–Tel. 26.35028	King's College Choir	* 23,008			
2–Tel. 26.35029	King's College Choir	* 23,010			
2–Tel. 26.35044	Harnoncourt	** 88,500			
2–Tel. 26.35045	Harnoncourt	* 71,500			
2–Tel. 26.35046	Harnoncourt	*584,001;	*584,002;	*584,003;	*584,013;
		*584,014			
2–Tel. 26.35052	Jürgens	* 4,100			
2–Tel. 26.35074	Adam, Schröter, Springer, Suitner	*924,750			
2–Tel. 26.35076	Richter	**111,525;	**111,526;	**111,527;	**111,528;
		**111,529;	**111,530		
2–Tel. 26.35077	Chapuis	*100,250			
2–Tel. 26.35082	Richter	**107,572;	**109,250		
2–Tel. 26.48002	Guglielmo, Pocaterra	*362,500			
2–Tel. 26.48006	Brüggen	*794,750			
2–Tel. 26.48007	Brüggen	*794,750			
2–Tel. 26.48008	Brüggen	*794,750			
2–Tel. 26.48009	Quadro Amsterdam	**289,500;	**289,750;	**290,000;	**290,250
3–Tel. 36.35008	Van Blerk	311,750			
3–Tel. 36.35009	Mauersberger	** 82,250			
3–Tel. 36.35018	Vienna Concentus Musicus	** 25,250			
3–Tel. 36.35020	Hansmann	930,750			
3–Tel. 36.35021	Ephrikian, Bologna	*384,250			
3–Tel. 36.35022	Harnoncourt	** 23,750			
4–Tel. 46.35048	Vandersteene, Souzay, Scovotti, Harnoncourt	*944,000			
5–Tel. 56.35017	Magnardi Danish Quartet	*333,250;	*333,500;	*333,750;	*334,000;
		*334,250;	*334,500;	*716,250;	*724,250

Turnabout

LABEL	PERFORMER	GUIDE NO.			
†Turn. 4489	Dercourt, Poulenc	*846,900			
Turn. 34003	Kunschak, Kladky	*526,200			
Turn. 34004		965,250;	988,800;	991,400;	991,450;
		991,600			
Turn. 34005	Faerber	*512,700;	*512,800;	*512,900	
Turn. 34006	Hautzig	*226,250;	*229,750		
Turn. 34009	Lemmen, Faerber	*574,078;	*574,083;	*574,266;	*574,288
Turn. 34010	Pohlers	*510,250			
Turn. 34017	Burgess	*174,000			
Turn. 34019	Polanska, Durand, Colte	** 20,100			
Turn. 34025	Bianchi, Santi	574,070			
Turn. 34027	Frankl, Faerber	*536,761;	*536,765		
Turn. 34029	Couraud	** 92,750;	*844,750		
Turn. 34032	Escribano, Ramor Quartet	*350,500			
Turn. 34035	Sous	*330,000;	*334,500		
Turn. 34042	Buckel	* 23,402			
Turn. 34049	Garaguly	*452,500			
†Turn. 34052E	Hye-Knudsen	401,500			
Turn. 34055	Ruf	**523,250;	**523,253;	**523,255	
Turn. 34057	Schneidewind, Pasch	492,500;	*531,250;	*574,075	
Turn. 34058	Burgess	** 21,100			
Turn. 34064	Brendel, Klien	**196,850;	**537,000		
Turn. 34065	Sandor, Reinhardt	*498,496;	*557,500		

ABEL	PERFORMER	GUIDE NO.			
ˉurn. 34070	Vienna Hofburg-Kapelle	** 3,800			
ˉurn. 34074	Isoir	**155,800			
ˉurn. 34077	Brendel	*116,250;	*116,500;	*116,750	
ˉurn. 34080	Brendel, Angerer	*536,767;	*536,769		
ˉurn. 34086	Reinhardt	587,250;	588,500		
ˉurn. 34087	Patero, Storck, Faerber	*196,500;	**536,000		
ˉurn. 34088	Grischkat	** 82,500			
ˉurn. 34089	Rilling	** 39,000			
ˉurn. 34090	Faerber	555,750			
ˉurn. 34095	Brendel, Böettcher	536,764;	*536,770		
ˉurn. 34096	Stoklassa, Sabo	*825,000			
ˉurn. 34097	Rilling	* 1,500			
ˉurn. 34099	Rilling	* 83,500			
ˉurn. 34129	Brendel, Angerer	*536,775;	*536,777		
ˉurn. 34130	Sandor, Reinhardt	*499,500;	*527,250;	557,250	
ˉurn. 34132	Gillesberger	* 55,000;	* 72,750		
ˉurn. 34134	Faerber	425,100;	*722,250;	715,000	
ˉurn. 34135	Haas, Faerber	*491,750;	521,014;	538,530	
ˉurn. 34136	Newman, Payne	*240,000; *241,000;	*240,250; *241,250;	*240,500; *241,500	*240,750;
ˉurn. 34137	Shaffer	* 300			
ˉurn. 34151	Glazer, Kohon Quartet	*371,250;	*575,250;	*575,750	
ˉurn. 34157	Kohon Quartet	*315,250;	*315,500		
Turn. 34164E	Novaes	*232,000; *234,750;	*234,000; *235,000;	*234,250; *236,250	*234,500;
ˉurn. 34167	Sandor	**113,000;	*114,500		
ˉurn. 34170	Kyriakou, Swarowsky	532,750;	534,000;	534,250	
ˉurn. 34173	Rilling	38,500			
ˉurn. 34175	Behrmann	* 42,250			
ˉurn. 34178	Klien	*196,000;	*200,250;	*536,774	
ˉurn. 34179	Soukupova, Zidek, Berman, Ancerl	*954,500			
ˉurn. 34182	Landau	453,500			
ˉurn. 34218	Westchester Symphony	643,000; 676,500	643,500;	676,000;	676,250;
ˉurn. 34221	Wallfisch, Faerber	*555,500			
ˉurn. 34229	Lautenbacher, Bunte	*570,750			
ˉurn. 34231	Grischkat	** 83,000			
ˉurn. 34233	Brendel, Angerer	536,772;	537,875		
ˉurn. 34234	Klien	*159,000			
ˉurn. 34235	Klien	*159,250			
ˉurn. 34236	Blees	*529,500;	*558,500		
ˉurn. 34241	Kyriakou, Klien	133,250			
ˉurn. 34264	Little	* 21,300			
ˉurn. 34271	Frankl	*133,750; *135,750	*133,800;	*133,850;	*133,900;
ˉurn. 34288	Wallfisch, Faerber	*566,000;	*566,500;	*568,000	
ˉurn. 34307	Pohlers, Kehr	*508,250;	*510,500;	*550,250	
ˉurn. 34309	Behrmann	10,200;	12,500;	13,200;	14,600
ˉurn. 34331	Woolf	846,000			
ˉurn. 34348	Zukerman, Faerber	526,400			
ˉurn. 34361	Maag	462,250;	462,500		
ˉurn. 34366	Sebestyén	241,750			
ˉurn. 34373	Sacher	716,500;	716,750		
ˉurn. 34378	Vintschger	*224,000;	*224,250;	*224,500;	*224,750
Turn. 34385E	Kempff	**185,750			
ˉurn. 34388	Cohen	*841,600			
ˉurn. 34397	Simon	*215,000;	*216,750		
ˉurn. 34398	Foss	614,250;	679,250;	752,250	
ˉurn. 34402	Brendel	*117,000			

LABEL	PERFORMER	GUIDE NO.			
†Turn. 34414E	Brendel	*186,500;	*186,507		
Turn. 34422	Rapf	127,750			
Turn. 34431	Behrmann	* 2,400			
Turn. 34447	Abravanel	*459,750;	*464,500		
Turn. 34449	List, Buketoff	*518,750			
Turn. 34459	Abravanel	597,000;	648,000		
†Turn. 34461E	Fournier	**281,000;	**281,250		
Turn. 34475	Brendel	**227,000			
Turn. 34481	Brendel	**226,500;	**226,501;	**226,502;	**226,503
		**226,504;	**226,700;	**226,701;	**226,702
		**226,703;	**226,704		
Turn. 34490	Vegh, Casals, Horszowski	**274,750			
Turn. 34503	Klien, Kehr	536,768			
Turn. 34507	Dorian Quartet	*298,000;	*314,500;	*342,000	
Turn. 34515	Fine Arts Quartet	965,800;	998,300		
†Turn. 34525E	Szell	**398,000			
Turn. 34534	Landau	404,000;	796,250		
Turn. 34536	Shields	987,400;	987,500;	987,800	
†3–Turn. 4111/3	Beecham	**934,500			
†3–Turn. 4117/9	Busch, Glynebourne	**933,250			

Vanguard

LABEL	PERFORMER	GUIDE NO.			
Van. HM–1 SD	Deller	15,500;	15,600		
Van. HM–2 SD	Gillesberger	3,000;	8,000		
Van. HM–3 SD	Noble	* 2,300			
Van. HM–4 SD	Deller	842,250;	843,250;	843,500	
Van. HM–9 SD	Venhoda	* 10,900;	* 11,400;	* 11,500;	* 11,600
		* 11,700;	* 11,800;	* 12,100;	* 12,300
		* 13,100;	* 13,300;	* 13,400;	* 13,800
		* 13,900;	* 14,100;	* 14,200;	* 14,400
		* 14,700;	* 14,900;	* 15,000;	* 15,100
Van. HM–16 SD	Stonic, Janigro, Solisti di Zagreb	*573,500;	*574,133;	*574,342	
Van. HM–22 SD	Prohaska	* 23,050			
Van. HM–23 SD	Janigro	**385,000;	**385,250;	**385,500;	**385,750
		**386,000;	**386,250;	**386,500;	**386,750
Van. HM–27 SD	Blum	**414,750;	**416,250		
Van. HM–29 SD	Griller Quartet, Primrose	*333,250;	*334,000		
Van. HM–31 SD	Wobisch	**508,750;	**544,750;	*574,075	
Van. HM–40 SD	Lardrot, Prohaska	*330,000;	*338,000;	*492,000;	520,500
		520,502;	*535,752		
Van. HM–42 SD	Griller Quartet	307,250;	307,500;	307,750	
Van. HM–43 SD	Schneider	*277,500			
Van. SRV–155 SD	Mahler	733,000;	733,250;	733,500;	733,750
Van. SRV–159 SD	Makanowitzky, Golschmann	572,504;	572,508;	572,509;	572,512
Van. SRV–160 SD	Fistoulari	631,251;	631,252;	*693,500;	*693,750
Van. SRV–166 SD	Wöldike	*424,750;	*425,000		
Van. SRV–187 SD	Wöldike	*424,000;	*424,250		
Van. SRV–194 SD	Griller Quartet, Primrose	*333,500;	*333,750		
Van. SRV–211 SD	Wöldike	*423,750;	*424,500		
Van. SRV–226 SD	Kalbhöfer	23,065			
Van. SRV–227 SD	Boatwright	* 50,750			
Van. SRV–228 SD	Boatwright	* 50,250;	* 50,500		
Van. SRV–229 SD	Boatwright	* 50,125;	* 50,625		
Van. SRV–274 SD	Abravanel	672,000;	711,750;	799,000	
Van. SRV–275 SD	Abravanel	518,750;	647,000;	648,250	
Van. SRV–280 SD	Cantelo, Deller	*847,000;	*847,250;	*847,500	
Van. SRV–284 SD	Schneider	*330,250;	*330,500		

LABEL	PERFORMER	GUIDE NO.			
Van. SRV–297 SD	Deller	* 66,500;	* 67,000;	*841,000;	*841,200
Van. VCS–10005	Yale Quartet	**267,000			
Van. VCS–10013	Farberman	678,000;	678,500;	680,250	
Van. VCS–10022	Deller	*844,000			
Van. VCS–10028	Davrath, Rudolf, Heiller	*851,625			
Van. VCS–10029	Harnoncourt	*289,000			
Van. VCS–10030	Takahashi, Simonovic	998,750;	998,850		
Van. VCS–10043	Brendel	*195,750;	*196,750;	*198,750;	*201,750
Van. VCS–10055	Hungerford	*121,500;	124,250;	*126,000	
Van. VCS–10057	electronic equipment	993,600			
Van. VCS–10062	Yale Quartet	**266,750			
Van. VCS–10064	Gomberg	284,000			
Van. VCS–10066	Blum	**718,750;	**719,000		
Van. VCS–10067	Somary	*652,000;	*653,000;	654,750;	*811,200
Van. VCS–10083	Stevens	* 18,800			
Van. VCS–10084	Hungerford	*118,500;	*118,750		
Van. VCS–10085	Hungerford	*119,250;	*119,500		
Van. VCS–10096	Yale Quartet	**266,500			
Van. VCS–10097	Yale Quartet	*263,000;	*267,250		
Van. VSD–2036	Lardrot, Prohaska	*492,000;	508,500;	520,504;	*523,500
Van. VSD–2094	Wild, Mester	509,500;	534,500		
Van. VSD–2095	Stokowski	*796,300;	*796,350		
Van. VSD–6536	Schickele	755,825			
Van. VSD–71126	Janigro	410,750;	411,000;	*664,750	
Van. VSD–71127	Janigro	*740,500;	*741,500		
Van. VSD–71145	Serkin	**354,000			
Van. VSD–71146	Schneider, Serkin	**354,500;	**355,000		
Van. VSD–71161	Blum	*416,000;	*417,500		
Van. VSD–71167	Brymer, Prohaska	512,000;	528,250;	575,250	
Van. VSD–71172	Hungerford	**125,750;	*126,250		
2–Van. SRV–282/3 SD	Sheppard	48,750			
2–Van. SRV–304/5 SD	Szigeti, Bartók	262,500;	**271,250;	**291,750;	**499,701
2–Van. VCS/10037/8	Abravanel	*754,250;	*754,500		
2–Van. VSD–719/20	Schickele	755,925			
2–Van. VSD–723/4	List	*176,000			
2–Van. VSD–2117/8	Abravanel	* 59,000			
2–Van. VSD–71141/2	Abravanel	**436,000			
3–Van. HM–24/5/6 SD	Wöldike	* 52,750			
3–Van. HM–37/8/9 SD	Tomasow, Boskovsky, Rossi	*571,005;	*571,008;	*571,010;	*571,011
3–Van. SRV–262/3/4 SD	Szigeti	*335,750;	*336,000;	**336,500	
3–Van. SRV–265/6/7 SD	Szigeti	*336,250;	*336,750;	*337,000;	*337,250;
		*337,500;	*337,750		
3–Van. VCS–10032/3/4	Farberman	430,250;	430,500;	430,750;	431,000;
		679,500			
†4–Van. SRV–300/1/2/3	Szigeti, Arrau	**269,250;	**269,500;	**269,750;	**270,000;
		**270,250;	**270,500;	**270,750;	**271,000;
		**271,250;	**271,500		

Vox

LABEL	PERFORMER	GUIDE NO.			
Vox SVBX–5407	Klien	202,250			
Vox. SVBX–5428	Klien	197,000;	197,250;	197,500;	197,750;
		198,000;	198,500;	198,750;	199,000;
		199,250			
Vox SVBX–5429	Klien	196,000;	196,950;	199,500;	199,750;
		200,000;	200,250;	200,500;	200,750;
		201,000			
Vox 510330	Van Remoortel	654,500;	654,750		

LABEL	PERFORMER	GUIDE NO.
†Vox 510940E	Novaes	*146,750; *147,001-024; *148,00(
†3–Vox SVBX–531E	Barchet, Elsner, Reinhardt	571,501; 571,512
3–Vox SVBX–549	Kohon Quartet	293,500; 293,750
3–Vox SVBX–556	Dekany Quartet	304,750
3–Vox SVBX–559	Dekany Quartet	305,750; 306,000; 306,250; 306,50(
3–Vox SVBX–568	Mannheim Trio	338,250; 338,500; 338,750; 339,00(339,250; 339,500
3–Vox SVBX–569	Pauk, Frankl	*352,500; 354,500; 354,750; 355,00(
3–Vox SVBX–573	Neumeyer	*181,502; *181,506; *181,508; *181,512 *181,513; *181,514
3–Vox SVBX–574	Kyriakou	181,521; 181,522; 181,540; 181,548 181,551
3–Vox SVBX–575	Klien	181,520; 181,534; 181,535; 181,536 181,537; 181,538; 181,544; 181,545 181,546; 181,552
3–Vox SVBX–576	Galling	181,527; 181,532; 181,549; 181,550
3–Vox SVBX–582	Schuster, Balsam	*326,000; *326,250; *326,500
3–Vox SVBX–595	Fine Arts Quartet	310,000
3–Vox SVBX–597	Fine Arts Quartet	306,750; 307,000
3–Vox SVBX–5100	Loewenguth Quartet	296,750; 296,850; 297,500
3–Vox SVBX–5211	Fahberg, Ewerhart, Santini	**931,000
3–Vox SVBX–5305	Kohon Quartet	990,200
3–Vox SVBX–5306	Concord Quartet	**318,000; **970,750; **973,000; **976,500 **981,000; **982,500; 987,700; 988,400 998,200; 998,250
3–Vox SVBX–5400	Kyriakou	*132,750; *133,000
3–Vox SVBX–5408	Sándor	*207,000; *207,250; *207,500; *207,750 *208,750; *209,000; *209,250
3–Vox SVBX–5425	Sándor	*113,800; *113,801; *113,802; *113,803 *113,804; *114,097; *114,100; *114,102 *114,109; *114,113; *114,120; *114,226 *114,227; *114,229; *114,231; *114,232 *114,235; *114,239; *114,250; *114,342 *114,344; *114,346; *114,350
3–Vox SBVX–5426	Sándor	**113,250; **113,500; **114,500; **114,750
3–Vox SVBX–5427	Sándor	*113,750; *115,000; *115,500
3–Vox SVBX–5433	Frankl	158,000; 158,250; 159,500; 159,750; 160,000; 160,250; 160,500; 160,750; 161,000; 161,250; 161,500; 161,750; 162,000; 162,250; 162,500; 162,750; 163,000; 163,250; 163,500; 163,750; 164,000; 164,250; 164,500; 164,750; 165,000; 165,250; 165,500; 165,750
3–Vox SVBX–5438	Galling	104,903; 105,800; 105,806; 105,807; 105,808; 105,809; 105,810; 105,811; 108,250
3–Vox SVBX–5445	Kraft	*102,640; *102,645; *102,646; *102,647; *102,648; *102,649; *102,650; *104,660; *104,669; *104,670; *104,675; *104,677; *104,678; *104,680; *104,682; *104,683; *104,684; *104,685; *104,687; *104,689; *106,750; *109,534; *109,536; *109,552
3–Vox SVBX–5448	Curtis	154,100; 154,200; 154,300; 154,400; 154,500; 154,600
3–Vox SVBX–5454	Rose	185,500
3–Vox SVBX–5455	Ponti	244,500
3–Vox SVBX–5457	Mourao	178,000; 178,250; 178,500; 178,750; 179,000; 179,500
3–Vox SVBX–5458	Mourao	178,000; 179,250
3–Vox SVBX–5459	Ponti	244,500
3–Vox SVBX–5468	Frankl	*230,250; 230,500; *231,250; *232,000; 233,750; 237,000; 237,250
4–Vox SVBX–5464	de Oliviera	990,500
6–Vox SVBX–5423/4	Crochet	167,000; 167,250; 167,500
9–Vox SVBX–527/9	Kraft	131,500; 132,500

Westminster

LABEL	PERFORMER	GUIDE NO.		
West. WGSO–8173–3	Rhodes, Bruck	939,500		
West. WGSO–8202–3	Forrester	*922,000		
West. WGSO–8205–3	Stich-Randall, Forrester	*921,750		
West. WGS–8110	Balanchine, New York City Ballet Company	984,800		
West. WGS–8156	List, Chávez	530,750;	530,752	
West. WGS–8165	Firkusny, Somogyi	**513,500		
West. WGS–8192	Scherchen	*592,750		
West. WGS–8206	Scherchen	26,500		
West. WGS–8216	Golden Age Singers	842,500;	842,750;	843,250

Reviews

3

The critic of musical performance must be extraordinarily versatile and open-minded. The musicologist who deals primarily with original scores and problems of historical interpretation may usually limit himself to meticulous inspection of a small slice of musical pie—a composer, school of composition, or era—whereas a critic may be entrusted with the task of sampling the yield of the entire musical bakery. The critic additionally must contend with a deadline. The high incidence of dyspeptic and superficial prose in music reviews may be due to aural indigestion induced by forced feedings of too many baked and half-baked musical goods. Criticism of sound recordings should be legitimized as a full-time occupation because a cosmopolitan familiarity with current trends and interpretive precedents, combined with an awareness of technical reproduction, packaging, and labeling standards should back up each judgment of a new release. Although the reviewer of live or recorded music is responsive to his readers' needs he must do more than reinforce their current listening habits. Pollination of interest, celebration and illumination of significant musical births or rebirths, a forthright leadership of taste—these are fair expectations. Above all, the critic should strive to appraise the relationship between the objective of the composer and its realization in performance. He should be able to detect embellishment, distortion, or omission in the performer's mirror of the original creative testament.

Only with the advent of machine-made music has it become possible to eliminate divergence from the composer's original inner conception in performance. Differences between two recorded versions of a programmed electronic work are not attributable to variations in interpretive imagination and feeling. As at the morn of Western music, the performing artist has again become a faceless functionary and the computer configuration bears a likeness to the medieval monastery that brought forth musical blossoms out of cloistered anonymity.

Nevertheless, despite the enlarged presence and popularity of electronic music, most contemporary scores require concert personalities to act as alter egos on behalf of composers. Instrumentalists, conductors, and singers may strive to identify with a composer in order to reconstruct the soundscape he sensed at the moment of creation *or* like plastic surgeons, they may apply the cosmetic of artistic license to prettify or reshape the original. We have no means of certifying fidelity to the composer's vision because the notes, dynamic markings, tempo, and phrasing indications in a score are an incomplete tran-

208

scription. Familiarity with the life and times of the composer, technical proficiency, and a selfless subordination of personal whim to the thought and will of a creative genius are united in any "inspired" performance. During such an occasion the concert artist incarnates the composer's spirit. It is *not* charisma or virtuosity that have made Rudolf Serkin, Benedetto Michelangeli, Dinu Lipatti, and Sviatoslav Richter giants of the pianistic world. Their repute is founded upon the universally intuited conviction that Beethoven, Debussy, Chopin, and Mussorgsky have been granted trenchant and truthful readings in their hands. This faithful transmission of messages is a blessing and affirmation of the continuity and communion of human thought and meaning. Assertion of continuity moves an audience because of music's vulnerable and evanescent nature. An analogy can illustrate this peculiar dependency of music. Pretend that no one had ever seen an original Giotto, Rembrandt, or Picasso and that only numbered color charts prescribing pigments and brush strokes to be applied by re-creative artists existed. In addition to this, imagine that all of the original canvases had been destroyed. It would then become mandatory for art critics to themselves be artists and art historians competent enough to see the relationship between reproductions and originals. There is indeed a parallel in music: The charts are scores; the canvases exist only in the minds of composers. Music is totally dependent upon a chain of empathic performances for its persistence in the public mind and it is the heavy responsibility of the critic to watch over and interpret the regeneration of signals from the past.

Book critics do not share this burden because dissimilarities between manuscript and finished book are editorially adjusted so that the emergent statement is settled and definitive. No middlemen are needed and each reader is his own interpreter. A second task, comparison of variant translations and editions, is rarely required of the book reviewer unless his audience is made up of literary scholars. Consequently, the new novel, poetry anthology, or literary essay can be described and analyzed as a single event. In contrast, a proper review of a recorded performance of a popular orchestral work such as Beethoven's Fifth Symphony, Tchaikovsky's *Romeo and Juliet,* or Mussorgsky's *Pictures at an Exhibition* necessitates reappraisal of the whole galaxy of recorded treatments because of the continuing availability of dozens of competitive versions among which a consumer must choose. In the record review business, neglect of comparative analysis is an unpardonable sin.

Appraisal of unfamiliar music is most difficult for the critic. When confronted by an enigmatic work he may be tempted to rationalize the wisdom of a "hit and run" hearing. He may argue that because concert hall audiences at premieres are not served second helpings of strange music, the critic should not give himself the unfair advantage of a sneak preview. Luddite logic is what we have here. The critic should be sympathetic to the listener's comprehension problem, but he should not use this as an excuse to evade homework. He must stay several steps ahead of his readers and if this requires advance study of the score and repeated auditing of the recording—so be it! There is no easier way out with honor. So long as music composition remains an art requiring intellectual muscle and absolute control of the medium, reviewers will owe each new work this courtesy. Only when composing ceases to be a craft will the critic's task change to suit changed conditions.

Beyond knowing his music history and composition, and being blessed with a discriminating ear, the critic must possess the patience and stamina to withstand an appalling amount of self-inflicted listening. Few individuals can fulfill the above requirements, create readable copy, and meet tight publication deadlines. Consequently most newspaper review columns contain pleasantries, not critical commentary. Unfortunately many of the reviews in prominent journals spread this same brand of low-grade fertilizer over a wider area. This becomes particularly offensive when it is used to nourish cultism or the marketplace success of already established recording personalities. Promotional highlighting of trendy offerings of the major recordings labels monopolizes space which might otherwise be occupied by critical appraisals of less prominent companies' productions. Though this policy may increase cash flow, it guarantees that Gresham's law dominates the marketplace. Recordings having the least intrinsic value force out of circulation those sought by music lovers with cultivated tastes. The recording manufacturers have determined that a substantial outlay of dollars for motivational advertising and promotion pays off better than a comparable investment in product development. In too many cases neither critic nor consumer controls the selection prerogative because too few reviewers grant the smaller labels an audition. Because these less affluent companies lack the resources to launch effective promotion campaigns, they may remain unknown to the average buyer until they go bankrupt or are cannibalized by competition. Their final dives to the bottom are heralded by panic-induced purgings of inventories at "drastic cost reductions" and this temporary visibility profits no one except the cannibals.

The six journals profiled immediately below provide the most consistently reliable, balanced, and comprehensive English-language coverage of sound recording activity. Their typical subscriber is the youthful, college bound or educated buyer with a liberal arts background, a person who enjoys the standard operatic, chamber, concert, and jazz repertoires. Each journal profile identifies approximate percentages of total criticism allocated to various categories, range of formats considered, and basic publication facts such as subscription office address, frequency and cost, and estimated number of reviews appearing each year. An annotation characterizes readership and distinguishing emphases and features.

Briefly annotated groupings of smaller-scale reviews which follow after the six profiles are divided into four categories: those which aim at the general public; address themselves to a special audience; focus upon a particular genre; or provide information for performers and music teachers. In a fifth category, an index of review opinion is identified because a large number of institutional buyers desire consensus support to justify their acquisitions decisions.

Major Review Journals

GRAMOPHONE

SUBSCRIPTION DATA:
    Address—General Gramophone Publications, Ltd.
        177–179 Kenton Rd., Harrow
        Middlesex HA3 OHA
        Eng.
    Frequency—Monthly.
        Cost—£6.60 (U.S. $16.50); Air edition $20.00; Air edition with index $20.90.

INDEX DATA: Composer-title index for each issue; yearly index (June–May) available for 90 cents plus postage. Annual index includes composers, works, artists, audio topics, collections, book reviews, stage and screen, and correspondence.
    Reviews analyzed in *MLA Notes* "Index to Record Reviews."

SOUND RECORDING REVIEWS BEGAN: 1923.

APPROXIMATE NUMBER OF REVIEWS PER YEAR: 2,500.

CODING AND GRADING SYSTEMS: None.

GENERAL ARRANGEMENT OF REVIEW SECTION: Classical reviews in orchestral, instrumental, choral and song, opera, Gregorian chant categories; spoken word; reissues, cassettes and cartridges; Nights at the Round Table (light music); popular LPs and singles; Latin American; nostalgia; stage and screen; jazz.

REGULAR FEATURES: Quarterly retrospective surveys; talks to major musical figures; exhibition reports; correspondence; audio commentary; equipment reviews; audio forum; classified advertisements.

PERCENTAGE OF REVIEWS PER CATEGORY: Early Music, 1; Standard Classical, 36; New and Experimental, 2; Jazz, 6; Folk, 2; Musicals, 5; Popular, 30; Prose, Poetry, and Drama, 1; Documentary and Historical, 2; Reissues, 15.

FORMATS CONSIDERED: All standard disc and tape configurations.

GENERAL DESCRIPTION: Most substantial, musically secure, comprehensive coverage of recorded sound. Twenty-four reviewers handle serious music recordings. Prominent musicologists, performers, and other notables are on *Gramophone* staff. Four reviewers are assigned to each of the sections which deal with popular music and jazz. All classical and jazz reviews are signed. The time lag is less than in American magazines and RCA, Columbia, Nonesuch, Vanguard, and other U.S. based manufacturers' output is picked up promptly. Though English labeling differs—e.g., HMV is Angel and Decca is London—it is easy enough to figure out equivalents in *Schwann*. Popular music is only superficially treated, not analyzed as in *Down Beat, Stereo Review, Crawdaddy, Rolling Stone,* or *Sing Out! Gramophone* is most conscientious in its attention to comparative analysis, reissues, historical aspects. Reviewers often discuss previous statements of other contributors. John Borwick's equipment reviews and

Alan Blyth's talks with musical luminaries are informative. *Gramophone* also publishes a series which is the British equivalent to the *Schwann* catalogs. These are quarterly classical and popular record catalogs, and an annual spoken word and miscellaneous catalog in which *Gramophone* review dates are given. In summary, *Gramophone* is essential for all collectors of classical and historically significant sound recordings.

HI-FI NEWS & RECORD REVIEW

SUBSCRIPTION DATA:
  Address—Hi-Fi News & Record Review
      Link House Publications Ltd.
      Dingwall Ave.
      Croydon CR9 2TA
      Eng.
  Frequency—Monthly.
      Cost—£7.50 (U.S. $18.00).

INDEX DATA: Composer-title-performer index for each issue [e.g., "Haydn: Symphonies 93 and 94 (Bernstein)."] Performer-album title index for popular reviews (e.g., "Grand Funk: *We're an American Band"*). Technical articles are cited in *British Technology Index.*

SOUND RECORDING REVIEWS BEGAN: 1935.

APPROXIMATE NUMBER OF REVIEWS PER YEAR: 1,500.

CODING AND GRADING SYSTEMS: Letters A–D designate audio quality; numbers 1–4 indicate very good to poor performance. Superlative interpretations are starred.

GENERAL ARRANGEMENT OF REVIEW SECTION: List of starred classical issues of the month, classical reviews, classical collections; other genres: light, popular, traditional, international, children's, poetry and drama, stage and screen, jazz, miscellaneous. Cassettes are intermittently reviewed in a separate section.

REGULAR FEATURES: Music on Record (compilations of best recordings of composers and interpreters), Historically Speaking, Soundings, Hints and Tips, Gramophile: The Record and Music Scene, articles on performing musicians, equipment reviews, Looking Back (Peter Gammond's column of "second thoughts, new discoveries, and old favorites"), readers' problems and letters, classified advertisements.

PERCENTAGE OF REVIEWS PER CATEGORY: Early Music, 1; Standard Classical, 41; New and Experimental, 2; Jazz, 3; Folk, 3; Musicals, 5; Popular, 27; Prose, Poetry, and Drama, 2; Documentary and Historical, 3; Reissues, 13.

FORMATS CONSIDERED: All standard disc and tape configurations.

GENERAL DESCRIPTION: Prosperous product of merger of John Crabbe's *Hi-Fi News* and Peter Gammond's *Audio Record Review* in 1970. Magazine is about evenly divided in its attention to hi-fi technology and record criticism. Glossy and less sober than *Gramophone.* Over twenty members of its staff concentrate upon classical recordings appraisal. One or two persons are assigned to each of the remaining sections. Review writers are all identified. Coverage of new and reissued recordings is very prompt.

The composer and performer retrospective cumulations of the "Music on Record" section are useful. Popular music receives more careful attention than in *Gramophone*. Photographs and drawings enhance the magazine's appeal. The technical articles and equipment reports are models of clarity and objectivity. Highly recommended for anyone concerned with the topical and technical aspects of sound recordings.

HIGH FIDELITY AND MUSICAL AMERICA

SUBSCRIPTION DATA:
Address—High Fidelity and Musical America
Subscription Dept.
1 Sound Avenue
Marion, Ohio 43302.
Frequency—Monthly.
Cost of *High Fidelity* alone is $7.95. Cost of *High Fidelity* and *Musical America* is $16.00.

INDEX DATA: No indexing of reviews.
Articles are picked up by *Abridged Readers' Guide to Periodical Literature, Readers' Guide to Periodical Literature,* and *Music Index.*
Yearly general index of articles (author and title) is provided. Reviews analyzed in *MLA Notes* "Index to Record Reviews."
SOUND RECORDING REVIEWS BEGAN: 1951.
APPROXIMATE NUMBER OF REVIEWS PER YEAR: 1,000.
CODING AND GRADING SYSTEMS: In the classical section, symbols designate "budget," "historical," and "reissued" recordings. In the popular section, asterisks indicate exceptionally fine performances. Because formats are integrated, symbols are used to specify various reel, cassette, cartridge, disc configurations.
GENERAL ARRANGEMENT OF REVIEW SECTION: Three or four review articles on major classical releases, classical reviews, recitals, and miscellany. The Lighter Side, theater and film, jazz, In Brief; The Tape Deck.
REGULAR FEATURES: Articles on current topics, music and musicians; "Audio and Video" (equipment reports, equipment in the news, news and views, inquiries from readers about hi-fi problems).
PERCENTAGE OF REVIEWS PER CATEGORY: Early Music, 1; Standard Classical, 50; New and Experimental, 4; Jazz, 7; Folk, 1; Musicals, 4; Popular, 26; Documentary and Historical, 3; Reissues, 4.
FORMATS CONSIDERED: All standard disc and tape configurations.
GENERAL DESCRIPTION: Most authoritative American review. Lively and learned comments from classical staff of about twenty musicologists, critics, program annotators including H. C. Robbins Landon, Robert C. Marsh, Alfred Frankenstein, and Harris Goldsmith. Eight reviewers are on lighter music, including the redoubtable John S. Wilson. Popular music comments are intelligent and free from coyness. Fullest treatment of jazz among general audience journals. Contributors are identified for reviews. Across all genres, *HF* provides the most complete coverage but biggest time lag before reviews appear. Comparative analyses and appraisals of

reissues and historically important items are particularly valuable. Subscription to the double publication is advised because *Musical America's* reportage of live music activities (performances, institutions, and personalities) enriches and relates to content of *HF*.

New equipment reports, four or five in each issue, are based upon test data and measurements obtained by CBS Laboratories. *High Fidelity* produces various annuals: a *Test Reports Buying Guide, Buyer's Guide to the World of Tape,* and *Consumer's Guide to Four-Channel Sound.* Its reviews are bound together each year as *Records in Review* annuals published by Scribners.

High Fidelity and these annual cumulations make up a necessary composite selection tool for the record collector.

MONTHLY LETTER

SUBSCRIPTION DATA:
    Address—Monthly Letter
            EMG Hand-Made Gramophones Ltd.,
            26 Soho Sq.
            W1V 6BB
            London, Eng.
    Frequency—Monthly.
        Cost—£3.00 (U.S. $7.20); Air edition £4.50 (U.S. $10.80).

INDEX DATA: No indexing of reviews.
    Reviews analyzed in *MLA Notes* "Index to Record Reviews."
SOUND RECORDING REVIEWS BEGAN: 1930.
APPROXIMATE NUMBER OF REVIEWS PER YEAR: 1,000.
CODING AND GRADING SYSTEMS: Letters indicate sonic quality on a scale ranging from superlative to substandard. Stars designate quality: Two stars indicate thorough recommendation of both performance and technical quality; one star expresses reservations about performance and/or reproduction; and omitted stars indicate many reservations.
GENERAL ARRANGEMENT OF REVIEW SECTION: New records and first reviews—orchestral, concertos, chamber music, organ, keyboard, vocal; transfers and reissues; late arrivals; best of the month list.
REGULAR FEATURES: None. Each issue is 6- x 8–inch pamphlet of approximately twenty pages completely filled with reviews.
PERCENTAGE OF REVIEWS PER CATEGORY: Early Music, 1; Standard Classical, 63; New and Experimental, 3; Musicals, 5; Documentary and Historical, 2; Reissues, 26.
FORMATS CONSIDERED: Disc recordings only.
GENERAL DESCRIPTION: The fastest appearing, most precise and pointed reviews among those printed in these six journals. Opinions are anonymously contributed by the EMG Hand-Made Gramophones Ltd. staff. In format and sponsorship, *Monthly Letter* is similar to the *New Records* (q.v.). Subscription to this journal in combination with the latest edition of the same publisher's the *Art of Record Buying* conveys a complete picture of the British perspective on current and retrospective record production. Its judgments are consistently discriminating, less cautious

and more scornful of poor quality than those of the other journals. It also provides the fullest treatment of reissues. *Monthly Letter* is a bargain which no record collector should bypass.

THE NEW RECORDS

SUBSCRIPTION DATA:
Address—The New Records
2019 Walnut St.
Philadelphia, Pa. 19103.
Frequency—Monthly.
Cost—$6.00.

INDEX DATA: No indexing of reviews.
Reviews analyzed in *MLA Notes* "Index to Record Reviews."
SOUND RECORDING REVIEWS BEGAN: 1933.
APPROXIMATE NUMBER OF REVIEWS PER YEAR: 750.
CODING AND GRADING SYSTEMS: None.
GENERAL ARRANGEMENT OF REVIEW SECTION: Introductory editorial; reviews divided into the following categories: orchestra, concerto, chamber music, opera, choral, vocal, piano, other solo instruments, jazz, miscellaneous; TNRs checklist of current favorites.
REGULAR FEATURES: None. Each issue is 6– x 9–inch pamphlet of approximately sixteen pages completely filled with reviews and editorial observations.
PERCENTAGE OF REVIEWS PER CATEGORY: Early Music, 1; Standard Classical, 69; New and Experimental, 7; Jazz, 2; Musicals, 8; Popular, 1; Prose, Poetry, and Drama, 1; Reissues, 11.
FORMATS CONSIDERED: Disc recordings only.
GENERAL DESCRIPTION: Frank, discerning, musically literate, highly readable, and compact reviews offered by five writers. Aversions and loyalties are unabashedly aired. The *New Records* is a house organ published by H. Royer Smith, Philadelphia record dealers since 1907. Subscribers may order *Schwann* catalogs through TNR. This is a very easy-to-consult, stimulating magazine deserving of its good name in record collecting circles.

STEREO REVIEW

SUBSCRIPTION DATA:
Address—Stereo Review
Circulation Dept.
P.O. Box 2771
Boulder, Colo. 80302.
Frequency—Monthly.
Cost—$7.98.

INDEX DATA: No indexing of reviews.
Articles indexed in *Music Article Guide.*
Reviews analyzed in *MLA Notes* "Index to Record Reviews."

SOUND RECORDING REVIEWS BEGAN: 1958.

APPROXIMATE NUMBER OF REVIEWS PER YEAR: 1,000.

CODING AND GRADING SYSTEMS: Each review is prefaced with a heading epitomizing performance and recording quality, and recordings of special merit are tagged. Because formats are integrated within a single alphabet, symbols are used to designate various reel, cassette, cartridge, and disc configurations.

GENERAL ARRANGEMENT OF REVIEW SECTION: Five or six large-scale reviews of "best of the month" recordings in classical and popular categories; reviews of popular discs and tapes (included are folk, spoken word, and jazz); reviews of classical discs and tapes.

REGULAR FEATURES: Martin Bookspan's "Basic Repertoire" series (comparative evaluations of available recordings of concert favorites), the continuing sequence of articles on American composers, Irving Kolodin's "Choosing Sides" (a seasoned, veteran critic's look at the state of the art of recording), technical articles and reports by Julian Hirsch, "Going on Record"—comments on the contemporary music and recordings scene by *SR* music editor James Goodfriend, Steve Simels' "Simels Reports" and letters to the editor.

PERCENTAGE OF REVIEWS PER CATEGORY: Early Music, 1; Standard Classical, 46; New and Experimental, 6; Jazz, 6; Folk, 2; Musicals, 3; Popular, 30; Prose, Poetry, and Drama, 1; Reissues, 5.

FORMATS CONSIDERED: All standard disc and tape configurations.

GENERAL DESCRIPTION: Regular features are exhilarating reading. Well-qualified classical reviewers include David Hall, Irving Kolodin, George Jellinek, Igor Kipnis, Eric Salzman, and Richard Freed. Five reviewers give popular music extensive and animated coverage. Writing throughout has a fashionably "in" flavor. Arrangement of magazine is uncluttered and convenient for the reader. *Stereo Review* has shown steady improvement over the past decade and is now one of the trio of top American publications dealing with sound recordings.

Other Journals with Reviews

General Audience Reviews

Audio (monthly)
134 N. Thirteenth St.
Philadelphia, Pa. 19107

400–500 reviews in all formats each year. Though most articles deal with audio, Associate Editor Edward Tatnall Canby offers a pithy, candid classical reviews column. Pop, jazz, blues receive selective treatment.

Consumer Reports (monthly)
Consumers Union of the
United States, Inc.
256 Washington St.
Mount Vernon, N.Y. 10550

About 50 reviews per year by an anonymous reporter who has musical intelligence and wit. Classical criticism predominates.

Consumers' Research Magazine
(monthly)
Consumers' Research, Inc.
Bowerstown Rd.
Washington, N.J. 07882

150–200 reviews per year of discs. Walter F. Grueninger's discriminating annotations rate interpretive qualities and sound fidelity. Limited to recordings of merit. Mostly classical.

New York Times—Sunday "Arts and Leisure" section of the newspaper
The New York Times Co.
229 W. 43rd St.
New York, N.Y. 10036

400–500 reviews each year. Fast appearing, trend-conscious criticism of LPs and tapes of all kinds of music. Early American composers, raga rock, John Wayne, theater discography, African music have been highlighted at different times by visiting and staff reviewers. Classical and pop get about equal space.

Records and Recording
(monthly)
Hansom Books Ltd.,
75 Victoria St.
Artillery Mansions
London SW1 HOHZ, Eng.

850–1,000 reviews in all formats. One of a family of seven journals produced by the same publisher. Other journals include *Music and Musicians, Films and Filming, Books and Bookmen.* Classical, jazz, folk, country and western, spoken word covered in a breezy style. More attention to sales and current musical movements than in *Gramophone* and *Hi-Fi News and Record Reviews.*

Saturday Review/World
(bi-weekly)
P.O. Box 2043
Rock Island, Ill. 61206

Only about 100 reviews a year. In the past, Irving Kolodin, Roland Gelatt, and guest reviewers wrote perceptive reviews across all categories. Kolodin now contributes to *Stereo Review* (q.v.) and presently *Saturday Review/World* concentrates most upon live music-making.

Sound & Picture Tape Recording Magazine (monthly)
Anglia Echo Newspapers Ltd.
16a Bevis Marks
London EC3A 7LN, Eng.

About 500 tapes, cassettes, and cartridges are briefly appraised as to sonic and interpretive qualities. Useful for the tape specialist.

Special Audience Reviews

MUSICIAN-SCHOLAR

Musical Quarterly (quarterly)
G. Schirmer, Inc.
866 Third Ave.
New York, N.Y. 10022

Highly respected journal formerly edited by Paul Henry Lang. About 15 very thorough reviews of significant music per volume. Validity of interpretation and score analysis receive careful attention.

Musical Times (monthly)
Novello and Co., Ltd.
U.S. Agent is:
Novello and Co., Ltd.
P.O. Box 1425
Long Island City, N.Y. 11101

Approximately 150 reviews each year. Crisp, erudite, signed criticism across a balanced front of classical music. Contemporary composers, especially English writers, are accorded excellent coverage.

Association for Recorded Sound Collections Journal
James B. Wright
Association for Recorded Sound Collections
Fine Arts Library
University of New Mexico
Albuquerque, N.M. 87131

An excellent source for comprehensive discographies (e.g., all of Leonard Bernstein on disc) and information regarding significant reissues, archival collections, figures, trends, and history of recordings.

Le Grand Baton (varies)
The Sir Thomas Beecham Society
664 South Irena Ave.
Redondo Beach, Calif. 90277

Best among the many journals which deal with great conductors out of the past. Valuable borrowings from other publications and original Beechamiania. Discographies of Sir Thomas and listings of contemporaries Rosa Ponselle, George Szell, Arthur Schnabel, Piero Coppola, et al. Rudolf Kempe is honorary president of the society and its offices are maintained on both sides of the Atlantic. The journal is free to members.

The Hillandale News
(bi-monthly)
"Salterns"
Seal Hollow Rd.
Sevenoaks, Kent, Eng.

For members of the City of London Phonograph and Gramophone Society. Deals principally with early phonographs and recordings. About a dozen items a year are considered. Mostly vocal, operatic, and jazz. An important source for the archivist.

Record Collector (bi-monthly)
17 Saint Nicholas St.
Ipswich 1P1 1TW
Suffolk, Eng.

Dedicated to connoisseurs of recorded vocal rarities. An essential magazine for collectors of early recordings of "immortal" singers.

Recorded Sound (quarterly)
British Institute of Recorded Sound
29 Exhibition Rd.
London S.W. 7, Eng.

Contains texts of the institute's lectures, special discographies, nontechnical retrospective articles, and book reviews.

Views and Reviews (quarterly)
633 W. Wisconsin Ave.
P.O. Box 4115
Milwaukee, Wis. 53203

This informal magazine focuses upon bygone flicks—Mae West, Rin Tin Tin, Hoot Gibson. . . . About a fourth of the space is given over to outstanding recordings with comparative analysis of major interpreters and composers. The critiques can be eccentric and effusive but the airing of information about lesser-known and budget labels is a valuable public service. Discographies prepared by the Koussevitzky Recordings Association and Toscanini Society are regular features. It's fun to read.

The Bruno Walter Society and Sound Archive
P.O. Box 921
Berkeley, Calif. 94701

This society publishes an irregular newsletter which provides data about privately and commercially sponsored Walter discs, many of which are available only through this source.

Other Journals

SCHOOL MEDIA SPECIALISTS AND LIBRARIANS

Booklist (bi-monthly)
American Library Association
50 E. Huron St.
Chicago, Ill. 60611

In 1970 *Booklist* advanced into the sound recordings field. About 100 spoken word and educational market disc and tape recordings are regularly reviewed. Guest contributors add annotated lists in other categories, both topical and musical. The most objective, competent reviews written for librarians.

Children's Record Critique
(bi-monthly)
Louisville Free Public Library
Fourth and York Sts.
Louisville, Ky. 40203

Between 50 and 100 disc recordings for juvenile listening are reviewed for quality and appropriate grade level. Barbara S. Miller, coordinator of Louisville Public Library is editor and primary evaluator.

Media and Methods (monthly
Sept.–May)
134 N. 13th St.
Philadelphia, Pa. 19107

Provides irregular coverage because current educational topics and subjects are targeted in multimedia listings which may or may not include sound recordings. A young, bustling magazine with more verve and alertness than its competition in the media field.

Previews (monthly, Sept.–May)
Non-print Software &
Hardware News & Reviews
1180 Ave. of the Americas
New York, N.Y. 10036

Short, casual statements on about 100 items a year. Picks up primarily faddish productions in all categories.

MUSIC RETAILERS AND ENTREPRENEURS

Billboard (weekly)
Billboard Publications, Inc.
9000 Sunset Blvd.
Los Angeles, Calif. 90069

Indispensable source of insight into the workings of the recordings industry. Buyer profiles, merchandising and marketing, distribution and promotion, music machines, and so on are covered in journalistic, high-pressured prose.

Cash Box (weekly)
119 W. 57th St.
New York, N.Y. 10019

An advance warning, periscope service for people in the business. Over a thousand 4–5 line notices of pops singles and albums estimate payoff potential for newcomers and established performers. Lots of chart data —the top 100 singles, number 1 albums of the week, the previous top ten, and so on.

Record Retailer (weekly)
7 Carnaby St.
London W1V 1PG, Eng.

British nephew of *Billboard*. About 1,700 recordings in all current formats are examined in terms of sales potential. An essential advisory service for English retail outlets.

Record World (weekly)
Record World Publishing Co., Inc.
200 W. 57th St.
New York, N.Y. 10019

Looks at over 2,000 discs with exclusive attention given to sales potential. Only music and spoken word recordings with mass audience appeal are considered. No classical, documentary, or educational market items are included.

219

Variety (weekly)
Variety, Inc.
154 W. 46th St.
New York, N.Y. 10036

Notices of over 1,000 pop productions appear each year in this financial newspaper. Grosses, hits, air plugs, other business action are described. Recordings share space with film, video, radio, music, and stage news.

Musical Genre Reviews

COUNTRY AND WESTERN

Bluegrass Unlimited (monthly)
Bluegrass Unlimited, Inc.
Box 111
Burke, Va. 22015

Good coverage of major label activity. In recent issues, has bestowed more attention upon amateur activities than in the past.

Pickin' Magazine (monthly)
Universal Graphics Corp.
1 Saddle Rd.
Cedar Knolls, N.J. 07927

About 100 reviews a year. Conscientious treatment of offbeat and local country and western labels. New and promising.

FOLK

English Folk Dance and Song
(quarterly)
The English Folk Dance and
Song Society
Cecil Sharp House
2 Regent's Park Rd.
London NW1, Eng.

Between 1 and 10 recordings of folk music are reviewed in each issue. Grade levels are suggested. Subscribers include musicians, teachers, librarians, and collectors.

Ethnomusicology (3 issues/yr.)
Society for Ethnomusicology
SEM, Inc.
Room 513
201 S. Main St.
Ann Arbor, Mich. 48108

About a third of each issue is entirely devoted to signed reviews of privately and commercially produced recordings. Contributors comprise an international gallery of ethnomusicologists. A world-wide mosaic of musical cultures is surveyed.

Sing Out! (bi-monthly)
595 Broadway
New York, N.Y. 10012

Looks at about 75 LPs each year across a wide spectrum of folk music. Concentrates upon offbeat labels ignored by other journals. New releases are posted in a "publications noted" column.

Western Folklore
California Folklore Society
University of California Pr.
Berkeley, Calif. 94720

Norm Cohen has a folk music on record review column which covers a diversity of styles and periods in concise essays. Privately produced and lesser-known labels' recordings of vintage hillbilly, bluegrass, railroad songs, and fiddle tunes are discussed. Bigoted and roseate sentiments alike are noted. Antiminority ditties, prowar songs, paeans of praise for former President Nixon are included along with standard expressions of mass culture.

JAZZ

Coda (6 issues/yr.; freq. varies)
Coda Publications
P.O. Box 87
Station J.
Toronto, Ontario MFJ 4X8
Canada

A vital, expertly edited, generously illustrated journal. John Norris, editor of *Coda*, is one of the pundits in the field. A mandatory magazine for the serious collector because of its first-rate discographical analyses.

Down Beat (fortnightly)
222 W. Adams St.
Chicago, Ill. 60606

Tops among American jazz review journals. Exuberant, relaxed, super-critics, about 25 strong, spin out about 400 reviews. Star ratings are used and everything is signed.

Jazz Hot (11 issues/yr.)
Charles Delaunay, Editor
14 rue Chaptal
Paris (9e), France

Began criticizing jazz recordings in 1935. Reviews between 300 and 600 discs each year. The magazine is addressed to mostly middle-aged people who were jazz buffs during their school and university years. Important for its attention to rare recordings.

Jazz Journal (monthly)
Novello and Co., Ltd.
The Cottage
27 Willow Vale
London W12, Eng.

Finest, all-round magazine in its territory. Reviews about the same number of recordings as *Jazz Hot*. Emphasis is current and all formats are considered. Also covers live events, equipment, and publications.

Matrix: Jazz Record Research Magazine (6 issues/yr.)
c/o Walter C. Allen
P.O. Box 1382
Highland Park, N.J. 08904

Essential for the jazz discographer. Has complete listings for individual artists' production on disc and reviews of limited edition pressings, e.g., Glenn Miller and Jimmy Yancey discographies and Billy Holiday alternative masters.

Storyville (bi-monthly)
Storyville Publications and Co.
63 Orford Rd.
London E17 9NJ, Eng.

About 60 to 70 historically important jazz recordings (LPs, 78s, open reel tapes) are appraised each year.

ROCK AND BLUES

Crawdaddy (monthly)
72 Fifth Ave.
New York, N.Y. 10011

Spectacularly successful magazine. More esoteric and adult than *Creem*. Examines the normal state of rock and jazz. Typical subscriber is 23-year-old adult so magazine soft-pedals transitory crazes. Over 800 reviews per year.

Creem (monthly)
Creem Magazine, Inc.
3729 Cass Ave.
Detroit, Mich. 48201

An omniverous review. *Creem* picks up country and western, rock, soul, experimental and middle ground music for its 18-year-old audience. Over 1,000 reviews each year.

Living Blues (bi-monthly)
917 W. Dakin St.
Room 405
Chicago, Ill. 60613

The accent is on black blues. Fascinating reportage of the ongoing tradition. Reviews are few but authoritative and insightful.

Rolling Stone (bi-weekly)
P.O. Box 2983
Boulder, Colo. 80302

This is the big one. About 1,100 recordings are looked at in a year with egalitarian attention to straight, rock, blues, and kinky offerings. A tough, thriving tabloid.

Zoo World (bi-weekly)
Zoo World, Inc.
Box 5728
Ft. Lauderdale, Fla. 33310

Calls itself a music megapaper. Aims to keep teenagers on top of it all. East coast competitor of *Rolling Stone* with spotlighting of contemporary musical personalities and productions.

CLASSICAL AVANT-GARDE

Melos: Zeitschrift für neue Musik (bi-monthly)
Verlag B. Schott's Söhne
Weihergarten
Postfach 3640
D-65 Mainz, W. Germany

Copiously illustrated, thorough treatment of modern music. Commentary on important premieres, theories and techniques, musical and choreographic analyses, and erudite reviews of recordings of new music make this an exemplary periodical.

Tempo: A Quarterly Review of Modern Music
Boosey and Hawkes, Inc.
30 West 57th St.
New York, N.Y. 10019

About 50 reviews each year. Lucid and authoritative. Produced by British music publisher. Contributors include notable composers and academics.

OPERA

Opera (monthly)
Seymour Press Ltd.
334 Brixton Rd.
London SW9, Eng.

British and continental emphases. Offers comparative, thorough appraisals of a dozen or so opera albums each year.

Opera/Canada (quarterly)
Canadian Opera Association
129 Adelaide St. W. Ste. 517
Toronto, Ontario M5H 1R6
Canada

About same number of reviews as *Opera*. Excellent illustrated coverage of Canadian performances.

Opera News (monthly May–Nov.; irreg. weekly Dec.–Apr.)
Metropolitan Opera Guild, Inc.
1865 Broadway
New York, N.Y. 10023

Published for guild membership. John Freeman evaluates about 3 new opera or aria recital albums in each issue. More informal and "star" conscious than the other two opera journals. Omnibus reviews of sound equipment components appear about once a year.

Reviews for Performers and Music Teachers

Many periodicals are produced specifically for amateur or professional performing musicians. Journals of interest to teachers of music in the schools are also represented in this group. The 14 titles listed below consistently review recordings. Their criticisms are brief, descriptive, few in number, and generally positive in tone because purportedly only the better productions have been picked for inclusion.

American Choral Review
(quarterly)
American Choral Foundation
130 W. 56th St.
New York, N.Y. 10019

American Recorder (quarterly)
Recorder Society, Inc.
141 W. 20th St.
New York, N.Y. 10011

American String Teacher
(quarterly)
American String Teachers
Association
c/o Anthony J. Messina
1745 Hannington Ave.
Wantagh, N.Y. 11793

*Clavier: A Magazine for Pianists
and Organists* (monthly)
Instrumentalist Co.
1418 Lake St.
Evanston, Ill. 60204

Guitar Player (monthly)
Guitar Player Magazine
348 N. Santa Cruz Ave.
Los Gatos, Calif. 95030

Guitar Review (2 or 3 issues/yr.)
Society of the Classic Guitar
409 E. 50th St.
New York, N.Y. 10022

Harpsichord (quarterly)
International Harpsichord
Society
Box 4323
Denver, Colo. 80204

Instrumentalist (monthly)
Instrumentalist Co.
1418 Lake St.
Evanston, Ill. 60204

*Music/AGO-RCCO Magazine/
A.G.O. Magazine*
American Guild of Organists
630 Fifth Ave., Suite 2010
New York, N.Y. 10020

Music Journal (10 issues/yr.;
annual in July)
370 Lexington Ave.
New York, N.Y. 10017

NATS Bulletin (quarterly)
National Association of Teachers
of Singing, Inc.
c/o Roger Scanlan
810 Pin Oak La.
Park Forest South, Ill. 60466

Pan Pipes of Sigma Alpha Iota
(quarterly)
George Banta Co., Inc.
Curtis Reed Plaza
Menasha, Wis. 54952

Piano Quarterly
Box 707
Melville, N.Y. 11746

STRAD: a monthly journal for
professionals and amateurs of
all stringed instruments played
with the bow.
Lavendar Publications Ltd.
Borough Green
Sevenoaks, Kent, Eng.

Reviewer Opinion Index

Notes: The Quarterly Journal of the Music Library Association
Executive Secretary: William J. Weichlein
343 S. Main St.
Room 205
Ann Arbor, Mich. 48108

Contains an index to record reviews. Two sections list composer and composite-recital recordings respectively. Sixteen major periodicals are interpreted by *Notes* and +, −, •, and other symbols are used to convey the gist of critical judgments. This service has been expanded to cover folk and popular music. A very handy source. About six months elapse between a review's publication and its citation in *Notes*.

Buying Sound Recordings 4

For the would-be purchaser who has compiled a list of desirable works taken from this guide and other sources, there remain three tasks: (1) identification of specific recorded versions of all titles, (2) selection of efficient and economical buying routes, and (3) preparation of purchase orders which clearly convey the customer's wishes to the vendor.

Lists

Keys and Indexes to Current Recordings
Schwann Catalogs
W. Schwann Inc. Publications, 137 Newbury St., Boston, Mass. 02116

Schwann–1 Record and Tape Guide. Monthly. $1.00/issue.
  This lists about 45,000 stereo LP records, 8–track cartridge tapes, and cassette tapes on over 800 disc and 250 tape labels.

Schwann–2 Record and Tape Guide. Semiannual supplement to *Schwann–1*. $.90/issue.
  This includes religious, spoken word, domestic popular music recordings which are more than two years old, international pop and folk music on U.S. labels, classical on lesser known labels, monophonic, and electronically simulated stereo recordings.

Schwann Artist Issue. 1970. $1.75/issue. Out of print.

Schwann Children's Record and Tape Guide. 1974–75 edition. Annual. $.40/issue.
  This includes over 1,400 mono and stereo recordings, 8–track cartridge, and cassette tapes on over 100 labels. Few of the music recordings deserve consideration because drab, technically disappointing renditions of overarranged classics or contrived pap predominate. However, this *Guide* is excellent for children's literature.

The Schwann family of publications is comparable to *Books in Print* in function and importance. *Schwann–1* and *Schwann–2* provide the most com-

prehensive and error-free inventory of recordings currently available through normal trade channels in the U.S.A. The high volume of production and rapidity of change in the industry makes a subscription to the pair of publications mandatory for all institutional purchasers of sound recordings. Since its inception in 1949, the Schwann organization has cataloged the LP record industry's growth. A complete description of the Schwann compilation and arrangement appears in the preface to each catalog. However, the following comments will be of interest to librarians:

1. Each *Schwann–1* provides a separate subsection of "New Listings" with contents analytics for composite composer-title discs and tapes. Regrettably, this very helpful feature has been drastically curtailed during recent years.
2. A manufacturers' price list appears in the back of each *Schwann–1* issue.
3. Items which have been cut out from manufacturers' catalogs are dropped as soon as Schwann has been notified of their discontinuance.
4. Birth and death dates accompany entries in the main composer sections of *Schwann–1* and *Schwann–2*.
5. Particular care has been given to verification of listings of contemporary American composers.
6. Electronic music is represented in a separate listing with cross references provided from the main composer section.
7. William Schwann, president and originator of the publication, retains his personal commitment to sustain the catalog's reputation as a dependable compiler and cultural catalyst for the recording industry. Readers' correspondence regarding errors or omissions is encouraged and conscientiously acknowledged.
8. The opera and ballet tables included in *Schwann–1* are handy for quick confirmation of work categories and for linking unknown composers to familiar titles.
9. Some public and radio station libraries, especially those with large holdings and closed stacks, have used Schwann listings as models for their cataloging and have shelved their recordings by manufacturer number.
10. The artist issues which have appeared sporadically (1963, 1966, 1970) are immensely valuable as tools for tracking down performances by pianists, string quartets, sopranos, percussionists, conductors, orchestras, and other executants. Which orchestras had Igor Stravinsky conducted? Are there recordings of Ravel or Rachmaninoff playing their own piano pieces? Where can one find koto, biwa, and zither recordings? What American composers had been performed by the Louisville Orchestra as of 1970? Answers to such questions are contained in this discontinued series of issues.

Record stores will supply courtesy copies of *Schwann–1* to regular customers. In the past, large discount houses had provided this same gratuitous service but this practice has ceased. Institutions and individuals must now pay for their subscriptions. Schwann prefers not to handle subscriptions but many of the record outlets do. The following dealers will accept orders: (1) Book Clearing House, Inc., 376 Boylston St., Boston, Mass. 02116; (2) National Record Plan, 44 W. 18th St., New York, N.Y. 10011; (3) The Record Hunter, 507 Fifth Ave., New York, N.Y. 10017; (4) A. H. Roemer Co., 1166 W.

Chestnut St., Union, N.J. 07083; (5) Rose Discount Records, Inc., 214 S. Wabash Ave., Chicago, Ill. 60604; (6) H. Royer Smith, 2019 Walnut St., Philadelphia, Pa. 19103; and (7) Schmitt Music Co., 88 S. 10th St., Minneapolis, Minn. 55403.

Harrison Tape Guide
143 W. 20th St., New York, N.Y. 10011.
Harrison Tape Guide. Bi-monthly. $1.00/issue; $5.50/yr.
This lists prerecorded tapes in all configurations; 8–track, cassette, open reel, quadraphonic, and so on. Dolbyized tapes are keyed. The majority of listings comprise popular, folk, jazz, shows, films, television, operetta, Hawaiian, and international popular categories with classical items occupying only about a fifth of the catalog's pages. Those who are also interested in discs should supplement Harrison with the two Schwann catalogs. The *Harrison Tape Guide* is recommended as a necessary and convenient tool for purchasers who are primarily interested in popular tapes. Catalogs may be obtained at most stores which sell prerecorded tapes (record shops, tape/hi-fi centers, automotive accessory outlets, music and camera shops).

Trade Service Publications, Inc.
One-Spot Publishing Division, 701 E. Prospect Ave., Mt. Prospect, Ill. 60056.
Weekly New Release Reporter. Weekly. $4.50/month.
This lists all new pop recordings; singles, EPs, and LPs, and is indexed by title and artist. New releases for the week are listed in the first part of each issue. Quarterly cumulations, designated as "Permanent File Editions," may be retained to provide a comprehensive listing of the reporting companies' popular music output for the year. Complete content analysis is provided for most albums in the "New This Week" and title sections.
Monthly Popular Guide. $5.00/month.
A comprehensive EP/LP index to the top pop singles, standards, specialties, and song titles most often requested from albums. About 400 labels are represented. This monthly index is issued in separate artist and title sections.
Numerical Index. Bi-monthly. $5.00/month.
The complete EP and LP catalogs, both classical and popular, for over 100 labels are listed in numerical, manufacturer number sequence. This looseleaf service documents the current production and is an effective reference, ordering, and inventory tool for depository institutions, archives, radio stations, and other organizations with extensive holdings. The content analysis of albums is very helpful.

Larger public libraries with a commitment to keep pace with popular trends should consider subscription to *New Release Reporter* and the *Monthly Popular Guide* because elusive titles, artists' repertoires, and various recordings of hits may be quickly traced through these indexes. The *Numerical Index* is most useful for organizations which shelve their disc recordings by manufacturer number.

Phonolog Publishing Division, Trade Service Publications, Inc.
2720 Beverly Blvd., Los Angeles, Calif. 90057.

Phonolog Reporter. Looseleaf with weekly replacement sheets. $11.00/month. The Los Angeles-based Trade Service Publications' *Phonolog Reporter* has been analyzing and indexing LP, EP, and 78 rpm recordings since 1948. Several times a week subscribers receive inserts to add to their looseleaf compendium. Currently *Phonolog* contains over 6,000 8½- by 11-inch pages with more than one million separate listings. The inserts are usually replacement sheets which include additions, changes, and deletions in manufacturers' catalogs. Deletions, because of the time it takes before dealer stocks are exhausted, are ordinarily not noted until six weeks have elapsed.

Phonolog is divided into six principal tabulated sections, three for popular and three for classical music. These groupings are "Pop Titles," "Pop Albums," "Pop Artists," "Classical Titles," "Classical Artists," and "Classical Composers." Unlike *Schwann*, in which the main entries are under composer names, the manufacturer numbers and contents breakdowns appear only within the titles sections with referrals from the other entries. Ten additional subsections cover the following categories: "Bands," "Christmas music," "Children's records," "Hawaiian," "Latin American," "Motion Pictures," "Sacred," "Show tunes," "Specialties and miscellaneous," and "Theme Songs."

The following features are especially useful for librarians:

1. A current and comprehensive listing of manufacturers' addresses is provided. Cross references from subsidiary labels and series to the parent labels facilitate convenient use of this directory.
2. Popular music titles and variant versions of children's classics, e.g., *Winnie the Pooh* and *Alice in Wonderland*, folk songs, recommended science and history recordings can be quickly located for order purposes.
3. Individual art songs, arias, instrumental and orchestral titles are represented. *Phonolog* is the best source for confirming trade data whenever one cannot cite a composer or parent work from which a title is excerpted.
4. The composer listing is more comprehensive than those in *Schwann* and *Harrison*. As in the latter two guides, birth and death dates are provided.
5. Instrumentalists, vocal artists, conductors, performing organizations are integrated within the "Classical Artists" section. It is therefore unnecessary to conduct multiple searches through various lists of conductors, oboists, choral groups, opera ensembles as it had been in the Schwann "Artists Issue" compilations.

In summary, most large public libraries with active audio-visual departments, radio station libraries, and urban school district media centers should find the *Phonolog Reporter* very helpful for reference, ordering, and inventory work. These institutions should send for a sample set of inserts and weigh the convenience gained versus the cost. Subscriptions from libraries, educational institutions, and radio networks are accepted only on an annual basis. The stand for the *Phonolog* and a complete accumulation of current inserts costs $35.00. Purchase of both the stand and inserts is advised with new subscriptions.

List-O-Tapes: All in One Tape Catalog. Looseleaf with weekly replacement sheets. $3.00/month.
List-O-Tapes indexes reel, cartridge, and cassette tapes in the same manner as its sibling service, *Phonolog Reporter* indexes disc recordings. Though a much smaller catalog than *Phonolog Reporter* with about one-twentieth the volume of entries, *List-O-Tapes'* dimensions and value will no doubt increase as the tape format's virtues are proven to the public and production volume rises. As in *Phonolog*, complete information is provided in the title sections with cross references from the artist and composer entries. *List-O-Tapes* is divided into five principal sections: "Pop Titles," "Pop Artists," "Classical Titles," "Classical Artists," and "Composers." Each week subscribers receive new pages to interfile within these sections and a report on new releases. Format and speed specifications for reels, cartridges, and cassettes are designated by symbols accompanying main title entries. Addresses of major producers of all labels with tape sources (e.g., Ampex, GRT, etc.) and suggested retail prices are given in a directory section. There are also reference lists which isolate selection titles alphabetically under eighteen different headings. Headings include "Children's," "Operas and Operettas," "Organ," "Spoken Word," "Christmas," "Folk Singers," and "Violin." The five convenience features noted above for *Phonolog* apply as well to *List-O-Tapes*.

Institutional buyers that anticipate a thousand dollar or higher annual expenditure on tapes should seriously consider *List-O-Tapes*. Subscriptions from libraries, educational institutions, and radio networks are accepted only on an annual basis. A binder complete with tabs and current inserts is provided to subscribers at no extra charge.

National Information Center for Educational Media.
University of Southern California, University Park, Los Angeles, Calif. 90007.
NICEM Index to Educational Records. $42.50 (book); $28.50 (microfiche). 3d edition 1974.
This is a selective bibliographical guide to more than 22,000 commercially produced educational records. Titles are given brief descriptive statements which include the following data: speed, number of sides, whether stereo or monophonic. In most cases, audience and/or grade level suitability is indicated. Titles are filed under curricular subject headings in a separate section to expedite the search for instructional materials. Producer and distributor addresses are appended to the catalog. Manufacturer numbers and prices are omitted and the universe of titles is limited to those produced by companies that send information to NICEM. Accordingly many companies with products of potential merit are missing. The main section of the *Index* is an "Alphabetical Guide to Educational Records" which is, in accordance with current practice, arranged by title. This results, especially in the case of classical recordings, in some arbitrary and confusing entries. Charles Ives and John Cage appear only under their first names; Bach, without any cross references, appears under J.S.; *La Bohème, La Traviata*, and *La Mer* cluster together under La. Typographical errors abound. It is hoped that these deficiencies will diminish in later editions

so that this source can become a more reliable and useful tool for those who seek to integrate media with school instructional programs.

NICEM Index to Educational Audio Tapes. $42.50 (book); $28.50 (microfiche) 3d edition 1974.

This is a selective bibliographical guide to more than 24,000 commercially produced audio tapes and cassettes. The kinds of data provided and demur expressed in connection with the *NICEM Index to Educational Records* apply with equal weight to this index. Running times to the nearest minute accompany about half of the entries. Presumably it should be useful for program planners to know that Pearl Buck and the Adlers take up eight and twenty-nine minutes respectively to answer questions about themselves and their books or that *Howard K. Smith, Codes, Ciphers, and Cryptanalysis,* and *Sir Thomas Beecham on Music* consume fifty-five, fifteen, and thirteen minutes each. Because of the proliferation of cassettes and lack of well-structured and current keys to what is relevant and available this NICEM index could become an indispensable professional tool if its initial shortcomings can be sufficiently diminished.

Because the NICEM index annotations are only descriptive and not critical, prospective purchasers must consult supplementary review sources and/or pre-audit all items prior to reaching acquisitions decisions.

One hopes that the federal government can in the future assume leadership in the cataloging of nonprint media. Technology, pending changes in copyright law, the ever-mounting chagrin and confusion among those who must contend with a maze of contradictory, incomplete, chaotically arranged, mutually inconsistent and out-of-date indexes make the assumption of federal responsibility in this area highly desirable.

Evaluative Listings in Books

The titles which appear in this section exclude pre-1970 publications because of the rapid ebb and flow in the recording market. The Cohn discography is cited because of the relative stability of contemporary classical music in comparison with less esoteric genres. All of the remaining books have established reputations and followings to insure their continuation in updated editions. Any serious record collector and all libraries desiring to maintain or create strong collections should own all titles.

Berendt, Joachim. *The Jazz Book: From New Orleans to Rock and Free Jazz.* New York: Hill and Wang, 1974.

This thorough, scholarly, lively guide is kept up-to-date by new editions. An extensive discography is provided by Dan Morgenstern in an appendix. In Europe, Berendt is considered the most authoritative history and guide in this genre.

Bookspan, Martin. *101 Masterpieces of Music and Their Composers.* New York: Doubleday, 1975.

Mr. Bookspan, former director of radio station WQXR in New York City and currently a contributing editor of the *Stereo Review,* has focused upon recorded interpretations of "basic repertoire" works for over a decade. His book contains a checklist of recommended disc and tape

versions of 101 concert favorites. Precisely stated and perceptive comparisons of two or more different interpretations are offered for most of the titles. The background annotations on the music and composers, and the bibliography make this useful for librarians and laymen who lack basic familiarity with classical music. Bookspan's opinions tend to mirror current, liberal American musical thinking.

Cohn, Arthur. *Twentieth-Century Music in Western Europe: The Compositions and the Recordings.* Philadelphia: Lippincott, 1965; Da Capo (reprint), 1972.
This is a dated but still useful discography by an eminent American composer, conductor, and observer of the contemporary musical scene.

Greenfield, Edward; Layton, Robert; and March, Ivan. *Stereo Record Guide.* London: Long Playing Record Library Ltd., 1961–74.
9 vols. (Available through Long Playing Record Library Ltd., Squires Gate Station Approach, Blackpool, Lancashire, England FY 82 SPU.) Vols. 5 and 6 were published in 1968, vols. 7 and 8 in 1972, vol. 9 in 1974.
Ivan March, director of the Long Playing Record Library Ltd. and editor of this series, has written more than a dozen books on sound recordings. One of his more recent publications, *Gramophone Record Librarianship in the Future,* deals with record library administration in depth and contains a section on practices in European institutions.
Later volumes in the *Stereo Record Guide* series are self-sufficient and meant to replace earlier numbers, some of which are now out of print. This series has been outstanding. Orchestral, vocal, instrumental, and humor categories are analyzed by contributors who have attained the bloom and vigor of a vintage Burgundy in the richness of their perceptions. The writing is lucid; the appraisals are sound. Triple star performances and notable failures are given evenhanded treatment. Although Arnold Bax, Michael Tippett, and other British composers receive proportionately more attention, American representation is not slighted. Comparative analysis of recorded interpretations is particularly strong. This series is highly recommended especially for home collectors.

Haggin, Bernard H. *The New Listener's Companion and Record Guide.* 4th ed. New York: Horizon Press, 1974.
Mr. Haggin has been reviewing musical performance on and off record for forty years. His *Music for the Man Who Enjoys "Hamlet"* and two books on Toscanini contain a wealth of witty, informed, and frank commentary on matters musical articulated by a mind and sensibility untouched by faddishness. Here you will find a concise and urbane introduction to musical form and precise summaries of Mozart's, Mussorgsky's, and Berlioz' contributions. His annotations for recordings pull no punches. Modernists may be startled by the conservative tone. Charles Ives, the aleatoric composers, and Béla Bartók are not Haggin favorites. The discographies in the latter half of the book are most valuable in the baroque, classical, and romantic repertoires. Versions "to be avoided" are cited and plentiful comparative analysis is provided.

Merriam, Alan P. *African Music on LP: An Annotated Discography.* Evanston: Northwestern University Pr., 1970.

This is a scholarly, comprehensive listing which should be purchased by large public and university libraries and all institutions and individuals interested in the recorded heritage of black history and folk music.

Roach, Helen. *Spoken Records.* 3d ed. Metuchen, N.J.: Scarecrow Pr., 1970.

Roach's annotated discography of American and English literature remains the best single, monographic source of critical commentary on nonmusical recordings. Suggestions for a basic collection are presented in the introduction and separate chapters deal with documentaries, authors' readings of their own works, actors' interpretations, and plays. Subsections treat public speeches, documentaries, Dickens, Bible and Shakespeare recordings. The criticisms are informal and brief. The introductory chapter's basic list of 40 recordings includes Homer's *Iliad*, Martin Luther King speeches, *Wind in the Willows*, Wodehouse's *Jeeves*, and "I can hear it now." A ninety page appendix contains eleven articles and essays among which the discussion of the oral study of literature by Algernon Tassin and G. Robert Vincent's history of the National Voice Library are particularly informative. Dr. Roach's selection of 28 children's recordings provides an excellent but limited and eclectic base from which to expand youngsters' tastes. Cute, contrived, unconvincingly projected performances are excluded because the author believes that "they are deadening to sensitive listening and may do more harm than is realized."

This book is admirable because of its impressive range, uncompromising critical standard, and illuminating discussion of performance and production pitfalls encountered by those who record the spoken word.

Publications Issued by Educational and Curricular Subject Specialists

(Appropriateness, sonic, and performance qualities of items listed in these sources should be corroborated by personal audition and/or favorable reviews.)

Gaver, Mary V. *The Elementary School Library Collection.* (6th ed. and suppl. Newark: Bro-Dart Foundation, 1974.

Approximately 500 sound recordings, mostly 33 rpm monophonic, are included. Conventional classical, folk and popular music, excerpts, arrangements, and anthologies suitable for curricular use predominate. Only about 5 percent of the representation is classical and much of it has been superseded by technically and artistically superior versions. Bartók, Debussy, Schubert, Haydn, Mendelssohn, and other composers who have penned music appropriate for elementary age listening have been overlooked. In contrast, the selection of spoken word is excellent. Biography, poetry, documentaries, and historical reenactments, children's literature, science, nature, mathematics, speech, Morse code, and sex instruction are areas which have been thoughtfully and thoroughly handled.

The *Collection* is an effective selection guide for school staffs charged with developing educational holdings for elementary media centers.

Association for Childhood Education. *Childhood Education.* Washington, D.C.: ACEI, 19–

> Sometimes contains useful discographies; six issues a year.

Music Educators National Conference. *Music in General Education.* Washington, D.C.: MENC, 1965.

National Center for Audio Tapes. *NCAT Catalog, 1970–1972.* Boulder: University of Colorado, 1972.

> This catalog lists over 12,000 audio programs in cassette and open reel formats suitable for use from the elementary level through to college.

National Council of Teachers of English. 508 S. Sixth St., Champaign, Ill. 61820.

> *Resources for the Teaching of English.*
> *Annotated List of Recordings in the Language Arts.*

New York Library Association. Children's and Young Adult Services Section. *Recordings for Children: A Selected List.* 3d ed. New York: N.Y. Library Association, 1972. rev. An adequate, balanced group of titles upon which to build a collection. Better in folk music and spoken word than in the classical genres.

Westinghouse Learning Corporation. *Learning Directory.* New York: Westinghouse Learning Press, 1970; supplement, 1973. 7 vols. and supplement.

> A detailed index by topic, audience level, and medium to titles of instructional resources in forty-seven different formats. Volume 8, the supplement, includes instructional materials issued after January 1971. Dates of production, running times, prices, publisher/producer facts are provided. This index has, to a lesser degree, the deficiencies noted in the previously described NICEM indexes.

Subject or Topical Guides

National Council of Churches. *Audio-Visual Resource Guide.* Cincinnati: Friendship Press, 1972.
(Order from Friendship Press, P.O. Box 37844, Cincinnati, Ohio 45237)

> This frequently revised compilation supports social studies subjects and value education. Critical evaluations with suggested age levels for all items. Abortion, Abraham, God, human rights, East Indian cultures are among the wide range of topics for which nonprint materials are listed.

Library and Special Repository Holdings Lists

Library of Congress. *Folk Recordings Selected from the Archive of Folk Song.* Washington, D.C.: Library of Congress, 1974.
(Available from U.S. Library of Congress, Music Division, Recorded Sound Section, Washington, D.C. 20540).

> Representation of 62 out of the more than 16,000 recordings in this very important archival collection. This list contains Anglo- and Afro-American folk music, animal tales, child ballads, railroad songs, American Indian music, and a series produced by John A. Lomax.

————. *Spoken Recordings Selected from the Archive of Recorded Poetry and Literature and the Archive of Hispanic Literature on Tape.* Washington, D.C.: Library of Congress, 1974. (Available from U.S. Library of Congress, Music Division, Recorded Sound Section, Washington, D.C. 20540).

> List contains recordings of twentieth-century poets reading their own poems, a 3-disc anthology of 46 poets reading 78 poems, a 5-record "Leaves of Grass" centennial issue of Walt Whitman poetry, interviews with Henry L. Mencken, and poems read by Pedro Salinas and Gabriela Mistral.

Library of Congress Catalog, Music, Books on Music, and Sound Recordings. Washington: Library of Congress, 1974–

> Catalog cards photographically reduced and in book form indicating the holdings of music and recordings at the Library of Congress.

"Recordings for Children." *Illinois Libraries,* April 1970. Periodically updated list of LPs for children which the Illinois State Library has for circulation. Other state libraries provide similar inventories of sound recordings. Some of the larger municipal libraries (e.g., Boston and New York) have outstanding recording collections in their music divisions.

Major Record Retailers That Provide Basic Lists

Chambers Record Corp., 97 Chambers St., New York, N.Y. 10007
Chesterfield Music Shops, Inc., 12 Warren St., New York, N.Y. 10007
Educational Record Sales, Inc., 157 Chambers St., New York, N.Y. 10007
Sam Goody, Inc., 46–35 54th Rd., Maspeth, N.Y. 11378
National Record Plan, 44 W. 18th St., New York, N.Y. 10011

The Record Hunter, 507 Fifth Ave., New York, N.Y. 10017. The "basic libraries" brochures distributed by these dealers are more promotional than objectively critical, but they can expedite the order preparation routine because manufacturer numbers usually accompany the basic composer-title data. Customers also get a clear indication of the depth and variety of the dealer's stock.

Special Audience and Connoisseur Labels

The following producers have established strength in specialized areas. The quality within the confines of their specialties is consistently high and deletion rates are low. These companies have developed reputations for artistic and technical excellence. Their catalogs may be used as adjunct tools for librarians and home listeners who wish to enrich their holdings in the special areas indicated opposite the labels.

LABEL	SPECIALTIES
Argo Record Co. 9 Albert Embankment London SE1 7SW, Eng. (distributed in the U.S.A. by Argo Sight and Sound Ltd., 539 W. 25th St., New York, N.Y. 10001)	A London subsidiary. Early, baroque, renaissance, contemporary vocal and choral literatures. Catalog incorporates Telefunken (definitive early music interpretations) and l'Oiseau Lyre listings as well.

LABEL	SPECIALTIES
C.M.S. Recordings Inc. (Chesterfield Music Shops) 12 Warren St. New York, N.Y. 10007	C.M.S. produces and distributes music and spoken word recordings which relate to the needs of public and school district libraries. Many first-rate though lesser-known American composers and performers are best represented in the Desto catalog which is available through C.M.S.
Caedmon Records, Inc. 505 Eighth Ave. New York, N.Y. 10018 (A Division of Houghton Mifflin, 110 Tremont St., Boston, Mass. 02107)	Authors' readings; theater, prose, and poetry. Has absorbed Shakespeare Recording Society and Theatre Recording Society catalogs.
Composers Recordings, Inc. 170 W. 74th St. New York, N.Y. 10023	Largest and oldest company dedicated exclusively to the recording of contemporary music. Includes 20 Pulitzer Prize winners recorded before they were Pulitzer Prize winners. This label has the largest proportional representation of women and black composers. No deletions.
Cornell University Laboratory of Ornithology 159 Sapsucker Woods Rd. Ithaca, N.Y. 14850	About 40 small but authoritative catalogs of disc and cassette recordings of song birds with slides to match. Records are also listed.
Droll Yankees Inc. P.O. Box 2447 Providence, R.I. 02906	American folklore and humor.
Folkways/Scholastic Records 50 W. 44th St. New York, N.Y. 10036	Folk music, nature, and science for educational use.
Louisville Recording Society 211 Brown Bldg. 321 W. Broadway Louisville, Ky. 40202	Premieres of American composers' works.
Newbery Award Records, Inc. c/o Miller-Brody Productions 342 Madison Ave. New York, N.Y. 10017	Readings of children's stories which have won Newbery Awards. First through fourth runners-up have also been recorded.
Nonesuch Records 15 Columbus Circle New York, N.Y. 10023	Outstanding, musically significant, budget-priced pressings of new electronic music and jewels of the baroque period.
Spoken Arts, Inc. 310 North Ave. New Rochelle, N.Y. 10016	Readings in foreign languages and English of contemporary and established masterpieces of poetry and drama. Many recordings of authors presenting their own works. Elementary and secondary school catalogs are available.

LABEL	SPECIALTIES
Vanguard Recording Society, Inc. 71 W. 23rd St. New York, N.Y. 10010	Notable strength in the Renaissance and baroque eras. Bach Guild, Cardinal, Everyman Classics, Surround Stereo labels have many fine offerings. Significant Newport Festivals, early Baez and Weavers, Mississippi John Hurt, and a superlative historical anthology (HM series) are included.

Major Manufacturers and Subsidiary Labels

Seven manufacturers and their subsidiaries, much like the "seven sisters" of the oil industry, control over ninety percent of the activity in the U.S. market. Accordingly their catalogs' contents are an accurate index of public taste and a helpful reminder of the numerous styles and forms of music and spoken word which may be purchased. In this respect, these listings resemble any other home order catalogs. It is possible to acquire a basic collection without straying beyond the limits of these seven producers but if one elects this route, the quality will be uneven and circumscribed by the lowest common denominator of prevailing general audience preference. Cambridge Records, Desto, CRI, Louisville, Vanguard, Nonesuch, the other specialty and connoisseur labels are necessary to create a cosmopolitan collection with adequate representation of younger artists and writers. Inevitably each large recording empire has its unique profile of strengths and weaknesses. The larger conglomerates cannot totally avoid bland or blank regions in one or more spoken word or musical categories, and so exclusive dependence upon only two or three companies is unwise. As a matter of cultural responsibility, one should reward the artistic courage of the smaller, independent producers and discourage the monopolistic drive of the giants in the field.

The summary which follows demonstrates the complexity of the network of interrelationships between parent corporations, manufacturers, and subsidiary labels.

PARENT CORPORATION	MAJOR MANUFACTURER	SUBSIDIARY LABELS
American Broadcasting Co. 1330 Ave. of the Americas New York, N.Y. 10019	Westminster Recording Co., Inc.	Audio Treasury, Award Artists, Back Beat, Bluesway, Command, Duke, Dunhill, Grand Award, Impulse, Jerden, LHI, Movietone, Music Guild, Peacock, Probe, Riverside, Senate, Simon Says, Song Bird, 20th Century Fox, Westminster Gold Label, Whitehall
Capitol Records, Inc. 1750 N. Vine St. Hollywood, Calif. 90028	Capitol Records Inc.	Angel, Apple, Burdette, Capitol/Pickwick, Hand, Harvest, Hot Biscuit Disc, Invictus, Island, Mango, Melodiya/Angel, Melodiya/Capitol, Melodiya/Seraphim, Seraphim, Shelter, Showtown, Uptown, Zapple

PARENT CORPORATION	MAJOR MANUFACTURER	SUBSIDIARY LABELS
Columbia Broadcasting System 51 W. 52d St. New York, N.Y. 10019	Columbia	Blue Sky, Columbia, Columbia Special Products Div., CBS, Epic, Gamble, Harmony, Invictus, Kirshner, Monument, Mums, Odyssey, Philadelphia International, T-Neck
Decca Record Company, Ltd. Decca House Albert Embankment London SE1 7SW, Eng.	London Records 539 W. 25th St. New York, N.Y. 10001	(Das) Alte Werk (*see* Telefunken), Argo, Ashley, Chapter One, Coliseum, Coral, Deram, Global Heritage Series, H1, London International, Mach (rock), MAM (Gilbert & Sullivan), Oiseau-Lyre, Orphic Egg, Parrot, Press, Phase 4 Stereo, Richmond, Sire, Stereo Treasury Series (classical budget), Telefunken, Threshold, Tribe, United Kingdom
RCA Corp. 30 Rockefeller Plaza New York, N.Y. 10020	RCA Corp. (owns National Broadcasting Company and has rights on early NBC performances, e.g., Toscanini, Rubinstein)	Amsterdam, Camden, Flying Dutchman, Erato, Grunt, Red Seal Stereo, Signature, Victor, Victrola
Polygram GmbH* Harvestehuder-Weg-1-4 Postfach 132266 D–2000 Hamburg 13, West Germany	Phonogram 1700 Broadway New York, N.Y. 10019	Mercury — Blue Rock, Dial, Golden Imports Series, Gregar, Intrepid, Fontana, Limelight, Pulsar, Smash, Vertigo, Wing, MGM Philips — Golden Classics
	Polydor 1700 Broadway New York, N.Y. 10019	Archive (classical), Deutsche Grammophon Gesellschaft (classical), People, Sire, Soul Classics, Spring

---

*Parent corporations of Polygram are Siemens A.G., specializing in electronics and electrical engineering, and Philips' Gloeilampenfabrieken, specializing in petroleum products.

Siemens A.G.
Postfach 103 D-8000
München, West Germany
also
D-1000 Berlin, West Germany

Philips'
Gloeilampenfabrieken, N.V.
Hoofdkantoor, Pieter Zeemanstraat
Eindhoven, Netherlands

PARENT CORPORATION	MAJOR MANUFACTURER	SUBSIDIARY LABELS
U.S. office: 450 Park Ave. New York, N.Y. 10022		
Vox Corp. 211 E. 43d St. New York, N.Y. 10017	Vox Corp.	Candide, Turnabout Historical Series, Turnabout Vox, Stereo Vox

Where to Buy

Record buying patterns and sales psychology are not what they were twenty years ago. In the 1950s, because of the openness and simplicity of customer approaches permitted by less aggressive and more specialized sales techniques, musically significant but commercially unpromising titles such as Vivaldi's *Four Seasons* and Berg's *Wozzeck* were able to achieve moderate profits for the industry. Within a small production stream their merit was easy for the public to discern. With bigness came the submergence of sympathetic and informative sales staffs. The formerly accepted practice of preauditing recordings before buying evaporated. (The musical literacy of sales staffs also waned.) Though there is presently a richer and more stimulating production of recordings than ever before, the merchandizing system has created a kink in the supply line between superior, small-scale producers and consumers with selective needs. It is hoped that the decline of the local record man can be halted because his store remains the best place where large and small companies alike can make accessible a representative cross-section of their entire production. The self-service racks in the supermarkets, drug, and department stores distribute fast-moving popular music and the most heavily promoted and least distinguished items of the leading five or six catalogs. They are not to be blamed because this is the only kind of stock which will insure a quick turnover. However, in this contact, the public is led by its nose and deprived of an opportunity to pick from the whole realm of recorded sound.

In summary, there is no doubt that if the staff is alert, experienced, and responsible, the preferred place for personal attention, convenience, and access to the greatest wealth of recordings remains the local record store. Despite the disparaging reports of deteriorating service at this level, it is recommended that this be the starting point for the home and small volume buyer with less than $250.00 a year to spend.

Bearing the foregoing remarks in mind, a procedure for testing the effectiveness of a local dealer is suggested. Draw up a list of disc and tape recordings and confirm their inclusion in the latest Schwann and Harrison catalogs. Then present the list to the dealer. He should be able to track down the recordings more quickly than the customer who must resort to direct correspondence with the companies and authorized distributors. If part of the order is out of stock, have the store order the records. If no local action has occurred

(e.g., no proof of letters sent out within a week after the request) and no records have arrived in response to the order after a month has elapsed, move on to another local dealer. Stick to a dealer until he proves himself deficient. If there are unresponsive record companies which ignore local retailer requests, the customer should be so informed. The local dealer cannot be blamed for failure to deliver the goods but he should pass along addresses of unresponsive distributors or companies so that the customer may take personal action. Quite often it is the manufacturer, not the local dealer that is being dilatory, or the company may be set up to handle only direct sales.

If local record buying cannot be accommodated, the next step is negotiation with one of the larger wholesale firms which cater to the bulk buyer. In most instances, these dealers will not discourage small orders but delays may result because of the higher priority attention they must reserve for established large-volume institutional customers. The capability of these jobbers can vary over time. Staff changes, conversions to automated operations, shifts in merchandising policy and in the profit/loss picture may directly affect service efficiency, and only a few firms have emerged as being dependable over the long term. In each case it should be evident that customer satisfaction will depend upon how closely matched are the contours of the customer's taste and the jobber's inventory. A jobber that performs well for school districts and public libraries in Boise, Idaho, will not necessarily be able to fill as easily the expectations of similar institutions located in eastern urban areas.

Any library with an anticipated annual purchase volume in excess of one thousand dollars could approach the following dealers all of whom have established moderately successful service reputations during this past decade. Needless to say, this list is selective and there are other firms which have or will have proven themselves worthy of inclusion. In future editions of this guide, this representation will be modified to reflect adjusted appraisal consensus among buyers.

Book Clearing House, Inc.
423 Boylston St.
Boston, Mass. 02116

Chambers Record Corp.
97 Chambers St.
New York, N.Y. 10007

Chesterfield Music Shops, Inc.
12 Warren St.
New York, N.Y. 10007

Sam Goody, Inc.
46–35 54 Rd.
Maspeth, N.Y. 11378

King Karol Records
Box 629, Times Square Station
New York, N.Y. 10036

National Record Plan
P.O. Box 568
New York, N.Y. 10008

The Record Hunter
507 Fifth Ave.
New York, N.Y. 10017

Rose Discount Records, Inc.
214 S. Wabash Ave.
Chicago, Ill. 60604

Schmitt Music Co.
88 S. 10th St.
Minneapolis, Minn. 55403

H. Royer Smith Co.
2019 Walnut St.
Philadelphia, Pa. 19103

A third alternative for the librarian and home recording purchaser is membership in a record club. Columbia, RCA, Capitol, the Musical Heritage Society, and numerous other companies preselect recordings for listeners who may have unusual tastes (drama, electronic, performances of legendary artists) or who demand resources to enhance religious, minority, ethnic, or professional identity. Club membership confers upon subscribers the option of guaranteed ownership of desirable recordings which might otherwise be overlooked or unavailable through normal trade channels. Typically a new member receives three to six recordings free of charge or in exchange for a nominal fee or commitment to comply with club rules. Members are usually required to purchase a set number of recordings each year. The advantages of the relationship are direct delivery and generous discounts off the list prices. The disadvantages are lack of diversity and consequently some forced buying after the initial infatuation has run its course. This latter hazard is documented by the often amusingly acerbic accounts of persons who have severed their connections with such clubs. The courting and marriage ceremonies are simple; the subsequent divorce proceedings can be trying and even traumatic. In summary, clubs are best suited for beginning collectors who buy by title and who are not adamant about performance requirements, or members of special groups and audiences for whom participation can lessen searching time, frustration, and delays. For others, a record club loses its value after the pool of desirable selections has been drained and choices must be made between humdrum alternatives.

How to Order

This section will deal with the major steps and logic of the purchase order preparation sequence. It is assumed that the purchaser already has prepared a list of desirable titles for which specific order information is required.

If cards have been extracted from a "recommended for purchase" file, they should be immediately replaced with fresh items culled from current review literature up to a point where the total file again represents an adequate shopping list if windfall money should materialize. This step should be taken because unpreparedness for unanticipated allocations can be embarrassing and used as justification for awarding a smaller slice of budgetary pie for recording purchases in the future.

Check each title against the appropriate trade tape/disc listings to confirm current availability and validate the manufacturer's number and list price. There is no unified trade directory apparatus comparable to the R. R. Bowker series of keys (*Books in Print, Publishers Trade List Annual, Publishers Weekly,* and *American Book Publishing Record*). This means that the buyer must consult the Schwann, Harrison and Trade Service Publications catalogs in conjunction with other sources to effectively confirm formats, manufacturers' numbers, prices, and market status. Many of the categories cf recorded

sound impose peculiar routes which must be followed to avoid frustration and error. These are summarized below:

Early Music

For music written by major composers such as William Byrd or Josquin Des Prez, look first in the main composers' section of the two Schwann guides. *Schwann–2* must be considered because a significant portion of early music is represented on minor labels or is available in monophonic only. The *Harrison Tape Guide* and Trade Service Publications catalogs are relatively ineffective supplementary sources because of the paucity of available cassettes.

For anthologies which constitute about one-third of the items in this category, consult the Collections section in the back parts of *Schwann–1* and *Schwann–2*. Within the section, early music is most apt to be found under the "Anthologies," "Choral," "Gregorian Chant," and "Vocal" subheadings. The very fine contributions of Victoria de los Angeles and Alfred Deller may be found under the latter subheading. The New York Pro Musica Antiqua under the sensitive and scholarly stewardship of the late Noah Greenberg has several landmark recordings listed under the subheading for this group.

Because of the dispersion of anthology titles in Schwann, it is easier to locate known titles in the *Phonolog Reporter* or to consult the *Numerical Index,* if the manufacturers' numbers are already in hand.

Choral Music

The majority of titles sought by purchasers are attributable to known composers. Therefore, the first stop should be the Composers section of *Schwann–1*. Popular excerpts from large choral masterpieces may be located under the "Choral" heading in the *Schwann–1* and *Schwann–2* Collections sections. The *Harrison Tape Guide's* Classical Works section may be consulted for taped versions.

Keyboard Music

The approach will be dictated by the purchaser's primary focus of interest, whether it be the work or the performer.

If the work is more important than a particular rendition, and the composer is known, the two Schwanns and the Harrison guide will suffice. Because of the relative unimportance of stereophonic sound in the recording of works for single instruments and presence of a vast quantity of artistically monumental early performances on prestereo, the *Schwann–2* guide is an indispensable verification source for the serious collector.

For those who are compiling orders of individual artists' recorded outputs, the 1970 *Schwann Artists Issue, Phonolog Reporter,* appropriate company or label catalogs, and catalogs of single artists' works are plausible sources. The *Schwann Artists Issue,* within its Instrumental Soloists section, displayed the complete recorded outputs (disc only) of pianists, organists, harpsichordists, clavichordists, and virginalists. In addition to showing all that Glenn Gould, Walter Gieseking, Raphael Puyana, or Carl Rogg had put on record as of

1970, the *Schwann Artists Issue* gathered together the performances of composers Dmitri Shostakovich, Maurice Ravel, Sergei Rachmaninoff, conductors George Szell and Leonard Bernstein, and other performing musicians. Unfortunately this catalog is now over half a decade old and has most value for the collector concernd with the history of recorded sound.

A second approach is through the Classical Artists sections of *Phonolog Reporter* and *List-O-Tape*.

For artists with a long standing affiliation with a record label, the most complete and reliable inventory of currently available recordings may be the manufacturer's catalog. Rachmaninoff's early recordings may be found in the RCA Victor and Klavier catalogs; Glenn Gould has been almost exclusively a Columbia property; Helmut Walcha, the amazing blind master of the baroque organ repertory, is fully represented in the Deutsche Grammophon Gesellschaft catalog.

Finally, especially for American composers, many of the recent biographies contain discographies. Charles Ives, Aaron Copland, Arnold Schoenberg, Scott Joplin, and John Cage have been served particularly well in this respect.

Chamber Music and Symphonies

The two Schwanns and the *Harrison Tape Guide* will turn up the necessary order data if the searcher has identified the composers.

Concerti and Other Works for Solo Instrument(s) and Orchestra

As stated for keyboard music preceding, selection of confirmation sources will depend upon whether the prospective purchaser is more interested in tracking down a performer or in verifying a preselected performance. In the latter case, the main composers sections of *Schwann–1* and *Schwann–2* will disclose the required data. For those who seek historical landmarks (Schnabel's Beethoven, Szigeti's Bach, Lipatti's Schumann) the more labyrinthine procedure delineated under keyboard music may be necessary.

Other Orchestral Works

Consultation of the Schwann main composer sections will usually suffice. However, for children's recordings of classical titles, there may be problems in cases where excerpts from unfamiliar works or pieces by unidentified composers are involved. Titles such as *Flight of the Bumblebee, Ritual Fire Dance, Gymnopédies, Greensleeves* and *Grand Canyon* Suite cannot be easily located in Schwann unless the searcher knows the composers. Because the *Flight of the Bumblebee* and *Ritual Fire Dance* are excerpts from larger works, awareness that Rimsky-Korsakoff and Falla are the composers will still not lead the searcher to a listing of recorded versions. The *Phonolog Reporter* and *List-O-Tapes* are the only sources that provide sufficiently comprehensive title listings to accommodate the person with limited knowledge.

Classical Vocal Artists

If one is searching for collections of a composer's arias, songs, or other selections sung by various artists, consultation of the *Schwann–1* and

Schwann–2 guides is advised. If anthologies of works by three or more composers are sought and both artist and album title are known, the Collections section of the Schwanns may produce the necessary order data. The *Phonolog Reporter* "Artist," "Title," and "Composer" sections are logical next steps for those who have at hand less complete preliminary facts. For those for whom market availability and stereophonic format are less important than enduring artistic merit, this search will be supplemented by reference to the many dealers who specialize in rare recordings. These specialists operate mainly in New York City.

If the manufacturer's label is known and the item is a recent issue or reissue, the *Numerical Index* may be the quickest pathway to confirmation.

Operas

The Schwann catalogs are the logical choice. The *Schwann–1 Guide* provides a listing of operas near the back of each issue. This is a most useful aide-mémoire for any person who is seeking an opera without knowledge of its composer. Looking here, *Pot of Fat* and *Pilgrim's Progress* may be immediately identified as works of Theodore Chanler and Ralph Vaughan Williams. *Phonolog Reporter* has a title listing and for store browsers is a more efficient place to look.

Classical Music by Contemporary Composers

Over four hundred composers born later than 1920 are represented in the Schwann guides. For the searcher with normal tastes and requirements, these guides will provide all that is needed. The dedicated contemporary music collector should additionally consult catalogs of all producers which specialize in new music. Notable labels with "contemporary" depth are Columbia, Composers Recording Institute (American writers), Desto, Deutsche Grammophon Gesellschaft (German composers), Nonesuch (Electronic music), and Louisville Recording Society (works commissioned for recorded performance by the Louisville Symphony Orchestra). Within *Schwann–1* and *Schwann–2* electronic music is placed in a separate section and listed by label and number. Whenever a recording includes traditionally scored as well as electronic music, a cross-reference is given to the listing in the Schwann composer sections. *Phonolog Reporter* provides a direct approach because all works, electronic and traditionally scored, are consolidated under composer headings so that double-searches for Milton Babbitt, Charles Wuorinen, or George Crumb who write in a variety of media can be circumvented.

Jazz

Go directly to *Phonolog Reporter*. Detailed and current listings of albums, singles titles, and artists across the entire spectrum of pops make this the right choice. The title index provided by *Phonolog Reporter* is its most useful feature and makes it indispensable for the jazz disc hunter. For any institutional purchaser that must be responsive to mass audience demand, access to the *Weekly New Release Reporter* and *Monthly Popular Guide* is also advised.

In contrast, if an artist or album title is known, the jazz sections of the two Schwanns will pick up the item *if* it has been designated by Schwann as "jazz."

243

Distinctions between jazz, folk, and popular music styles being as fuzzy as they are, Schwann can create confusion and frustration for any searcher who is at all unsure or un-Schwann in his interpretation of genres.

Finally, for the collector of jazz classics, the advice given the seeker of vocal rarities is valid. Contact stores with stocks of "oldies" located in New York City. The Manhattan telephone directory contains current addresses.

Folk Music

A thorough search for folk music could try a saint's patience. Fortunately, the main stream of saleable American folk music (the commercial, scrubbed up, cleverly transcribed kind) can be located in the Current Popular section of *Schwann–1,* unless it was issued more than two years ago. Older items, if still available, appear in *Schwann–2.* If the folk music is other than American, it is necessary to consult the *Schwann–2* International Pop and Folk Music section. Note that Indian (American) folk music has been expatriated and appears as foreign folk music between India and Indonesia. In this relatively new Schwann compartment, the album titles are listed under each country whereas in the current and noncurrent Popular sections, the album titles appear under the artists.

Buyers interested in national or regional folk music should send for producers' catalogs. Folkways/Scholastic embraces the whole field; Monitor (Slavic), Lyrichord (Japan), Grecophon (Greece), and Tikva (Israel) have strength in the indicated nationalities. Local record dealers should be able to provide current addresses or leads to these labels.

Musical Theater

This in unproblematical. Most current Broadway musicals are listed alphabetically by show title in *Schwann–1* in a separate section, Musicals, Movies, TV Shows, in which soundtracks and original cast productions are coded. If the recording should be a special audience version or perennial favorite, e.g., *My Fair Lady* in Yiddish or *Lady in the Dark* with Gertrude Lawrence, *Schwann–2* should be examined as well.

Phonolog Reporter provides several avenues for title pursuit: (1) a reference section which lists show tunes under musical shows and operettas arranged in alphabetical order; (2) a "Pop Album" subdivision; and (3) a Pop Title section.

Popular Music

Phonolog Reporter is again favored because detailed analytics of popular artist, album, and title entries facilitate identification. Schwann's orientation and arrangement make it unsuitable for this purpose. Fullest possible coverage of the popular field would be afforded by having access to the *Phonolog Reporter, Weekly New Release Reporter,* and *Monthly Popular Guide.* Schwann's telegraphically abbreviated listings, mostly under performers, will adequately serve those for whom popular music is of only minor importance.

244

Foreign-Language Instruction

The knowledge of language experts, friends' and relatives' learning experiences, curricular guidelines, and personal acquaintanceship with a company's offerings should weigh heavily when selecting this kind of material. After receiving advice from one or more advisory sources, purchasers should (in most instances) deal directly with a manufacturer or authorized distributor. For those who desire a bird's eye view of possibilities, the *Schwann–2 Guide* contains within its Spoken and Miscellaneous section listings under the heading "Language Instruction." Over forty languages from Arabic to Yiddish are represented. The *NICEM Index to Educational Records,* though it lacks manufacturer number and price information, sorts out the major languages into separate groupings and addresses of producers are represented.

Berlitz, Caedmon, Conversaphone (produces greatest number of recordings for persons learning English as a second language), C.M.S. Records, Inc., Cortina, Folkways/Scholastic, Four Continents, Linguaphone, and Monitor are firms with extensive foreign language instruction catalogs. Up-to-date addresses may be confirmed in *Library Journal*'s annual purchasing issues, R. R. Bowker's *Audio-Visual Marketplace*, with your local record retailer, or in the Manhattan telephone directory as most of the companies have headquarters in New York City.

Prose, Poetry, Drama

The *Schwann–2 Record and Tape Guide*, within its Spoken and Miscellaneous section, provides subheaded categories for "Plays" and "Poetry, Prose, Speech" recordings. As in the case of foreign language recordings, one should have at hand producers' catalogs. Those of Argo, Caedmon, Folkways/Scholastic, Spoken Arts, and the Library of Congress should be within reach of anyone with a lively interest in the language arts.

Documentary, Historical, Technical

Although the *Schwann–2 Guide* contains about a page of documentary titles in its Spoken and Miscellaneous section, institutions will find the NICEM indexes, *Westinghouse Learning Directory*, discographies appended to articles and monographs concerned with topical and historical treatments, the *Elementary School Library Collection*, A.L.A.'s *Booklist* recordings reviews, and company catalogs are necessary supplementary tools to satisfactorily survey this cluttered field. The promotional brochures compiled by educational market firms such as Educational Record Sales, Enrichment Teaching Materials, and C.M.S. should also be considered. In areas such as science and mathematics instruction, the publications of the American Association for the Advancement of Science and specializing journals such as *Arithmetic Teacher* and *Mathematics Teacher* review recordings.

The preceding confirmation procedures, though elaborate, are essential whenever a retrospective list, "basic collection," or other dated cumulation is used as the source of items to be purchased. The lazy alternative of simply shooting out the order and "hoping for the best" is unwise because the high number of

"out of stock," "no longer available," "deleted" and other dead end responses will eventually consume more time and money than careful preliminary checks. Also, clients' confidence and patience may be eroded. Dependence upon current reviews is a way to minimize this effort. If a recording has been evaluated within the past year in a reputable journal which keeps pace with production, the confirmation procedure may be bypassed because a year's lifetime in a manufacturer's inventory is a fairly secure expectation for classical titles.

The reader may note that tape has been underplayed in the above point by point checking procedure. This is due to the transitional character of existing tape indexes. Experimental designs and technological breakthroughs are still occurring as industry strives to combine the virtues of simplicity, high fidelity, compactness, and durability in this medium. During this time, readers should avail themselves of the keys to the tape literature, using them to supplement the steps delineated above as dictated by prevailing need and practice.

Decide upon the appropriate purchase source. Should it be a local dealer or wholesale jobber? The decision to pick a wholesale firm should be based upon a consideration of the following factors:

a. The volume of orders should be sufficient to justify bypassing local record sales outlets.

b. The order should be confined to recent additions to company catalogs and/or items currently represented in Schwann, Harrison, or Trade Service Publications. If rare or discontinued recordings are sought, the purchaser should go to outlets which cater to the rare recording collector.

c. The purchaser must recognize that gains in order fulfillment efficiency and price markdowns may be offset by loss of close contact with the vendor. Informal adjustments and personalized service cannot be expected from most large, wholesale operations.

d. Accuracy and completeness of order responses achieved by various vendors should be checked out in advance. At least three other institutions with similar buying programs should be queried regarding their experience with the dealer being considered. The purchase schedules, categories, and quantities of titles should be as similar as possible to lend credence to the results of the inquiry.

e. After a vendor has been chosen, the agency should be granted sufficient time to prove itself. Unfortunately many institutions are subject to fiscal regulations which force them to automatically solicit fresh bids each year. This procedure is valid only if the bid specifications are precise and realistic in the definition of acceptable quality service. Order response time, accuracy of order completion, percentage of order fulfillment, order adjustment and substitution options, sturdiness of shipping containers—these are a few of the factors to be prescribed in addition to competitive pricing. Too many libraries have erred by prematurely jumping from a strong to a weak jobber solely upon the basis of low bid allure. It should also be apparent that firms which have automated their inventory, service, and delivery functions can be disadvantaged by the annual bid procedure. This is because machine processing of added customer accounts requires a start-up period and initial programming may involve delays and errors which are compensated for in increased efficiency only after an operation has

been set into motion. This observer has seen disgruntled librarians switch vendors only to relive their negative experience with a new wholesaler.

f. The searcher for offbeat recordings must pick purchase avenues to suit the quest. Historical documentaries for the high school, foreign-language instruction for those learning English as a second language, 78 rpm records of Bunk Johnson or Nellie Melba, readings for the blind, and many other specials can rarely be purchased through any one source with the possible exception of Record Hunter in New York City.

Features to be noted in the illustrated form include:
Verification—All data were confirmed in a current Schwann or Harrison guide.

Physical Description—Because there are at least half a dozen different audio formats or "configurations" on the market, partitioning by format is advised to avoid confusion.

Manufacturer Number—These are listed as they appear in Schwann or Harrison. The buyer should transcribe all letter and number prefixes because companies rely upon these to distinguish between their many product sequences.

Authorization to Substitute—If a desired title is available in several acceptable performances in the required format, the supplier should be given the opportunity to provide alternate versions. The *s*'s immediately preceding the manufacturer numbers in the purchase order illustration authorize substitutes for the Haydn, Liszt, and Saint-Saëns items.

Performance Description—Data should be sufficiently complete to confirm the correctness of the manufacturer number and provide enough guidance so that if a substitute is permissible, the vendor will be able to comply without rechecking with the purchaser.

Direct Orders—The items in this section should be ordered from authorized distributors or manufacturers. Educational market materials are often sold only by firms which deal directly with school districts. These companies may discourage sales through other agents so that they can concentrate upon a marketing system geared to school needs.

Prepare the purchase order so that it clearly conveys buying needs. A book rationale which seeks to limit salient features to the author, title, and subject cannot be applied to the sound recording medium. The key characteristic of a recorded work may be its composer, a performer or performing organization, geographical place name, title, or instrumentation. Accordingly, the best way to arrange a purchase order is by *manufacturer's number*, using the label and series abbreviations found in the Schwann and Harrison catalogs. An accessions file set up in this manner also safeguards the buyer against accidental duplications in future orders. Because major record distributors store their inventories by manufacturer and label numbers, incoming orders compiled in this way can be more quickly and accurately processed than those arranged by composer or title.

An illustration of a purchase order containing sufficiently explicit information follows.

Recordings to Be Ordered from Distributors

FORMAT	CATALOG NO.	PERFORMANCE DESCRIPTION	NO. OF ITEMS	LIST PRICE
Stereo LP	Ang. S–35937	De los Angeles, Victoria/Cantos de Espana	1	$6.98
Stereo LP	Ang. S–36071	Foster/Songs/Wagner Chorale	1	$6.98
Stereo LP	Ang. S–36786	Varèse/Déserts-Density 21.5/ Simonovitch	1	$6.98
Stereo LP	Argo ZNF–1	Britten/Noye's Fludde/Rex, Brannigan	1	$6.98
Stereo LP	Argo ZRG–720	Stravinsky/Mass/Preston	1	$6.98
Stereo LP	Argo ZSW– 520/1	Saint-Exupery/Little Prince/ Ustinov	1	$6.98
Stereo LP	Col. MS–6218	Schubert/Sym5/Walter	1	$6.98
Stereo LP	Col. MS–6497	Copland/Old Amer. Songs/ Copland&Warfield	1	$6.98
Stereo LP	Col. M–31512	Handel/Hpsi Suites 1–4/Gould	1	$6.98
Stereo LP	CRI S–308	Imbrie/Sym3/Farberman, LonSymOrch	1	$6.95
Stereo LP	CRI S–321	Brün/Gestures for 11/Electronic Studio	1	$6.95
Stereo LP	2–Desto 7179/80	Beeson/Sweet Bye & Bye/Patterson, Kansas City	1	$13.96
Stereo LP	2–DG 2707028	Schubert/Winterreise/Fischer-Dieskau	1	$15.96
Stereo LP	s Lon. CS 6385	Haydn/Quartet Op3–5/Janacek Qr	1	$6.98
Stereo LP	Lon. OS 25821	Berlioz/Nuits d'été/Crespin, Ansermet	1	$6.98
Stereo LP	Lon. STS–15052	Bizet/L'Arlésienne Suites/Ansermet	1	$3.98
Stereo LP	Lon. STS–15162	Wilbye/Madrigals/Pears, Wilbye Consort	1	$3.98
Stereo LP	2–MCA 2–10008	Play of Herod/NY Pro Musica	1	$13.96
Stereo LP	None. H–71209	Ives/Songs/Nixon/w.Goehr& Schürmann	1	$3.98
Stereo LP	None. H–71225	Wuorinen/Time's Encomium/ Synthesizer	1	$3.98
Stereo LP	Oiseau OLS–159	Shakespeare Dances/Dart&Boyd Neel Orch	1	$6.98
Stereo LP	Phi. 6500532	Mozart/Syms1,4,10/Marriner,St.M in Fields	1	$7.98
Stereo LP	Phi. 6558001	Fanshawe/African Sanctus/Hughes, Ambrosian	1	$7.98
Stereo LP	Tel. S–9591	Monteverdi/Lamento d'Arianna/ Schlean	1	$6.98
Stereo LP	Van. VCS– 10097	Beethoven/Quartet 16/Yale Qr	1	$6.98
Stereo LP	Van. 79327	Hurt, Mississippi John/Last Sessions	1	$6.98
Stereo LP	s 2–Van. 703/4	Haydn/Sym45/Janigro,Zagreb/ w.Tr con, Sym 100	1	$6.98
Mono LP	Folk. 5524	Eleanor Roosevelt/Human Rights	1	$6.98
Mono LP	Pathways 1027	Winnie Ille Pu-Vol.I	1	$5.98
Mono LP	Sera. 60161	Shostakovich/Con 1 for Piano/ Shostakovich	1	$3.98

248

FORMAT	CATALOG NO.	PERFORMANCE DESCRIPTION	NO. OF ITEMS	LIST PRICE
Quad LP	Col. MQ–32791	Bach/Organ Favorites/Biggs	1	$7.98
Quad LP	s RCA ARDI–0484	Saint-Saëns/Sym3/Fox, Ormandy	1	$6.98
Quad LP	Van. VSQ–40027	Sainte-Marie/N.Amer Child Odyssey	1	$7.98
Open Reel Tape	Lon. L–90113	Stravinsky/Renard, Mavra, Scherzo Russe	1	$7.95
Open Reel Tape	RCA EPPA–3766C	Jefferson Airplane/Surrealistic Pillow	1	$7.95
Cassette (stereo)	Ang. 4XS–36580	Haydn/Cello Con in D/DuPré, Barbirolli	1	$6.98
Cassette (stereo)	Apple 4XT–2576	Beatles/Revolver	1	$6.98
Cassette (stereo)	Caed. CDL–5320	Sophocles/Antigone/Tutin; Adriann; Brett	1	$7.95
Cassette (stereo)	Lon. M–31099	Gilbert and Sullivan/Mikado	1	$6.95
Cassette (stereo)	Van. E5310	Morath/World of Scott Joplin	1	$8.95
Cartridge (stereo)	Atl. TP–1305	Mingus/Blues and Roots	1	$6.97
Cartridge (stereo)	Caed. CDL–51218	Service/Poetry	1	$7.95
Cartridge (stereo)	Peters 8PP–4011	Villa, Claudio	1	$6.98
Cartridge (stereo)	s RCA R8S–1231	Liszt/Opera Transcriptions/Bolet	1	$6.95
Cartridge (quad)	Col. GAQ–30997	Miles Davis/Bitches Brew	1	$7.97
Cartridge (quad)	Col. MAQ–31019	Subotnick/Touch	1	$7.98
Cartridge (quad)	Col. MAQ–32160	Boulez/Marteau sans maître/Minton,Boulez	1	$7.98
Cartridge (quad)	RCA PQ8–1895	Rich, Buddy/Live in London	1	$7.95

s indicates customer's willingness to accept a substitute performance in the same format

Recordings to Be Ordered Directly from Producers

FORMAT	CATALOG NO.	PERFORMANCE DESCRIPTION	NO. OF ITEMS	LIST PRICE
Stereo LP	Musical Heritage Society MHS–1714	Buxtehude/*Singt dem Herrn*	1	$4.25
Open Reel Tape 2tr. 3¾	Imperial Prod.s	*The Lad Who Went to the North Wind*	1	$6.00
2tr. 3¾	Imperial Prod.s	*Paddy's Christmas*	1	$6.00
Cassette (mono) 1⅞	Miller–Brody 1005C	*All about the Alphabet*	1	$7.95
1⅞	Miller–Brody F4505	*Perez and Martina*	1	$7.95

Classification, Cataloging,   5
and Care of Sound
Recordings

Classification

Most libraries with extensive holdings of sound recordings have devised their own shelf arrangements or modified the Dewey Decimal or Library of Congress systems to accommodate their patrons' searching and browsing behavior. The diversity of recording classification schemes in U.S. libraries is a virtue, evidence that practicing librarians realize that differing collections, publics, programs, and circulation systems require localized solutions of the problem.

Contents, creative responsibility, appeal of recorded sound and printed word share insufficient common elements to justify universal application of the L.C. or D.D.C. systems. Although integration of the media would simplify the cataloger's task, the public would not benefit. Music recordings can be classified in the 780s or L.C.'s M division, but they cannot be approached, analyzed, consulted, or appreciated like composers' biographies, sheet music, and musicological treatises. Recordings are like short stories and novels, being sought mainly for their recreational, aesthetic, or emotionally therapeutic values. Recordings are often bringers of pleasure, seldom carriers of cold facts. Because the human eye can scan print with efficiency and flexibility while recorded transcription imposes both a set order and sluggish pace upon the listener, "publication" of strictly informational transactions in this medium is gross foolishness. The conference-on-a-cassette craze of recent years has demonstrated our miscalculation of the shortcomings of recorded sound. On the other hand, the taping of music, dramatic enactments, psychiatric conferences, business meetings, or court proceedings during which the intonation and implication, subtlety and valence of human dialogue are important—they are legitimate employments of the medium. In summary, many considerations should condition the selection of a classification. Format, required playback equipment, user motivation, and content should be reviewed. Whenever all these factors are examined, it becomes apparent that physical integration of musical information carriers—scores, books, *urtext* facsimiles, journals, and recordings—makes sense only in the music institute or conservatory. In this very special case, there would be a need for the student or scholar to follow a recorded performance with score in hand. Even here however, the written word should probably be separated from the scores and recordings.

250

If separate classification is preferred, there are innumerable schemes from which to choose. Six shelf arrangements that work reasonably well, whenever the factors of collection size, content, and use are in appropriate conjunction, are described below:

Accession Number

This does *not* bring together like forms, genres, or similar works of a composer nor does it cluster all recordings of a title. All it does is provide an arrangement geared for those interested in recent acquisitions. As newer records in any library are less worn and closer to popular trends, they are in higher demand than the rest of the collection. Also many patrons enjoy random browsing and arrive at the library with no specific preference in mind. Finally, the system does not impose upon the librarian's organizational skill. The countervailing disadvantage is that all users with predefined requirements are forced to consult the card catalog in order to locate desired recordings. Unless the collection contains less than 200 discs and/or tapes, the time required to sequentially thumb through the holdings is prohibitive. It is also important to bear in mind that any browser is limited to contact with "in" items and may leave with a completely false impression of the library's holdings. Only if a staff is totally ignorant of musical culture and the organization of nonprint materials, the collection is small, and the cataloging can compensate with a sufficient richness in analytics, should the accession number arrangement be used. As soon as holdings surpass the 500-item mark, composers, uniform and popular titles, performers, and categories must be represented in the card catalog to permit adequate access. With a collection of this magnitude, a compromise system may be considered by the cataloger who is insecure with music. Arrangement by accession number within broad categories may narrow the number of recordings to be scanned by the searching user to a manageable quantity. The categories might include I Orchestral Sound, II Chamber Music, III Opera, IV Spoken Word, V Keyboard Instruments, VI Jazz, VII Shows, VIII Folk, IX Popular-Vocal, X Popular-Instrumental, and XI Electronic. Examples of call numbers generated by this compromise system are illustrated below:

AC I
18

    AC I = an audiocassette in category I, Orchestral Music.
    18   = Eighteenth acquisition in category I
        Recording is: Bruckner, Anton
          Symphony no. 4 in E flat (*Romantic*)
          DG3300328
          Daniel Barenboim, conductor; Chicago
          Symphony Orchestra

AD IX
26

    AD IX = an audiodisc in category IX, Popular-Vocal.
    26   = Twenty-sixth acquisition in category IX
    Recording is: Jim Croce, vocals and guitar
          I Got a Name
          ABC 797

The Bruckner would require entries for Bruckner, Barenboim, and *Romantic Symphony*. In the Chicago area or wherever interest in performing organizations justifies inclusion, there could be an added entry for the Chicago Symphony Orchestra.

The Jim Croce recording would require representation of Jim Croce, the performer, and separate entries for each band title only if local demand justified the effort.

Manufacturer's Number

For a very large collection containing over 25,000 physical units, arrangement by manufacturer's number is workable if access can be limited to the staff or other special clients who will use the recordings on the premises. Record wholesalers, large public libraries, and broadcasting companies have successfully adopted this arrangement. Very full and explicit cataloging with a profusion of analytics is required to accommodate effective usage. Record sales outlets may depend upon the Trade Service Publications to perform this function but libraries must develop their own catalogs to cover retrospective as well as current holdings. Files should be established for the following entries:

1. *Titles*. Works with distinctive titles should be represented in the original language if it is one of the five common Western tongues (German, English, French, Italian, or Spanish) or Latin, and if the works are listed the same way in the *Schwann–1 Guide*. Popular translated opera arias should be represented in the language in which they are sung *and* two other languages if the original libretto is in German, French, or Italian. Mozart, Verdi, Puccini, and Wagner arias which are frequently sung in other than the original tongue are eligible for this treatment.

   For a collection of large magnitude, title entries will be of most value to the average patron. If titles, composer, and performer headings are interfiled, color coded cards can simplify the searcher's task.

2. *Composers*.

3. *Performing artists and ensembles*. This file should include accompanists and singers, featured soloists of the big bands such as Count Basie's or Woody Herman's various "herds," and individual members of ensembles such as the Budapest Quartet because stylistic shifts occur as personnel changed.

4. *Classification headings*. Headings should be descriptors which target topics and kinds of recordings commonly requested by the library's constituency. "Seasonal music," "local composers," "sound tracks," "ballet music for children," "educational recordings" are examples.

5. *Authors-librettists-lyric writers*. W. H. Auden, Emerson, Ogden Nash, Heine and Rimbaud, Gertrude Stein and Walt Whitman, Thoreau and Emily Dickinson have been set to music by Saint-Saëns, Walton, Hindemith, Stravinsky, Schubert, Debussy, Copland, and Ives. Particularly for art songs, it is necessary to establish a file for collaborators and inspirers of vocal settings if local patrons are partial to art songs and lieder. This

file can serve as a vehicle for igniting a program planner's imagination by revealing unexpected combinations and interrelationships.

6. *Instruments.* Patrons seeking recordings of unusual instruments such as the biwa, sitar, dulcimer, or electronic synthesizer will be grateful for directional guidance. Whenever instruments or vocal parts (soprano, tenor, treble, bass, etc.) have prominent parts in compositions, they should be represented in a separate file.

Among the preceding files, the first four are essential if the library intends to encourage borrowing by a general public with normal tastes, motivations, and levels of familiarity with music. The fifth and sixth files permit even fuller advantage to be taken of the collection's potential.

LC or DDC Number

Standard book classifications are not recommended unless scores and recordings are shelved side by side. The score as a musical blueprint may be classified on the basis of its intellectual content; the recording must be treated differently.

ANSCR Classification

This system, though imperfect, is better than any other available at present. Performance is recognized as the distinctive feature of recordings and the differences between genres are dealt with head on. *ANSCR*'s major shortcomings are: First, the system does not adequately distinguish between musical forms, functions, genres, instrumentations, and levels. *Alexander Nevsky*, a choral cantata conceived as a sound track, may be placed in either category. An electronic jazz organ piece could be placed in any one of three locations.

Second, there are too many categories. Twenty-three divisions and thirty-six subdivisions permit excessive overlapping and compartmentalization. According to *ANSCR*, Stravinsky's *Symphony of Psalms* should be classified as a choral work because of its form, not its scoring. Its form *is* actually symphonic so *ANSCR* has it placed correctly for the wrong reasons. This same composer's *Renard* has been called an opera, burlesque, and dance scene and could be classified as a choral, operatic work, or ballet.

Third, the notation is neither mnemonic nor expressive. E is Orchestral Music, R is Holiday Music, P is Folk Music, F is Chamber Music, and so on. The lack of mnemonic clues means that additional explanatory labeling of the shelves is imperative for any library which adopts the system.

Fourth, chamber music is ineptly treated. Debussy's set of sonatas is fragmented. The Sonata for Flute, Viola, and Harp is classified in F, Cello Sonata in GS, and Violin Sonata in GV. Stravinsky's Concertino for Twelve Instruments, *Dumbarton Oaks* Concerto, and *Ragtime* for Eleven Instruments, are not considered chamber music because they are all scored for more than nine instruments. Mozart's Serenade no. 10 in B flat for 13 Wind Instruments, K. 361 (a chamber piece) joins John Philip Sousa in category H (Band Music).

Fifth, the rules for call number construction result in contradictions between the denotive functions of the four *ANSCR* level identification codes. Illustrations of this inconsistency follow:

ANSCR Call Number	Recording
GO BACH TOC B 61	Bach: Toccata and Fugue in d. E. Power Biggs, Organist. Columbia MS 6261
GO FOX VD F 57	*Vale of Dreams* (selection of various composers' works). Virgil Fox, Organist. Capitol SP 8557
C HAND MES H 92	Handel: *Messiah*. Harper, Watts, Wakefield, Shirley-Quirk; Colin Davis, London Symphony Orchestra and Chorus. Philips PHS 3–992
C MORM LP M 68	*The Lord's Prayer* (various choral pieces) Mormon Tabernacle Choir; Richard Condie, conductor. Columbia MS 6068

Note that conductors, composers, and performing groups are used as second level abbreviations; individual artists, performing organizations, and concluding digits are represented by the fourth-level term.

For the above cited and other reasons, the *ANSCR* system must be modified and accompanied by explanatory guidelines for it to function effectively as a shelf arrangement scheme.

Arrangement by Composer or Predominant Characteristic

Eric Bryant has proposed a simplified composer and/or performer shelf arrangement because, in his opinion, patrons are primarily attracted by these two elements. Their listening interests and the commercial media place the stress upon composers and artists so that any kind of categorical arrangement impedes the user's effort to locate desired recordings. Hence gathering together classical composers' works regardless of instrumentation and form is preferred in a medium-sized collection. Only after more than 50 different items accrue to a composer does this solution become unwieldy for the user. This 50–title limit is usually surpassed first by a prolific composer; such as Mozart, Beethoven, Haydn, or Bach. In the larger collection, it becomes necessary to divide composer production into categories; orchestral works, operas, chamber music, and so on to safeguard against the growth of the file to inhibiting proportions. It is better to do this than to interpose between borrower and recording a hurdle in the form of systematized classification rules for forms and genres which may do violence to musical judgment and common sense. For example, the *ANSCR* system with its arbitrary definitions of chamber music and other form and instrumentation divisions could be comprehended only if the user himself participated in the classification process. For the middle-sized,

expanding collection, a more serviceable and simple solution is subdivision of holdings into the categories used by the *Gramophone Classical Record Catalogue*. These divisions are I Orchestral, II Chamber, III Instrumental, IV Vocal and Choral, and V Stage Works. Because the Gramophone Catalog has been designed to display the total current output of discs, cassettes, open-reel tapes, and cartridges reviewed in *Gramophone* (the journal), the hospitality of the arrangement is a foregone conclusion. The five-part division is general, unambiguous, musically correct, and functional. Popular and jazz recordings are included in the *Gramophone Popular Record Catalogue* and the *Spoken Word and Miscellaneous Catalogue* (published annually in the autumn) completes the three-way coverage. These catalogs may be used to corroborate category assignments by comparing local and Gramophone designations. For a large majority of public libraries, this could be a sensible way of coping with classification.

Arrangement by Category for Large Collections

The academic, junior college, or very large public library browsing collection could consider the following shelf scheme. All sound recordings would be shelved by composer or key descriptor.

CATEGORY	MAIN ENTRY USED FOR SHELVING ORDER	SUGGESTED ADDED HEADINGS FOR CATALOG
1. Early Music (written by composers born before 1550 A.D.)	Composer or School of Composition	Performer(s); Titles; Instruments
3. Choral Music	Composer	Performer(s); Titles
5. Keyboard Music	Composer	Performer(s); Instrument(s); Title(s)
7. Chamber Music	Composer	Performer(s); Form Classification; Instruments
9. Symphonies	Composer	Conductor; Orchestra; Popular title
11. Concerti and Other Music for Four or Fewer Instruments and Orchestra	Composer	Soloist(s); Conductor; Orchestra; Popular title
13. Other Orchestral compositions	Composer	Popular title; Conductor; Orchestra
15. Opera	Composer	Conductor; Key Cast Members; Orchestra; Chorus; Librettist

CATEGORY	MAIN ENTRY USED FOR SHELVING ORDER	SUGGESTED ADDED HEADINGS FOR CATALOG
17. Art Songs, Lieder, Arias	Composer (recitals may be filed under singer)	Composer(s) not used as main entry; Titles; Performers; Accompanists; Poets and Librettists
20. New Directions	Composer	Titles; Performers; Electronic Music Studios; Instrumentation
F. Folk Music	Region or Country; or Performer	Titles; Style Classification
J. Jazz	Performer	Titles; Instruments
P. Popular Music	Title or Featured Performer	Titles; Performers
A. Drama, Poetry, Prose, Ballads in English	Author	Authors not used as main entry; Titles; Subjects; Performers
B. Drama, Poetry, Prose Ballads in Foreign Languages	Author	Authors not used as main entry; Titles in original language and English; Subjects; Performers
C. Documentary, Scientific, and Instructional		Title within subclassification to suit local purpose and audience
H. Humor		Title or Performer

Summary

Basic decisions have to be made before selecting, modifying, or creating a classification scheme for a library or personal collection. Should the classification be utilitarian or academically respectable? Should it lead the user to the object of his quest or should it conform to an absolutist conception of music as an intellectual construct? It cannot do both! If the librarian seeks a system that will serve as an inventory or visible index to holdings or as an auxiliary reference map for the scholar and musicologist, the music schedules of the L.C. and D.D.C. will suffice. If assistance to the general user is the aim, other means will be required to attain that goal. In this case, the essential elements of import to the user of the collection must be assessed. What are the ordering elements which count most within the recorded literature to be classified?— authors, creators, interpreters, performers, geographical locales, dates, forms,

titles, languages, or subjects? Analysis of content and leading features of recordings to be arranged must proceed in conjunction with analysis of users' motives, perspectives, and levels of comprehension. If these grounds are accepted and one's action is governed by the following logical guidelines, a workable scheme can be produced.

1. Classification notation must be compact and simple. A mixture of letters, numbers, and punctuation allows for more concise notation than a strictly alphabetical or numerical system. The superior precision of the British as against the American postal zip code attests to this fact.

2. Expressiveness of notation should be given a high priority. For example, the Vocal Works, Opera, and Spoken Word categories could be V, O, and S. A lack of mnemonic aids is a serious defect in any classification.

3. Space between major divisions of the classification should allow for insertion of unborn sibling division or products of existing divisions which have split into two or more parts not at a lesser level of importance than the parent.

4. Pertinence to audience level and locale is important. A borrowed system must be modified to suit the library's constituency. As a case in point, the *ANSCR* system with minor adjustments could work within a medium-sized public library. The same classification would be ill-suited for a conservatory collection.

5. A vocabulary/title/authority file is essential to maintain internal consistency. Dependence upon recording container spellings of composers' names and work titles is not advised because of the notorious variations in transliterations and unevenness of documentation behind the data.

6. Mutual exclusivity of categories should be maximized. The system must be simple. Do not permit categories to proliferate because as they do so, the opportunity for overlapping and confusion increases. An upper limit of twelve or thirteen major divisions is advised. After this number is surpassed the mixture of genres, forms, and other categories becomes unmanageable.

7. If confronted with a recording of twenty or more different pieces, by nineteen different composers, performed by ten different artists, do not select the main entry on the basis of physical characteristics. The percentage of recording space committed to a piece or its placement on a recording have no proven bearing upon significance or appeal. Whenever in doubt, one should solicit expert advice instead of relying upon catalogers' terminology.

8. Create special categories if access and usage can be enhanced by their addition to the system. For example, a local performing organization should have its recordings grouped together. Visual guides can be used to alert patrons to the new category.

9. Color codes for categories are helpful directive aids. Physical containers of recordings can be striped, tagged, or flagged to assist customers and staff in locating and reshelving recordings.

Cataloging

Two decisions must be made before local cataloging can commence: (1) Should entries for sound recordings be maintained in a separate file or should they be integrated with those for other nonprint and printed materials? and (2) How much specificity and detail will be required to furnish adequate internal control and guidance for the users of the collection? The conventional wisdom of media specialists stresses that subject matter is the superordinate concern of the patron and that format distinctions should be translated or delimited so that a standardized card layout can prevail. Integration supposedly permits the user who is conducting a comprehensive subject search to track down his quarry without resorting to more than one key. Also, the integrated catalog may introduce nonprint components of the collection to users who might otherwise remain ignorant of their existence.

The integration argument fails because listening habits and motivations of users seeking recordings are dissimilar to the reading habit and motivation of persons looking for nonfiction subject coverages. It is perverse to force the record hunter's nose into an omnium-gatherum directory in which printed materials, graphics, scores, filmstrips, biographies, realia, recordings, and other media are comingled. Before reaching the catalog he runs the additional risk of getting caught in a traffic jam with other searchers. Several years ago, color coding of nonprint entries had been employed by many school libraries to simplify the look-up process. However, this practice has been placed on the endangered species list because colors are not machine readable. Therefore, a separate catalog for sound recordings is recommended for any library with a collection exceeding 500 items which is not physically integrated with other formats and printed materials.

The second decision should be governed by the needs and searching style of the library's clientele. Although increased efficiency and scope of retrieval through comprehensive analytics of composers, titles, performers, instruments, librettists, lyricists, and genres is desirable, the time and technical ability needed for their preparation are seldom available. It is certain that in many settings with unsophisticated users, much of this analysis could be superfluous and even confusing. Therefore, cataloging between the two extremes is proposed for public and school librarians.

Academic and music libraries with primarily classical recordings should instead stay with the Library of Congress or Dewey Decimal systems and *Anglo-American Cataloging Rules.*

Simplified Cataloging Rules

The outline of the classification entitled Arrangement by Category for Large Collections (pages 255–56) is used as a basis for the simplified cataloging rules that follow. Although this cataloging is minimal, it is sufficient for most public and school district libraries.

I. Number of Entries

A. There is a minimum of three entries for categories 1 through 20. Main entry is under name of composer; subject entry is under the musical medium or form (see medium of performance headings on pages 268–69); an added entry is provided for the key performer or performing organization.

B. Categories A and B are treated as if in book form with entries determined in accordance with *AACR* rules.

C. Category C generally have the main entry for title or focal subject of the documentary, scientific topic, or foreign language presented on the recording.

D. Category F have the main entry for the performer, performing group, or nationality.

E. Category J have the main entry for the performer or performing group; an added entry for the album title.

F. For the above categories, added entries may be selected from the list of suggested added headings on pages 255–56. The number of added entries will be conditioned by size of the collection, requirements of the library public, purposes for which recordings are used, and the effectiveness of ancillary keys such as the shelf arrangement, brochures, directional guides.

II. Descriptive Cataloging Requirements

A. Main Card (for categories 1–20 only)
The main heading is determined by the relative importance of the creative and recreative (performance) content of the sound-recording form, i.e., disc(s), cassette(s), cartridge(s) within the physical container or album identified as the unit of entry.

    1. Single works by one composer comprise total content. Recordings fitting this description are entered under the name of the composer.

    2. Two or more comprising compositions or excerpts from the works of

        a. One composer
        The main entry for this type of sound recording will be under the name of the composer.

        b. Two or more composers
        The main entry for this type of sound recording will be under the most important composer as defined by standard biographical directories. All other composers will have added entries. If there are more than three composers *and* their works are recondite, the main entry will be under the collective title as represented in *Schwann–1*, some other standard authority source, or from the sound recordings container. Descriptive notes on the container will be accepted only as the reference of last resort.

Examples. Examples in the Library of Congress and proposed simplified format follow:

259

Schubert, Franz Peter, 1797-1828.
   [Symphony, D. 944, C major] Phonodisc.
   Symphony no. 9 (The great C-major). Angel S 36044
[1970].
   2 s. 12 in. 33 1/3 rpm. stereophonic.
   Slipcase title: Dr. Szell's last recordings.
   Cleveland Orchestra; George Szell, conductor.
   Duration: 46 min., 21 sec.
   Program notes by Klaus G. Roy on slipcase; "A
special commemorative leaflet" ([5]p. illus.)
inserted.

*Library
of Congress
Example 1*

Schubert, Franz Peter, 1797-1828.
   [Symphony, D. 944, C major] Phonodisc.
   Symphony no. 9 (The great C-major)...card 2

   1. Symphonies. I. Szell, Georg Andreas, 1897-
1970. II. Cleveland Orchestra. III. Title: Dr.
Szell's last recordings.

*Simplified
Example
1a*

ADS 9   Schubert, Franz
S384   Symphony No. 9 in C, "The Great," D. 944
00009   Angel S 36044; stereo LP disc
36044   Ed. level: Sec.
       George Szell, conductor; Cleveland
    Orchestra
       Duration: 46 min.
       1. Symphonies. I. Szell, George.
    II. Cleveland Orchestra.

Mozart, Johann Chrysostom Wolfgang Amadeus, 1756-1791.
   [Quartets, flute & strings] Phonodisc.
   The Mozart flute quartets. Columbia M 30233.
[1971].
   2 s. 12 in. 33 1/3 rpm. microgroove. stereo-
phonic. (Columbia masterworks)
   Jean-Pierre Rampal, flute; Isaac Stern, violin;
Alexander Schneider, viola; Leonard Rose, violoncello.
   Duration: 12 min., 36 sec., 10 min., 45 sec.,
8 min., and 15 min., 8 sec.
   Program notes by Piero Weiss on slipcase.

Mozart, Johann Chrysostom Wolfgang Amadeus, 1756-1791.
   [Quartets, flute & strings] Phonodisc.
   The Mozart flute quartets...card 2

   CONTENTS: D major, K. 285.-A major, K. 298.-G major,
K. 285a.-C major, K. 285b.
   1. Quartets (Flute, violin, viola, violoncello)-To
1800. I. Rampal, Jean Pierre. II. Stern, Isaac, 1920-
III. Schneider, Alexander, 1908- IV. Rose, Leonard.

*Library
of Congress
Example 2*

```
ADS 7    Mozart, Wolfgang Amadeus
M939         Quartets, flute and strings; K. 285,
QUAFL    K. 285a, K. 285b, K. 298.
30233        Columbia M 30233; stereo LP disc
             Ed. level: Elem.
             Jean-Pierre Rampal, flute; Isaac Stern,
         violin; Alexander Schneider, viola; Leonard
         Rose, violoncello
             Durations: K. 283-13 min., K. 285a-8 min.,
         K. 285b-15 min., K. 298-11 min.


                      continued on next card
```

```
             ADS 7    Mozart, Wolfgang Amadeus
             M939         Quartets, flute and strings; K. 285,
             QUAFL    K. 285a, K. 285b, K. 298.
             30233                                    (Card 2)
                          1. Quartet - Instrumental.  2. Flute.
                      I. Rampal, Jean-Pierre.  II. Stern, Isaac.
                      III. Schneider, Alexander.  IV. Rose, Leonard.
```

Simplified
Example 2a

Note the changes and omissions in the simplified examples:

1. Composer names conform with *Schwann–1* and the general vernacular. Birth and death dates are omitted.
2. The work title is as it appears in *Schwann–1*. French, German, Italian, Spanish, and Latin titles are retained in the original languages unless Schwann, as the mirror of general practice, has translated them into English. For example, *Prélude à l'après-midi d'un faune, I Lombardi alla prima Crociata,* and *Des Knaben Wunderhorn* remain in the original language; *L'Apprenti sorcier, Pini di Roma,* and *Die Zauberflöte* are translated into English.
3. In the Mozart flute quartets, the reader is immediately made aware of Köchel listings and specific works contained on the disc without having to refer to the contents note for these data. Thematic index numbers (e.g., D. 944 and K. 285a) are the most reliable work indicants for composers Johann Sebastian Bach (Schmieder), Wolfgang Amadeus Mozart (Köchel), Domenico Scarlatti (Longo), Franz Schubert (Deutsch), and Antonio Vivaldi (Pincherle). For other composers, opus numbers, ordinal numbers of works created in a specific form (e.g., Symphony no. 39 and Quartet no. 15), and key signatures are used in combination to the extent necessary to avoid vagueness.
4. Production dates are omitted because the practice of multiple studio "takes" has nullified the former value of this information and it is considered inconsequential by most users. The exception to the rule is the occasional recording of an historically significant session or performance.
5. The physical description is compressed and placed on the same line as the manufacturer's number, and terms comprehensible to the common reader replace the cataloger's abbreviations for sides, diameter, and playing speed. Sound recordings of the same size and format are usually shelved together as a homogeneous group rendering this information superfluous.
6. Duration to the nearest minute should be sufficient for schools or libraries which anticipate use of recordings for scheduled events.

7. The performance medium headings (e.g., Bassoon, Cello, Spinet, Quartet —Instrumental) are taken from the list at the end of this section.
8. The selection of performers to be given added entries is a matter of local discretion. In the preceding Mozart example, Jean-Pierre Rampal, the flutist, must be represented; the three string players, though eminent musicians, could be omitted in public and school library catalogs.

Aside from these distinctions in layout, some general recommendations are offered:

1. A separate shelf list should be maintained. Numbers in parenthesis in the lower right quadrant of each of these unit cards could indicate accession number and acquisitions date. This information's inclusion would depend upon the degree of locally required accountability.
2. The rules for main entry promulgated by the Association for Educational Communications and Technology should be disregarded. If the librarian chooses to accept the AECT recommendation that all audiovisual materials be entered under title, trivial, misleading, and imprecise information will be highlighted. In the field of sound recordings, composer, genre, and performer are generally more meaningful to the patron than title. Main entry by title is more than a misplaced emphasis. The title, if taken from the container in accordance with AECT instructions, may be the product of promotional imagination and an inaccurate representation of content. The cataloger's role should be to ease access to information and not to clutter the patron's path with the slogans of record wrapper designers.
3. A unit card is recommended because (1) sound recordings require three or more entries in the vast majority of cases, and (2) the searcher is more likely to succeed even if his interpretation of the most important elements of a recording differs from that of the cataloger. His chances are better because all descriptive data will be found under the title, composer, performer, classification number, or wherever else he looks without making a detour to some other point in the catalog. (3) Xerographic duplication of unit cards can save clerical time and an aide or other nonprofessional assistant can be enlisted to copy the unit cards and add tracings.

More illustrations of the simplified layout follow:

```
ADM11    Mozart, Wolfgang Amadeus
M939        Concerto for Horn No. 2, K. 417
HORN2       Seraphim 60040; mono LP disc
60040       Ed. level: Sec.
            Dennis Brain, horn; Walter Susskind, con-
         ductor; Philharmonic Orchestra
            Duration: 13 min.
            With: Dukas, Paul. Villanelle-6 min.
         Beethoven, Ludwig van. Sonata for Horn &
         Piano, Op. 17-15 min. Mozart, Wolfgang
         Amadeus. Divertimento No. 16 in E flat,

                    continued on next card
```

```
ADM11    Mozart, Wolfgang Amadeus
M939         Concerto for Horn No. 2, K. 417
HORN2                                              (Card 2)
60040
             K. 289 (Minuet and Adagio only)-6 min.
         Dittersdorf, Karl Ditters von.  Partita in D
         (Minuet and Trio only)-3 min.  Schumann,
         Robert.  Adagio & Allegro for Horn, Op. 70-
         8 min.  Haydn (Franz) Joseph.  Symphony No.
         31 in D, "Hornsignal" (Allegro only)-4 min.
             1. Horn.  2. Wind Instruments.  I. Brain,
         Dennis.

                               continued on next card
```

```
ADM11    Mozart, Wolfgang Amadeus
M939         Concerto for Horn No. 2, K. 417
HORN2                                              (Card 3)
60040
         II. Moore, Gerald.  III. Matthews, Denis.
         IV. Haas, Karl.  V. Westrup, Jack A.
         VI. Susskind, Walter.  VII. Dukas, Paul.
         VIII. Beethoven, Ludwig van.  IX. Dittersdorf,
         Karl Ditters von.  X. Schumann, Robert.
         XI. Haydn, (Franz) Joseph.  XII. Villanelle.

                         (1833-021176)
```

In the immediately preceding illustration, assisting pianists Gerald Moore and Denis Matthews; conductors Haas, Susskind, and Westrup could be omitted because for most users, horn virtuoso Dennis Brain would be the main attraction of this particular album. On the other hand, it is more likely that there could be persons seeking early Haydn symphonies or the rarely heard Schumann Adagio and Allegro. For this reason, extra tracings are advised. Readers should realize that this illustrates an abnormal profusion of titles, composers, genres, and performers.

Whenever two or more works are on the same recording, the main entry should be for the first and/or largest work only if the librarian cannot ascertain the relative importance of the represented items. A "with" note identifies the remaining works on the recording.

The elements of the unit card should be as spare as possible without compromising accuracy and completeness of description.

1. *Composer.* Use of the version of the name appearing in *Schwann–1* is recommended. The latest edition of the *Baker's Biographical Dictionary of Musicians* is an excellent secondary confirmation source.

2. *Title.* The use of a standardized title is recommended to insure consistency and avoid dispersion of various designations for the same work throughout the catalog. The *Schwann–1 Record and Tape Guide* is suggested as an adequate authority. Supplementary sources are listed at the conclusion

of this section. The "conventional" or "uniform" title in its brackets is a distracting catalogers' ceremonial which may be dispensed with in school and most public libraries.

3. *Performer, performing organizations, conductors. Baker's Biographical Dictionary*, the *Library of Congress, Music, Books on Music, and Sound Recordings* catalog, and *Schwann Artist Issue* may be utilized as confirming sources for names.

4. *Label data.* Use no abbreviations if the likelihood of ambiguity or confusion with other labels exists. Columbia, Colgems, Colosseum, Colonial Williamsburg, and Colonial all begin with Col. Therefore, Columbia should be spelled out in full. Deutsche Grammophon Gesellschaft in its abbreviated form, DG, is not as vulnerable to misinterpretation.

5. *Physical description.* This information must be included if different formats or various configurations of the same format are to be represented in the same catalog. Different formats would include a mixture of discs, cassettes, and open reel tapes. Various configurations include 8, 16, 33⅓, 45, and 78 rpm discs; monophonic, stereophonic, and quadraphonic cassettes; differing track combinations on tapes, and so on. The physical description is also indicated in the top term of the call number. The following code for various formats is used in the illustrations:

ABM = monophonic cartridge
ABS = stereophonic cartridge
ACM = monophonic cassette
ACS = stereophonic cassette
ACQ = quadraphonic cassette
ATM = reel-to-reel monophonic tape
ATS = reel-to-reel stereophonic tape
ADM = monophonic 33⅓ rpm disc
ADS = stereophonic 33⅓ rpm disc
ADQ = quadraphonic 33⅓ rpm disc
AEM = monophonic 45 rpm disc
AES = stereophonic 45 rpm disc
AFM = 16 rpm disc
AGM = 8 rpm disc (for blind listeners)
ASM = 78 rpm disc

The detail provided in the physical description will depend upon the number of different kinds and forms of recording which are available through the catalog. The data must be sufficient to inform the user whether his home equipment can play the recording. For tapes, cassettes, and cartridges, the number of tapes, diameter in inches, speed in inches per second, number of tracks, and phonic data (is the tape stereophonic, monophonic, quadraphonic?) may all have to be stated to avoid ambiguity. This information should be placed on the same line and immediately following the label data.

6. *Educational level.* This may be indicated on the line below the label data. If level designations are deemed desirable, the elementary, secondary, and adult categories usually provide sufficient specificity. Local educational jurisdictions can devise abbreviations to denote appropriateness for nursery, kindergarten, primary, intermediate, middle school, junior and senior high school, and adult listening.

7. *Notes*

a. Descriptive pamphlets or leaflets accompanying recordings should not be mentioned unless they are instructional manuals or integral correlative materials such as opera libretti, musical scores, or historical commentaries.

b. The language of the performance, if not apparent from the vernacular title, may be indicated.

c. The historical importance of the performance or happening should be noted. Typically such notes are phrased "Recorded during a live performance at . . ." or "Contains spoken commentary by the composer." This kind of note is most often associated with jazz recordings.

d. Any major alteration of the original composition should be brought to the user's attention. This kind of note applies only to categories 1–20. Alterations include arrangements, abridgements, orchestrations, transcriptions. The name of the reviser should be included if it is not given within the body of the card entry.

e. Sources from which readings are taken and which are integral to a recorded presentation should be cited for categories A and B.

f. If special materials or equipment are required in conjunction with use of recordings, this information should be noted.

g. A twenty-five- to fifty-word summary may be included to explicate content. Such summaries can assist patrons with limited time and background information.

Shelf List Card

This is the librarian's inventory control. The shelf list serves as a comprehensive representation of the collection as it stands on the shelves. Color banded cards indicating items awaiting future purchase in each category may be interfiled within the shelf list. If this is done, a quick visual inspection may reveal approximate balances within the collection whenever this information is needed. Accordingly, the shelf list may serve as auxiliary acquisitions tool and inventory control.

File Arrangements for the Public Catalog

Cards should be filed in four separate sections; (1) Classical (categories 1–20), (2) Folk Music (Category F), (3) Jazz and Popular Music (Categories J and P), and (4) Nonmusical Recordings (Categories A, B, C, and H). The Classical section will be a dictionary arrangement with the composer, title, medium of performance, performer, and author/lyricist/librettist entries intermixed. The Folk Music entries may be divided by country or region and subdivided by performer, or they may be arranged in dictionary catalog fashion. If the collection is heavily weighted in national and regional folk music, the first arrangement is preferable. If popular American folk music predominates, the dictionary arrangement may be more effective. Categories J and P will have intermixed performer and title entries. Within these two categories, performers tend to retain their place in the public mind for a longer period of time than do individual titles. Because of this, as a collection expands and ages, it may be beneficial to create a separate performer file for jazz and popu-

lar music artists. Nonmusical recordings with a closer content affinity with printed resources may be integrated into the main public catalog. Author, title, subject, performer entries will be best displayed in a dictionary catalog with the possible exception of category H, Humor. Well-known humorists, stand up comedians, and impressionists might in a very large collection assume enough dimension to justify establishment of a separate file.

Authority Sources

For libraries which depend upon other than the *Library of Congress Music, Books on Music, and Sound Recordings* catalog to confirm composer, title, performer, and author-lyricist-librettist entries, the following sources are suggested as name authorities. Categories for which they should prove useful are indicated.

American Music Center, Inc., 2109 Broadway at 73rd St., New York, N.Y. 10023.

The American Music Center maintains a tape library of commercial and private recordings of composers who have deposited copies in their collection. The center also has lists of scores suitable for performance in the schools. Useful for category 20.

American Society of Composers, Authors, and Publishers. *ASCAP Biographical Dictionary of Composers, Authors, and Publishers.* 3d ed. New York: ASCAP, 1966.

ASCAP is considering a fourth edition for 1977 as their membership has doubled since 1963. A complete membership list is published each year and is available free of charge from ASCAP, 1 Lincoln Plaza, New York City, N.Y. 10023. Useful for category 20.

Baker's Biographical Dictionary of Musicians. 5th ed. with 1971 suppl. Nicolas Slonimsky, reviser. New York: G. Schirmer, 1971.

This reliable work has been periodically revised by Slonimsky, a lexicographer-musicologist universally respected for his meticulous scholarship. Useful for categories 1–20.

Berkowitz, Freda P. *Popular Titles and Subtitles of Musical Compositions.* New York: Scarecrow Pr., 1975.

Most of the titles in this source should be represented in the public catalog. Popular and nickname titles ranging from the *Academic Festival Overture* to George Crumb's *Fantasy Pieces after the Zodiac for Amplified Piano (Makrokosmos)* are included in this handy monograph. Useful for categories 3–17.

B.M.I.: The Many Worlds of Music, 10 issues/year.

Informative biographical summaries of currently active musicians. This publication of Broadcast Music Inc. is offered free of charge to qualified individuals. Inquiries should be sent to the Public Relations Department at B.M.I.: 40 W. 57th St., New York City, N.Y. 10019. Useful for categories 20, J, and P.

Catalogs of Record Companies
Columbia, Composers Recordings, Inc., Nonesuch, Orion, Louisville, Deutsche Grammophon Gesellschaft, London Records publish catalogs which may be used for confirming data. Consider for categories 1–20.

Chilton, John. *Who's Who of Jazz: Storyville to Swing Street.* Philadelphia: Chilton, 1972.
Useful for category J.

Coover, James, and Colvig, Richard. *Medieval and Renaissance Music on Long-Playing Records.* (Detroit Studies in Music Bibliography no. 6) and *Medieval and Renaissance Music on Long-Playing Records: Supplement, 1962–1971.* (Detroit Studies in Music Bibliography no. 26) Detroit: Information Coordinators, Inc., 1964 and 1973. Useful for category 1.

DeCharms, Désirée and Breed, Paul F. *Songs in Collections: An Index.* Detroit: Information Services, Inc., 1966.
Useful for category 17.

Ewen, David. *New Encyclopedia of the Opera.* New York: Hill and Wang, 1971.
Useful for categories 15 and 17.

Lawless, Ray McKinley. *Folksings and Folksongs in America: A Handbook of Biography, Bibliography and Discography.* New rev. ed., New York: Meredith Pr., 1965.
Useful for category F.

Mattfield, Julius. *Variety Music Cavalcade, 1620–1969, A Chronology of Vocal and Instrumental Music Popular in the U.S.* 3d ed., Englewood Cliffs, N.J.: Prentice-Hall, 1971.
Useful for categories J and P.

Record jackets and accompanying descriptive notes.
Useful for all categories.

Schwann–1 Record and Tape Guide.
Useful for categories 3–17.

Sears, Minnie Earl. *Song Index and The Song Index Supplement.* (Reprint of the original 1926 edition and its 1934 supplement). Hamden, Conn.: Shoe String Pr., 1966.
An amazingly comprehensive index of songs and opera arias extant at the time of its compilation. Useful for categories 15 and 17.

Stahl, Dorothy. *A Selected Discography of Solo Song: A Cumulation Through 1971.* (Detroit Studies in Music Bibliography no. 24) Detroit: Information Coordinators, Inc., 1972.
Useful for category 17.

Stambler, Irwin. *Encyclopedia of Popular Music.* New York: St. Martin's Pr., 1965.
Useful for category P.

Stambler, Irwin, and Landon, G. *Encyclopedia of Folk, Country, and Western Music.* New York: St. Martin's Pr., 1969.
　　Useful for category F.

Medium of Performance Headings

The following headings are suggested for Instrument and Medium of Performance added entries (for categories 1–20 only):

Accordion
Aleatoric Music (see Chance Music)
Alto Voice
Bagpipes
Balalaika
Banjo
Baritone Horn
Baritone Voice
Baryton
Bass Voice
Basset Horn
Bassoon
Bells
Bells—Church
Bells—Tubular
Biwa
Brass Instruments
Brass Trio
Bugle
Carillon
Castanets
Celesta
Cello
Chamber Ensemble
Chamber Symphony
Chance Music
Child's Voice
Cimbalon
Clarinet
Clarinet—Bass
Clavichord
Coloratura Voice
Concertina
Contra Bass (see Double Bass)
Contrabassoon
Contralto Voice
Cornet
Countertenor
Cymbals
Double Bass

Drum
Drum—Bass
Drum—Kettle
Drum—Side
Drum—Tenor
Duet—Instrumental
Dulcimer
Electronic Equipment
English Horn
Ensemble—Instrumental
Ensemble—Vocal
Euphonium
Falsetto
Female Voice
Flute
Flute—Alto
Flute—Bass
French Horn (see Horn)
Glasses—Musical
Glockenspiel
Glockenspiel—Keyed
Gong
Guitar
Guitar—Spanish
Guitar—Electric Amplified
Happenings (see Chance Music)
Harmonica
Harmonium
Harp
Harpsichord
Horn
Hornpipes
Hurdy-Gurdy
Jew's Harp
Koto
Lute
Lyra
Male Voice
Mandoline
Marimba

Mechanical Music
Mezzo-Soprano Voice
Music Box
Musical Clock
Narrator
Nonet—Instrumental
Novachord
Oboe
Oboe d'amore
Octet—Instrumental
Ondes Martenot
Opera Company
Orchestra
Organ
Organ—Hammond
Organ—Mechanical
Organ—Wurlitzer
Percussion Instruments
Phonola
Piano
Piano—Prepared
Pianola
Piccolo
Pipes
Pipes—Bamboo
Player Piano
Prepared Music
Quartet—Instrumental
Quartet—Vocal
Quintet—Instrumental
Quintet—Vocal
Rattle
Recorder—Alto
Recorder—Bass
Recorder—Soprano
Recorder—Tenor
Saxhorn
Saxhorn—Bass
Saxophone
Saxophone—Alto
Saxophone—Baritone
Saxophone—Soprano
Saxophone—Tenor
Septet—Instrumental
Septet—Vocal
Sextet—Instrumental
Sextet—Vocal
Sitar
Snare Drum

Soprano Voice
Sousaphone
Spinet
Stochastic Music
String Quartet
String Trio
Strings
Tambourine
Tenor Voice
Theremin
Timpani
Toy Instrument Orchestra
Trautonium
Treble Voice
Triangle
Trio—Instrumental
Trio—Vocal
Trombone
Trombone—Bass
Trumpet
Trumpet—Bass
Tuba
Tuba—Bass
Ukelele
Vibraphone
Viol
Viol—Alto
Viol—Bass
Viol—Division
Viol—Double Bass
Viol—Soprano
Viol—Tenor
Viola
Viola da gamba (see Viol)
Viola d'amore
Viola di bordone (see Baryton)
Violin
Violoncello (see Cello)
Virginal
Welte-Mignon
Whip
Whistle
Whistle—Vocal
Wind Instruments
Wind Band
Woodwind Instruments
Xylophone
Zither

Sample Catalog Cards

The following sample cards illustrate application of the above described simplified procedure.

```
ADM F     Seeger, Pete
S451          American folk songs for children
AMERI         Folkways FT 1501; mono LP disc
01501         Ed. level: Elem.
              Pete Seeger, singer
              Contents: Jim along Josie-2 min., There
              was a man and he was mad-2 min., Clap your
              hands-3 min., She'll be coming 'round the
              mountain-2 min., All round the kitchen-
              2 min., Billy Barlow-3 min., Bought me a
              cat-3 min., Jim crack corn-2 min., Train

                          continued on next card
```

```
ADM F     Seeger, Pete
S451          American folk songs for children
AMERI                                          (Card 2)
01501

              is a-coming-3 min., This old man-2 min., Frog
              went a-courting-4 min.
                  From Ruth Crawford Seeger. American Folk
              Songs for Children: A Book of Musical Nota-
              tions and Notated Guides, for Home and School.
              New York: Doubleday, 1956.

                                    continued on next card
```

```
ADM F     Seeger, Pete
S451          American folk songs for children
AMERI                                          (Card 3)
01501

                  1. Folk songs - America.  I. American
              folk songs for children.
```

```
ADM     Mexico
M611       Folk Music of the Americas
MEXIC      Library of Congress, Division of Music,
00019   Recording Laboratory AFS L19.
           Contents: Cora tribe-Son del elote;
        Son del vanada; Son de la siembra.
        Seri tribe-Cancion del maginero-cansado;.
        Cancion de Dios; Cancion del curandero.
        Tarahumara tribe-Fiesta del peyote; Fiesta de
        la calabaza; Fiesta de los enfermos.

                       continued on next card
```

```
ADM     Mexico
M611       Folk Music of the Americas
MEXIC                                        (Card 2)
00019

           Tzotzil and Tzeltal tribes-Son de San Juan;
        Son de fiesta; Son de carnaval; Anuncio de
        carreras de caballos; Son de Semana Santa.
           Program notes (6p., illus.) by editor.
           Recorded in Mexico, 1944-1946, for the
        Library of Congress in cooperation with the
        Inter-American Indian Institute and Mexico
                             continued on next card
```

```
ADM     Mexico
M611       Folk Music of the Americas
MEXIC                              (Card 3)
00019

        Department of Education. Performed by
        members of Indian tribes, in part with
        accompaniment of wind and percussion
        instruments.
           Henrietta Yurchenco, compiler and
        editor.
           1. Indians of Mexico - Music.  2. Folk
        songs - Mexico.
                          continued on next card
```

```
ADM     Mexico
M611       Folk Music of the Americas
MEXIC                               (Card 4)
00019

           3. Percussion Instruments.  4. Wind Instru-
        ments.  I. Yurchenco, Henrietta, comp.
```

```
ADM J    Herman, Woodrow Charles
H551        Woody Herman - 1963
WOODY       Philips PHM200-065; mono LP disc
00065       Ed. level: Elem.
            Contents: Mo-lasses-7 min.-(Solos: Sal
         Nistico, tenor saxophone; Bill Chase, trumpet)
         Blues for J.P.-3 min.-(Solos: Paul Fontaine,
         trumpet; Gene Allen, baritone saxophone).
         Don't get around much anymore-4 min.-(Solos:
         Paul Fontain, trumpet; Phil Wilson, trom-
         bone; Gene Allen, baritone saxophone).

                            continued on next card
```

```
ADM J    Herman, Woodrow Charles
H551        Woody Herman - 1963
WOODY                                    (Card 2)
00065
            Tunin' in-4 min.  Sister Sadie-3 min.-(Solo:
         Sal Nistico, tenor saxophone).  Sig EP-4 min.
         -(Solos: Larry Cavelli, tenor saxophone; Paul
         Fontaine, trumpet).  It's a lonesome old town
         (when you're not around)-3 min.-(Solo: Phil
         Wilson, trombone).  Camel walk-8 min.-(Solos:
         Gordon Brisker, tenor saxophone; Phil Wilson,
         trombone).
                            continued on next card
```

```
ADM J    Herman, Woodrow Charles
H551        Woody Herman - 1963
WOODY                                    (Card 3)
00065
            Recorded October 1962.
            Personnel: Woody Herman, clarinet and
         leader; trumpets - Bill Chase, Paul Fontaine,
         Dave Gale, Ziggy Harrell, Gerry Lamy; trom-
         bones - Phil Wilson, Eddie Morgan, Jack Gale;
         saxophones - Sal Nistico, Larry Cavelli,
         Gordon Brisker, Gene Allen; rhythm - Nat

                            continued on next card
```

```
ADM J    Herman, Woodrow Charles
H551        Woody Herman - 1963
WOODY                                      (Card 4)
00065
            Pierce, piano, Chuck Andrus, bass, and Jack
         Hanna, drums.
                Ralph J. Gleason, notes on record jacket.
                1. Saxophone - Tenor.  2. Saxophone -
         Baritone.  3. Trombone.  4. Trumpet.  I.
         Nistico, Sal.  II. Chase, Bill,  III. Allen,

                                  continued on next card
```

```
ADM J    Herman, Woodrow Charles
H551        Woody Herman - 1963
WOODY                                   (Card 5)
00065
         Gene.  IV. Fontaine, Bill.  V. Wilson, Phil.
         VI. Cavelli, Larry.  VII. Brisker, Gordon.
         VIII. Title: Woody Herman - 1963.  IX. Mo-
         lasses.  X. Blues for J.P.  XI. Don't get
         around much anymore.  XII. Tunin' in.  XIII.
         Sister Sadie.  XIV. Sig Ep.  XV. It's a
         lonesome old town (when you're not around).

                              continued on next card
```

```
ADM J    Herman, Woodrow Charles
H551        Woody Herman - 1963
WOODY                                      (Card 6)
00065
            XVI. Camel Walk.

                              (826-121375)
```

```
ADS 1    Jannequin, Clement
J34        Le Bataille de Marignan
BAT        Vanguard SRV-298SD; stereo LP disc
00298      Ed. level: Sec.
           Deller Consort
           Duration: 6 min.
           With: Jannequin, Clement. Le chant des
        oiseaux-6 min., Ce moys de may-1 min., Le
        chant de l'Alouette-3 min., O joly boys-2 min.
        Des Prez, Josquin. Parfons regretz-3 min.,

                        continued on next card
```

```
ADS 1    Jannequin, Clement
J34        Le Bataille de Marignan
BAT                                    (Card 2)
00298
        Le deploration de Jehan Okeghem-5 min.
        Lassus, Orlandus (Roland de). Mon coeur se
        recommande a vous-2 min., Le nuit froide et
        sombre-3 min. Passereau. Il est bel et bon-
        1 min. Costeley, Guillaume. Mignonne, allons
        voir-2 min., Allons, gay Bergeres-2 min.
        Machaut, Guillaume de. Comment qu'a moy-
        2 min. Grimace. Alarme, alarme-2 min.
                    continued on next card
```

```
ADS 1    Jannequin, Clement
J34        Le Bataille de Marignan
BAT                                    (Card 3)
00298
        Anon. Or sus dormez trop-1/2 min.
           1. Countertenor.  2. Ensemble - Vocal.
        I. Deller, Alfred.  II. Deller Consort.
        III. - VIII. (composers)  IX. - XXIII.
        (titles)
                        (19-030470)
```

```
ADM A     Cummings, E.E.
C971          EIMI, Lenin's Tomb
POEMS         Caed. TC-1017; mono LP disc
01017         Ed. level: Sec.
              E. E. Cummings reader
              Duration: 13 min.
              With: Cummings, E. E. HIM, the acrobat
          passage-6 min., SANTA CLAUS, Scene Three-8
          min., when serpents bargain for the right to
          squirm-1 min., dying is fine but Death-1 min.,

                          continued on next card
```

```
ADM A     Cummings, E.E.
C971          EIMI, Lenin's Tomb
POEMS                                        (Card 2)
01017
              why must itself up every of a park-2 min.,
          when god decided to invent-1 min., nothing
          false and possible is love-1 min., Hello is
          what a mirror says-1 min., who were so dark
          of heart they might not speak-1 min., i say
          no world-2 min., life is more true than
          reason will deceive-2 min., o by the by-

                          continued on next card
```

```
ADM A     Cummings, E.E.
C971          EIMI, Lenin's Tomb
POEMS                                        (Card 3)
01017
          1 min., one's not half two. It's two are
          halves of one:-2 min., hate blows a bubble of
          despair into-2 min., yes is a pleasant
          country-1 min., i thank You God for most this
          amazing-1 min., "sweet spring is your-2 min.,
          true lovers in each happening of their hearts-
          1 min., when faces called flowers float out of

                          continued on next card
```

```
ADM A     Cummings, E.E.
C971          EIMI, Lenin's Tomb
POEMS                                        (Card 4)
01017
              the ground-2 min.
                  Recorded in New York City on May 28,
          1953.
                  1. American poetry - 20th century.
              I. - XX. (titles).
```

```
ACM C    Thomas, Norman Mattoon
T459        The constant rebel; Socialist leader
PHILO    Norman Thomas discusses his philosophy and
12111    career.
            Forum Assoc.s 020 12111; mono cassette
            Ed. level: Sec.
            Norman Thomas, speaker
            Duration: 28 min.
            Includes bibliography
               1. Socialist Party (U.S.).  2. U.S. -
            Politics and Government - 20th century.

                                    (1836-050372)
```

Care of Sound Recordings

Discs

LP recordings are susceptible to four sources of damage: the factory, poorly maintained or inadequate equipment, mishandling by the user, and adverse environmental conditions. Each of these origins of trouble can be defined and countermeasures taken by the consumer to protect himself.

Damage originating at the factory is more of a problem in America than in Europe because of (1) the enormous size of the U.S. recording industry, and (2) the American propensity to compromise quality control whenever profit margins shrink. European pride of craftsmanship is reflected in insistence upon high standards and can be proved by comparing the sleek, silent surfaces of DGG, Philips, and London with their American counterparts. As with automobiles and the resolution capability of television receivers, the American customer gets no more than he demands and hardly ever what he needs or deserves. Consequently there are many freshly minted, factory-sealed recordings that are warped and pock marked, have clicks and crackles (induced by excessive electrostatic charges built into the plastic), off-center holes, incorrect labels, and other assembly-line defects. However, it is not fair to accuse the manufacturer until you have selectively explained away possible causes within your playing equipment. Make sure that the record, not the equipment, is blemished. Once you have determined that the disc and not the equipment is faulty, return it immediately to the dealer not only to rid yourself of a useless purchase but to corroborate whether the failure is *serial* or *singular* in nature. Sometimes a complete pressing will be tainted, in which case the local man cannot be blamed as everyone everywhere has been faced with the identical flaw. If the replacement you receive is "clean," the trouble is probably confined to that particular disc and the middleman might be responsible, though this is a remote possibility because the former practice of trial listening in record shops has almost completely ceased. If you suspect that prelistening has occurred and your suspicions border on the paranoic, order your popular and jazz discs from classical record stores and buy your classical recordings from places where the "top of the charts" crowd congregates. In other words, pick

a dealer who will put up with paranoia or a store where your kind of recording holds little allure for the customers.

Poorly maintained or cheap equipment is the greatest enemy of recordings and among components the dirty or worn stylus is most often responsible for disc deterioration. A moistened stylus cleaning brush, resembling a child's toothbrush, should be used to remove dust. As with cleaning teeth, a gentle back-and-forth motion is effective. Ethyl alcohol is the ideal cleansing fluid; vodka is an acceptable substitute if it can be diverted from other channels. Proper protection of recordings requires self-control and vigilance in a household with small children and pets. The elaborate detoxification rituals required of returning astronauts seem no more rigorous than the precautions imposed by dedicated audiophiles. White gloves, pre- and post-cleansing, and a strictly choreographed set of motions are part of the playing-listening ceremony. A no-smoking ordinance for listeners is justifiable today as it was not in the past because equipment components in the upper-price ranges have been so perfected that air pollution in the forms of automobile exhaust fumes, cooking and tobacco smoke, and not normal wear through playing, is usually responsible for sound deterioration.

The mechanics of handling a disc are important. When removing a record from its container, bow the jacket to minimize abrasion and keep the fingers off the playing surface. Before replacing the disc within its cover, make sure that the inner transparent-plastic slipcover opens toward the inside of the outer jacket to lessen the entry of dust. Always put away a record as soon as it has been played. If it is not removed from the turntable, it will pick up both floating atmospheric particles plus downward spiraling dust in air eddies generated by the rotating turntable. Each time, before playback or repacking, a detergent (ethyl alcohol or chemically pure ethylene glycol with distilled water) should be applied to the disc surface. A hair dryer may be used to hasten evaporation.

Obviously the above described steps broach upon manic fastidiousness. The public library could not, without negating its cordial image, urge or force its clients to observe such complicated precautions. Because of this good-natured leniency, most public library records are unplayable after less than a year. Also because of this, clever borrowers with valuable collections at home use two plug-in phonocartridges. Their better and more sensitive cartridge is saved for their first-class home collection; the middling quality cartridge is reserved for borrowed recordings.

Environment, primarily because of user error and neglect, plays a major role in record decay. Shelving, temperature, relative humidity, and light are all crucial factors to consider. To provide adequate storage, several factors should be taken into consideration. If records are shelved on a normal bookstack, there should be separators no more than six inches apart to assure that no more than twenty discs are stored within a group. If there are more than this number, leaning or excessive pressure will produce surface distentions and undulations, i.e., warped records. A bit less effective than permanent compartmentalized wooden shelving is a steel bookstack with adjustable slotted separators. The disadvantage is that shelvers can change widths and create sections which permit leaning and slipping. In the home, cabinets should be constructed to conform to these restrictions and doors should be provided to keep out dust.

Removal from close proximity to radiators or exposure to direct sunlight is essential. Partially full vertical shelving should be shored up with dummy fillers so that the records never have enough leeway to cascade down upon one another.

The most convenient and protective style of storage is the browser bin or rack. Record jackets, which often provide useful clues for the would-be borrower, are easily viewable. The leafing-through procedure is less harmful to a collection than the grasp-and-grind motion necessitated by "normal" shelving. Most library furniture manufacturers have browser bins in their catalogs, and laminated plastic, lettered guides can be utilized to create self-sufficient display and storage units. Within a 5-foot wide, 3-foot high unit, it is possible to shelve and display upwards of 250 records. Custom-built units consisting of racks on rollers can accommodate up to three times this number in approximately the same amount of space.

The other great enemy of discs is the natural environment. The combination of warm climate, high humidity, and an environment hospitable to organic growth can stimulate the growth of fungi and degradation of the polyvinyl chloride. PVC in these conditions releases hydrochloric acid. Fortunately, this kind of deterioration is very gradual, taking over a century to occur even in the adverse atmosphere of the unair-conditioned library. A more immediate and harmful emission of corrosive acid occurred several years ago when shelves and books were eaten away by fumes from vesicular microfilm (same chemical structure) stored in overheated and dank environments in public and academic libraries. The ideal temperature for long-term storage is 55 degrees Fahrenheit but 68 degrees is adequate for all libraries except those with archival responsibility. Fifty percent relative humidity is considered optimal. Polyvinyl chloride is a plastic compound with poor resistance to high temperatures (above 80 degrees F.), light, imprints and abrasion, dust, fingerprints, grit, or water. If relative humidity is too low during the winter months, a humidifier or bowl of water may be kept near the turntable with an immersed foam rubber sponge or piece of flannel to promote evaporation.

Avoidance of dust contamination is an extension of good housekeeping practice. This means that (1) the rubber mat on the turntable must be periodically dusted, washed, and dried along with the surrounding playing area; (2) whenever the turntable is not in use, its dust cover should be replaced; (3) records should be kept in their containers when not being played; (4) fluff and sludge on the stylus should not be flicked off with the fingers because body oil can cause more damage than the dust it displaces; and (5) the record surface should not be blown upon to remove flecks of dust because saliva is no substitute for alcohol and any static tendency is further aggravated.

Because static electricity is the natural ally of dust, luring it to the record surface, much inventive effort has been expended by manufacturers in battling this nemesis, from the first breakthrough in 1954 of Cecil Watts' Dust Bug on up to the fairly recent Parastat machine. Collectors reported that the Dust Bug tripled the life expectancy of their recordings, and the other devices further inflated that figure. Static electricity is a subtle nuisance. It may be embedded in the plastic back at the point of manufacture. The friction of removal of records from envelopes adds a charge which is again reinforced when records are cleaned with a dry cloth.

Devices used to combat dust and static electricity fall into two categories, the hand held and the automatic. The dry cleaning cloth is the simplest dust remover. The Bib Record and Stylus Cleaning Kit sold through Revox Corporation (155 Michael Dr., Syosset, N.Y. 11791 and 3637 Cahuenga Blvd. West, Hollywood, Calif. 90068) consists of two cleaning cloths and a stylus brush. The main disadvantage of the dry cloth is of course the static caused by friction. The Watts Preener distributed by Elpa Marketing (New Hyde Park, N.Y. 65201), and the Discwasher (available from Discwasher, 909 University, Columbia, Mo. 65201) add liquid to increase surface humidity. The Preener is a double layer of velvet pad with two brushes of finely tipped nylon bristles in between. As the record is rotated in this velvet sandwich, the brushes remove dust from its grooves while simultaneously applying a thin film of antistatic compound. This protective film can remain on the record for the rest of its playing life. The Discwasher operates in a similar fashion with capillary action conveying particulate matter onto a "uni-directional" brush fiber. A third kind of hand-held cleaner is the ubiquitous velvet pad or brush. Decca has recently developed a super brush with over one million fine bristles.

The Watts Dust Bug remains the most popular of the automatic dry cleaners. Its action is the same as that of the cowcatcher on a locomotive. A small, plush pad, treated with antistatic ethylene glycol or ethyl alcohol in tandem with a nylon brush, sweeps and cleans the grooves in advance of the stylus. Bib Sales (represented in the United States by Revox Corporation) has marketed several models based on this same principle, the Groov-Kleen Model 42, a separate cleaning arm for turntables, and Groov-Kleen Model 45, a record-changer arm attachment. The latter (velvet pad, brush, and carrier) weighs less than three grams so that heaviness is not a problem. On most of the better machines, the arm playing weight can be readjusted to compensate for the attachment's extra bulk; on cheaper equipment the proportional weight increase will be insignificant and those owning inexpensive components are unlikely to purchase this accessory. The Groovac Vacuum Record Cleaner is a composite miniature vacuum cleaner and feather weight arm. A seven-tenths-gram tracking nozzle with extra fine hairs sucks pollutants off the record surface. This device has a larger, expensive cousin for industrial applications, the Keith Monks vacuum pump used by professional record cleansers in England. The Keith Monks machine pumps a mixture of alcohol and distilled water onto the record surface, and the vacuum head draws up the loosened deposits leaving behind a bone-dry, pristine disc.

Still another startling, avant-garde solution to the static problem is the Zerostat ionization pistol (available for about twenty dollars from Zerostat, Nuffield Road, Industrial Estate, St. Ives, Huntingdon. St. Ives 62225 Eng.) This handgun emits positive ions after developing high voltage. After this, negative ions are released so that the charge on the disc surface is completely neutralized. There are numerous other accessories available on the market, some of which should be avoided. Almost without exception, special soaps, silicon-coated cloths, sprays, mists, and gels leave more unwelcome residue than they remove. Also, the sprays tend to become habit forming because deposits they leave behind convince the user that more and not less of the same treatment is needed. It would be more sensible to store records in the refrigerator because of the environmental isolation and optimal temperature. Whenever

the record is removed for playing, moisture condensation guarantees a static-free surface.

In summary, this writer recommends that most institutions should opt for either of the first two types of manual cleaner over the velvet pad or brush because of the latter's greater susceptibility to misuse and dirt accumulation. There should also be, as part of the ongoing inventory procedure, a listening check performed on all recordings every four years to confirm their listenability.

Home listeners should pick a cleaning device compatible with their budget, attitude towards their collection, and quality of hi-fi components.

Tapes

Sources of tape damage are multiple. The factory, an inferior tape formulation, a careless user, a mechanically unsound tape player are all potential causes of malfunctions and deterioration. Reel-to-reel tape, because of its generally higher quality and that of the associated playback equipment, is usually received and maintained in better condition than cassette and cartridge tapes. Although the cassette tape as a sealed unit has a higher resistance to mishandling by children and clumsy adults, the format is disadvantaged by the relative instability of the equipment. Cassette tape has improved in its playback fidelity, and the quality of the hardware is catching up to that of the traditionally superior open-reel machines. However, the mechanical alignment in tape transport systems remains an area of palpable neglect. Record/play head guides, erase head guides, capstans, pinch rollers are too easily jounced askew. After one pass through a unit with an incorrect tracking geometry, a tape can be rendered unlistenable. This problem is not negligible because about half of the cassette recorders that come off manufacturers' shelves have improper alignments. Unfortunately, correction of this fault requires special equipment, care, and skill. If misalignment is suspected, it is best to consult an expert and refer to *Audio* magazine, manufacturers' manuals, and technical guides for assistance.

General tape-equipment maintenance is simpler. Dust, stray magnetic fields, high temperature, and dampness are the main dangers. The tape-deck heads should be cleaned regularly to deter dust from settling on and around the moving parts of the unit, especially the tape guides, magnetic head, capstan, and rubber pressure roller. Tape dust can be removed with alcohol. Cue tips or kitchen matches wrapped in soaked cotton may be used to clean around the guide pins and head channel. No metal tool should ever be employed for this purpose. Bib Sales, represented in the United States by Revox Corporation, provides a variety of tape-care accessories, including cassette and cartridge-head cleaning tapes and maintenance, care, editing, and salvage kits for broken cassettes.

Another problem is created by the incremental magnetification of the tape recorder as each tape is played. Tape which is audited after machine parts have become magnetic has an unacceptable amount of hiss. To avoid this unpleasantness, the magnetic head channel and capstan should be demagnetized after every fifty or so plays by passing a degausser (demagnetizing device) with a stroking motion over all parts which contact the tape. Be sure to remove

any tape from the unit in advance because the degausser will also erase recorded sound if moved in close proximity.

Tape storage requirements are dictated by the medium's sensitivity to environment. Because all current bearing wires have magnetic fields, storage units should be at least two yards from any electrical appliances. Also, most tapes should be stored at approximately 50 percent relative humidity. Tape is sensitive to humidity and becomes brittle if subjected to prolonged storage in a damp environment.

As is the case with disc recordings, ideal storage conditions for tape are uncomfortably cool for humans, ranging between 40 and 60 degrees Fahrenheit. Archival institutions should store master tapes within these temperatures and permit only their copies to be used by the public. Copying is common practice because high-speed duplicators and even coin-operated cassettes are now available and their presence is guaranteed to increase until a much more restrictive copyright law than is in force at present is enacted. Ideally, any tape recordings in the general-access category should be stored as a separate group on narrow, special shelving, slightly angled to the rear.

Another simple means of extending cassette and reel-to-reel tape life and of discouraging annoying print-through is to leave played tape *un*rewound after each hearing. Immediate rewinding permits the tape to remain in an overly taut and compressed position for too long a period of time. This supposed courtesy to the next user therefore has greater implications.

Finally, open-reel tapes that are to be used by the public should be stored side by side like disc recordings within containers designed for this purpose, which are available through most library-equipment supply houses. Pancake pile storage is not recommended because tape spool flanges can become warped from the stress of vertical stacking pressure. Tape storage units suitable for school library use are listed and described in a section of the current edition of the National Audio-Visual Association's *Audio-Visual Equipment Directory* (National Audio-Visual Association, Inc., 3150 Spring St., Fairfax, Va. 22030).

Equipment and 6
Environments for Listening

Listening equipment is usually selected with little care given to specifications and to conditions of use. At one end of the spectrum is the person or institution that chooses equipment that will surpass the intended audience's means and ability to appreciate. The fifty-year-old listener with limited hearing ability who insists upon having recordings played on a 700-watt quadraphonic system with a flat response from 16 through 35,000 Hz is as irrational as the elderly driver who uses a 440 horsepower sports car for short jaunts around town. No less misguided is the school librarian or parent who buys cheap, unsafe, and low-fidelity equipment for children. Three kinds of specifications should enter into any purchase decision: (1) the technical specifications corroborated by independent laboratory tests; (2) specifications dictated by local usage conditions; and (3) specifications predicated entirely upon personal judgment. Relative weighting of their importance will depend upon the purchaser's priorities and experience. The secondary-school library will be concerned primarily with usage-dictated specifications—e.g., durability, pilferage resistance, portability, and compatibility with other district-owned equipment. Taken to an extreme, this emphasis can result in equipment which endures but creates unendurable sound and cripples recordings. In contrast, an affluent private listener may purchase components which satisfy his taste and listening style. Between these two extremes is the person or institution responsible to a governing authority who must rely upon objective findings confirmed by laboratory instruments and written up in *Consumer Reports, Educational Products Information Exchange, High Fidelity,* or some other source. Equipment which receives a favorable laboratory report should not be considered unless local availability of parts and service can also be demonstrated. Otherwise, missing parts, mechanical failures, and the locusts of customer discontent will devitalize the new venture.

The following review of the nature of sound, acoustical phenomena, and human hearing capability is offered before entering into a discussion of audio equipment.

We are awash in an ocean of noise, bathed in undulating particles of air. Sound vibrations have been injected in small increments into our daily existence and have enslaved our conscious so that silence has become difficult to accept. Ironically, as our displeasure over jet, traffic, and city construction noise has become more intense, our tolerance of the din in private spaces has steadily increased. The level of television, appliance, and other machine originated sound has risen. Noxious substances *in* the air produce smarting eyes, emphy-

278

sema, and unsightly and harmful residues. To this visible pollution we react with indignation and corrective measures. Audio pollutants are more insidious. Frayed nerves, digestive disorders, and permanent hearing impairment have been miseries ascribed to noxious substances *on* the air. Lately scientists have speculated that waves in the lowest part of the sound spectrum, below 16 cycles per second, though not heard by the human ear may cause sympathetic vibrations to occur within the body with sufficient intensity to induce internal bleeding. It has been conjectured that infrasonic waves may also be responsible for the heightened irritability or "under the weather" feeling that overtakes people before earthquakes, tornadoes, and sudden atmospheric changes. As for sounds we *can* hear, they are often used as a screen to block out other noises or the silent voice of inner consciousness. The portable or car radio is a surrogate for human companionship, a consoling insulation from silence, or a substitute for other noise. Most of the sound equipment we listen to is worthy neither of our capability nor of the original performance which it recreates. As Abraham Maslow and Henry Thoreau have said, man and environment exercise upon each other a reciprocal raising-lowering effect. If the environment decays, so does the man.

Finally, one could reject background music on strictly legalistic grounds. Music in the supermarket, office, maternity ward, funeral parlor, and points in between is an infringement of liberty and the right to privacy. If we were forced to wear mood-setting glasses in shopping centers and offices to accelerate our spending and productivity, there would be a general outcry and resistance to this manipulation. Sound is universally used for these purposes without public dissent because it is fluid and more devious than sight, having many guises like alcohol. It can be an uncomplicated intoxicant or the transformation of natural live matter into mellow and heartening substance, a dry martini or a noble burgundy. It can be a security blanket for the "sonicolic" as is the bottle for the alcoholic. Because of the variability of tastes, motivations, and tolerance, listening prerogatives should be privately exercised. Any sound other than one's own sound is "noise." If others enjoy it, they are nonetheless being distracted by an attractive nuisance; if they dislike it, they are being bullied.

Every sound heard within an enclosed space has four characteristics: frequency, amplitude, timbre, and reverberation time. Frequencies of sounds formerly designated in "cycles per second" are now called "Hertz." One hundred Hz equals 100 cycles per second. Middle C on the piano keyboard is 256 Hz, and the piano's frequency range extends from 27 Hz to 4096 Hz. The organ's range, the widest of any musical instrument, covers 16 through over 16,000 Hz. The nonscientific and subjective equivalent of frequency is pitch. Young children can hear from 20 Hz on up as far as the top of the organ's range, or in excess of 16,000 Hz. The length or distance from node to node of the wave projected by the bottom note of the piano (27 Hz) is 41 feet! Middle C is about 4 feet long and the highest note on the piano is only 3 inches long. Like large swells on the ocean surface, the longer and lower frequency sounds bypass or flow around small objects. Any experienced concertgoer can attest to this bending effect. Similarly, the rumble of a subway is heard and felt regardless of intervening baffles, but the shriek of brakes or a factory whistle attains its full effect only if the sound source is unobstructed.

279

The timbre of sound is caused by subtle and complex interrelationships between fundamentals and overtones. Timbre is the personality or fingerprint of a sound, analogous to a blend of color and tint in the visible spectrum. The clarinet (buttercup yellow), flute (daffodil yellow), and viola (mustard yellow) may all produce the same fundamental pitch, a 440 Hz A (yellow), but the three instruments remain easily identifiable. For the same reason, sounds produced by close friends and relatives, famous singers, or a Stradivarius are immediately recognized by familiar listeners.

The amplitude of sound identifies its intensity, indicating whether it is a ripple, white cap, or tidal wave. Amplitude is a measure of the width or strength of a sound's vibrations. The most familiar measure of relative loudness is the decibel, or one-tenth of a bel, the common logarithm of a power ratio. One decibel (or dB) is approximately the smallest discernible difference in loudness which the human ear can identify. A whisper at ten paces approximates 10 dB; the reference room of a large research library may reach about 25 dB. Other estimated levels are: living room = 30–40 dB; normal office = 40 dB; piano in living room = 60–80 dB; supermarket on a Saturday afternoon or school playground during a recess = 60–80 dB; chamber music = 70 dB; electric typewriter = 72 dB; door slam = 75 dB; noisy vestibule in city restaurant = 85 dB; heavy traffic or typical cocktail party = 80 dB; fire-engine siren and fortissimos produced by a full symphony orchestra = 90 dB; pneumatic drill = 100 dB. Above the 90 dB mark, one should use ear stopples or protective headsets to avoid pain or permanent hearing damage. Amplified rock bands frequently surpass the 100 dB level and, to no one's surprise, permanent hearing loss has been endemic among performers and many of the listeners to these groups. Not only is the volume of sound they produce set at an intentionally intolerable level but also manufacturers of this music prefer distorted or "dirty" sound at the lower end of the sound spectrum as it increases the harmonic turbulence and muddiness. Low-quality amplification systems heighten the tension and psychic pain (and pleasure?) experienced by the audience.

A fourth characteristic which conditions our response to sound is the environment in which it is heard. Out-of-doors reverberation time carried to an extreme is called an echo. Indoors, its length is determined by the size of the listening enclosure; sound absorbent characteristics of walls, ceilings, and floors; dispersion and placement of sound absorbers within the space; interference patterns and resonances. Reflection angles and reverberation time are the key elements to consider in the design of indoor areas. Outdoor listening facilities are much easier to plan. The sound usually comes directly from the source, whereas within an interior listening environment the sounds that are heard are a compound of direct, reflected, and diffused vibrations which have bounced off glass, walls, ceilings, and other intervening listeners and objects. The optimal design for an outdoors auditorium was first suggested by Greek geometricians, later by the sixteenth-century Jesuit mathematician, Athanasius Kircher, and reconfirmed by contemporary architects. All have agreed that a parabolic shield placed in front of an orchestra would reflect the sound equally to all members of a listening audience. The Blossom Music Center outside Akron, Ohio, reaffirms the reliability of this ancient model. Acoustically inefficient outdoor structures are rare.

Weather conditions, not poorly constructed sheds, shells, or stadia, are responsible for the spectacularly sour sound which audiences sometimes hear in open-air summer concerts. The sound wave lengths propagated by woodwinds, organ pipes, and brass instruments remain constant because they are dictated by the unchanging dimensions of the instruments. They cannot be adjusted (as can the human voice or violin) to compensate for environmental conditions and sound wave velocity automatically increases as the temperature and humidity rise. Because velocity is the product of wave length times frequency, the pitch of the instruments rises whenever the air becomes warm and more humid. Romantic woodwind and band music suffer most from the vagaries of weather. An extreme illustration of velocity acceleration occurs if one inhales helium or hydrogen gas. The sound velocity is increased so that the normal pitch produced by the human vocal cords shifts upwards several octaves producing a comical effect. To a lesser degree this change is what accounts for faulty intonation during open-air concerts on humid summer evenings.

The reverberation rate is of utmost importance in the design of a suitable interior listening space. Unfortunately, what is desirable for speech is unsatisfactory for music. Even within music, the characteristics of optimal listening enclosures vary according to the tempo, orchestration, and style of works being heard.

In the spaces in schools, the diffusion of intelligible sound from area to area is undesirable, and a relatively dead sound is preferred so that speech articulation is as clear as possible. The ideal reverberation time in the classroom is about .67 seconds. If the space is more live, there is difficulty in understanding normal conversation. The rate of sound decay becomes so slow that one or more syllables hang on the air and overlap. In an extremely live room, ideal for music listening, this muddying of sound applies not only to the wanted sounds but also to intruding sounds, whether from the room itself or from external sources, which may compound the confusion. The conflicting sounds can emanate from heating and ventilating units or worn baffles in fluorescent fixtures. Or they can originate from neighboring spaces, being caused by moving objects or people, impacts of trays, feet, scraping, scuffling, or other distracting sources. Within the schools, intelligible interference is even more annoying than unintelligible interference. Open schools, which are planned so that sounds over 50 feet distant are blended into a general hum, are preferable to installations where distant conversations or music are clearly etched in the ear. In short, classrooms or teaching spaces require short-distance clarity and a low reverberation rate, while music listening requires long-distance definition and a relatively high reverberation time.

Optimal reverberation time depends upon the size of the space and kind of sound presented. An optimal reverberation time for a 10-by-10-by-10-foot space approximates one second. This goes up to 1.5 seconds for a 10,000 cubic foot enclosure and approximately 1.7 seconds for a large hall. Reverberation times should be adjusted to suit various performances. Modern music demands more clarity than romantic music. It has been suggested that 1.48 seconds is the optimal for modern music, 2.07 seconds for romantic and choral works, and 1.54 seconds for classical. A crowded concert hall is always less reverberant than a sparsely populated one, so that modern music is usually played in an overly live environment but Tchaikovsky and Brahms, who customarily

281

fill the house, are played in a relatively dead space. The result is adverse modification of acoustics for both kinds of music and so provides ammunition for those who advocate listening in the home. A common situation illustrates this conflict between speech and music requirements. In a large church or cathedral, the organ tone, because of the extreme reverberation, may be enhanced while the minister's sermons remain almost entirely unintelligible unless loudspeakers beam his words simultaneously to all corners of the church. In these cases, echo effects usually becloud the speech.

For the listener at home, experimentation is advised. If a living room is too live, one can try the expedient of gradually bringing in pillows, carpets, heavy drapery, and friends until an acceptable level of deadness is achieved. Sound-absorbency characteristics for various substances are expressed as coefficients. The higher the coefficient from .000 to 1.000, the more sound a substance will absorb. A chair with a hard seat and back rates .038, a soft-seat chair with cloth back raises this value to .16. The same chair with a sitting listener has a coefficient of .49. Cotton-cloth drapery has a coefficient of .35 while a brick wall and mirror have .07 and .04 respectively. An open window rates a 1.00 because *all* of the sound directed towards it escapes into outer space.

Localized listening can be accommodated in an open-school environment only if the damping of transmitted sound is effective and the focus of radiated sound blurs as it moves towards other people in the space. Sometimes, despite extremely low noise levels in libraries, even a whisper will carry a relatively great distance and irritate others. A clever way of handling such a problem is by masking or enveloping humans' intermittent sounds within a random "white" noise signal with no rhythmic pulse or timbre. This denatured noise drowns out both natural and any other association-laden, man-made sounds.

The effects of acoustical conditioning merge into our daily experience. Mental images of gymnasia, corridors, classrooms, and office and library areas are flavored as much by their acoustical properties as by their visual attributes. A cocktail party or banquet in a gymnasium would be a trial of endurance because whenever the general sound level is too high due to insufficient boundary absorption by drapery, carpeting, or other softening materials, people almost instinctively talk more loudly than in a heavily draped, noise-inhibiting enclosure. This tendency in turn increases the general noise level in a rising spiral until finally the guests are literally shouting without achieving satisfactory intelligibility. In contrast, acoustically calming spaces by their very presence elicit muted behavior from students and teachers. Many schools have media centers which fail only because they frustrate the listening, viewing, and studying activities of their occupants. There is no excuse for this situation because acoustics can be designed into a school with amazing precision. Educational Facilities Laboratories reports and a substantial technical literature confirm this point.

Inner human hearing, however, remains far less amenable to definition. Cultural conditioning, individual hearing ability, and climate filter and add to what one hears. Young children can usually hear tones from 16 Hz to as high as 20,000 Hz, while persons over fifty years of age are limited to a constricted range of about 40 Hz to 5,000 Hz. Intelligible speech covers the 100–5,000 Hz range, while music extends from 16 Hz through 20,000 Hz. Most of what the ear hears is around the 3,000 Hz mark; our sensitivity to loudness is acute

in this midrange sector. Keenness of hearing has been linked to mental and physical health. A dyspeptic, hypochondriacal, or tense individual is more sensitive to sound and has a lower tolerance for noise than the average listener. While the "sonicolic" indiscriminately basks in sound, his nervous neighbor is being bruised and violated. The inventory of common disturbing sounds has been ranked and found to include, in order of annoyance, jet aircraft, followed by young children, followed by domestic appliances, and other people's television and radio sets. There is increasing speculation that the health hazard of noise is at least as serious as that posed by polluted air or water.

Beyond the psychic and physiological differences between individuals there is the conditioning of local culture. For example, East Indian students who have been unexposed to scale steps of Western music have an inordinately difficult (by occidental standards) time identifying directions in pitch change. A frequency change of 4 percent (more than a semitone at C below high C) which is easy for even the untrained Western ear to discern cannot be identified by an individual nurtured in a culture which has encouraged other kinds of acuity, such as awareness of rhythm or timbre. It is possible that many more listeners would have absolute pitch if transposition from one key to another had not become an experience ingrained from an early age. We have no trouble seeing distinctions among reds, yellows, blues, and greens, and composers, notably Wagner, Rimsky-Korsakoff, and Scriabin, have assigned traits to the chroma of keys. G is green and sentimental, C is bright and white, D is yellow and open, and B minor is purple and melancholic. The implication is that we are musically imprecise because of the escape from the need to relate all of music's spectrum to a single fixed tone (do) or polar star in the sonic firmament. Similar to this decay is the erosion investigators have noted in visual perception. As we became less dependent upon sight cues to forewarn us of natural predators, our interpretive ability lessened as it became an incidental rather than imperative condition of survival.

Despite this attrition of ability, most of which has been circumstantially and culturally inspired, the human ear is still more sensitive than the most advanced electronic apparatus for sensing, analyzing, and responding to the nuances of sound propagation. For this reason, the very finest reproduction equipment within budgetary limits is mandatory for those who wish to extend and enrich their lives with recorded music.

Specifications Preparation

A fundamental error is made by those who select equipment after having only heard A-B comparisons in a hi-fi salon. Preparation of specifications in advance is required of any institutional purchaser who is buying on behalf of others and is also strongly advised for the home purchaser. As with automobiles, encyclopedias, and insurance policies, selection should be predicated

upon a careful study of alternatives, local requirements, the credibility of the sales organization, and qualities of the offered products. Specifications may be divided into three types: performance, situational, and subjective. Performance specifications have by now been very precisely defined in the sound-equipment field. Frequency response, total harmonic distortion (THD), the ratio of desirable signal to noise (S/N), speed accuracy, power output, and vertical tracking force (VTF) are rated by independent laboratories and subsequently published in *Audio*, *Gramophone*, *Consumer Reports*, and other popular journals. The buyer can scan and compare reports on components being considered and check findings against his own minimum specifications.

Situational specifications do not relate to sound reproduction capability; they refer to a component's or system's usefulness within a particular context. They define durability of case material, portability, service conditions in the purchaser's locality, price, ease of use, repair frequency, convenience and simplicity of operation, resistance to rough handling, cost of replacement parts, and safety features.

Subjective specifications are personal opinion. For example, speakers A and B may have equally outstanding performance specifications, but experienced listeners divide into two camps, the A and B advocates. Speaker A is liked because of its silky, sleek sound by those who collect electronic and popular music, while B is the overwhelming favorite of the chamber music listeners because of its more patrician, mellow sound. There are also components which are popular because of performance deficiencies which produce pleasurable distortion and masking at points in the sonic spectrum where many prefer haze to clarity. Although all three kinds of specifications should inform any equipment purchase decision, librarians rely primarily upon subjective and improvisatory judgments because of their lack of mechanical literacy and traditional indifference to technology. The writing of performance specifications for supportive equipment in the schools is scandalously devoid of stringency. While situational specifications have assumed a high priority, performance qualities have been neglected. There are three markets for equipment manufacturers as there are for automobile manufacturers. There is the utility vehicle or stripped-down, basic transportation/maximum durability taxicab/pickup truck (*situational* specifications are uppermost); there is the series of passenger cars for the average consumer (*performance* specifications are crucial); there is the custom vehicle for the person who wants to drive something out of the ordinary (*subjective* specifications dominate). Because the school market falls into the first category, industry has developed inexpensive, sturdy, no-nonsense equipment with low-performance specifications to meet the needs of the economy/durability conscious clientele.

As one examines the equipment in the National Audio-Visual Association's *Audio-Visual Equipment Directory*, one is struck by the overriding concern with *situational* specifications: low cost, teacher convenience, and features to please the accountability-minded purchaser. However, the attention to fidelity requirements for the reproduction of fine music is minimal. Compliance, distortion, frequency response, power, and evenness of production quality across the sonic range, specifics about cartridge, stylus, vertical tracking force, tone-arm weight, speaker sound characteristics are absent or deficient. The public, academic library, and typical consumer are more alert to performance specifi-

cations. These markets are more competitive, less incestuous, not as inclined to box themselves into contract commitment corners. Finally, for those who seek near perfect sound and have time and money to indulge themselves, there are luxury, ultrarefined components such as the Revox tape decks, Dayton-Wright XG–8 speaker, and Phase Linear 700 amplifier.

Consumers of equipment at any level should balance their attention to the three kinds of specifications because lack of attention to any one set of criteria will result in a purchase blunder. Poorly performing equipment is a double disaster; distorted sound is forced upon the listener and the recording collection's depreciation rate will increase. If we are concerned about the fidelity of art reproductions and corrective lenses in glasses, we should be equally concerned about the ability of phonographs and tape players to reproduce the content of discs and tapes. Poor equipment, not the user, is most responsible for record wear. Some examples of inadequate *performance* specifications can illustrate this.

First, there is the sapphire stylus, commonly found in schools. The sapphire has a maximum playing life of only 12 hours before its point deteriorates into a jagged, gouging instrument. This deterioration is rapid in schools because the tracking weight of their units' tone arms usually far exceeds the 5-gram maximum pressure to which both disc and needle should be exposed. In contrast, a diamond stylus, exerting a vertical tracking force of less than 2 grams, can traverse upwards of 1,000-hours worth of surfaces before it becomes a menace to records. An insidious factor is the willingness of the human ear to ignore deterioration of sound quality. The ear, like the eye or nose, can develop an allusion of adequacy or indifference to environmental spoilage which to an outsider or to one who has freshly met the situation, seems intolerable. Familiarity is more likely to breed acceptance than skepticism.

Another threat to discs is the poorly designed record changer. For any person aware of the multiple possibilities for record wear and improper groove-stylus interface, the cheap changer is an anathema; this detestation is justifiable. First, when records are stacked and slapped onto other records, the vinyl surfaces rub against one another and abrasion occurs. Second, as each record is added to the stack, the angle of contact with the record surface shifts so that the tracking of the grooves becomes uneven and incomplete. One distressing consequence is that records played consistently as singles, develop over time a differing wear pattern than those stacked in the third or higher positions. Also the needle will modify its original shape to conform with the angle of impact. After a while its contour will fit best the grooves in the bottommost record because single discs are played most frequently. Consequently, the upper records will suffer more from wear. Third, there is the problem of the horizontal angle between the contact point of the tone arm and the disc. Records are cut on a lathe-like machine but played back by an arm with a fixed pivot. The pivot should move with the stylus as it tracks from the outer to inner edge of the playing surface so that the whole tone arm slides in toward the center. Only the better turntables and the Dual, Elac, Miracord, BSR, and Garrard top line models have found ways of solving this geometry problem. Fourth, inexpensive changers inflict damage in yet another way. Their tracking weights are generally excessive enough to hasten wear, and the pressure of the stylus against the side of the groove mounts as the arm moves towards the center of the

disc. An increase in lateral pressure is required to activate a change cycle. Therefore, most records that have been played on changers develop a tell-tale muddiness at the beginning and end of each side. Worn center holes develop, the playing speed fluctuates, and an annoying wobble results. A "swinger" has been born.

Although it is not assumed that the average school or library can afford the very best, it also cannot afford the worst. Performance standards for equipment should be carefully developed by experts, enforced, and updated at least every two years.

The *subjective* specification is important because the ear, despite advances in modern electronics, remains the most accurate and sensitive audio pattern analyzer. The ear reacts to sound across the time dimension which the machine cannot differentiate and interpret. No oscillograph can distinguish between sounds created by a master pianist and a competent child, but the musician or musically sensitive ear easily senses the difference. The magnitude of artistic persuasion cannot be measured by electronic instruments. Likewise, the adequacy of hi-fi equipment's response to variations in texture or the blending of orchestral colors is best appraised by the human ear. One must continually remind oneself that fidelity is just that—the degree to which the reproduction creates in the listener the illusion that what is heard is *un*recorded or live. To further compound the complexity of subjective demand, there is a host of other factors, each differing for each listener as conditioned by the times and environments in which the listening experiences occur. Health, temperament, acoustics, age, time of day, and other variables are among these additive effects. Yet despite all of these *subjective* imponderables, the prospective buyer should draw up minimal performance and situational specifications before setting forth on a purchase expedition.

Sample Specifications and Sound Systems

Five cost levels are treated in this section: (1) phonographs for three- to seven-year-old children's personal use ($25–90); (2) listening equipment appropriate for the elementary school library media center ($90–200); (3) equipment for secondary school libraries and small public libraries ($200–350); (4) equipment for larger public, academic, and music libraries, and enjoyment in the home ($350–700); and (5) components for the connoisseur ($700–   ).

Phonographs for Three– to Seven–Year–Old Children ($25–90)

Performance specifications: Maximum tracking force of 5 grams. Sapphire stylus. Ability to play 33⅓ and 45 rpm monophonic recordings. Correct speed within a half-tone and freedom from distracting flutter (sustained piano tone should not waver).

Situational specifications: Pliable and durable plastic case. Portable (less than 15 pounds weight). No exposed live recesses within reach of a child's fingers or hairpins. Undetachable parts except for the stylus. Sapphire stylus. Underwriters Laboratories approval for electrical and mechanical safety. Speaker should be reasonably well protected from exploratory probes. Undetachable power cord (otherwise child can electrocute self at live end of plugged-in cord). Safety flange on power plug. Clamp-on arm rest. On-off and volume controls only.

Subjective specifications: Reproduction quality should be such that music recordings give pleasure to the child and minimal displeasure to adults. Fuzzy, tinny, fluttery sounding phonographs should be avoided. Because of wide variations among individual units bearing the same model designation, preexamination prior to purchase is advised.

Although no phonograph was capable of meeting all specifications as of 1975, the Panasonic Funnygraph Model SG200 had imaginatively solved the problem of modifying fragile machinery to withstand the brusque movements of young children. The Funnygraph tone arm is preset in playing position within the cover of the machine and does not touch the disc surface until the machine is closed. Arm skittering-skating accidents are circumvented. To its disadvantage, this cleverly conceived phonograph has high flutter, an arm which tracks too heavily, a speaker cone within reach of curious fingers, and a stylus which is too easily removed.

Purchase of a phonograph for a preschooler is at best a mixed blessing. Such a machine offers a child pride of ownership, independent listening opportunities, and a headstart on the road to music appreciation. However, the supply of worthwhile monophonic recordings is minuscule, the sound is execrable by adult standards, machinery of this sort is short-lived and has more than its share of mechanical ailments, and addiction to the listening habit will mean harassment for all adults within earshot.

Equipment for the Elementary School Library Media Center ($90–200)

Portable Stereo Record Player

Performance specifications: Maximum tracking force of 4 grams. Wow and flutter less than .20 percent. Rumble more than 40 dB down. Both channels reproduce 100–10,000 Hz plus or minus 4 dB. IM distortion less than 4 percent. THD less than 4 percent. Negligible speed error; no more than a quarter tone off pitch. 8 watts power with no clipping. Diamond stylus for stereo discs. Magnetic cartridge. Can play 7-, 10-, and 12-inch discs. Has two 12-inch round or 4-by-6-inch built-in oval speakers. Separate tone controls for bass and treble. Automatic shutoff after record side is completed.

Situational specifications: Tone-arm drop guard. Tone-arm lock for support. Finger lift for tone arm. Rubber mat turntable. 10-inch or wider diameter turntable. Fine speed adjustment. 2 input and 2 output jacks. Headphone jack. 2 microphones and mixer. Sufficient speaker cord to permit at least 8 feet separation of speakers for stereo projection. Built-in 45-rpm adaptor. Shock mounted feet. 3-conductor, nondetachable power cord exceed-

ing 6½ feet in length *or* self-storing 15-foot power cord. Maximum weight of 35 pounds. Durable cover with storage space within case. Clear instruction manual; instructions should also be embossed on machine or in case lid. 1-year warranty. Parts and service locally available. Underwriters Laboratories label. Simple and clearly marked controls.

Subjective specifications: Ability to reproduce satisfactorily the spoken word and musical recordings acquired by the library media center.

The better machines within the above category will disappoint those who look for full-range and distortion-free reproduction of orchestral and operatic music. For folk music, spoken word, light rhythmic, and program music such equipment will suffice.

There are several stereo record players which meet most performance specifications but may not hold up under rough handling in districts. Poorer sounding but more ruggedly constructed models may be preferred in such situations. Specifications of the VM 296 AV which offers adequate fidelity are offered below to illustrate acceptable equipment in this range.

VM (Voice of Music) 296 AV ($149.50)

Performance specifications: Tracking force of 5 grams. Wow and flutter is .16 percent. Rumble is 43 dB down on both channels. Both channels reproduce about 120–10,000 Hz. Negligible speed error; less than ⅛ tone off pitch. 8-watts maximum power without clipping. Diamond stylus for LP discs. Ceramic cartridge (below specification). Plays 16⅔, 33⅓, 45, and 78 rpm discs. Plays 7-, 10-, 12-inch diameter discs. 2 separate speakers. Separate tone controls for bass and treble. Automatic shutoff after record side is completed.

Situational specifications: Tone-arm drop guard only partially effective because protective bumper does not extend far enough to prevent stylus from striking deck next to tone arm rest. Tone-arm lock for support. Finger lift for arm. Stylus may also be lifted by pressing down on rear portion of tone arm behind fulcrum. Rubber mat turntable. 10–inch diameter turntable. No fine speed adjustment (a disadvantage). 2 input jacks and 4 output jacks—2 speaker outputs (pin plug jacks) and 2 headphone outputs (¼–inch stereo phone jacks). Built-in 45-rpm adaptor. Sufficient speaker cords to permit minimum of 8 feet between speakers for stereo separation. Unit rests on 4 rubber feet. 3-conductor, nondetachable, 6½–foot power cord. Weight of 32 pounds. Durable case of ⅜-inch wood covered with vinyl. Storage space for power cord in back. Case corners protected with metal corner guards. Plastic carrying handle and skid bumpers to prevent scuffing of exterior finish opposite handle. Clear instruction manual—covers identification of all components, usage and function of each control, use of arm rest and lock, stylus selection and replacement, auxiliary input, warranty terms, and includes an assembly diagram. 1-year warranty with labor at no charge for 90 days. Parts and services locally available. Underwriters Laboratories label. Pilot light. Simple and obvious controls. Tracking pressure may be adjusted to zero grams.

Subjective specifications: Ability to reproduce satisfactorily spoken word and musical recordings acquired by the library media center.

Other companies, for example Newcomb and Audiotronics, manufacture units which, while they compromise sound fidelity, promise superior endurance in active school environments.

Headphones for Portable Stereo Record Players

For those unwilling to accept the expedient of purchasing equipment which compromises either sound or durability requirements, there is the option of private listening units; that is, phonographs without external loudspeakers. For fine arts and music departments of public libraries, study carrel locations in schools, or wherever private listening stations can be used, this alternative makes sense. Much better sound, lower distortion and wider frequency response, can be built into equipment by the manufacturer when the power requirement of external speakers is eliminated. For less than $200, a set which does not offend the discriminating ear can be selected. The Shure Model SA–10 is such a self-contained sound system that integrates several superior components within one unit. A Garrard 4-speed automatic turntable, Shure amplifier, and high-quality cartridge are combined and the aforementioned fidelity specifications are exceeded. For example, instead of delivering 100–10,000 Hz plus or minus 4 dB called for in the specifications, the Model SA–10 puts out 20–19,000 Hz plus or minus 3 dB. Its tracking force can be adjusted down to 3 grams, there is no discernible rumble, and the controls have a spartan simplicity as there are only three functions: on-off, volume, and turntable speed selection. Headphones to go with the model SA–10 or any other private listening unit should meet the following minimum specifications:

Performance specifications: 10–10,000 Hz + or − 3 dB. 8–16-ohm impedance. Stereo.

Situational specifications: 27-ounce maximum weight. Adjustable steel headband with plastic cover. Nontoxic, vinyl-covered cable. Volume control on headset. Tangle-free coil at least 10 feet long. Power cord with standard 3-conductor phone plug. Around-the-ear–circumaural fitting headset.

Subjective specifications: 30 minutes of sustained listening provides a pleasant experience. A try-on session should allow for comparison with at least two other units at the same price level.

Before deciding to invest in a headset, the buyer should determine whether or not awareness of outside sound is required during listening sessions. For example, it may be advisable for the user to be able to respond to external signals such as crying children, telephones, coworkers' or teachers' voices. In these cases, the on-the-ear rather than around-the-ear style headphone is preferable. The Sennheiser Electronic Corporation produces clean-sounding and relatively inexpensive sets that permit one to pick up peripheral noise while listening to recorded sound. For the person who seeks isolated communion with his recordings, the Koss Pro 4AA headphone is an excellent choice. AKC (North American Philips Corporation) and Lafayette have good around-the-ear phones in this same price range. The purchaser should look for discounts on these top-rated models as the difference in quality between them and units costing $20 less is sufficiently dramatic to make the search worthwhile.

289

Cassette Tape Recorder

Within this same price bracket for equipment suitable for middle and secondary school applications, the following minimum specifications are suggested:
Performance specifications: IM distortion of less than 3 percent. THD of less than 3 percent at full output. Maximum output to exceed 4 watts. Tape head temperature to not exceed 120 degrees Fahrenheit. S/N ratio to exceed 40 dB.

Situational specifications: Carrying case of scuff-and-dent-resistant plastic. Storage space within case for cassettes, headphones, and essential accessories. 2 or more outputs for headphones. Cassette ejection device to minimize user frustration and forcing of tape or transport mechanism. Piano key controls, *not* rotating knobs or T shifts. Jam-proof controls, so that if 2 or more controls are used simultaneously no damage occurs. 3-conductor, nondetachable power cord over 6½ feet long. Underwriters Laboratories approval label confirming mechanical and electrical safety. Dual track capability. Index/tape counter. VU (volume unit) meter. Simple but thorough instruction manual, which is very helpful if key usage steps are embossed or imprinted on tape recorder as a convenient memory aid. Pause control, essential if language study, dictation, editing are anticipated. Volume and tone controls. 10-millimeter spacing between miniphone (microphone) and submini plug (remote control), on-off, combination jack. Availability of local service and parts.

Subjective specifications: Should reproduce satisfactorily prerecorded cassette tapes similar to those used in the school or library media center. Should be able to record local events with acceptable fidelity. Should be approved by all staff who will be heavily involved with its use.

Two models are cited below as examples of units which meet and/or surpass the preceding specifications. Both are good choices for general school district applications.

Sony/Superscope TC-180 AV ($179.95)
In addition to meeting the preceding specifications, this model has the following additional features:

1. An end-of-tape alarm.
2. Automatic recording level. The recorder adjusts itself to levels of incoming sound precluding the need for human monitoring of the VU meter. This feature is not desirable for recording music as orchestral climaxes and very soft passages are flattened out and lose their dynamic contours. Ideally this feature should be an *optional,* separate control which can be activated when needed to tape conferences, conversations, plays.
3. Provision for audible or headphone monitoring of recording input.
4. Ability to mix input from 2 microphones.
5. Public address capability.
6. Locking and/or momentary controls for fast forward and rewind.

Sharp RD–465U ($94.95)
This model is an excellent buy for the money. Although its wattage and frequency response capability are not comparable to the power and fidelity of

the Sony/Superscope 180 AV, the Sharp has established an excellent reputation among users and has been favorably reviewed by EPIE (Reports 56 and 59). This particular model has an automatic level control, built-in microphone, and easily viewable, full-size, record level meter which also indicates battery condition. The controls have braille markings and are color coded, the construction is fairly solid, and an automatic end-of-tape stop feature cuts down on machine wear.

Equipment for Secondary Schools, Small Public Libraries ($200–350)

Within this range exists equipment suitable for situations where tonal quality and solid construction weigh equally in the purchase decision. A cassette tape recorder which illustrates qualities one may expect at this magnitude of expenditure is the Telex Communications Telex 529. It meets or surpasses all performance specifications indicated in range level 2 for cassette tape recorders. The situational specifications also extend beyond those enumerated for the previous level. The extra refinements are asterisked in the listing below:

Situational specifications: Cassette ejection button. Very detailed, clear, explicit instruction manual. Unjammable controls—if 2 keys are depressed at the same time, no functions are activated. Underwriters Laboratories label. Permanently attached power cord is 6 feet, 8 inches long and has a safety ground. *AC 2-prong wall adaptor is provided with the unit. Dual track capability. Record level meter. *Pause control device. Index-tape counter. Molded plastic, durable case. Headphone, speaker, and auxiliary outputs provided. Storage space in case to accommodate microphone, cord, and spare cassettes. Tape head temperature rises no higher than 74 degrees Fahrenheit. Automatic level control. *Input may be monitored while recording. *Portions of tape may be reviewed by rewinding (with the review key) without taking the recorder out of the play mode. *Unit may be table mounted. *Controls are color coded and marked in braille. *Microphone and microphone stand are included within the purchase price. *Automatic end-of-tape shut-off.

Cassette tape recorders are fast becoming refined instruments, and it is now possible to select from a growing number of models which integrate high-performance quality with the utilitarian sturdiness desirable in a school setting. In contrast, the phonograph fails to offer anywhere near the variety of models of acceptable worth within this same price range. Three firms which have dominated the school market for the past decade have seemingly conspired to drag their heels rather than move ahead in the area of performance specifications. They may have done too little because insufficient pressure has been applied by customers who are indifferent to or ignorant of performance standards. Although efficient service, tamper-proof construction, ruggedness, and simplicity of controls have been achieved, the performance quality of phonographs has remained disappointing. The comparisons in table 3 pinpoint this gap between technically feasible performance specifications and the lower-order characteristics of two relatively expensive models offered by companies which currently dominate the school product market.

Before paying this much money for subminimal performance and the certainty of hastened wear and depreciation of disc holdings, the school consumer

Table 3. Comparison of Performance Specifications

Specification Elements	Preferred	Model A ($240)	Model B ($250)
Tracking force	3 grams	6 grams	5 grams
Wow and flutter	less than .15	.12	.12
Rumble	40+ dB down	34 dB down	40 dB down
Frequency response	30–16,000 Hz ±3 dB	97–10,400 Hz ±3 dB	100–11,000 Hz ±3 dB
IM distortion	less than 3%	28%	17%
THD	less than 3%	4.2%	7%
Wattage	minimum 8 watts without clipping	5 watts maximum	10 watts maximum
Stylus	diamond	sapphire	sapphire
Cartridge	magnetic	ceramic	ceramic
Type of power	transistorized	transistorized	vacuum tube

should investigate equipment made for the general consumer. KLH, Zenith, Sony, Lafayette, and Sylvania have marketed units which are kinder to both records and the human ear, even though these companies are not represented in the National Audio-Visual Association's *Audio-Visual Equipment Directory.* Only if student use of equipment is very loosely supervised should educators feel constrained to limit their exploration to listening units of the standard manufacturers that serve schools. In contrast to the drab sonic quality of most existing school equipment, the KLH 34 FM, a phono and FM combined system priced at less than $350, includes a Garrard changer, Pickering cartridge, a 10–watt per channel stereo receiver, and matching 2-way speakers. The package provides aural satisfaction unattainable from educational market products costing upwards of $450.

Equipment for Larger Public, Academic, and Music Libraries ($350–700)

The equipment considered here is for planners of sound systems for public and academic libraries with demanding and urbane patrons or for situations in which music appreciation is an essential curricular element. Controlled use, adequate security, and a listening schedule crowded enough to justify the investment are necessary preconditions for purchase. At this point, subjective specifications begin to assume more importance as selection criteria. Accordingly, specification illustrations are omitted for this and the next range of equipment pieces. Instead, three groupings of sound system components to satisfy all but the most severely discriminating tastes are cited. These components have been judged superior by a consensus of equipment critics and their quality has been corroborated by personal listening tests.

COMPONENTS	GROUP 1	GROUP 2	GROUP 3
Speakers	Advent 2-Way	Hegeman H-1	AR-5
Amplifiers and receivers	Dynakit SCA-80Q amplifier and Dynakit FM-5 tuner	Marantz 2230 receiver	Kenwood KR5200 receiver
Automatic changers	Dual 1229 Automatic	Elac/Miracord 770H Automatic	Garrard Zero 100 Automatic

Components for the Connoisseur ($700–   )

For those persons whose high-fidelity tastes are unfettered by price limits, three component groups are listed below which are "state of the art" quality, coming very near to reproducing absolute sonic reality. Although specific model designations will change, these manufacturers will probably continue their production of such components for the audio connoisseur.

COMPONENTS	GROUP 1	GROUP 2	GROUP 3
Speakers	AR Magneplanar Tympani IIIa	KLH 9	Quad or Infinity Servo-Statik 1
Power amplifiers	Phase Linear 700B	Crown DC-300A	AR Dual 76 or Harmon/Kardon Citation 12
Preamplifiers	Phase Linear 4000	Crown IC-150	AR SP-3a or Harmon/Kardon Citation 11a
Tuners	Marantz 10B	Sequerra Model 1	Harmon/Kardon Citation 14
Turntables	Panasonic SP-10 with Rabco SL-8E tonearm	Thorens TD-125 with SME 3009II arm	Sony TTS-3000A
Cartridges	ADC/XLM	Ortofon M-15E Super	Shure V15 Type III
Headphones	Koss ESP-9	Stax SR-3	Stax SRX
Tape decks	Revox A-77 MkII	Braun TG-1000	Nagra IV S

Equipment Reviews

Equipment selection is safer if one's actions are guided by reliable reports rather than by impulse, salesmen's preachments, hi-fi salon demonstrations, or hearsay evidence. The sources listed below provide appraisals independent of bias, technically thorough, and generally comprehensible to the layman.

SOURCE	AUDIENCE
The Absolute Sound. Quarterly. $8/yr. Subscription address: P.O. Box 115, Sea Cliff, N.Y. 11579.	Perfectionists with the money to indulge their tastes.
Audio. Monthly. $7/yr. Subscription address: 134 N. 13th St., Philadelphia, Pa. 19107.	Persons with an uncommon interest in the technical aspects of sound reproduction.
Consumer Reports. Monthly. $11/yr. Publisher, Consumers Union of United States, Inc. Subscription address: P.O. Box 1000, Orangeburg, N.Y. 10962.	Consumers seeking an unbiased review of a wide spectrum of products. Reviews are more thorough and uncompromising on performance than those in *EPIE* and *LTP* (q.v.) but less attentive to situational specifications.
EPIE Educational Product Reports. Membership service of the Educational Products Information Exchange Institute, 463 West St., New York, N.Y. 11014. Five "In Depth" Reports and four "In Brief" Reports are published between October and June of each year. Membership $50/yr. Nonmembers may purchase "In Depth" *Reports* for $10 each and "In Brief" *Reports* for $3 each. EPIE is a nonprofit educational corporation chartered in 1967 by the Regents of the University of the State of New York. P. Kenneth Komoski is the institute's executive director.	Elementary and secondary school purchasing agents, curriculum/instructional planners, teachers, librarians, and administrators. Provides very useful situational specifications and performance data.
Gramophone. Monthly. $17.40/yr. with index; $20.90/yr. via airmail. Subscription address: General Gramophone Publications Ltd., 177–179 Kenton Rd., Harrow, Middlesex, HA3OHA Eng.	All persons interested in recorded sound. The "quality" amongst periodicals which deal with audio recordings.
High Fidelity/Musical America. Monthly. $16.00/yr. with *Musical America* inbound. Subscription address: P.O. Box 14156, Cincinnati, Ohio 45214.	General listeners. Nontechnical tutorials often included for those who seek basic knowledge of hi-fi terms.
Library Technology Reports. Bimonthly. $100/yr. American Library Association, 50 East Huron St., Chicago, Ill. 60611.	Librarians. An expensive but valuable advisory service. School districts and smaller public libraries should cooperatively purchase this. No academic library can afford to bypass it as a very wide range of supplies and equipment is objectively appraised.

SOURCE

Stereo Review. $7.98/yr. Subscription address: Stereo Review, Circulation Dept., P.O. Box 2771, Boulder, Colo. 80302.

AUDIENCE

General listeners and equipment fanciers. Magazine is geared slightly more to the technically oriented than *High Fidelity/Musical America.*

Equipment Selection Procedure

The procedure for equipment selection can be simple and direct. The first requirement is that the buyer familiarize himself with equipment and current sound-reproduction technology. This self-tutorial step may be accomplished by scanning *Library Technology Reports, EPIE,* and the other previously cited sources. It is beneficial if this research is supplemented by informal discussions with persons whose listening habits are similar to those who will be using the equipment. A professional musician's opinions can also be extremely revealing, particularly if one is considering range 3–5 levels of equipment expenditure. Visits to local dealers to discuss component purchase options should follow only after one has built-up a comfortable knowledge of ratings of models in the price range being considered. It is possible to uncover and eliminate at this stage dealers who are not sensitive to the performance or situational specifications established as minimal. More valuable data can come out of these exploratory visits if the prospective purchaser will let the vendor do the talking so that his expertise or ignorance can be more quickly displayed. It is advisable to open bid offers to all firms which sell products within the range established. The bid form should list the desired specifications in a center column. Most of the specifications should be minimal, but a small percentage (about a tenth) should be desirable features which can count as partial compensation for insufficiency in other essential specifications. Two columns containing numbered blank lines in the same order should parallel the specifications column; one column for listing features and specifications which are less than those called for in the bid form and a second column for identifying features and specifications above the cited minima. At the end of the form, there should be space for the bidder to describe unique attributes of his equipment which should be drawn to the prospective purchaser's attention.

Bids should be carefully appraised from several perspectives. Most important to any institutional purchaser should be the existing and past levels of satisfaction expressed by other customers with the bidder's installations and equipment. Institutions with similar facilities, programs, schedules, patrons, and collections are the preferred sources for this kind of reference. A second criterion is the quality of workmanship. This quality measure does not apply unless custom cabinetry is required. In these cases, external appearance, compatibility with other furnishings and equipment, ease of access to parts for emergency repair, adequate ventilation for heat generating tubes or motors, and proper placement of controls in relation to the intended users are funda-

mental considerations. The third value to be reviewed is the bidder's conformance with minimal specifications. In this regard it is advisable to establish priorities and numerical weightings for each specification and determine *in advance* which compensatory "extra" specifications may be traded off as acceptable alternatives for noncompliance with basic specifications. As much quantification as possible is urged to simplify and expedite judgments of this criterion. A fourth factor is price. In the opinion of this author, lowest price should never weigh more than one-third in any final acceptance/rejection decision. A fifth element is the bidder's service and warranty package. For simple equipment a "call as needed" arrangement is customary, but for complex and potentially more temperamental installations a preventive maintenance schedule is desirable.

A qualification chart may be prepared before bid opening, and final award can be determined on the basis of highest composite score. Table 4 illustrates a bid acceptance decision and may be useful as a model for local adaptation.

Firm E was awarded the contract despite firm A's low bid. The recommendation for acceptance of the firm E offer was accompanied by documentation of the five firms' qualifications across the five criteria. Although this process may seem overly elaborate to readers not familiar with bid procedure, the savings in averted equipment failures and gain in enduring patron satisfaction are worth the extra effort.

Table 4. Sample Bid Acceptance Form

	Firm A	Firm B	Firm C	Firm D	Firm E
Customer satisfaction with existing installations	3.0	2.5	2.5	2.5	4.0
Cabinetry—quality of workmanship and attractiveness. Concern with internal structural relationships, ventilation, mounts, tolerances	3.0	1.0 (D.S.)	2.0 (D.S.)	3.0	4.0
Conformance with specifications	2.0	3.0	1.0	3.0	4.0
Price	4.0	1.0	1.0	3.0	2.0
Service and warranties	3.0	2.0	2.0	3.0	3.0
TOTAL SCORE	15.0	9.5	8.5	14.5	17.0

Code: 2.5 = average; 1 = poor; 2 = marginally acceptable; 3 = good; 4 = outstanding. D.S. indicates that cabinetry is responsibility of subcontractor.

Maintenance of Recording Equipment

Proper maintenance of hi-fi equipment is as important as proper care of an automobile. Audio equipment may run smoothly and sound fine yet hover on

the brink of serious malfunction. If oil or brake fluid are dangerously low, the unwary motorist may suddenly lose control or suffer severe engine damage without any advance warning. With repeated listening the human ear develops an illusion of adequacy which is sustained as the quality of sound reproduction decays. The usual source of this deception is the stylus. The typical sapphire stylus with which school units are equipped should in optimal conditions last up to fifty hours. However, with the heavy tracking arms (often in excess of 12 grams) and rough usage in the usual institutional setting, this figure is shaved down to no more than ten to twelve hours of maximum life per stylus. Another factor in deterioration is the recording level in the grooves of discs. A stylus which tracks chamber music and piano pieces will last up to one and one half times as long as one which must ride the more convoluted ridges which contain loud orchestral or popular music. Therefore, a sapphire stylus should be inspected for deterioration after every ten hours of playing time; a diamond stylus after eight hundred.

Most users of equipment have no sure way of determining how many plays a particular stylus has absorbed. Recently, however, stylus timing gauges have been developed by Pickering and other manufacturers so that a fairly accurate approximation of accumulated playing time can be read off. The Pickering Model PST–1 stylus timing gauge ($13.96) has a color-coded scale that indicates the status of the stylus at a glance. Green shows while the stylus is safe (under 200 hours); yellow indicates that microscopic examination is advisable (200–500 hours); pink is a warning that replacement may be necessary, registering between the 500 and 1,000 hours. This gauge is a helpful accessory for the hi-fi fan at home and its use could save needless record wear in school and public libraries. However, its novelty, easy removal from the turntable, and small size make its survival in an institution unlikely.

Another factor to be checked is vertical tracking force. Neither an overly light nor excessively heavy (over 3 grams) tracking weight should be tolerated. Among audiophiles a pressure between 1 and 1.5 grams is considered optimal. Granted a compliant cartridge, low-tracking error, and this magnitude of tracking pressure, a diamond stylus may be expected to yield up to 1,000 plays (that is 2,000 sides) of standard, stereo LP discs. If tracking pressure is insufficient, the arm will skitter across the record surface and fracture the grooves. The Shure SFG–2 ($4.95) is a very handy, vertical-tracking force gauge which should be purchased by buyers of range 4 and 5 equipment mentioned earlier in this chapter. The gauge is calibrated in .05-gram steps and measures weights between .5 and 3 grams.

Something else that can cause considerable damage is hum. Hum is dangerous because its vibrations can convert the pickup stylus into a cutting edge. In other words, the needle's sympathetic movement in the groove can be forceful enough to impress the sound of the hum into the record surface so that it thenceforth becomes audible and offensive whenever the disc is played on any other phonograph. There are many causes of hum. An overly taut or slack spring on the turntable motor, inadequate or faulty grounding, reversed leads, and an amplifier too close to the turntable motor are common sources.

Other electrical-mechanical problems which arise should usually be referred to an audio-technician. A careful reading of the series of technical articles in

Audio and *Stereo Review* can greatly increase one's ability to cope independently with minor technical difficulties.

Very little of the maintenance required by cassette tape recorders can be performed outside of the repair shop. Analogous to the damage inflicted by worn or chipped needles upon disc recordings is the damage to recorded tapes perpetrated by dirty replay heads that need cleaning and defluxing (or degaussing). If replay heads accumulate foreign matter, they add background noise to all tapes that are played. Cleaning, demagnetization of the heads, and tape transport adjustment should be done periodically in accordance with instructions which accompany the cassette tape recorder. Broken drive belts and battery corrosion are other hazards common to machines used in schools and libraries. These are remediable by proper local maintenance. Batteries should always be removed from machines not in use, and broken drive belts can be replaced by persons with only minimal mechanical competence.

Conclusion

The listening experience reinforces, focuses and expands consciousness. The recording's power resides in its ability to transcend time and thereby escape from the confinement of locally imposed culture and circumstance. A sound recording, by preserving the past, can retain and transmit elements common to the human psyche at an ontological level. The recording of a "definitive" performance of a composer's or poet's work allows the listener to experience something of the same feelings as those of the creative artist when he was possessed by the demon and had to confine, domesticate, and transubstantiate that experience within the crucible of form. On such an occasion, the full force of the creator's intellectuality, language, and being flow towards the listener. This experience constitutes a forward leap for the listener, a move towards the more sensible and beautiful, a move away from oppressive inhibition and the denigration of consciousness and a turning towards the light of infinity. Portals are opened to realms which dwarf and defy the human capacity to measure and condition or logically define. The sound recording can provide direct access to the artistic soul, and this is its best reason for being. As Alexander Solzhenitsyn wrote in his Nobel lecture:

> The task of the artist is to sense more keenly than others the harmony of the world, the beauty and outrage of what man has done to it, and poignantly to let people know, in failure as well as in the lower depths— in poverty, in prison, in illness—the consciousness of a stable harmony will never leave him . . . .
>
> Art warms even an icy and depressed heart, opening it to lofty spiritual experiences. By means of art we are sometimes sent—dimly, briefly— revelations unattainable by reason. Like that little mirror in the fairy tales —look into it, and you'll see not yourself but, for a moment, that which passeth understanding, a realm to which no man can ride or fly, and for which the soul begins to ache . . . .

A Glossary of Audio Terms

The following glossary includes basic terms which laymen and librarians should find helpful in their negotiation of equipment purchase and management decisions.

Amplifier

An electronic device that increases the strength of electrical impulses received from a phono cartridge, tuner, or tape deck so that they can drive or activate a loud-speaker.

Balance

The relationship between high- and low-frequency levels of an audio signal, or the stereo-preamplifier control which adjusts relative sound output of two speakers. This convenience feature permits a listener to equalize or set to his personal taste the volume outputs from speakers of differing efficiency.

Cartridge (also called "eight-track")

An eight-track endless loop of tape housed within a casing more bulky than that of the cassette. Push it in and it starts; pull it out and it stops. Tamper proof and convenient. Has adequate fidelity for popular tunes and background listening. Therefore, this format is preferred for installation in automobiles. It is not suitable for selective listening because of the continuous loop and the inferior quality of sound reproduction.

Cassette

A sealed plastic housing enclosing two reels of permanently attached tape. A cassette can be snapped in and out of a cassette tape recorder very easily. The tape can be recorded in stereo or mono. To play or record the second side of tape, the user removes the cassette, turns it over and snaps it back in. Cassettes come in four standard lengths; C-30 (15 minutes on each side), C-60 (30 minutes on each side), C-90 (45 minutes on each side), and C-120 (total playing time of two hours). The C-30 and C-60 have higher fidelity than the C-90 and C-120 and are worth the inconvenience of shorter recording times if quality of sound reproduction is important. Cassettes are small and easier to store than LP records or open-reel tapes but the prerecorded cassette costs about $2 more than the typical 33⅓ rpm disc. Cassettes could replace LPs as LPs superseded 78s.

Channel

A separate and isolated strand of sound. In stereophonic systems, two separate audio signals move from the program source to loudspeakers. The program source consists of two channels either in the form of recorded tracks on magnetic tape or trenches cut into an LP's surface. Quadraphonic sound is produced through four channels. Although "discrete" and "matrix" systems are both advertised as quadraphonic, only the discrete system permits true four-channel separation. The matrix system reduces the four channels to two during the recording process, and subsequent resynthesis of the four channels for reproduction does not entirely restore their original character.

Compliance

The ability of a phono cartridge to respond freely to the undulations of a record groove or "give" of the stylus suspension. Has been superseded by the more meaningful term "minimum recommended tracking force," a characteristic which includes several other performance specifications as well as compliance. The compliance figure should always be compatible with the mass of the tone arm. It is possible for an improperly matched phono cartridge and arm to produce their own resonance. What is created thereby is unpleasant distortion and increased record-surface degradation.

Cross talk

The opposite of channel separation. 30 dB at 1 kHz (1,000 Hz) is a minimal quality specification for an adequate phono cartridge.

Cueing

The raising and lowering of a tone arm to play at any point on a record by means of a manual lever or push button control on the turntable. The term "damped cueing" refers to hydraulic cushioning of the arm's descent towards the disc surface.

Decibel (dB)

One-tenth of a bel. One dB is approximately the smallest discernible distinction between the intensity of two sounds by the human ear. A whisper at ten paces approximates 10 dB; a busy supermarket on a Saturday afternoon or school playground during recess may reach 60 dB; a pneumatic drill or rock band can attain 100 dB. Above 115 dB pain and/or permanent hearing loss occurs.

Deck, tape or cassette

A tape recorder/player without a power amplifier and loudspeaker. It must, therefore, be added on to an existing sound system. At the time of this compilation, the only route to sonically adequate reproduction of music on cassettes was with a cassette deck because most portable recorders were mediocre in tone quality.

Discrete

A four-channel system which permits four strands of sound to retain their unique identities all the way from recording to loud speaker reproduction.

300

Open-reel four-channel tapes and Q-8 eight-track cartridges are the only formats to accommodate true discrete reproduction.

Distortion

False or blurred reproduction of sound due to changes which occur as the impulses elicited from tape or disc surface move through a system toward their destination, the hearer. Stylus cartridge, turntable, tape transport mechanism, amplifier, speaker, all contribute increments to the total distortion which reaches the human ear. Ideally, a hi-fi system should provide no additive to the sound already present within the audio recording surface.

Dolby

A two-step extraneous-noise suppression process originated by Ray Dolby. First, the sound level of quiet passages of music is raised before being recorded or transmitted. Later, during playback or broadcast, the original soft-loud dynamics are restored so that the hiss that formerly blighted soft music during transmission or playback is circumvented. Most stereo cassette tape decks have built-in Dolby Type B noise-reduction circuitry, and its incorporation in portable players may soon become standard. Many FM stations have also adopted the system. Accordingly, it is important that prospective cassette-deck purchasers realize that only models with Dolby B circuitry permit optimal reproduction of the many Dolbyized tapes now on the market. Dolbyized cassettes and tapes are keyed in the *Harrison Tape Guide.*

Dynamic range

The distance (expressed in decibels) between the softest and loudest sounds in a live or recorded piece of music. A Mahler symphony or Wagner opera may fluctuate from a low of 30 decibels to a high of 100 decibels. A good audio system can reproduce a range of 60 decibels, nearing but not quite achieving the range heard in live performance.

Efficiency

The measure of how effectively an energy-conversion device operates. In high-fidelity parlance, the term usually refers to speaker systems. Most speakers are remarkably inefficient because for every 100 watts of amplifier power ingested they yield only about 1 watt of sound energy. The compact acoustic suspension speakers are relatively more inefficient than the larger home systems, which may return in excess of 10 watts for every 100 watts of amplifier input.

Electrostatic speaker

A thin diaphragm pulled tight in a frame between two metal plates. High voltage from the amplifier makes the plates vibrate in response to an audio signal and the sound radiates into space through perforations in the plates. Although effectively utilized in high-frequency tweeters and in some of the newer headphone designs, the electrostatic speaker becomes exorbitantly expensive to operate when employed for full frequency-range reproduction. The expense, inefficiency, and cumbersome size of the full-range electrostatic reproducers mitigate against their consideration by the average buyer.

301

Feedback

Cumulative interaction between microphone and loudspeaker. The cause of the electronic humming and screeching produced when platform speakers are projected over an improperly set-up public address system.

Flat response

Ability of an audio system to reproduce all tones (low and high) in their proper proportion. A superior sound system may be characterized as having a fairly flat response, plus or minus 2 dB from 30 to 15,000 Hz. Consequently, no frequency differs in loudness output from any other frequency by more than 4 dB. The perfect frequency-response performance specification would read 30 to 15,000 Hz ±0 dB.

Fletcher-Munson effect

The human ear's uneven sensitivity to frequencies across the audible spectrum. Low frequencies and, to a lesser degree, higher ones are not heard as well as middle-range sounds. Bass tones must be projected with disproportionate intensity for music to satisfy the human ear. Consequently, a *loudness compensation* or *loudness control* circuit is provided in most amplifiers and receivers to maintain the illusion of natural balance by boosting low and some high frequency output as the volume is turned down. (*See also* Loudness control).

Flutter

See Wow and flutter.

Frequency modulation

The sending and receiving of radio waves so that their amplitude remains constant while their frequency varies along with the sound being transmitted. The FM band runs from 88 to 108 megahertz, with stations assignments placed at 400 kilohertz intervals in any listening locality. AM (amplitude modulation) radio does not extend beyond 5,000 Hertz; FM encompasses a range of 30 to 15,000 Hertz. Because noise is produced mainly by amplitude modulation, FM remains free of the static which often disrupts AM reception. FM stations must use the upper frequencies to accommodate wide-band transmission. The short wave lengths used for these frequencies are lost in space and do not bounce off the upper layers of atmosphere as do AM radio waves. Therefore, FM stations lack AM radio's range, being limited to line-of-sight distances not extending beyond the horizon.

Head (tone arm)

The part of the tone arm that holds the cartridge and stylus or styli.

Head (tape recorder)

The small, ring-shaped element in the tape machine that reads the signal from the tape for reproduction or provides energy to magnetize the iron oxide or chromium dioxide particles into special patterns. The more expensive open-reel machines have separate erase, record, and playback heads, each specifically designed to perform its own function. Cassette decks usually have two heads; one for recording and playing, the other for erasing.

Hiss

In a tape recorder, a noise originating in the amplifier or tape, especially noticeable in the pre-Dolby era. The hiss will increase if tape heads are not periodically degaussed or demagnified. If this maintenance is not performed, hiss will be unintentionally recorded on tape whenever it is being audited.

Hum

Low-pitched background noise caused by poor shielding, inadequate grounding, or mismatched impedances. Usually identifiable as an annoying 60-Hz monotonic "mmm" sound picked up from electrical power wires. Three-pronged polarized plugs help to minimize this problem.

Hz (Hertz)

Synonym for "cycles per second," named after Heinrich R. Hertz, the German physicist who discovered electromagnetic waves in the late 1880s. In 1960 the Hertz was officially adopted as an international standard of measurement. The oboe A, sounded by orchestral musicians when they tune up, has a frequency of 440 Hz or 440 cycles a second, and middle C on the piano keyboard vibrates at 256 Hz. The piano frequency range is 26–4,096 Hz; that of the organ is 16–16,384 Hz. The subjective, musician's term for frequency is "pitch."

Impedance

The resistance in an electrical circuit to the flow of current. Impedance expressed in ohms is one indicator of compatibility between components in a sound system. A 4-ohm speaker should be hooked up to a 4-ohm amplifier. In systems which include preamplifiers and power amplifiers, the input impedance of the amplifier should fall within the range of impedances which can be driven by the output circuits of the preamplifier. Impedance incompatibility may cause distortion, a decrease in volume output, loss of high or low frequencies, fuse popping, and other malfunctions.

Integrated amplifier

A combination of power amplifier, preamplifier, and controls (bass, treble, volume, loudness compensation, etc.) within a single unit.

Intermodulation distortion (IM)

Interaction between wave forms. Whenever this occurs, original wave shapes are altered and new harmonics are produced. These machine created sounds are more serious than harmonic distortion because they are more noticeable and annoying to the listener.

IPS (inches per second)

The speed at which a tape moves past over a magnetic head. The usual speeds are 1⅞, 3¾, 7½, and 15 ips. The faster speeds are better for music and the slower ones more convenient with fidelity adequate for speech recording and playback.

Jack

A socket into which an appropriate plug can be inserted to interconnect equipment. Phono jacks (small dome-shaped sockets with outer metal shells and insulated central holes) and phone jacks (designed to receive the standard headphone plugs) are most often encountered in consumer and educational market products. Jack boxes, especially popular in schools, afford several inputs so that eight or more headphones may be plugged into a single program source at the same time.

Loudness control

A circuit that boosts bass and treble automatically when the volume output is reduced. This control compensates for the tendency of the human ear to lose bass and treble faster than the mid-range sounds. On some units the loudness control, or compensation, cannot be turned off. This lack of control is undesirable because the listener should be able to adjust the contours of the sound to suit his or her personal taste.

Loudspeaker

The device which transforms electrical impulses from the amplifier into sound waves. Usually called "speaker."

Manufacturer's number

The number, commonly preceded by a prefix of two or three letters, by which a disc or tape recording is listed in the Schwann, Harrison, or Trade Service Publications catalogs. This identification tag appears on the label pasted on each recording and its container. Because the larger manufacturers produce various series (bargain, regular, historical, special, landmark, and so on), it is necessary to cite all of the alpha-numerical characters in the manufacturer's number whenever ordering a recording.

Matrix number

The number scratched onto the disc surface between the grooving and center label; usually the same as the manufacturer's number. Sometimes used to determine "Side A" and "Side B" in cataloging but not used when ordering. Makes it possible to identify mislabeled discs.

Open reel

The traditional audio tape wound on a large spool as compared with tape sealed within a cartridge or cassette. Remains the aristocrat of the tape field.

Patch cord

Connecting cable with a plug on each end for convenience in connecting two pieces of audio equipment.

Phono cartridge

The very sensitive box-shaped device in the tone arm which contains the stylus and a minute electrical generating system. This delicate and versatile component converts mechanical movements of the stylus into an alternating electric voltage which is boosted by the amplifier. Ceramic cartridges are often

used in low-priced record players. Because the magnetic cartridges supply better frequency response and stereo channel separation, they are preferred for most medium- and high-priced record players. The important criteria of cartridge performance are frequency response, stereo separation, sensitivity, vertical tracking force requirement, freedom from intermodulation, immunity to hum, and tracking ability.

Preamplifier

The component which increases the signal from the phono cartridge so that it is strong enough to be detected by the amplifier.

Receiver

A component combining the functions of the tuner, preamplifier, and amplifier. This intergrated unit is more economical and less complicated in its wiring requirements than a combination of the three separate components. Most amplifiers in receivers supply sufficient power (about 75 watts) for all except those who want to recreate the Bayreuth Festival in their basements. However, separate components permit more flexible and sophisticated controls, may be updated as needed, and place the buyer on the road to the ultimate in high-fidelity technology.

Rumble

Heavy, low-pitched noise produced by vibration in the moving parts of the turntable or changer, picked up and transmitted through the rest of the system.

S/N

The amount of desirable signal divided by the amount of noise. S should be as large as possible and a ratio of 50 dB is a minimal requirement for acceptable amplification quality.

Stroboscope

A device to verify the speed of a turntable. Most medium- and high-priced changers and turntables have built-in speed indicators or stroboscopic cards. Viewed under a fluorescent or incandescent light, the lines on a rotating "strobe disc" seem motionless when the speed setting is correct. One can check the speed of any turntable with a separately purchased strobe disc (costs less than a dollar).

Stylus

The finely contoured point which traces the record groove and transmits its undulating motion through a metal shank to the phono cartridge. Most styli today are elliptically shaped diamonds. The changeover from the former conical to an elliptical shape allows for a more precise contact between stylus and grooves. The improvement in fidelity is noticeable to the human ear.

THD (total harmonic distortion)

The sum of all harmonics produced by a distorting element. Harmonic distortion is measured by feeding a pure sine wave into an audio system, observing the amplitude of harmonics produced with relation to the amplitude of the fundamental, and expressing this as a percentage.

Tone arm

The pivoting playing arm which holds the phono cartridge and stylus or styli.

Tracking

The action of the phono cartridge when following the record groove.

Transducer

A device for converting energy from one form to another; e.g., from electrical to mechanical, or vice versa. A microphone is a transducer which converts variations of air pressure (sound waves) into variations of electric current; a loudspeaker is a transducer which transforms variations of electric current into variations of air pressure (sound waves).

Tuner

The component or circuit that picks up radio signals and turns them into audio signals, which are then amplified to drive a loudspeaker. A tuner combined with a preamplifier, amplifier, and speaker is called a radio.

Turntable

The revolving platform upon which a record is played. It must be level and run at accurate speed. The term includes the motor that drives the platform.

VTF (vertical tracking force)

The principal cause of record wear. The weight which the stylus must bear on the record in order to follow the groove. A tracking force of more than 4 grams is undesirable in moderately priced and inexpensive phono cartridges. Better quality turntables and changers accommodate a VTF of 2.5 grams or less.

VU meter

Device for measuring levels (volume units) of sound being picked up by a tape recorder or amplifier.

Wow and flutter

Recurring change in the speed of the record originating from the turntable or from up-and-down arm movement, making the pitch of the music wavery or unstable. Wow is flutter with a very low frequency.

Title Index to Composer-Title List

This is an index to the *Composer-Title List* (pp. 45–150). Included are songs; arias; operas; orchestral titles such as *Tapiola, Romeo and Juliet, Boléro,* and *Orpheus*; popular names such as the *Minute Waltz, Dumky* Trio, *Tempest* Sonata; striking and distinctive titles such as *Play of Daniel, Pictures at an Exhibition,* and *Silver Apples of the Moon.* Index entries include the following: title, musical form if needed for clarification, musical category number (see key at the foot of each page), composer name, and guide number.

Abdelazer Suite (7) Purcell 733,000
Abduction from the Seraglio Overture (7) Mozart 716,000
Abendempfindung (8) Mozart 844,250
Abraham and Isaac (8) Britten 823,502
Abschied (8) Schubert 852,000
Abu Hassan Overture (7) Weber 809,000
Academic Festival Overture (7) Brahms 604,000
Acceleration Waltz (7) Strauss, Johann 769,750
Ach bleib' bei uns, Herr Jesu Christ (3) Bach, J. S. 102,649
Ach Elslein, liebes Elselein (1) Rhaw 15,900
Ach, Ich fühl's from *Magic Flute* (9) Mozart 892,100
Achorripsis (11) Xenakis 998,500
Ach, Weh mir unglückhaftem Mann (8) Strauss, Richard 870,500
Ach wie flüchtig, ach wie nichtig (2) Bach, J. S. 23,026
Acis and Galatea (2) Handel 48,500
Adagio for Strings (8) Barber 584,500
Addio, del passato from *La Traviata* (9) Verdi 900,000
Addio fiorito asil from *Madame Butterfly* (9) Puccini 893,600
Adelaide (8) Beethoven 815,200
Adieu, m'amour, adieu ma joie (1) Dufay 3,300
Adieu, mes amours (1) Des Prez 1,800
Adieu, notre petite table from *Manon* (9) Massenet 890,850
Les Adieux Sonata (3) Beethoven 124,750
Adjuro vos filiae Motet (1) Palestrina 10,900
Ad nos Fantasia and Fugue (3) Liszt 186,250
Aeolian Harp Étude (3) Chopin 135,050
Aeterna Christi munera Mass (1) Palestrina 9,900
Afferentur Motet (2) Bruckner 37,250
Again, As Before, Alone (8) Tchaikovsky 877,000

Age of Anxiety (5) Bernstein 382,250
Age of Gold (7) Shostakovich 761,250
Agon (7) Stravinsky 782,000
Ah! fors' e lui from *La Traviata* (9) Verdi 900,100
Ahi che quest'occhi miei Madrigal (1) Palestrina 9,200
Ahi, dispietate morte Madrigal (2) Marenzio 63,500
Ahi, gia mi discoloro Madrigal (2) Gesualdo 45,500
Ah non credea mirarte from *La Sonnambula* (9) Bellini 887,300
Ah! sì ben mio coll'essere from *Il Trovatore* (9) Verdi 900,500
Ah, vous dirai-je, Maman Variations (3) Mozart 202,000
Aïda (10) Verdi 957,750
Aïda Ballet Music (7) Verdi 801,100
Aïda Grand March (7) Verdi 801,000
Air on the G String (7) Bach, J. S. 584,013
Akrata (11) Xenakis 998,550
A la bataglia (1) Isaac 4,400
El Albaicin (3) Albéniz 97,500
Albert Herring (10) Britten 909,000
Alborada del gracioso (7) Ravel 735,750
Album für die Jugend (3) Schumann 230,250
Alceste (10) Gluck 919,750
Alcina (10) Handel 921,000
Alcina Ballet Music (7) Handel 659,000
Aldebaran (11) Ivey 988,150
Alexanderfest Concerto (7) Handel 659,800
Alexander Nevsky (2) Prokofiev 75,750
Alexander's Feast (2) Handel 48,750
Allégez-moy (1) Des Prez 1,800
Allegro Barbaro (3) Bartók 113,000
L'Allegro ed il Penseroso (2) Handel 49,000
Allein Gott in der Hoh' sei Ehr (S.675) (3) Bach, J. S. 104,675

Musical Category Key: 1 Early/2 Choral/3 Keyboard/4 Chamber/5 Symphonies/6 Concerti
7 Orchestral/8 Songs and Lieder/9 Arias/10 Operas/11 New and Experimental

Allein Gott in der Hoh' sei Ehr (S.677) (3) Bach, J. S. 104,677
Alleluia (8) Rorem 850,000
Allerseelen (8) Strauss, Richard 870,750
Allmacht (8) Schubert 852,250
Allmächt'ge Jungfrau from *Tannhäuser* (9) Wagner 902,600
Allon, gay Bergères (1) Costeley 1,700
Alma redemptoris Mater (1) Ockeghem 8,100
Almería from *Iberia* (3) Albéniz 97,000
Eine Alpensinfonie (5) Strauss, Richard 473,750
Also Sprach Zarathustra (7) Strauss, Richard 778,750
Alte Laute (8) Schumann 865,000
Altenberg Lieder (8) Berg 816,400
Alternating Thirds (no. 129) from *Mikrokosmos* (3) Bartók 114,229
Alto Rhapsody (2) Brahms 31,000
L'altra notte il fondo from *Mefistofele* (9) Boito 887,800
Amahl and the Night Visitors (10) Menotti 928,250
Am Camin from *Kinderscenen* (3) Schumann 234,750
America (3) Ives 183,750
American Festival Overture (7) Schuman 759,000
American in Paris (7) Gershwin 640,000
American Quartet (4) Dvořák 294,000
American Salute (7) Gould 648,000
Amériques (7) Varèse 799,000
Amid Nature Overture (7) Dvořák 626,000
El amor brujo (8) Falla 831,400
Amores for Prepared Piano and Percussion (11) Cage 971,500
L'amour est un oiseau from *Carmen* (9) Bizet 887,600
Amour, viens aider ma faiblesse from *Samson et Dalila* (9) Saint-Saëns 895,800
Am stillen Herd from *Die Meistersinger* (9) Wagner 902,400
Anakreons Grab (8) Wolf 878,750
An Chloe (8) Mozart 844,500
Ancient Airs and Dances, Set 1 (7) Respighi 739,750
Ancient Airs and Dances, Set 2 (7) Respighi 740,000
Ancient Airs and Dances, Set 3 (7) Respighi 740,250
Ancient Voices of Children (11) Crumb 976,250
Andante and Variations (3) Haydn 181,000
Andante favori (3) Beethoven 116,000
An den Sonnenschein (8) Schumann 865,250
And God Created Great Whales (7) Hovhaness 673,000
An die ferne Geliebte (8) Beethoven 815,600
An die Laute (8) Schubert 852,500
An die Leier (8) Schubert 852,750
An die Musik (8) Schubert 853,000
And On the Seventh Day Petals Fell in Petaluma (11) Partch 992,100
Andrea Chénier (10) Giordano 919,250
Anima mea (1) Victoria 17,000
Animus II (11) Druckman 980,750
Anna Bolena (10) Donizetti 913,875

Années de pèlerinage (3) Liszt 185,000–185,750
Annen Polka (7) Strauss, Johann 770,000
Ann Street (8) Ives 835,300
An Sylvia (8) Schubert 853,500
Antar Symphony (5) Rimsky-Korsakov 459,000
Antarctica Symphony (5) Vaughan Williams 481,500
An Wasserflüssen Babylon (3) Bach, J. S. 103,653
Apocalypse (11) Dockstader 978,000
Apollo (Apollon Musagète) (7) Stravinsky 782,200
Apothéose de Lully (7) Couperin 616,500
Appalachian Spring (7) Copland 611,750
Apparitions (11) Tate 996,900
Appassionata Sonata (3) Beethoven 124,000
Arabella (10) Strauss, Richard 952,250
Arabeske (3) Schumann 231,250
Arabesques (3) Debussy 158,000
Arcana (7) Varèse 799,200
Archduke Trio (4) Beethoven 275,000
Ariadne auf Naxos (10) Strauss, Richard 952,500
Ariodante Ballet Music (7) Handel 659,000
L'Arlésienne Suite 1 (7) Bizet 599,000
L'Arlésienne Suite 2 (7) Bizet 599,250
Armida Overture (7) Haydn 664,500
Artists Life Waltz (7) Strauss, Johann 770,250
Art of the Fugue (7) Bach, J. S. 583,000
Art of the Fugue (3) Bach, J. S. 100,000
Ascendens Christus in altem (1) Victoria 17,100
Ascendo ad patrem Mass (1) Palestrina 10,000
L'Ascension (11) Messiaen 990,400
As pants the hart (Chandos Anthem 6) (2) Handel 50,750
Assempta est Maria Mass (1) Palestrina 10,100
Asturias (*Leyenda*) (4) Albéniz 246,500
A Teo cara from *I Puritani* (9) Bellini 887,150
Atlas (8) Schubert 853,750
At the Ball (8) Tchaikovsky 877,100
At the River (8) Ives 835,400
Aubade (6) Poulenc 542,250
Auch kleine Dinge (8) Wolf 879,750
Auf dem Kirchhofe (8) Brahms 818,000
Auf dem Wasser zu singen (8) Schubert 854,000
Auf der Jagd Polka (7) Strauss, Johann 770,500
Auf ein altes Bild (8) Wolf 881,750
Auf einer Wanderung (8) Wolf 882,000
Auf Flügeln des Gesänges (8) Mendelssohn 840,000
Auf meinen lieben Gott (partita on the chorale) (3) Buxtehude 131,750
Aufschwung (3) Schumann 233,000
Aufträge (8) Schumann 865,500
Das Augenlicht Cantata (2) Webern 93,500
Au joly boys (1) Jannequin 4,500
Auprès de cette grotte sombre (8) Debussy 827,701
Aus den Liedern der Trauer (8) Strauss, Richard 871,000
Aus tiefer Not schrei' ich zu dir (3) Bach, J. S. 104,687
Automatic Descriptions (3) Satie 218,250
Autonno from *The Four Seasons* (6) Vivaldi 572,003

Musical Category Key: 1 Early/2 Choral/3 Keyboard/4 Chamber/5 Symphonies/6 Concerti

Autumn (7) Glazounov 642,500
Autumn Evening (8) Sibelius 870,000
The Autumn Wind (8) Britten 824,751
Available Forms I (11) Brown 970,250
Avant de quitter from *Faust* (9) Gounod 889,300
Avant dernières pensées (3) Satie 218,000
Ave Maria (1) Morales 7,200
Ave Maria (1) Ockeghem 8,200
Ave Maria (8) Schubert 854,250
Ave Maria (1) Victoria 17,200
Ave Maria from *Otello* (9) Verdi 898,800
Ave Maria Motet (2) Bruckner 37,500
Ave Maris stella Mass (1) Des Prez 2,100
Ave Maris stella Motet (1) Palestrina 11,000
Aventures (11) Ligeti 989,000
Ave Regina Motet (1) Palestrina 11,100
Ave, verum corpus (1) Byrd 500
Ave, verum corpus (2) Mozart 72,000
Avodath Hakodesh (8) Bloch 817,400
Away with these self-loving lads (8) Dowland 828,000
Azerbaijan Mugam (7) Amirov 579,750

Baal Shem for Violin and Piano (4) Bloch 276,250
Baba Yaga (7) Liadov 691,000
Bachianas Brasileiras no. 2 (7) Villa-Lobos 802,000
Bachianas Brasileiras no. 5 for Soprano and 8 Celli (8) Villa-Lobos 877,600
Bachianas Brasileiras no. 6 (4) Villa-Lobos 366,500
Le baiser de la fée (7) Stravinsky 782,400
Ballade (3) Liszt 186,000
Ballade for Piano and Orchestra (6) Fauré 515,500
Ballet mécanique (7) Antheil 580,000
Ballo delle ingrate (10) Monteverdi 930,000
Un Ballo in maschera (10) Verdi 958,000
Banalités (8) Poulenc 846,750
Banditen Galopp Polka (7) Strauss, Johann 770,750
Barber of Seville (10) Rossini 946,250
Barber of Seville Overture (7) Rossini 747,250
Barcarolle (3) Fauré 167,000
Barcarolle from *Tales of Hoffmann* (7) Offenbach 727,200
Barkarole (8) Strauss, Richard 871,250
Barque sur l'océan (7) Ravel 736,000
Les Barricades mystérieuses (3) Couperin 154,300
Barstow-8 Hitchhiker Inscriptions from a Highway Railing at Barstow, California (11) Partch 992,150
Bartered Bride: Dance of the Comedians (7) Smetana 765,500
Bartered Bride: Furiant (7) Smetana 765,750
Bartered Bride: Overture (7) Smetana 766,000
Bartered Bride: Polka (7) Smetana 766,250
Le bataille de Marignan (1) Jannequin 4,600
Bataille de Martinestie Symphony (5) Neubaur 452,000
Batti, batti, bel Masetto from *Don Giovanni* (9) Mozart 891,650

Battle of the Huns (7) Liszt 692,250
Bear Symphony (5) Haydn 419,500
Béatrice et Bénédict (10) Berlioz 907,250
Beatrice di Tenda (10) Bellini 905,750
Beautiful Dreamer (8) Foster 833,200
Beautiful Galatea Overture (7) Suppé 788,500
Bedlam (8) Rorem 850,100
Die beiden Grenadiere (8) Schumann 865,750
La Belle Excentrique (7) Satie 754,250
La Belle Hélène (10) Offenbach 936,000
La Belle Hélène Overture (7) Offenbach 727,250
The Bells (2) Rachmaninoff 77,500
Bells of Zlonice Symphony (5) Dvořák 396,000
Bell Song from *Lakmé* (9) Delibes 888,050
Bel raggio lusinghier from *Semiramide* (9) Rossini 895,700
Belshazzar's Feast (2) Walton 93,250
Benedicite (2) Vaughan Williams 89,500
Berceuses du chat (8) Stravinsky 876,500
Berenice Overture (7) Handel 659,200
Berliner Symphony (5) Weill 485,000
Betrothel in a Convent (10) Prokofiev 939,250
Biches ballet suite (7) Poulenc 729,500
The Big Chariot (8) Britten 824,752
Billy Budd (10) Britten 909,250
Billy the Kid (7) Copland 612,000
Bist du bei mir (8) Bach, J. S. 813,750
Black Angels for electric string quartet (11) Crumb 976,500
Black key Étude (3) Chopin 134,850
Black Maskers suite (7) Sessions 761,000
Black Roses (8) Sibelius 870,100
Blow, Blow thou Winter Wind (8) Arne 812,500
Bluebeard's Castle (10) Bartók 905,000
Blue Danube Waltz (7) Strauss, Johann 771,000
Le Boeuf sur le toit (7) Milhaud 711,000
La Bohème (10) Puccini 940,500
Bohor I (11) Xenakis 998,600
Boîte à joujoux (7) Debussy 617,000
Boléro (7) Ravel 736,250
La Bonne Chanson (8) Fauré 832,100
Book of the Hanging Gardens (8) Schoenberg 851,750
Boris Godunov (10) Mussorgsky 935,500
Botschaft (8) Brahms 818,250
Bourgeois gentilhomme (7) Strauss, Richard 779,000
Bourrée fantasque (3) Chabrier 132,750
Bourrée fantasque (3) Chabrier 608,500
Boutique Fantasque (7) Respighi 740,750
Bowery Bum (11) Mimaroglu 991,400
Brandenburg Concerti (7) Bach, J. S. 583,251–583,256
Breit über mein Haupt (8) Strauss, Richard 871,750
Bridal Procession from *Coq d'or* (7) Rimsky-Korsakoff 744,500
Brigg Fair (7) Delius 621,750
Brindisi from *Lucrezia Borgia* (9) Donizetti 888,650
Browning Overture (7) Ives 678,000
Buffoon Suite No. 1 (7) Prokofiev 730,500
Bulgarian Rhythm (no. 113) from *Mikrokosmos* (3) Bartók 114,113

7 Orchestral/8 Songs and Lieder/9 Arias/10 Operas/11 New and Experimental

Burleske for Piano and Orchestra (6) Strauss, Richard 556,000
Burning Fiery Furnace (10) Britten 909,500
La Buscarle (11) Messiaen 991,100
Butterfly from *Lyric Pieces* (3) Grieg 178,250
Butterfly Étude (3) Chopin 135,150

Cäcilie (8) Strauss, Richard 872,000
The Cage (8) Ives 835,500
La Calisto (10) Cavalli 911,500
Calm Sea and Prosperous Voyage Overture (7) Mendelssohn 707,000
Les Calotins et les calotines ou la Pièce à tretous (3) Couperin 155,300
La Calunnia e un venticello from *Barber of Seville* (9) Rossini 895,200
Cambiale di Matrimonio (10) Rossini 946,500
Campanella (*Transcendental Etude* no. 3) (3) Liszt 189,000
Canary Cantata (2) Telemann 88,000
Candide Overture (7) Bernstein 597,000
Can She Excuse My Wrong (8) Dowland 828,250
Cantantibus organis Motet (1) Palestrina 11,200
Cantata (2) Stravinsky 86,000
Cantata (2) Webern 93,750
Cantata Academica (2) Britten 33,000
Cantata Misericordium (2) Britten 33,500
Cantata Profana (*Enchanted Deer*) (2) Bartók 26,000
Canti de Prigionia (11) Dallapiccola 976,750
Cantiones sacrae (1) Tallis 16,400
Cantiones sacrae (2) Schütz 82,250
Cantiones sacrae in 5 and 6 voices (1) Byrd 600
Cantos de España (3) Albéniz 94,750
Capriccio (10) Strauss, Richard 952,750
Capriccio for Piano and Orchestra (6) Stravinsky 557,250
Capriccio brillant (6) Mendelssohn 532,250
Capriccio espagnol (7) Rimsky-Korsakoff 743,750
Capriccio italien (7) Tchaikovsky 790,000
Caprices for Solo Violin (4) Paganini 341,000
Le Carillon de Cythère (3) Couperin 155,100
Carmen (10) Bizet 907,750
Carmen Fantasy for Violin and Orchestra (6) Sarasate 550,750
Carmen Suite (7) Bizet 599,500
Carmen Suite no. 1 (7) Bizet 599,750
Carmina Burana (*Benediktbeurn Manuscript*) (1) 19,200 and 19,300
Carmina Burana (2) Orff 73,500
Carnaval (3) Schumann 232,000
Carnival of the Animals (7) Saint-Saëns 753,250
Carnival Overture (7) Dvořák 626,250
Caro mio ben from *Andrea Chénier* (8) Giordano 888,750
Caro nome from *Rigoletto* (9) Verdi 899,300
Carry Nation (10) Moore 931,500
Cartridge Music (11) Cage 972,000
Casta Diva from *Norma* (9) Bellini 887,100
Castor et Pollux (10) Rameau 944,000
Catalogue d'Oiseaux (11) Messiaen 990,500
Catalogue d'Oiseaux (11) Messiaen 991,100
The Cat and the Mouse (3) Copland 152,000

Cathédrale engloutie (3) Debussy 162,750
Catulli Carmina (2) Orff 73,750
Caucasian Sketches (7) Ippolitov-Ivanov 676,000
Cavalleria Rusticana (10) Mascagni 927,250
Cavalleria Rusticana Intermezzo (7) Mascagni 704,000
Celeste Aïda from *Aïda* (9) Verdi 896,500
Ce Moys de May (1) Jannequin 4,900
La Cenerentola (10) Rossini 946,750
La Cenerentola Overture (7) Rossini 747,500
Central Park in the Dark (7) Ives 678,250
Céphale et Procris (7) Grétry 651,000
Ceremony of Carols (2) Britten 34,000
La Cetra (Concerto no. 4) (6) Vivaldi 572,504
La Cetra (Concerto no. 8) (6) Vivaldi 572,508
La Cetra (Concerto no. 9) (6) Vivaldi 572,509
La Cetra (Concerto no. 12) (6) Vivaldi 572,512
Chamber Concerto (7) Berg 593,000
Chamber Symphony (5) Kupferman 433,000
Champagne Polka (7) Strauss, Johann 771,250
Chandos Anthems (2) Handel 50,125–50,750
Change of Time (no. 126) from *Mikrokosmos* (3) Bartók 114,226
La Chanson d'Ève (8) Fauré 832,200
Chanson d'Orkenise (8) Poulenc 846,751
Chansons de Bilitis (8) Debussy 826,750
Chansons madécasses (8) Ravel 849,250
Le Chant de l'Alouette (1) Jannequin 4,700
Le Chant des oiseaux (1) Jannequin 4,800
Chapters turned every which way (3) Satie 218,500
Charlie Rutlage (8) Ives 835,600
Chasseur maudit (7) Franck 633,500
Che farò senza Euridice? from *Orfeo* (9) Gluck 889,150
Che gelida manina from *La Bohème* (9) Puccini 893,000
Ch'ella mi creda libero from *La fanciulla del West* (9) Puccini 894,000
Cheminé e du Roi René (4) Milhaud 327,000
Chester (2) Billings 30,000
La Chevelure (8) Debussy 826,751
Chichester Psalms (2) Bernstein 29,500
Child of our Time (2) Tippett 89,000
Children's Corner Suite (3) Debussy 158,250
The Children's Hour (8) Ives 835,700
Choëphores (2) Milhaud 65,500
Choral Hymns from the Rig-Veda (2) Holst 57,750
Chôros no. 1 for Guitar (4) Villa-Lobos 366,750
Christe, alle Welt trost (3) Bach, J. S. 104,670
Christian Wolff in Cambridge (11) Feldman 981,750
Christ lag in Todesbanden (2) Bach, J. S. 23,004
A Christmas carol (8) Ives 835,800
Christmas Concerto (7) Corelli 616,258
Christmas Concerto (7) Locatelli 696,000
Christmas Eve Suite (7) Rimsky-Korsakov 744,000
Christmas Oratorio (2) Bach, J. S. 23,750
Christmas Oratorio (2) Schütz 82,500
Christ, unser Herr, zum Jordan kam (S.684) (3) Bach, J. S. 104,684

Musical Category Key: 1 Early/2 Choral/3 Keyboard/4 Chamber/5 Symphonies/6 Concerti

7 Orchestral/8 Songs and Lieder/9 Arias/10 Operas/11 New and Experimental

Musical Category Key: 1 Early/2 Choral/3 Keyboard/4 Chamber/5 Symphonies/6 Concerti

Dumky Trio (4)) Dvořák 295,250
Duo Concertant for Violin and Piano (4) Stravinsky 361,000
Duo ubera tua Motet (1) Palestrina 11,700

Easter Oratorio (2) Bach, J. S. 24,000
Easter Oratorio (2) Schütz 83,000
Ebony Concerto (7) Stravinsky 783,400
Ecce ego Joannes Mass (1) Palestrina 10,300
Eccentric Beauty (3) Satie 219,250
Mass *"Ecce nunc benedicite Dominum"* (1) Lassus 5,300
Ecce sacerdos Motet (2) Bruckner 37,250
Ecce tu pulcher es Motet (1) Palestrina 11,800
Ecco moriro . . . Madrigal (2) Gesualdo 46,000
Echoes of Time and River (11) Crumb 976,500
Economy Band (11) Van Vactor 997,750
Egmont Overture (7) Beethoven 590,750
Egyptian March (7) Strauss, Johann 771,500
Die Ehre Gottes aus der Natur (8) Beethoven 815,800
1812 Overture (7) Tchaikovsky 792,750
Eight Russian Folksongs (7) Liadov 691,250
Eight Songs for a Mad King (11) Davies 977,750
Eine Kleine Nachtmusik (7) Mozart 724,250
Ein feste Burg ist unser Gott (2) Bach, J. S. 23,080
Der Einsame (8) Schubert 855,000
An Election (8) Ives 835,850
Elégie for Cello and Orchestra (6) Fauré 515,750
Elegies (3) Busoni 130,500
Elektra (10) Strauss, Richard 953,250
Elijah (2) Mendelssohn 65,250
L'elisir d'amore (10) Donizetti 914,500
Eljen a Magyar Polka (7) Strauss, Johann 771,750
Ella giammai m'amò from *Don Carlos* (9) Verdi 897,500
Elsa's dream from *Lohengrin* (9) Wagner 902,200
E lucevan le stelle from *Tosca* (9) Puccini 894,400
Emperor Concerto (6) Beethoven 500,002
Emperor Quartet (4) Haydn 308,500
En blanc et noir (3) Debussy 159,000
Enchanted Deer (*Cantata Profana*) (2) Bartók 26,000
The Enchanted Lake (7) Liadov 691,500
L'Enfance du Christ (2) Berlioz 28,250
L'Enfant et les sortilèges (10) Ravel 944,750
English Folk Song Suite (7) Vaughan Williams 800,000
English Suites for Harpsichord (3) Bach, J. S. 105,800–105,811
En habit de cheval (7) Satie 754,500
Enigma Variations (7) Elgar 630,000
En Saga (7) Sibelius 764,250
Entflieht auf leichten Kähnen (2) Webern 94,250
Entführung aus dem Serail (10) Mozart 933,500
Entführung aus dem Serail Overture (7) Mozart 716,000
Entlaubet ist der Walde (1) Rhaw 16,000

Entrance of the Gods in Valhalla from *Das Rheingold* (7) Wagner 805,500
Entropy (11) Trythall 997,400
Eonta (11) Xenakis 998,750
Épigraphes antiques (3) Debussy 159,250
L'Épineuse (3) Couperin 155,600
Epiphanias (8) Wolf 879,000
Epiphanias (8) Wolf 879,000
Epiroticos (Greek Dance) (7) Skalkottas 765,250
Epitaphs (8) Chanler 825,400
Epos (11) Donovan 980,250
L'Épreuve villageoise Ballet music (7) Grétry 651,500
Eritaña from *Iberia* (3) Albéniz 97,750
Der Erlkönig (8) Schubert 855,250
Ernani (10) Verdi 958,500
Ernste Gesänge (8) Brahms 819,000
Eroica Symphony (5) Beethoven 377,500
Eroica Variations and Fugue (3) Beethoven 126,500
Erschallet, ihr Lieder (2) Bach, J. S. 23,372
Erwartung (8) Schoenberg 851,800
Escales (*Ports of Call*) (7) Ibert 675,500
L'Espagnole from *Les Nations* (4) Couperin 289,750
España (7) Chabrier 609,000
Estampes (3) Debussy 159,500
Estancia (7) Ginastera 641,000
Estate from *The 4 Seasons* (6) Vivaldi 572,002
Estote fortes in bello (1) Victoria 17,300
L'Estro Armonico no. 5 (6) Vivaldi 571,005
L'Estro Armonico no. 8 (6) Vivaldi 571,008
L'Estro Armonico no. 10 (6) Vivaldi 571,010
L'Estro Armonico no. 11 (6) Vivaldi 571,011
Et exspecto resurrectionem mortuorum (11) Messiaen 990,800
Études symphoniques (3) Schumann 237,000
Eugen Onegin Polonaise (7) Tchaikovsky 790,500
Eugen Onegin (10) Tchaikovsky 955,750
Eugen Onegin Waltz (7) Tchaikovsky 794,250
Euryanthe Overture (7) Weber 809,150
Evangelimann: Selig sind die verfolgung leiden (9) Kienzl 890,300
Evening (8) Ives 835,900
Events (11) Powell 993,400
Evocación from *Iberia* (3) Albéniz 96,250
Exaltabo te Motet (1) Palestrina 11,900
Exalta est Sancta Dei Genitrix Motet (1) Morales 7,700
Exit Music I: The Wasting of Lucrecetzia (11) Gaburo 984,400
Exit Music II: Fat Millie's Lament (11) Gaburo 984,600
Exotica (11) Schubel 994,300
Exsultate, Jubilate (8) Mozart 844,750
Extended Voices (11) Ichiyanagi 987,900
Exultate Deo Motet (1) Palestrina 12,000

F Sharp (11) Schubel 994,350
Façade (7) Walton 808,200
Facsimile (7) Bernstein 597,500
Fair Melusina Overture (7) Mendelssohn 707,250
Fairy Queen (10) Purcell 943,250
Faithful Shepherd Suite (7) Handel 660,000
Falstaff (10) Verdi 958,750

7 Orchestral/8 Songs and Lieder/9 Arias/10 Operas/11 New and Experimental

Musical Category Key: 1 Early/2 Choral/3 Keyboard/4 Chamber/5 Symphonies/6 Concerti

Funeral Ode Cantata (2) Bach, J. S. 23,398
Für Elise (3) Beethoven 117,250
Furiant from *Bartered Bride* (7) Smetana 765,750

Gaîté Parisienne (7) Offenbach 727,500
Galanta Dances (7) Kodály 686,250
Galop from *Comedians* (7) Kabalevsky 683,500
Galop from *Masquerade* Suite (7) Khachaturian 685,250
Ganymed (8) Schubert 856,750
Il gardellino concerto (6) Vivaldi 573,003
Gargoyles (11) Luening 989,800
Der Gärtner (8) Wolf 882,250
Gaspard de la nuit (3) Ravel 215,000
Gaudent in coelis (1) Victoria 17,400
Gayne Ballet suite (7) Khachaturian 684,000
La Gazza Ladra Overture (7) Rossini 747,750
Gebet (8) Wolf 882,500
Geheimes (8) Schubert 857,000
Gelobet seist du, Jesu Christ (3) Bach, J. S. 101,604
General William Booth Enters Heaven (8) Ives 836,200
Genoveva Overture (7) Schumann 760,250
German Dances (7) Mozart 719,500, 720,250
German Dances (3) Schubert 226,250
German Dances (7) Schubert 757,750
German Organ Mass (3) Bach, J. S. 104,660–104,689
German Requiem (2) Brahms 31,250
Gesang der Jünglinge (11) Stockhausen 995,000
Gesangscene (6) Spohr 555,000
Gesang Weyla's (8) Wolf 882,750
Ghost Trio (4) Beethoven 273,500
Gianni Schicchi (10) Puccini 941,000
Gigues (7) Debussy 618,250
La Gioconda (10) Ponchielli 938,500
Giselle (complete ballet) (7) Adam 577,250
Giselle: Suite (7) Adam 577,300
Gleich wie der Regen (2) Bach, J. S. 23,018
Gli uccelli (7) Respighi 742,000
Gloria (2) Poulenc 74,750
Gloria (2) Vivaldi 92,750
Gloriana: Courtly Dances (4) Britten 284,250
Die glückliche Hand (10) Schoenberg 949,500
Gnossiennes (3) Satie 221,750
Goethe Lieder (8) Wolf 878,500
Goldberg Variations (3) Bach, J. S. 107,988
Golden Spinning Wheel (Symphonic Poem) (7) Dvořák 626,500
Gondoliers (10) Gilbert and Sullivan 917,250
Good Friday Music from *Parsifal* (7) Wagner 804,750
Good-humored Ladies (Ballet suite) (7) Tommasini 797,000
Gordian Knot Untied (Suites 1 and 2) (7) Purcell 733,250
Götterdämmerung (10) Wagner 961,500
Gottes Zeit ist die allerbeste Zeit (2) Bach, J. S. 23,106
Gott heiliger Geist (3) Bach, J. S. 104,671
Gott Vater in Ewigkeit (3) Bach, J. S. 104,669
Goyescas (3) Granados 177,000

Graduation Ball (Ballet suite) (7) Strauss, Johann 768,750
Granada (4) Albéniz 246,000
Grand Canyon Suite (7) Grofé 656,000
Grand Duchess of Gérolstein Overture (7) Offenbach 727,750
Grande Messe des Morts (2) Berlioz 28,500
Grand Fantasy on Polish Airs (6) Chopin 507,750
Grand March from *Aïda* (7) Verdi 801,000
Great Consort (4) Lawes 322,000
Great Mass (2) Bruckner 37,000
The Great Mass (2) Mozart 72,500
The Great Symphony (5) Schubert 463,500
Greensleeves (7) Vaughan Williams 800,150
Greeting Prelude (7) Stravinsky 784,400
Gretchen am Spinnrade (8) Schubert 857,250
Grillen (3) Schumann 233,500
Grosse Fuge (7) Beethoven 591,200
Gruppe aus dem Tartarus (8) Schubert 857,500
Gruss (8) Mendelssohn 840,000
Gurre-Lieder (2) Schoenberg 80,000
Gwendoline Overture (7) Chabrier 609,500
Gymel (11) Castiglioni 976,000
Gymnopédie no. 1 (7) Satie 754,750
Gymnopédie no. 2 (7) Satie 755,000
Gymnopédie no. 3 (7) Satie 755,250
Gypsy Baron (10) Strauss, Johann 952,000
Gypsy Baron Overture (7) Strauss, Johann 769,000

Haffner Serenade (7) Mozart 723,500
Haffner Symphony (5) Mozart 450,000
Halloween (7) Ives 679,500
Halt im Gedächtnis Jesum Christ (2) Bach, J. S. 23,067
Hamlet (7) Liszt 692,000
Hamlet (7) Shostakovich 762,000
Hamlet Fantasy Overture (7) Tchaikovsky 791,000
Hamlet (Film Music) (7) Walton 808,350
Hammerklavier Sonata (3) Beethoven 125,500
Hansel and Gretel (10) Humperdinck 924,750
Hansel and Gretel Overture (7) Humperdinck 674,250
Hansel and Gretel (prayer) (7) Humperdinck 674,500
Harmonics from *Mikrokosmos* (3) Bartók 114,102
Harmoniemesse (2) Haydn 56,500
Harmonies (11) Ligeti 989,100
Harmonies poétiques et religieuses (3) Liszt 186,507
Harmonious Blacksmith (3) Handel 180,500
Harold in Italy (6) Berlioz 502,000
Harp Quartet (4) Beethoven 265,750
Harvest Home Chorales (2) Ives 59,500
The Harvest of Sorrow (8) Rachmaninoff 847,700
Háry János (10) Kodály 926,250
Háry János Suite (7) Kodály 686,500
Havanaise for Violin and Orchestra (6) Saint-Saëns 549,750

7 Orchestral/8 Songs and Lieder/9 Arias/10 Operas/11 New and Experimental

315

Musical Category Key: 1 Early/2 Choral/3 Keyboard/4 Chamber/5 Symphonies/6 Concerti

n dulci jubilo (3) Bach, J. S. 101,608
n ecclesiis benedicite Domino (2) Gabrieli 44,500
nextinguishable Symphony (5) Nielsen 453,000
n fernem Land from *Lohengrin* (9) Wagner 902,300
nferno (11) Grauer 985,000
n festis apostolorum Mass (1) Palestrina 10,400
n London Town (*Cockaigne* Overture) (7) Elgar 629,750
n Memoriam (7) Moore 713,000
n Memoriam Dylan Thomas (8) Stravinsky 876,700
nnsbruck, ich muss dich lassen (1) Isaac 4,100
n questa reggia from *Turandot* (9) Puccini 894,700
n Riding Habit (3) Satie 219,750
ntégrales (7) Varèse 799,400
ntemerata Dei Mater Motet (1) Ockeghem 8,900
ntermezzo from *Cavalleria Rusticana* (7) Mascagni 704,000
n the Beginning (2) Copland 40,000
n the Lord I Put My Trust (*Chandos Anthem* 2) (2) Handel 50,250
n the Silent Night (8) Rachmaninoff 847,750
n the Steppes of Central Asia (7) Borodin 603,000
n the Style of a Folk Song from *Mikrokosmos* (3) Bartók 114,100
n the Village from *Caucasian Sketches* (7) Ippolitov-Ivanov 676,250
ntroduction and Allegro (4) Ravel 348,000
ntroduction and Allegro for Strings (7) Elgar 630,500
ntroduction and Polonaise for Piano and Cello (4) Chopin 287,250
ntroduction and Rondo Capriccioso (6) Saint-Saëns 550,000
ntroduxit me rex Motet (1) Palestrina 12,300
ntroduzione teatrale no. 5 (7) Locatelli 696,500
nvan dunque, o crudele Madrigal (2) Gesualdo 46,250
nveni David Motet (2) Bruckner 37,250
J'inverno from *The 4 Seasons* (6) Vivaldi 572,004
nvitation to the Dance (7) Weber 809,450
olanthe (10) Gilbert and Sullivan 917,750
onisation (7) Varèse 799,600
o son ferito Madrigal (1) Palestrina 9,600
o tacero, ma nel silentio mio Madrigal (2) Gesualdo 46,500
phigénie en Aulide Overture (7) Gluck 646,500
rmelin Prelude (7) Delius 622,250
saw my lady weep (8) Dowland 829,200
slamey (*Oriental Fantasy*) (3) Balakirev 112,000
L'Isle joyeuse (3) Debussy 161,750
sle of the Dead (7) Rachmaninoff 734,000
srael in Egypt (2) Handel 51,500
ste sanctus pro lege Dei (1) Victoria 17,600
taliana in Algeri (10) Rossini 947,000
taliana in Algeri Overture (7) Rossini 748,000
talian Concerto (3) Bach, J. S. 108,250

Italian Serenade (7) Wolf 811,400
Italian Symphony (5) Mendelssohn 438,750
Italienisches Liederbuch (8) Wolf 879,500–881,000
Itene o miei sospiri Madrigal (2) Gesualdo 46,750
It's All I Have to Bring (8) Bacon 814,250
It Was a Lover and His Lass (8) Morley 842,500
I Will Magnify Thee (*Chandos Anthem* 5) (2) Handel 50,625

Jardin sous la pluie from *Estampes* (3) Debussy 159,750
Jauchzet Gott in allen Landen (2) Bach, J. S. 23,051
Jeannie with the Light Brown Hair (8) Foster 833,300
Jenufa (10) Janáček 925,500
Jephtha: Sinfonia (7) Handel 660,750
Jephte (2) Carissimi 39,000
Jeremiah Symphony (5) Bernstein 382,000
Jérez from *Iberia* (3) Albéniz 97,750
Jesu Christus, unser Heiland (3) Bach, J. S. 104,689
Jesu der du meine Seele (2) Bach, J. S. 23,078
Jesu dulcis memoria (1) Victoria 17,700
Jesu, joy of man's desiring (2) Bach, J. S. 23,347
Jesu, meine Freude Chorale Prelude (3) Bach, J. S. 101,610
Jesu, meine Freude Motet (2) Bach, J. S. 25,000
Jesu Rex admirabilis Motet (1) Palestrina 12,400
Je tremble en voyant ton visage (8) Debussy 827,703
Jeu de cartes (7) Stravinsky 784,600
Le jeu de Robin et Marion (1) Adam de la Halle 100
Jeux d'eau (3) Ravel 215,225
Jeux d'Enfants (7) Bizet 600,000
Jeux-Poème dansé (7) Debussy 618,750
Je veux vivre from *Roméo et Juliette* (9) Gounod 889,550
Jewel Song from *Faust* (9) Gounod 889,400
Job (*A Masque for Dancing*) (7) Vaughan Williams 800,350
Jolie Fille de Perth Suite (7) Bizet 600,250
Jonny spielt auf (10) Křenek 926,500
Jorsalfar Suite (7) Grieg 652,750
Jota Aragonesa (7) Glinka 644,000
Joyeux Noël (11) Schubel 994,450
Jubilate in D (2) Purcell 76,500
Julius Caesar (10) Handel 921,250
Jüngling an der Quelle (8) Schubert 858,750
Jüngling und der Tod (8) Schubert 859,000
Jupiter Symphony (5) Mozart 451,500

Kaddish Symphony (5) Bernstein 382,500
Kaiser Waltz (7) Strauss, Johann 772,000
Kakadu Trio (4) Beethoven 274,000
Kamarinskaya (7) Glinka 644,250
Kammermusik no. 2 (4) Hindemith 311,500
Kammermusik no. 3 (4) Hindemith 311,750
Kammermusik no. 4 (4) Hindemith 312,000
Karelia Suite (7) Sibelius 762,500
Die Kartenlegerin (8) Schumann 867,000

7 Orchestral/8 Songs and Lieder/9 Arias/10 Operas/11 New and Experimental

Katerina Ismailova (10) Shostakovich 950,750
Kennst du das Land? (8) Wolf 879,250
Kettledrum Mass (2) Haydn 55,250
Khovantchina Prelude to Act I (7) Mussorgsky 725,250
Kikimora (7) Liadov 691,750
Kinderscenen (3) Schumann 234,000–235,000
Kindertotenlieder (8) Mahler 839,000
King Arthur (10) Purcell 943,750
King Lear Overture (7) Berlioz 595,250
King Lear Suite (11) Luening and Ussachevsky 989,650
King of Denmark (11) Feldman 982,500
The King Shall Rejoice (*Coronation Anthem*) (2) Handel 49,500
King Stephen Overture (7) Beethoven 591,250
Das klagende Lied (2) Mahler 63,000
Klavierstück IX (11) Stockhausen 995,300
Klavierstück XI (11) Stockhausen 995,400
Klefticos (Greek dance) (7) Skalkottas 765,250
Kleine geistliche Konzerte a 1-5 (2) Schütz 83,250
Kleine Kammermusik, Op. 24, no. 2 (4) Hindemith 312,250
Eine kleine Nachtmusik (7) Mozart 724,250
Des Knaben Wunderhorn (8) Mahler 839,100
The Knot Garden (11) Tippett 997,000
Knoxville: Summer of 1915 (8) Barber 814,750
Kol Nidrei for Cello and Orchestra (6) Bruch 506,250
Komm, heiliger Geist (3) Bach, J. S. 103,652
Komm, heiliger Geist–Fantasia (3) Bach, J. S. 103,651
Kommst du nun, Jesu, vom Himmel herunter (3) Bach, J. S. 102,650
Konzertstück for 4 Horns and Orchestra (6) Schumann 553,250
Konzertstück for Piano and Orchestra (6) Weber 576,000
Krakowiak Rondo for Piano and Orchestra (6) Chopin 508,000
Kreisleriana (3) Schumann 235,750
Kreutzer Sonata (4) Beethoven 271,250
Der Kuss (8) Beethoven 816,200
Kyrie Le roy (1) Taverner 16,800

Lachen und Weinen (8) Schubert 859,250
La donna è mobile from *Rigoletto* (9) Verdi 899,500
Lagrime d'Amante al Sepolcro dell'Amata (8) Monteverdi 841,000
Lagrime d'Amante Madrigal (2) Monteverdi 66,500
Lakmé (10) Delibes 913,750
Lamentabatur Jacob (1) Morales 7,300
Lamentatione Symphony (5) Haydn 411,000
Lamentations of Jeremiah (1) Tallis 16,500
Lamentatio sanctae matris (1) Dufay 3,200
Lament for Beowulf (2) Hanson 53,750
Lamento d'Arianna (8) Monteverdi 841,200
Lamento della ninfa (8) Monteverdi 841,400
Land of Lost Content (Song Cycle) (8) Ireland 835,200

The Lark Ascending (Romance for Violin and Orchestra) (6) Vaughan Williams 570,250
The Lark Quartet (4) Haydn 307,000
Lass Fürstin, lass noch einen Strahl (2) Bach, J. S. 23,398
Last Spring (7) Grieg 653,000
Latin American Symphonette (7) Gould 648,25
Lauda Sion salvatorem (1) Victoria 17,800
Lauda Sion salvatorem Motet (1) Palestrina 12,500
Laudate pueri (2) Monteverdi 70,500
Leçons de Ténèbres (*Lamentations of Jeremiah* (8) Couperin 826,000
Légende for Violin and Orchestra (6) Wieniawski 576,500
Lehn' deine Wang' (8) Schumann 867,250
Leiyla and the Poet (11) El Dabh 981,250
Lemminkäinen's Return (7) Sibelius 762,750
L'Enfance du Christ (2) Berlioz 28,250
Lenin Symphony (5) Shostakovich 470,250
Leonore Overture no. 1 (7) Beethoven 591,50?
Leonore Overture no. 2 (7) Beethoven 591,502
Leonore Overture no. 3 (7) Beethoven 591,503
Let thy hand be strengthened (*Coronation Anthem*) (2) Handel 49,750
Liebesbotschaft (8) Schubert 859,750
Liebe schwärmt auf' allen Wegen (8) Schubert 859,500
Liebeslieder Waltzes, Op. 52 (2) Brahms 31,50?
Liebeslieder Waltzes, Op. 65 (2) Brahms 31,75?
Liebestod from *Tristan und Isolde* (7) Wagner 807,000
Liebestod from *Tristan und Isolde* (9) Wagner 902,900
Liebestraum no. 3 (3) Liszt 187,250
Liebst du um Schönheit (8) Mahler 839,302
Liebster Gott, wann werd' ich sterben (2) Bach, J. S. 23,008
Lied eines Schiffers an die Dioskuren (8) Schubert 860,000
Liederkreis (op. 24) (8) Schumann 867,500
Liederkreis (op. 39) (8) Schumann 867,750
Lied von der Erde (8) Mahler 839,200
Lieutenant Kijé Suite (7) Prokofiev 731,000
Light Cavalry Overture (7) Suppé 788,750
Lilacs (8) Rachmaninoff 848,000
Lilacs (7) Ruggles 752,000
Lincoln Portrait (7) Copland 613,250
Lindenbaum (8) Schubert 860,250
Linz Symphony (5) Mozart 450,250
Lions? (8) Rorem 850,300
Litanei auf das Fest Aller Seelen (8) Schubert 860,500
Litaniae de beata Virgine (1) Victoria 17,900
Litaniae de beata virgine Maria Motet (1) Palestrina 12,600
Little Symphony (5) Schubert 463,000
Little Elegy (8) Rorem 850,400
Little Organ Mass (2) Haydn 55,000
Little Russian Symphony (5) Tchaikovsky 475,750
Little Symphony (5) Effinger 398,750
Little Symphony (5) Sanders 461,000

Musical Category Key: 1 Early/2 Choral/3 Keyboard/4 Chamber/5 Symphonies/6 Concerti

Little Train of the Calpira (7) Villa-Lobos 802,200
Liturgique Symphony (5) Honegger 428,250
Lob des Leidens (8) Strauss, Richard 873,750
Lobgesang Symphony (5) Mendelssohn 438,250
Lohengrin (10) Wagner 961,750
Lohengrin: Prelude to Act I (7) Wagner 804,000
Lohengrin: Prelude to Act III (7) Wagner 804,250
Lo, here the gentle lark (8) Bishop 817,200
Lola from *Cavalleria Rusticana* (9) Mascagni 890,500
London Overture (7) Ireland 677,000
London Suite (7) Coates 611,250
London Symphony (5) Haydn 425,000
London Symphony (5) Vaughan Williams 480,250
Look Down, Fair Moon (8) Rorem 850,500
The Lord of Salisbury his Pavin (3) Gibbons 174,000
Loreley (8) Schumann 868,000
Die Lotosblume ängstigt sich (8) Schumann 868,250
Louisiana Story: Acadian Songs and Dances (7) Thomson 796,250
Loup Ballet (7) Dutilleux 625,500
Love for Three Oranges (10) Prokofiev 939,750
Love for Three Oranges Suite (7) Prokofiev 731,250
Lucia di Lammermoor (10) Donizetti 915,250
Lucrezia Borgia (10) Donizetti 915,500
Lullaby from *Gayne* (7) Khachaturian 684,500
Lulu (10) Berg 906,750
Lulu Suite (7) Berg 593,250
Luna Park (11) Dockstader 978,500
Lux Aeterna (11) Ligeti 989,200
Lydia (8) Fauré 832,600
Lyric Suite (4) Berg 275,750
Lyric Suite (7) Grieg 653,250
Lyric Symphony (5) Kupferman 433,250

Ma bouche rit (1) Ockeghem 8,300
Macbeth (10) Verdi 959,500
Machet die Tore weit Cantata (2) Telemann 88,250
Machine Music (11) Hiller 987,400
Ma dall' avido stelo divulsa from *Un ballo in maschera* (9) Verdi 897,200
Madame Butterfly (10) Puccini 941,250
Madamina! il catalogo e questo from *Don Giovanni* (9) Mozart 891,950
Mädchenlied (8) Brahms 819,750
Madrigali guerrieri et amorosi (2) Monteverdi 68,500
Mad Scene from *Lucia di Lammermoor* (9) Donizetti 888,450
Magic Fire Music from *Walküre* (7) Wagner 807,500
Magic Flute (10) Mozart 934,500
Magic Flute Overture (7) Mozart 720,750
Magnificat (2) Vaughan Williams 90,000
Magnificat septimi toni (1) Morales 7,400

The Maiden Returned from Her Tryst (8) Sibelius 870,300
Die Mainacht (8) Brahms 820,250
Major Seconds Broken and Together (no. 132) from *Mikrokosmos* (3) Bartók 114,232
Maladetto sia l'aspetto (8) Monteverdi 841,600
Málaga from *Iberia* (3) Albéniz 97,750
Ma maitresse (1) Ockeghem 8,400
Ma Mère l'Oye (7) Ravel 737,250
Ma Mère l'Oye (4-hand piano suite) (3) Ravel 215,500
La Mamma morta from *Andrea Chénier* (9) Giordano 888,850
Mamma quel vino from *Cavalleria Rusticana* (9) Mascagni 890,550
Mandoline (8) Debussy 827,400
Manfred Overture (7) Schumann 760,500
Manfred (symphonic poem) (7) Tchaikovsky 791,250
Man in the Moon (10) Haydn 923,000
Manon (10) Massenet 927,750
Manon Lescaut (10) Puccini 941,500
Manzoni Requiem Mass (2) Verdi 91,750
Marche Joyeuse (7) Chabrier 609,750
Marche militaire (7) Schubert 758,000
Marche Slave (7) Tchaikovsky 791,500
March of the Dwarfs (3) Grieg 178,500
Maria Theresa Symphony (5) Haydn 414,250
Marosszék Dances (7) Kodály 686,750
Marriage of Figaro (10) Mozart 934,750
Marriage of Figaro Overture (7) Mozart 722,000
Married Beau Suite (7) Purcell 733,500
Marteau sans maître (11) Boulez 968,250
Martern aller Artern from *Abduction from the Seraglio* (9) Mozart 891,500
Martha (10) Flotow 916,750
Martibus suis dixerunt Motet (1) Palestrina 13,000
Masonic Funeral Music (7) Mozart 722,500
Masquerade Suite (7) Khachaturian 685,000
Mass (2) Stravinsky 86,750
Mathis der Maler Symphony (5) Hindemith 426,000
Le Matin Symphony (5) Haydn 406,750
Mattinata (Aubade) (8) Leoncavallo 836,500
Mausfallensprüchlein (8) Wolf 881,250
Mavra (10) Stravinsky 954,250
May Night Overture (7) Rimsky-Korsakov 745,500
Mazeppa (7) Liszt 694,000
Medea (10) Cherubini 912,000
Medea (ballet suite) (7) Barber 585,000
Medea's Meditation and Dance of Vengeance (7) Barber 585,250
Meditations on Ecclesiastes (7) Dello Joio 624,000
The Medium (10) Menotti 928,750
Meeresstille und glückliche Fahrt (2) Beethoven 27,250
Mefistofele (10) Boito 908,500
Meine Seele erhebt den Herren Cantata (2) Bach, J. S. 23,010

7 Orchestral/8 Songs and Lieder/9 Arias/10 Operas/11 New and Experimental

Meine Seele erhebt den Herren Chorale Prelude (3) Bach, J. S. 102,648
Meistersinger Prelude (7) Wagner 804,500
Die Meistersinger von Nürnberg (10) Wagner 962,000
Me, me and none but me (8) Dowland 829,250
Men and Mountains (7) Ruggles 752,250
Menuet antique (7) Ravel 737,500
Mephisto-Waltz (7) Liszt 694,250
Mephisto-Waltz (Version no. 1) (3) Liszt 187,500
Mephisto-Waltz (Version no. 3) (3) Liszt 187,600
La Mer (7) Debussy 619,000
Mercè, dilette amiche from *I Vespri Siciliani* (9) Verdi 901,000
Mercury from *The Planets* (7) Holst 670,750
Mer hahn en neue Oberkeet (*Peasant Cantata*) (2) Bach, J. S. 23,412
Merle noir (11) Messiaen 990,900
Merry Andrew (no. 139) from *Mikrokosmos* (3) Bartók 114,239
Merry Wives of Windsor Overture (7) Nicolai 726,000
Mesa (11) Mumma 991,650
Messiah (2) Handel 51,750
Metamorphosen (7) Strauss, Richard 780,000
Métastasis (11) Xenakis 998,850
Mi chiamano Mimi from *La Bohème* (9) Puccini 893,200
Le Midi Symphony (5) Haydn 407,000
Midsommarvaka (*Swedish Rhapsody*) (7) Alfvén 579,500
Midsummer Marriage (10) Tippett 957,500
Midsummer Marriage: Ritual Dances (7) Tippett 796,750
Midsummer Night's Dream (10) Britten 910,250
Midsummer Night's Dream: Incidental Music (7) Mendelssohn 707,750
Mignon (10) Thomas 956,750
Mignonne, allon voir si la rose (1) Costeley 1,700
Mignon Overture (7) Thomas 796,000
Mikado (10) Gilbert and Sullivan 918,000
Mikrokosmos (3) Bartók 113,800–114,350
Mikrophonie I (11) Stockhausen 995,600
Mikrophonie II (11) Stockhausen 995,700
Military Polonaise (3) Chopin 145,250
Military Symphony (5) Haydn 424,000
Minor Seconds, Major Sevenths (no. 144) from *Mikrokosmos* (3) Bartók 114,344
Minute Waltz (3) Chopin 148,506
Miracle Symphony (5) Haydn 423,000
The Miraculous Mandarin ballet (7) Bartók 587,250
Mir ist ein feins brauns Maidelein (1) Rhaw 16,100
Miroirs (3) Ravel 215,750
Missa Ave Maris stella (1) Des Prez 2,100
Missa brevis (2) Britten 34,500
Missa brevis (2) Kodály 61,250
Missa brevis (2) Mozart 72,750
Missa brevis (1) Palestrina 10,500
Missa Caput (1) Ockeghem 8,500

Missa carminum (1) Isaac 4,200
Missa choralis (2) Liszt 62,250
Missa Ecce ancilla (1) Ockeghem 8,700
Missa Fortuna desperata (1) Obrecht 7,900
Missa Hercules dux Ferrariae (1) Des Prez 2,200
Missa L'Homme armé (1) Des Prez 2,300
Missa in tempore belli (2) Haydn 55,250
Missa Mi-mi (1) Ockeghem 8,800
Missa Noe, Noe (1) Arcadelt 200
Missa Pange Lingua (1) Des Prez 2,400
Missa Papae Marcelli (1) Palestrina 10,600
Missa pro defunctis (2) Anerio 22,000
Missa Quaeramus cum pastoribus (1) Morales 7,500
Missa sine titulo ad quator voces inaequales (1) Tallis 16,600
Missa Solemnis (2) Beethoven 27,500
Missa Solemnis (2) Haydn 55,750
Missa Sub tuum praesidium (1) Obrecht 8,000
Missa super o praeclara (1) Isaac 4,300
Missus est Gabriel angelus (1) Morales 7,600
Moldau (*Vltava*) (7) Smetana 766,500
Moments musicaux (3) Schubert 227,000
Mon coeur se recommende à vous (1) Lassus 5,100
Der Mond (10) Orff 937,750
Mondnacht (8) Schumann 868,750
Monodia (11) Nono 991,900
Monumentum pro Gesualdo (7) Stravinsky 784,800
Moonlight Sonata (3) Beethoven 121,750
Morgen (8) Strauss, Richard 874,000
Mörike Lieder (8) Wolf 881,500–884,000
Morning, Noon and Night in Vienna Overture (7) Suppé 789,000
Morning Papers Waltz (7) Strauss, Johann 772,250
Mort de Cléopâtre (8) Berlioz 816,600
Moses and Aaron (10) Schoenberg 949,750
Moto perpetuo for Violin and Orchestra (6) Paganini 541,000
Le Moucheron (3) Couperin 154,400
Movements for Piano and Orchestra (6) Stravinsky 558,000
Musensohn (8) Schubert 860,750
Musical Joke (7) Mozart 722,250
Musical Offering (7) Bach, J. S. 583,500
Musical Sleigh Ride (7) Mozart, Leopold 715,000
Music for a While (8) Purcell 847,500
Music for Six (11) Donovan 980,000
Music for Strings, Percussion, and Celesta (7) Bartók 587,500
Music for the Theater (7) Copland 613,500
Music from the Venezia Space Theatre (11) Musgrave 991,700
Music of the Spheres Waltz (7) Strauss, Josef 778,500
Musique de Table (suites) (7) Telemann 794,750
My Beloved is Mine (8) Britten 823,501
My Bonnie Lass, She Smileth (8) Morley 842,750
My Days Have Been So Wondrous Free (8) Hopkinson 835,000

Musical Category Key: 1 Early/2 Choral/3 Keyboard/4 Chamber/5 Symphonies/6 Concerti

My Fatherland (*Ma Vlast*) (7) Smetana 766,750
My Home Overture (7) Dvořák 626,800
My Old Kentucky Home (8) Foster 833,500
Mysterious Mountain (7) Hovhaness 673,500

Nabucco (10) Verdi 959,750
Die Nacht (8) Strauss, Richard 874,250
Les Nations (4) Couperin 289,500–290,250
Nativité du Seigneur (11) Messiaen 991,000
Vein, junger Herr (8) Wolf 880,500
Nelson Mass (2) Haydn 55,750
Nessun dorma from *Turandot* (9) Puccini 894,800
New England Triptych (7) Schuman 759,750
New Hungarian Folk Song (no. 127) from *Mikrokosmos* (3) Bartók 114,227
New World Symphony (5) Dvořák 398,250
Night Crow (8) Rorem 850,600
Night Music (11) Musgrave 991,675
Night on Bald Mountain (7) Mussorgsky 725,500
Nights in the Gardens of Spain (6) Falla 515,000
Night Speech (11) Roussakis 994,050
Night Waltz from *Rodeo* (7) Copland 615,250
Nigra sum Motet (1) Palestrina 13,100
Nimmersatte Liebe (8) Wolf 883,250
Nobles Seigneurs, salut! from *Les Huguenots* (9) Meyerbeer 891,250
Les Noces (2) Stravinsky 87,000
Nocturnal for Guitar (4) Britten 284,500
Nocturne for Violin, Cello, and Piano (4) Schubert 352,000
Nocturne no. 10 (3) Fauré 167,250
Nocturne no. 13 (3) Fauré 167,500
Nocturnes (*Nuages, Fêtes, Sirènes*) (7) Debussy 619,250
Noël des enfants qui n'ont plus de maisons (8) Debussy 827,600
None But the Lonely Heart (8) Tchaikovsky 877,300
Non piangere, Liù from *Turandot* (9) Puccini 894,900
Non più andrai from *Marriage of Figaro* (9) Mozart 892,400
Non sa che sia dolore (2) Bach, J. S. 23,409
Noonday Witch (7) Dvořák 627,000
No Pagliaccio non son from *I Pagliacci* (9) Leoncavallo 890,350
Norfolk Rhapsody (7) Vaughan Williams 800,500
Norma (10) Bellini 906,000
North American Time Capsule (11) Lucier 989,500
Norwegian Dance no. 2 (7) Grieg 653,750
Norwegian Moods (7) Stravinsky 785,000
Notre-Dame Mass (1) Machaut 6,900
Notre Dame Organa (1) Le Jeune 5,900
La notte (Concerto for Flute and Orchestra) (6) Vivaldi 573,002
Notturno (3) Grieg 178,750
Notturno (7) Grieg 653,500
Notturno (no. 97) from *Mikrokosmos* (3) Bartók 114,097
Nouvelles aventures (11) Ligeti 989,300
Novelettes (3) Schumann 236,000
November Steps (11) Takemitsu 996,600

Now Is the Month of Maying (8) Morley 843,250
Noye's Fludde (10) Britten 910,500
Nuages from *Nocturnes* (7) Debussy 619,500
Nude Paper Sermon (11) Salzman 994,200
Nuit des Tropiques (symphonic poem) (7) Gottschalk 647,000
La nuit froide et sombre (1) Lassus 5,100
Nuits d'été (8) Berlioz 816,800
No. 9 Zyklus (11) Stockhausen 995,900
Nunc Dimittis (1) Byrd 1,400
Nun ist das Heil und die Kraft (2) Bach, J. S. 23,050
Nun komm der Heiden Heiland (S. 599) (3) Bach, J. S. 101,599
Nun komm der Heiden Heiland (S. 659) (3) Bach, J. S. 103,659
Nun lass uns Frieden schliessen (8) Wolf 880,750
Nursery (song cycle) (8) Mussorgsky 846,000
Der Nussbaum (8) Schumann 869,000
Nutcracker (complete ballet) (7) Tchaikovsky 791,750
Nutcracker Suite (7) Tchaikovsky 792,000

O beau pays de la Touraine from *Les Huguenots* (9) Meyerbeer 891,300
O Be Joyful in the Lord (*Chandos Anthem*) (2) Handel 50,125
Oberon Overture (7) Weber 809,600
Obras de musica para tecia (1) Cabezon 1,500
The Oceanides (7) Sibelius 763,000
O, Cease Thy Singing Maiden Fair (8) Rachmaninoff 848,250
Octandre (4) Varèse 366,250
Ode for St. Cecilia's Day (2) Handel 52,000
Ode for St. Cecilia's Day (2) Purcell 77,000
Ode to Napoleon (8) Schoenberg 851,850
Oedipus Rex (10) Stravinsky 954,500
O'er the hills and far away (8) Hopkinson 835,100
O Ewigkeit du Donnerwort (2) Bach, J. S. 23,060
Offrandes (7) Varèse 799,800
Of Wood and Brass (11) Ussachevsky 997,550
O grief! Even on the Bud (8) Morley 843,500
Oh, patria mia, mai piu ti rivedro from *Aïda* (9) Verdi 896,700
Oh! quand je dors (8) Liszt 837,000
Oiseaux Éxotiques (11) Messiaen 991,100
O Lamm Gottes unschuldig (3) Bach, J. S. 103,656
Old American Songs (8) Copland 825,600
Old Dog Tray (8) Foster 833,800
The old lute (8) Britten 824,756
Old Sequins and Old Cuirasses (3) Satie 220,000
O liebliche Wangen (8) Brahms 820,750
O magnum mysterium (1) Morales 7,800
O magnum mysterium Mass (1) Victoria 18,400
O magnum mysterium Motet (1) Palestrina 13,200
O magnum mysterium (motets and hymns) (1) Victoria 18,100

7 Orchestral/8 Songs and Lieder/9 Arias/10 Operas/11 New and Experimental

Ombre leggiera from *Dinorah* (9) Meyerbeer 891,200
O Mensch, bewein' dein' Sunde gross (3) Bach, J. S. 101,622
O Mistress Mine (8) Morley 843,750
Ondine (3) Debussy 165,000
On Hearing the First Cuckoo in Spring (7) Delius 622,500
O Paradiso from *L'Africaine* (9) Meyerbeer 891,150
Ophelia's Mad Scene from *Hamlet* (9) Thomas 896,350
O quam gloriosum Mass (1) Victoria 18,500
O quam gloriosum (motets and hymns) (1) Victoria 18,200
L'Orfeo (10) Monteverdi 930,750
Orfeo ed Euridice (10) Gluck 920,250
Organ Symphony (5) Saint-Saëns 460,500
Organum (7) Ruggles 752,500
Orgelbüchlein (S. 599–644) (3) Bach, J. S. 101,000–101,622
Orient-Occident III (11) Xenakis 998,900
Orlando Paladino Overture (7) Haydn 664,750
L'Ormindo (10) Cavalli 911,750
O rosa bella (1) Dunstable 3,600
Orpheus (7) Liszt 694,500
Orpheus (ballet) (7) Stravinsky 785,200
Orpheus in Hades Overture (7) Offenbach 728,000
Orthogenesis (11) Malovec 990,050
Osculetur me Motet (1) Palestrina 13,300
Os justi Motet (2) Bruckner 37,250
Ostinato (no. 146) from *Mikrokosmos* (3) Bartók 114,346
Otello (10) Verdi 960,000
Otello (ballet music, Act III) (7) Verdi 801,400
Otello Overture (7) Dvořák 627,250
O tu che in seno agli angeli from *La Forza del Destino* (9) Verdi 898,200
L'Ours Symphony (5) Haydn 419,500
Our Town (suite) (7) Copland 613,750
Outdoor Overture (7) Copland 614,000
Outline for Flute, Percussion and String Bass (11) Oliveros 992,050
Out of Doors (3) Bartók 114,500
Over the Hills and Far Away (7) Delius 622,750
Over the Pavements (7) Ives 679,750
Overture, Scherzo, and Finale (7) Schumann 760,750
O vos omnes Motet (2) Gesualdo 47,000
Oxford Symphony (5) Haydn 422,000

Pacific 231 (7) Honegger 672,000
Pagan Poem (7) Loeffler 697,000
Pagliacci (10) Leoncavallo 927,000
Paladins (suite for Horn and Strings) (7) Rameau 735,250
Pange lingua Motet (2) Bruckner 37,250
La Pantomine (3) Couperin 155,700
Papae Marcelli Mass (1) Palestrina 10,600
Papillons (3) Schumann 236,250
Parable of Death (2) Foss 43,500
Parade (7) Satie 755,500
Parfons regretz (1) Des Prez 2,600

Paris (7) Delius 623,000
Paris Symphony (5) Mozart 449,000
Le Parnasse (Apothéose de Corelli) (7) Couperin 616,750
Parsifal (10) Wagner 962,250
Parsifal: Good Friday Music (7) Wagner 804,750
Parsifal: Prelude (7) Wagner 805,000
Partita for Orchestra (7) Walton 808,400
Pas d'acier (suite) (7) Prokofiev 731,750
Passacaglia (3) Satie 220,250
Passacaglia on Vermont Folk Tunes (11) Donovan 980,250
Passacaille (3) Couperin 154,600
Passion According to St. Luke (11) Penderecki 992,900
La Passione Symphony (5) Haydn 414,500
Pastoral Sonata (3) Beethoven 122,000
Pastoral Symphony (5) Beethoven 378,250
Pastoral Symphony (5) Vaughan Williams 480,500
Pastorale (3) Franck 169,500
Pastorale d'été (7) Honegger 672,250
Pastor fido (4) Vivaldi 369,250–370,500
Il Pastor Fido: ballet music (7) Handel 659,000
Pathétique Sonata (3) Beethoven 120,250
Pathétique Symphony (5) Tchaikovsky 476,750
Les Patineurs (ballet) (7) Meyerbeer 710,500
Patrie Overture (7) Bizet 600,500
Paukenmesse (2) Haydn 55,250
Pavane (7) Fauré 632,750
Pavane pour une infante défunte (3) Ravel 216,000
Pavane pour une infante défunte (7) Ravel 737,750
P.D.Q. Bach (7) Schickele 755,825
Peacock Variations (7) Kodály 687,000
Pearl-White Moments Antiphonie III (11) Gaburo 984,000
Peasant Cantata (Mer hahn en neue Oberkeet) (2) Bach, J. S. 23,412
Péchés de vieillesse (8) Rossini 851,000
Les Pêcheurs de perles (10) Bizet 908,000
Peer Gynt Suite no. 1 (7) Grieg 654,000
Peer Gynt Suite no. 2 (7) Grieg 654,250
Pelléas et Mélisande (10) Debussy 913,500
Pelléas et Mélisande (7) Fauré 633,000
Pelléas et Mélisande (7) Sibelius 763,250
Pelléas und Mélisande (7) Schoenberg 756,500
Peloponnisiaskos (Greek dance) (7) Skalkotta 765,250
La Péri (7) Dukas 625,000
Per la S.S. Assunzione di Maria Vergine (Concerto for Violin, 2 String Choirs, 2 Harpsichords) (6) Vivaldi 573,500
Perpetual Motion (7) Strauss, Johann 769,500
Perpetuum Mobile (no. 135) from *Mikrokosmos* (3) Bartók 114,235
Per pietà from *Così fan tutte* (9) Mozart 891,600
Peter and the Wolf (7) Prokofiev 732,000
Peter Grimes (10) Britten 910,750
Peter Grimes: 4 Sea Interludes and Passacaglia (7) Britten 606,000
Petite camusette (1) Ockeghem 9,000

Musical Category Key: 1 Early/2 Choral/3 Keyboard/4 Chamber/5 Symphonies/6 Concerti

Les Petits Riens (ballet music) (7) Mozart 722,750

Petrouchka (complete ballet) (7) Stravinsky 785,400

Petrouchka: Suite (7) Stravinsky 785,600

Pezzi sacri (2) Verdi 91,500

Phantasy for Violin and Piano (4) Schoenberg 350,000

Der Philosoph Symphony (5) Haydn 410,750

Piangerò, la sorte mia from *Guilio Cesare* (9) Handel 889,850

Pictures at an Exhibition (3) Mussorgsky 203,000

Pictures at an Exhibition (7) Mussorgsky 725,750

Pièce heröique (3) Franck 169,750

Pièces de claveçin (3) Rameau 214,000

Pièces de claveçin en concert (4) Rameau 346,000–347,000

Pièce en forme de Habañera for Violin and Piano (4) Ravel 348,250

La Piémontaise from *Les Nations* (4) Couperin 290,250

Pierrot Lunaire (8) Schoenberg 851,900

Pinball (11) Ivey 988,100

Pines of Rome (7) Respighi 741,250

Pique Dame (10) Tchaikovsky 956,250

Pique Dame Overture (7) Suppé 789,250

Pirates of Penzance (10) Gilbert and Sullivan 918,250

Pithoprakta (11) Xenakis 998,950

Pizzicato Polka (7) Strauss, Johann 772,750

The Planets (7) Holst 670,500

Play of Daniel (1) 15,700

Play of Herod (1) 15,800

Plectra and Percussion Dances: Castor and Pollux (11) Partch 992,150

Pleurez! pleurez, mes yeux! from *El Cid* (9) Massenet 890,800

Pli selon pli (11) Boulez 968,500

Plow that Broke the Plains (7) Thomson 796,300

Le plus que lente (3) Debussy 162,000

Poème d'Extase Symphony (5) Scriabin 466,500

A Poem in Cycles and Bells (11) Luening and Ussachevsky 989,700

Poet and Peasant Overture (7) Suppé 789,500

Pohjola's Daughter (7) Sibelius 763,750

Poised Antiphonie IV (11) Gaburo 984,250

Poissons d'or (3) Debussy 161,500

Polifonica (11) Nono 991,900

Polish Symphony (5) Tchaikovsky 476,000

Polovtsian Dances from *Prince Igor* (7) Borodin 603,750

Pomp and Circumstance Marches (7) Elgar 630,751–630,755

Poppy Nogood and the Phantom Band (11) Riley 993,900

Porgy and Bess (10) Gershwin 917,000

Porgy and Bess (symphonic picture) (7) Gershwin 640,500

Portals (7) Ruggles 752,750

Portsmouth Point Overture (7) Walton 808,600

Posthorn Serenade (7) Mozart 723,750

La Poule Symphony (5) Haydn 419,750

Pour l'amour de ma doulce amye (1) Dufay 3,300

Pour le piano (suite) (3) Debussy 162,250

Prague Symphony (5) Mozart 450,500

Prairie (7) Sowerby 767,750

Preciosa Overture (7) Weber 809,750

Prélude à l'après-midi d'un faune (7) Debussy 620,250

Prelude and Fugue on B-A-C-H (3) Liszt 188,000

Prélude, Choral, et Fugue (3) Franck 170,000

Preludes for Piano (3) Gershwin 173,000

Les Préludes (7) Liszt 694,750

Pribaoutki (8) Stravinsky 876,800

La primavera from *The 4 Seasons* (6) Vivaldi 572,001

Prince Igor (10) Borodin 908,750

Prince Igor Overture (7) Borodin 603,500

Prince Igor: Polovtsian Dances (7) Borodin 603,750

Prince of Denmark's March (*Trumpet Voluntary*) (6) Clarke 508,750

Princess Ida (10) Gilbert and Sullivan 918,500

Printemps (7) Debussy 620,500

Prison (8) Fauré 832,700

Procession of Bacchus from *Sylvia* (7) Delibes 621,250

Procession of the Sardar (7) Ippolitov-Ivanov 676,500

Le Promenoir des deux amants (8) Debussy 827,700

Prometheus ballet music (7) Beethoven 591,750

Prometheus Overture (7) Beethoven 592,000

Prometheus Symphony (5) Scriabin 466,750

Prophecy of the Suffering and Death of Jesus Christ (2) Demantius 42,250

Prophetiae Sibyllarum (1) Lassus 5,700

Proporzioni for Solo Flute (11) Evangelisti 981,500

Psalm 24 (2) Schütz 84,125

Psalm XLVII (2) Schmitt 79,000

Psalm 103 (2) Scheidt 78,000

Psalms of David (2) Schütz 84,000

Psalms 24, 67, 90, 100, 150 (2) Ives 59,750

Psalmus Hungaricus (2) Kodály 61,500

Puerta del Vino (3) Debussy 165,250

El puerto from *Iberia* (3) Albéniz 96,500

Pulcinella ballet (7) Stravinsky 785,800

Pulcinella: Suite (7) Stravinsky 786,000

Puppets are Dancing (3) Satie 220,500

I Puritani (10) Bellini 906,250

Quam pulchri sunt Motet (1) Palestrina 13,400

Quando le sere al placido from *Luisa Miller* (9) Verdi 898,600

Quando m'en vo' soletta from *La Bohème* (9) Puccini 893,400

Quartermass (11) Dockstader 978,750

Quartettsatz (4) Schubert 353,000

Quashed Culch (11) Schubel 994,500

Quatuor pour la fin du temps (11) Messiaen 991,200

Questa o quella from *Rigoletto* (9) Verdi 899,800

Quiet City for Trumpet, English Horn, and Orchestra (6) Copland 510,000

Qui la Voce from *I Puritani* (9) Bellini 887,200

Quintette en forme de Chôros (4) Villa-Lobos 368,750

Rackoczy March (7) Berlioz 595,300
Radetzky March (7) Strauss, Johann, Sr. 775,750
Rage over a Lost Penny (3) Beethoven 117,750
Ragtime for Piano (3) Stravinsky 242,500
Rainbow in Curved Air (11) Riley 993,950
Raindrop Prelude (3) Chopin 147,015
Rake's Progress (10) Stravinsky 955,000
Rape of Lucretia (10) Britten 911,000
Rapsodie espagnole (7) Ravel 738,000
Rastlose Liebe (8) Schubert 861,500
Rasumovsky Quartets (4) Beethoven 265,000–265,500
Raymond Overture (7) Thomas 796,050
Recondita armonia from *Tosca* (9) Puccini 894,500
Red Pony Suite (7) Copland 614,500
Red Poppy (ballet suite) (7) Glière 643,000
Reflets dans l'eau (3) Debussy 161,000
Reformation Symphony (5) Mendelssohn 439,250
Refrain (11) Stockhausen 996,300
Regata Veneziana (8) Rossini 851,250
La Reine Symphony (5) Haydn 420,250
Rejoice in the Lamb (2) Britten 35,000
Relâche (7) Satie 755,750
Réminiscences de Don Juan (3) Liszt 188,250
Renard (10) Stravinsky 955,250
Requiem (2) Delius 41,500
Requiem for the Empress Maria (1) Victoria 18,600
Rest Sweet Nymphs (2) Pilkington 74,500
Resurrection Symphony (5) Mahler 434,750
Retablo de Maese Pedro (10) Falla 916,250
Réveil des Oiseaux (11) Messiaen 991,100
Rêverie (3) Debussy 165,500
Revolutionary Etude (3) Chopin 134,900
Rhapsody in Blue (6) Gershwin 517,250
Rhapsody on a Theme of Paganini (6) Rachmaninoff 545,750
Das Rheingold (10) Wagner 962,500
Das Rheingold: Entrance of the Gods in Valhalla (7) Wagner 805,500
Rhenish Symphony (5) Schumann 465,500
Rhine Journey from *Götterdämmerung* (7) Wagner 803,750
Ride of the Valkyries from *Walküre* (7) Wagner 807,250
Rienzi Overture (7) Wagner 805,750
Rigoletto (10) Verdi 960,250
Rimes pour différentes sources sonores (11) Pousseur 993,200
Der Ring des Nibelungen (10) Wagner 962,750
Rite of Spring (*Le Sacre du Printemps*) (7) Stravinsky 786,200
Ritmica (11) Nono 991,900
Ritorna vincitor! from *Aïda* (9) Verdi 896,900
Il ritorno d'Ulisse in patria (10) Monteverdi 931,000
Ritter vom Steckenpferd from *Kinderscenen* (3) Schumann 235,000
Ritual Fire Dance from *El Amor Brujo* (7) Falla 631,500

The River (suite) (7) Thomson 796,350
Rodelina (10) Handel 921,750
Rodeo (7) Copland 614,750
Le Roi David (2) Honegger 59,000
Roman Carnival Overture (7) Berlioz 595,500
Romance in C for String Orchestra (7) Sibelius 764,000
Romantic Symphony (5) Bruckner 390,750
Romantic Symphony (5) Hanson 403,500
Romantica Symphony (5) Chávez 393,250
Romanze from *Eine kleine Nachtmusik* (7) Mozart 724,500
Romeo and Juliet (7) Diamond 624,500
Romeo and Juliet (7) Prokofiev 732,250
Romeo and Juliet (7) Tchaikovsky 793,000
Romeo and Juliet (complete ballet) (7) Prokofiev 732,500
Roméo et Juliette (2) Berlioz 28,750
Roméo et Juliette (10) Gounod 920,750
Rondes de Printemps (7) Debussy 618,500
La Rondine (10) Puccini 941,750
Rondo brillant for Piano and Orchestra (6) Mendelssohn 534,000
Rondo brillant for Violin and Piano (4) Schubert 354,500
Rondo capriccioso (3) Mendelssohn 192,250
Rosamunde (incidental music) (7) Schubert 758,750
Der Rosenkavalier (10) Strauss, Richard 953,750
Rosenkavalier: Suite (7) Strauss, Richard 780,250
Rosenkavalier: Waltzes (7) Strauss, Richard 780,500
Roses from the South Waltz (7) Strauss, Johann 773,000
Le Rossignol-en-amour (3) Couperin 155,000
Rossiniana (7) Respighi 741,500
Le Rouet d'Omphale (7) Saint-Saëns 754,000
Roumanian Folk Dances (7) Bartók 587,750
Roumanian Rhapsody no. 1 (7) Enesco 631,250
Roumanian Rhapsody no. 2 (7) Enesco 631,250
La Roxolane Symphony (5) Haydn 416,750
Royal Fireworks Music (7) Handel 660,500
Ruddigore (10) Gilbert and Sullivan 918,750
Rugby (7) Honegger 672,500
Ruhe, meine Seele (8) Strauss, Richard 874,500
Ruins of Athens (incidental music) (7) Beethoven 592,250
Russian Dance from *Petrouchka* (7) Stravinsky 785,650
Russian Easter Overture (7) Rimsky-Korsakov 746,000
Russian Sailors' Dance (7) Glière 643,500
Russlan and Ludmila Overture (7) Glinka 644,500
Rustic Wedding Symphony (5) Goldmark 402,750
Ruy Blas Overture (7) Mendelssohn 708,500

Sacred Service, Avodath Hakodesh (8) Bloch 817,400
Le Sacre du printemps (7) Stravinsky 786,200
Saga-Dream (7) Nielsen 727,000
Sailor's Song (8) Haydn 834,700
St. Cecilia Mass: Messe Solennelle (2) Gounod 48,000

Musical Category Key: 1 Early/2 Choral/3 Keyboard/4 Chamber/5 Symphonies/6 Concerti

7 Orchestral/8 Songs and Lieder/9 Arias/10 Operas/11 New and Experimental

Silver Apples of the Moon (11) Subotnick 996,400
Simon Boccanegra (10) Verdi 960,500
Simple Symphony for Strings (5) Britten 389,250
Sine nomine Mass (1) Palestrina 10,700
Sinfonia (11) Berio 967,750
Sinfonia Concertante, K. Anh. 9 (6) Mozart 538,000
Sinfonia Concertante, K. 364 (6) Mozart 538,250
Sinfonia da Requiem (7) Britten 606,900
Sinfonia Expansiva (5) Nielsen 452,750
Sinfonia India (5) Chávez 393,000
Sinfonia: Janiculum (6) Persichetti 542,000
Sinfonia Semplice (5) Nielsen 453,500
Signor Bruschino Overture (7) Rossini 749,000
Singulière Symphony (5) Berwald 383,250
Si puo? (prologue) from *I Pagliacci* (9) Leoncavallo 890,400
Sirènes from *Nocturnes* (7) Debussy 620,000
Si tra i ceppi from *Berenice* (9) Handel 889,800
Six Little Pieces for Piano (3) Schoenberg 224,250
Six Pieces for Orchestra (7) Webern 810,600
Skaters Waltz (7) Waldteufel 807,800
Skyscrapers (7) Carpenter 608,000
Slätter (Norwegian Peasant Dances) (3) Grieg 179,500
Slavonic Dances, Op. 46 (7) Dvořák 628,500–628,508
Slavonic Dances, Op. 72 (7) Dvořák 628,751–628,757
Slavonic Mass (2) Janáček 60,500
Sleeping Beauty (complete ballet) (7) Tchaikovsky 793,500
Sleeping Beauty (excerpts) (7) Tchaikovsky 793,600
Socrate (8) Satie 851,500
Le Soir Symphony (5) Haydn 407,250
Solomon (2) Handel 53,250
Somadsah (11) Matsudaira 990,100
Some Trees (8) Rorem 850,700
Sonate éccossaise (Fantasy in f sharp) (3) Mendelssohn 192,000
Song of India from *Sadko* (7) Rimsky-Korsakov 746,500
A Song of Orpheus for Cello and Orchestra (6) Schuman 552,250
Song of Summer (7) Delius 623,250
Song of the Flea (8) Mussorgsky 846,250
Song of the Forests (2) Shostakovich 85,500
Song of the Nightingale (7) Stravinsky 786,800
Song of the Wood Dove from *Gurre-Lieder* (2) Schoenberg 80,250
Songs and Dances of Death (8) Mussorgsky 846,500
Songs My Mother Taught Me (8) Dvořák 831,200
Songs of a Wayfarer (8) Mahler 839,400
Songs of the Auvergne (8) Canteloube 825,200
Songs without Words (3) Mendelssohn 192,750
Sonic Contours (11) Ussachevsky 997,650
La Sonnambula (10) Bellini 906,500
Sonntag (8) Brahms 821,750

Son vergin Vezzosa from *I Puritani* (9) Bellini 887,250
Sorcerer's Apprentice (7) Dukas 625,250
Sorrow, stay (8) Dowland 829,750
Souvenir de Florence (4) Tchaikovsky 363,250
Spanish Dances (3) Granados 177,500
Spem in alium (1) Tallis 16,700
Spirituals for Orchestra (7) Gould 648,500
Sports and Entertainments (3) Satie 220,750
Spring Sonata for Violin and Piano (4) Beethoven 270,250
Spring Symphony (2) Britten 35,500
Spring Symphony (5) Schumann 465,000
Spring Symphony (5) Stamitz 473,250
Stabat Mater (2) Dvořák 42,500
Stabat Mater (2) Pergolesi 74,250
Stabat Mater (2) Poulenc 75,500
Stabat Mater (2) Rossini 77,750
Stabat Mater Motet (1) Palestrina 14,000
Ständchen (8) Brahms 822,000
Ständchen (8) Schubert 862,750
Ständchen (8) Strauss, Richard 875,000
Statements for Orchestra (7) Copland 615,750
Still Falls the Rain (8) Britten 823,503
Stoned Guest (7) Schickele 755,825
Story of Babar the Elephant (7) Poulenc 730,000
La stravaganza (Concerti for solo Violin) (6) Vivaldi 571,501–571,512
Structures for String Quartet (11) Feldman 982,500
Structures for 2 Pianos (11) Boulez 969,250
Stücke (5) im Volkston for Cello (4) Schumann 358,000
Suggestion Diabolique (3) Prokofiev 208,750
Suite bergamasque (3) Debussy 158,750 and 165,750
Suite española (7) Albéniz 578,500
Suite for Piano (3) Schoenberg 224,500
Suite française (7) Milhaud 712,000
Suite française (7) Poulenc 729,750
Suite Pastorale (7) Chabrier 610,000
Su le Sponde del Tebro (8) Scarlatti 851,625
Sumer is Icumen in, Lhude Sing Cuccu (1) Rhaw 16,200
Summer (11) Wolff 998,200
Summer Music for Woodwind Quintet (4) Barber 259,000
Summer Night on the River (7) Delius 623,500
Sun-Treader (7) Ruggles 753,000
Suor Angelica (10) Puccini 942,000
Sure on this Shining Night (8) Barber 815,000
Surgam et circuibo civitatem Motet (1) Palestrina 14,100
Surge, amica mea Motet (1) Palestrina 14,200
Surge illuminare Motet (1) Palestrina 14,300
Surprise Symphony (5) Haydn 422,500
Survivor from Warsaw (2) Schoenberg 80,750
Swanee River (Old Folks at Home) (8) Foster 833,900
Swan Lake (complete ballet) (7) Tchaikovsky 794,100
Swan Lake (excerpts) (7) Tchaikovsky 794,200
Swan of Tuonela (7) Sibelius 746,500

Musical Category Key: 1 Early/2 Choral/3 Keyboard/4 Chamber/5 Symphonies/6 Concerti

Swedish Rhapsody (7) Alfvén 579,500
Sweet Nymph, O Come to Thy Lover (8) Morley 844,000
The Swimmers (8) Ives 836,100
Les Sylphides (7) Chopin 610,750
Sylvia: Procession of Bacchus (7) Delibes 621,250
Sylvia: Suite (7) Delibes 621,500
Symphonia domestica (5) Strauss, Richard 474,000
Symphoniae Sacrae (2) Schütz 85,000
Symphonia Serena (5) Hindemith 426,250
Symphonic Dances (7) Grieg 654,500
Symphonic Dances (7) Rachmaninoff 734,250
Symphonic Etudes (3) Schumann 237,000
Symphonic Metamorphoses of Themes by Weber (7) Hindemith 669,000
Symphonic Variations (7) Dvořák 629,000
Symphonie espagnole (6) Lalo 528,750
Symphonie fantastique (5) Berlioz 381,250
Symphonie funèbre et triomphale (5) Berlioz 381,750
Symphonies of Wind Instruments (7) Stravinsky 787,400
Symphonies pour les soupers du roi (7) Lalande 688,000
Symphony for Strings (5) Schuman 464,000
Symphony no. 1 in One Movement (5) Barber 375,750
Symphony of a Thousand (5) Mahler 436,250
Symphony of Psalms (2) Stravinsky 87,500
Symphony on a French Mountain Air (6) D'Indy 512,600
Synchronisms (11) Davidovsky 977,500
Syrinx for Flute Unaccompanied (4) Debussy 292,000

Il Tabarro (10) Puccini 942,250
Table Music (suites) (7) Telemann 794,750
Tacea la notte placida from *Il Trovatore* (9) Verdi 900,900
Der Tag des Gerichts (2) Telemann 88,500
Tales of Hoffmann (10) Offenbach 936,750
Tales from Vienna Woods (7) Strauss, Johann 773,250
Tambourin (3) Rameau 214,750
Tam O'Shanter (symphonic ballad) (7) Chadwick 610,250
Tancredi Overture (7) Rossini 749,500
Tannhäuser (10) Wagner 963,250
Tannhäuser Overture (7) Wagner 806,500
Tapiola (7) Sibelius 764,750
Tarantella from *Italian* Symphony (5) Mendelssohn 439,000
Tarantelle styrienne (7) Debussy 617,500
Taras Bulba (7) Janáček 681,500
Tasso-Lament and Triumph (7) Liszt 695,000
Te Deum (2) Berlioz 29,000
Te Deum (2) Bruckner 38,000
Te Deum (2) Purcell 77,250
The Telephone (10) Menotti 929,000
Tell me, true love (8) Dowland 830,000
La tempesta di mare Concerto, P.415 (6) Vivaldi 572,005

La tempesta di mare Concerto, P.261 (6) Vivaldi 573,001
Tempest Sonata (3) Beethoven 122,500
Le Temple de la Gloire Suite (7) Rameau 735,500
Tender Land (orchestral suite) (7) Copland 616,000
Terminus (11) Ivey 988,150
Terpsichore (Dance Pieces) (7) Praetorius 730,250
Testament to a Big City (*Short Symphony*) (5) Bazelon 376,000
Textures (11) Takemitsu 996,650
Thanksgiving Day (5) Ives 430,000
Theme and Variations for Band (7) Schoenberg 756,750
Theresien-Messe (2) Haydn 56,000
Thesis Symphony (5) Cowell 395,250
Thieving Magpie Overture (7) Rossini 749,750
Things to Come: Suite (7) Bliss 601,000
Three-Cornered Hat (ballet) (8) Falla 831,600
Three-Cornered Hat (complete ballet) (7) Falla 631,750
3 Distinguished Waltzes of the Disabused Affected Man (3) Satie 221,000
Three Penny Opera (10) Weill 964,500
3 Pièces faciles (3) Stravinsky 243,500
Three Pieces for Piano (7) Schoenberg 224,750
Three Places in New England (7) Ives 680,000
Three Songs of Night (11) Ivey 988,150
Threnody for the Victims of Hiroshima (11) Penderecki 993,000
Thunder and Lightning Polka (7) Strauss, Johann 773,500
Le Tic-toc-choc, ou Les Maillotins (3) Couperin 155,200
Till Eulenspiegel (7) Strauss, R. 781,000
Time Cycle (11) Foss 983,500
Time's Encomium (11) Wuorinén 998,400
Timor et tremor (2) Gabrieli 45,000
Tintagel (7) Bax 589,500
Toccanta for Soprano, Flute, Cello, and Piano (8) Cowell 826,250
Toccata for Percussion (7) Chávez 610,500
Tod und das Mädchen (8) Schubert 863,000
Le Tombeau de Couperin (3) Ravel 216,500
Le Tombeau de Couperin (7) Ravel 738,250
Tombeau d'Edgar Poe (11) Mimaroglu 991,600
Tombeau de M. de Chambonnières (3) D'Anglebert 98,500
Tombeau de M. de Chambonnières (3) Couperin, Louis 156,000
Torre bermeja (4) Albéniz 246,750
Torvaldo e Dorliska Overture (7) Rossini 750,000
Tosca (10) Puccini 942,500
Tota pulchra es Motet (1) Palestrina 14,400
Totentanz for Piano and Orchestra (6) Liszt 530,250
To the Children (8) Rachmaninoff 848,750
To the Spring (3) Grieg 179,000
Touch (11) Subotnick 996,450
Toy Symphony (5) Haydn 425,100
Tragic Overture (7) Brahms 604,750

7 Orchestral/8 Songs and Lieder/9 Arias/10 Operas/11 New and Experimental

Tragic Symphony (5) Schubert 462,500
Tragoedia (11) Rudin 994,100
El Tra-la-la y el Punteado (8) Granados 834,400
Transcendental Etude no. 3 (*Campanella*) (3) Liszt 189,000
Transcendental Etudes (3) Liszt 188,750–189,250
Transición II (11) Kagel 988,350
Trauermusik (6) Hindemith 526,000
Trauer Symphony (5) Haydn 413,250
Traum durch die Dämmerung (8) Strauss, Richard 875,250
Traümerei from Kinderscenen (3) Schumann 234,500
Travail du Peintre (8) Poulenc 846,900
Traveling Music (11) Dockstader 979,000
La Traviata (10) Verdi 960,750
Traviata: Prelude Act I (7) Verdi 801,500
Traviata: Prelude Act III (7) Verdi 801,600
Trepak from *Nutcracker* (7) Tchaikovsky 792,250
Très douce dame (1) Machaut 6,800
Trial of Harmony and Invention (concerti from op. 8) (6) Vivaldi 572,000–572,012
Triana from *Iberia* (3) Albéniz 97,250
Tristan und Isolde (10) Wagner 963,500
Tritsch Tratsch Polka (7) Strauss, Johann 773,750
Trois Ballades de François Villon (8) Debussy 827,800
Trois Chansons de Charles d'Orléans (2) Debussy 41,250
Trois Gymnopédies (3) Satie 222,250
Trois morceaux en forme de poire (3) Satie 222,500
Trois pièces brèves (4) Ibert 314,500
Trois Poèmes Juifs (7) Bloch 601,750
Trois Valses romantiques for 2 Pianos (3) Chabrier 133,250
Trois visages de Liège (11) Pousseur 993,300
Trout Quintet (4) Schubert 354,000
Il Trovatore (10) Verdi 961,000
Les Troyens (10) Berlioz 907,500
Trumpet Voluntary (*Prince of Denmark's March*) (6) Clarke 508,750
Tsar Saltan: Suite (7) Rimsky-Korsakov 746,750
The Tsar's Bride (10) Rimsky-Korsakov 946,000
Tua Jesu dilectio Motet (1) Palestrina 14,500
Tu che di gel sei cinta from *Turandot* (9) Puccini 895,100
Tu es Petrus Motet (1) Palestrina 14,600
The Tulip Tree (8) Rorem 850,800
Turandot (10) Puccini 942,750
Tarangalila Symphonie (11) Messiaen 991,300
Turco in Italia Overture (7) Rossini 750,250
Turkish March from *Ruins of Athens* (7) Beethoven 592,500
Turn of the Screw (10) Britten 911,250
Tu, tu piccolo iddio from *Madame Butterfly* (9) Puccini 893,700
Twelve Poems of Emily Dickinson (8) Copland 825,800
Two Elegiac Melodies (7) Grieg 654,750
Two Fragments from Apocalypse (11) Dockstader 979,250

Two Portraits for Orchestra (7) Bartók 588,250
Tzigane for Violin and Orchestra (6) Ravel 546,500

Uirapurú (7) Villa Lobos 802,400
Um Mitternacht (8) Mahler 839,305
Unanswered Question (7) Ives 680,250
Un bel di, vedremo from *Madame Butterfly* (9) Puccini 893,800
Under Palm Tree from *Cantos de España* (3) Albéniz 95,500
Under the Greenwood Tree (8) Arne 813,250
Und willst du deinen Liebsten sterben sehen (8) Wolf 881,000
Unfinished Quartet (4) Haydn 310,000
Unfinished Symphony (5) Schubert 463,250
Unpleasant Glimpses (3) Satie 221,250
Unser dummer Poebel meint Variations (3) Mozart 202,250
Ut queant laxis (2) Monteverdi 71,000

Valse from *Façade* (7) Walton 808,300
La Valse (7) Ravel 738,500
Valse-Fantaisie (7) Glinka 645,000
Valses nobles et sentimentales (3) Ravel 216,750
Valses nobles et sentimentales (7) Ravel 738,750
Valse triste from *Kuolema* (7) Sibelius 765,000
Variaciones Concertantes (7) Ginastera 641,500
Variations for Orchestra (7) Webern 810,800
Variations for Piano and Orchestra (6) Riegger 547,000
Variations on America (7) Ives 680,500
Variations on a Recitative for Organ (3) Schoenberg 225,000
Variations on a Rococo Theme for Cello and Orchestra (6) Tchaikovsky 560,000
Variations on a Theme by Frank Bridge (7) Britten 607,500
Variations on a Theme by Haydn (7) Brahms 605,250
Variations on a Theme by Tchaikovsky (7) Arensky 580,500
Variations sérieuses (3) Mendelssohn 193,000
Vater unser im Himmelreich (S.682) (3) Bach, J. S. 104,682
Vater unser im Himmelreich (S.683) (3) Bach, J. S. 104,683
Vaticini di Pace (Christmas cantata) (8) Caldara 825,000
Das Veilchen (8) Mozart 845,500
Veni sancte spiritus Motet (1) Palestrina 14,800
Veni sponsa Christi (1) Victoria 18,300
Veni sponsa Christi Mass (1) Palestrina 10,800
Veni sponsa Christi Motets and Hymns (1) Palestrina 14,900
Venusberg Music from *Tannhäuser* (7) Wagner 806,750
Verborgenheit (8) Wolf 883,750
Vergebliches Ständchen (8) Brahms 822,500
Vergine bella (1) Dufay 3,200
Vergnügte Ruh', beliebte Seelenlust (2) Bach, J. S. 23,370
Veritable Flabby Preludes (3) Satie 221,500
Verklärte Nacht (7) Schoenberg 757,500

Musical Category Key: 1 Early/2 Choral/3 Keyboard/4 Chamber/5 Symphonies/6 Concerti

Das verlassene Mägdlein (8) Wolf 884,000
Verschwiegene Liebe (8) Wolf 878,250
Vesperae Solennes de Confessore (2) Mozart 73,250
Vespri Siciliani Overture (7) Verdi 801,700
Vespro della Beata Vergine (2) Monteverdi 71,500
Vestiva i colli Madrigal (1) Palestrina 9,800
Vetrate di Chiesa (7) Respighi 742,500
Vida breve (10) Falla 916,500
Vida breve: Dance no. 1 (7) Falla 632,000 and 632,250
Vida breve: Interlude (7) Falla 632,250
Viderunt Omnes (1) Perotin 15,600
Vienna Blood (7) Strauss, Johann 774,000
Vienna Bons Bons (7) Strauss, Johann 774,250
A Village Romeo and Juliet (2) Delius 42,000
Vineam meam Motet (1) Palestrina 14,700
Virtuous Wife: Suite (7) Purcell 733,750
Visions fugitives (3) Prokofiev 209,250
Vissi d'arte from *Tosca* (9) Puccini 894,600
Vitebsk, Study on a Jewish Theme (4) Copland 288,250
Viva il vino from *Cavalleria Rusticana* (9) Mascagni 890,600
Vive le Roi (1) Des Prez 1,800
Vocalise (11) Avni 965,250
Voces intimae Quartet (4) Sibelius 360,000
Die Vögel (8) Schubert 863,250
Vogel als Prophet from *Waldszenen* (3) Schumann 237,750
Vogelfänger bin ich ja from *Magic Flute* (9) Mozart 892,250
Voice in the Wilderness (6) Bloch 503,000
Voices of Spring (7) Strauss, Johann 775,000
Voi che sapete from *Marriage of Figaro* (9) Mozart 892,550
Voiles (3) Debussy 164,000
Volumina (11) Ligeti 989,400
Vom Himmel kam der Engel Schar (3) Bach, J. S. 101,607
Von deinen Thron (3) Bach, J. S. 103,668
Von fremden Ländern und Menschen from *Kinderscenen* (3) Schumann 234,000
Von Gott will ich nicht lassen (3) Bach, J. S. 103,658
Von Heute auf Morgen (10) Schoenberg 950,000
Vox dilecti mei Motet (1) Palestrina 15,000
Voyage à Paris (8) Poulenc 846,754
Vulnerasti cor meum Motet (1) Palestrina 15,100

Wachet auf! (2) Bach, J. S. 23,240
Wachet auf, ruft uns die Stimme (3) Bach, J. S. 102,645
Waldseligkeit (8) Strauss, Richard 875,500
Waldstein Sonata (3) Beethoven 123,500
Waldszenen (3) Schumann 237,500
Walk to the Paradise Garden (7) Delius 623,750
Walküre (10) Wagner 963,750
Walküre: Magic Fire Music (7) Wagner 807,500
Walküre: Ride of the Valkyries (7) Wagner 807,250

Walt Whitman (8) Ives 836,400
Waltz of the Flowers from *Nutcracker* (7) Tchaikovsky 792,500
Der Wanderer (8) Schubert 863,750
Wanderer Fantasie (3) Schubert 230,000
Wanderers Nachtlied (8) Schubert 864,250
War Requiem (2) Britten 36,000
Warsaw Concerto (6) Addinsell 491,500
Warum? from *Fantasiestücke* (3) Schumann 233,250
Warum betrubst du dich (3) Bach, Johann Christian 99,250
Washington's Birthday (5) Ives 429,250
Washington's Birthday (7) Ives 680,750
Was mir behagt, ist nur die muntre Jagd (2) Bach, J. S. 23,408
Wasps (Incidental music) (7) Vaughan Williams 800,800
Water Music (11) Dockstader 979,500
Water Music (7) Telemann 795,750
Water Music (complete) (7) Handel 661,000
Water Music: Suite (7) Handel 662,000
Waverly Overture (7) Berlioz 595,750
Wedding Cantata (*Weichet nur, betrübte Schatten*) (2) Bach, J. S. 23,402
Wedding Day at Tröldhaugen (3) Grieg 179,250
Wedding March from *Midsummer Night's Dream* (7) Mendelssohn 708,250
The Weeping Babe (2) Tippett 89,250
Weichet nur, betrübte Schatten (*Wedding Cantata*) (2) Bach, J. S. 23,402
Welcome to the Queen (7) Bliss 601,250
Wellington's Victory (7) Beethoven 592,750
Well-Tempered Clavichord (3) Bach, J. S. 111,846–111,893
Wenn du zu den Blumen gehst (8) Wolf 886,250
Wenn wir in höchsten Noten (3) Bach, Johann Michael 99,500
Wer nur den lieben Gott lässt walten (3) Bach, J. S. 102,647
Wesendonck Songs (8) Wagner 877,800
The western wynde Mass (1) Taverner 16,900
West Point Symphony (5) Gould 403,000
What if I never speed (8) Dowland 830,250
What Sparks and Wiry Cries (8) Rorem 850,900
When Jesus Wept (2) Billings 30,750
Where the Bee Sucks (8) Arne 813,500
Where the Citrons Bloom (7) Strauss, Johann 775,250
Widmung (8) Schumann 869,500
Wie bist du meine Königin (8) Brahms 822,750
Wiegenlied (8) Brahms 823,000
Wiegenlied (8) Strauss, Richard 876,000
Wie Melodien (8) Brahms 823,250
The Wild Bull (11) Subotnick 996,500
William Tell (10) Rossini 947,500
William Tell Overture (7) Rossini 750,500
Willow Song from *Otello* (9) Verdi 899,100
Willst du dein Herz mir schenken (8) Bach, J. S. 814,000
Wilt thou, unkind, thus leave me (8) Dowland 830,500
Wine, Women and Song (7) Strauss, Johann 775,500

7 Orchestral/8 Songs and Lieder/9 Arias/10 Operas/11 New and Experimental

Winter Dreams Symphony (5) Tchaikovsky 475,500
Winterreise (8) Schubert 864,500
Winter Winds Etude (3) Chopin 135,200
Wireless Fantasy (11) Ussachevsky 997,700
Wir glauben all' an einem Gott (3) Bach, J. S. 104,680
Wise Virgins (ballet suite) (7) Walton 808,800
Wo die schönen Trompeten blasen from *Des Knaben Wunderhorn* (8) Mahler 839,500
Wooden Prince (7) Bartók 588,500
Wo soll ich fliehen hin (3) Bach, J. S. 102,646
Wozzeck (10) Berg 907,000
Wurst of P.D.Q. Bach (7) Schickele 755,925

Xerxes (Serse) (10) Handel 922,000

The Yeomen of the Guard (10) Gilbert and Sullivan 919,000
Young Person's Guide to the Orchestra (7) Britten 607,800
Youth (sextet for wind instruments) (4) Janáček 317,000

Zadok the Priest (2) Handel 50,000
Zampa Overture (7) Herold 667,000
Zefiro torna (8) Monteverdi 841,800
Zigeunerlieder (2) Brahms 32,250
Zigeunerweisen for Violin and Orchestra (6) Sarasate 551,000
Zion spricht (2) Schein 78,600
Zueignung (8) Strauss, Richard 876,250
Zyklus (11) Stockhausen 996,300

Musical Category Key: 1 Early/2 Choral/3 Keyboard/4 Chamber/5 Symphonies/6 Concerti 7 Orchestral/8 Songs and Lieder/9 Arias/10 Operas/11 New and Experimental

Subject, Proper Name, and Composer Index

Composers with recordings in the *Composer-Title List* (pp. 45–150) are in capital and small capital letters. Numbers in parentheses following their names indicate musical categories (see key at foot of each page); other numbers are page references. Composers mentioned in the text are in regular type.

Musical Category Key: 1 Early/2 Choral/3 Keyboard/4 Chamber/5 Symphonies/6 Concerti 7 Orchestral/8 Songs and Lieder/9 Arias/10 Operas/11 New and Experimental

Musical Category Key: 1 Early/2 Choral/3 Keyboard/4 Chamber/5 Symphonies/6 Concerti

7 Orchestral/8 Songs and Lieder/9 Arias/10 Operas/11 New and Experimental

Musical Category Key: 1 Early/2 Choral/3 Keyboard/4 Chamber/5 Symphonies/6 Concerti

7 Orchestral/8 Songs and Lieder/9 Arias/10 Operas/11 New and Experimental

Musical Category Key: 1 Early/2 Choral/3 Keyboard/4 Chamber/5 Symphonies/6 Concerti

7 Orchestral/8 Songs and Lieder/9 Arias/10 Operas/11 New and Experimental

Musical Category Key: 1 Early/2 Choral/3 Keyboard/4 Chamber/5 Symphonies/6 Concerti

7 Orchestral/8 Songs and Lieder/9 Arias/10 Operas/11 New and Experimental

Musical Category Key: 1 Early/2 Choral/3 Keyboard/4 Chamber/5 Symphonies/6 Concerti 7 Orchestral/8 Songs and Lieder/9 Arias/10 Operas/11 New and Experimental

D0914620